THE WARS OF THE
ROOSEVELTS

THE WARS OF THE
ROOSEVELTS

The Ruthless Rise of America's
Greatest Political Family

WILLIAM J. MANN

HARPER ⬤ PERENNIAL

NEW YORK • LONDON • TORONTO • SYDNEY • NEW DELHI • AUCKLAND

FOR T.D.H.

THE WARS OF THE ROOSEVELTS. Copyright © 2016 by William J. Mann. All rights
reserved. Printed in the United States of America. No part of this book may
be used or reproduced in any manner whatsoever without written permission
except in the case of brief quotations embodied in critical articles and reviews.
For information, address HarperCollins Publishers, 195 Broadway, New York,
NY 10007.

HarperCollins books may be purchased for educational, business, or sales pro-
motional use. For information, please email the Special Markets Department at
SPsales@harpercollins.com.

FIRST HARDCOVER EDITION PUBLISHED 2016.
FIRST HARPER PERENNIAL EDITION PUBLISHED 2017.

Library of Congress Cataloging-in-Publication Data has been applied for.

ISBN 978-0-06-238334-1 (pbk.)

17 18 19 20 21   LSC   10 9 8 7 6 5 4 3 2 1

Contents

AUTHOR'S NOTE

The story of the Roosevelts is well-trod territory. Its various chapters have been masterfully chronicled by H. W. Brands, Ken Burns, Blanche Weisen Cook, Doris Kearns Goodwin, Joseph Lash, David McCullough, Edmund Morris, Geoffrey Ward, and many others. This is not an attempt to duplicate what these excellent historians have done. Rather, my goal is to tell a story that has been embedded, entwined, in some ways hidden in plain sight, within the larger Roosevelt narrative. I set forth the family's rise to power and prestige not as a record of politics and public policy, but rather as a series of personal contests (even, at times, as a blood sport) beginning with the rivalry between the brothers Theodore and Elliott Roosevelt and then passed down to the next generations. That the Wars of the Roosevelts, like the Wars of the Roses, was a dynastic struggle between two distant branches of a family has been documented before. What's been less acknowledged is the fact that the battles went far deeper and were more personal than that, raging between parents, children, siblings, and spouses.

The rise of the Roosevelts is the story of a family at war, of survival of the fittest, where the strong devoured the weak and where the nonconformist—such as Elliott; his illegitimate son, Elliott Roosevelt Mann; the renegade James ("Taddy" or "Jimmie") Roosevelt; and the tragic Kermit Roosevelt—were brutally relegated to nonexistence.

In this book, I view these rebels through a new lens, corrected for class privilege and outmoded moral judgments, allowing for their so-called transgressions to be reconsidered and their family's responses reevaluated. And the most appropriate eyes through which to view this dynastic battlefield are those of Theodore's niece Eleanor, as she was there from the beginning and, as much as any of them, experienced the personal costs of the Roosevelt ambition.

This is new information based on new research. For the first time, I tell the full account of the struggles of Elliott Roosevelt, including the unknown backstory of the shady lawyer appointed to deal with Elliott's mistress and illegitimate son. In most previous accounts, Theodore Roosevelt's actions in 1891–1894, when he did his best to commit his brother to an asylum, even if that meant splitting up Elliott's family, have been presented as noble and inevitable. I take a somewhat different view. Also for the first time, I have fleshed out the life of Elliott Roosevelt Mann (no relation to my own family), who was as much a Roosevelt as any of the others, with the same ambition and skill, even if he was denied their surname and privilege of birth.

Likewise, the story of Franklin's nephew Jimmie is told with many new details; my discovery that his wife, Sadie, was Jewish sheds fresh light on why the family was so opposed to her. I also reveal considerable new information about the lives of Kermit and Ted Roosevelt and the heretofore forgotten political scandals of Alice Roosevelt. Finally, I have attempted to bring a twenty-first-century understanding to Eleanor's sexuality and her alternative, polyamorous marriage with Franklin—successful for the most part, although not without its challenges and difficulties.

I have not fictionalized these events. All scenes described come from primary sources: the thousands of letters written by the principals (which provide extraordinarily rich detail to recreate their worlds) as well as diaries, datebooks, telegrams, court records, FBI reports, contemporary newspaper accounts, maps, photographs, and daily weather bulletins. Nothing has been created simply for dramatic sake, and I do not venture carelessly into the minds of my subjects. If I write of inner thoughts or feelings, I'm basing my descriptions on letters or memoirs written by the subject in question, wherein such emotions, attitudes, or motivations have been disclosed or can be deduced. Full citations and explanations can be found in the notes. Anything in quotation marks comes directly from a primary source.

THE WARS OF
THE ROOSEVELTS

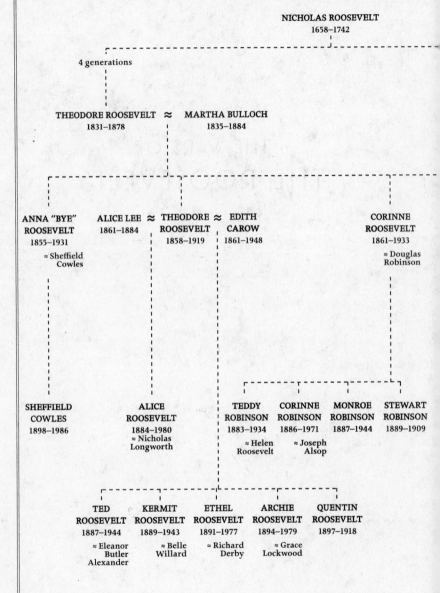

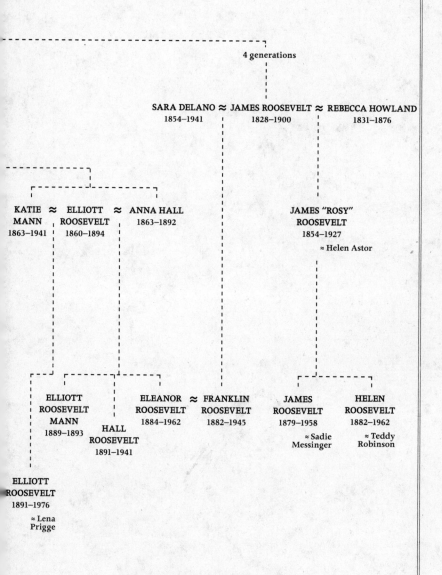

4 generations

SARA DELANO ≈ JAMES ROOSEVELT ≈ REBECCA HOWLAND
1854–1941   1828–1900   1831–1876

KATIE   ≈ ELLIOTT   ≈ ANNA HALL   JAMES "ROSY"
MANN   ROOSEVELT   1863–1892   ROOSEVELT
1863–1941   1860–1894   1854–1927

                                              ≈ Helen Astor

ELLIOTT   ELEANOR   ≈ FRANKLIN   JAMES   HELEN
ROOSEVELT   ROOSEVELT   ROOSEVELT   ROOSEVELT   ROOSEVELT
MANN   HALL   1884–1962   1882–1945   1879–1958   1882–1962
1889–1893   ROOSEVELT
            1891–1941   ≈ Sadie   ≈ Teddy
                                                    Messinger   Robinson

ELLIOTT
ROOSEVELT
1891–1976

  ≈ Lena
  Prigge

≈ = *marriage and/or child with symbol*

PROLOGUE:
THE LARGER PICTURE

1960

The old woman walked with her head thrust forward, as if she were in a hurry to get where she was going. The low-heeled shoes on her long, narrow feet were more practical than stylish, a smart choice given how much walking she did around the city. On her head she wore a kerchief, as a light rain had begun to fall. The sidewalks of New York's Greenwich Village were wet and slippery that April morning, and the air was cool, not even fifty degrees.

As she walked, the old woman was lost in thought, a habit for which her friends frequently admonished her. For most of her seventy-five years, a barrage of ideas, hopes, desires, and regrets had been in constant collision in her mind. Something was always brewing, ready to burst. Ever since she was a small girl she'd been possessed of extraordinary drive and purpose, and while her body might be slowing down, her mind churned as fast as ever, light-years away from the mundane world around her. That week, she was consumed by thoughts about how to "unite American women for decisive action against the threat of worldwide nuclear slaughter" and how to pass laws to "prohibit discrimination based on race, religion or national origin," as she wrote in her nationally syndicated newspaper column. So it was no surprise that when she stepped off the curb at Eighth Street, she failed to notice a car that was backing up toward her. Nor, unfortunately, did the driver see her.

The car struck her in the hip. Like an ancient tree, the woman fell onto the asphalt. A screech of brakes rent the air as the driver, a young man, realized what had happened. He jumped out of the car and ran around back.

The old woman seemed unhurt. With some effort, she got to her feet, clutching her purse and conscious of the stares of passersby. Her sharp blue eyes fixed on the driver. She told him he should go, drive away, before someone came along and made a fuss.

Did the young man recognize her? He might easily have, as the old woman with the braided gray bun was very familiar to most Americans in 1960, and to many people around the globe. For more than forty years she had lived in the public eye. Millions loved her for her work; some hated her for it. The widow of a president, the niece of another, she was also, finally, a stateswoman in her own right, a latter-day accomplishment few would ever have predicted when she was a neglected and ridiculed child.

If the driver of the car knew he had hit Eleanor Roosevelt, he never let the fact become public. He simply did as he was instructed. He got back in his car and sped away. Eleanor was glad of it. She didn't want to be the cause of any trouble for the young man. She'd tell a friend the driver was "a Negro," and she knew the trouble policemen could sometimes make for Negro boys.

Limping across the street on a swollen ankle, Eleanor arrived at the salon of François de Paris, the celebrity hairdresser, where she'd been asked to speak at a cancer fund luncheon. Despite her discomfort, she soldiered through the event, but afterward she gave in and allowed her doctor to wrap her ankle. That was all the coddling Eleanor would allow herself: she adamantly declined the doctor's request that she cancel the rest of her day's schedule. Hobbling in on a crutch to another fund-raiser that night, the former First Lady and current UN ambassador was clever enough to use her injury to her advantage. She told a friend later that when people saw she was in pain, they coughed up more cash.

The lightheartedness, however, belied the ache. Over the course of her seven decades, Eleanor had learned how to live with pain, how to manage it, even how to use it. That didn't mean she didn't feel it.

That sprained ankle, inconsequential on its own, marked the beginning of a long decline for Eleanor. Days later, she received a far more serious diagnosis from her doctor. She was suffering from aplastic anemia, for which there was no cure. It was the most basic of diseases, striking the bone marrow, the very core of what kept the body running. The diagnosis explained the increasing pain and fatigue Eleanor had been feeling, which she understood now would only get worse. Over the ensuing months, she would endure hospitalizations, transfusions, fevers, painkillers, and depression.

One night, hooked up to tubes in her hospital bed, with a machine to help her breathe constantly beeping in her ears, she awoke from a nightmare. Her brother Hall and her son Elliott, both deeply troubled men, had metamorphosed into one creature—"like a Picasso drawing," Eleanor described it to a friend—and were trying to smother her. If, in her delirium, she dreamed of her brother and her son, she might well have dreamed of others, too: her husband probably, her cousins, her uncle, her lover quite possibly, her father almost certainly. Eleanor's past was rushing in at her, unfinished and unresolved.

The world had come to think of Eleanor Roosevelt as a very wise woman, and she was, but she was also lonely and deeply conflicted, haunted by family secrets and lies that had followed her for decades. The Roosevelt family had changed America, rising to prominence at the end of the nineteenth century and profoundly shaping the twentieth. They had not achieved their influence without struggle and cost. Eleanor had observed (and participated in) the internecine family battles as first her uncle and then her cousins and husband strove for power. She had witnessed the battles for supremacy; she'd seen firsthand how the strong and ambitious had utterly annihilated the weak and nonconformist. Indeed, Eleanor herself might have been one of those destroyed, but she had been tested in the fire and had emerged the strongest of them all, mastering politics and public policy as few women before her had done, negotiating confidently with presidents and prime ministers. Yet, in some ways, her family (the immediate and the extended, as her children and cousins would attest) always remained out of her reach, beyond the capacity of her understanding.

So, in the short amount of time she had left, Eleanor decided she needed to revisit the extraordinary life she'd lived. At the same time that she was making plans for her burial—in a plain wooden coffin, without embalming—she would also attempt to make sense of her story. She'd written three previous memoirs, but this one, she hoped, would go deeper. She hired a woman to help her, Elinore Denniston, a fifty-nine-year-old freelance writer who, being unmarried, could devote all her time to the enterprise. To get started, Denniston met Eleanor at her cottage, Val-Kill, nestled in the woods of Hyde Park, on the Hudson River, a place that had once hosted ambassadors and senators and a steady parade of friends, but that now stood mostly quiet, save for the woodpeckers rapping on the roof. Eleanor tried valiantly to learn how to use the modern tape recorder Denniston brought with her, but she never quite got the hang of it.

Her task was never going to be easy. She set out to reshape and reconsider the story of her life, cutting out all that was no longer relevant and adding material that "seemed necessary for a better understanding" of her story. Yet while her publisher was clamoring for a behind-the-scenes exposé of Washington politics, Eleanor, facing death, was no longer interested in the "big important things" of her life; what drew her now were the "small and personal." In telling her story this final time, she had two simple objectives. One was "to give a picture of the world in which I grew up and which today is changed in many ways." The second, and more important, was "to give as truthful a picture as possible of a human being."

Could she do it? Was she strong enough? Could she make peace with her ghosts? Sifting through the residue of her life, Eleanor relived not only the triumphs of her family, of which there were many, but also the tragedies, of nearly an equal number. Her uncle Theodore had established the modern American presidency, and left behind a more equitable, meritocratic, and verdant nation. Yet in his climb to the top, he'd also found it expedient to destroy Eleanor's father, ripping open a hole at the center of his niece's life that would never be filled. He'd also left behind a brood of bruised, bullied children forever in competition with one another and with their cousins for custody of their father's mantle; the Wars of the Roosevelts would pile more bodies on top of that of

Eleanor's father. Her husband, Franklin, had ended the Great Depression and won a world war, but on a personal level he'd failed Eleanor grievously, leaving a wound she thought was healed, only to find it torn open again at his death. Also, instead of learning from her own unhappy childhood, Eleanor had in some ways failed herself: her own children remained distant and estranged from her.

The effort of reconsidering her life took its toll on Eleanor. One day, after strenuous attempts to collect her thoughts, she said to Denniston, her hands trembling, "I can't work." She was full of apology. "I don't understand it. And you have come so far."

Time was running out for Eleanor. For all her sincere desire for honesty, how could she really tell the truth, given how the public had come to revere her and her family? How could she possibly tell the stories of the husband who had both uplifted and betrayed her; of the uncle who had shattered her young life in the cause of his own ambition; of the cousins who had tormented her and upon whom she had wrought a regrettable revenge; of the lover she had abandoned; of the brother she had failed and the brother she had refused to acknowledge; and most critically, of the father who had been everything to her and whose loss was never overcome?

Eleanor was astute enough to know that to tell her personal history, so intertwined with the rise of the Roosevelts, she would need "the framework of a larger picture." Yet could she really attain this? Extraordinary distance would be needed from the events of her life if she were to understand not only what had been done to her but also what she had done to others. Very deep soul searching was going to be necessary to grasp how and why her fabled empathy and compassion could make a difference in the lives of millions of people around the globe, but hadn't been able to rescue her own siblings and children. At this late date, was it even possible for her to construct such a complete and honest perspective on her life?

As always, Eleanor did her best. It was a Sisyphean task, though, and some part of her must have known that. To be truly successful, she would need to become omniscient, somehow gain insight into the lives of people she had never met or had barely known, yet whose lives had so imprinted hers. She would need to possess the ability of total recall, to summon up the words and phrases she'd heard swirling around her as a child in order to decode the mystifying events that shaped her early life. She would need to become a time traveler, to transcend the decades and find herself back in the world of which she wrote so fondly, a time when the Roosevelts were just coming to power, a time before automobiles and breathing machines and tape recorders, a time before the terrible demands of living in the public eye, a time before all the pain.

PART I

CAIN AND ABEL

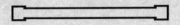

1890–1891

Like a colossus, Theodore Roosevelt stomped down the marble steps of the atrium of the courthouse, his footsteps echoing up into the vaulted ceiling. When he was like this, everyone knew to get out of his way.

He was not a very big man, standing just five nine, with a square face and a straggly mustache that looked like a plant in need of water, but he had intense blue eyes that squinted behind his spectacles whenever he wanted to emphasize something, which was nearly all the time, and broad shoulders and muscular arms and a powerful barrel chest. Throughout the capital, stories swirled of Roosevelt fighting off grizzly bears and surviving buffalo stampedes at his hunting ranch in North Dakota. Once, he'd pursued thieves up the Little Missouri River, capturing them and standing guard over them for forty straight hours, reading Tolstoy to stay awake. As civil service commissioner, Roosevelt's legend was nearly as compelling: he'd publicly taken on various government officials in his much-publicized quest to reform political appointments and abolish patronage.

Yet it was not Washington politics that enraged him on this day. Rather, it was something far more personal. It was his brother, the brother with whom he'd been competing since boyhood and who now jeopardized all Theodore's plans.

In the voluminous letters he wrote to his older sister, Bye (sometimes several a week, keeping her apprised of his accomplishments in the capital), Theodore made much of how he frequently walked between his office and his home, even in the coldest weather. Striding out on a brisk winter evening, Theodore would make his way west on Louisiana Avenue; in those days, the street ran roughly where Indiana Avenue runs today. Off to his left, shining above the trees that then covered the National Mall, rose the white obelisk of the Washington Monument. The capital was far more orderly than Theodore's hometown of New York City, which was why his wife, Edith, preferred living there.

"Quiet and tree-lined," his daughter, Alice, would describe the Washington of her youth, with "the atmosphere of a postbellum Southern town."

Theodore appreciated Washington for a very different reason: in its past he saw his future. On his way home, he strolled through squares named for Benjamin Franklin, General McPherson, and Admiral Farragut. When the spirit moved him, he took a detour to pass directly in front of the Executive Mansion. Whenever he did so, he admitted, his "heart would beat a little faster."

Someday, he vowed, he would live there. Someday he would be president of the United States. In these plans, he was supported and encouraged by Bye, his chief booster and unofficial adviser. Bye, whose real name was Anna, was originally called "Bamie," short for "Bambina," her father's nickname for her. She'd become "Bye" when she started traveling frequently: "Hi, Bamie. Bye, Bamie." Still unmarried at the age of thirty-six, Bye possessed what many of her peers called the most brilliant mind in the family: if she'd been a man, many thought, she would have run for president herself. Yet Bye wasn't a man, so she lived vicariously through Theodore, and she knew as well as he did that their shared dreams of glory were increasingly threatened by the behavior of their brother, Elliott.

Theodore had recently received a letter from the New York law offices of William Howe and Abraham Hummel, lawyers best known for defending prostitutes, chorus girls, and saloonkeepers. They were claiming that Theodore's brother, Elliott, had gotten one of the chambermaids in his house pregnant, and the woman was in dire need of money. Theodore had no idea if the woman was telling the truth or was merely a con artist, but it was indicative of the kind of life Elliott led that such a claim could even have been made. Theodore's brother drank too much and showed no respect for proprieties. For the past few years he'd been embarrassing the family at dinner parties and other social gatherings. At one soiree thrown by Bye, he'd been rude to her guests, finding them insufferably snooty. "It is a perfect nightmare about Elliott," Theodore told his sister after getting a report of the evening. "I am distressed beyond measure."

This couldn't keep up. At the moment, Elliott was in Europe, living beyond his means with his extravagant wife, Anna, who in Theodore's view only exacerbated the problem. Anna, Theodore declared, was "Chinese" in her "moral and mental" standards—in other words, she did not act like a good Christian woman. Although not deeply religious, Theodore was keenly aware of decorum and discretion, as any man with his eye on the presidency would be. He knew careers could be derailed in the drawing rooms of New York society, where Elliott and Anna had made themselves infamous. People would be very reluctant about backing a candidate with a black sheep such as Elliott in his family.

It was only seven years earlier, after all, that the cries of "Ma, Ma, where's my pa?" threatened to derail Grover Cleveland's campaign for president. Taunted about stories of an illegitimate son, Cleveland barely won an election he was supposed to have taken handily, eking out a win in the popular vote by just one quarter of one percent. (He did far better in the electoral vote tally.) Until the end, a Cleveland win remained in doubt, with preachers blasting him from their pulpits and the Republican press publishing frequent heartrending affidavits from the mother of the little boy.

Such dishonor could not attach itself to Theodore. After years of government corruption, he was positioning himself as a new kind of politician: moral, principled, incorruptible. His whole public persona was predicated on his integrity and character. He'd made his first mark as a New York state assemblyman at the age of twenty-four, when he exposed a corrupt judge in a railroad investment scandal. His intolerance of backroom deals was well known: Theodore refused to countenance patronage, misconduct, or disrepute of any kind. That was why Elliott's shenanigans were potentially so dangerous.

Yet for all his crusading against patronage, Theodore's own appointment had been a political plum. As a Republican Party operative in New York, he'd worked hard for the election of Benjamin Harrison in 1888, ensuring the defeat of the libertine Cleveland. Harrison thanked him by appointing him to the Civil Service Commission; it was, party bosses promised, a stepping-stone. Still smarting over his loss in the New York mayoral race in

1886 (a humiliating defeat, since he'd come in third, behind both the Democrat *and* a third-party candidate), Theodore yearned for redemption. The party bosses promised him his time would come.

Yet he was in a hurry. He was thirty-two years old. He didn't want to be some gray-bearded codger when he finally grabbed the brass ring. He didn't want to be President Harrison, in other words, "the little gray man in the White House," as Theodore called him, who looked on "with cold and hesitating disapproval" at his civil service commissioner's efforts at reform.

By seizing the mantle of change and winning the admiration of press and public for doing so, Theodore had essentially checkmated the president of the United States. The previous month, in Boston, he delivered a well-publicized speech to a group of businessmen, arguing that "civil service had a moral as well as a business side." He told the group that he followed the Ten Commandments in his work as much as any party manifesto. Fairness for all was his goal, "from the fourth-class postmaster to the Census Enumerator." The American way, Theodore declared, was achieved only through "honesty and manliness." The next day, nearly every paper in the country reported on "Roosevelt's reform speech." With appearances like these, Theodore was making a name for himself far more effectively than he would have if he'd followed the party's advice to toil for a decade as an anonymous, loyal bureaucrat. He wasn't about to let anything get in his way now.

The walk home from the courthouse took about half an hour. Theodore's town house, at 1820 Jefferson Place, Northwest, was small and cramped but quite comfortable, warmed by a fire and lit by flickering gas lamps. His three children routinely greeted him at the door: Alice, just about to turn seven; Theodore Junior, three; and Kermit, still in his nursemaid's arms at the age of one. Wife Edith, as Theodore wrote to Bye, was always ready with the tea when he came home from the office.

Edith, in fact, had been a ready and willing partner to him in every way. They had taken Washington society by storm, turning themselves into one of the most popular young couples in the capital. On one recent night, they dined with Vice President Levi

Morton; on other nights, they entertained "thoroughly respectable, unimportant congressmen," as Theodore privately called them, men such as James W. Wadsworth of New York and John F. Andrew of Massachusetts. Their importance, however, might reveal itself later, when it was time to call in favors to accelerate his rise to the top.

Theodore's ambition was deeply personal, rooted in a lifelong desire to excel, but it also grew out of an altruism instilled in him by his father, who saw in their class privilege a duty to do good in the world. For all his self-aggrandizement, Theodore truly wanted to make the nation a better, more equitable place; he simply believed he was the best and the right man for the job. "I am very glad to have been in this position," he wrote to Bye after settling into his role as commissioner. "I think I have done good work— and a man ought to show that he can go out into the world and hold his own with other men."

Exactly the lesson his brother Elliott had failed to learn.

Alone at night, after Edith and the children had gone to bed, Theodore sat at his desk and wrote letters to Bye back in New York, ruminating over their reckless brother. The problem with Elliott, Theodore firmly believed, was that he had let himself go soft. Nothing stopped Theodore when he wanted something. When he rode to the hounds, he always came in first, no matter what. Even when, on one horrific occasion, his horse slammed into a stone wall, smashing Theodore's eyeglasses into his face and breaking his arm so badly that it resembled "a length of liverwurst," he remounted and carried on, coming in behind only the huntsman. "I don't grudge the broken arm a bit," he quipped to a friend. "I'm always ready to pay the piper when I've had a good dance."

In contrast, when Elliott broke his leg during an amateur charity circus, he took to his bed, getting hooked on morphine, laudanum, and an expanding supply of alcohol.

Yet, when they were younger, it was Elliott who was the stronger brother. Riding, hunting, climbing, swimming—all these came naturally to Elliott, whereas Theodore, until the age of eleven, was a frail, asthmatic child. He was his mother's precious little "Teedie," forever being rushed out of their Manhattan town house and into the countryside, or to the beach, or on a grand tour of Europe, whenever the first crackle of a wheeze was heard in his voice. Teedie's sudden fits, usually late at night, terrified his parents, who kept the boy secluded in his room, treating him as if he were a fragile piece of china, liable to shatter if handled too hard.

Then, one day, his father, a wise old Knickerbocker, had had enough. He called his son in to see him. "Theodore," he said, eschewing the childish family nickname, "you have the mind, but you have not the body, and without the help of the body the mind cannot go as far as it should." It was time for the boy to take control over his illness. "It is hard drudgery to make one's body," Father Roosevelt acknowledged. "But I know you will do it."

So Theodore started to run. He lifted weights. He spent hours assaulting punching bags. Creating his own gym on the piazza of the family's five-story brownstone on East Twentieth Street, between Broadway and Fourth Avenue, he set out to widen his chest, presumably to give his lungs more room to breathe. He was terrified of being a pretender, of not being a man at all, as in Robert Browning's poem "The Flight of the Duchess." In it, Browning describes an effete young aristocrat as "The pertest little ape / That ever affronted human shape." Theodore saw himself in that verse: after so many generations of comfortable living, with mansions and carriages and servants to chop the wood, his family line had grown soft, he believed, detached from the rigors that made men men.

So he willed himself to get stronger, to reclaim the manhood his people had lost. Eventually his shoulders thickened, his arms bulked up, and his chest widened just as he'd hoped it would. Slowly his asthma disappeared. If his parents had continued to coddle him, Theodore was convinced he would have died—or worse: he would have ended up a pampered patrician, propped up on pillows, dependent upon servants who were more men than he. Rather like his brother, Elliott.

How cavalier Elliott had been with his natural-born gifts, wasting all the strength and vitality Theodore had once envied. Their competition began in earnest the moment Theodore made himself strong. When Elliott came to visit him while Theodore was a student at Harvard, spending a few days in sporting and athletic activities, Theodore kept score in his journal: "As athletes we are about equal: he runs best, I row best. He can beat me sailing or swimming; I can beat him wrestling and boxing. I am best with the rifle, he with the shotgun." A decade later, out on Long Island, the rivalry continued. Racing their horses, Theodore noted that Elliott won the half-mile dash, while he came in fifth; in the quarter-mile dash, Elliott came in second, which would have evened things up, except that Theodore came in third. He wasn't pleased.

Yet, to family members, Theodore insisted that while he was driven to "show up" every man around him, the one exception was Elliott, for whom he professed to feel no jealousy. After all, he'd dedicated his book *Hunting Trips of a Ranchman* to him: "To that keenest of sportsmen and truest of friends, my brother, Elliott Roosevelt." Yet the very existence of the book (Theodore's second, and there had been five since) was enough to "show up" Elliott, who'd never been able to publish a word. Theodore seemed unconscious of that fact, or of the weight his words might carry when he asserted that a grizzly bear was bigger and stronger than any tiger, since it was the head of a grizzly that hung on his wall and the skin of a tiger that lay across Elliott's floor.

Elliott had also been the better-looking brother, carrying on a string of romances from his young teens. "All the girls," Theodore would recall wistfully, "from Helen White and Fanny Dana and May Higham used to be so flattered by any attentions from him." Theodore, on the other hand, had few romantic adventures in his youth, until he met the woman who'd become his wife. (Not Edith: there was a wife before her, though Theodore did his best not to think about his first wife.) Elliott's luck with women was, in fact, legendary, and that luck, apparently, had continued. How many other chambermaids might come forward? Such sexual impropriety offended Theodore to his core.

When he underwent his physical transformation, he acquired more than just a strong body. He also emerged with a rigid set of principles. There was good and bad, right and wrong, strong and weak. Such an ironclad worldview often made him difficult to please. "If I were to do something Theodore thought was weak or wrong," his younger sister, Corinne, explained to her husband, "he would never forgive me, whereas Elliott no matter how much he might despise the sin would forgive the sinner."

Yet Theodore was never going to apologize for having standards. Although he liked a pretty girl as well as any man, he was married, and that was that: any excess energy, he believed, could be worked off by a swim or a hike. All the thrills and passion he needed in life could be obtained at his ranch in North Dakota, to which he repaired every summer to herd cattle and hunt elk. That was how a real man, a good man, a *decent* man, lived.

Also, a decent man needed a decent wife. Elliott's wife, Anna, was no Edith. She was foolish and frivolous, Theodore thought, and her extravagance had "eaten into her character like an acid." Whether she'd stand by her man if the claims of the chambermaid were proven true remained to be seen. So far, though, Anna had been an eager and equal accomplice in Elliott's high living. The time had come to put an end to their games.

Since Elliott had abdicated his responsibilities, Theodore wrote to Bye, they needed to step in. The first thing Elliott had to do was get rid of his doctor. No matter that Dr. William T. Lusk was head of the faculty at Bellevue Medical College and president of the New York State Medical Association. To Theodore, Lusk was a "fool" because he hadn't yet insisted Elliott check himself into an insane asylum. The fact that Lusk was a Yale man probably didn't help.

Instead of Lusk, Theodore wanted Elliott to "put himself completely in the hands of some first-rate man of decision," he told Bye, ideally Dr. William M. Polk, the son of a lionized Confederate general, a bishop in the Episcopal Church, and a man well known in Roosevelt social circles. Elliott needed to be put away, Theodore firmly believed, preferably in England or France, where he could do no harm to himself or anyone in his family. Either that or he should "be sent on some long trip, preferably by sea, with a doctor as companion." If Elliott were under a reliable doctor's care, Theodore wrote to Bye, it would be easy to get a court to commit him. "Most people know he is out of his head," he told his sister.

From here on in, Theodore intended to seize the reins of Elliott's life. In his letter to Bye, he dictated the terms. "Anna and Elliott must live apart," he decreed. That Anna had recently announced she was pregnant complicated matters but did not change them. "They have no right to have children now," Theodore insisted. "It is a dreadful thing to bring into the world children under circumstances such as these. It must not be done. It is criminal."

What had made the situation so urgent was the letter from attorneys Howe and Hummel alleging the liaison with the chambermaid. If the charge was true, Elliott's wife and his mistress were pregnant at the same time. A public scandal could erupt at any moment. So Theodore told Bye he was sending a trusted doctor, Gerardus H. Wynkoop, another scion of an ancient Dutch family, out to Brooklyn to examine the woman, named Catherina Mann, an immigrant from Bavaria. "Wynkoop is going to try to get the truth," he wrote. No one stood in the way of Theodore Roosevelt's ambitions—not his wayward brother, and certainly not some Bavarian chambermaid.

GRAZ, AUSTRIA

Thrice a day the bell inside the Glockenturm rang one hundred one times, a reminder that it had been cast from as many Turkish cannonballs, a defiant declaration of the city's indestructibility. The bell tower had withstood the Turks and Napoleon, and the city of Graz below it had prospered, its Renaissance-era streets and structures still standing after three hundred years. Protected by the Alps to the north, the city lay within a basin open only to the south, allowing the air of the Mediterranean to rush in. In Graz, the sun shone longer than it did in Vienna or Salzburg, and the rain and wind came less frequently. In Graz, there was a feeling of safety, protection, refuge.

Not for Elliott Roosevelt, however, who had come to the city seeking precisely those things and who, so far, had turned up short. Elliott was in exile. His whole family, it seemed, had turned against him. Letters from back home arrived regularly scolding him for overspending his trust fund and dipping into the family capital. Yet Elliott had run out of options. He couldn't go home. He was unwilling to live under the thumb of his brother, Theodore, any longer. For too long Theodore had looked down his nose at Elliott's friends and askance at the parties Elliott and his wife, Anna, threw at their Long Island summer home. "I do hate his Hempstead life," Theodore had written to Bye. "It is certainly very unhealthy, and it leads to nothing."

Elliott was well aware that he didn't contribute to society in the ways Theodore did, with all his political work and commissions, but he had never possessed Theodore's public spirit. He was a playboy, a bon vivant. "Live and let live," Elliott would write in an unpublished short story he kept among his papers, whose protagonist seems modeled on him: "Never miss an opportunity of enjoying life, no matter what the cost." Elliott might not be the philanthropist Theodore was, but charity, to his mind, was an instrument used by the civic-minded and the ambitious. He was neither. He lived for "pleasure only," he wrote, and never did anything he disliked when he could avoid it. "And when the end comes," he concluded, he would "take it cheerfully. Strauss is going to be played at my funeral, no funeral march for me."

Despite his devil-may-care approach to life, Elliott had taken steps to respond to his family's criticism. Most significantly, since fleeing to Europe, he'd stopped drinking; letters between Anna and Bye during these months attested to that fact. "Elliott has been a perfect angel," Anna stated plainly. Also, by removing himself entirely from New York society, where Theodore feared he'd be an embarrassment, he had given in to his brother's fervent demand that he "get away [from the] club and social life." In Europe, Elliott hoped, he could find a fresh start away from his family's control.

Even with all that, the criticism still came: Theodore wanted him to stop relying on Lusk, a doctor Elliott trusted completely. So it was with a great deal of bitterness that Elliott viewed his family back home. "I am not going to speak of this all again," he wrote to Bye from Berlin, when he first arrived on the Continent in the summer of 1890. "I am too sad and need no friends."

All he needed now, Elliott believed, was his wife and children, a girl, Eleanor, age six, and a boy, Elliott Junior, not quite two. While he remained unhappy about the schism within his family, he found, to his great pleasure, that his seven months abroad had rejuvenated his marriage and home life. Elliott hadn't always been faithful to Anna; the previous summer, he had dallied with the family's chambermaid, an immigrant girl named Catherina Mann. How much Anna knew about Catherina would never be entirely clear, but it was soon after the affair that the family abruptly closed the house and sailed for Europe. The children, however, had liked Catherina well enough; from the spa town of Bad Reichenhall, Germany, Elliott had sent his erstwhile mistress a photograph of Eleanor as a remembrance. Perhaps it was his way of ending the relationship on good terms.

Since then, Elliott had fallen in love with his wife all over again. To Bye, he called Anna "noble [and] beautiful." To his mother-in-law, he wrote, "She is my only friend, my precious Wife," describing the long walks they took together every morning. In Paris they'd ridden "a jolly little pair of ponies . . . along the banks of the Seine." Once more they were very much a couple in love.

Just as special had been Elliott's time with his daughter. Eleanor was an odd child, awkward and gangly. She had inherited none of her mother's beauty. Anna sometimes seemed at a loss to know what to do with the dreamy, imaginative little girl, but Elliott adored her, playing with her on the beaches of Italy and building her snowmen in the mountains of Germany. For all the fears Elliott's family had about the "intemperate influence" he might have on his children, Eleanor would remember only happiness with her father. He was always "kind and loving and charming," she said, ruled by his heart and not his head.

The happy family, in fact, was about to get bigger. Anna had recently discovered she was pregnant with their third child. Elliott was delighted, but his brother's reaction (no surprise) could be heard from across the Atlantic. Adding another child to the mix, Theodore grumbled, was just going to drive Elliott's costs higher. For once, Elliott had to admit his brother was right.

He knew he couldn't go on much longer without some sort of

rapprochement with his family back home. While it wouldn't be easy reaching out to Theodore, Elliott knew it would be prudent. Now that a new baby was on the way, he was going to need his family's financial help. So he swallowed his pride and scratched out a warm, friendly missive to his brother.

They didn't have much in common, these two brothers, at least not anymore, but they did have their daughters, born just a few months apart seven years earlier. "Tell Alice," Elliott wrote, "that Eleanor takes French lessons every day and tries hard to write so she won't be far behind her when we return."

There it was: the competitive urge that had burned between Elliott and Theodore for decades. Now it had been bequeathed to their daughters.

Once, Elliott had loved his brother. Theodore was sixteen months older than he, but for the first decade of their lives, it had been Elliott who was stronger, more dependable, and more level-headed. In those days, "Teedie" was always coughing and wheezing, frequently reliant on his brother just to get up and down stairs. During the family's grand tour of Europe in 1870, it fell to Elliott, who was called "Nell," to provide a shoulder on which Teedie could lean. Many years later, Nell's daughter, Eleanor, would cherish the stories that were passed down from that trip, describing her father's "consideration and thoughtfulness to his brother, Theodore, who, at the time, was far from being the strong person that he later made himself."

Then Teedie started to swim and ride and lift weights, and the asthma faded. Suddenly he was beating Nell in athletic contests; in a series of fifteen bouts waged between Teedie, Nell, and several male cousins in the second half of 1875, Teedie won fourteen and tied the fifteenth. Almost overnight, the brothers' roles were reversed; now it was Nell who experienced fainting spells and fits. He would suffer from a form of epilepsy for years; some suspected the ailment was more emotional than physical. Hoping to toughen him up, Roosevelt *père* sent Elliott to a military camp in Texas. He also kept him regularly informed of Teedie's continued progress in packing on the muscle and triumphing over the delicacy of his youth. Nell seemed painfully aware that he was now the inferior son. "You are right about Teedie," he wrote to his father. "He is . . . a boy I would give a good deal to be like in many respects." Still, he added a *cri de coeur*: "Oh, Father, will you ever think *me* a noble boy?"

Elliott did his best at the camp to make his father proud. He learned to ride and shoot expertly. Athletic prowess and coordination had always come naturally to him, while for Theodore it had taken real courage and effort; perhaps that was why Theodore's accomplishments always seemed to matter more to their father than Elliott's. It was also why "the strenuous life" mattered more to Theodore. For all his inherent gifts as a sportsman, Elliott found more appeal in indoor pleasures. It was at the Texas camp, as a teenager, that he started to smoke and drink, and he proved very popular with the ladies of the frontier. In contrast to Theodore, with his blunt features, Elliott was quite handsome, with dark hair, striking blue eyes, a broad forehead, and a round face. At five ten, he stood an inch taller than his older brother, though he wasn't nearly as muscled as Theodore.

When the brothers met again upon Elliott's return from camp, their rivalry only accelerated. They were forever blackening each other's eyes in boxing matches and dropping to the floor to wrestle. An inveterate hiker and hunter, Theodore had taken to studying, stuffing, and classifying the wildlife of upstate New York, but Elliott had a plan to outdo his brother's foxes and hawks. Soon after his twentieth birthday, the younger Roosevelt embarked on a glamorous adventure to India, promising to bring back the tusks of an elephant and the hide of a tiger. Despite falling very sick in the Indian jungle and needing to be carried out on a litter by servants, Elliott succeeded at his goals. A letter he received from his mother telling him of "the pride Theodore had taken" in learning of Elliott's slaughtered beasts likely made all his suffering worthwhile.

Still, in every other case, his brother outclassed him. While Elliott used his inheritance from his father to go to India, Theodore used his to go to Harvard, from which he would graduate magna cum laude. Theodore published a catalogue, *The Summer Birds of the Adirondacks*, but every time Elliott tried to write about his

Indian expedition, he lost interest and went out riding and drinking with his pals instead. In the next decade, Theodore would write many other books, including an account of the War of 1812. He was called a prodigy, and was groomed for politics. Elliott tried joining the Republican Club, but his older brother was such a giant presence there that he eventually stopped going.

When Elliott chose to marry the beautiful Anna Hall, one of New York's most popular socialites, Theodore didn't approve. Anna's love of fun and her disregard for convention matched her perfectly with Elliott, which left Theodore concerned. Elliott wooed Anna outside the normal protocol, sending her gifts even before they were fully acquainted. Writing to thank him for one such present, Anna admitted it was "very wicked" of him, but added, "I must tell you how much pleasure it gave me." They were married soon afterward.

Theodore, at least from his brother's perspective, had grown into sort of a prig, so it was no surprise when he was outraged at Anna's spending spree during the couple's first trip to Europe. Elliott wrote jovially to their sister Bye that his wife had a "dissipated time buying dresses, hats and the Lord knows what . . . I don't know what will become of [my] credit." Neither did the family.

Although the brothers both purchased summer homes on Long Island less than twenty miles from each other, they rarely visited; their circles didn't overlap. Of the gay parties Elliott threw in Hempstead, Theodore did not approve. There was entirely too much wine and song.

Rapprochement was not going to be easy. Still, Elliott made a valiant effort. Writing to his brother from Graz, he presented himself as sedately as he could. He kept his letter light, filled with carefree little details such as Eleanor throwing snowballs with her German friends. His goal seemed to be to convince Theodore that he was serious and sober now, and that his brother should withdraw his controlling hand—not to mention release the monies necessary to continue their life abroad and care for a new baby.

What Elliott did not mention in his missive to his brother were the nights he sank into what Anna called "a melancholy from which nothing moves him." The family scorn, which Elliott argued he had done nothing to deserve, had nonetheless left its mark. Especially now that he was no longer drinking, he often lapsed into deep despair, lamenting his loss of esteem within the family structure. His dark moods terrified his wife, who, quite unbeknownst to him, had taken pen to paper herself.

Some weeks before, Anna had written to Bye, and while she'd rejoiced over "how very much better" Elliott was, she was desperately frightened by how depressed he sometimes became. Anna told Bye that Elliott believed he had "irretrievably disgraced himself" in his family's eyes with his lifestyle, and therefore could never go home again. What he needed, Anna said, was a gesture from Theodore. So would Bye ask Theodore "to write him, praising him for keeping straight and for pulling himself together?" That would make all the difference, Anna believed.

No such letter ever came.

By that point, it was perhaps too late to convince Elliott that the great and accomplished Theodore Roosevelt could ever find anything admirable about him again. So he continued to brood, gripped by some inchoate fear, as Anna told Bye, that "something dreadful" was lurking. They did not know yet of the letter Theodore had received from Catherina Mann's attorneys, but Elliott seemed to sense that doomsday lay around the corner, and he could do nothing except wait for it to arrive.

MANHATTAN

Sometime in the middle of March 1891, a very heavily pregnant young woman and her aged mother walked up the steps of a single-family, two-story wooden structure at 32 East Thirteenth Street. Much of the street was vacant or under construction, but number 32 was bracketed by a saloon on one side (at the corner of University Place) and an inn on the other. The neighborhood had once been stately and aristocratic, but by 1891 it had fallen on hard times: a year later, the proprietors of the inn would be hauled into court on charges of running a "disorderly house." One of its previous residents, however, Dr. Gerardus Wynkoop, was attempting to rebuild and upgrade much of the block.

The little house at 32 East Thirteenth would be Catherina Mann's home for the last few weeks of her pregnancy. The place might not have been elegant, but it was far more private than the Brooklyn tenement where she had been living. The house had likely been secured for her by Wynkoop, since, against all odds, the wealthy society doctor had taken the servant girl on as a patient. Catherina was hardly typical of Wynkoop's clientele: more often he treated the likes of the Cunard and Collier families. Yet, after being sent to see the immigrant chambermaid by Theodore Roosevelt, Wynkoop had begun treating her and, with his connections to the neighborhood, had apparently also found her a place to live.

That alone was a de facto admission by the Roosevelt family that they believed the child Catherina was carrying was one of theirs. There was further evidence of their belief, though: the house chosen for her "lying-in" was owned by a member of the family. Not a very near relation—that would have been taking too much of a risk if the young woman's identity ever leaked—but the family knew it could trust the nearly ninety-year-old Clinton Roosevelt, a second cousin twice removed to Theodore and Elliott, who'd owned a large portion of the block since 1854. Originally the property was part of a sprawling eighteenth-century farm belonging to James (Jacobus) Roosevelt, Theodore's great-grandfather, back in the days when little more than cornfields and pastureland stretched between Union Square and Canal Street. Yet even across such an expanse of generations, family ties remained: just two years earlier, Theodore, Elliott, and Clinton Roosevelt were all in attendance at the gala society wedding of another distant cousin.

Closer family connections could be found nearby as well. As Catherina settled into her new home, a glance out her eastward windows, across University Place, would have revealed the edge of the gardens that once belonged to C. V. S. Roosevelt, the grandfather of Theodore and Elliott. C.V.S. had owned the entire end of the block between Thirteenth and Fourteenth Streets along Broadway. There, Elliott's grandmother had once sung him lullabies in Dutch. Yet as Catherina had sadly come to realize, Elliott wouldn't be making any return visits to the old family neighborhood.

When she'd arrived in the United States six years earlier, at the age of twenty-three, on board the SS *Habsburg*, Catherina (whose friends called her Katie) was an idealistic young woman. According to the stories passed down by her family, she looked forward to a new life in America. Born in Grünstadt, on the northern border of the Palatinate Forest, she'd immigrated with her widowed mother. Katie's brothers had already settled in the new country: Rudolph, a baker, and Bernhard, a barber, were raising large families. Katie hoped to do the same. She wanted, her descendants said, to find "someone to marry, have babies, and live in a house with a garden all her own."

Soon after her arrival, she took a job as a servant to a wealthy family at 29 East Thirty-Eighth Street, accompanying them to their house on Long Island occasionally as well. At the time, Katie had no idea that the Elliott Roosevelts were part of such an important clan. She knew only that they were rich enough to offer her room and board, which was helpful. At first, she spoke little English; she picked up words and phrases by overhearing governesses teaching the little Roosevelt girl, Eleanor, who was fond of Katie. In fact, everyone was very kind to Katie, especially the handsome gentleman of the house. Occasionally, at night, he would come by her room to talk.

Very quickly Katie fell in love with the charming, handsome Elliott Roosevelt. She came to believe that he loved her, too, which was why, one night, she gave herself to him. Elliott made quite the show of professing his devotion to her, giving her gifts and writing her letters. At one point, her family would reveal, they even pledged their troth to each other. Katie was left dazed and besotted. "Katie Mann was the victim of a mock marriage," her granddaughter would say years later, "an immigrant girl who was confused and [who] believed the drunken Elliott Roosevelt when he 'married' her." Elliott called Katie his "spiritual wife."

Then, apparently, his actual wife discovered their rendezvous, because all at once the family packed up, closed the house, and sailed off for Europe. Not only was Katie out of a job and bereft of her lover, but a short time later, she discovered she was pregnant. From Bad Reichenhall, Germany, she received a photo in the mail of little Eleanor, and most likely, according to her family, she tried replying to the letter. Yet Elliott was constantly moving, so no word ever reached him of her condition. Living in a small flat in Brooklyn with her mother, Katie took in laundry, barely making the rent. She felt desperate.

For as long as she could, she held on to the dream that when Elliott learned of her predicament, he'd come to her aid. She held on to the letters he had written to her expressing his devotion, and around her neck she wore a locket that he had given her, containing his picture. According to her family, Katie hung on to the belief that if Elliott knew she was pregnant, he'd leave his wife and be with her. Eventually, though, that belief faded.

What a naïve child she'd been, she came to realize by March 1891. When Elliott had made his protestations of love, Katie had disregarded the smell of alcohol on his breath. She'd believed what she wanted to believe. Now she saw the truth. Not one word had come from him since her lawyers contacted his family. No longer could she deny that he had deceived her. The man she loved had used her and discarded her.

Still, would he really abandon his child? Katie thought not. She remained hopeful that Elliott would take care of her and their baby.

In moving her to Thirteenth Street, Dr. Wynkoop promised her a safe and sterile delivery. To such an offer, Katie's lawyers hadn't objected; in fact, according to her family, they thought it was the least the Roosevelts could do, and they expected them to do much more. Ten thousand dollars was the amount Howe and Hummel were demanding. Raising a child as a single parent was going to be extraordinarily difficult on a laundrywoman's wages, after all. Besides, the child was a Roosevelt: shouldn't that be enough to entitle him or her to a comfortable life? Katie's lawyers believed she had a solid case.

Howe and Hummel had rather shady reputations as defenders of prostitutes and striking workers, but usually they had their clients' best interests at heart. Rarely did they represent hardened criminals or con artists. Underneath their flamboyance and silver tongues lay a real sense of honor. Judge Charles Van Brunt said that he'd rather have Howe's word on something than a sworn affidavit, as Howe was a master at using every technicality he could find to weasel around the law, but his own word was sacrosanct. "Howe was the soul of honor," Van Brunt said, "if you put him upon his honor." Howe and Hummel promised that the Roosevelts would do right by Katie.

During that cold and rainy March of 1891, Katie and her mother settled into the house on Thirteenth Street. Although Katie was by now proficient in English, her mother, Elisabeth Köhler Mann, still spoke mostly German, and was becoming very frail. Katie, her youngest, was born when Elisabeth was past forty, and now the old woman moved slowly, suffering from arthritis and heart trouble. A tattered Lutheran prayer book, her family would remember, was usually in the pocket of her dress.

On the morning of March 11, after rain for four days straight, the sun finally broke through the clouds. The temperature edged past fifty degrees, the warmest it had been all month. Inside 32 East Thirteenth Street, Katie delivered a healthy baby boy. She named him Elliott Roosevelt Mann.

Yet when Dr. Wynkoop filled out the birth certificate the next day, he did not dare write the boy's name. All he reported was a male child born to Katie Mann; in the blank reserved for the father's name, he scrawled just two letters: "O.W." *Out of wedlock*. That, Wynkoop hoped, would keep the child forever consigned to anonymity.

GRAZ, AUSTRIA

Nearly four thousand miles across the ocean, a little girl had no idea that she had a newborn baby brother. All that six-year-old Eleanor Roosevelt knew was that she had one brother and another on the way, or maybe it would be a sister. Her mother was seven months pregnant and, cooped up in their little house, often tired and crabby. Now, in the early spring of 1891, Auntie Bye had come to stay with them, and things were a little better, because Auntie Bye was never crabby. Still, the girl wished that her father hadn't gone away.

Her mother had never been very tender with Eleanor. Anna Hall Roosevelt always seemed resentful of the child, disappointed in her somehow. Maybe it was because her daughter wasn't as pretty as the other girls in the Hall family, all of whom were renowned for their beauty and grace. Eleanor, in contrast, was lanky and awkward, with a weak chin and an overbite. Her eyes, however, cerulean blue and full of soul, enchanted her father. Elliott discerned possibilities in Eleanor that everyone else seemed to miss. He looked upon her "shortcomings with a much more forgiving eye," Eleanor would remember. He gave her "warmth and devotion," she said, and "some badly needed reassurance."

Elliott meant the world to little Eleanor. A few years later, she'd pen a third-person description of their relationship. "I knew a child once who adored her father. She was an ugly little thing, keenly conscious of her deficiencies, and her father [was] the only person who really cared for her." No wonder she was so sad he'd gone away.

Until now, they'd been having a magical time in Europe. In Venice, her father took her out in a gondola, singing to her as they wound through the canals. She was his "Little Nell," which pleased her very much, since "Nell" had been her father's nickname, too. At the top of Mount Vesuvius, they tossed in pennies. Along the Lido, on the mighty Adriatic Sea, they enjoyed "watching the gray surf and catching funny little crabs." Wandering across the Continent with her father had been heaven for Eleanor.

In all that time, only once would she remember his ever being cross with her. They were traveling by donkey over country roads, led by guides, when Eleanor suddenly balked at descending a steep cliff. "I never knew you were a coward," her father snapped, and went off on his own. His sharp words stung, but from them, Eleanor took a lesson: if she were to get ahead in the world, she would need to conquer her fears. That would be difficult for a girl who admitted she was "always afraid of something: of the dark, of displeasing people, of failure." Still, she vowed to try.

Now that her father had gone away, Eleanor was expected to be brave and strong. If she cried, she would upset Mother, and

Mother must never be made upset, given her nerves. So Eleanor spent her days as quietly and dutifully as possible. In the morning, she had a French governess; and in the afternoon, Auntie Bye read to her—that was, if Auntie Bye wasn't at the hospital with Father.

Just why her father had gone to a hospital Eleanor had no clue. Of the troubles that surrounded her, she had only "a strange and garbled idea," gleaned from snippets of whispered conversations among the adults. One day, they'd all been happy, heading off to Paris to meet Auntie Bye. Then, when they got back to Graz, Father had disappeared.

How Eleanor worried about her father. A few years earlier, he broke his leg performing in a charity circus, and his pain greatly upset the little girl. Watching him "hobbling out on crutches," Eleanor "dissolved in tears," sobbing her heart out "for hours." The only way she could make sense of her father's current troubles was to believe that they came from lingering effects from that "terrible ordeal." Eleanor had no idea of the truth.

Up in the hills above the village of Graz, though, Elliott Roosevelt, confined to a sanitarium, had faced the facts all too clearly. Soon after his sister Bye arrived, ostensibly to join them on holiday, Elliott realized the true nature of her visit. Their brother, Theodore, wanted Elliott committed, and Bye had come to do his dirty work. With the birth of Katie Mann's child, the family seemed spurred to action, fearful of the scandal that might erupt at any moment.

At first, Elliott denied that the child was his, and vehemently refused Theodore's plea to make some kind of settlement on Katie. Weary of his brother telling him how to spend his money, Elliott insisted that he wanted nothing to do with his former mistress. Theodore countered that if it were just the two of them, he "should advise fighting her as a pure blackmailer." Yet this was more than just the complaint of one woman against one man, Theodore argued. "It would create a great scandal," he said, "and much would be dragged out that we are very desirous of keeping from the public." He framed his argument as being protective of Elliott's reputation: "You were very sick, and for hours at a time were out of your head." Elliott, however, was undoubtedly savvy enough to know whose reputation his brother was most concerned about.

He couldn't deny the truth of the child's paternity for long, however. Perhaps he felt some guilt; perhaps the warm feelings he'd had toward Katie, the feelings that had prompted him to send her the photo of Eleanor from Bad Reichenhall, resurfaced. No matter what caused his change of heart, Elliott eventually consented to pay Katie some money. He didn't have the ten thousand her lawyers were asking for, but he agreed that she deserved something. He wrote Theodore and gave him permission to negotiate on his behalf.

That was the first step in repairing the fissure that had split the family. Still, Elliott knew if he really wanted to win back Theodore's trust, there was one more thing he had to do. He needed to go away.

Until now, he'd resisted the idea. He wasn't drinking, after all, and Anna was standing by him, regardless of Katie Mann's story, and opposing any efforts to send her husband away. Even Bye had written to Theodore's wife, Edith, that Elliott had "kept perfectly straight." It didn't matter. He needed to go. Elliott came to the realization that his family (or at least his brother) would not be satisfied until he paid some sort of penance for what had happened.

So Elliott had agreed to enter the sanitarium at Graz of his own accord. His commitment would last three months. That was plenty of time, he believed, to rest and heal. Writing from New York, Dr. Lusk concurred. Would Theodore?

Elliott understood the threat he posed to his brother. He was as familiar with Theodore's ambitions as anyone. They'd been in competition with each other for a very long time. So their struggle had come to this: a spartan room behind a locked door in an Austrian asylum.

Elliott would put in his time, but he deeply resented having to do so. From the evidence of his letters and his behavior from this point forward, it is clear that he never overcame his resentment at being forced to agree to this confinement. He accepted its necessity in order to perform his penance and appease his brother and, should the current troubles with Katie Mann become public, to give the family some cover for having taken control of the situation. But Elliott's bitterness only deepened.

Never again would he come out on top. Never again would he experience the sort of victory over his brother that he'd scored that one glorious day three years earlier on the polo field on Long Island. That day remained vivid in the minds of everyone who was there. Meadow Brook, Elliott's club, had taken on Oyster Bay, where Theodore held court, for the annual Challenge Cup. Hundreds had gathered to see the Roosevelt brothers go head to head.

To the cheers of the crowd, Elliott and Theodore mounted their ponies, the sun catching the similar auburn highlights in their hair. The umpire tossed out the ball, and in the blink of an eye, both teams were off, charging down the field, the riders holding the reins in their left hands and gripping their long wooden mallets in their right. When the ball came toward Elliott, Theodore charged, but Elliott was too skilled a player to succumb to such a stunt. He easily maneuvered his pony out of his brother's way, hit the ball, and galloped toward the goal. Then Theodore was at his heels again.

Behind the fence, their sister Corinne kept watch. "Theodore rushed after Elliott at terrific speed as he took the ball downfield," she'd write to Bye, providing an eyewitness account. "There was a thump of horseflesh as brother tried to ride brother out. Suddenly—no one saw how—Theodore was thrown."

Sprawled out on the grass, he was "perfectly limp and senseless," as he'd later admit with some embarrassment. The game was halted. Elliott dismounted and stood over his fallen brother, as Edith gathered her skirts and came running out onto the field, distraught. Theodore's pulse was taken.

He was alive but unconscious. Carried into the clubhouse, he awoke some minutes later but remained dazed for an hour. Insisting he was fine, Theodore staggered back home. Still, his "infernal tumble," as he'd call it, had worked its "mischief." Only a few on the field that day knew that Edith was pregnant. A week later, she suffered a miscarriage.

If Elliott ever suspected a connection between the two events—

that Edith's terror over Theodore's injury had caused her to lose the baby—he never left any record of it. Yet perhaps he remembered that day now, as he brooded in his somber little room in the hills above Graz.

WASHINGTON, DC

Easter Sunday morning, March 29, dawned bright and warm in the nation's capital, the sun seeming to burn away the last remnants of a long, angry winter. Inside the small town house at 1820 Jefferson Place, the two eldest Roosevelt children, Alice and Ted Junior, were spending an "ecstatic half hour" discovering "the numerous eggs and small toys laid by the Easter Bunny in divers corners of the library and parlor." With obvious pleasure, their parents watched from the sidelines, applauding as each egg was lifted from its hiding place. Once all the treasures had been deposited into their Easter baskets, Alice and Ted scampered upstairs, while their father, adjusting his pince-nez, sat down at his writing desk. It was time to check in with Bye.

In giving his sister the latest news from the capital, Theodore reported that he and Edith had recently enjoyed "a very pleasant dinner" with John Hay, one of the grand old men of the Grand Old Party. Hay's career dated back to President Lincoln; now he was one of Washington's premier kingmakers, possessing the money and the influence to advance people's careers. Theodore, naturally, made sure to pay homage. Reading of her brother's dinner with Hay would have reassured Bye that Theodore's political ambitions were still moving forward—but only if they took care of Elliott.

Nearly two months earlier, Theodore had sent his trusted sister to Europe with the goal of institutionalizing their brother. Elliott, Theodore had declared, was either "insane and should be confined, or else not insane and therefore acting with vicious and criminal selfishness." If the wise, shrewd Bye couldn't get Elliott committed, no one could. "My dearest sister," Theodore wrote to her just before she sailed, "what a terrible trial you have to go through. But I will not speak more of this, for it has to be done."

And now it was. Bye wrote triumphantly from Graz claiming that her mission was a success. Elliott had committed himself.

Yet still Theodore wasn't satisfied. Three months in an asylum, he told Bye, was not enough—"useless as far as a permanent improvement goes." Elliott, he insisted, needed to be put away for a number of *years*.

No matter how sanely Elliott spoke or acted, Theodore could not be shaken in his belief that his brother was clearly out of his mind—or else he would never have fathered that child with that chambermaid. While much of Theodore's campaign against Elliott seemed driven by fear of potential political scandal, another part emerged from his unsparing sense of personal morality; he was deeply offended by the whole affair. Elliott, to his mind, was "evidently a maniac morally no less than mentally," as he would describe their brother to Bye.

Elliott's immorality, however, did not excuse the behavior of Katie Mann. More than a decade later, Theodore would write in his autobiography, "Public opinion and the law should combine to hunt down the 'flagrant man swine' who himself hunts down poor or silly or unprotected girls. But we must not, in foolish sentimentality, excuse the girl from her duty to keep herself pure."

Katie, in Theodore's view, was impure, and therefore just as guilty—perhaps even more so for demanding money to keep quiet. Theodore knew that those shysters Howe and Hummel weren't going to back down in their request for ten thousand dollars. Since Elliott was far too deep in debt to pay such an amount and Theodore wasn't willing to part with the money himself, he began inquiring of his attorneys about other ways of dealing with Katie Mann. Bye suggested they speak with her lawyer, a man named Frank Weeks, a skilled barrister trusted by some of the most prominent families in New York.

As for Elliott, now that the child was born, there was only one option, Theodore declared. Their brother needed to be committed for a long period, and Anna needed to divorce him. There could be no further argument about it, Theodore told Bye. Anna had "*no right*," he decreed, underlining the words in his letter to Bye, "to live with [Elliott] henceforth."

No longer was it enough simply to lock Elliott away. Now his wife and children had to be permanently taken away from him as well. It didn't matter that the family was happy, or that no one was complaining of their situation. Elliott had made their lives improper, and Theodore would not stand for it.

"I regard it as little short of criminal for Anna to continue to live with him and bear his children," he wrote to Bye. "She ought not to have any more children, and those she has should be brought up away from him. He has no claim on them." He wrote these words about his brother with his own children, Alice, Ted Junior, and baby Kermit, secure in their rooms upstairs. It was the cruelest fate one father could wish on another.

Yet Elliott had brought this on himself, Theodore believed. Scandal was unavoidable now, he told Bye. The only course left to them was to tend to appearances. If Elliott were locked away and his wife and children removed from him, then the actions of the family would be adjudged decent and appropriate to the situation. "If the worst comes to the worst," Theodore wrote, "next fall let him come back and we will put him in an asylum here." They could easily get a court order in New York, Theodore believed, so long as Anna agreed to leave his brother.

Bye had just one objective now, Theodore charged: as soon as Anna gave birth, Bye was to whisk mother and children straight back to America. Abandon Elliott in the asylum; he no longer mattered. "Elliott is only secondary," Theodore wrote to Bye. The safety of Anna and the children, he wrote high-mindedly, should now be their only concern—except for Theodore's career, of course, though that hardly needed to be said.

MANHATTAN

The lawyer who came to see Katie Mann in May 1891 was tall and mostly bald, with a long, droopy moustache. He rarely smiled, because when he did, he revealed many gaps amid rotten, uneven teeth.

He introduced himself as Frank Weeks and told Katie he'd come in response to a letter that her attorneys, Howe and Hummel, had

sent to the Roosevelt family. The letter described how her relationship with Elliott had come to be and how it was carried out,
and revealed particulars that only someone with an intimate understanding of the man and his family would have known. When
he read the letter, Theodore had hit the roof, vowing never to
yield "a houndsbreadth to a case of simple blackmail," but Katie
knew too much for him to dismiss her out of hand. Accordingly,
on Bye's suggestion, he'd turned to Frank Weeks to make this
vexing woman go away.

Katie let the lawyer inside to hear him out. Weeks assured her
that he was not there on behalf of the Roosevelts, despite the fact
that his cousins (who spelled their name "Weekes") did, on occasion, represent Douglas Robinson, the husband of Corinne Roosevelt. The only reason he'd come, he told Katie, was because he
believed he could settle all this unpleasantness much more quickly
than Howe and Hummel, who seemed determined to go to trial.
Did Katie really want her son to grow up against the background
of salacious headlines?

No, she did not, Katie replied, as her family would tell the
story. So she listened to what Weeks had to say.

In a letter to Bye dated May 10, 1891, Theodore revealed that he
was behind Weeks's visit to Katie. "I shall write you as soon as I
get Weeks' report," he promised his sister. Douglas Robinson, he
added, would "put a stop" to the troublesome Howe and Hummel.
Just how Douglas would manage that wasn't clear, but Weeks's
call on Katie, it would seem, was an integral part of the process.
The plan appeared to be to bring everybody under the central
control of the Roosevelt family. Weeks's cousins Harry and Frederic Weekes were not just Douglas's lawyers. They were also representing Elliott in the paternity case, though Weeks likely didn't
mention that detail to Katie.

From his letters, it was clear that Theodore felt he could trust
Frank Weeks. The Weeks family was an old and respected one;
a branch had a house in Oyster Bay, not far from Theodore's
summer house. They were, in other words, his people, unlike the
immigrant, working-class Katie Mann.

Frank Weeks certainly came with the highest recommenda-
tions. Despite the droopy moustache and bad teeth, the lawyer
was quite charismatic. Many of New York's most prestigious families swore by his brilliance. At the moment, Weeks was managing the estates and trust funds of John Jacob Astor Bristed, Mrs.
Nicholas Fish, Countess Isabel von Linden, and many illustrious
others. He had an uncanny knack for investing their trust funds
and making their investments grow by leaps and bounds.

Clearly, that day he visited Katie so soon after her son's birth,
Weeks worked his charms on her. He made the case that he could
avoid the circus sideshow that Howe and Hummel would cause in
the courtroom. This, according to Katie's family, proved the deciding factor for the young mother. She agreed to fire her lawyers
and switch over to Weeks. That meant that members of the same
family, all of them allies of the Roosevelts, would now represent
both plaintiff and defendant in the case. The goal of control had
been achieved.

Katie wasn't entirely swayed, however. She did *not* promise
never to go to trial. She still had Elliott's letters and his locket at
her disposal. She also had the testimony of other servants, who'd
"chaffed her about Elliott's being devoted to her, and asked her
once if they had not heard him in her room." If she did not get
support for her son, Katie said, she would use whatever means she
had to get it.

When Weeks reported back to Theodore, he told him he
thought three or four thousand dollars might be enough to keep
Katie quiet, but he couldn't be sure. After all, he warned, if
they had to settle this in a courtroom, they were sunk, as juries
tended to side with the woman in these cases. Moreover, Theodore knew that Elliott on the stand would be an unmitigated
disaster. A cross-examination would reveal that he was "apt to
get drunk, or to be under the influence of opiates, or to go out
of his head and become irresponsible," as Theodore wrote Bye.
"It would tell heavily against him"—and against Theodore's political ambitions. Better to just pay the woman, he decided, and
pray she went away.

NEUILLY, FRANCE

Postmarked WASHINGTON, the envelope was sure to raise Elliott's suspicions if he saw it. So when it arrived one day in late May at the little house Anna had leased for them outside Paris, Bye made sure to open it when no one was watching. Now that Elliott was home from the asylum, she had to be careful. Her brother's distrustful eyes followed every move she made. He was convinced that his family hadn't been mollified by his three-month exile and that they were continuing to plot against him.

He was right.

To throw Elliott off the scent, Theodore had taken to writing two letters, the first one chatty and innocuous, the second, tucked behind the first, containing his latest directives. This way, when Elliott asked to read what Theodore had written, which he did often, Bye could hand him the first letter and smile without any worry as he read it. If Theodore mentioned Elliott at all in his cover letters, his tone was offhand and casual.

His private letters, however, revealed a far different frame of mind. Elliott's three months in the asylum, Theodore believed, were woefully inadequate. He was still determined to break up his younger brother's family. "Even if Elliott does not drink," Theodore wrote to Bye, "he is sure now and then to have some attacks. A dozen years of his life leave effects which can not be gotten rid of in any short time." Elliott, he declared, must "live alone and in gloom unless he can learn to stand by himself."

Not surprisingly, Elliott refused to accept such a bleak decree. Whenever Bye raised concerns that the family still had about his welfare, he would produce a doctor's statement declaring that he was sane and could not "be shut up against his will." The statement infuriated Theodore, who dismissed the Austrian doctor as he had earlier dismissed Lusk: as a fool. "If we could get Elliott back on this side," he mused to Bye, "we could shut him up at once without the slightest difficulty. Then we could have a hold on him at last."

That his family was preparing another assault wasn't lost on Elliott. Weary and resentful of their interference, he was increasingly irritable and quick-tempered. On the journey back to Paris from Graz, he'd been impatient with how often they had to stop and rest, given Anna's pregnancy. Bye, of course, cited his boorishness as yet more evidence of madness. How could a sane man, she wrote to Theodore, treat his wife so inconsiderately?

Once settled in Neuilly, Elliott decided to stake his claim as master of the house. He ruled there, he announced, not Theodore, and if he wanted to drink in his own home, he would. No doubt he was aware that, late at night, in the privacy of her room, Bye was conveying all this in her letters to their brother. That only made Elliott angrier, especially when he caught Bye in whispered conferences with Anna. He demanded to know if his sister and brother would now turn his wife against him. At times, he raged: if Anna left him, he'd cut her off without a cent. On other occasions, he became despondent, vowing to kill himself if he ever lost Anna and the children. For Bye, Elliott's mood swings were still more proof that he needed to be committed. She seemed to have no awareness that she and Theodore, through their scheming, might have been making the situation worse.

Their only hope, Theodore concluded, was to get Elliott home. "Once here," he told Bye, "I'll guarantee to see that he is shut up."

In the meantime, they had Katie Mann to deal with. Theodore had written to Elliott that, according to Weeks, three or four thousand dollars would get "a quitclaim" from her, meaning she would ask for nothing more and would disappear. She would also be required, Theodore said, to sign a paper admitting "on her own plea she must have been a willing, or even inviting, party." He lamented how she had them over a barrel: "She has chosen her time with great skill."

Elliott, consumed with self-doubt, could make no decision. Instead, he flailed about the house and, at least once, gave in to his cravings and got drunk. Increasingly he bickered with Anna, who found her loyalty to him wavering, worn down as she was by Bye and the ongoing drama of Katie Mann.

The only consolation left to Elliott, therefore, was his darling little Eleanor, in whose eyes he could do no wrong. Yet even Eleanor was now largely denied him. As tensions in the house intensified, Anna and Bye had deemed it wise to send the six-year-old off to school at a nearby Roman Catholic convent, ostensibly so she could learn French. Yet even at such a young age, Eleanor understood it was mostly to keep her "out of the way."

The first day of school arrived. Dressed somberly, Eleanor was led out to the carriage. Her mother accompanied her for the short ride through the French countryside. All the way there, Anna seemed pensive. At last she turned to Eleanor and admitted she was worried about their future, a frightening thing for a little girl to hear, especially on her first day of school. When they pulled up in front of the convent's gate, Anna gave her daughter a mournful look. "You have no looks," she lamented, "so see to it that you have manners." With that, she sent Eleanor out of the carriage and into a gaggle of black-robed nuns who spoke a language the little girl didn't understand.

Incense permeated the old stone structure. The muffled sounds of prayer left Eleanor bewildered. "Keenly conscious" of being an outsider, the child was miserable. Watching as her classmates knelt around a shrine to the Virgin Mary, Eleanor "longed to be allowed to join them," but as a Protestant, she was kept apart. She had never felt more alone.

One day, when a little girl caused a stir by accidentally swallowing a penny, bringing all the nuns fluttering in concern to her side, Eleanor, craving the same sort of attention, announced that she had swallowed one herself. Her lie was quickly discerned, however, and her mother was sent for. All the way home in the carriage, Anna scolded her. Yet what her mother did not understand, Eleanor would say later, was that sometimes a lie grows out of fear.

Back home, Elliott was just as frightened, but he was also angry. He'd had enough of spying eyes and cold shoulders. One day, he lost his temper over something inconsequential, and Anna began to cry. That was just the opportunity Bye needed. Taking Anna aside, she relayed Theodore's latest admonition. Stressing that he chose his words "with scientific exactness," Theodore said it was "both maudlin and criminal" for Anna to continue living with Elliott, "false to her duty and to her children." Even more, it was "shamefully immoral." Broken at last, Anna agreed that Elliott needed to go, and that she would sign whatever papers were needed to commit him.

Bereft of his last ally, Elliott capitulated. He accepted another short-term stay at a sanitarium, this one at Suresnes, about three miles away, on the other side of the Seine. While that was not going to be enough to satisfy Theodore, for the moment it was the best Bye could accomplish. No announcement was made to his children that Elliott would be leaving again. One day, Eleanor returned home from school and simply found him gone. His absence was wrenching. "He was the only person," she said, "who did not treat me as a criminal."

Exultant, Bye wrote to Theodore that she, Anna, and the children were now free to return to New York as soon as the baby was born. If Elliott followed, which seemed likely, then Theodore could arrange for someone to nab him at the pier. Frank Weeks was certain they could get a judge's order to commit him. For a brief moment, Bye and Theodore thought they had won.

Then, just as Anna went into labor, things changed. She still loved Elliott, Anna declared, and wanted him with her when their baby was born. A message was sent to Suresnes, and a doting, contrite Elliott hurried to his wife's side for the birth, on June 28, of their son Hall, their second and his third. Flush with renewed confidence, Elliott told Bye that no matter what she and Theodore planned next, he would never again leave his family's side. Bye was terribly upset, but for little Eleanor, there was nothing but joy.

MANHATTAN

The offices of DeForest and Weeks were located in the Equitable Life Assurance Building at 120 Broadway, a nine-story structure between Cedar and Pine Streets. On the hot, muggy afternoon of July 7, Theodore, having made the trip up from Washington, met with Frank Weeks and his cousin Harry Weekes. He was there to put an end, at long last, to their troubles with Katie Mann.

Harry Weekes, as Elliott's attorney, expressed some discomfort at being present, since he knew that, once the Mann case was settled, considerable conflict would remain between the two Roosevelt brothers. Frank Weeks, despite nominally being Katie's attorney, had no such qualms over a conflict of interest.

Enormous metal fans rattled in the windows as the temperature outside approached eighty degrees. Theodore was feeling just as hot-headed. Events in Paris were quickly spinning out of control, and soon, he feared, everything would be lost. How foolish Anna had been to allow Elliott to return to her side when the baby was born. In Theodore's mind, his brother was "simply a selfish, brutal and vicious criminal," and needed to be treated as such. Making matters worse was the fact that other members of the family were not as convinced as he and Bye that Elliott needed to be institutionalized. Corinne was ambivalent, and Uncle Jimmie Gracie, their mother's sister's husband and the closest the family had to a patriarch, was absolutely furious with Theodore's efforts to commit Elliott. Still, none of their opinions deterred Theodore in his plans.

Writing to Bye, he warned her to be wary lest Elliott try to kidnap the children. Everything had to be done carefully to get them and Anna home, and then, if need be, he and Bye should be prepared to testify against their brother in divorce court. "Let Elliott know that the Katie Mann affair gives us a complete hold over him if Anna chooses to use it," Theodore warned.

Still, Elliott refused to be intimidated, and his obstinacy pushed his brother into a purple rage. Theodore asked the attorneys what could be done.

Frank Weeks thought it was possible that Elliott could be declared "judicially insane" even without being physically present in New York. Harry Weekes expressed his doubts, and his continued discomfort at the direction of the conversation, but Theodore wasn't listening to him. He was, instead, heartened by Frank Weeks's confidence that he could "almost certainly shut Elliott up and have him adjudged incapable of taking care of his property." That was the sort of talk he liked. More and more, he trusted Frank Weeks. The lie that Weeks was representing Katie

Mann's best interests was made plain that day in the Equitable Building.

Theodore apparently hoped there might still be a way out of paying Katie any money. He'd asked a police detective to pay a call on the young mother, as one letter to Bye would reveal. By now, Katie had returned to Brooklyn with her baby, doing her best to support him on her meager earnings. No doubt she was surprised when Detective William Frank Cosgrove appeared at her door.

Cosgrove was a local celebrity of sorts, the apprehender of famous murderers and embezzlers, and now here he was, at the tiny flat of Katie Mann on Park Avenue in Brooklyn. "He went over to Brooklyn believing the case one of mere blackmail," Theodore reported to Bye, but one glance at the nearly four-month-old baby in Katie's arms changed the detective's mind. "He came back convinced from the likeness that K.M.'s story is true," Theodore wrote. It was Cosgrove's "business," Theodore added, "to be an expert on likenesses."

So this was their lot, then. They would have to find a way to take care of Katie and then to take care of Elliott—to make them both go away. Frank Weeks was promising to do the former, but Theodore, increasingly impressed with the attorney, thought perhaps that Weeks was capable of helping with the latter as well. Until now, he'd assumed that one of the usual family lawyers, Joseph Choate, a Republican Party loyalist and an old friend of Theodore's father, would lead the insanity suit against Elliott. Now Theodore wrote to Bye that he didn't think Choate was "at all the right man." The right man was sitting across from him at the Equitable Building. Frank Weeks could be the answer to all their problems.

What Theodore had no way of knowing—what no one could possibly have known at this point—was that Frank Weeks was a full-fledged hustler who'd been profiting off fraudulent investment schemes for the past ten years. All that money he'd supposedly made for his rich clients by investing their trust funds was, in fact, no longer in their accounts—except on paper. Instead, it was being used by Weeks to subsidize land speculation in the Midwest, and to purchase two yachts, the *Iola* and the *Montauk* ("the fastest schooner of her size afloat"), and an elaborate home in Cold Spring, Long Island, not far from Theodore's place, along with all the "equipages and horses necessary to an establishment of the kind," as one newspaper account would describe it.

What drove Frank Weeks, who hailed from the "poor" side of the Weekes family, wasn't money or material acquisitions: it was *status*. "His chief aim," one report would say, "was to pose in the social world." Few men had more associations in New York than Weeks. He belonged to the Metropolitan, Century, City, Union, University, St. Anthony's, Democratic, and Player's Clubs, and the New York Bar, the Seawanhaka and Oyster Bay Yacht Clubs, and the Downtown Association. He sat on the boards of the American Museum of Natural History and the Metropolitan Museum of Art. Such enviable, illustrious status had been achieved by deftly draining the estates of some of the most prominent suckers in New York society—to which list Weeks had just added the name of Theodore Roosevelt.

BROOKLYN

A network of clotheslines stretched from the backs of the tenements on Park Avenue across the alley to the backs of the tenements on Floyd Street, in the heart of Brooklyn's German village. An army of washerwomen ran out their clothes every day along these lines, pinning newly laundered shirts and shifts to the threadbare rope and shouting to their counterparts across the way, sharing news of the weather or some juicy neighborhood gossip, nearly always in their guttural native German. Katie Mann and her mother were often among them, and in a little crib, never out of Katie's sight, was baby Elliott.

Katie had every reason to believe things were going to turn out all right for her son. Frank Weeks had assured her that he would get her at least three thousand dollars, possibly four. It was considerably less than the ten thousand Howe and Hummel had promised her, but Weeks had guaranteed she'd get that much or more in the end: he was planning to invest the money and pay her a little at a time, he explained. That way, he said, when Elliott was old enough to go to college, they'd have quite the savings. Katie didn't understand financial matters, but there was no question that Weeks had made a lot of money for people who did. So maybe, despite Elliott's abandonment, things would still be fine for Katie and her child—providing Elliott's brother approved. He, apparently, had the final say.

At long last, Theodore Roosevelt would be coming to get a first-hand look at the child. He was a very important man, Katie was told, working for the president of the United States. People said he might even be president himself one day. None of that intimidated Katie. She had no objection to Roosevelt's visit, family members recalled. In fact, she welcomed it.

Monday, July 13, was an extremely warm day, with a high of ninety-one degrees. In the tenements, it was often even hotter than that. Theodore Roosevelt, accompanied by his brother-in-law Douglas Robinson, walked into Katie's flat. He was a big, barrel-chested man who seemed to take up all the space in the room. For the first time, the commissioner and the chambermaid stood face-to-face. From behind his spectacles, Theodore's beady eyes glared at Katie. So this was the girl who had caused him so much trouble.

Then Katie presented him with his nephew. Evidently Theodore's reaction was much the same as Detective Cosgrove's. He looked at Elliott, took in the shape of his face and his firm little jaw. He made no further objection to paying Katie some money.

Katie had to do something for him in return, though. She needed to give her word that she would make no further claims on the family and that she would never tell anyone who the boy's father was.

Katie replied that she had no desire for a scandal. All she cared about was her son's future.

Weeks would take care of that, Theodore assured her. But from here on in, all communication between them needed to cease. Did he have her word? Katie assured him that he did.

PARIS

Auntie Bye told her that soon they would be going home, that they'd be boarding one of the great ships, like the one that had brought her to Paris, and returning at last to New York. The thought carried no excitement for Eleanor. She didn't like ships. She especially didn't like water. She would be safe, she believed, only if her father were with her, but her father had gone away again.

The little girl's fear of water went back to the night of May 19, 1887, when she was not quite three years old. She was in her father's arms, and her mother, her aunt, and her nurse were at their side. They were standing on the deck of the SS *Britannic*, some 110 miles east of Sandy Hook, New Jersey, and they were being told that their ship was sinking. The ship's whistles had been screeching ever since the sickening thud made by the collision with the SS *Celtic*. From steerage came the screams of children whose limbs had been severed by the prow of the other ship. Pandemonium was raging.

They were being moved from the *Britannic* onto the *Celtic*. Lifeboats were waiting. Peeling Eleanor from his shoulder, her father handed her over to a crewman. At the separation, Eleanor panicked. Her father stepped down into the lifeboat. Holding his hands up in the air, he told the crewman to drop the little girl to him.

Eleanor could see the roiling dark waters far below. She was terrified that she would miss her father's arms and plunge straight into the ocean. She screamed, refusing to let go of the crewman's neck.

Her father spoke gently to her, reassuring her.

The crewman let her go. For a second, Eleanor was in free fall. Dark water rushed up to claim her. Then her father, her savior, caught her. From then on, he would always be the one she loved best in the entire world.

As it turned out, the *Britannic* didn't go down. Both damaged ships made it back to New York safely, where Eleanor's parents simply dusted off their portmanteaux and secured new tickets to

« « «

resume their trip to Europe. As they were about to board their new vessel, though, Eleanor suddenly cried so pathetically that her "gentle and patient" aunt Annie Gracie, who had come to see the family off, took her in her arms and promised to watch over her during her parents' absence. When the whistles blew and the ship bearing Father and Mother steamed out across the harbor, Eleanor was left behind.

"Where is Baby's home now?" the little girl asked Aunt Annie, who assured her that she had a home with her and Uncle Jimmie Gracie. Yet when they took Eleanor out in the carriage toward Long Island Sound, the child became terrified. "Baby does not want to go into the water," Eleanor cried. That fear of water never left her—and now she would have to get on a ship without her father there to protect her.

What Eleanor didn't know was that her uncle Theodore had brought the whole sorry comedy to an end by threatening to come over to Paris himself, and if he came, he warned Bye, "I come to settle the thing once and for all. I come to see that Elliott is either put in an asylum against his will or not, or else to take you, Anna, and the children away, and to turn Elliott loose to shift for himself."

Fear of her brother-in-law finally turned Anna against her husband. She began preparing to return home without him. Not surprisingly, this set Elliott off. Words flew; in his anger, Elliott even asked if baby Hall was really his son. "Elliott's hopeless misconduct and outrageous behavior," as Theodore would call it, resulted in the asylum at Suresnes being called and the men in the white suits arriving. Bye told Theodore that Elliott entered the facility willingly; Elliott, on the other hand, would claim he was "kidnapped."

However things transpired, on August 1, at the port of Le Havre, Bye, Anna, and the children boarded the sparkling new ship *La Touraine*, the fifth-largest steamer in the world, and sailed for home. For the little girl trembling on the deck, watching as France disappeared on the horizon, one fear was likely at the forefront of her mind: if their ship was hit as the other one had been, and they all had to scramble down into lifeboats, her father would not be there to catch her.

MANHATTAN

On the morning of August 18, 1891, the headline on the front page of the *New York World* screamed in big black ink: ELLIOTT ROOSEVELT INSANE. A scandalized city devoured all the details about the glamorous young playboy who had once been a regular name on the society pages. "The unfortunate man now confined in a Paris chateau . . . ," "Excessive indulgence in drink . . . ," "Entertained lavishly, went out in society too frequently . . . ," "The petition is believed to have been instigated by his wife to protect his estate."

While it was true that Anna had given her consent, the instigation, of course, was Theodore's right from the start. He pushed and prodded and cajoled and chastised until what had been a happy ensemble in February was a roiling battleground by June.

With Bye at his side, he had trooped down to the Supreme Court in Lower Manhattan on August 17 and filed the petition against his brother. In this, he was represented by DeForest and Weeks, though, to keep up some pretense of objectivity in the Katie Mann matter, Frank himself did not appear in court, handing over that duty to his nephew Henry DeForest and his cousin Archibald Weekes. Standing before Judge Morgan J. O'Brien, Theodore told his sad family story, testifying about Elliott's unsound mind. "How far this was produced or aggravated by his excessive indulgence in drink and how far by other causes, I am unable to state," he declared, making his point regardless. After Bye stepped up to offer similar testimony, the judge granted "a *writ de lunatico inquirende* to inquire into the lunacy of the said Elliott Roosevelt." A commission of investigators was named to interview the doctors at the Suresnes asylum about the condition of the "alleged lunatic" in their care.

The newspapers ran with the story, gleefully digging up tales of Elliott's escapades. "The fact that Elliott Roosevelt has been drinking to excess has been well known among the inner circle of society and club men in this city for more than two years," the *World* reported. "But little comment was made, partly because of the frequency of such complaints and principally on account of the family." Even worse, for Elliott anyway, was the salt the newspaper rubbed in his wounds: "Unlike his distinguished brother, he has chosen the quieter paths of life, and has neither mingled in politics or dipped into literature."

Yet the family could be thankful for one thing: there was no mention of Katie Mann or the child. Theodore hadn't been able to avoid scandal, but he *had* contained it. For this much, at least, he'd been prepared. "If some frightful scandal arises," he'd written to Bye a couple of months earlier, "it should be widely known that we regarded him as irresponsible, that Anna had left him with the children, and that we stood by Anna."

To Theodore's mind, he'd made the best of a very bad situation. No matter the difficulties his actions now placed upon his brother's wife and children, the situation was far better, he was convinced, than if they'd been permitted to stay with him and remain a family. "Any poverty would be better for the children," he wrote to Bye, "than to be brought up in that degradation of association with Elliott."

For the rest of her life, Eleanor would passionately disagree. Her childhood would be delineated by the theft of her father: a time before and a time after. Leaving him behind in Paris changed everything for her. Nothing was ever the same. Just two years earlier, on her fourth birthday, her parents had thrown her a party, and her father showered her with presents and kisses. She was the apple of his eye, his darling, the happiest of little girls. After the party, a delighted Elliott wrote to Bye that his daughter had gone to bed declaring she "loved everybody and everybody loved her." Never again would Eleanor feel that way.

PART II

EVERYTHING TO FEAR

1893–1894

The path to the sea was overgrown with bayberry and cattail, redolent of a salty low tide. From the reeds, a band of children came parading single file, following their leader, a big man wearing pince-nez and a bathing suit shot through with holes. Shrieking war whoops, the children beat their skinny chests with tiny fists. Wheezy little Ted tried, as usual, to keep to the front of the pack; handsome, thoughtful Kermit sometimes made bird-calls as he marched; and bright-eyed Alice, singing at the top of her lungs, ceded nothing in volume or imagination to the boys. Only the child bringing up the rear, spindly, awkward Eleanor, remained quiet. To those who would remember her from these family "scrambles," as they were called, it seemed as if Eleanor weren't there at all.

Bare feet squished in mud. The children trudged through the quicksand instead of going around it. They marched through the frothy salt chucks heedless of the depth. That was the Way, the Truth, that had been hammered into their heads since they were babes: Always keep to the path. Take no detours. Indulge no delays. Keep your eyes on the prize.

That day in the summer of 1893, their prize was the sea. Mollusk shells and sea lavender were trampled underfoot. Through Fleet's Pond the children sloshed, fiddler crabs scampering sideways into the sea grass. Up ahead, Eleanor's uncle, with an almost febrile energy, called for them to hurry. The tide waits for no man! The white-hot sun reflected off his spectacles.

Nearing the Sound, Cold Spring Harbor, the children began to run. Bare feet slapped against the old wooden pier. One after another, small bodies cannonballed into the sea. Doffing his glasses, Uncle Theodore dove in as well, causing a minor tsunami. The children laughed. Only Eleanor remained on the pier, a tiny bird perched precariously at the edge, her beak pointing down.

She was eight years old, the senior of most of the others already in the water. Watching her was a firing squad of ferocious blue eyes. They were her cousins: first cousins Ted, Kermit, and Alice, and second cousins from farther back on the sprawling Roosevelt family tree. It was a rare visit for Eleanor to Uncle Theodore's house on Long Island for a few days of fun and games.

Despite all the whooping and laughter that went on, it was never entirely clear how much fun some of the children had on these outings. Ted coughed water through his nose when he exerted himself too hard. Kermit sometimes withdrew into melancholic silences. Alice was a coiled snake, keenly aware that she came from a different mother from her brothers'. None of them could quite comprehend their timid cousin Eleanor, who tended to shy away from their games, and who now stared down at them from the pier, seeming bolted to the spot.

Uncle Theodore was growing impatient. He urged Eleanor to jump, but the little girl was afraid. "I never knew you were a coward," her father had said to her once.

Eleanor took a breath and then jumped. In an instant, the world disappeared. All sound ceased, except for the bubbling in her ears. Weightlessly, Eleanor tumbled through the water, the nightmare of the *Britannic* come true. Her father hadn't saved her—her father was gone, taken to a place far, far away from her. Her mother was dead, some said of a broken heart. No one was left to watch over Eleanor.

Suddenly there was light. Eleanor bobbed upward and broke the surface of the water. Sound rushed back in, the laughter of children, the booming voice of her uncle commending her for her bravery. Eleanor tried to suck in a breath but found it wasn't possible. Hands were upon her, pushing her, overwhelming her. Her cousins appeared above her in a blur, the boys laughing, Alice's eyes dancing. They took hold of her. They shoved her back down. Eleanor was helpless. She went under again.

For Ted, the eldest son of Uncle Theodore, the "crown prince" as some called him, dunking Eleanor was what was expected of him, a Roosevelt ritual. Ted himself had been dunked plenty of times. Before he was even able to swim, his father tossed him off the pier. A Roosevelt had to be tough, Ted knew; a Roosevelt couldn't be coddled; a Roosevelt had to learn fast and hard. Ted had survived the experience: like a little frog, he'd swum back to the pier, delighting his father, even if his mother worried about all the coughing he did later, his throat and nostrils burning. Ted was often sick; illness seemed as normal to him as eating or sleeping or learning his spelling. He accepted his colds and fevers and headaches with a forbearance that seemed more mature than his tender years. Ted, everyone agreed, was a smart little boy. He understood that being dunked underwater might not be pleasant, but tradition mattered. Custom was to be respected—and the weakest kid was always dunked.

For Kermit, the second son, dunking Eleanor was simply fun, and when Kermit was in the mood for fun, he went all in. He would throw himself into somersaults and cartwheels; he would ride his scooter at breakneck speed; he would transform a household dust mop into his favorite toy. Better looking than Ted, far more imaginative, Kermit nonetheless could turn very dark. The cartwheels would cease, and he would spiral down into silence and seclusion, refusing all company except his mother's. So when Kermit could have a little fun, he seized the moment—or, in this case, his cousin's hair.

For Alice, dunking Eleanor was something else entirely. Alice had no patience for those who were afraid to stand up for themselves. She and her brothers would laugh at the ugly black knee socks and old-fashioned ankle-high shoes Eleanor's grandmother forced her to wear, and which she was too spineless to refuse. It was this slavish obedience to authority that Alice seemed to loathe about Eleanor, not her fear. Alice understood the fear.

Not so long before, she herself had trembled as her father shouted at her, "Dive, Alicy, dive!" In that moment, her father was nothing more to Alice than "a horrible sea-monster" peering at her, nearsighted without his glasses, his mustache glistening wet in the sunlight. How Alice would cry when her father insisted she dive. The family would joke that after a diving lesson, Alice's tears made a perceptible rise in the tide. Alice cried; she shook her head; she stamped her feet. No one could throw a tantrum quite like Alice Lee Roosevelt. Then, at last, her terror of her father the sea monster overcame her terror of the water, and

Alice, like Eleanor, jumped—not out of duty, not out of pressure or a desire to be obedient, but out of simple fear.

How very different these Roosevelt children were, yet how very much the same.

On another scramble, possibly during that same visit, the children followed their leader out to Cooper's Bluff, a two-hundred-foot sand dune with a sheer drop to the beach. Once again, Eleanor moved at her own pace, occupied by her own thoughts, weighed down by a melancholy everyone noticed. "I was a solemn child," she would admit, "without beauty and painfully shy . . . I seemed like a little old woman entirely lacking in the spontaneous joy and mirth of a child." Certainly that summer of 1893, Eleanor had cause to be solemn: her mother's death the previous winter; the death of Elliott, the elder of her two brothers, the past spring; the isolating household of her grandmother, where she'd been sent to live after her mother's death; and her father's continued exile and separation from her.

Uncle Theodore had tremendous affection for Eleanor: he once hugged her so tightly that he popped the buttons off her dress. His fondness seems to have been brewed from a mix of grief, pity, and possibly (deep down and unacknowledged) guilt. He was clear-eyed enough to know that the girl's unhappiness was due largely to his own actions; had he not broken up her family, she might still have been living with her father, a situation, Eleanor would make plain, she longed for. Still, in Theodore's view, such a scenario would have been far more deleterious to her than her current woes. He believed he'd done what he needed to do—and if he'd had to do it over, he almost certainly would have done exactly the same thing.

Two years since separating his brother from his family, Theodore still smarted over his failure to get him officially committed to an asylum. He'd effectively ended his brother's carousing, of course, and severely limited the scandal he had caused, but getting him locked up had proven utterly impossible. Theodore had faced strong opposition from Uncle Jimmie Gracie, who persuaded Corinne and her husband, Douglas, to oppose Elliott's commitment as well. The doctors hadn't cooperated, either. The initial court-appointed investigators contacted the doctors at Elliott's various sanitariums and actually found him competent. So Theodore tried again, with a different judge in a different court. Still, the second commission came to the exact same conclusion as the first: after discussing his case with his doctors, Elliott was deemed "mentally capable of transacting his own affairs."

Fools, all of them.

So Theodore had ended up doing what he'd threatened to do all along: in January 1892 he sailed to Paris and confronted Elliott himself. He knew he had to tread carefully; as he warned Bye, with the doctors ruling in Elliott's favor, their brother could turn the tables on them and sue them for conspiracy. "He is so sane," Theodore marveled, "and yet so absolutely lacking in moral sense." With his wife gone, Elliott had taken up with a woman, a scandalous divorcée whose name had been in all the papers several years back, a woman whose reputation for drink and carefree living matched his own. It was imperative that they get Elliott back to America before they had another bastard to deal with—and this time from a woman far wiser in the ways of the world than Katie Mann.

Face-to-face with the brother he'd been competing with since childhood, Theodore prevailed. Elliott "surrendered completely," he wrote to Bye, describing his younger brother as "utterly broken, submissive and repentant." Theodore's letter to Bye recounting the episode began with a single word: "Won!" For Theodore, this was one last wrestling match with Elliott, and he'd come out on top.

From here on in, Theodore intended to lay down the law. Elliott was to follow his orders in everything. Even though he was sober and had completed the program at Suresnes, he was ordered to go through another five-week "cure," at the Keeley Center in Illinois. After that, Theodore instructed, Elliott was to remain out of sight for two years; it went without saying that he could not see his children. If, after this probation, he had proven himself, he could resume his place in the family.

To keep Elliott busy and away from civilization, Douglas Robinson hired his brother-in-law to scout and settle a vast tract of land he'd recently purchased in Abingdon, Virginia. For a time, Elliott did quite well in the position; he even managed to repay debts he owed Bye. Then Anna got sick with diphtheria, and died in December 1892. Her death, followed so soon by the death of his eldest son and namesake, little Ellie, in the spring of that year, left Elliott shattered, especially because he was prevented from seeing them. Perhaps not surprisingly, word reached Theodore that his brother had turned to the bottle once again. "He admits that he drank heavily on his last spree," Theodore wrote wearily to Bye. There were also reports that he was seeing that divorcée again. So they were right back to where they'd started, worrying about a scandal involving Elliott.

At least now Elliott's children Eleanor and Hall were under Theodore's control, and his bastard, Elliott Mann, was hopefully gone for good.

They reached the top of Cooper's Bluff. Eleanor, as usual, brought up the rear. Far below, the sea crashed. At high tide, a headlong descent down the sheer side of the bluff inevitably ended up in the water. Indeed, that was Uncle Theodore's mad plan. Instructing the children to link hands, he readied them for a race to the bottom.

Eleanor would remember being "desperately afraid." She wished she were back at the house, where sometimes Uncle Theodore would take them up to his "gun room," on the third floor, and read them stories. How much happier Eleanor would have been there, safely hunkered down in an old leather chair, listening to the exploits of Ivanhoe, rather than here, two hundred feet above the sea and preparing for a terrifying plunge to what seemed like certain death.

The boys, however, were clamoring to go, so they all took a deep breath and ran as fast as they could down the steep incline of sand. Soon one, then two, then more went down, pulling the others down with them, rolling and slipping down the bluff and into the surf. Eleanor, all spindly arms and legs, came tumbling after them. She ended up soaked.

Yet something strange and wonderful occurred during her roll down the bluff. Once she'd picked herself up and shaken the sand out of her hair, she had a revelation. "It was not so bad as I thought," she would later say, "and then we clambered up again." Indeed, the tumble had been (something Eleanor didn't often experience) *fun*. A rare sound bubbled up from her throat as she and the others came sliding back down for a second time: *laughter*. Eleanor, as it turned out, was made of more than just her fear.

BROOKLYN

Thirty miles and a world away to the east, another Roosevelt child grappled with his own set of insecurities. He wasn't afraid of water, or heights, or his father's disapproval: he didn't even know his father. Rather, two-year-old Elliott Roosevelt Mann lived with a more existential fear, absorbed from his mother, who every morning wondered if they'd be tossed out onto the street.

Pans of ice melted quickly in the windowsills, a futile attempt to keep cool in the middle of a hot summer. Everyone had their windows open, the smells of sauerkraut and sausage braiding with the leather and dyes from the shoemaker who lived on the first floor of the building. Katie Mann had hoped that, by now, she and Elliott would be far away from this place, having used the money from the Roosevelts to find themselves a home. She didn't hope for anything elaborate, just a couple of rooms, with enough land for a garden, maybe near a river or a lake, so Elliott, like his Oyster Bay cousins, could take a swim when it was warm.

Yet in two years, Katie hadn't seen a dime. As her family would recall, she made the trek from Brooklyn into Manhattan several times to see Attorney Weeks, and on each visit he promised her that the money was coming. If Katie were only patient, Weeks told her, she would find herself a very rich woman. So she would return to Brooklyn to eke out a living for her son and her mother as best she could.

Her brothers were beginning to worry that Katie had been cheated. If she'd gone to court as Howe and Hummel had been prepared to do, her brothers argued, she would have been well taken care of by now. She would also have been branded a whore, she argued back, and Elliott a bastard. As it was, most of Katie's neighbors thought she was a widow, and they had only sympathy for her little boy. For that reason alone, Katie would never regret not going to trial.

Still, she was worried. At some point that summer, she put on a clean dress, tied up her hair, and rode the sooty elevated train once more into the city. DeForest and Weeks had relocated its offices a couple of blocks east, to 62 William Street, but Katie would have noticed that wasn't the only change. The gold lettering on the door now read DEFOREST BROTHERS. Only the doormat, which still read DEF. & W, gave any hint that Frank Weeks had ever worked there.

Inside the office, Katie was told what all Weeks's clients were being told: He was no longer a member of the firm. He had not been seen or heard from since May.

Franks Weeks's schemes had at last caught up with him. The previous February, an investigation had been started into his management of the Land and River Company of Wisconsin. In May, he resigned as treasurer of the company, sent letters of resignation to all his clubs, and promptly disappeared. Various reports placed him in Canada, the Windward Islands, and Cuba. The court now considered Weeks a fugitive from justice, and had turned his accounts over to an assignee.

"He was quite a borrower of money," the assignee told the press after a review of the books. When Weeks had found it "impossible to secure sufficient accommodation" for his various land management projects, he'd tapped into his wealthy clients' trust funds—and maybe those of some of his not-so-wealthy clients as well. Yet the assignee eventually determined that while Weeks's liabilities were close to one million dollars, he appeared to have enough assets to "meet every one of his obligations." That reassured Katie, at least for the time being.

Still, as more claims piled up, the enormity of Weeks's crimes became apparent. It appeared he had embezzled seventy thousand dollars from the Bristed estate and eighty thousand from the Fish family. In an attempt to get some of that money back, the court had attached several of Weeks's properties. Katie, of course, didn't need seventy or eighty thousand. She just wanted the three or four she had been promised. Were there truly enough assets to cover Weeks's debts?

Then came the news that the American-born countess Isabel von Linden had learned that "none of the securities belonging to her estate could be found." In all, the countess was missing about two hundred thousand dollars. Weeks's assets were quickly being wiped out.

Week after week, Katie made the trip into Manhattan to visit the offices of the DeForest Brothers, but no one seemed able to give her an answer. The young mother grew desperate. If she didn't hear soon, she might have to break the promise she'd made to Theodore Roosevelt. She might be forced to contact the family once again.

OYSTER BAY, LONG ISLAND

The house called Sagamore Hill sat high in the center of a sandy peninsula, bathed in sea air and sunshine. Cold Spring Harbor sparkled off to one side; Oyster Bay slumbered on the other. This was Theodore's castle, his refuge from New York and Washington. Shuttered for much of the cold Long Island winters, the place looked weathered and ancient, despite the fact that it had stood for less than a decade. Sedate in its lines, the house was nonetheless pervaded by a certain unexpected gaiety. A band of mustard-colored wooden shingles rose above the red brick of the first floor, and the trim was painted pink. From the southernmost gable a pair of elk antlers protruded, a touch of whimsy for the children but also a declaration of conquest by the hunter who lived within.

Separating Sagamore Hill from the water was a gnarled grove of fruit trees the children called the Fairy Apple Orchard, over which Alice claimed dominion, charging her brothers and cousins a penny to pass through. Horses, some sleek and fast, others fat and old, chewed hay in the stables. A couple of rat terriers were always racing across the lawn.

The beauty of the place could sometimes overwhelm Theodore. "The violets dotted the ground in great beds, so as to make patches of light blue in the green expanse," he wrote to Bye one fine day. "The dogwood is in full bloom and the orchards are masses of white blossoms."

Inside, the house was just as fragrant, suffused with leather, tobacco, and the carnauba oil used on the mahogany chairs and tables. At night, gas lamps gave the house an amber glow. Presiding over the entrance hall on the first floor were the heads of mounted beasts killed by Theodore on his hunting expeditions out west: wolf, eland, oryx, antelope, buffalo—all staring down with their dull, glassy eyes at whoever entered the house.

Despite its youth, the house was steeped in history. "Sagamore is the offspring of the years as surely as is a reef of coral," Theodore's son Ted would reflect. Each room told "a story in the same fashion as the rings in the trunk of a great tree." Here rested a footstool from Theodore's childhood home on Fourteenth Street; there stood a rosewood desk from Edith's great-aunt. "To understand a family," Ted wrote, "it is necessary to know . . . their house."

At Sagamore, books were everywhere: in the library, in the living room, in the second-floor nursery, in the bedrooms, in the great and mysterious gun room on the third floor—old travelogues of Europe, nature guides, the classics. On cluttered tables, Chinese porcelain vases stood beside bronze statues of lions; and carved ivory ashtrays rested on the arms of Chippendale chairs. On dark paneled walls hung oil paintings of Gothic cathedrals and city streets. From the mantel in the library, a mahogany clock resounded through the house every hour on the hour, Cambridge chimes on eight bells.

Those chimes sometimes went unheard, however, in the cacophony of the place. On any given day during the summer months, there could be up to eighteen children howling through the rooms, wearing Indian headdresses or smuggling rabbits in under their jackets: Theodore's four, his brother Elliott's two, his sister Corinne's four, the others the offspring of his Roosevelt cousins Alfred and Emlen, who also had homes in Oyster Bay. The older children were envied by the younger for their outings with Theodore: Ethel (Theodore's baby) and Hall (Eleanor's brother) were just two years old, so they were kept closer to home, never far from their nannies' skirts. Still, their proving time would come, and soon. Theodore Roosevelt did not believe in coddling children for too long—least of all his eldest son.

Early in the mornings, as the sun peeked above the dunes, Theodore would be up and dressed, rushing about the house and calling for his "bunnies," his name for the children. He enjoyed romping with them, but keeping them physically fit and constantly challenged was a greater motivator for him, the only way to ensure that their bodies kept pace with the development of their minds. "A life of slothful ease," he would say later, in his famous speech about the "strenuous" life, "which springs merely from lack either of desire or of power to strive after great things, is as little worthy of a nation as of an individual." For him, children needed to be "so trained that they shall endeavor not to shirk difficulties, but to overcome them; not to seek ease, but to know how to wrest triumph from toil and risk."

When all the bunnies had gathered, he'd line them up by height. A pity that Ted, one of the oldest, was not also among the tallest. At nearly seven years of age, he was hardly yet the specimen Theodore hoped he would someday become: frail and underweight, the boy was also slightly cross-eyed and had a bit of a stammer. "He wears big spectacles," Theodore wrote to his mother-in-law, "which only make him look more like a brownie than ever." Most of the time, on their walks back from Cooper's Bluff, Ted would tire out and need to ride piggyback on his father. His father's back was, in fact, one of Ted's favorite places. He was small enough that he could crawl up onto Theodore as he sat writing letters at his desk and fall fast asleep on his shoulders, like a cat.

As dear as that was—or as "cunning," as Theodore liked to say—it didn't change the fact that Ted needed toughening up. While Theodore boasted to Bye that his son "plays more vigorously than anyone I ever saw," and likened him to one of P. T. Barnum's "little seals," the child was plagued by headaches, which struck him with the same terrible unpredictability that asthma had once struck his father. Although he was not without sympathy for Ted—during one of the boy's illnesses, he kept an anxious forty-eight-hour vigil at his bedside—Theodore was uncannily reminded of the fits that befell his brother at a young age, compelling their father to send Elliott out West to get him into shape. That was Theodore's response to his son as well: the strenuous life was the only way to proceed, he believed. Ted needed to follow his example and vanquish his Achilles' heel through sheer will and effort. Row it off. Hike it off. Swim it off. Otherwise he might end up soft and dissipated like his uncle Elliott.

"Sickness," Theodore told his brood, "is always a shame and often a crime." For the children, then, shame would always accompany pain, as well as a vague fear of retribution if they complained. They would be criminals, after all, if they let the malady win.

So Theodore put his bunnies through their paces. A whistle blew, and off they went, playing a game they all knew very well: Over, Under, or Through, But Never Around. Across the lawn they marched, right through the Fairy Apple Orchard, keeping to the straight line they had set for themselves. If they came to a tree, they climbed it; if they came to a bog, they swam it; if they came to a fence, they scaled it. *Over, under, or through, but never around.* At the end, when they had circled back home, the children were tired, scratched, muddy, and a little bruised, but for those who had found no fence too high, no bog too deep, there was triumph, made all the sweeter by the clap of Theodore's hand on their backs. For those who had faltered, however, who had committed the sin of Going Around, there was only shame. For all the high spirits that launched them on their treks, there was also, underneath, for all of them, a goodly dose of fear.

Yet this is what made them, Theodore believed. This is what taught the girls perseverance and turned the boys into men. Competition was important for building character: at one point he declared he'd "disinherit" any son who did not participate in competitive sports. "In so strenuous a household," family friend Hermann Hagedorn wrote, "someone was always getting hurt, and learning to take it in stride." That, of course, was precisely the lesson. "Don't let anyone impose on you," Hagedorn would remember Theodore telling his sons. "Don't be quarrelsome, but stand up for your rights. If you've got to fight, fight, and fight hard and well." A coward was the only thing "meaner than a liar."

The previous spring, Theodore had visited the Groton School in Massachusetts, an exclusive college preparatory institution backed by some of the most affluent, influential families in America. Groton was committed to turning out graduates who would pursue the public good, not merely personal enterprise, which fit exactly Theodore's worldview. Life at Groton consisted of cold showers, spartan cubicles, stringent academic expectations, and rigorous physical training, including highly prized competitive sports teams—all of which also conformed to Theodore's ideals. Yet, as he wrote to Bye, he'd need to get them ready: "I'll have to have Ted and Kermit well-trained first, or they will never get in."

Later, Theodore would admit he "pushed" his boys, but always, he said, with the best intentions. He was teaching them, he believed, about such things as stamina and honor. When a neighboring boy threw apples at the younger children, Theodore insisted that Ted go over and fight him, even though the aggressor was bigger and stronger. Staggering back somewhat worse for the wear, Ted had nonetheless learned what was expected of him as the senior son and namesake: no slight to the family could go unchallenged. For a boy like Ted, however, frail and often sickly, playing defender of home and hearth wouldn't always be easy. His father's cousin West Roosevelt commented that even baby Ethel seemed sturdier and less "nervous" than her eldest brother. Still, better to push and prod the boy to overcome that nervousness than allow him to turn into his uncle Elliott.

For all the pressure he faced, Ted did not resent his father. He idolized him. One night, his governess overheard him conjuring up a picture of his father, who had been away from home for a while: "A nice little moustache, and white teeth, and black hair, very short, and a nice smell of cologne, and wears glasses and gray trousers—nice gray trousers, and white feet with bones in them and red slippers, and that's my Papa." Ted could sometimes be spotted emulating his father's speeches, and more than once he articulated his wish to grow a "mufstache" like Papa. When Theodore picked Kermit up in his arms, Ted would sometimes cling to his leg, as if to make sure he wasn't forgotten.

Kermit, like the others, had been thrown off his share of piers into deep water and forced to run sprints, but his position as second son largely spared him from the front lines. Kermit's hide, therefore, didn't grow quite as thick as Ted's; his need to prove himself was never as strong. Slighter in build than his older brother, angelic of face, Kermit seemed at times almost ethereal: "pale and yellow-haired," his sister Ethel would describe him, "dreamy [and] detached." Far more likely to sit daydreaming in a windowsill than to run around and climb trees, Kermit didn't chase after his father the way Ted did. Instead, he'd sit quietly beside his mother, Edith, who was always the boy's preferred company. "Odd and independent," she would describe her son, who became her favorite.

Yet Kermit might actually have been more naturally athletic than Ted: his father noted with pleasure that his younger son was agile enough to scratch his nose with his toes and place the soles of his feet against his cheeks. He was, Theodore declared, a "sturdy little scamp."

Both sons understood that their father's life was the model by which they should live. When they disappointed him, they knew it from a glance, but when they pleased him, they knew that, too. Theodore was not stingy with praise as some other fathers of his class tended to be. When his sons rose to his challenges, he lifted them up on his shoulders and beamed his approval for all to see.

There was no such praise for his eldest daughter. Alice had been too young, at three, to remember much about her brother Ted's birth, but surely she still felt the reverberations from it. A preponderance of female births in recent years had left the extended Roosevelt family feeling "cursed," Edith recalled, so there was much rejoicing at Ted's birth, with one uncle joyriding through the streets, "the dashboard of his wagon decked with goldenrod and an orange ribbon in his whip." With great ceremony, this uncle presented Theodore with a gold piece "because a Dutch boy had come."

No surprise, then, that when Ted had his hair cut that summer to look like a little man, and received his father's gaze of approval for doing so, Alice stepped forward and "announced a strong desire that she, too, might have her hair cut and wear trousers," as Theodore wrote humorously to Bye.

Alice, of course, intended no humor in her remark. If cutting her hair got her father to notice her, to appreciate her, to invest in her the kind of capital he'd invested in Ted, then she would gladly have wielded the scissors herself. She was painfully aware that she stood apart in the family. Edith was not her birth mother, after all, a fact that hung over all of them, even if it was implicitly forbidden for them ever to mention it—except once, and that was a harrowing moment for Alice.

After the death of her mother, Theodore's first wife, of whom he never spoke, Alice was, by necessity, fed by a wet-nurse. One day, Ted overheard that fact being discussed among the adults, and he went running through the house shouting, "Sissy had a sweat nurse!" Alice was mortified, less for the words than for their implication: she'd been exposed as an alien.

To directly acknowledge Alice's difference, however, was prohibited. The fact that she had grandparents the other children did not have, who came from Boston a couple of times a year to take her away for brief holidays, was accepted but never explained. At her maternal grandparents' house, Alice felt privileged: "Everything belonged to me. I would come in and jump up and down on the sofa," something she would never have done in her stepmother's house. Yet even these grandparents never spoke of Alice's mother. Only her Irish governess dared, urging the little girl in whispers to pray for her mother's soul in heaven.

If Edith ever resented raising another woman's child, she never made that apparent: she did her duty by her stepdaughter, as she recorded regularly in her diary. She took Alice to buy Valentines, bought her new shoes, accompanied her to riding lessons. When Alice needed a brace for her legs, Edith learned how to fasten the contraption, how to oil it, and how to remove it. Alice called Edith "Mother" just as Ted, Kermit, and Ethel did. Still, there was distance. Alice found her stepmother "withdrawn, rather parched," as she'd later recall. "She had almost a gift for making her own people uncomfortable."

One time, Alice overheard Edith discussing how she and Theodore had been childhood sweethearts. They planned to be married, Edith said. Only after they quarreled did Theodore marry his first wife. In other words, Alice realized, her father had married her mother only on the rebound.

On another occasion, Edith let slip, this time in front of little Ted, that "it was just as well that [Alice's] mother had died" because Theodore "would have been bored to death staying married to her." Impishly, Ted carried the tale back to Alice; it cut her deeply. The insinuation was clear: her mother had been a flighty socialite whom her father never really loved.

Yet, in some ways, the dead woman was no more Alice's mother than Edith was. The only mother Alice had ever known was Auntie Bye—"the only one I really cared about," she'd later admit. Until the age of three, Alice lived with Bye as her aunt's "blue-eyed darling." For three happy years she didn't need to compete with a household of other children for affection and attention. Then her halcyon childhood came to an end, when she was claimed by a proficient but distant stepmother and a father preoccupied with sons and indifferent to daughters. She came to understand that if she were ever to win her father's attention away from her brothers, she was going to have to fight.

She had limited means to do so of course, but she did her best. One night, she and Ted had been playing with little toy monitor warships that Theodore had made for them out of pasteboard. Alice crowed in triumph when she caused Ted's monitor to sink. Content that she had won, she trooped off to bed, but Ted, taught by his father never to give up, retrieved his sunken boat and kept on playing. "And now," he shouted, "bang goes a torpedo— Sister's monitor sinks!" Indignant, Alice sat up in bed and announced, loud enough for her father to hear, "No, it didn't sink at all. It went to bed just before it had time to sink. My monitor always goes to bed at seven, and now it's three minutes past!"

Alice had learned an important lesson: the boys could get by on their physical prowess, but she would have to rely on a shrewd and calculating mind.

The antics of his "bunnies," including Ted's valiant attempts to keep up with Alice's sharp little retorts, always made Theodore laugh. He repeated them in letters to his sisters, his friends, his in-laws. Yet he never quite seemed to recognize the deeper emotional implications in his children's words and actions. Subtlety, of course, would never be his stock in trade.

Bulldozing his way through life (wolfing down a dozen eggs at breakfast, riding his horse at top speeds), Theodore also romped vigorously with his children, pushing them to run and jump and dive, urging them to beat whatever personal best they'd set the time before. That was the only way to prepare a child for a future in a ruthless world, he believed. Life, to Theodore, was an antelope waiting to be wrestled to the ground—and then gutted, beheaded, and mounted on the wall.

"I am fairly reveling in Edith and the children," he wrote to Bye shortly before returning to Washington in the summer of 1893. Revel he certainly did, for by the time he boarded the train south, Edith was pregnant with their fifth child.

MANHATTAN

With a barely noticeable limp, Bye Roosevelt made her way through the gilded lobby of the Hotel Savoy. She was well known at the Savoy, and at the nearby Plaza, and at most of the fine establishments in the city. Often she would preside over charity auctions and society banquets held at these places, and her dining partners would frequently be European counts or the wives of millionaires. Today, however, her companion would be someone even more important, at least to her: her brother Theodore. They had much to discuss.

That afternoon, July 28, 1893, Theodore had just arrived from Washington; he came to the Savoy directly from the train station. He was filled with updates about his work and eager to share them with his sister, who, as always, remained his sharpest adviser and most enthusiastic strategist.

The year before, Democrat Grover Cleveland had won back the presidency, ousting President Harrison. He'd retained Theodore on the Civil Service Commission, however; by now he was too popular with the public to dismiss. Still, Cleveland proved to be only nominally more supportive of Theodore's antipatronage campaigns. "As far as my work is concerned," Theodore wrote to his friend, Sen. Henry Cabot Lodge of Massachusetts, "the two Administrations are much of a muchness."

For Theodore, the same old political fights were wearing thin. "Mean, sneaking little acts of petty spoilsmongering" no longer held his interest. His work, initially stimulating, had become stultifying. By now he was supposed to have been *somebody*. He'd fought off mountain lions, shot grizzly bears, survived cattle stampedes, but in politics he was still just one of three commissioners toiling, often anonymously, for a secondary federal agency. He had been promised that his position on the commission would lead to bigger things. Nearly five years later, though, nothing beckoned but a lifetime as a cog in the Washington machine. He was restless.

Bye encouraged him to keep finding ways to get out of the capital and be seen and heard around the country. While his exposés of corruption hadn't made him popular with Washington insiders, they had turned him into a hero in the press. At a recent speech at Northwestern University, in front of an assembly of students, teachers, and (most important), newspapermen, he railed about "the selfish indifference of the educated classes." To them much was given, he said, so *of* them much should be required. Yet too many of these educated elites, he argued, shirked "the responsibilities that belong to their position." The applause that followed reached up into the rafters. The *Chicago Journal* opined, "Mr. Roosevelt is a worthy example of what the college graduate may be and do for his country. He is an influence for virtue, courage and American manhood wherever he happens to be, on the ranch or platform." The campaign slogans were practically writing themselves.

Bye was nearly as eager as Theodore to advance his career. "She was ambitious," wrote a family friend some years later, "but only and always for Theodore." A woman couldn't vote then, let alone run for public office, so she used her brilliant political acumen for her brother's sake. She had no family to distract her. At thirty-eight, she had settled into what was then called spinsterhood, so she had the time to devote to Theodore's career.

For a brief and beautiful moment in her life, however, Bye hadn't been so alone. For two years, she had a daughter: Theodore's eldest child, golden-haired, blue-eyed little Alice, whose mother had died just hours after giving birth to her. Theodore had given Alice to Bye to raise, convinced he'd never marry again. So Bye taught the little girl to walk and tie her shoes; she played games with her in the garden and kissed her bruised elbows when she fell. Then, all too suddenly, motherhood was over. Theodore did indeed marry again, and Edith, his new wife, declared it wouldn't be seemly for Alice to stay with Bye. So, one terrible day, Theodore and Edith arrived in their carriage to claim Bye's little girl. It was best, Bye agreed, that Alice go with them, but she made sure she wasn't home when the little girl left. She couldn't bear to say good-bye.

Part of the reason Bye had never married, perhaps, was the curved spine she was born with, which left her with a slight limp, though this was disguised by special shoes. No amount of shawl collars or lacy scarves, though, could completely disguise the forty-five-degree angle at which Bye's head sat on her neck. Little was ever said in the family about her condition, though her nieces Alice and Eleanor would both be fitted with braces when doctors called their young bones brittle, and their parents were terrified they might have inherited their aunt's affliction. Much *was* made, however, of the series of "beaux" who flattered Bye and asked her to dance at society cotillions. Indeed, Theodore liked to kid his sister about all the hearts she had broken. Did she ever dream of all her rejected suitors, he asked, "stretching from Gussie of Egypt and Johnnie of Oyster Bay through Samuel the Uncertain of Utterance"?

He was being kind. The cold, hard truth was that no man had ever been serious about Bye. Her younger sister, Corinne, slender and pretty and perfectly shaped, had been married for nearly nine years now, with four children running about. Bye, everyone concluded, would remain simply "Auntie."

Yet one man, many years ago, had looked fondly upon her. One man had courted her and even asked for her hand in marriage. That man was James Roosevelt, a fourth cousin once removed, a charming country squire from Hyde Park, New York, in the northern Hudson River Valley. For perhaps the only time in her life, Bye received love letters in the mail. "I hope you will not think me too bold," Mr. James (as he was called) wrote, before pouring out his loneliness to her. He was a widower hoping to find someone with whom to share his life, someone who didn't think only of money and "so-called society." In his letters, Mr. James made much of his gracious house, Springwood, set on several acres of wooded land overlooking the Hudson, a house that would, of course, become the home of whatever woman he married. Despite the difference in their ages—Mr. James had a son who was just nine months older than Bye—he expressed "such a longing" to be with her. For Bye, it was a new and heady experience.

Yet her head was not so easily turned. Sensible and practical, Bye knew her suitor wasn't really in love with her; he was looking for companionship. Also, despite his declared indifference to money and society, marrying into the far wealthier Manhattan branch of the family would have benefited the Hyde Park Roosevelts a great deal. Bye's grandfather C. V. S. Roosevelt, the founder of Chemical Bank, had been one of the wealthiest men in New York, worth $7 million when he died (hundreds of millions in today's money). Mr. James's total worth (at the time of his courtship of Bye) was around $160,000 (which converts "only" into tens of millions today). No matter her crooked neck and limp, Bye Roosevelt was undeniably a catch.

Yet Mr. James was kind and sweet, so Bye gave his offer some thought before, graciously and inevitably, declining. Instead, she suggested he meet a friend of hers, Sara Delano, another wealthy heiress; she even arranged a meeting for them in the city. Mr. James promptly fell in love. "I am beaming over with happiness," he wrote to Bye soon after Sara agreed to marry him. "Each day of our lives seems only to add to the conviction that we are perfectly matched." For Bye, the letter was no doubt bittersweet. She had, to all appearances, just forfeited her one chance at marriage.

She remained close to Mr. James, however, and it was through him that she came to hire Frank Weeks and later to recommend him to Theodore. Mr. James had named Weeks as a trustee on the will of William Howland, a member of his first wife's family, but now more than one hundred thousand dollars of the Howland trust was gone, and Mr. James had sued Weeks in court. According to the newspapers, "Mr. Roosevelt says that, owing to the standing of Mr. Weeks at the bar, he had trusted him implicitly, and no formal accounting was ever made." To the list of Frank Weeks's victims, the name of James Roosevelt of Hyde Park was now added.

The Frank Weeks scandal rocked New York. On the day of Bye's lunch with Theodore at the Savoy, it was in all the newspapers. So many people they knew had trusted the lawyer and were now out thousands of dollars. Had Bye, like her friends, lost money through Weeks? Had Theodore? Even if they hadn't, every few days more people were coming forward who had; Bye and Theodore couldn't have missed their stories. The very day after their lunch, the New York *World* printed the names of dozens of Weeks's victims, a list that included some of New York's most prominent families. It was an incomplete list, though. There was no mention of Katie Mann.

That day at the Savoy, according to their letters, Bye and Theodore had many things to discuss: politics, careers, family. Almost certainly, however, they also discussed Frank Weeks. The topic was simply unavoidable. Given their close involvement with the lawyer, they must have wondered whether the money that had been earmarked for Katie (*and for their nephew*) had ever been received, or if it had disappeared like Mr. James's investments— and John Jacob Astor Bristed's, and the Countess von Linden's. If either Bye or Theodore ever made inquiries, though, neither left any record of doing so. Katie's family believed they never inquired. Apparently, it was best not to ask questions when they did not want to know the answers.

TIVOLI, NEW YORK

The thick foliage on the riverbanks was striped with the white bark of aspens. At Tivoli, some three hours north of Manhattan, the dark blue Hudson River was three quarters of a mile wide, with willows on either side weeping into the waters. A couple of times a week, Eleanor went rowing down the river with her Aunt Pussie (whose real name was Edith Hall) to collect their mail at the post office. Pussie was twenty years old, artistic, and temperamental, and as beautiful as her late sister, Anna, Eleanor's mother. Aunt and niece would row in and out of the willows to the village. On the best of days, a letter from Eleanor's father would be waiting, her name written out in his familiar, comforting script.

Returning upriver, Eleanor and her aunt would tie the boat at the little wharf and hike through the woods back to the Hall family mansion, called Oak Terrace, a three-story, twenty-two-room Second Empire structure with a mansard roof and asymmetric square tower. Being so far north on the Hudson and surrounded by such a dense virgin forest, the Halls were isolated from nearly everyone and everything. No surprise, then, that Eleanor loved her trips into the village, even more so when they resulted in a letter from her father. His letters reconnected her to the world and, more important, to him.

On a warm day in late August 1893, Eleanor settled down to read her father's latest missive. "Do not forget your Father entirely," he wrote, as if that were even remotely possible. For Eleanor, life was spent waiting for his next communication. His letters, like the man himself, could sometimes quiver with self-pity, but they could also be insightful and charitable, providing windows on the world for his daughter. That summer, Elliott told Eleanor about the economic crisis gripping the country. In May, stocks had collapsed; unemployment had soon shot up to a million people. The Panic of 1893 was under way, the worst economic depression to hit the United States until that time.

For the little girl dressed in ribbons and lace, who was served breakfast, lunch, and dinner by a series of bustling servants, the crisis would have seemed far away. Her father brought it home to her. There was "great distress all through this country," Elliott told her. While he had experienced some financial difficulties himself, he told his daughter, he was more concerned for "the poor miners in the coal field who are absolutely, for lack of employment, starving." Reading her father's letters, savoring every word and ruminating over every idea he raised, Eleanor was stirred by the first inklings of a social conscience and the first glimmer of awareness of her privilege.

Yet she didn't understand why she could never see her father. "I must go to New York in a few days on business," Elliott wrote that summer, "but I shall not ask Grandmama to bring you down to see me, as I think it foolish for you to come to the city for a visit that way." Eleanor wouldn't have thought it foolish.

There was something else Eleanor didn't know: the family, led by Uncle Theodore, had forbidden Elliott from seeing his children. The last time she laid eyes on her father had been right after her mother's death, the previous December. The loss of her mother hadn't traumatized Eleanor the way her father's ongoing absence had. Eleanor had loved her mother out of a sense of duty, not from the heart, as she loved her father. When a cousin came to tell her that her mother had died, the news was tempered by the happier report that accompanied it. "One fact wiped out everything else," Eleanor would remember. "My father was back and I would see him soon."

Their reunion, after all those terrible months apart, took place at Grandmother Hall's home on West Thirty-Seventh Street in Manhattan. When told that her father had come, Eleanor hurried down the stairs in anticipation. She found him waiting for her in the high-ceilinged, dimly lit library on the first floor, sitting in an enormous armchair and dressed all in black. He held out his arms to her (those same arms that had once saved her from certain death on the *Britannic*) and pulled her tightly to him. For several moments they were quiet, father holding daughter, hearts beating in the center of their embrace.

After a while, her father spoke softly in Eleanor's ear. He explained that they needed to become a team. They needed "to keep close together" now. It was almost as if she were being asked to take her mother's place in her father's life and heart. Someday, he told Eleanor, she would make a home for him again.

"Somehow," Eleanor realized, in the vision of their future her father described, "it was always he and I." If her brothers were included in the vision at all, it would be as children whom she and her father would raise. That day started a feeling, Eleanor said, that would never leave her: that she and her father were inextricably linked, and that someday they would build a life together, and from their union, all happiness would flow.

"He told me to write to him often," Eleanor remembered, "to be a good girl, to study hard, to grow up into a woman he could be proud of." He would come to visit, he promised, whenever it was possible.

She hadn't seen him since.

He'd sent her a pony last spring, however, with a note wishing he could be there to teach her himself how to ride, "but that cannot be." Once more, Eleanor was waking in the middle of the night to overhear hushed words through the walls. "Something was wrong with my father," she realized yet again, even if, from her point of view, "*nothing* could be wrong with him." It was a conundrum no one took the time to explain to her, and about which she knew instinctively not to ask.

After her mother's death, she and her brothers had been sent to live with their widowed maternal grandmother. Mary Livingston Ludlow Hall was imperious, often autocratic, and deeply religious. Morning and evening, she gathered everyone in the house, including the servants, for prayers. In between, the old woman spent most of the day in her bedroom, the curtains drawn against the sunlight, continuing her meditations. Grandmother Hall intended to keep Eleanor similarly sheltered from the corrupting influences of the world. The girl was dressed in clothes more appropriate for a five-year-old than someone almost nine. She was also ordered to walk up and down the path outside the house with a rod across her shoulders, her arms hooked over it at the elbows, as a way of improving her posture.

Eleanor made no protest. She was always obedient to a fault. When an aunt brought some candy for her, she resisted the urge to taste it right away because, as she wrote to her father, "I do not eat between my meals." To disobey or act out might jeopardize the agreement she had with him, which was to be good, to follow orders, to maintain the status quo. In this way, she would always be ready for him when the moment came for their reunion. His letters continued to promise that he would come for her someday: "Because Father is not with you is not because he does not love you . . . Soon I'll come back well and strong and we will have such good times together, like we used to have."

In the meantime, Eleanor was lonely. Her sense of displacement meant an outsize dependency on her father. "I needed my father's warmth and devotion more perhaps than the average child, who would have taken love for granted and not worried about it," she would write. Her often cheerless existence contrasted greatly with her memories of living with her father: stealing into his dressing room in the morning and dancing for him, "intoxicated by the pure joy of motion, twirling round and round until he would pick me up and throw me into the air and tell me I made him dizzy!"

There was no dancing at Oak Terrace. While Eleanor enjoyed her aunts Pussie and Maude (especially Maude, who spoke to her as if she were an adult, not a child) and her uncles Eddie and Vallie, both of whom were tennis champions, they were constantly in and out of the house, high-spirited young people who tousled their niece's hair and blew her kisses but generally lived their own lives. Meanwhile, her brother Elliott, who'd been closer to Eleanor in age, had died of diphtheria this past spring, the same illness that had claimed their mother. Little Hall, barely two, could hardly be considered a companion for his older sister. So Eleanor was left mainly with tutors and governesses.

Most of them were kind to the lonely child, but Madeleine Bell was Eleanor's bête noir. Twenty-four, born in France, Madeleine was a cold disciplinarian who pulled her charge's hair and took her to task over simple chores. If socks were not darned to Madeleine's satisfaction, she would cut large holes in them, making repair doubly difficult for Eleanor. To little Hall, Madeleine spoke kindly and gently, but to Eleanor, her words were curt and dismissive. The little girl became "desperately afraid" of Madeleine, but she never let anyone see her cry.

Far too obedient to be openly defiant, Eleanor could nonetheless be willful in her own way. She chose to detach from uncomfortable situations, to look through people, to seem not to care—to vanish right before them and into a world of her own. Such behavior bewildered her cousins at Sagamore Hill, and caused them to laugh at and pick on her. It also exasperated her grandmother, and likely infuriated Madeleine, who would have preferred to get a rise out of her charge. Yet Eleanor had learned how to evade her adversaries, how to deny them satisfaction, by taking refuge in a fantasy life. There, no one could reach her. There, she lived happily in the future, with her father beside her, and they both were happy and strong.

"They always tried to talk to me," Eleanor would say of the people in her grandmother's house, but "I wished to be left alone to live in a dream world in which I was the heroine and my father the hero. Into this world I retired as soon as I went to bed and as soon as I woke in the morning, and all the time I was walking, or when anyone bored me."

She lived for her father's letters. They gave her hope and inspiration, and in many ways they set her on the path she would follow in life. In one letter, her father suggested that Eleanor watch some workmen building a house, "one stone after another." She should think of the stones as "funny little workmen called 'ideas,'" Elliott said. These "ideas," in turn, carried smaller stones called "facts," and together they could build many things, using "Persuasion," "Instruction," "Love," and "Truth" as guides. All these wonderful stones, her father concluded, would "build a beautiful house called 'Education.'"

Sometimes, however, there would be stones Eleanor didn't want to carry, he warned her. That was why he introduced to his story a character named "Discipline," who would give her the ability to succeed. All these attributes Eleanor took deeply to heart; all would become intrinsic parts of who she was. Still, her father stressed the importance of one quality above all the others. "Of all the forces," he wrote, "Father and you, too, Little Witch, probably like Love best."

When sometimes weeks passed and no letters came, Eleanor worried. On occasion, she received notes from Elliott's valet, explaining that her father wasn't well enough to write himself (an attack of "la grippe"), but he wanted to assure her "as ever of his love." No matter who signed them, Eleanor kept all her father's letters, reading them again and again, until they were nearly memorized.

Yet Elliott didn't have the grippe. He suffered from something far more chronic. Eleanor didn't know it, but when the summer ended and she and Grandmama's household packed up and returned to Manhattan, her father was no longer nearly seven hundred miles away from her in Virginia, but rather, just sixty-four blocks north. Elliott had leased a three-story limestone town house at 313 West 102nd Street, between West End Avenue and Riverside Drive. The agent for the house had known him only as "Mr. Eliot"; Elliott's intention was to live there as anonymously as possible. Only his sister Corinne and her husband, Douglas, had any contact with him. The reason for Elliott's seclusion: he was drinking more than ever before, and seemed no longer to care about making a change in his life.

His wife's death, followed so quickly by his son's, had destroyed him. His family had been ripped away from him, and he'd been forced to watch from the sidelines as the two died before he was able to make peace with them. Elliott no longer had any fight left. Fighting had gotten him nowhere. Immediately after the scandalous headlines, when Theodore attempted to commit him, Elliott had tried punching back, sending a letter of outrage to the newspapers, denying his brother's charges and declaring that he was simply "taking the cure" (as so many socialites did when overworked) at "an établissement hydrothérapeutique." Elliott's letter was published in the Paris edition of the *New York Herald*, but the damage had been done. He'd been branded a lunatic. Charges like that didn't go away, even if two court-appointed commissions declared him sane.

Before Theodore brought him back to America, Elliott had tried living on his own in Paris. He took comfort there in the company of Florence Bagley Sherman, a woman very much like him. Divorced by her husband and slandered in the newspapers as an alcoholic, Sherman was, in truth, a highly independent woman and spiritual seeker—she followed the teachings of Hindu monk Swami Vivekananda. Like Elliott, she had little patience for the social niceties. Sherman's husband had accused her of sleeping with other men, basing his charge on his wife's habit of discussing "intemperate" topics with male visitors, such as Émile Zola's novel *Nana*, about a high-class Parisian prostitute. Even worse, her husband charged, Florence "spoke in an indelicate way of the marriage relation in general." In other words, Florence was that rare nineteenth-century woman not embarrassed by sex. Such nonconformity ensured that she was banished from polite society after her divorce, but with Elliott Roosevelt she found a soul mate. Both of them rejected the "unintelligent, petty, common, timid" ways of proper society, Sherman would say. Her relationship with Elliott, she'd write, was "the great emotion" of her life.

Yet their time together was brief. Sherman witnessed Elliott's capitulation to his brother in January 1892, writing in her diary, "This morning, with his silk hat, his overcoat, his gloves and cigar, E. came to my room to say goodbye. It is all over. Now my love was swallowed up in pity—for he looks so bruised, so beaten down by the past week with his brother. How could they treat so generous and noble a man as they have? He is more noble a figure in my eyes, with all his confessed faults, than either his wife or brother."

Elliott had always had a way with women—he'd convinced both Katie Mann and Florence Bagley Sherman that he loved them—but his great love always remained his wife. Although he was back in the United States for several months by the time Anna fell ill, he'd been forbidden from seeing her, a fact he deeply resented. He was sober, he was working hard at rehabilitation, and Douglas was sending glowing reports about his work in Virginia, yet still he was kept away from his wife and children. Anna abided by the edict. "I cannot understand," Elliott wrote in desperation to his mother-in-law, "what influence can have been brought to bear upon [Anna] to make her feel the way she evidently does to me." That was just rhetoric, though. Elliott knew full well it was his brother and sister who had exerted that influence on his wife.

Could it have been otherwise, if Theodore and Bye had left Elliott and Anna and their children alone? Elliott obviously believed so; Eleanor, in the way she wrote so longingly about her father for the rest of her life, seemed to feel the same. Once his wife and son were dead, however, Elliott merely confirmed his siblings' worst opinions of him: he returned to the bottle, no longer seeming to care what anyone thought about him. He seemed to decide that, since he'd been called a drunk and a maniac for so long, he'd finally become a drunk and a maniac. He still pined for his children, however, especially Eleanor.

The second week of October 1893 was fair and warm, with temperatures in the upper sixties. On Wednesday the eleventh, Eleanor turned nine. Presents came from Grandmama and Eleanor's aunts and uncles, but the gift she most wanted to receive arrived unexpectedly one afternoon as she was walking down the street with her governess on the way to a sewing class.

Her father, riding in the back of a hansom cab, spotted Eleanor on the sidewalk and ordered the driver to rein in his horse and pull up alongside her. Eleanor was delighted. Against her governess's wishes, she climbed into the cab beside her father. Elliott brushed aside any concerns, insisting he'd take Eleanor to her lesson. So off they flew into the warm afternoon, chattering happily like a couple of magpies.

Only in stolen moments like these could Elliott see his daughter. Other times, he'd find a way to pick her up in his own carriage, and they'd ride off through Central Park, the wind in their hair. Eleanor was always so surprised to learn that her father was in the city. "We would go on rather mad chases," she would remember. Elliott had a spirited horse named Mohawk, and if they got stuck behind other carriages in the park, he'd tell his daughter that he only had to whisper "Hoopla!" in Mohawk's ear to make the stallion rise up like Pegasus and magically fly over all the other carriages. The idea both thrilled and terrified Eleanor.

On these rare outings with her father, she came alive. Sitting beside him as they careened through the city, laughing at the top of her lungs, Eleanor experienced what she called the "high points" of her existence. In those moments, her fantasy world at last became real.

JERSEY CITY, NEW JERSEY

A crowd was waiting inside the cavernous Pennsylvania Railroad Station in Jersey City, New Jersey, as the *Southern Express* from New Orleans arrived on the afternoon of November 3, 1893. Black smoke filled the air as the train's engines chugged to a halt. Crowds of people surged forward as blue-uniformed policemen wielding billy clubs did their best to keep them back.

From the rear platform of the second car, a little man stepped into view accompanied by two police detectives. Catcalls rang out as the crowd recognized him. Frank Weeks looked very different from before he disappeared: gaunt and haggard, his face pale, his drooping mustache merged into a long black beard streaked with gray. When he left New York, he'd taken only the clothes on his back, and from the looks of him, he hadn't changed them since. His overcoat was wrinkled and soiled, his shoes dirty and worn. The derby hat on his head was gray with the dust of travel.

In early September, Weeks had been discovered in Costa Rica. Securing his extradition had taken some time, but finally he'd been sent back to the United States via New Orleans. That gave plenty of time for those he'd swindled—and given the size of the mob, there were many hundreds of them—to be there waiting at the station when his train arrived.

As he moved through the crowd escorted by the detectives, Weeks, "the despoiler of women's and children's fortunes," as one newspaper called him, never made eye contact with anyone. Certainly he never smiled, keeping those hideous teeth concealed. Except for "a tremor now and then at the corner of his mouth," he gave no indication that he heard the jeers from his victims or the questions shouted by reporters. The detectives quickly hustled Weeks onto the ferry for the trip to Manhattan.

Across the Hudson, another crowd was waiting at the Desbrosses Street ferry station. Among them, trying to catch a glimpse of Weeks over the heads of others, was Katie Mann. Her family remembered that Katie still held out some preposterous hope that she might finally get her money now that Weeks had been captured. That was why she'd headed down to the ferry station that day, perhaps expecting the man who had been so nice to her to write her a check on the spot.

Yet the newspapers were printing the cold hard facts: less than $60,000 remained of the $1.4 million Weeks had embezzled. Surely his more powerful clients were going to get first dibs on the little that was left. What chance did Katie stand against a countess?

Moreover, the publicity surrounding Weeks's capture had brought the crazies out of the woodwork. As the crowd followed the embezzler's carriage to police headquarters on Mulberry Street, people were shouting for blood. Some of them had truly been cheated by Weeks; others were con artists. One older woman pushed her way past police and into the office of the district attorney, where she announced that Weeks had been entrusted with her dowry sixty years earlier; it was worth in the millions by now. Weeks, of course, was only forty-nine. The woman was ushered out of the office, dismissed as "a crank."

Katie's brothers told her she'd be called the same if she pressed her claim. After all, she was just a poor Bavarian immigrant. No one was going to back her up if one of the city's richest, most influential families denied the story she told.

The economic downturn, of course, made everything more difficult. If Katie was suffering, so were the Roosevelts: over the past few years, Theodore had lost considerable money on his Dakota ranch, so his accounts were already overdrawn when the Panic hit. Not wanting to tap into the family trust, he sold six acres surrounding Sagamore Hill to make up the deficit. Paper money got so scarce that Edith had to pay the servants in gold. She also tightened the household budget; in the past, she'd been able to trim the butcher's bill from $165 a month to $110 and the grocer's bill from $95 to $75. Still, other bills loomed: "The repair of the carriages," Edith lamented, "hangs over me like a nightmare." Theodore feared "the poorhouse was impending."

Katie Mann, of course, had nightmares about things far more dire than carriage repairs, and a $75 grocer's bill could have made a yearlong feast. For her, the poorhouse was not hyperbole. Yet no one in the Roosevelt family was asking about Katie Mann, not even Bye, who was always so solicitous of nephews, nieces, cousins. At the moment, Bye was making plans to relocate to London, where her beloved Mr. James's son, also named James but called Rosy, was the first secretary of the American embassy. His wife, the former Helen Astor, had just died, leaving Rosy with two young teenage children. "Would it help if I came over to be with you for a while?" Bye had cabled Rosy, who quickly and gratefully accepted her offer. So, by the end of the year, Bye would be in London, entertaining Rosy's guests and helping to rear his children—finally a "Mrs. James Roosevelt" in all but name. "You are an angel, as usual," Mrs. Henry Cabot Lodge wrote to her, "to go and take care of all the poor forlorn things in the world."

Not all of them seemed to give no thought at all to her brother's child, who was certainly much poorer and more forlorn than the heirs to the Astor fortune. POOR LITTLE ROOSEVELT CHILDREN, one newspaper headlined ironically, publishing the "sermon on the benefits of economy to the rich" that was delivered by a judge to Rosy when he complained that his children's allowance from their mother's trust fund was being cut from thirty thousand to fifteen thousand per annum.

Katie Mann, according to her family, sometimes lamented the fact that she'd left Howe and Hummel, that she'd allowed herself to be swayed by Frank Weeks, who, she now realized, had been in the pocket of the Roosevelts. The man once lauded by Theodore as the answer to all the family's problems pled guilty to embezzlement and other crimes on November 8, 1893, and was sentenced to ten years of hard labor at Sing Sing Prison. Yet Katie didn't spend much time brooding over regrets. She couldn't, her family said. She had a little boy to raise.

MANHATTAN

Upstairs in her grandmother's house on Thirty-Seventh Street, Eleanor tried to keep her mind on her lessons and suppress the excitement she felt. Yet every time the doorbell rang she abandoned her books and hurried out onto the landing to lean over the bannister to see if "the person she loved best in the world" had arrived. This day in early 1894 was a very special one for

Eleanor. Her father was being permitted a rare visit, and the girl was beside herself with anticipation.

At last she heard his voice. Bounding down the stairs, she flew straight into the arms of her handsome, well-dressed father. The visit had been arranged by Eleanor's grandmother, probably without Elliott's brother's knowledge. Theodore would not have approved. The brothers had not been in communication for the past few months; Theodore was greatly offended by Elliott's co-habitation with a new mistress, a Mrs. Evans, at the 102nd Street town house. Word had reached Theodore, too, of a recent accident Elliott had suffered in his carriage, in which he struck a lamppost and fell on his head. Only sister Corinne kept up any regular contact with their estranged brother, a fact that irritated her other siblings: "I do wish Corinne could get a little of my hard heart about Elliott," Theodore wrote to Bye. "She can do, and ought to do, nothing for him."

Elliott had grown accustomed to the way his family, "with averted gaze, would have him know his unworthiness," as Mrs. Evans would later describe it to Corinne. Likewise, when Elliott encountered friends from his past, and they spoke of the old days, he would afterward "be lost in gloom," as Mrs. Evans described him. Moved by the woman's stories, Corinne would compose a poem about Mrs. Evans's life with Elliott. Her brother's mistress, Corinne wrote, came from a "strange world" that the Roosevelts could never know: a "'half-world' with its glamour and its glare, its sin and shame." Yet Elliott had saved Mrs. Evans's "vagrant and despairing soul," and in turn she had taken care of him as his addiction grew worse.

Like all Elliott's women, Mrs. Evans loved him fiercely. Her defense of him, turned into poetry by Corinne, would ring down through the ages: "You, who have never known the fierce, hot fumes / That rise and choke the very soul of man / . . . How can you judge of him? / . . . I who knew the evil of the world / Could never shrink before so sad a thing."

In March 1894, Elliott's name was back in the newspapers. On the night of the nineteenth, he hailed a cab outside the Knicker-bocker Club and asked to be taken to Harlem. James Healey, the cabman, said he "didn't seem quite certain where he wanted to be driven." At first Elliott asked to be dropped at 100th Street and Madison, then changed his mind to 101st. "When that point was reached," the *New York World* reported, "Mr. Roosevelt changed his mind again and told the cabman to go to One Hundred and Third Street." Growing suspicious, Healey asked for payment and discovered that Elliott had no money. So the cabman drove him directly to the police station.

There, a belligerent Elliott insisted that his name was McCullagh, but a search of his pockets revealed his card and his true identity. "He was very much intoxicated," the *World* revealed, "and was locked up for the night."

The next day, he was released. Friends of Elliott had paid Healey's fare, so no complaint was filed. The headlines, of course, were bad enough. MR. ROOSEVELT DISCHARGED—OUTCOME OF A DESULTORY RIDE WHICH ENDED IN A STATION-HOUSE.

Theodore was surely outraged when he read the article. At the moment, he was being urged to consider another run for the mayor's office, to take on corrupt Democratic mayor Thomas Gilroy. Finally, Theodore might have a chance to redeem himself after his embarrassing third-place finish in the New York mayoral race of 1886, but not if Elliott kept acting up this way. Theodore's brother was a nightmare that just wouldn't end. Even as his drinking got worse, his constitution remained "so marvelous," Theodore told Corinne, that he'd likely "continue indefinitely" as he was. "If only *he* could have died," Theodore mused darkly in a letter to Bye, "instead of Anna."

OYSTER BAY, LONG ISLAND

It was summer again, and Theodore spent as much time as possible in the sunshine and clear air of Sagamore with his "blessed bunnies," who now numbered five: baby Archie had been born the previous April. Alice was now ten, Ted was nearly seven, Kermit was four, and Ethel three. Summer, Theodore believed, was the ideal time to teach his brood the virtues of the strenuous life.

Onto a spirited new pony Ted was plopped. When the animal

reached around and took a bite out of Ted's leg, the child was reduced "not unnaturally to much woe," his father admitted. Still, Ted was "plucky about it," Theodore added in his account of the incident to Bye, and continued on with the riding lesson. Of course he did: the boy knew what was expected of him. Although Theodore praised his son for being "manly and very bright," he admitted to Bye that Ted was also "clumsy in spite of his quickness."

That summer, Kermit was excused from most physical activities. He'd complained of pain in his knee (something his older brother would never have done) and, like his sister Alice, was fitted with a metal brace. "Little Kermit tends to be fretful and peevish under the strain," Theodore told Bye. A week later the boy was so irritable that he picked a fight with three-year-old Ethel: standing on his head, he gave her a good whack with his metal leg. Once again Kermit was demonstrating behavior Ted would never have indulged in: the older Roosevelt boy endured his frequent headaches and illnesses stoically, with a determined cheer that made Theodore proud. Kermit seemed unable to help his moods and was never as eager as his brother to please his father.

On that task, Alice had given up nearly completely.

Out in the harbor that summer, Theodore gave his two eldest children advanced swimming lessons. "Both are entirely fearless in the water," he informed Bye, though this appeared to be wishful thinking on his part. While Ted did indeed dive and dog-paddle as fast as possible, even if he ended up wheezing, Alice remained nervous in the water and resisted her father's "perfectly awful endurance tests masquerading as games." The girl was becoming increasingly willful. Alice seemed to reason that since her father was never going to pay attention to her the way he did to her brothers, she'd need to find other ways to get him to notice her. Negative attention was better than none at all. Shouting at Alice to dive off the pier or forcing her to run down Cooper's Bluff (where she once cut her head and had to be rushed to the doctor) would be father and daughter's most common sort of interaction.

Her stepdaughter's obstinacy unnerved Edith. "I do feel

quite . . . sorry for the poor child," she confided to Bye, "for she realizes something is wrong with her, and goes through a real mental effort trying to get straightened out."

Of course, the only thing "wrong" with Alice was that she felt she didn't fit in with the family, and neither Edith nor Theodore did anything to disabuse her of the notion. On some level, Edith seemed to understand the part she played in Alice's distress. "I'm afraid I do not do rightly in adapting myself more to her," she wrote to Theodore. "I wish I were gayer . . . Alice needs someone to laugh and romp with her instead of a sober and staid person like me." Edith's natural reserve was always going to be a hindrance in her relationship with her stepdaughter, but the problem went deeper: she could never quite bring herself to fully embrace the daughter of her disliked predecessor. Years later, Alice would acknowledge both the "enormous effort" Edith made with her and her own sense that her stepmother "was bored by doing so." Edith's disapproval was impossible to disguise, especially to a girl as sharp as Alice.

So Alice developed a tough, defiant nature: "Early on," she would recall, "I became hard-minded and learnt to shrug a shoulder with indifference. I certainly wasn't going to be a part of everyone saying 'the poor little thing.'"

Such sentiments were more commonly expressed about her cousin Eleanor, but Elliott's daughter was not with her cousins at Sagamore that summer. Nor would she be returning anytime soon, if Edith had her way. "Elliott has sunk to the lowest depths," Edith wrote to her sister. "Consorts with the vilest of women . . . I live in constant dread of some scandal of his attaching itself to Theodore." Edith subscribed to the social Darwinist idea that weakness and immorality could be passed from generation to generation; the only hope for Eleanor to overcome the "bad blood" of her father, therefore, was a good school, but even then, Edith wasn't optimistic. "I do not feel [Eleanor] has much chance, poor little soul," she wrote to Bye.

So it was better, Edith believed, to keep Eleanor away from her brood of children. Now that the bad blood in the family had been exposed, Edith felt that all contact between Eleanor and her family should end. "I never wished Alice to associate with Eleanor," Edith told her mother, "so shall not try to keep up any friendship between them."

She might disapprove of her stepdaughter's obstinacy, but Edith made sure Alice always compared favorably to Eleanor. Alice needed to dress well, Edith explained, because otherwise she'd "look quite as forlorn as Eleanor in makeshifts." Edith pitied Eleanor for being so homely: "Her mouth and teeth seem to have no future," she quipped, rather famously, to Bye, though she did concede "the ugly duckling may turn out to be a swan."

Theodore made little effort to reach out to his brother's children that summer of 1894, as he was more distracted by career plans than ever. Talk of the New York mayor's race had escalated. The party bosses wanted Theodore to run, and he was raring to go. Sick to death of his civil service job in Washington, he wanted desperately to be back in politics. To his friend Sen. Henry Cabot Lodge, he'd confided that he regretted not being with him "doing the real work." To Theodore's mind, elected office was the only way one could really make a difference. What was more, he craved the crowds and the campaigning and the speeches and the applause and the kind of personal affirmation that only a triumph on Election Night could provide.

He also wouldn't have minded a pay raise. With a new baby at home and the economy still weak, Theodore concluded that a low-paying government job was no longer "the right career for a man without means." Means, of course, was relative. Ambition, at least of the kind Theodore possessed, was not. His destiny, he was convinced, awaited.

Unless, of course, Elliott acted up again—but so far, rather miraculously, Theodore had escaped being tainted by his brother's misdeeds. When congressman Lemuel Quigg remarked that it was unfortunate Theodore was so stained with "such a variety of indiscretions, fads and animosities," he was being sarcastic; the opposite was in fact true. Theodore was still seen as the virtuous, honorable reformer, a man of the people. Weary of corrupt Tammany Hall politics, New York voters were ready for a change. Theodore, every strategist agreed, would be elected mayor overwhelmingly.

Yet Edith wouldn't hear of it. What if he lost? He'd be out of work, she argued, with five children to feed and a house full of servants to pay. Besides, Edith loved Washington and didn't like the idea of returning to grimy New York. She scolded Theodore and said that he had to put the needs of his family before his personal ambition. So the matter was decided.

Theodore fell into a dark depression. "I would literally have given my right arm to make the race, win or lose," he wrote to Lodge. "It was the one golden chance, which never returns." His decision not to run, he was convinced, "meant the definite abandonment of going on in the work and life for which I care about more than any other." So much, apparently, for his great destiny.

When Bye found out what had happened, she was furious. If she hadn't been in London, she would have encouraged Theodore to go for it. Bye blamed Edith. An undercurrent of tension had long simmered between the two women. Edith resented her sister-in-law's political influence over her husband, and Bye resented Edith's attempts to keep her at arm's length. Now that hostility bubbled to the surface. Edith's intransigence, Bye believed, had cost Theodore his big chance. Worse, it had left him convinced that his entire future had "ended in consequence of this decision," as she wrote to Lodge, a development Bye found "frightful." Full of anger, she dashed off a letter to Edith rebuking her for her opposition, which led to a rare moment of humility and regret on Edith's part. "I cannot begin to describe how terribly I feel at having failed him at such an important time," she wrote Bye in response. "He never should have married me, and then would have been free to take his own course quite unbiased."

She was being melodramatic. As many of her letters would document, Edith believed firmly that she and Theodore were soul mates and that their marriage was fated. In fact, Edith was not always entirely genuine in her pronouncements—as ten-year-old Alice discovered around this time.

On a day that would forever change Alice's view of her family and her place in it, Uncle Jimmie Gracie delivered to her some papers that his late wife had wanted her to have. Two small pieces of vellum were covered with Auntie Gracie's fine, spidery handwriting; along with them were mementos of Alice's deceased mother. "This lock of hair and this little piece of paper," Auntie Gracie had written, "I wish the little girl to have if I die before she is old enough for me to tell her." What her aunt wanted Alice to know was how much her mother had "loved and longed for" her. Yet, perhaps even more significantly for Alice, Auntie Gracie also revealed how much her father had loved her mother.

Outside the room where his wife's body lay, Theodore had walked up and down, consoled in his grief by Auntie Gracie. "What little I know about the whole matter," Alice would later write, "I learnt from my Aunt Gracie." The image of her grieving father was very different from the one Alice had always imagined, the one that was based on stories she'd overheard and been told— stories that originated with Edith. Alice had thought her mother bored her father! She had never visualized him grieving for her.

This new information did not appear to comfort her, however. It seemed only to embitter her more. "My father never told me anything about this . . . which was absolutely wrong," Alice lamented years later. "The whole thing was handled very badly. It was awfully bad psychologically."

At some point, Alice would learn more details. A friend's mother revealed how Theodore had stayed with them after his wife died, pacing the house and filled with grief. In his diary, he wrote, "The light has gone out in my life." Two days later he added, "For joy or sorrow, my life has now been lived out."

So he *had* loved her mother. She hadn't been merely an indiscretion, a detour on the path back to his true love, Edith. Sharp as she was, Alice would realize that the reason her father never spoke of her mother was because, even now, it was too difficult for him to remember her—a memory made even more complicated by the presence of the devoted, if less passionate, Edith.

So Alice finally understood why her father had needed to subsume her into his new family and erase her mother from history. "My father obviously didn't want the symbol of his infidelity around," she would reflect years later. "His *two* infidelities, in fact: infidelity to my stepmother by marrying my mother first, and to my mother by going back to my stepmother after she died." Alice would come to discern the emotional labyrinth through which her family (and she herself) was forever navigating. "It was all so dreadfully Victorian," she said, "and mixed up."

BAR HARBOR, MAINE

From the schooners and yachts moored in Frenchman Bay, flags and pennants flapped in the strong breeze. Horses and carriages were unloaded from the ferry to be claimed on the dock by their wealthy owners. Bar Harbor was a favorite summer destination for northeastern society. The "cottagers," as they were called, included Rockefellers, Morgans, and Vanderbilts. John Jacob Astor always made a grand show arriving on his yacht. That season, Lord and Lady Randolph Churchill were spending part of the month at the Malvern Hotel.

That July of 1894, however, given the economic downturn in the country, the social whirlwind was a bit more subdued than usual. While the elegant summer homes—the term *cottage* was consciously ironic—were all occupied, the hotels were not operating at full capacity. So, as a gesture of good taste, the cottagers decided to take their parties down a notch. "There are probably not many cottagers at Bar Harbor whose income is much smaller than it was last year," observed a newspaper reporter, "but they seem to have an idea that times are going to be hard, and that they ought to economize. That is what makes it dull here."

One cottager, however, didn't find Bar Harbor dull. Nine-year-old Eleanor Roosevelt, on holiday with her grandmother, was having a wonderful time. In a series of letters to her father, she wrote about catching six fish off a boat ("Don't you think I did well for the first time?") and hiking up Kebo Mountain—though she lamented how she'd had "to find the paths all alone." How much better her adventure would have been if her father had been with her. Instead, her main companion was her brother Hall, who'd recently turned three but whose stride had yet to match hers.

If Eleanor was writing a flurry of letters, the responses she received were becoming fewer and fewer. Characteristically, she never chided her father for his silence; she seemed to take it as a matter of course. After all, Elliott Roosevelt was a busy man: "Father would write you a long letter if he could," he'd explained a while back, "but he is very busy and even to send off these few lines is more than he should do." Men, Eleanor understood, had concerns and obligations that women did not.

There was also the fact to consider that her father was often sick. Sometimes he'd blame his malaise on "a return of my Indian fever," the sickness he contracted all those years ago when he was a young man hunting big game in India. To Eleanor, the explanation seemed credible, and she clung to it, even into her adult life.

Yet Elliott wasn't suffering from Indian fever. From the reports Theodore was getting from his brother's valet, Elliott was knocking back "whole bottles of anisette and green mint" (probably absinthe, known as *la fée verte* by the city's demimonde). He was also drinking brandy and champagne, Theodore was told, "sometimes a dozen [glasses] a morning." Worse, he was using stimulants, likely cocaine. That would explain his constant wandering of the neighborhood. He was "never still," Theodore reported to Bye, and was frequently dashing off letters and telegrams to his family. At one point he asked Theodore to help him get his account of his Indian expedition finally published; when Theodore agreed to work on it, Elliott sent back a response that was both "incoherent and grateful," his brother said. Even after all these years, Elliott still seemed to hope he could do something to make his brother proud.

Yet for all the chaos he created, his house was neat and orderly, thanks to Mrs. Evans. Beside his bed rested his Bible. Photographs of Anna hung on walls and stood on tables, including in the room Elliott shared with his mistress. He often lapsed into reveries about his wife and children and the life they'd lived.

Whether he ever spoke of his son Elliott Mann isn't known, but at some point early that summer, he at least would have had to face the boy's existence: Katie Mann paid him a visit. Learning his location from the newspaper account of his night in jail, Elliott's former mistress decided to make a direct appeal to the father of her son. Katie had always believed that Elliott, when confronted personally with his child's welfare, would step up and help—and he might have, if she had managed to catch him a couple of years earlier, before this final disintegration.

Yet the man Katie saw before her now was virtually unrecognizable. His face was bloated, his eyes sunken. This was not the dashing, handsome man she had so foolishly fallen in love with four years earlier in stolen moments in her room, under his wife's nose. Elliott might not even have understood who Katie was or what she was asking of him. All that would be known of her visit would come from a letter Theodore wrote to Bye, reporting that Corinne's husband, Douglas Robinson, had revealed that "Katie Mann was again bothering Elliott." How much bother she actually caused would be debatable. Katie's family would insist that she once again came away empty-handed.

Elliott, of course, had no money to give. He lived in a world of delusion. He wandered along the street convinced he was showing his dog to his dead eldest son. On another occasion, he walked up the steps of a neighbor's house, knocked on the door, and politely inquired "if Miss Eleanor Roosevelt were at home." When he was told she wasn't there, he replied, "Tell her her father is so sorry not to see her," then frantically ran away.

More than anything or anyone else, it was Eleanor who seemed to occupy Elliott's thoughts that agonizing summer. Her regular updates from Bar Harbor had gone unanswered, but on August 13 he finally managed to pen a reply. "What must you think of your Father who has not written in so long, but we seem to be quits about that. I have, after all, been . . . quite ill, at intervals not able to move from my bed for days." Attempting to lighten the mood, he told his daughter a funny story about his "darkey" coachman building a cart to be pulled by dogs. He asked about the pony he'd given her, and inquired after little Hall. Then he signed the letter, "With tender affection, ever devotedly, your Father, Elliott Roosevelt." It was the last letter Eleanor would ever receive from him.

Elliott had reached the end he had so long fantasized about, but he was not taking it cheerfully, as he had once predicted, but wretchedly. "My life has been a gamble," he'd written in the short story that would be found among his papers, "a frivolous, useless thing." He was defiant in the story, however, insisting he'd never done "anyone any harm" but himself.

The hardship and adversity his three surviving children had to endure gave the lie to his claim, of course. But Elliott was not entirely wrong to believe that he had been sinned against as much as he had sinned.

Sometime during the afternoon of August 14, 1894, Elliott climbed up onto the sill of his parlor window and attempted to jump out onto the street. He was caught by Mrs. Evans and his valet, and safely brought back to his bed. That night, however, he suffered a series of violent convulsions. Finally, at ten o'clock, after a great deal of crying and thrashing about, he died. He was thirty-four years old.

WASHINGTON, DC

On the morning of August 15, through the snarl of private carriages and hansom cabs, Theodore rushed to the Baltimore and Ohio Railroad station at New Jersey Avenue and C Street. From a block away, the majestic dome of the U.S. Capitol loomed against the blue sky. The morning was fair and already quite warm. The train to New York was running its engines as Theodore took his seat. The trip would take just under four hours. That was plenty of time for him to think.

Early that morning, he'd gotten word of Elliott's death. The news was "a fearful shock," he'd tell Bye later, even though he hadn't been unprepared. The day before, he'd received a telegram from Elliott's valet, informing him that his brother was deteriorating. Theodore had heard such reports before, and chosen not to go. So his brother had died without his family around him, with only his mistress and his valet at his side.

Those four hours to New York couldn't have been easy for Theodore. Still depressed over his decision not to run for mayor, he had no clue, at that particular moment, what came next for him, if anything. In his letters to Bye and Henry Cabot Lodge, he worried that he'd squandered his last best chance for advancement.

Bye was still convinced that his destiny remained the Executive Mansion, but just how he would get there no longer seemed clear.

Yet Theodore was a popular speaker, his sister and his friends assured him. His vision of America seemed to resonate for many in this time of great change and innovation. A few years earlier, *The Nation* had reviewed his book on the history of New York: "[Roosevelt] lays down the singular proposition that a feeling of broad, radical, intense Americanism is necessary if good work is to be done in any direction." In his full-throated, heartfelt calls for service and duty, Theodore routinely embodied the tenets of American exceptionalism that had been growing as the country pushed its boundaries west during the second half of the nineteenth century. In that time, such marvels had been achieved: elevators, telephones, electric stoves, light bulbs, phonographs. Railroad travel had exploded to every corner of the nation, and many predicted personal conveyances called automobiles within a few years. What might America create in the twentieth century? A man such as Theodore, so young, so full of energy, confidence, and moral purpose, was the right sort of man to lead it.

For the moment, however, he wasn't likely dwelling on such things. In the wake of his brother's death, he was consumed by grief, loss, doubt, regret. This was something he had to go through alone. As Lodge wrote to Bye, only "time will help him out." For now, there was "nothing else to be done"—except to bury Elliott.

For all his desire to be a force for good and for change in the world, the ironic dichotomy of Theodore Roosevelt would be his often brutal control of his family and his inability to countenance different worldviews, such as the one his brother had held. Arriving in New York, he made his way to Elliott's home on 102nd Street. There he found a realm quite alien to his own. Elliott's friends from the saloons had come to pay their respects. Working-class men, laborers, and immigrants passed through the rooms. Mrs. Evans grieved like a widow. Theodore looked upon his brother's mistress in a sort of wonder, as one might an exotic animal at the zoo. Her relationship with Elliott, Theodore wrote to Bye, was "just as strange as everything else." He seemed thunderstruck by the realization that the lower social classes might have the same emotions as he did, and that they were capable of forming genuine attachments with those of his kind.

Having finally had a glimpse into his brother's life, Theodore struggled to make sense of it, and ultimately failed: "The absolute contradiction of all his actions and of all his moral even more than his mental qualities, is utterly impossible to explain." Even in the face of the tender care that he acknowledged Mrs. Evans had provided to Elliott, Theodore couldn't help but conclude, "The terrible mixture of madness and grotesque, grim evil continued to the very end." In his eyes, the proletariat congregating in Elliott's house was an assembly not of mournful friends, but of "grim" and "evil" outsiders.

Theodore was sincerely egalitarian in his public life and in the public policies he supported. Nonetheless, he believed in the inherent rightness of a moneyed, educated Anglo-Saxon ruling class. In a few years' time, when working-class populations were booming, he would criticize declining birth rates among the Anglo-Saxon aristocracy, calling it "race suicide." So he instinctively saw Elliott's struggle through a prism of class: the only way his brother could have saved himself from "evil" was if he had given up both the bottle *and* Mrs. Evans—or, as Theodore called her, "the woman." Alcohol, in Theodore's view, was not the only vice that had turned Elliott into a maniac; it was also his association with "those people."

In 1894 there was little understanding of the physical or psychological causes of addiction, and therefore little compassion. Theodore saw only the scandal of it. Had Elliott lived another forty-eight hours, Theodore told Bye with an obvious measure of relief, he would have been trussed into a straitjacket and taken away. The headlines would have been devastating.

Theodore never accepted any responsibility for the trajectory of his brother's last years. To his mind, Elliott had brought everything on himself. He'd allowed himself to go soft; he'd given in to temptation and self-indulgence; he'd married a woman of "questionable" morals; he'd consorted with inferior classes. He was, quite possibly, in Theodore's view, born defective, a common belief among those who accepted the idea that "bad blood" could exist. "I suppose," Theodore wrote to Bye, "he has been doomed from the beginning." That was the last word he is known to have uttered on the whole tragic affair.

It was left to others to offer more compassionate eulogies. "I know it is best," Corinne wrote to Bye in London. "I know it had to come sooner or later. I know it makes his memory possible to his children. I know all, and yet my heart feels desperately sad for the brother I knew, the Elliott I have loved and known, which all that has passed cannot efface."

Theodore wasn't immune to grief, however. Standing by Elliott's bed, looking down at his brother's lifeless face, he let more than three decades of emotion come to the surface. Elliott was no longer the "stricken, hunted creature" he had been, Theodore thought, but instead "looked very peaceful, and so like his old, generous, gallant self of fifteen years ago."

Corinne was there as Theodore said his good-bye. "He was more overcome than I have ever seen him," she reported to Bye. After years of pent-up emotion, of bottled rage and regret, the tears finally came for Theodore. He stood at his brother's bedside, Corinne said, and "cried like a little child for a long time."

BROOKLYN

Elliott's funeral cortege wound its way over the bridge and through the narrow streets of Brooklyn to Green-Wood Cemetery. The day was warm and abundant with sunshine. In the front carriage, Theodore rode with Corinne and her husband, Douglas Robinson. Edith did not accompany them. Both Alice and Ted had doctor's appointments that day, and Edith hadn't wanted to cancel them. Besides, after all the ignominy her brother-in-law had caused, it was probably deemed best that she keep her distance.

At the Episcopal Church of the Holy Communion at Sixth Avenue and West Twentieth Street, "a large number of relatives and friends" filled the pews. The altar was decorated with calla lilies and lilies of the valley, and despite what he wrote in his short story, in which he called for a marching band, it was a solemn funeral dirge that played for Elliott, a choir of mixed voices singing

"Rock of Ages" and "Just as I Am"—about as far from Strauss as one could get.

Afterward, dozens of carriages made the journey out to Brooklyn. Theodore found it "grotesque" that one carriage was reserved for "the woman and two of her and his friends"—working people again. Still, he couldn't deny that Mrs. Evans and the others "behaved perfectly well, and their grief seemed entirely sincere." Once more he appeared eminently surprised.

Elliott was laid to rest in the family plot, beside his parents and Theodore's first wife. That wasn't where he'd wanted to be buried: he'd asked to be placed next to Anna and his little son, who were interred near Tivoli. Anna's family had wanted that, too, but Theodore was horrified by the idea. "I promptly vetoed this hideous plan," he told Bye, ruling that Elliott would be buried at Green-Wood, "beside those who are associated with only his sweet innocent youth." Even in death, he intended to keep Elliott and his family apart.

After the funeral, Douglas Robinson returned to his office at 500 Madison Avenue. A real estate developer, he often acted as the Roosevelt family's unofficial financial adviser, and as a favor, he was looking over the settlement of Elliott's estate. Frederic Weekes, the unindicted cousin of Frank, was handling the various open claims, one of which greatly concerned Theodore.

Mrs. Evans was asking for $1,250 in reimbursements. After all, for several months she had cared for Elliott, cleaned his house, bought his food, and cooked for him. Weekes was recommending that, rather than deduct the amount from the meager inheritance going to Elliott's children, Theodore and Corinne should split Mrs. Evans's claim. When presented with the idea, however, Theodore refused absolutely. "The woman," he admitted, had "a fair claim to the money," but it was not his or Corinne's affair to deal with. His view: let the children pay. This stunning lack of generosity only continued. Elliott's devoted valet, who'd acted as guardian and sick nurse, should be paid "five dollars for each night he sat up," Theodore declared. Though even that, he said, could be "pared down" when the final check was written.

At least Mrs. Evans and the valet got something. Not everyone did. That afternoon at his office, just hours after Elliott's funeral, Douglas looked up to see he had a visitor. In fact, he had two. Katie Mann had come in from Brooklyn to see him, and she'd brought with her three-year-old Elliott, who looked so much like his father.

One last time Katie was trying for justice. She had tried to keep her promise not to approach the family again, but the family had not kept its promise. She'd been working as a seamstress, she explained, doing what she could to support her son. Still, it wasn't enough, she told Douglas. So, reading about Elliott's death in the newspapers, she'd brought her son with her to plead for "mercy from his father's family."

Douglas made no promises, but it appears he did not completely reject Katie's request, either; he would, obviously, need to consult with Theodore. Yet Theodore's position had not changed. He told Douglas that no further money was to be paid to Katie. Whether she had been swindled out of her settlement by Frank Weeks seemed not to matter. In fact, Theodore was now backtracking on whether he believed Elliott Mann to be his nephew at all, despite having previously accepted Detective Cosgrove's (and his own) positive identification. He wrote to Bye, "Katie Mann came in to Douglas' office with the child which she swears was [Elliott's]. I have no idea whether it was or not . . . but her story may have been partly true. We cannot know." Of course, keeping alive the possibility that Katie was a con artist made it easier to deny her financial support. "Well," Theodore concluded his letter to Bye, "it is over now."

Not quite. For Katie Mann, the struggle was only beginning. She returned to Brooklyn to raise her child as best she could, entirely on her own, without a penny of support from anyone. "She was a bad woman," Theodore told Bye, without any justification, without knowing a thing about Katie or her character or her motivations, judging her from a distance, through a cloud of presumption and intolerance, hiding behind his own fears.

Katie never contacted the Roosevelts again. The same, however, would not be true of her son.

TIVOLI, NEW YORK

In the shuttered, echoing darkness of her grandmother's house, Eleanor was told that her father had died. She responded calmly, as if the news carried no real surprise. "I did want to see Father once more" was all she said.

Death, of course, had been a regular visitor to Eleanor's family: first her mother, then little Ellie, and now her father. Yet her father's passing changed everything for her. Although Elliott had been largely absent from Eleanor's life for more than two years, there had always been the possibility that he might show up unexpectedly on the street to whisk her away in his carriage. Even when months went by and she failed to see him or even get a letter from him, she had been sustained by her father's promise that one day he would return to claim her and set up their family once again. That dream was now shattered.

She became even more withdrawn. "The poor child has had so much sorrow crowded into her short life she now takes everything very quietly," her grandmother wrote to Corinne Robinson.

One night, as Eleanor would describe in a story scrawled in a notebook given to her by Aunt Pussie, she sat up in bed, awakened by ghostly whispers all around her. "He has broken his word," the voices taunted. "He has broken his word." In desperation, Eleanor called out to her father, and he came to her, she wrote, standing over her and placing his cool hand on her hot head. At the end of her story, Eleanor indulged in some wish fulfillment. When those "who had never understood" came to her room the next day, they found her dead, taken by her father to live with him beyond "this earthly sphere."

Not easily or willingly would Eleanor surrender her father's ghost. "Dead people did not come back [but] her father had promised to come," she wrote, referring to herself in the third person. "She could not bear to hear him spoken of as dead, but at last she grew accustomed to it. They were making a mistake but what was the difference? The years went by and she still believed."

She would live with her father in death, Eleanor said, even

"more closely than I had when he was alive." Nightly she still scratched out letters to him, keeping them hidden in her drawer. She could tell no one of this dream world of hers, because in the real world her father's name was never spoken. It was as if Elliott had never existed. So Eleanor was forced to file away fragments of memory, in her notebooks and in her mind, so that she might one day tell others about the man who had been her father. "He never accomplished anything which could make him of any importance to the world at large," she would write much later, "unless a personality which left a vivid mark on friends and associates may be counted as important."

She cherished one family story because she believed it explained the mystery of her father's life. When Elliott was just a boy of seven, he insisted on giving his coat to a cold and ragged urchin he passed on the street. "He never could learn to control his heart with his head," Eleanor said, as if that simple sentiment justified everything he had done, and not done, in his thirty-four years. "With him the heart always dominated." The challenge for Eleanor now was to live up to her father's heart.

PART III

POPULAR AND POWERFUL

1903–1905

The tall, handsome young man with the sharp blue eyes soaked up the sights of the recently refurbished Executive Mansion, better known these days as the "White House," a colloquialism made popular by the well-liked, plainspoken president. On this New Year's Day of 1903, the renovations, executed under the demanding eye of the First Lady, were being revealed to the public for the first time. As "the sunshine of a perfect winter day" cascaded into the rooms, sparkling off gilt frames and crystal chandeliers, more than two thousand invited guests explored the first floor of the mansion, marveling over the silken walls of the Blue Room and newly hung portraits of George and Martha Washington. In a break from the past, the only blooms on display were poinsettias; the modern, more minimalist First Lady had banished "flowers in the old-time quantities."

At the stroke of eleven, just as the Marine Band struck up a rousing rendition of "Stars and Stripes Forever," the young man's eyes turned to the newly constructed East Stairs, reserved for the exclusive use of the First Family. Down the stairs bounded the president, flashing his toothy grin, his genteel wife on his arm. "The personality of the Chief Magistrate of the nation and his attractive wife naturally dominates in everything about the executive mansion," wrote a reporter from the Washington *Evening Star*, "and was never more marked than when President and Mrs. Roosevelt came down to receive and return the greetings of the New Year with the representatives of nearly every nation under the sun and of the great American public."

With almost hero worship, the young man gazed over at the president, who was, he was proud to report, his fifth cousin. Franklin Roosevelt was twenty years old, a Harvard upperclassman, and every bit as ambitious as the young Theodore Roosevelt had been. Making his way through the line, Franklin eagerly shook his kinsman's hand. "The President was in his usual cordial mood," the *Star* disclosed, "and his handclasp was as hearty as ever." For a fleeting moment, Franklin basked in the president's glow. His cousin was his inspiration.

With careful note, Franklin had watched Theodore's path to the White House. Just when Theodore began to despair of his political future, he made a series of strategic decisions that had put him back on track. In 1895 he accepted the position of president of the New York City Police Commission and immediately began reforming and modernizing the police force. With muckraking journalist Jacob Riis, he formed a partnership to improve the lives of impoverished immigrants in the city. Even with his staff of servants and his summer home on Long Island, Theodore was acclaimed as "a man of the people," praised for making a difference in the lives of the poor and disenfranchised.

Republican Party bosses finally had a place for him. Theodore was an ideal man to bring into the new administration of William McKinley, who'd won the presidency back for the GOP in 1896. Appointed assistant secretary of the navy, largely due to his writings about the War of 1812, Theodore quickly transferred his reputation as a take-charge leader from New York to Washington.

Just how much he would take charge, however, McKinley couldn't have guessed. Despite the president's rather pacifist politics, Theodore was one of the leading agitators for war with Spain after the USS *Maine* was sunk in Havana Harbor in 1898. Whether the explosion was the work of Spanish saboteurs or an internal failure on board the ship would never be fully clear, but Theodore, and most American newspapers, strongly believed the former. When war was declared, Theodore resigned his civilian post and formed a regiment of volunteers to fight in Cuba, dubbed the "Rough Riders" by the press. Five months later, he returned a war hero, and won the governorship of New York that fall.

In Albany, Theodore continued the populist mandate that had served him so well: demanding public responsibility for corporations, regulating trusts and railroad rates, mediating between capital and labor, conserving natural resources, and protecting the disadvantaged through governmental programs. It was a new and somewhat radical approach for the conservative, traditionally probusiness party, but there was no denying Theodore's ability to get votes. So popular had he become that Republicans chose him to fill the vacancy created by the death of Vice President Garret Hobart when McKinley ran for his second term in 1900. Their gamble paid off: the McKinley-Roosevelt ticket crushed Democrat William Jennings Bryan, and Theodore moved back to Washington—and, six months later, into the Executive Mansion, when an anarchist's bullet left President McKinley fatally wounded in Buffalo.

Except for that last development, Theodore's rise to power was a textbook model for Franklin to follow if he, too, wanted the nation's top job, which he very much did. Making Theodore's success even more appealing to the college-age Franklin was this fact: he had accomplished all this by the age of forty-two, making him the youngest president in American history.

Franklin had come to the White House as a guest of the president's daughter Alice, now eighteen. Alice had turned into a strikingly beautiful young woman. As Franklin watched, she made the rounds of the foreign ambassadors and Cabinet ministers in a dress of black velvet and cream-colored lace, a strand of white pearls around her neck. Her second cousins Christine and Elfreda Roosevelt wore "girlish white dresses," according to the *Star*, and mingled through the crowd as well. Yet it was another cousin whom Franklin most noticed, the plain, lanky Eleanor, who dressed without the eye to fashion the other girls possessed and who, instead of moving coquettishly among the guests, assisted discreetly in the distribution of biscuits, cheeses, and fruits.

After a slow start, Franklin was developing an eye for the ladies, and found to his pleasure that they had an eye for him as well. He stood six two, which meant he looked down at the president when he shook his hand. He wasn't as muscular as Theodore, however, but rather slender, almost willowy. His mother, who doted on him, noted in her diary around this time that Franklin weighed one hundred sixty-one and one-half pounds "in his silk pajamas and barefoot." He was classically handsome, and his face retained a summer glow all year round. All in all, Franklin was a package women found irresistible.

Even Alice, his fifth cousin once removed, had had a crush on

him when they were young teenagers, making her feelings en-
dearingly plain in a letter cowritten with Franklin's niece Helen
(though, given the closeness in their ages, Helen was more like
Franklin's cousin). "I want to know the name of the girl . . . you
[are] stuck on instead of me," Alice demanded. "I suppose James
[Helen's brother and Franklin's nephew] told you all the pleasant
little things I said about you. They are all true." Goaded by Helen,
Alice added, "I hope you have given me up, if not you had better."
Another boy, she explained, had dedicated a poem to her.

If the flirty little missive was intended to make Franklin jealous, it probably didn't work. Until recently, Franklin hadn't been
very sophisticated when it came to the opposite sex. Before he
entered Groton at the age of sixteen, he knew very few girls—
very few boys, either, for that matter, as his mother had rarely
allowed him to wander very far without her. Not until he arrived
at Harvard in 1900 did he really begin to notice girls and attempt
to make contact with them—but even then, Sara Delano Roosevelt
was always quick to douse the flames. When Franklin asked if he
might invite some friends home, including three girls, his mother
squelched the idea of a coed holiday. She told Franklin about another boy they knew who invited only male friends home. "[He]
prefers it and I daresay you will also," Sara said. Without any objection, Franklin obeyed his mother. He was nineteen at the time.

His mother had always been protective, but in the past two
and a half years since the death of his father, Franklin had felt her
grip tighten. He was all she had now, a fact of which she often reminded him. For a time, Sara took an apartment in Boston, just to
be closer to Franklin at school. From across the Charles River she
scratched out a flurry of letters admonishing him to study hard,
to "systemize his time," to get plenty of sleep, and not to let others
keep him up too late. In the letters Franklin sent back across the
river, he made sure to profess his undying love to her—while
never, *ever* mentioning the girls he was increasingly taking out for
late-night carriage rides.

He especially never mentioned Alice Sohier. A year earlier,
Franklin had fallen hard for the pretty blue-eyed girl with the
nose described on her passport as "retrouseé," or delicately

turned up. The daughter of a wealthy Boston lawyer, Alice was only sixteen, yet nearly as tall as Franklin. She seemed hardy enough to bear lots of children, which was a good quality, since Franklin wanted six. So much did he like Alice that one day he forgot propriety and made a pass, getting a slap across the face for his presumption. Alice felt he was moving too fast. Besides, she didn't want to be "a cow" birthing all those children, as she'd tell people later. Her parents sent her to Europe for a season. Franklin saw her off at the pier, and their relationship ended.

Five months later, Franklin was still heartbroken. Nonetheless, he was back in the social swirl, doing his best to keep up with his more famous cousins. That New Year's Eve, after the festivities wrapped up, "Miss Roosevelt and the younger members of the party" made their way to the theater, as one newspaper noted. Alice attracted notice wherever she went, and as part of her retinue, Franklin would have gotten a firsthand look at the sort of celebrity bestowed by the White House. Newspaper reporters noted that in Alice's wake came Christine, Elfreda, and, a couple of steps behind them, Eleanor. The Roosevelt girls had become social trendsetters ever since their coming-out parties the previous fall, "so pleasantly calling attention to the family name." The night before, Christine's aunt, the sister of Sen. John Kean of New Jersey, had hosted a New Year's Eve party, and of course the entire younger Roosevelt generation had been there to sip champagne and dance in the cotillion—though, if Franklin had looked closely at Eleanor, he might have discerned that the smile on her face was a bit strained.

He was, in fact, looking more closely at Eleanor these days. They'd known each other all their lives (Eleanor's father had been Franklin's godfather), but they'd seen each other only rarely. After a Christmas party in 1898 at Corinne Robinson's, Franklin came away thinking Eleanor had a "very good mind," but it was only in the last few months that they had started running into each other with any regularity. On a train heading to Hyde Park, Franklin, strolling through coach class, recognized Eleanor, whom he hadn't seen in four years. Sitting by herself reading a book, she was just back from school in London. For two hours

Franklin sat and talked with her, eventually bringing her up to the parlor car so she could say hello to his mother. Sara was cordial to Eleanor, recalling how fond she and her late husband had been of her father.

A few months later, Franklin was again in Eleanor's company, for dinner at Sherry's restaurant in New York, and later in his half-brother Rosy's box for a horse show at Madison Square Garden. By the time of the New Year's gala in Washington, the two young people had become well acquainted. "Sat near Eleanor," Franklin wrote in his diary after one White House event. "Very interesting day."

Of course, it wasn't just the fine mind of his fifth cousin once removed that he found interesting during his stay in the nation's capital. The whole experience (the parade of foreign ambassadors, the glittering renovations of the Executive Mansion, the crush of newspaper reporters, the dinners with the president and First Lady) had left Franklin invigorated. He seemed born to this.

Certainly his childhood had been exalted enough. Both Franklin's parents had doted on him, as had the large staff of servants. Although his father (Bye's beloved Mr. James) had an older son from his first marriage—Rosy was twenty-eight years Franklin's senior—Franklin was, in essence, an only child, and was indulged in every way.

Mr. James did not come from the sort of money that his Oyster Bay cousins enjoyed, but he quickly made up for it through the institution of marriage. Bye's introduction to Sara Delano proved very advantageous. Sara hailed from one of the wealthiest families in New York, and now the Roosevelts of Hyde Park lived like English aristocracy. The sleigh in which they rode across the snowy grounds of Springwood had been a gift from Czar Alexander II to Napoleon III. Buying it at auction, Mr. James added the Roosevelt crest beside the imperial standard. As one biographer wrote, Franklin, as a young boy, sat by himself in the back of the sleigh, "where the Empress Eugénie had once ridden as she glided through the Bois de Boulogne." Up front, his parents sat shoulder to shoulder "to shield him from the cutting wind."

When the family traveled by train, Mr. James had his own private car hitched up to separate them from the riffraff. Decorated in brass and mahogany, the car had its own sleeping quarters and sitting rooms, and of course its own private porter. Sailing was just as exclusive. On one transatlantic trip onboard the *Adriatic*, seven-year-old Franklin came down with typhoid, so the captain gave him his own private room on deck and set the staff scurrying to meet his every need. When the ship docked, Franklin was met by a special tender arranged by no less than Thomas Ismay, the founder of the White Star Line. Such treatment instilled in the boy a heightened sense of his and his family's importance. To his mind, everything that came to him was his due.

When, on occasion, the world was *not* handed to him, or he was not treated with the deference he'd come to expect, he could turn sharp and argumentative. Playing with another little boy on the grounds of Springwood, he was overheard by his mother barking out orders left and right. Sara gently advised her son that his companion might occasionally want a turn at making decisions. Franklin looked at her as if she were mad. "Mummie," he said, "if I didn't give the orders, nothing would happen."

Sara would tell this story, eagerly and repeatedly, to illustrate her son's natural-born leadership qualities, but in fact, Franklin's playmate that day was not his peer, but "a little boy on the place," as Sara described him, the son of a servant. The children of the help were occasionally allowed to fraternize with the little master, who most of the time had no playmates his own age. So in his romps with the other boy, Franklin wasn't just displaying signs of future management or organizational skills. He was behaving appropriately to his class. Like his father, mother, and older brother, Franklin told other people what to do.

Growing up, he had very little consciousness of his privilege, or of any responsibility that might come with it. His father could deliver fiery lectures at the St. James Guild, exhorting his fellow bluebloods to "help the poor, the widow, the orphan," but the same message wasn't conveyed at home. Franklin grew up in a bubble. At Harvard, one friend would recall, "He did not have the 'common touch' at all. [He] seemed ill at ease with people outside of his group."

In this, Franklin departed dramatically from his role model Cousin Theodore, who, although eased through life with nearly as much privilege, had nonetheless been brought up with a sense of noblesse oblige, a message he'd been thundering from podia for years. Despite his belief in the inherent superiority of the "Anglo-Saxon" races, Theodore was never comfortable with the idea of an American aristocracy or with his own membership in it. At one society event, seated next to Mrs. John Jacob Astor IV, he was bemused by the grand dame's reaction to the assassination of the Russian czar. "They are attacking us all over the world," Mrs. Astor said—a use of the pronoun Theodore would never have thought to employ himself. Franklin, however, might have.

If his famous kinsman's populism had yet to make an impact on him, Franklin was following in his footsteps in other ways. As a boy, he hunted, classified, and stuffed birds much as the young Theodore did. He attended Groton, the school where Theodore sent his own sons, and then moved on to Harvard, Theodore's alma mater. For a while, Franklin even sported pince-nez. At Harvard, he joined the Republican Club, even though his father had always been a Democrat. When Theodore was elected as McKinley's vice president, Franklin celebrated on campus with his friends. Still, he sometimes had to admit that the president wasn't his uncle or even a close cousin; when pressed, Franklin was forced to acknowledge that he wasn't one of "*the* Roosevelts."

He did his best to blur that distinction, however. For a long time, Franklin believed that the best way of proving his mettle was to be accepted into the Porcellian Club, the most exclusive student club at Harvard, and where Theodore was once a notable member. Yet apparently the Porcellian membership saw something they didn't like—perhaps he came off as too eager or presumptuous— and they rejected Franklin's request to join. The young man was shattered. "The greatest disappointment in my life," he would call it. Twenty years of entitlement, a lifetime of access and advantage, had not prepared him for such a rejection. For the first time, he was stopped at the gate and refused entry. Not even a Roosevelt, he discovered, was automatically admitted into the highest ranks—not so long as there were others with more power ahead of him. It was a realization that changed his life.

One college friend traced Franklin's ambition from the moment he was denied by Porcellian. After that, the friend said, Franklin became determined to make himself "popular and powerful." No one would ever refuse him again—which was precisely why he was in Washington that New Year's Day. When he returned to school, he could tell his classmates all about his meetings with the president and his privileged peek inside life at the White House. He could boast to his colleagues on the *Harvard Crimson*, where he served as secretary, about his connection to the most important man in the country. What Franklin wouldn't let on, however, was that the president's family disliked him, that they called him names behind his back.

To the rambunctious Ted and Kermit, who'd spent their childhoods jumping off piers and climbing trees, Franklin was a spoiled mama's boy. They'd heard the stories of how their Hyde Park cousin was kept in long curls and lace dresses until he was six, and even then his mother expressed regret that his golden curls were shorn "long before they should have been." At Groton and Harvard, Franklin was never the sort of sportsman Cousin Theodore was priming his sons to be; indeed, Franklin's only athletic ribbon was for managing the baseball team. Ted and Kermit played football and various other sports.

Six years before that New Year's Day, in the summer of 1897, the Oyster Bay cousins had gotten a close-up look at Franklin and his demeanor and abilities, when he joined them for the Fourth of July. Franklin had long hoped for an invitation to Sagamore Hill, and when it finally came, he defied his mother's wishes by attending. Yet it was quickly revealed that, even at fifteen, he wasn't nearly the athlete that nine-year-old Ted or even seven-year-old Kermit was. Even worse were his affectations. When meeting a lady, Franklin bowed from the waist, and he spoke with a sort of pseudo-British accent acquired from spending summers abroad. He was rather a dandy in the clothes he wore, too, delighting in capes and other elegant accessories. One Harvard friend went so far as to say that Franklin possessed a "characteristically feminine quality" and resorted to charm instead of reason to get his way. Later, the journalist Marquis Childs would comment on Franklin's personal vanity, calling it "the quality of an actor, the man who could be photographed always with just the perfect camera angle."

After that Fourth of July visit, Franklin's Oyster Bay cousins would always laugh behind his back and consider him "nancy." His initials, F.D., they declared, stood for "Feather Duster." The daughter of Corinne Roosevelt Robinson, also named Corinne, recalled how they all thought Franklin resembled the dandified gentlemen pictured on ladies' handkerchief boxes.

Even Alice, who'd had a crush on Franklin and who didn't mind her handsome, well-dressed distant cousin occasionally joining her entourage, could be two-faced about him, especially around her brothers. "He was the kind of boy whom you invited to the dance but not the dinner," she'd later say, "a good little mother's boy whose friends were dull, who belonged to the minor clubs and who was never at the really gay parties."

One party, however, was plenty gay for Franklin: the soiree his half-brother, Rosy, threw for him in New York to celebrate his twenty-first birthday late that same January of 1903. "Very jolly!" Franklin recorded in his diary. A favorable assessment of the gathering was perhaps inevitable as, much to Franklin's pleasure, Rosy had thought to invite Eleanor Roosevelt. Neither as pretty nor as socially skilled as Alice Sohier, Eleanor nonetheless had that "very good mind" Franklin so admired—and five months after having his heart broken by a girl much younger than he, a little intelligence and maturity seemed to make all the difference to Franklin.

MANHATTAN

It took some getting used to, this world of high society.

On a night in March 1903, Eleanor sat alongside her cousin Alice in the Astor family box at the Metropolitan Opera House, part of the glittering "Diamond Horseshoe" of seats owned by New York's wealthiest families. She took care to smile, to look interested, and to be on her guard against making a social faux pas. She was aware that people were watching her through their opera glasses, eager for a glimpse into the lives of the rich and famous. It was almost as if Eleanor were onstage herself. "Every box in the Diamond Horseshoe," wrote the socialite Elizabeth Drexel Lehr, "would present the spectacle of two women superbly gowned and bejeweled sitting in the front row." This night, Eleanor and Alice were the spectacle, and while Alice basked in the limelight, Eleanor fidgeted.

Ever since she returned from London the previous summer, she'd been doing her best to fit into the beau monde, keeping an exhausting schedule of dinners, parties, and cotillions. Her grandmother explained that this was expected of a girl of her social status. After the New Year's celebrations, Eleanor was formally received at the White House by her aunt Edith; she then returned to New York for a party given by Mrs. Edward Haney, for her daughter, who, like Eleanor, was one of the season's debutantes. A short time later, Eleanor was herself fêted by Dr. and Mrs. H. P. Loomis at their home on East Thirty-Fourth Street. She was also obliged to make appearances at the Metropolitan Club and at the home of Mrs. W. Bayard Cutting, for parties in honor of other girls. On January 20, a gala was held at Sherry's restaurant for all the debutantes. It was Cousin Alice, however, called "Princess Alice" in the newspapers, who, as usual, excited the newspapermen the most.

Now, a few weeks later, Eleanor was with Alice once again, this time in the Astor box at the Metropolitan to see Meyerbeer's *Le Prophète*. The First Daughter, dressed in a glittering white gown, "attracted much attention" from the other theatergoers, as the newspapers reported. Eleanor would remember watching with "great awe" as her cousin navigated the crowd. Moving from the box through the velvet curtain, Alice paused in the small private sitting area, where an attendant helped her into her fur wrap. In the corridor, she stopped to chat with important people. Never was Alice at a loss for words, flirting with ushers and aristocrats alike. Hands reached out to touch her, and Alice didn't flinch; people shouted her name, and Alice responded with a gracious smile, lifting her gloved hand to wave.

Eleanor exhibited no such poise in social settings. She was awkward and uncomfortable. Even her own coming-out party, the previous autumn, had been "utter agony" for her. She worried no one would dance with her at the event—and while that fear turned out to be groundless, she harbored no illusions about herself: "By no stretch of the imagination could I fool myself into thinking that I was a popular debutante." Of her steady schedule of social obligations, she despaired; she felt like a fraud when she tried to be witty or demure or gay. People expressed surprise at her obvious unease: after all, her mother had been one of the legendary belles of society. Anna once feared her daughter would be a disappointment. That fear had come to pass.

How different Cousin Alice was, reveling in the attention. Much to her father's discomfort, Alice considered the high-society set her people. "They were tribal friends," she explained, people whose money, influence, and breeding bonded them together and set them apart from the lower classes. Eleanor, for her part, could never quite adjust to her own membership in the tribe. To her, Alice seemed "so much more sophisticated and grown-up" than she was, and while she admired Alice, she admitted she was "afraid of her" as well. After all, Eleanor was almost like a lady-in-waiting to her cousin at these events, and at any moment, Alice might ask her to perform some duty on her behalf, speak with a gentleman or lead the dancing, and Eleanor worried she would freeze.

Of course, her fear of Alice stretched back well beyond their current social obligations, back to the days when Alice and her brothers would dunk her underwater or taunt her for her attire. The persecution hadn't ended there. After her father's death, Eleanor saw little of her Oyster Bay kin, but every Christmas, her grandmother sent her to Aunt Corinne Robinson's holiday party, where Eleanor's outdated dresses (still above the knees like a little girl's, with embarrassingly high socks) elicited the same old laughter. "I knew that I was different from all the other girls," Eleanor would recall, "and if I had not known, they were frank in telling me so!"

According to Corinne's daughter, known as "Little Corinne,"

Eleanor heard the whispers of "ugly duckling." She was terribly self-conscious that she was the first "Hall girl not to be the belle at every party." Gatherings of her Roosevelt cousins, Eleanor said, "were more pain than pleasure." The others all knew one another better than they knew her, and were usually out skiing, sledding, or skating on the grounds. "I rarely coasted and never skated," Eleanor said, "for my ankles were so weak." More giggling, whispering, and finger-pointing ensued.

Yet here she was, almost nineteen years old, fresh from London, and supposedly more cosmopolitan and worldly, attending Alice like a lady-in-waiting at various events around town. These days, Eleanor's clothes were more fashionable; they had to be, if she were to be seen in the company of her cousins at Sherry's and the opera house. Still, she was the last one to get the joke, especially if it was a bit naughty—and what fun Alice had making Eleanor blush when the conversation turned to sex! Once, when they were both staying at Auntie Bye's, Alice tried explaining just what the Bible meant when it reported someone begat someone else. Eleanor, mortified, leapt at her, trying to smother her with a pillow and scolding her for being blasphemous. "She probably went to her wedding not knowing anything about the subject," Alice said, looking back. "It was just that kind of difference between us from the start." Another time, Eleanor lectured Alice against accepting jewelry from gentlemen. "I listened to her earnest discourse," Alice remembered, "fingering all the while a modest string of seed pearls that an admirer had given me the week before."

For Eleanor's naïveté, Alice had little patience, and her cousin's "ugly duckling" reputation drove her to distraction. She believed Eleanor traded on it for sympathy. In fact, Alice thought, Eleanor wasn't all that unattractive. "Tall, rather coltish-looking," she described her cousin, "with masses of pale, gold hair rippling to below her waist, and really lovely blue eyes." While it was true that Eleanor's "chin went in a bit," Alice said cattily, that wouldn't have been a problem "if only her hateful grandmother had fixed her teeth."

Yet Eleanor possessed something that Alice most decidedly did not: a Continental education. Grandmother Hall may have been derelict in some ways in Eleanor's upbringing, but four years earlier she had made a decision that forever changed the life of her ward and the way she would see the world. In New York, Eleanor was the pitiful cousin, always dull, drab, and bereft. Her only chance, as starchy Aunt Edith had told her sister-in-law Bye, was for her to attend a good school. Auntie Bye knew just the place for her: Allenswood, at Wimbledon Park, just outside London, whose formidable founder and headmistress, Marie Souvestre, had taught Bye some two decades earlier. Allenswood educated the daughters of European and American elites, but not in the usual old, stodgy society traditions. Rather, Allenswood students were trained to think independently and to take personal responsibility. That approach had appealed greatly to Bye, and she thought it would appeal to Eleanor as well.

Eleanor sailed for London in 1899, shortly before her fifteenth birthday, utterly unprepared for what she would find there. At Allenswood, students were permitted only three baths a week, none lasting more than ten minutes. Every night at dinner, students were required to confess any words they had spoken in English during the course of the day (lessons were all conducted in French). Physical exercise was mandatory—and for a girl as uncoordinated as Eleanor, this was a major adjustment, indeed.

Mlle. Souvestre proved as much of a revelation as the school. In her late sixties, small and stout, with her snow-white hair worn in a twist at the back of her head, she struck Eleanor with her intensity right away. "Her brilliant speech darted here and there with the agility and grace of a hummingbird," one former student, Dorothy Strachey, described her, in a roman à clef published several decades later. If Souvestre found a student's answers facile or unconsidered, she might sternly upbraid her, but she also inspired a pursuit of excellence not often found in the education of girls at the time. To every idea, she brought "a sort of hammering logic," another student remembered, and she would smash the idea into pieces "unless it be of very sound metal." Never before had Eleanor encountered someone so charismatic. "Every subject," Strachey wrote, "however dull it had seemed in the hands of others, became animated in hers. The dullest of her girls were stirred into some sort of life in her presence; to the intelligent, she communicated a Promethean fire which warmed and colored their whole lives."

Eleanor was one of the fortunate recipients of that fire. From the start, her intelligence and seriousness, cultivated during those lonely days and nights reading and studying in her room at Tivoli, stood her apart from the others. Back home, Eleanor quaked beside Alice, thinking her cousin so much more mature than she, but at Allenswood, it was a very different story. "I remember the day she arrived at the school," one of her classmates would recall. "She was so very much more grown up than we were, and at her first meal, when we hardly dared open our mouths, she sat opposite Mlle. Souvestre, chatting away in French."

Eleanor found the older woman "beautiful, with clear-cut, strong features, a very strong face and broad forehead." Yet it was her mind that was even more captivating to the young, impressionable girl. Souvestre was part of a group of radical thinkers who challenged notions of gender, family, society, and religion. Among her confederates were Leslie Stephen, the writer, reformer, and father of Virginia Woolf; John Morley, the liberal, anti-imperialist statesman; and Jane, Lady Strachey, the author and advocate for women's suffrage. So strongly did Strachey believe in Mlle. Souvestre's worldview that she sent four of her own daughters, including Dorothy, to be educated by her. Among the headmistress's most notable former pupils was Natalie Clifford Barney, the American expatriate poet and playwright now living in Paris, who made no secret of her love affairs with women.

In the midst of the prevailing patriarchy of the times, Mlle. Souvestre chose not to prepare her students for marriage. Instead, she got them ready for *life*. It was a very different message from those that had been imparted to Eleanor by her mother and grandmother, for whom a woman's place was always behind a man, well-dressed and demure. Within days of her arrival at Allenswood, Eleanor blossomed. During her time at the school, she grew proudly into her full six feet. Her chin was held high, her eyes lifted from the floor to look straight ahead. The childish clothes that had made others laugh at her were discarded: Mlle.

Souvestre encouraged her to buy a daring red dress made by a Parisian couturier, and Eleanor wore it to school dances, where the other girls always vied to be her partner. Most dramatically, she overcame her clumsiness and reticence toward outdoor activities, making the first team in field hockey—"one of the proudest moments of my life," Eleanor said. When she scored a goal for her team and basked in the cheers and embraces of her teammates, the little lost girl, the object of so much pity back home, was reborn.

She also found her courage. For much of her first fifteen years, Eleanor had lived in a state of constant terror, avoiding confrontation at all costs. No longer. "For the first time in all my life," she said, "all my fears left me." During her freshman year, she developed a crush on a girl she would identify later only as "Jane." Jane was "fascinating" and "brilliant," Eleanor thought. The daughter of a wealthy Texas landowner, Jane had "a real personality," Eleanor wrote, unlike the artificial façades of so many of the girls back home. In history class, Eleanor recalled, "There were perhaps eight other girls, but as far as I was concerned there was no one but Jane." Yet her beloved Jane had a temper. One day, angered about something, Jane tossed a bottle of ink at her German teacher. Mlle. Souvestre lost no time in expelling her from the school.

Eleanor was furious. Marching to the headmistress's office, she pleaded with Souvestre to change her mind. She wept, she wrung her hands, she raised her voice in anger. Challenging authority was not in Eleanor's experience; such behavior would have been unthinkable back home. Her grandmother would have punished her severely, but Mlle. Souvestre sat patiently and listened, admiring the passion her student displayed. Respectful challenge and honest inquiry were things Souvestre encouraged; mindless obedience was useless. While Souvestre did not relent and pardon Jane, neither did she penalize Eleanor for trying to save her friend. Eleanor learned that speaking up for herself did not equal disaster. Presenting her truth, as it turned out, could be empowering.

Her time at Allenswood was filled with rigorous learning experiences. There was a reason her cousin Franklin would praise her "very good mind." Well-read as a child, Eleanor was exposed to a wide swath of ideas and philosophies at Allenswood. Classroom studies tended to be conventional, with a focus on history, literature, and the arts. In Mlle. Souvestre's informal library, however, lively discussions ranged in topic from the dangers of colonialism and the limits of capitalism to the emancipation of women and the evils of anti-Semitism. In all these discussions, Eleanor participated eagerly, her hand constantly in the air. Her intellectual ardor made her a particular favorite of her teacher.

She was also a favorite of her classmates. During her time at Allenswood, Eleanor was the popular girl, a position completely alien to her in her previous life, but one to which she now took easily and graciously. "The purity of heart, the nobleness of her thought," Souvestre wrote to Eleanor's grandmother, "has been verified by her conduct among people who were at first perfect strangers to her. She is full of sympathy for all those who live with her and shows an intelligent interest in everything she comes in contact with." During Eleanor's last year at Allenswood, her cousin Corinne Robinson matriculated at the school and was immediately struck by how Eleanor was "everything" to her classmates. "She was beloved by everybody," Little Corinne remembered. "Young girls have crushes and you bought violets or a book and left them in the room of the girl you were idolizing. Eleanor's room every Saturday would be full of flowers because she was so admired."

In her roman à clef, Dorothy Strachey would write unambiguously of the romantic love that existed among many of Mlle. Souvestre's students, a passion that was not discouraged and was even tacitly promoted by their teacher. For some girls, the crushes evaporated once they returned home; for others, including Strachey and Natalie Barney, they awakened a self-affirming, lifelong lesbian orientation. For Eleanor, the love between women at Allenswood was natural, liberating, and empowering. It would become an integral part of who she was.

But after two years, her grandmother summoned her home. Immediately all the wretchedness of her childhood came rushing back at her. Oak Terrace had become a house of horrors, a refuge for broken dreams. Both her uncles, once great tennis champions, were now bitter alcoholics; Uncle Vallie sometimes shot his rifle out the window at people. In some ways, the saddest of all was Aunt Pussie. Nearing thirty and unmarried, her heart had been broken by a series of men and her plans for an artistic career had collapsed. Soon after Eleanor arrived from London, Aunt Pussie turned cruelly on her niece, telling her she'd "never have the beaux the rest of the family had" because she was so ugly. That was bad enough, but there was even worse to come. Pussie was in a rage. She spilled all the family secrets about Elliott's unhappy last years: the boozing, the asylums, the opiates, the suicide attempts, the women, and, presumably, the fact that Eleanor had a ten-year-old half-brother out there somewhere.

Did she tell Eleanor who her father's mistress was? If so, did the name "Katie" ring a bell for Eleanor, conjuring up the kind, pretty face of the family chambermaid of whom she'd been fond when she was six, the one to whom she sent a photograph of herself from Germany?

No matter which details she learned, Eleanor was crushed. "Painful and distressing" was how she would describe the experience, and surely that was an understatement. Eleanor's sainted image of her father had been smashed with all the savagery of a rock hurled through a stained-glass window. The Elliott described by Pussie was impossible for Eleanor to make sense of, especially when she reread his loving, inspiring letters, something she did often. Still, other relatives reluctantly confirmed what Pussie had told her. For Eleanor, it was a terrible homecoming, and she wanted only one thing: "to get back to England to school." Her grandmother, likely out of sympathy, granted her one last year with her cherished Mlle. Souvestre.

The Eleanor who finally returned home for good on July 16, 1902, on board the *Kronprinz Wilhelm*, was stronger for the ordeal, but no less heartbroken. She avoided Oak Terrace as much as possible, preferring to stay at her grandmother's house on West Thirty-Seventh Street in Manhattan. That meant, of course, that she was expected to play the part of a socialite and show up for every engagement.

Throughout the spring and summer of 1903, obligations on the society calendar continued unabated. As the weather warmed, the beautiful people moved out to Newport, Rhode Island, where Eleanor spent "the greater portion" of the month of July. Next it was a stay in the Adirondacks, where she met Lord Minto, the governor-general of Canada, and his wife and daughter. There were also frequent visits to Washington, to be received at the White House by Uncle Theodore. Eleanor wasn't just any socialite; she was also the niece of the president of the United States, so her calling card was in great demand by party planners.

She hated it. She hated every curtsy, every forced smile, every awkward attempt at small talk. She did not feel a part of the tribe, and the tribe did not fully embrace her, either. She would remember "struggling through formal society each night," but at the same time feeling she "would not have wanted to be left out." She was still "haunted" by the lessons of her childhood that had taught her that "what was known as New York Society was really important." The pressure and conflict she felt in these first months back home nearly brought her to a "nervous collapse."

This was not the world she had prepared for at Allenswood. Where were the thinkers? Where was the challenge to authority, the intelligent inquiry, the probing curiosity, the upending of the status quo?

"Give some of your energy, but not all, to worldly pleasures," Mlle. Souvestre had warned her. "Bear in mind that there are more quiet and enviable joys than to be among the most sought-after women at a ball." The goal should always be, as Souvestre wrote elsewhere, "a life intelligently lived."

That was precisely Eleanor's dilemma. How did she achieve such a goal flitting from party to party? Thankfully, when she was in Washington, she could stay with Auntie Bye, who had also been a student of Mlle. Souvestre's and who had never defined herself by how popular she was at a ball. Indeed, Auntie Bye's position as chief adviser to her brother was common knowledge now that he was president. "Uncle Theodore made no major decision in foreign or domestic policy," Eleanor said, "without first discussing it with Auntie Bye."

Bye was recognized as the doyenne of Washington politics, sought out by members of both parties for counsel and favors. Her three-story brick home at 1733 N Street Northwest was dubbed "the little White House" because the president often sent over-flow diplomatic guests to stay there. Bye also invited various movers and shakers to her drawing room on her own, when she thought she might be able to finesse a tricky political negotiation or advance some cause of her brother's. That spring of 1903 alone, the newspapers were filled with items about her meetings with businessman George Vanderbilt, Sen. Chauncey Depew of New York, and the Japanese ambassador Takahira Kogorō. Sightings of Bye riding around the city in an open surrey with Takahira at her side became part of Washington folklore, the ambassador's pigtail flying behind them in the wind. Theodore joked that his sister "oversees the entire nation."

By example, Bye taught Eleanor what a serious woman could do in the world. She might not be able to vote, but she could nev-ertheless be critically engaged in political and cultural affairs—in those "quiet and enviable joys" that Mlle. Souvestre had written about. Always interested in original ideas, Bye frequently found occasions to promote new information about the world—such as the time she hosted Yamei Kin, a well-known (and female) Chinese physician, who lectured to a rapt audience on Chinese plays and novels and the experience of Chinese women. Eleanor was spend-ing time with Bye then; if she wasn't present for Dr. Kin's lecture, she was certainly aware of it.

Her uncle's campaign for vice president in 1900, however, had "meant very little" to Eleanor, since she'd been away at school in London. Even his ascendancy to the White House after McKin-ley's assassination had been a faraway event for her. "I lived in a totally nonpolitical environment," Eleanor would remember, with only "a faint conception" of how politics worked. All she really knew was the glitz and glamour of White House receptions. At Auntie Bye's house, however, she witnessed a woman who had, through her brother's position but also through her own intelli-gence and actions, claimed some political power of her own. At Auntie Bye's, "the talk was always lively," Eleanor said, reminis-cent of Mlle. Souvestre's library salons. "I loved to be with her."

At some point, she asked her aunt for advice. Although in her recollections she does not divulge exactly what she asked Bye about, it would seem likely that it concerned her struggle over her place in the world, the pressure she felt from her grandmother to be a socialite, and the sense, instilled in her at Allenswood, that there was more to life than that. "I had a great curiosity about life and a desire to participate in every experience that might be the lot of a woman," Eleanor would recall of this period. That curiosity might be encouraged by Auntie Bye, but it displeased Eleanor's grandmother and others. "Do not be bothered by what people say," Bye counseled, "as long as you are sure that you are doing what seems right to you." The most important thing, Eleanor's aunt insisted, was that "you face yourself honestly."

Where Auntie Bye differed from Mlle. Souvestre, however, was that she no longer moved through life as a single, independent woman. Surprising her whole family, in 1895, at the age of forty, she had married Cmdr. William Sheffield Cowles, a naval attaché and a portly, genial fellow nine years her senior. Finally, Bye was no longer just "Auntie"; she was also "Mother" to young Sheffield, now five years old, born when Bye was forty-three. For all her involvement in society, politics, and culture, Bye had seemed to find her spinsterhood deficient, or perhaps she was simply lonely. Whatever her reasons for marriage, when she told Henry Cabot Lodge of her plans, the senator jokingly asked why she'd want to do such a thing, when she had both him and Theodore to look after? The flush on Bye's face gave him his answer. The next day, a chastened Lodge presented her with a sapphire brooch as an engagement present.

Even Eleanor, just eleven at the time, had found Bye's upcoming nuptials difficult to make sense of: "It seems so funny to think that you are engaged," she wrote her aunt. Bye saw nothing amusing about it, and married Cowles, whom she warmly called "Mr. Bearo," in a simple ceremony in London.

Love, affection, and companionship, Eleanor came to understand, were not necessarily incompatible with a life intelligently lived.

So, with some hesitation and tremendous awkwardness, she accepted the attentions of her fifth cousin once removed. She liked

Franklin. His parents, after all, had loved her father, and anyone who'd loved her father was immediately virtuous in her book. Elliott had served as Franklin's godfather; the heavy watch fob Franklin wore had been a gift from him. When Eleanor was very little, her parents had taken her to visit Hyde Park; she'd ridden around on Franklin's back playing horse. Franklin, therefore, had a connection to her past, to those long-ago happy days, which meant a great deal to Eleanor.

She also, significantly, sensed the alienation Franklin felt. Despite his wealth and privilege, he was not quite accepted into the "inner clique," as Eleanor called it—the world of Porcellian, the world of Princess Alice. That was definitely something she could relate to.

Moreover, in his interactions with her, Franklin was polite, even chivalrous, a novelty for a girl who had never had a beau. In fact, in her darkest days before she left for Allenswood, it was Franklin who rescued her from one of her worst nightmares. At one of Aunt Corinne's gatherings, Eleanor stood apart, an awkward wallflower, until Franklin came up and asked her to dance. He didn't ask Alice or any of the other, prettier girls. He asked *her*. Perhaps he did so out of pity, spotting the gangly girl in the old-fashioned skirt and ridiculous knee socks cowering in the corner. Regardless of his reasons, he asked her, and Eleanor was very grateful. She had never forgotten that kindness.

Still, Eleanor believed a man as handsome as Franklin couldn't be seriously interested in a woman as plain as she was. His attentions had to be platonic. All her life Eleanor had been conditioned not to see the obvious: "It was understood that no girl was interested in a man or showed any liking for him until he had made all the advances," she explained. "I had painfully high ideals and a tremendous sense of duty entirely unrelieved by any sense of humor or any appreciation of the weaknesses of human nature." For all Franklin's courtly conversation and gallant gestures that spring of 1903, Eleanor would not allow herself to imagine their relationship as anything other than friendship.

Little did she know that, after she spent a few days in June as part of a group of six friends visiting Hyde Park, taking hayrides with Franklin and lying with him in the grass under the trees, her besotted admirer would write in his diary (in code, so that his mother couldn't decipher it), "Eleanor is an angel."

OYSTER BAY, LONG ISLAND

On Sunday, August 23, 1903, an exquisitely beautiful, warm, sunny day, the president of the United States and his wife filed out of Christ Church and made their way, posthaste, back to Sagamore Hill. They had such little time to themselves, now that Theodore had attained the presidency, that they were going to make sure every moment of this glorious day counted.

Theodore helped Edith into the rowboat and pushed it off the shore before stepping in himself. Dropping the oars into the calm blue waters, he rowed them across Oyster Bay to Lloyd Neck. Katydids sang from the marshes; it wasn't uncommon for herons to burst from the tall reeds in a blur of flapping wings.

Once onshore, Edith spread out a blanket and opened a picnic lunch. After she and her husband ate, they spent a couple of blissful hours reading books "and looking out over the beautiful Sound and at the headlands and the white beaches of the coast," Theodore mused. It was just the two of them: no children, no Cabinet members, no Secret Service men. "Heaven," the president wrote. Finally, it was time to pack up and head home. "We rowed back," Theodore wrote to his son Ted, "through a strange shimmering sunset."

His beloved Sagamore was no longer the private refuge it had once been. Summer was no vacation from the duties of high office. "I have seen a great many people who came to call upon me on political business," he wrote to his sister Corinne that summer. "I have had to handle my correspondence, of course, and I have had not a few worrying matters of national policy." He was also receiving frequent updates from Bye on press speculation about whom he planned to appoint as secretary of war now that Elihu Root had resigned. Theodore told Bye it was going to be William Howard Taft, a progressive Republican like him.

Two years into the job, the "progressive" label had become crucial to Theodore. Government, he believed, had an active, positive role to play in the life of the nation. In his first address to Congress, he insisted that the federal government should protect and preserve wilderness and natural resources "for the use and benefit of our people as a whole." Months later, he named Oregon's Crater Lake as the first of several national parks he'd establish, and just this past March, he proclaimed Pelican Island in Florida the first federal bird preserve. Theodore's love of the natural world, acquired as a young boy trying to overcome his asthma, was being codified into national policy.

Not everyone saw this as a good thing. Progressives, their critics charged, were all about regulation and control. It was overreach, they argued, to deny Americans the right to develop land for their own individual gain. Theodore's view that national resources belonged to all citizens was abhorrent to McKinley's probusiness supporters, who grew only more suspicious of the president after his Department of Justice announced that the Northern Securities Company (a subsidiary of J.P. Morgan) would be prosecuted for violating the Sherman Antitrust Act. Many of these antitrust laws had been on the books for years, but not until Theodore took office were they rigorously enforced. Many in his party felt betrayed. Theodore was not the president they'd expected.

By establishing the progressive wing of the Republican Party, Theodore had taken positions he felt a new century demanded: progress in science and culture; technological change; and more equitable economic policies. His work with Jacob Riis for the betterment of the poor of New York seemed to have instilled in him a greater sympathy, even empathy, for the working classes than he had possessed at the time of his brother's death. As president, he made plain his support for the rights of workers, leaving many in the Republican (and Democratic) old guard uneasy.

Yet the hostility directed at him by "the very wealthy," he insisted, was unreasonable. Explaining his policies to his son Ted, he wrote, "I wish to make the rich man feel that I am not in the least against him because he is rich, that all I am striving to do is to protect him while he handles his wealth aright, and merely to prevent his using that wealth for sinister purposes; and similarly I wish to make the poor man feel that all I can do in his real interest will be done."

Few rich men were convinced. In March, the report of the Anthracite Coal Strike Commission, which Theodore had appointed to investigate the mining industry, came back with a conclusion that further alienated probusiness interests: workers could not be discriminated against due to their union membership. Theodore, in fact, was changing the nation in a deeply fundamental way—and, he realized, he could do so much more if he won election the following year in his own right.

That summer, he was feeling cautiously optimistic about his electoral prospects. The country loved him and his straightforward, dynamic style, his rushing from place to place saying "bully" this and "bully" that. Much of his popularity, however, was owed to his large, boisterous, headline-grabbing family, the youngest brood of children ever to live in the White House at one time. "Princess Alice," of course, in her fashionable hats and gowns, was a regular in society columns and Sunday photogravures. "Alice has been at home very little," Theodore wrote to Corinne, "spending most of her time in Newport and elsewhere, associating with the Four Hundred—individuals with whom the other members of her family have exceedingly few affiliations." He remained uncomfortable with being part of an American aristocracy—the pretentiousness of "the Four Hundred," the exclusive club of the highest of high society, was repellent to him—but he clearly recognized that Alice's celebrity among the readers of popular newspapers and magazines helped him politically.

Meanwhile, the athletic and academic achievements of Ted and Kermit, now sixteen and thirteen respectively, and enrolled at the Groton School, drew their own glowing coverage. Yet it was the three youngest children who won the nation's tender affection: tomboy Ethel, twelve; sharp-witted Archie, nine; and the baby, Quentin, who'd been born six years earlier. Stories of mischievous Quentin, just three when his father became president, being chased across the White House Lawn by "long-suffering Secret Service men," as Theodore called them, delighted the public.

For the first time, the concept of a "First Family" came into vogue. The Roosevelts represented a new world for a new century—indeed, a new order based on youth, energy, commitment, and high ideals. The previous fall, the newspapers had been filled with the story of "Teddy and the bear"—how the president, while on a hunting trip in Mississippi, refused to shoot a bear that had been tied to a tree to make the hunt easier for him. To do so, he said, would have been unsportsmanlike. Cartoonists couldn't resist, and soon dozens of depictions of a gallant, noble Roosevelt sparing the life of a frightened, adorable little bear appeared in American newspapers; that Christmas, stuffed "Teddy bears" sold in the millions. The fact that the actual bear had been an old one, and that Theodore had asked for it to be put down, and had then feasted on it, was not part of the narrative. A myth was born that would endure for a century; in the short term, it would also, his supporters hoped, guarantee Theodore reelection.

Yet being president was grueling work, and often hazardous. The previous September, Theodore was thrown from a carriage, permanently damaging his leg. He was in a wheelchair and then on crutches for months. Not long after that, he fractured his arm while playing tennis. While just forty-four, the youngest president ever, Theodore was nonetheless feeling his age. Since coming into office he'd had "a tendency to rheumatism, or gout, or something of the kind," he lamented to Ted, "which makes me very stiff." A large part of the problem was a reduction in opportunities for physical exercise due to the pressures of his office. "I feel rather aged and feeble," he admitted to Kermit, "and I should awfully like to get off for three weeks or so in the mountains."

He lived vicariously through his sons' reports of their own activities. Ted, as always, was especially determined to measure up to his father's example, and by now, as Theodore admitted to Henry Cabot Lodge, he'd actually surpassed him in some ways. "He can do better than I can at almost all outdoor sports except shooting," Theodore wrote, "and when it comes to high-jumping on horseback he can certainly beat me too, if only on account of his weight." Such an admission, however, would not be made to his son anytime soon.

Both Ted and Kermit were doing well at Groton, the school

chosen to turn them from boys into men. With regard to that transformation in his sons, Theodore had undergone a significant change of his own. Where once he had declared belligerently that he would disinherit any son who did not excel in competitive sports, now he was more careful with his words. Five years earlier, he'd sat across from a doctor who relayed a very painful truth to him: it was *he*, Theodore Roosevelt, the man with supposedly all the answers about manhood, childrearing, and the strenuous life, who was the cause of Ted's terrible headaches. The revelation had washed over Theodore. He had pushed his son too hard; the pressure on the boy had been too much. "Hereafter," he vowed, "I shall never press Ted in body or mind. The fact is the little fellow, who is peculiarly dear to me, has bidden fair to be all things I would like to have been, and it has been a great temptation to push him."

For all his bullying of his family, for all his occasional ferocity, Theodore was not without a conscience, especially concerning his children. He made the decision to back off from Ted. Still, the temptation to push and prod did not entirely go away.

The fact remained that, no matter how strong, quick, and eager Ted had become, he still weighed only one hundred or so pounds and was very prone to sickness. The previous year, he was knocked down by a severe case of pneumonia. Edith hurried up to Groton to tend to him. PRESIDENT'S SON STRICKEN BY ILL-NESS blared the front-page headlines. Every update on Ted's condition, no matter how trivial, was announced in the newspapers. When the teenager finally got better, the *Washington Times* bannered CONDITION MUCH IMPROVED, and reported on Ted's arrival in Washington on the train "bundled in overcoats and traveling wraps which permitted but a glimpse of his pale face." Thousands of congratulatory notes flooded into the White House, including one from Kaiser Wilhelm II, so worldwide did the story spread.

Ted, of course, would never admit just how frail his health was. During another illness, he wrote to Alice that despite being in the Groton infirmary for three days, he had not been "very sick." Sickness, after all, was a crime—at least if you were the son of Theodore Roosevelt.

Although Theodore had vowed not to push his sons as he had in the past, it was, in fact, too late to reverse course: the message had been imprinted on the boys' minds early in their childhoods, and it would never completely go away. This was a father who, after all, lived by the hunt, demonstrating his superior strength, cunning, and stamina in tracking down and killing wild beasts, and then displaying their heads and skins as trophies on his walls. For Theodore's children, the only worthwhile example to follow was his. Their idealized father was never sick, never weak, never unsure, never outflanked, never intemperate, never frivolous, never afraid.

So Ted spent all his energy trying to be exactly like his father. During Theodore's campaign for the vice presidency, the thirteen-year-old had stood on the front porch of Sagamore Hill mimicking his father, lecturing the groundsmen on the dangers of free silver. Like his father, he kept track of all his personal bests and was constantly moving his goalposts forward. During his first year at Groton he was very proud to report to Alice, "I passed my swimming exam day before yesterday in the river, a swim of about 100 yards. It is the first time I have ever swum in fresh water." In boxing, he kept a record of when he was beaten and by whom, so he could analyze the reasons. In the "hop-skip-and-jump" exercise, he came in a disappointing third. "There are from twenty to thirty in each class so third is not so bad as it seems," he wrote to his father, trying to justify his performance.

For Theodore, the urge to instill "manliness" in his son proved impossible to contain. During the early fall of 1903, he sent Ted out to the Black Hills of South Dakota for a few weeks of training under Sheriff Seth Bullock. Called the "last of the pioneers," Bullock had tamed the lawless frontier town of Deadwood and later served as a Rough Rider under Theodore's command during the Spanish-American War. He would, without question, be one tough taskmaster. "I feel the trip will teach you a lot in the way of handling yourself in a wild country," Theodore wrote to Ted, "managing horses, dealing with frontiersmen, etc."

Despite his thin frame and lazy eye—his father fretted that it "converged" with the other—Ted performed quite ably out west.

Bullock called him "hard as nails," praise that Theodore happily passed on to Ted. "He said there was good leather in you," he wrote proudly to his son.

Yet Theodore harbored no illusions about his son's robustness. A boy as slender and sickly as Ted needed to be careful, so Theodore frequently expressed his doubts about the teenager's abilities, urging him not to go "out of his class" by trying for the varsity squad. The message Ted heard, of course, was not one of pragmatism and common sense, but rather the cold, hard truth that, unlike his father, he was not varsity class in anything. Ted was determined to change that perception. The activity he chose to make his point was *football*—the one sport his father had never excelled in. "I greatly admire football," Theodore had told him, "though it was not a game I was ever able to play myself."

Despite Ted's resolve, however, his father's doubts proved strong enough to hold him back. When a letter arrived at the White House from Groton in late September 1903 with "Hurry! Hurry!" scrawled across the envelope, Theodore took his time replying. Inside, Ted was pleading for permission to play football again that season, but his father, remembering the broken collarbone the boy had suffered the previous year, wasn't sure—or, at least, he made a great show of seeming unsure. "I have sympathized so much," Theodore finally wrote his son, "with your delight in physical process and have been so glad at the success you have had that sometimes I have been afraid I have failed to emphasize sufficiently that of course one must not subordinate study and work to the cultivation of such process." The value of work and the development of character should always come before athletic ambition, Theodore counseled, a message he feared had been lost with all his emphasis on the strenuous life.

In the end, however, he let Ted play. He gave his blessing, Theodore insisted, in order to keep Ted from being disappointed. Yet surely it was also his own disappointment he wanted to avoid. The bottom-line truth was that Theodore would rather have had his son break his collarbone than sit on the sidelines. Manliness could be proved only in the arena. "I believe in rough, manly sports," he told Ted, and the pleasure he took from his son's willingness to risk injury in the pursuit of that manliness was impossible to disguise.

And so, that warm fall of 1903—a sort of "Indian summer," as the newspapers described it, with "blue sky, warm sun, invigorating air"—Ted set out to show what he could do. With football the new rage, students and townsfolk thronged the Groton campus to sit on the hill and cheer for the players. Stars were made on the football field. The boys came running out in their moleskin knickers and turtleneck jerseys bearing the school letters G S. On their heads they wore no helmets, and only the thinnest pads protected their shoulders, elbows, forearms, and knees. It was considered unmanly to wear too much padding, even though the game could get very violent. Every year, several students were hospitalized. That was partly what drew the crowds: everyone wondered who'd go down, what limbs would be snapped in two. In 1903, football was a blood sport.

Ted came running out onto the field. His friends on the sidelines cheered. But when the ball came his way, he fumbled it, and then found himself tackled by several members of the opposing team. Ground into the earth by the weight of the other players on top of him, he shattered a tooth and broke his nose. He had to sit out the next game. So much for proving himself to his father on the gridiron.

Theodore's lectures likely didn't help. In another letter to Ted that fall, the elder Roosevelt counseled, "A man must develop his physical process up to a certain point"—that point being his maximum potential. Once that point was reached, however, then "other things [should] count more." But *only* when that point was reached. The message was clear: Ted had not yet reached his maximum potential. So the boy was being tacitly commanded to continue trying to prove himself.

Kermit was also playing football that fall, but no one, including him, expected him to excel. He played on the third squad, not even the second, where Ted was busy trying to keep up. (At one point, Theodore suggested Ted drop down to third, which surely offended the boy terribly: play with *Kermit*?) Between the two brothers there was an ocean of difference. Kermit didn't push himself the way Ted did; nor was their father as tough on him. That didn't mean the younger son didn't feel any pressure. Playing tennis at Sagamore that summer, Kermit and his second cousin Philip Roosevelt were beaten in two straight sets while Theodore acted as umpire. To make matters worse, they were beaten by Ethel, a girl, and second cousin Oliver Roosevelt, who was a year younger than Kermit. Theodore was surprised by Kermit's loss, as he wrote to Ted. No doubt Kermit watched glumly as his father handed out penknives as prizes to the winners.

The fact was neither of his sons was quite what Theodore had hoped he would be by this point. When Corinne told him that her son Stewart planned to study medicine, Theodore responded with some regret: "I wish any of my boys had developed a genuine taste for a pursuit in life." Neither Ted nor Kermit had expressed a clear ambition for what he wanted to do once he finished school. By contrast Theodore, by the time he was Ted's age, had already decided he wanted to serve the public. His sons seemed content to just follow what he told them to do, without any driving ambitions of their own.

Backing off on expectations for his sons ultimately proved a futile endeavor for Theodore. The pressure to achieve, to "be a man," was now passed down to Archie. That fall of 1903, Theodore wrote glowingly to Ted of "the ferocious scrap" he'd witnessed between Archie and Oliver; he was impressed that it had lasted a full fifteen minutes. "I am rather glad to say that Archie fairly stood Oliver off," Theodore wrote, as giddy as his nine-year-old son. "He believed he would have scored a more decisive victory if not hampered by riding boots."

In a handwritten postscript, Theodore added that he'd just beaten a friend himself in two straight sets of tennis. "Ha! Ha!" he scrawled. "Aren't you glad you didn't play your venerable father that final match?" The urge to compete could not be suppressed. The tiger simply couldn't change his stripes.

Despite all his creaky joints, Theodore held on to the belief that he was still a fighter, still a winner. He had to be. Everything was focused now on his reelection. Conservative Republicans were trying to deny him the nomination, angling to replace him with

Sen. Mark Hanna of Ohio. "I enjoy being President," Theodore wrote to Kermit that fall, still a year away from the polls, "and I like to do the work and have my hand on the lever. But it is very worrying and puzzling, and I have to make up my mind to accept every kind of attack and misrepresentation." He had no regrets about the actions he'd taken in the last two years as president, even if they had alienated sections of the party. "As far as I can see," he told Corinne around the same time, "these policies have been right."

The world was changing, and Theodore was in the thick of it. In late October 1903, he hosted a group of Episcopalian bishops at the White House, and among them were "a colored archdeacon from North Carolina and a colored clergyman from Maryland," as he wrote to Ted. Theodore had not yet forgotten "the howl that was made in the South" when he invited the black educator Booker T. Washington to dinner at the White House two years earlier. This time, though, no objection was raised over the bishops' reception. "Why in the name of Heaven," he wrote his son, "these big, bad children—for that is just what many Southerners are—should be perfectly willing to have these two colored clergymen come with the white clergymen and their wives and daughters, and object to a colored educator or a colored official coming here, is more than I can fathom."

He still rode his horse around Washington, but increasingly he found himself surrounded by shiny new automobiles that "swarmed" into the city, as he described them. Speeding and honking, the motorized vehicles terrified the president's poor old horse. "A live experience," Theodore wrote to Kermit after his ride. He was a nineteenth-century man charging headfirst into the twentieth.

BALTIMORE, MARYLAND

Black smoke still rose from the charred buildings of the central business district nearly a week after a fire devastated the city, scorching an area of some one hundred forty acres. With much of Baltimore still smoldering, police were roping off the downtown area, allowing only a select few to pass; women were strictly forbidden from entering the fire zone. Then, on the morning of February 13, 1904, Brig. Gen. Lawrason Riggs received a call from Washington: President Roosevelt was sending his daughter Alice to tour the disaster area as his representative. The no-women rule would need to be suspended.

At 3:30 that afternoon, in an open barouche, Alice arrived at the courthouse, which had been miraculously spared by the fire. Wearing a wide-brimmed hat and white gloves that would soon turn sooty, the First Daughter was received by General Riggs and the fire marshal. Alice expressed her father's deepest concern. That was, in fact, the best she could offer: there was not yet any federal disaster assistance that a president could provide a devastated city. With a battalion of Red Cross workers around her, Alice was escorted into the fire zone. Riggs told her that he would take her only as far as Fayette Street, "where a fairly good view could be obtained." Alice agreed. She saw enough of the devastation to give her father a detailed report when she returned home.

Although it was largely symbolic, Alice's tour of Baltimore demonstrated to the nation that the president *cared*. It was a new, twentieth-century role for the nation's leader: "commander in grief" when the country mourned. In 1904 it was also still a novelty for the president to employ family members as surrogates, and a beautiful, fashionably dressed twenty-year-old daughter was a popular surrogate indeed. Newspapers were agog over Alice's visit. BEAUTY AMONG THE RUINS, one headline proclaimed. PRINCESS ALICE WATCHES SMOKE.

In the three years Theodore had been president, a "cult of Alice" had arisen. Her coming-out party at the White House in 1902 was a national sensation. Ferdinand Sabathil composed the "Alice Roosevelt Waltz," and women copied Alice's hats, shoes, and gowns. She almost always wore blue, to set off her eyes, and colorists painstakingly attempted to match the hue exactly for magazine illustrations. America's princess received marriage proposals from all over the world. One admirer, from Denmark, wrote asking for her photograph: "I think you are divine. If you fulfill my prayer, I shall protect and keep holy your image." Alice was, in a very real sense, the first teen idol.

Everything she did was noticed. "Miss Alice Roosevelt launched still another fad in Washington," wrote the *Gazette* of Billings, Montana, when she showed up wearing a silver wishbone around her neck "to bring her luck." Another time, she carried a gold-tipped cane, "and the girls of Washington adopted it without a murmur." The *Washington Times* called Alice "a mistress of the occult and black arts" for the sleight-of-hand parlor tricks she was fond of performing at White House parties. It could also have been for the way she had bewitched a nation.

Her popularity continued to prove useful to her father. Baltimore was only the latest in Alice's public duties. The previous spring, she traveled as her father's emissary to Puerto Rico, receiving considerable praise for her diplomatic poise. Before that, wearing a gown of blue velvet, she famously christened the Kaiser's American-built yacht, the *Meteor*, in front of five thousand spectators, including her father and the Kaiser's son. The event was memorialized in a series of photographs on front pages all across the country. When the president called for three cheers for the Kaiser, Prince Henry responded by calling for three cheers for Alice. "She has become one of the most regarded women in the world," the *New York Tribune* editorialized after the christening, "replacing the young Queen of Holland in popular favor. She is seemingly unaffected by the sudden notoriety thrust upon her, but stands in the glare of the footlights without flinching."

Yet the dutiful daughter who smiled so prettily for the newspaper photographers would return to the White House after excursions such as the one to Baltimore in a very different temper, retreating to her room and keeping her distance from her family. She had been very excited at the start of her father's presidency to assume her public role; indeed, when she heard that McKinley had been shot, she put on a sad face in public but admitted in private that she "did a little jig." The reality of life as First Daughter, however, had turned out not to match her hopes. In the privacy of her room, Alice let her unhappiness flow in her diary. "Lunch at Mrs. Congressman [Charles] Joy's, given in my honor—or rather to give the wives and daughters of congressmen the pleasure of meeting not me but the 'President's daughter.'" She was fully conscious that she was playing a role, that the "Princess Alice" image was an illusion.

Ever since she discovered the truth about her father's first marriage and the fact that he had hidden and suppressed his love for her mother, Alice had been rebelling in various ways. In the years before the White House, when Theodore was police commissioner and then governor, Alice regularly broke curfews. She rode around on her bicycle with her feet on the handlebars, her lacy white slips exposed for the whole world to see. She hung around with boys, meeting them in stable lofts, much to Edith's despair. When Alice was forbidden to see her boyfriends without a female companion, she arranged to have one of her pals dress up like a girl and come calling for her. Theodore rebuked his daughter as a "guttersnipe" and sent her off to stay with Auntie Bye for a while in the winter of 1898. It was the banishment from the family that Alice long believed was coming and that she had finally made a self-fulfilling prophecy.

Now, as First Daughter, the rebellion continued, even if in public she played her father's devoted emissary. She was often caught smoking outside the Executive Mansion, sometimes by reporters, at a time when the idea of tobacco use among women was considered déclassé at best and immoral at worst. Alice smoked like a fiend, both pipes and cigarettes. After a meal, she'd get "quite nervous" until she had a smoke, observed secretary of war William Howard Taft. Alice herself recalled, "The family remonstrated with me on the subject from time to time, though they never actually ordered me not to smoke." She was told only that she couldn't smoke "under their roof," so she'd go up *on* the roof to light up. Unbeknownst to her parents, she even got her brother Kermit hooked, presenting him with a corncob pipe all his own. Kermit would remember a song Alice taught him: "Sweet cigarettes, why did you teach me to love you so, when I have to pretend that I don't know you?"

Her association with the opposite sex also continued unabated. One day, at Auntie Bye's Connecticut house, Alice allowed a man into her canoe, which was daring enough, but it also turned out to be foolhardy, since the man "hadn't the vaguest idea about how to stear [sic] and at one time he nearly took us over the mill-dam!" Other times, Alice rode around unchaperoned in automobiles, frequently at the wheel herself, scandalizing society and her parents. If she was to be called a guttersnipe, she seemed to think, then she'd act like one.

Alice's irreverent personality was, of course, part of the reason she was so popular with the public. One time, continually interrupting a meeting between her father and the novelist Owen Wister, she caused Theodore famously to quip, "I can be President of the United States, or I can attend to Alice. I cannot possibly do both." Alice's unpredictability, her impish smirk, her parlor magic tricks, made for colorful copy. Yet few knew the extent of the First Daughter's shenanigans. With other high-spirited girls such as Eleanor "Cissy" Patterson (daughter of the influential *Chicago Tribune* correspondent Robert Patterson) and Marguerite "Maggie" Cassini (daughter of the Russian ambassador to the United States), Alice, not yet twenty-one years of age, would show up at Washington parties to drink alcohol and smoke cigarettes with men much older than she. At night, in her diary, she'd record the "fearfully naughty stories" they whispered in her ear.

The dichotomy between her public and private lives could make Alice depressed, and she poured out her woes in her diary, lamenting the inauthenticity of it all. Still, performing as her father's ambassador did have its upside. The work gave her a rare opportunity to receive Theodore's acknowledgment and affirmation. Alice didn't box or swim or play football as Ted and Kermit did, so she never got the same sorts of letters they did praising their accomplishments. The best she could hope for were letters like the one she received after her state visit to Puerto Rico, in which her father called her "blessed girl" and told her how "very much pleased" he was with her: "You were of real service down there because you made those people feel that you liked them . . . and your presence was accepted as a great compliment." What was missing from her father's letters, however, was the sort of inside information he'd sometimes share with Ted or Kermit about his duties as president or issues he was grappling with. To Alice, he'd write only about "Mother's" health or his scrambles with Quentin or the antics of their menagerie of pets.

This was absurdly ironic, since Alice knew far more than her brothers about who was who in Washington and which way the political winds were blowing, since many of the players she actually considered friends. Her circle was Washington's young "in crowd," and they had connections everywhere.

She was always rushing off to one party or another. On the evening of January 20, 1904, she braved a light rain falling over Washington to head across town. She walked alone: only the youngest children had Secret Service bodyguards. "There was a village quality about Washington in those days," Alice recalled, "and nobody bothered one." After a long, frigid cold wave, temperatures had climbed back above freezing, and for the first time in nearly a week, many in the nation's capital, despite the drizzle, were venturing outside. Alice was bundled up in a wrap of fox fur, her hands kept warm in a muff made of mink. Her destination was the brownstone town house on Connecticut Avenue occupied by popular freshman congressman Nicholas Longworth of Ohio. Nick, as Alice called him, threw the very best dinner parties and invited all the most exciting people in town.

Under the pinkish glow of the electric chandelier, the conversation was witty, gay, and a little risqué. Nick, a bachelor and fifteen years Alice's senior, flirted with her but also made eyes at Cissy and Maggie. Alice's heart, however, was set on Charles "Charly" de Chambrun, the handsome secretary of the French embassy, who, in a never-ending game of romantic musical chairs, spent much of his time that night paying attention to Maggie. Alice turned back to Nick, who, as the night wore on and the champagne flowed, bet her fifty dollars she couldn't find out if a fellow guest was wearing a toupee. He quickly learned that Alice Roosevelt never backed down from a dare. "He said I couldn't find out, but I did," she wrote that night in her diary, though she neglected to say just how she discovered the truth. Still, she definitely made sure to collect her bet.

Back at the White House, Theodore was fuming. Alice's revelries did not please him. "Sister continues to lead the life of social excitement," he wrote to Ted on the very night of Nick Longworth's party, "which I think is all right for a girl to lead for a year or two, but which upon my word I do not regard as healthy from the standpoint of permanence. I wish she had some pronounced serious taste. Perhaps she will develop one later."

"Serious taste" bored Alice. Musing about her future, she wrote in her diary, "I pray for a fortune. I care for nothing except to amuse myself in a charmingly expensive way." Her father frequently took her to task for "gallivanting with society and for not knowing more people like my cousin Eleanor." After one afternoon lunching with socialites, Alice returned to the White House to face "a talking-to" from her parents "on having no interests in life." The lecture was, she told her diary, "not at all unexpected nor yet in the least undeserved. Only I am afraid I just don't care. I wish I did." She ended her entry: "No hope for Alice."

She just didn't care. That was a critical insight in understanding Alice. She wasn't acting out just for the fun of it. She was acting out to pay her parents back for their perceived injustices to her. Even if she never fully articulated that motivation in her diary, it was clear from her actions. Later she'd admit, "All the fun in having it is *taking* it, and doing one's best to defy one's parents." Despite repeated parental lectures, Alice never changed her ways. She continued her rounds of parties, gallivanting from place to place without her lady's maid, which irked Edith to no end. "You must keep Anna until you reach Auntie Bye's," Edith harangued her before one excursion. "I would not be willing to have you rambling about the country like Mrs. Leslie's Escorted Lady"—a reference to the collection of popular short stories by Eliza Leslie. Once again, Alice ignored her stepmother's warning, ditching Anna at the first possible opportunity. Edith was furious. "Your folly in allowing Anna to get separated from you has worried me very much, because you really know better," the First Lady scolded. "You are being trusted with a great deal of liberty and you must be careful not to abuse it." Again, Alice simply *did not care.*

In another letter, Edith had more advice to offer: "I meant to warn you about talking continually about yourself. It is quite the natural subject for a girl of your age but, except with your family, is neither well-bred nor wise."

Her maternal grandparents, with whom she still stayed a couple of times each year, were softer touches, especially her grandfather. At one point, when her parents refused her money, Alice wheedled a thousand dollars out of her grandfather, though it came with a cautionary note: "You say that you don't really think you are as bad as you seem. You are not bad at all in my estimation. But you lead such an exciting, undomestic life that you will come to grief, physically, before you are twenty-one years old. Of course it is all right to 'go it whilst you are young,' but I am afraid you are overdoing it and you will regret it later. You go with people who have money to burn and, I fear, lead you into extravagances. But as you are going to turn over a new leaf and reform, I won't find anymore fault with you now."

Clearly Alice had needed to make some promises to get the thousand bucks, but "reform" was hardly on her agenda. For the rest of the winter and spring of 1904, her diary was a litany of parties and flirtations. In Newport, her flamboyant behavior set tongues to wagging. Alice carelessly exposed her slip when she danced; when off-color jokes were told, she laughed a little too heartily. Also, once again she was unchaperoned. In the gentleman's club the Reading Room, there was even talk that she used "stimulants" in the private quarters of some of the more reckless millionaires. Gossip of this kind rarely deterred Alice, but on this particular occasion, the scuttlebutt in the Reading Room was overheard by someone, who passed it on to the society scandal sheet *Town Topics*, which filed it away for future use.

If her diary reflected only fun and lightheartedness, then Alice's rebellious lifestyle and her defiance of her parents' wishes could be explained simply as the behavior of a high-strung, independent young woman. Instead, her diary frequently reflects depression, anger, and despair. Her misbehavior was her revenge for feeling rejected as a child—and *revenge* was a word she often scrawled across the pages of her diary in large letters whenever someone crossed her. And the one who had caused her the greatest offense was her father.

"Father doesn't care for me," Alice wrote in her diary, "that is to say one-eighth as much as he does for the other children . . .

and Lord why should he? We are not in the least congenial, and if I don't care overmuch for him and don't take an interest in the things he likes, why should he pay any attention to me or the things that I live for?" With brutal candor, she admitted she didn't love anyone "overmuch" except for herself. As for her father, she loved him only as much as she could, with "the love that I am so far capable of."

The resentment that festered within her meant that the young woman who could be so charming and gay at parties could also turn mean and cruel. Jealousy was the one emotion Alice couldn't seem to suppress. When she learned that her cousin Christine had fifteen suitors pursuing her, she dismissed the men as "all more or less stupid." When she discovered that her cousin and close friend Helen, the daughter of Rosy Roosevelt, was serious about Aunt Corinne's son Teddy, she callously spread stories of the couple's looming engagement. For once, Alice's insensitivity prompted a rebuke. "I do not care for myself what you say," Teddy Robinson wrote to her, "but I don't want Helen's name talked of . . . It is all very well to fool about such matters but some people take them seriously . . . Please don't say any more about us to anyone."

Alice's hard exterior was, of course, a mask. The most famous girl in the world, the recipient of marriage proposals from around the globe, the glamorous beauty of the pictorial magazines, was, in fact, feeling unwanted and unloved. Charly ultimately chose Maggie over her; Christine had beaux right and left; Helen and Teddy were madly in love; but she, supposedly so desirable, was alone. "No one ever comes to see me," Alice lamented in her diary. "Oh what wouldn't I give to be a most marvelous belle and be more run after than any other girl." All the attention she received wasn't really for her, she believed, but rather for the "president's daughter." Sometimes Alice fantasized about running away and going into "seclusion." In her diary, she named those whom she would take with her: friends Johnnie Saltonstall, Margaret Dix, and Jean Reid; Helen and Teddy; and her cousin Eleanor.

Eleanor, at least, could never compete with her. Eleanor, at least, was every bit as alone as Alice felt. This was what made Eleanor such an ideal member of her entourage: she never tried to show Alice up. Eleanor was always lingering in the background, waiting on Alice's orders. When in New York, Alice often stayed with Eleanor at her grandmother's house. Her mousy cousin was acquiescent when Alice suddenly announced she wanted to pay a call on Margaret Dix, or have lunch with cousin Elfreda, or seek out a fortune-teller to predict their futures. Eleanor never objected to anything Alice suggested. Nothing about Eleanor intimidated Alice, which she couldn't say about someone as tempestuous and beautiful as Maggie Cassini. Nothing about Eleanor made Alice feel inferior—except, of course, the fact that Eleanor had been educated at Allenswood. That much her cousin had on her.

Significantly, just as Eleanor was finishing up her time at Allenswood, Alice took it upon herself to write Mlle. Souvestre a letter, using her very best French. The missive contained nothing of significance, just a rather boring account of Alice's visit to the Adirondacks. Perhaps Auntie Bye had suggested that Alice write to Souvestre to demonstrate that she, like Eleanor, was fluent in French and that she, like Eleanor, was bright and cultured. Yet any need to impress Mademoiselle was no longer all that urgent now that Eleanor was back home.

What Alice did not know, however, was that her shy, unassuming cousin—like Maggie, like Christine, like Helen—had a beau. Cousin Franklin had, in fact, asked Eleanor to marry him. That early spring of 1904, Alice remained blissfully unaware that homely, awkward Eleanor had landed a man before she had. Still, she'd find out soon enough.

MANHATTAN

On the corner of 106th Street and Broadway, the young man had reached the limits of his patience. The boor standing across from him had insulted his wife for the last time, so the young man hauled off and slugged him, knocking him to the ground. These sorts of altercations happened all the time on the streets of New York, but this one would make the newspapers, because the name of the man who'd thrown the punch was Roosevelt.

James R. Roosevelt Jr. was the son of Franklin's older half-brother, Rosy. He was once the beloved ward of Bye Roosevelt, after she stepped in to help care for him following his mother's death. His sister was Helen Roosevelt, the good friend of Alice Roosevelt and the paramour of Teddy Robinson. His family called him "Taddy," though his friends called him "Jimmie"—fitting, since he seemed a different person to different people. Jimmie didn't move in the same rarefied circles that his Roosevelt relatives did. The man he'd just struck was a saloonkeeper, and the wife he'd so gallantly defended was formerly known as "Dutch Sadie," a popular figure in the red-light district of the Tenderloin and the "resorts" of Twenty-Eighth and Twenty-Ninth Streets. Jimmie didn't take kindly, however, when someone called her "Dutch Sadie" now that she was his wife.

A policeman arrived and dispersed the crowd, telling the fallen saloonkeeper to get up and get moving. No charges were filed. Mr. Roosevelt took the arm of his wife, and they continued, heads held high, down the street. They lived at 343 Riverside Drive, a deluxe five-story "American basement house" built just two years earlier, for which Jimmie had paid $61,000. Sadie Roosevelt was, as always, dressed to the nines. She was a beautiful woman, with bright hazel eyes, "a profusion of bronze hair," as one newspaper described her, and cheeks of a "clarity and tint any woman might envy." She wore extravagant fur coats and a $7,500 diamond collar. The Jimmie Roosevelts were flashy and unconventional. This wasn't the first time their names would make the newspapers, and it wouldn't be the last.

On the eve of launching a political career of his own, Franklin Roosevelt had something else in common with Cousin Theodore. Just as Theodore had lived in fear for more than a decade that his brother, Elliott, might embarrass him and jeopardize his political ambitions, Franklin worried the same thing about his nephew— and his response to his kinsman would have echoes of Theodore's to his.

Early in 1904, Franklin was on top of the world. He'd just won election as chairman of his Harvard class committee, taking 168 out of the 253 votes cast—not a landslide by any means, but it was his first electoral victory, the first of many, he hoped. Franklin had already completed his undergraduate degree, but had remained on campus to jump-start his graduate courses (and to serve as editor of the *Harvard Crimson* newspaper). This would help accelerate a career he hoped would match Theodore's. "[Franklin] had more on his mind [in college] than sitting in the Club's front window, doing nothing and criticizing the passersby," a classmate would recall. He wasn't like others "who thought that the world belonged to them and who did not want to change anything in it." Rather, Franklin aggressively mapped out the steps he needed to take to achieve his goals. He'd been accepted by Columbia Law School for the fall, and from there he planned to sit for the New York State Bar before running for state office. Eleanor had agreed to marry him, which was a definite advantage; he'd need a good wife if he were to rise in politics. So, that early spring of 1904, Franklin had every reason to feel that he was on his way. That was, so long as his nephew didn't do something outlandish to tarnish the family name.

Franklin and Taddy were more closely connected than typical uncles and nephews. In fact, Taddy, the nephew, was actually three years older than Franklin, the uncle. They were raised together, at nearby estates in Hyde Park, more like cousins, with Taddy and his sister, Helen, frequently joining Franklin for holidays. Yet the two boys couldn't have been more different. Taddy shared none of Franklin's interest in books or studying. Instead, he was a mischievous, rascally sort of boy: Alice Roosevelt would remember that he always pulled her hair when he visited. On the playground, he proved to be bigger, faster, and stronger than his effete uncle, who—no surprise—recoiled at the idea of playing with him. From an early age, after one too many attempts at roughhousing, Franklin kept his distance.

When Taddy was thirteen, he and his sister went off with their parents to live in London, where, soon after their arrival, their mother died, a loss Taddy would never quite get over. Cousin Bye Roosevelt came to live with them for a while, providing a much-needed mother figure, but then she, too, left, marrying Admiral Cowles, and Taddy, at sixteen, was pretty much left to fend for himself.

Unlike Franklin, Taddy had never known the involved hand of a parent. Sent by his indifferent father back to America to attend school at Groton, he didn't share with Franklin the luxuries of visits back home or care packages that arrived during exam times. He was, effectively, an orphan. "I have not heard from my father for over a month," he wrote to Bye during the spring of 1897, "and have no idea of his whereabouts. One paper said he had sold all of his horses and had started for Paris. The papers seem evidently more informed on the subject than we are." He didn't even get to see his sister very often, lamenting to Bye that he and Helen might have only "an hour or two" together the next month. When Sara, Franklin's mother, sent Taddy an Easter card one year, he told Franklin she was "much kinder to him than his own family."

That didn't mean Sara liked the boy. "Do not let Taddy convince you choir-singing is a bore," she wrote to Franklin while both boys were at Groton. "Many things in life bore him and he will lose a great deal by having such ideas."

Taddy chafed against the regimentation of school. Choir singing was indeed a bore to him, as were mathematics, football, exams, and student clubs. What wasn't boring to Taddy was machinery: he was forever building and fixing machines. Automobiles, those newfangled moving machines, especially fascinated him. He loved racing them, polishing them, tinkering with them. It was hardly a hobby appropriate for a Roosevelt, though, and Taddy was scorned by his peers for his working-class interests. "A queer sort of boy," one former Grotonian would recall, "much made fun of by his classmates."

For Franklin, Taddy proved to be the bane of his existence, at both Groton and Harvard. He blamed Taddy at least in part for his own trouble fitting in. When Taddy was put on academic probation at Harvard, Franklin wrote to his parents, "I have never heard of such asininity. Everyone up here thinks him a fool." Something needed to be done, Franklin urged, lest Taddy continue tarnishing the family name. "He may be off on a bat right now for ought I know," Franklin told his mother. "I think the very strictest measures should be taken"—starting, he suggested, with cutting Taddy's allowance in half.

Yet Taddy was not a bad boy. At Groton, the headmaster had found him "troublesome, occasionally eccentric and difficult to deal with," but added that he definitely had a conscience. Mr. James, the boy's grandfather, called him a "good-natured, well-intentioned young fellow," though he admitted that when it came to studies and social obligations, Taddy could be "lazy."

In the highly ordered, regulated world of the upper class, there would always be those who bristled at the rules and expectations. To them, blind allegiance to authority, strict adherence to convention, and unquestioning compliance with tradition went against the very fiber of their beings. They didn't care about such things as club memberships and college loyalties. They rejected the very notion of divisions between the classes. Some, such as Taddy (and Elliott Roosevelt) simply could never fit into the world of their parents and siblings, and no room was ever made for their idiosyncrasies. In working-class worlds, far more leeway was allowed for people to carve out singular paths. Yet within the aristocracy, no such accommodation was possible, lest one risk the collapse of the whole delicate, artificial structure.

Both Theodore and Franklin had bought into the system. They fundamentally believed in its intrinsic righteousness. They used its practices and protocols to further their own desires and ambitions. For Taddy and Elliott, however, so inherently different from the others, there really was no other choice for them but to act out, to rebel, if they were ever to find some measure of authenticity in their lives. For Taddy, that meant shedding the family-imposed nickname and becoming Jimmie, a man of his own creation, in New York's Tenderloin.

Reformers referred to the vast area between Twenty-Third and Fifty-Seventh Streets as "Satan's Circus," and claimed it was populated by gamblers, gangsters, and prostitutes. In fact, there were many honest, industrious people living and working in the Tenderloin, adhering to their own standards and codes of honor. Not to them was dancing sinful; not to them was betting on a card game a ticket to hell; not to them was a woman expressing her sexuality shameful. In this world, Jimmie Roosevelt, at twenty years old, finally found a place he could call home.

Jimmie was quite popular in the Tenderloin, always quick to peel bills off his bankroll to pay for a round of drinks. His mother's Astor fortune, doled out in installments of over three hundred dollars a month (about ten thousand in 2016 dollars) kept him flying high. His friends at the Haymarket Dance Club were very different from the stuffy, entitled Harvard students he'd left behind. Now his best chum was Douglass Brown, twenty-one, a dry goods clerk and the son of a middle-class box manufacturer. Unlike Jimmie's classmates, Douglass didn't judge him for missing lectures or skipping the latest cotillion at Newport.

In the Tenderloin, Jimmie also fell in love. Sadie Messinger was a buxom redhead five years younger than Jimmie (not older, as the newspapers would insist) whose voice retained a trace of her native Hungarian, adding a certain "piquancy to her manner," one listener thought. Sadie had come to the United States with her family in 1895; they settled in the Lower East Side of New York. Her father was an accountant and real estate broker, but the whole family worked. Sadie toiled in a shop making neckties; her sisters worked alongside her making waistcoats. Another sister rolled cigarettes at a tobacco factory. The Messinger women were unlike the careful, measured, proper debutantes Jimmie had grown up with. Sadie spoke her mind; she was quick to laugh; she didn't pretend to be shocked by risqué jokes or crude language. In other words, she was just the sort of woman Jimmie would fall madly in love with.

From the perspective of Jimmie's family and aristocratic friends, however, Sadie's worst "crime" was probably not her working-class background. It was the fact that she was Jewish. For the bluebloods of Hyde Park, this was beyond the pale. To marry a factory girl was scandalous enough; to marry a *Jewish* factory girl unthinkable.

Jimmie didn't care. On the afternoon of June 14, 1900, without telling his father or grandfather, he hired two coupes, the first for him and Sadie and the second for Douglass Brown and a friend of the bride's, and headed to City Hall. Not surprisingly, the Marriage Bureau clerk was struck by the name Roosevelt, since Theodore was governor of New York at the time. He also noticed how expensively both parties were dressed, especially the woman, whose clothing he called "flashy" and "not in the best of taste." He asked no questions, though; the ceremony was performed, and the newlyweds departed City Hall in their coupes to celebrate their nuptials in the Tenderloin.

Less than two months later, Jimmie turned twenty-one, and his full Astor inheritance of $1.5 million flowed into his coffers. That gave him about $25,000 to live on per year, which, in current dollars, would be about $1 million. With this windfall, Jimmie purchased a luxurious suite at 124 West Eighty-Fourth Street and contracted a downtown furniture company "to furnish the apartments suitably." Sadie wore "expensive gowns . . . imported hats [and] lots of jewelry," according to one newspaper, and carried a purse with her initials engraved in gold.

For five months Jimmie managed to keep his new life a secret from his family, but word inevitably reached Hyde Park. On October 14 his father learned of the marriage and set off for the city in a rage. At the Eighty-Fourth Street apartment there was "a scene," with Sadie first in tears and then spitting with anger. "She scolded her father-in-law and her youthful husband," one newspaper reported, "and defied the former to take the latter away from her." Rosy did just that. With great reluctance, Jimmie acquiesced and returned to his despised former life.

That might have been the end: the family was working on an annulment on the grounds that Jimmie—Taddy to them—had been a minor at the time of the marriage. Given their clout, they might very well have secured what they wanted. Then, on October 18, 1900, the news went public. With Theodore running as vice president that fall, the story was leaked to the press, possibly by a political opponent. Virtually all the New York newspapers reported on the marriage, with illustrations of the "scarlet woman" and headlines such as ASTOR SCION'S BRIDE WON IN DANCE HALL. The gossip weekly *Town Topics* was all over the story, running a satirical poem:

When everything is said and done
Society is out for fun.
And should morality arise,
As an issue on the side,
And should they raise their saintly eyes,
It cannot be denied
That many social dames there are
Who, by such judgment, we should bar.

The implication of the poem was that some society women were just as morally compromised as Sadie—but, in fact, the real slander here was against Sadie. In the wake of her marriage to Jimmie, the implication in much of the press coverage was that Sadie had been a prostitute, a smear that would be repeated for decades without the slightest evidence. Apparently the fact that she was called "Dutch Sadie" in the Tenderloin was proof enough for those who'd already been conditioned to believe the worst about poor, immigrant women. In the newspapers, Sadie was portrayed as a hard older woman of loose morals who had seduced the innocent Jimmie for his money—when, in fact, none of those descriptors were true. Yet for those of Jimmie's social class, no defamation was too unjust when used against the working-class immigrant Jew who'd dared marry one of their own.

But Sadie, as it turned out, could handle herself. When reporters came nosing around Eighty-Fourth Street, she seemed at first to fear, not unreasonably, the combined power of the Roosevelts and the Astors, and tried, feebly, to deny that any marriage had taken place. Then, confronted with her marriage certificate, she quickly reasserted herself. "I'm just as good as any of those friends of Jim's," she declared loudly, "and I'll tell John Jacob Astor and Teddy Roosevelt so, too!"

Jimmie agreed. Turning his back on his family—and his class, and on what Alice called their "tribe"—he left Hyde Park and returned to New York to live with his wife. He had the means to do so of course: his father might have disowned him, but his mother's will guaranteed him a sizeable income. In this, Jimmie was very different from Elliott Roosevelt, who had tried to reject the tribe but remained dependent upon his family for money. Ultimately, Elliott was destroyed by his family's attempts to control him. Jimmie, on the other hand, was free to live his life as he pleased, his family be damned.

Two nights after all the publicity, on October 20, 1900, Mr. James suffered a heart attack. He'd been stressed by work pressures for some time, but "the dreadful and disgraceful business about Taddy was the last straw," Sara wrote to Franklin. "Your father cannot get out of his mind the thought that his grandson has been leading a wicked life for months. His marrying the creature brings it before the public." To Franklin, she passed on Mr. James's heartfelt plea to "never be like Taddy."

Six months later, Mr. James died. Franklin would forever blame Jimmie for his father's death. "One can never again consider him a true Roosevelt," Franklin declared. So he banished Jimmie as utterly as Theodore had banished Elliott. Never again would Franklin speak Jimmie's name; nor would he permit him to attend family gatherings. If Franklin knew of the life Jimmie and Sadie continued to lead, openly and unapologetically right there in New York (in 1902 they sold the Eighty-Fourth Street residence and moved to a swankier, more exclusive residence on Riverside Drive, where they entertained friends lavishly and employed a couple of German-born servants), he never made mention of it.

Some small comfort could be taken in the fact that Jimmie's latest stunt, punching the saloonkeeper for insulting Sadie, hadn't made the major newspapers. If it had, the story might have been picked up and carried all across the country as news of his marriage had been. It's also possible that Franklin was spared seeing any mention of the altercation at all, for during several weeks in the early part of 1904, he was off on a Caribbean cruise with his mother. The reason he was on that cruise might have provided him some insight into his reaction to Jimmie, if he'd been open-minded enough to see it.

The previous November, Franklin had asked Eleanor to marry him. He loved her not only for her character and compassion and "very good mind," but also for her strength: he'd always relied on a strong woman to support him, and he would need a strong woman if he were ever to break free of his mother. To his great delight, Eleanor had said yes—but then had come the task of his telling his mother.

He gave Sara the news on Thanksgiving Day 1903. She wasn't pleased. To Sara's mind, a man ought to marry only after he "had made a name and place for himself," as she'd write later in her memoir. At twenty-one, Franklin was still too young, she believed, to be thinking of marriage. Of course, much of her resistance to the marriage was because she was not yet ready to lose her beautiful boy, her companion at dinner and social events. Now that Mr. James was dead, it was Franklin who always sat opposite her at the dining table.

Sara also had some reservations about Eleanor. As smart and respectable as she was, Eleanor was not the woman Sara would have chosen for her son. While she'd been quite fond of Eleanor's father, Sara had not forgotten that Elliott scandalized his family: people had long memories for such things.

Stalling for time, Sara begged Franklin to keep the engagement a secret for a year. Reluctantly, Franklin agreed—and Eleanor, counseled by her grandmother that their first priority in all this was not to hurt Sara's feelings, went along with the plan. Such adherence to an antiquated set of social proprieties made the courtship of Franklin and Eleanor very different from that of Jimmie and Sadie, neither of whom would ever have considered the first priority in their relationship to be the protection of *someone else's* feelings.

Sara then arranged to take Franklin on a cruise, with the hope that during their five weeks at sea her son would have time to "think this matter over," as Eleanor later realized, and find his ardor cooling. Sara also made sure that the timing of their departure precluded a chance for the young lovers to say good-bye.

That, however, was more than Eleanor could take, and she let Franklin know her displeasure: "I don't quite think your Mother quite realizes what a very hard thing she was asking me to do, for I am hungry for every moment of your time." Franklin felt the same way, and for once he stood up to Sara, insisting that Eleanor visit them at Springwood before they left. He made clear to his mother that this was the woman he loved, and he would not be kept away from her.

He did not see Jimmie's situation in the same way at all. Yet on its most obvious level, Jimmie's crime had been to fall in love with the wrong woman, which was precisely what Sara now considered Franklin to have done. Of course, in Jimmie's case, there were obvious differences in social status, and that was enough for Franklin to have rendered any comparisons invalid. In his view, it was appropriate for him to fight for the woman he loved because she came from the same class as he did; it was not appropriate for his nephew because his ladylove was riffraff. Like Cousin Theodore, who had never viewed either Katie Mann or Mrs. Evans as a truly equal human being with his brother, Franklin believed fundamentally in an innate inequality of the classes. Mr. James needn't have worried: Franklin could never "be like Taddy." In Franklin's view, just as it was in Theodore's, class mixing was a crime against not just society, but nature itself.

WASHINGTON, DC

In the drawing room of Auntie Bye's house in Washington, in front of the tiled fireplace and highly polished carved oak mantel, Eleanor welcomed Franklin back from his cruise. From a distance, Bye kept a proper, watchful eye on the couple. Their engagement had not yet been officially announced, so a certain formality had to temper their reunion. Still, to anyone watching, it would have been obvious that these two young people had missed each other deeply and were very happy to be together again. Their talk in front of Auntie Bye's warm fire provided Eleanor with the reassurance she'd been craving: that Franklin, despite his mother's most ardent hopes, had not forgotten her during his many weeks away.

She hadn't been so sure. When days passed between his letters, Eleanor had worried, just as she did when she was a child and failed to hear from her father. "I cannot tell you the awful fear which came over me when no letter came," she wrote Franklin. "I suppose women are always fools about the people they love and I know you will laugh at me for worrying so."

The exact words Franklin used in his reply would never be known; years later, Eleanor would destroy all his letters. Yet, from the tone of her letters to him, which Franklin carefully preserved, it would be clear that he did not laugh at his fiancée's worries, but rather, dismissed them and set her mind to rest. Sometimes Franklin's reassurances took the form of poetry from Elizabeth Barrett Browning: "How do I love thee? Let me count the ways . . ." Sometimes they came from Bible lessons: "Fear nothing" and "Be faithful unto death." Eleanor rejoiced at such words. Not since her father had anyone cared enough to reassure her. Mlle. Souvestre had taught her how to be strong and stand up for herself, but Franklin offered another, equally important gift. He gave her a shoulder to lean on when she needed it.

At twenty years of age, Eleanor had come to understand what was expected of her as a woman of her class. She was to be submissive without appearing fragile, and intelligent without seeming competitive. She could grow and prosper and succeed, within some constraints, but she must never allow any change in herself to become too apparent, lest she appear to have outclassed any man. Mlle. Souvestre had created a utopian world for women at her school, but in the real world, Eleanor learned, a woman was required to operate within a tightly controlled sphere. In her second year back home, she came to accept those limits as an unchangeable reality. "Perhaps it is just as well we haven't the power of fulfilling our desires," she wrote to Franklin, "for we would do so many things which we ought not to do."

Her use of *we* was not intended to refer only to women. But in fact, the pronoun did not apply equally to Franklin or to any man: men *did* have the power to fulfill their desires, even when those desires led them toward things they "ought not do." Franklin enjoyed the intellectual conversations he and Eleanor shared, but he saw her strength in terms of how she could bolster his: "Dearest," she wrote to him at school, "if you only knew how happy it makes me to think that your love for me is making you try all the harder to do well!"

Eleanor was not unsatisfied. If her goal was a life intelligently lived, such an arrangement as she'd found with Franklin was perhaps the best a woman could hope for in 1904: a supportive spouse who would permit her intellectual and cultural pursuits even if her primary purpose was to support him. Besides, after so many years of feeling like an ugly duckling, Eleanor seemed to be awfully grateful just to have a man in love with her.

Her changed outlook on the world was evident. Her letters, not only to Franklin but to everyone, lost their pervasive tone of despondent self-absorption. She no longer felt alone in the world. Until Franklin came into her life, she'd been virtually homeless, bereft of a family: Grandmother Hall was a shut-in at Tivoli, her uncles were alcoholic and unpredictable, Aunt Pussie was increasingly erratic, and her other aunts and cousins had their own lives to lead. Her relationship with her uncle Theodore and his family, while cordial, was largely ceremonial. So Eleanor had no one—except, that is, her brother Hall.

Now thirteen years old, Hall was the child born during those last terrible weeks in Paris just before Eleanor's father was snatched away from her. Hall was in some ways all she had left of Elliott, and she had developed an increasing sense of duty toward her brother, who had recently departed their grandmother's house for the Groton School. "I loved him deeply," she said, "and longed to mean a great deal in his life."

That spring of 1904, Eleanor took the train up to Groton, where Hall was the less famous Roosevelt alongside his cousins Ted and Kermit. She made it a point to visit Hall once every term, "which was what all good parents were expected to do," she'd recall. She also wrote to him several times a week. "I want him to feel he belongs to somebody," she explained to a friend. Her father had, after all, imagined a day when they would all be together, with Eleanor playing the role of mother to her brother. As best she could, she was fulfilling that vision now.

Of course, her father had had another son, who was now the same age as Hall. Eleanor most likely knew of Elliott Mann's existence, either from Aunt Pussie's diatribe or from one of the other relatives she had approached to confirm what her aunt had told her. Whether Eleanor ever wondered about this other brother—where he lived, where he went to school—would never be known.

Then again, her father had never asked her to look after this child the way he had with Hall, since he'd never looked after the boy himself.

For Eleanor, it was better to direct her charity elsewhere, toward less personal, less charged endeavors. Many of her peers that season were joining the newly formed Junior League, an organization of high-society young women dedicated to advancing the cause of social reform among the working classes. While many of the League's members signed up because it was the thing to do and restricted their involvement to meetings and financial contributions, Eleanor dirtied her hands with actual work. She taught calisthenics and dancing (courtesy of her training at Allenswood) at the Rivington Street Settlement House, on the Lower East Side. Her students were the children of Italian and Jewish immigrants, and they adored her. One day a little girl pleaded with Eleanor to come home with her after class. "Her father wanted to give me something because she enjoyed her classes so much," Eleanor said. She didn't go home with the child because she didn't want a gift, but nonetheless she felt "a glow of pride" run through her.

"I can't say it was very important work," she'd later write about her time at the settlement house, "for I was not a trained worker, but it kept children off the streets and it taught me an understanding of a side of life that might have remained to me a closed book if I had not come in close contact with settlement work." Once again, she was doing what she thought her father would have wanted. When she was a very young girl, Eleanor had helped her father serve Thanksgiving dinner to homeless newsboys; her father had always shown an interest in the poor.

Her friends were often driven down to the Lower East Side in chauffeured carriages, but Eleanor rode the streetcars, mingling with the hoi polloi. The children of the working class interested her "enormously," she said. There were so many of them, chattering in a Babel of different languages, none of which Eleanor understood: Italian, Yiddish, Polish, and Russian had not been taught at the Allenswood School. The children lived in cramped tenements where only the rooms on the street got any light or air. Many of them panhandled, dressed in rags. Their parents, it seemed, worked all the time, laboring from dawn to dusk in factories, leaving the children to fend for themselves.

Disturbed by the conditions she witnessed, Eleanor joined the Consumer League, which advocated for better conditions for workers. If the lives of the parents were improved, Eleanor reasoned, the children would benefit. Always accompanied by a more experienced, older woman, Eleanor toured the factories in the Garment District, observing girls her age and much younger working the looms and the giant sewing machines, sweating profusely and sometimes hurting themselves. "It had never occurred to me that the girls might get tired standing behind counters all day long, or that no seats were provided for them," Eleanor said. She was struck by the less-than-sanitary conditions in the lavatories. With tremendous understatement, she'd write that her visits taught her about "some of the less attractive and less agreeable sides of life."

Her family was appalled by her volunteerism. When Eleanor showed up to one family gathering, a cousin expressed fear she might catch some immigrant disease from her. Yet it was Franklin's opinion that Eleanor cared about. Would he support her work or call it unseemly for a woman of her social status?

So far, he'd been tolerant. In her letters to him at school, describing her work, Eleanor occasionally asked him not to laugh at her. He never did. The big test, however, came one night when he was in New York and agreed to meet her at the Rivington Street house. What would his reaction to the neighborhood be?

Franklin was far more conscious of his place in society than Eleanor was of hers. Not long before, he'd taken a trip out west (a part of the country in which Theodore regularly found rejuvenation) and recoiled at the coarse manners and primitive living conditions of what he called "real Americans" (implying, even in jest, that his own social world was the artificial one). To a friend he joked, "I was saved, but it was an awfully narrow escape." Would he feel the same need to be "saved" at the Rivington Street Settlement?

Lumbering team-pulled drays stacked high with beer barrels and fast-moving single-horse wagons making deliveries of ice and milk clattered noisily through the streets. Sooty laborers trudged home from the factories on the straw-covered sidewalks. Everywhere was the smell of raw fish and boiled cabbage. Newsboys hawked their papers on the corners, and old women with dried-apple faces sold flowers for a penny apiece. In the midst of all this, Franklin pulled up in his expensive carriage.

Eleanor's students knew that Franklin was her "feller" (a term she'd never heard before) and had affectionately teased her about him. On this night, though, no one was smiling. When Franklin arrived, he found one of the little girls sick, and Eleanor distraught. The child couldn't make it back to her family's apartment on her own. Eleanor told Franklin he'd have to carry her.

Wearing a fashionable frock coat—Franklin always dressed elegantly—he lifted the girl in his arms. Out onto the street they went, Eleanor leading the way. The tenements of the Lower East Side loomed over them, five and seven stories tall and built close together. In the winter, a blizzard of black soot puffed up from the coal furnaces and fell over everything; in the summertime, the heat could be stifling inside the unventilated rooms. Franklin carried the child up the steep, narrow steps. Very little electric light had been installed in these places; people made their way in the dark using candles. The stench of raw sewage seeped into the walls, since minimal indoor plumbing existed and most waste was collected in chamber pots, to be dumped into the East River later. Inside the girl's apartment, the light would have been dim and the furniture sparse and threadbare. Most apartments consisted of just two or three small, often windowless rooms, with several people sleeping in each. How very different this world was from Franklin's in Hyde Park.

"My God," he said to Eleanor when they came back outside. "I didn't know anyone lived like that."

In a way, the girl's illness proved fortuitous. "I wanted him to see how people lived," Eleanor would later tell a friend. "And it worked. He saw how people lived, and he never forgot."

Franklin would pay several visits to Rivington Street to meet Eleanor. He saw the work she did, and admired the passion and the commitment she brought to improving the lives of these people. He encouraged her to keep on with her efforts, no matter what anyone might say.

This was why Eleanor loved him. In a world where women could accomplish only so much, she would need a partner, a man, to help her do the sorts of things required for a life intelligently lived. Franklin would be an ideal partner. He was, in every way, much more than Eleanor could have ever hoped for: handsome, charming, intelligent, committed to similar values—or, at least, persuadable to those values. Just as important, he was committed to *her*. Franklin was, in a very real sense, her father come back to life.

One threat still loomed over Eleanor's happiness, however: her mother-in-law-to-be. Eleanor did her best to win over the formidable lady. "I do so want you to learn to love me a little," she'd written to Sara soon after Franklin gave her the news of their engagement. "You must know that I will always try to do what you wish for I have grown to love you very dearly." Much like Sara herself, Eleanor insisted she had only Franklin's best interests at heart: "It is impossible for me to tell you how I feel toward Franklin," she wrote. "I can only say that my one great wish is always to prove worthy of him." Sara was not fully convinced, and remained hopeful that this year of delayed gratification would snuff the romance out.

For all Franklin's support and reassurance, the delay kept Eleanor insecure. To her cousin Ethel she confided that she was worried she "would never be able to hold him, he is so attractive." Franklin had become Eleanor's ticket to happiness. "I am so happy," she told him, "so very happy in your love, dearest, that all the world has changed for me. If only I can bring to you all that you have brought to me all my dearest wishes will be fulfilled and I shall know that you too will always be happy." She signed her letters to Franklin "Little Nell," just as she had her letters to her father.

On June 18, 1904, Eleanor and Franklin attended the wedding of Helen Roosevelt and Teddy Robinson at the quaint stone church of St. James in Hyde Park. Franklin was an usher and Eleanor a bridesmaid, sharing the honor with her cousin Alice. The bridesmaids wore white muslin and lace, with garden hats trimmed with pink tulle and pink roses. Uncle Theodore and Aunt Edith arrived late to the church, bringing everyone to their feet as they were seated. After the ceremony, a "small" reception, as the newspapers called it, was held for about three hundred guests under a canopy on the south lawn of Rosy's house, attended by dozens of waiters and busboys. The invitations were "confined to members of the family and intimate friends."

Not the entire family was present: Jimmie Roosevelt, the bride's brother, and his wife, Sadie, were conspicuously absent. According to Franklin, they were no longer Roosevelts at all.

WASHINGTON, DC

On the morning of October 20, 1904, in parlors and drawing rooms of the upper classes all over the Northeast, refined ladies and gentlemen opened the inky newsprint pages of *Town Topics* to read the latest tittle-tattle in the column "Saunterings." Few could believe what they were reading. Ever since publisher Col. William D. Mann had turned the society newspaper into a scandal sheet more than a decade ago, they'd gotten used to reading scuttlebutt about Astors and Vanderbilts and Schermerhorns. But *the President's daughter?*

"From wearing costly lingerie to indulging in fancy dances for the edification of men was only a step," the paper reported.

And then came—second step—indulging freely in stimulants. Flying all around Newport without a chaperon was another thing that greatly concerned Mother Grundy. If the young woman knew some of the tales that are told at the clubs at Newport she would be more careful in the future about what she does and how she does it . . . I was really surprised to hear her name mentioned openly there in connection with that of a certain multi-millionaire of the colony and with certain doings that gentle people are not supposed to discuss. They also said she should not have listened to the risqué jokes told her by the son of one of her Newport hostesses.

Only her first name was used at the start of the item, but most everyone knew it was Alice Roosevelt *Town Topics* was reporting on. For the few clueless souls who remained, *Collier's* magazine, several days later, named her plain. Ostensibly the magazine was taking Alice's side against "the most degraded paper of any prominence in the United States," but its defense only worsened things. *Collier's* made it clear that the *Town Topics* broadside had been "an attack on a young girl who happens to be the daughter of the President"—and, with its own eye perhaps on newsstand sales, the magazine reiterated the salacious charges against her. "All the errors that hurt a woman most," the article declared. Decent people, *Collier's* urged, should stop reading *Town Topics* and shun Colonel Mann, whose standing was "somewhat worse than that of an ordinary forger, horse-thief or second-story man." The damage, however, was now compounded.

Three weeks before the presidential election, northeastern elites were abuzz with talk about the scandal of Theodore's daughter—the same movers and shakers from whom he had once feared judgment over his brother's similar antics. "*Town Topics* was supposed to be read avidly only below stairs," Alice recalled, "but upstairs took pretty long peeks at it as well." Spoken gossip was one thing; *printed* gossip was something very much worse. Princess Alice's behavior had now crossed a line: she'd become one of those "social dames" whom *Town Topics* criticized back in 1900 as not being any better than the likes of "Dutch Sadie" Roosevelt. "Crazier than ever," her cousin Eleanor called Alice in a letter to her fiancée, Franklin, around this time. "I saw her this morning in Bobbie Goelet's auto, quite alone with three other men! I wonder how you would like me tearing round like that!"

Years later, Alice would remember the scandal this way: "*Town Topics* said I did dance on the roof of Grace Vanderbilt's house in Newport clad in a chemise for the benefit of millionaires. It was utter nonsense." Yet time had apparently dimmed her memory. In the fall of 1904 the scandal was hardly "nonsense," but was, rather, deeply worrisome for Theodore. Alice had dragged him smack into the middle of a tabloid war between *Town Topics* and its rival gossip rag, the *New-Yorker*. Continually trying to outdo each other, the editors of the two publications regularly collected thousands of dollars from intimidated socialites, ostensibly for publication of society registers in which they would be featured, but actually as hush money to keep them out of the columns. The publisher of *Town Topics* called its proposed society register *Fads and Fancies*, but in three years nothing had been published. According to Colonel Mann, among the prominent people who had subscribed to *Fads and Fancies* was President Roosevelt, who a few years earlier had sent a photograph of himself to be used. Most likely, Theodore sent more than that: as would eventually be discovered, people such as Mrs. Jacob Astor and Sen. Chauncey Depew paid $2,500 to the *Fads and Fancies* fund. No one could get into the fund, and enjoy the protection it ensured, for free.

Clearly, the fact that Theodore had colluded with Mann before this latest development suggested he had ongoing concerns about the family's reputation: perhaps, even three years earlier, Alice's hijinks made him nervous. It was also possible that Theodore's "subscription" payment was made out of fear of an older scandal. The lawyers for *Town Topics* were none other than Howe and Hummel, who'd carried the secret of Katie Mann and her son for more than a decade now. The president of the United States would not have wanted it implied that he had a nephew living from hand to mouth in the tenements of Brooklyn. Mrs. Astor had paid $2,500 to keep her skeletons hidden; Theodore would likely have paid even more than that if he'd needed to. To add to the irony, it was once again a person by the name of Mann who threatened to expose his secrets, although there was no relation between Katie and the colonel.

The immediate problem was Alice: how badly had she damaged him in the weeks before he faced the voters at the ballot box? Once, his daughter had been an asset to him; now, as a headstrong, independent adult, she could prove to be a powerful liability. Not long before, Alice had been spotted taking money from a bookie; only due to the efforts of "a great friend" of Theodore's had the story been kept out of the papers, as Alice would reveal many years later.

In response to her misbehavior, Theodore drafted a letter to his daughter that "scorched the paper on which it was written," as Alice would remember. "It enumerated the iniquities that I had committed, and my sins of omission too—that I had all but stopped writing to the family, that I did not appear to have a particle of affection for any of them, that I thought only of my own pleasure." Theodore accused her of actually seeking out such publicity to show him up. Even though Alice had admitted as much in her diary, she was infuriated by the accusation. "One of the greatest experts in publicity there ever was," she'd say, referring to Theodore, "accusing me of trying to steal his limelight."

Still, she understood the seriousness of the situation. Her reply to her father was courteous, and she promised to mend her ways. Afterward, however, she tossed her father's letter into the fire, "in a temper at being interfered with," she remembered.

Alice denied the *Town Topics* report, at least the part about the stimulants: "I have never had the faintest inclination toward stimulants other than tea and coffee." Her spirits were high enough already, she argued, so she avoided alcohol so "no one could say my gaiety came out of a bottle." Her statement, however, was directly contradicted by the secretary of war, William Howard Taft, in a letter to his wife: "She likes a strong drink occasionally and Nick [Longworth] always helps her, though such a habit ought not to be formed in one as highly strung as she is."

Alice had become a ticking time bomb. The best strategy was to ignore *Town Topics* (and, perhaps, pay the rag some more money) and hope the talk died down. After all, there wasn't yet a full-fledged industry fueled by gossip and sensation as there would be in another couple of decades. *Town Topics* and the *New-Yorker* were the only major players; *Collier's* called them "sewer-like sheets." The strategy seemed to work: as Election Day neared, all talk of Alice's antics disappeared from the press. Theodore was undoubtedly relieved.

Yet Alice hadn't exactly reformed. The scandal would have a second act, even if none of them knew it quite yet.

OYSTER BAY, LONG ISLAND

From the house, the crunching of wheels on gravel could be heard as a barouche filled with top-hatted gentlemen rolled up the driveway, drawn by a pair of horses. The family rushed to the windows to watch the show that was about to take place. Dressed similarly in top hat and frock coat, Theodore strode out the front door and greeted his visitors. Hats were lifted and smiles exchanged. The men had come to officially announce that Theodore was the Republican Party's nominee for president. Bowing graciously, the president launched into a formal speech of acceptance, though from inside the house his exact words couldn't be heard. The women, especially, were prevented from being outside for this bit of political theater—"hidden out of sight like *houris* in a harem," Alice would remember, "while the men performed their stately minuet outside . . . tribal rites in which we had no part."

Politics was a man's business, after all, and by the fall of 1904 the men of the Republican Party had united around Theodore as their standard-bearer. His main threat for the nomination, the conservative Mark Hanna, had died unexpectedly, and no further challengers were seriously considered after that. Now, with conventions over and nominations officially made, he set about the task of winning.

There was still so much that Theodore wanted to accomplish as president. His triumph at the Supreme Court in the dissolution of the Northern Securities Company had furthered his resolve to continue trust-busting throughout the country. What was foremost in his thoughts that fall, however, was the canal he was having built through the isthmus of Panama, finally linking the Atlantic and Pacific Oceans. In March he'd ordered his engineers to "make the dirt fly," but delays had kept the work from commencing. Now digging wasn't set to start until after the election. Theodore wanted very much to be the president who presided over the opening of the Panama Canal.

He was cautiously confident of victory. The scandal over Alice had been successfully tamped down, and his Democratic opponent, Judge Alton Parker, had failed to ignite much interest outside the South. Theodore ran his campaign largely from the front porch of Sagamore Hill, meeting with newspapermen and putting out statements to his supporters. It was not considered seemly for incumbent presidents to barnstorm around the country looking for votes. So while rallies for the Republican ticket were held from California to Maine, the candidate at the top wasn't present. Even so, from the size of these gatherings, and from the less impressive turnouts at Democratic rallies, most political watchers were predicting a Roosevelt victory.

Still, Theodore wasn't counting any chickens. "Nobody can tell anything about the election," he told Bye. "Things look favorable at present and I hope we shall win, but we won't be able to tell until the votes are in." To Kermit he wrote, "If things go wrong remember that we are very, very fortunate to have had three years in the White House, and that I have had a chance to accomplish work such as comes to very, very few men in any generation, and I have no business to feel downcast or querulous merely because when so much has been given me I have not had more."

Early on Election Day, November 8, the president voted in Oyster Bay, then returned to Washington. He sat down to a quiet dinner at the White House with Edith, Bye, the children, and a few Cabinet members. The gathering could "be turned into a festival of rejoicing or into a wake, as circumstances warrant," Theodore told Bye. A telegraph office had been set up in the Executive Wing to receive returns from each state.

They didn't have to wait long. By 7:30 it was clear that Theodore had won, and won decisively. Victories were being wired in from everywhere. Few had dared to imagine he could win this big. Theodore took every state outside the solidly Democratic South, piling up 336 electoral votes to his Democratic opponent's 140. That night in the White House, reading each telegram (run over to him by an excited ten-year-old Archie), Theodore was overcome. He called to his secretary, William Loeb. He needed to put out a statement.

The question many had been asking throughout the fall was whether Theodore was running for his first or second term. Since George Washington, the two-term limit for presidents had been the custom, even if it was not the law. For the past three years, however, Theodore had been merely filling in for the murdered McKinley; surely, some argued, he was entitled to a full term all his own, which opened up the possibility that he could run again, for his second term, in 1908. Conceivably, Theodore could hold power into the next decade, fundamentally reshaping the nation according to his own progressive values and vision.

On Election Night, though, flush with noble feeling, he made a decision he would live to regret. At 10:30 he strode over to the Executive Wing and spoke with the newspapermen who'd been gathering there all evening. In front of the assembled press, Theodore told Loeb to take down his statement, which he dictated in a loud and clear voice so all could hear:

"I am deeply sensible of the honor done me by the American people," the president said. "I appreciate to the full the solemn responsibility this confidence imposes on me, and I shall do all that in my power lies not to forfeit it."

He went on: "On the fourth of March next I shall have served three and one-half years, and this three and one-half years constitutes my first term. The wise custom which limits the President to two terms regards the substance and not the form. Under no circumstances will I be a candidate for or accept another nomination."

In that one impulsive, emotional decision, intended to demonstrate that he hadn't allowed success to go to his head, Theodore tied his own hands. Behind him as he spoke, both Edith and Alice blanched at his words, which took them completely by surprise. Edith would later admit she recognized right away the problems Theodore would face trying to get his agenda passed now that he'd made himself a "lame duck" for the next four years. Alice, for her part, simply couldn't fathom how someone could so willingly relinquish power and prestige. She would never do something that foolhardy.

MANHATTAN

The horns, drums, bagpipes, and cheers from the 1905 St. Patrick's Day parade marching down Fifth Avenue echoed off the brick and brownstone buildings. The clamor threatened to drown out the ceremony that was being conducted inside the stately town house at 8 East Seventy-Sixth Street.

After a long year of waiting, Eleanor was finally wearing her white satin wedding gown with its pearl collar (the latter a gift from her future mother-in-law) and the rose-point Brussels lace veil that had been her mother's—appropriate, since March 17 was her mother's birthday. Unfortunately, with the parade blocking the entrance to the street, "a few irate guests" were stranded outside, and would end up missing the ceremony, as Eleanor would remember.

There was the additional problem of security: Madison Avenue was also blocked off by police, due to the imminent arrival of the president, who was making the trip from Washington to give the bride away. That the wedding had come off at all, after months of wrangling and negotiations, was a wonder in itself. For Eleanor, the past few months hadn't been easy. Soon after their engagement was announced, Eleanor, stressed and anticipating more stress to come, got sick. "Very weak and looks like a shadow," Sara recorded in her diary about her daughter-in-law-to-be. Eleanor was confined for several weeks.

Meanwhile, the papers were full of the news of the Roosevelt-Roosevelt union. "A trip to Europe and an automobile are offered to any subscriber who will solve the Roosevelt matrimonial problem," joked the *Minneapolis Journal*. "Miss Eleanor Roosevelt, daughter of Elliott Roosevelt and niece of Theodore Roosevelt, is to marry the son of Mrs. James Roosevelt, who is a half-brother to J. Roosevelt Roosevelt, and whose half-niece, Miss Helen Roosevelt, married a nephew of President Roosevelt. These facts being as they are, how much did Great-Grandfather Roosevelt get for cordwood?"

Eleanor and Franklin had, of course, let the White House know of their plans ahead of time, and Theodore and Edith quickly expressed their congratulations. "We are rejoiced over the good news," Theodore wrote to Franklin. "I am as fond of Eleanor as if she were my daughter; and I like you, and trust you, and believe in you . . . May all good fortune attend you both, ever." To Eleanor he was even more effusive: "You know how fond your Aunt Edith and I are of you, and how we like and respect Franklin; we should have been much pleased to know that you were in love with and betrothed to any good man whom we thought worthy of you; but we are much more than merely pleased now, for we think the lover and the sweetheart are worthy of each other. Dear girl, I rejoice deeply in your happiness." He signed himself, "Your attached uncle."

Whether Eleanor actually knew how fond her aunt and uncle were of her would never entirely be clear. Memories of Aunt Edith's aloof disapproval likely hadn't faded in the past ten years, and while Uncle Theodore was always affectionate in his letters to her, Eleanor was never quite so effusive in return.

Significantly, she did not ask her uncle to give her away immediately. As her late father's only brother, Theodore was the obvious choice, but she understood the strategic negotiations that would need to take place to ensure his presence at the event. So, in the days after the engagement was announced, a flurry of letters flew back and forth between Theodore and Bye about what dates would work for him. He could attend, he told his sister, if the wedding took place before March 17, but after that he would be simply too busy. Three dates were best for him, he told Bye: February 11, February 14, and March 16. Looking over the list, Eleanor chose March 16, the most distant date and therefore the one that would give her the most time to plan. Only when that was settled did she ask her uncle to give her away.

"Indeed I shall be very, very glad, very dear girl, to do as you wish," Theodore wrote in response. "March 16 goes down as the date, and only some utterly unforeseen public need will keep me away."

Of course, it would have been more convenient if he hadn't had to travel up to New York for the ceremony, so a few days after Christmas, Edith penned a note to her niece on White House stationery. "My dear Eleanor, your uncle and I have thought and talked so much of your wedding and he feels that on the day he stands in your father's place, he would like to have your marriage under his roof and make all the arrangements for it." In this way,

Edith pointed out, Eleanor could pick any date for the wedding that she wanted—except for Thursdays, the First Lady qualified, "when we could not conveniently have a wedding on account of the large evening entertainments which come always then." Any other date, though—that was, any time before March 17—they would be glad to host Eleanor's wedding at the White House.

Eleanor lost little time in turning their offer down. Although her reply did not survive the years, no doubt she expressed gratitude and humility. A White House wedding, for many brides a dream come true, held little appeal for her. Her aunt's warm words may well have seemed hollow to Eleanor, after the years of Edith's disparaging her father. The little girl whose mouth and teeth had once had "no future," according to Edith, was not eager to accept her aunt's belated beneficence now. For that matter, while she embraced the role of Uncle Theodore as her father's representative at the ceremony, she was also not willing to turn over "all the arrangements" of her happiest day to him. Eleanor had lived through Uncle Theodore's "arrangement" of her life before and wasn't eager to give him that power again.

Once Eleanor had declined their offer, Edith wrote back that, since the president would therefore need to travel, the date of the marriage would have to be changed. March 18 now suited him better than March 16. Eleanor agreed to the new date. Then, a week later, Edith wrote again, requesting that since the president had to leave New York no later than three o'clock on the afternoon of the eighteenth, could Eleanor change the date once more, this time to the seventeenth? Edith explained that since Theodore had to be in New York that night anyway, to speak to the Society of the Friendly Sons of St. Patrick, he could fit Eleanor's wedding in around "3:00 or a little later" that afternoon. Once again, Eleanor altered her plans.

On the day of the wedding, the house on Seventy-Sixth Street (belonging to a maternal cousin of Eleanor's) was modestly decorated. The caterer, according to a spy for *Town Topics*, was an Italian with little recognition among the higher ranks of society. Likewise, the flowers came from a Madison Avenue florist "of no particular fame." The narrow staircase in the house allowed only one person to ascend or descend at a time. It was a far cry from the elaborate White House wedding Eleanor could have had, but it was her own.

The place was packed with family and friends. Auntie Bye was there. So were Aunt Corinne and Uncle Douglas Robinson, and Grandmother Hall in somber black velvet. Sara Roosevelt made a grand entrance in white silk and black lace. Aunt Pussie, perhaps still unconvinced about Eleanor's looks, advised her niece to drink strong tea, without milk or sugar, to raise her color before her march down the aisle. Eleanor's brother Hall, however, remained at school. Just before the ceremony, a telegram arrived from Mlle. Souvestre that contained just one word: "Bonheur."

Among Eleanor's bridesmaids, dressed in white silk and tulle and carrying pink roses, were her cousins Alice and "Little" Corinne. As groomsmen, Franklin chose mostly Harvard classmates. His half-brother, Rosy, was ill, and his nephew Taddy, of course, no longer existed.

Theodore and Edith arrived by special train. "Cheering and waving of hats and handkerchiefs greeted the President whenever crowds caught a glimpse of him," the *Tribune* reported. The same sort of attention awaited him at Seventy-Sixth Street. To the curious well-wishers who'd gathered along the block, the Roosevelt wedding took on "the semblance of a 'National Event,'" a reporter positioned outside the house observed. The nuptials were made especially noteworthy by "the presence of President Roosevelt, the bride's uncle, Miss Alice Roosevelt and Mrs. Roosevelt." One woman on the sidewalk, dazzled by all the rich and famous people going in and out, said it was "very much like a royal alliance."

Yet when Theodore emerged from an anteroom with Eleanor, who was taller than he was by a head, it was the bride who grabbed everyone's gaze. Aunt Pussie needn't have worried. Eleanor looked radiant, her blue eyes shining. At last she was a belle—but the focus didn't stay on her for long. By the time they reached the front of the room and the officiant, the Rev. Endicott Peabody, the headmaster from Groton, asked "Who gives this woman?" Theodore boomed out, "I do!" and reclaimed the attention of the crowd. "My father lived up to his reputation of being the bride at every wedding and the corpse at every funeral and hogged the limelight unashamedly," Alice recalled. At the front of the room, Theodore handed Eleanor over to Franklin and stepped temporarily to the side.

The bride and groom exchanged their vows. Resplendent in his morning coat, Franklin had caught the eye of several women outside, who remarked how handsome he was. "Surprising for a Roosevelt," someone else replied. Yet even the dashing Franklin couldn't draw the limelight entirely away from the president. After Peabody pronounced them man and wife, and Franklin leaned in to kiss his wife, Theodore clapped his new nephew-in-law on the back and said, loudly enough for everyone to hear, "Well, Franklin, there's nothing like keeping the name in the family!" Then he turned and rushed off to the reception in the library, eager to eat and drink and get on to his next event.

As Eleanor and Franklin watched, most of the crowd hurried after him. Eleanor would remember that the newlyweds were left "standing alone." While a few guests did stop long enough to offer their congratulations, most "were far more interested in the thought of being able to see and listen to the President." So Eleanor and Franklin did the only thing they could have done: they followed the crowd. In the library, they found Theodore holding forth, the entire room riveted to his stories and laughing at his jokes. "I do not remember being particularly surprised at this," Eleanor would say, looking back years later, "and I cannot remember that even Franklin seemed to mind."

They'd both mind soon enough, however. On that happy St. Patrick's Day in 1905, they weren't yet focused on competition, but their days of being eclipsed by Theodore and his family were fast coming to an end.

LATONIA, KENTUCKY

The largest crowd ever assembled at the Latonia Race Track leapt to its feet nearly in unison as the Foreman, a maiden colt, beat out its competitors to win the mile-and-a-half Latonia Derby by a nose. Cheers erupted and hats were tossed into the air. The thoroughbred's jockey raised his arms in triumph.

On that warm day in early June 1905 a group of distinguished spectators watched the races from a corner of an upper veranda of the clubhouse roped off from the other guests. A number of U.S. congressmen were in attendance, and at one point Kentucky governor J. C. W. Beckham joined them, but the "centre of attraction" at the Derby that day, the newspapers reported, was Miss Alice Roosevelt, wearing a lavender linen suspender gown and a lavender straw polo turban crested with ostrich feathers. Alice had watched the races with great interest, climbing over the low railing at one point to get a better view. She bet five dollars on the wrong horse, and was rather nonplused when she was handed her ticket instead of the cash. Alice Roosevelt wasn't used to losing.

She was at the Derby as the guest of Nick Longworth, who made a point throughout the day to introduce her to several other politicians. "Everyone presented to Miss Roosevelt was led to her through several of the inner rooms and a large window opening on the veranda," one newspaper reported. "Mr. Longworth made all the presentations and remained by her side throughout the afternoon, looking after her comfort."

Since April, the newspapers had been speculating about a romance between the pair—MISS ROOSEVELT IN LOVE, read one headline—but the White House continually shot down the rumors. After a visit to Cincinnati during which Alice spent time with Nick's mother, however, the press started drawing its own conclusions. "It is generally held here," one Ohio paper reported, "that Miss Roosevelt and Congressman Longworth are engaged to be married."

Those who remembered Alice's casual flirtations with Nick, as well as with half a dozen other bachelors in Washington, might have scoffed at the stories: Alice and Nick were just pals, many thought. Yet, over the past few months, the friendship had metamorphosed into something else. The previous fall, Alice's mentions of Nick in her diary were the same as they'd ever been: casual and lighthearted. Then, soon after Eleanor announced her engagement to Franklin, things changed. "Lunch [with] Mr. Williams and Nick," Alice wrote. "Talked to Nick. Oh my." A few days later, after supper at Nick's house, she wrote, "Nick and I in a very dark corner afterwards. It was quite wonderful."

Whether the two events, Eleanor's engagement and Alice's falling in love with Nick, had any connection to each other would never, of course, be known or proven. The fact remained, though, that just as Eleanor was preparing for her wedding (with Alice's father set to give her away), the nation's vivacious First Daughter was suddenly, madly, passionately in love for the first time in her life. Little notes on White House calling cards now flew down Pennsylvania Avenue to the U.S. Capitol, "personal and private" scrawled on the envelopes. "My own beloved Nick," Alice wrote. "Today has been very dull and wretched because I haven't seen you once. And I haven't been able to think of anything else. Last night when you kissed me I was so happy."

Yet like so many young people in love for the first time, Alice was insecure. In her diary, she worried whether Nick honestly cared for her, or if he still loved Maggie Cassini. Her own feelings for him had become overpowering: "I love Nick more than I can think and I know I let him see it pretty plainly. Oh, will you keep on liking me Nick? I want to be first for you, my darling Nick."

There was one way, of course, that Alice could make sure she was first for him. Nick Longworth was an ambitious politician. At that point in his career, he was less interested in falling in love and settling down than he was in getting ahead: Nick wanted someday to be Speaker of the House. An alliance with the president's daughter would definitely be an advantage in his rise to power. Even if Theodore had lost some of his political muscle by ruling out a run in 1908, he remained popular in Washington and around the country. Nick was glad to hitch his wagon to Theodore's star. The fact that the president's twenty-two-year-old daughter was a looker, and fifteen years Nick's junior, didn't hurt, either.

Nick had come to Washington after a fast rise in Ohio politics, where he'd been a protégé of Republican party boss George Cox. Things had always come rather effortlessly to the smart and clever Nick. Born to a prominent family of old Cincinnati money, he was a classical violinist at a young age, and at Harvard, unlike Franklin, he was warmly welcomed into the Porcellian Club. "His good head," said one Harvard classmate, "made it easy for him to get perfectly respectable marks without doing much of any work." In Washington, however, Nick found himself just one of 386 congressmen, and he was anxious to find a way to stand out. To climb up through the ranks, he'd need other members to assist him, not compete with him. Alice Roosevelt could help with that.

"My darling little girl," Nick wrote to her, once it was clear that Alice's own feelings for him had reached a fever pitch, "I simply can't stay away from you any longer." They planned to attend a party at one of the clubs together, but Nick told her, "If we get tired, we can adjourn to my well-furnished study." During a recent trip to Ohio, he'd heard so many wonderful comments about her: "You really are the most popular person in the world," he told her. "I simply love to bask in the rays of your reflected glory . . . And it isn't only the people in society that say nice things about you but everybody, including all my really toughest friends." He closed with a vow that the "last thing that would ever be left" in him would be his "wholly absorbing love" for her.

Nick was especially enjoying Alice's "reflected glory" that day at the Latonia Derby. At one point, he introduced her to two of the racetrack's owners: his Ohio mentor George Cox and his fellow congressman Joseph T. Rhinock. The forty-year-old Rhinock had been elected the previous November to represent Kentucky's Sixth District, which bordered on Nick's district in Ohio. The two men had been "warm friends" for years, despite the fact that Rhinock was a Democrat. Meeting the president's daughter would have been beneficial to any freshman member of Congress. In Rhinock's case, though, it carried some particular prospective benefits. Along with Cox, Rhinock was in the midst of overseeing the largest merger of racetracks in the country—"a gigantic combination," one newspaper would call it—with a total property value of three million dollars. In addition, the congressman had plans to "organize a mammoth company to disseminate racing news," a projected six-million-dollar-a-year business. Also with Cox, he was an investor in the Shubert theatrical syndicate, an organization many critics considered a "trust" and wanted to see dissolved—critics such as Alice's father.

Nick Longworth was not at heart a progressive Republican. He believed in the right of American businesses to organize, to conglomerate, to control markets in order to maximize services as well as profits. He knew that it would only benefit like-minded friends such as Cox and Rhinock to make the acquaintance of Princess Alice. She might speak well of them and their projects to her father. Even if the president didn't change his policies, it was always useful to have influence and inroads with him. Alice could indeed be very useful to Nick and his friends on many different levels.

"Nick impresses no one with his sincerity," William Howard Taft would write about the romance between Alice and Nick. For her part, Alice was spellbound. It didn't matter that Nick was so much older than she, or a little paunchy and prematurely bald. She was drawn to older men—"a father complex coming out," she admitted. Also, he made her laugh; he made her feel special. He let her be who she was, without any criticism or censure. Best of all, he promised to take her away from her parents.

Alice was no naïf, of course: she wasn't blind to the politics involved or the fact that part of Nick's attraction to her was tied up in what she could do for him. In the past, she rued the distinction between "the president's daughter" and herself, but in the three years since she had spilled that heartache in her diary, she'd reconciled those two parts of her identity. Her birthright gave her power, and she was prepared to use it.

So when Nick asked her to marry him, she said yes. "I don't see any reason why you shouldn't be the lady representative from the east half of Cincinnati for some years to come," he told her. Alice liked the sound of that—so long as they didn't actually have to *live* in Cincinnati, of course. Nick's destiny, she believed, was right there in Washington, first as Speaker of the House, then possibly as senator, then—who knew?

In March, Nick had accompanied her to New York for Eleanor's wedding. In her diary, Alice wrote barely a word about her cousin's engagement, and offered only the thinnest of details about the ceremony itself—except for one key moment that no doubt filled her with glee: she found the ring in the wedding cake. According to custom, that meant she'd be the next one married.

Still, an announcement of her engagement to Nick would have to wait. Alice had agreed to act as her father's ambassador on a tour of the Far East, accompanying William Howard Taft and a group of senators and congressmen. She'd never been west of the Mississippi, so the trip, with stops in the Philippines, China, and Japan, promised plenty of excitement—especially since she'd persuaded Nick to go along. So the gossip about their romance could keep bubbling for a few months longer. Alice was used to people talking about her.

That June, though, the talk turned dark.

A few days after Alice's appearance at the Latonia Derby, the *New-Yorker* ran with a huge story headlined AN INSULT TO MISS ROOSEVELT, calling out Nick's influence peddling in introducing Rhinock and Cox to Alice. The tabloid also alleged that Congressman Rhinock had once been arrested for theft, which made his introduction to the president's daughter doubly inappropriate. Rhinock, recognizing the damage that such allegations could have on not only his political career but also his ambitious merger plans, promptly pressed charges against the *New-Yorker*'s editor, Robert W. Criswell.

Given the connections of all involved (two congressmen, a prominent businessman, and even, indirectly, the president of the United States), the case was investigated posthaste by New York County district attorney William Travers Jerome, an ardent progressive Republican and supporter of the current administration. On July 11, Criswell was arrested on a charge of criminal libel and held on a thousand dollars' bail. Criswell's arrest, however, only blew the story up bigger. Newspapers across the country bannered the scandal—SLUR AT MISS ROOSEVELT LED TO LIBEL SUIT, read one headline—and furthered the allegation that Nick was seeking "political advancement by introducing his supposed fiancée, Miss Roosevelt, to politicians." Now Nick was being smeared as well.

The DA had other reasons to go after Criswell, however. He wanted to nail both the *New-Yorker* and *Town Topics* for their extortion of politicians and society figures through their phony "social register" funds. So Alice's earlier scandal was now dredged up by the investigation into her latest.

That summer, Jerome finally exposed the gossip rags' racket for what it was. "Solicitors told the men of wealth whom they approached for subscriptions that to purchase the book would insure the absence of their names from the columns," the DA's charges stated. Much of the newspaper coverage included speculations about the president's actions in the matter. Theodore had allegedly "agreed to have a pleasant article written describing his favorite recreations and amusements," while former president Grover Cleveland had pointedly refused any participation in the scheme. Had Cleveland taken the high road and Theodore sold out—or, more accurately, *paid* out?

No evidence would ever be found to prove that suspicion: when the list of names of those who had paid into the fund to avoid negative coverage was published on July 24, it included Mrs. Astor, Senator Depew, Reginald Vanderbilt, and dozens of others, but not Theodore. If indeed there was a record of any payment made by him to *Town Topics*, Jerome, a supporter of the president, wasn't likely to embarrass him by publicizing it. (Just that past winter, Jerome had publicly defended Theodore against his conservative critics in Congress, who, the DA felt, were unfairly "isolating" him.) Still, the mere mention of the president's name in connection with such dishonorable activity was bad enough.

Then, in August, the whole sordid affair reached an appropriately ghastly conclusion. On the night of August 3, editor Criswell, out on bond and facing not only the libel charges against him but the various extortion investigations, entered the Seventy-Second Street subway station. Half a dozen people were waiting on the platform for the downtown express train. One young woman noticed the way Criswell stood poised at the edge of the platform. Just as the train pulled into the station, Criswell leaped, hitting the front of the car and becoming entangled under its wheels. His head was severed and went rolling down the tracks. The young woman on the platform fainted dead away.

Criswell's suicide, Rhinock declared, was evidence of his guilt. The libel investigation, and any further scandal for the Roosevelts associated with it, ended there, but the extortion cases with both *Town Topics* and the *New-Yorker* kept on. Colonel Mann eventually published his long-promised *Social Register*, settled most of the libel suits against him, and continued to publish *Town Topics* for another couple of decades. The *New-Yorker*, however, folded not long after the arrest of its new editor, four months after Criswell's suicide.

The scandal Alice had unwittingly unleashed had concluded in the ugliest way imaginable, but she was spared the worst of it. She and Nick had conveniently sailed for the Far East three days before Criswell's arrest, but surely she learned all about it. Others might have been abashed by the scandal, and withdrawn from political intrigue, but Alice's passion for the game only intensified after she returned to the United States.

The *New-Yorker* scandal was different from the sort of gossip that had previously dogged her. Those stories had concerned girlish things: parties and flirtations and showing too much of her slip. The controversy with Rhinock, however, was about influence peddling and the power Alice could wield. When she'd stood inside the screen door at Sagamore watching her father outside receiving the news of his nomination from the barouche full of top-hatted men, she'd felt cut out from the political rites of men, and had "fantasized about what effect it would have if the screen doors flew open and the ladies of the harem tumbled out in a giggle." She was beginning to find out.

Even so, her power, at least for now, could come only through partnership with a man who could facilitate her achieving her own ends. Nick wasn't the only one, therefore, who would benefit from their arrangement. Theodore might have been willing to give up his command after four years, but Alice had no intention of disappearing when he did.

So she'd marry Nick, and together they would control the town. After a childhood spent feeling as if she didn't matter, Alice was determined never to be powerless again.

The wars begin. The rivalry between Theodore Roosevelt and his brother Elliott was passed down to their children. *(TR Center, Dickinson State University)*

The extraordinary Anna "Bye" Roosevelt might have been president instead of Theodore if she had been born a man. *(TR Center, Dickinson State University)*

Theodore's star-crossed elder children: Kermit, Alice, Ethel, and Theodore Junior. The crossed eyes would be the first of Ted's challenges to overcome. *(TR Center, Dickinson State University)*

The family grew: Theodore, Archie, Ted (now with glasses), Alice (standing apart as always), Kermit (already a dreamer), Edith, and Ethel. *(TR Center, Dickinson State University)*

Sagamore Hill in Oyster Bay, Long Island. *(TR Center, Dickinson State University)*

Elliott with his daughter, Eleanor. Their relationship defined her life. *(Franklin D. Roosevelt Presidential Library and Museum)*

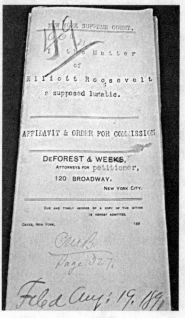

Anna Hall Roosevelt, Eleanor's mother *(Franklin D. Roosevelt Presidential Library and Museum)*

Court records from Theodore's unsuccessful attempt to commit Elliott to an asylum. *(New York Surrogate Court, author collection)*

Francis H. Weeks.

Theodore thought highly of Frank Weeks, until the lawyer was arrested for embezzlement. The money promised to Katie Mann was never delivered. *(Author collection)*

Katie Mann worked as a seamstress and laundress to support her son with Elliott. Elliott Roosevelt Mann is seen in the background, about the age of six or seven. *(From the collection of the Biles family)*

Elliott Mann (second row from the bottom, fifth in from the right) graduated from Public School 55 in 1906. *(From the collection of the Biles family)*

Katie Mann's mother, Elisabeth Köhler Mann, at their apartment in Brooklyn. *(From the collection of the Biles family)*

Pampered and protected, little Franklin (left) grew up with his aunt Helen and uncle Taddy, who were his same age. Taddy called himself Jimmie after he rebelled against the family and was banished. *(Franklin D. Roosevelt Presidential Library and Museum)*

Franklin (back row, third from left) didn't make the Porcellian Club at Harvard as Theodore's sons did, but he was editor of the *Harvard Crimson*. *(Franklin D. Roosevelt Presidential Library and Museum)*

The only son of "Mr." James and Sara Delano Roosevelt, Franklin took his father's place in his mother's life after the Roosevelt patriarch died. *(Franklin D. Roosevelt Presidential Library and Museum)*

President Theodore Roosevelt made the First Family a national treasure, and his boisterous brood helped his popularity: Quentin, Theodore, Ted, Archie, Alice, Kermit, Edith, and Ethel. *(TR Center, Dickinson State University)*

Theodore won handily in 1904, but he'd live to regret his hasty announcement on Election Night not to run again. *(TR Center, Dickinson State University)*

PRESIDENT'S SON ILL.

Theodore Junior Stricken With Pneumonia at New England School.

MOTHER HASTENS TO HIM.

Possible That His Boy's Illness May Cause the President to Abandon His Proposed Trip to the Charleston Fair.

Washington, Feb. 8.—Owing to the illness of Theodore Roosevelt, Jr., who, it is said, is suffering from pneumonia at Groton, Mass., Mrs. Roosevelt has gone to Groton. She has been obliged to recall her invitations for a tea next Monday and also to cancel all her engagements in Washington for the present.

It is not known yet whether the proposed trip of the president to Charles-

THEODORE ROOSEVELT, JR.

ton will be abandoned. It is known that he will go if his son's condition will warrant it, and much will depend upon Mrs. Roosevelt's report after she reaches the young man's bedside.

Young Roosevelt is quite ill, but his condition is not as yet considered alarming.

Ted was better known to the public for his boyhood illnesses than for any great athletic or academic achievements. *(TR Center, Dickinson State University)*

Kermit was the dreamer, the wanderer, the "different" son. *(TR Center, Dickinson State University)*

LESLIE'S WEEKLY

Copyright, 1902, by Judge Company, No. 110 Fifth Avenue

Vol. XCIV. No. 2421   New York, January 30, 1902   Price 10 Cents

MISS ALICE ROOSEVELT,

THE CHARMING DAUGHTER OF THE PRESIDENT, WHO HAS BEEN ASKED BY EMPEROR WILLIAM TO CHRISTEN HIS NEW YACHT—HER LATEST PHOTOGRAPH, TAKEN IN HER DEBUTANTE GOWN, AND WEARING THE NECKLACE WHICH WAS THE GIFT OF THE PRESIDENT.—Copyright, 1901, Frances Benjamin Johnston.

Princess Alice was the first teenage celebrity, prompting an "Alice mania" across the country. *(Author collection)*

Eleanor's coming-out portrait. She hated every minute of the experience, but a generation later didn't protect her daughter from the same ordeal. *(Franklin D. Roosevelt Presidential Library and Museum)*

Elliott Mann's teenage years were hardscrabble and enterprising, a world away from his privileged siblings and cousins. His mother always made sure he dressed well. *(From the collection of the Biles family)*

Franklin and Eleanor at Helen Roosevelt's wedding to Teddy Robinson, a year before they tied the knot themselves. No photographs would survive from their own wedding. *(Franklin D. Roosevelt Presidential Library and Museum)*

By 1912 Franklin was an up-and-coming politician whose looks brought women flocking to his campaign events. *(Franklin D. Roosevelt Presidential Library and Museum)*

PART IV

A SHOT

1912

The man with the heavily lidded eyes stood in the crowd, doing his best to blend in, waiting for his chance.

The night of October 14, 1912, was crisp and clear. A throng of people had gathered outside the Hotel Gilpatrick on North Third Street after word got around that Theodore Roosevelt was inside. An open touring car waited on the street to whisk him to the Milwaukee Auditorium, where he was set to give a speech. The former president, known these days as "Colonel Roosevelt," was in the midst of a campaign to win back the White House as an independent candidate, challenging both the incumbent Republican, President William Howard Taft, and the Democrat, Governor Woodrow Wilson of New Jersey. He was trying to make up for the blunder he'd made on Election Night 1904, when he impulsively ruled out running again.

Roosevelt's independent campaign was the reason the man with the hooded eyes had come to the Hotel Gilpatrick that night. It was also the reason he had pursued the former president from Charleston to Atlanta to Chattanooga to Nashville to Louisville to Chicago, and finally here, to Milwaukee.

The man stationed himself near Colonel Roosevelt's car and waited. At a little past eight o'clock, Theodore emerged from the front doors of the hotel. The crowd burst into cheers. Shaking hands all around, the ex-president reveled in the applause and the shouts of good luck. He was in unusually fine spirits. Approaching his fifty-fourth birthday, he was no longer the robust champion he'd once been—slimmer, grayer, but he'd withstood the rigors of the campaign as well as a man half his age. A few months earlier, sitting on the rear platform of a train flying through a dusty stretch of Arkansas, Theodore had told reporters that he was "feeling like a bull moose"—which quickly became the nickname for his independent Progressive Party. The "Bull Moose Party" still seemed a long shot to challenge the entrenched two-party system, but it had certainly upset the political landscape.

With an extremely popular, much-lauded former chief executive as its standard-bearer, the Progressives, some thought, might just go all the way.

Theodore wanted very much to be back in the White House. Taft, his carefully chosen successor, whose nomination and election he had worked so tirelessly to achieve, had proven to be a shattering disappointment. Soon after leaving office in March 1909, Theodore went off with Kermit on a safari to Africa; at the end of the hunt, he met up with Edith in Khartoum for a European tour. Yet, all the while, he was receiving dispatches from allies in the United States detailing Taft's perfidy. Bit by bit, from conservation efforts to trust-busting, the new president was undoing all the progressive gains Theodore had made during his time in office. The conservative, probusiness wing of the party was now back in power. Theodore felt deeply, personally betrayed.

Before Taft was even in office for a year, a movement arose to draft Theodore to run for another term—either his second or his third, depending on one's point of view. In New York, some newspapermen formed a Back from Elba Club, toasting their dream of Theodore's restoration at each gathering. Yet Theodore, who had settled into an editorship at *The Outlook* magazine after his European tour, was not initially very enthusiastic about a political comeback, despite his disillusionment with Taft. When it became clear that progressives within the party were angling to draft Theodore to challenge Taft's renomination, the former president rebuffed the plan. To one supporter he wrote, "Everything must be done by you and all the other people to stop any possibility of a stampede to me. This is the one thing that must not happen." To his son-in-law, Congressman Nick Longworth, he gave strict orders that all movements on his behalf were to be squashed.

Still, friends kept nudging him. Henry Cabot Lodge reported the talk going around Washington: "He made Taft president. He made the Republican Party nominate him. He owes us something now to get us out of our troubles." Lodge knew that this would play to Theodore's finely tuned sense of personal responsibility. "This may not be logical," Lodge wrote, "but it is very human."

What really rankled Theodore was the resurgence of the old

party bosses. During that summer of 1912, his nephew Teddy Robinson, Corinne's son, launched a run for the New York State Assembly as a Progressive Republican. T.R.'S NEPHEW BUCKS MACHINE, read the headlines. Not long afterward, the machine struck back: Teddy's nomination was overturned on a technicality. The conservative old guard wasn't eager to accept another radical Roosevelt into their ranks. Enraged, Theodore counseled his nephew on his next steps. "I have sent Teddy the very rough draft of what I should tentatively recommend in the way of a proclamation," he wrote to Corinne. "He has been defrauded by a piece of as outrageous political scoundrelism as I have ever known." He blamed "big businessmen, the great conservatives and the professional intellectuals" who had never supported him while he was president, either—and who were the very people now running the Taft administration.

What Theodore advised his nephew to do was simple and direct: he should fight back. It proved sound advice, as a court reinstated Teddy's nomination and he went on to win office in November. Teddy's example was not lost on Theodore. If his nephew could fight back and win, why couldn't he?

So, finally, he agreed to challenge Taft. When he failed to wrest the Republican nomination away from the president, though, he gave in to his supporters' most ardent wishes: he accepted the nomination of a new third party, the National Progressive Party, which held its first convention in August. For the first time in history, female delegates were welcomed to a party convention. The Progressives declared their support for women's suffrage, a position neither of the two major political parties had yet taken. Social activist Jane Addams enthusiastically seconded Theodore's nomination.

Yet even if they shared the liberal philosophy espoused by the Progressives, few high-ranking Republicans bolted the party, unwilling to risk possible career suicide. Theodore was deeply disappointed with many former allies who sided with Taft, but he gave a pass to one of them: Nick Longworth.

"Of course you must stand straight by Taft and the Administration," Theodore reassured his son-in-law. The president was

Nick's constituent, after all, hailing from his district in Ohio; to oppose him would have been, as Nick argued, extremely "awkward." Theodore accepted the argument, but cautioned, "Do keep yourself clear to stand for progressive policies." He liked Nick, trusted him, and assumed they were simpatico. He assumed wrongly.

When Nick asked for Alice's hand in marriage, Theodore had given his assent enthusiastically—and not just to get his publicity-prone daughter married and out of the headlines. Nick was a Harvard man and, even better, a Porcellian: they called each other "Brother Roosevelt" and "Brother Longworth," leaving Alice rolling her eyes. Yet if Theodore believed that Nick shared his progressive values and vision of leadership, he was eventually disabused of that belief: Nick was a politician, after all, skilled at telling people what they wanted to hear. He was a progressive when it was expedient to be one; now the conservatives offered him a better chance to hang on to power.

If few Washington insiders trusted that Theodore and his Progressive Party could prevail, that wasn't the case among the true believers, who brought "a fairly religious fervor" to the campaign, Theodore thought. He tapped into that passion to great effect. "We stand at Armageddon," he told his followers, "and we battle for the Lord!" Galvanized by their belief in a noble cause, Progressives wanted to break the hold of big money over American politics, level the playing field for all citizens, and do away with the corrupt, corporate control over nearly every facet of American life. Not surprisingly, the Progressives' goal of fundamentally transforming the country unnerved the powers-that-be. "Every corrupt boss and every corrupt financier in the country," Theodore said, "and all the newspapers they control are engaged in the effort to beat me at all costs." For Progressives, Theodore was their great hope, the one who had given their movement a capital *P*. When Theodore accepted the party's nomination, delegates cheered him for a full hour before he could speak, and then, after applauding for him for two more hours during his rousing speech, still "wanted more," as Theodore proudly told his son Kermit.

For all that, he knew the odds remained stacked against him.

"I do not for a moment believe that we shall win," he confided to Kermit. "The chances are overwhelmingly in favor of Wilson." Pitted against the Progressives, he pointed out, was "all the money, the organization, all the press, nearly all the political and business leadership." What he hoped for, at least, was to come in "a little ahead" of Taft, who, he felt, had betrayed him.

Still, he allowed himself to dream of victory, especially as the campaign rolled on and large crowds greeted him at every stop. Progressive leader William Allen White found the candidate "full of animal spirits, exhaustless at all hours, exuding cheer and confidence." He was, after all, not only a popular ex-president, but also a Nobel Prize winner, the first American to win the award, which had been given to him for his help in negotiating peace between Russia and Japan in the fall of 1905. No former president had ever retained as much influence and clout, in the nation and around the world. So, very cautiously, he revised his estimates upward: "There is a very slight chance," he'd recently admitted to Kermit, "that we will develop enough strength to win."

Certainly he was fighting for victory as hard as he'd ever fought for anything, propelled by his belief in the cause, his anger at Taft, and his regret over that impulsive decision not to run for office again in 1908. At every stop, the love from the crowds was palpable, and Theodore basked in it.

Outside the Hotel Gilpatrick in Milwaukee, the love seemed especially ardent. Taking his seat in the open automobile, Theodore was so moved by the outpouring of support from the crowd that he stood up once again to graciously acknowledge his fans. That was when the man with the heavily lidded eyes saw his chance. From his pocket, he withdrew a .32-caliber Colt revolver and readied his finger on the trigger.

The man's name was John Schrank. He'd been dreaming, quite literally, of this moment for weeks. He was a thirty-four-year-old German-born American citizen and former saloonkeeper from Manhattan. Living off the rents from several properties he owned, Schrank spent his time reading and obsessing over the increasingly hostile coverage Theodore received in the *New York World*. The newspaper was outraged that Colonel Roosevelt should defy tradition and seek what it was calling a "third term." Sometimes they didn't refer to Theodore by name, but only as "the third-termer." Schrank clipped hundreds of newspaper articles that accused the former president of treason, corruption, militarism, and more. He became convinced that Theodore was "trying to get perpetual power and dictatorship" for himself. In a manifesto that he carried on his person, Schrank wrote, "We have allowed an adventurer to circumtravel [sic] the Union with military escort with the torch of revolution in his hands to burn down the house we live in." Schrank was determined to "defend tradition of his country against violation." It was God's will, he believed, that he should act.

Shortly after President McKinley's death, Schrank had dreamed of the murdered chief executive sitting up in his coffin and accusing his successor, Roosevelt, of being his true murderer. The dream had recurred since then, and Schrank had become convinced that he was on a divine mission to kill the would-be dictator Roosevelt. "God has called me to be his instrument," Schrank wrote. "Let it be the right and duty of every citizen to forcibly remove a third termer." To those who called him crazy, Schrank replied, "I presume you would declare Joan d'Arc, the Maid of Orleans, insane because the Holy Virgin appeared to her in a vision. God appeared to Moses in the shape of a burning thorn bush, then again as a cloud . . . Why then in cases of dire national needs should not God appear to one of us in a vision?"

Schrank was not the first (nor would he be the last) highly suggestible person to embrace extremist beliefs and conspiracy theories after being influenced by highly partisan, sensationalistic news media. To many people, Theodore was a much-needed agent for social change, but Schrank saw that change as destructive of traditional American values—"burning down the house," as he wrote in his manifesto. Theodore personified big government, an image that frightened conservatives, individualists, and loners such as Schrank. As New York City police commissioner, Theodore had closed down those saloons not in compliance with municipal codes, and Schrank's family's bar had been one of them. Two decades later, Schrank remained bitter over this "encroachment on his right" to do business. It was time, he declared in his manifesto, to "be a man" and stop the tyrant in his tracks before he destroyed the country.

For once, Theodore was the hunted. For once, someone else had the gun.

Schrank had been lurking in the crowds when Theodore spoke in Atlanta and in Chattanooga, but both times his prey had escaped him. "He did not come out the way I expected," Schrank later told investigators. "He went out a different way and [so] the man got away."

Not any longer. Finally, outside the Gilpatrick Hotel, Schrank had a clear shot. "A man that wants a third term," he believed, "has no right to live." He pulled the trigger.

The sound of the shot echoed off the surrounding brick buildings. For a millisecond, there was stunned silence. Then people began to scream. Theodore gasped and gripped his chest before falling back against the car seat.

Instantly the Colonel's bodyguards were on Schrank like a pack of dogs. One got his hands around the man's neck, fully intending to kill him, but Theodore called out to let his assailant go. Sitting back up in the car, he was still clutching his chest but apparently not hurt fatally. He asked that Schrank be brought over to him. The two men looked into each other's eyes. Later Theodore would recall the deadness he saw in Schrank's gaze.

As the would-be assassin was taken away by police, Theodore's aides discovered he'd been hit in the right side of his chest and was bleeding through his shirt. He could breathe easily, however, and when he coughed into a handkerchief, he saw no blood, which convinced him the bullet had missed his lung. Refusing medical treatment, he announced he'd continue with his plans. "You get me to that speech," he told his aides.

Ever since he became president eleven years earlier, Theodore had been prepared for an assassination attempt; a gunman's bullet, after all, had brought him to the White House. He'd thought through all the "possible contingencies in advance" and decided "that if I was shot when I was about to give a speech or anything of the kind I should go on with the speech or whatever I was doing, because two or three hours always elapse before a man is so incapacitated by a wound as to make it physically impossible for him to do his work." His speech that night at the Milwaukee Auditorium turned out to be one of the great spectacles of political theater of all time.

"Friends," Theodore addressed the crowd, "I shall ask you to be as quiet as possible. I don't know whether you fully understand that I have been shot." He unbuttoned his waistcoat to reveal his bloody shirt. The crowd gasped. "But it takes more than that to kill a bull moose," he declared, prompting raucous cheers. He withdrew his speech from his jacket. It was folded in two, punctured through by the bullet. Theodore held it up for the crowd to see. His speech, along with his dented spectacles case, had slowed the bullet enough to keep it from his lung. His words, quite literally, had saved his life.

Gathering his strength, he launched into his usual tirade, going after the millionaires, the heads of big business, the corrupt party bosses. The crowd listened in a state of shock, as if Lazarus himself stood at the podium. As Theodore spoke, the color drained from his face; his shirt became steadily pinker. Finally, after a full hour, he concluded his words, accepted the thunderous applause, and agreed to go to the hospital.

"Indomitable courage," declared the *New York Times*. "No thought of self," bannered the *Sun*. A cartoon in the *New York Herald* depicted Theodore reading from his bullet-torn speech. "We are against his politics," the newspaper declared, "but we like his grit."

>———<

Upon learning the news, Theodore's family rushed to his side. Only the two youngest, Archie, eighteen, and Quentin, fourteen, remained at school. Edith, Ted, and Ethel hurried from New York, meeting Alice, who came in from Cincinnati. X-rays showed that the bullet was lodged against a rib. "Temperature and pulse normal," the family wired to Bye. "General condition good. One rib broken by bullet. Blood pressure coming down." Theodore was transferred by train to Mercy Hospital in Chicago, where doctors concluded it was better to leave the bullet where it was rather than risk cutting it out. Theodore would carry the slug of metal inside him for the rest of his life.

Meanwhile, so many roses and lilies of the valley were arriving at the hospital from Bye that they filled four vases. "Dearest Bamie," Edith wrote, using her sister-in-law's childhood nickname, "Theodore looks perfectly well but it will still be some time before he is free from discomfort and I know he ought not to use his right arm as much as he does. Last night he slept well and was able to turn on the right side so he is very bright today. The doctor suggested he should only have a glass of milk for lunch, and a hearty breakfast and dinner, which is a good plan because he had gained much in weight."

For Alice, it had been an especially fraught few days. She got the news of the shooting while eating breakfast with Nick at his family's home in Cincinnati and made plans to go to her father right away. Nick did not accompany her, but promised to join her later. Her husband was, of course, in the midst of running his own reelection campaign, and supporting a man other than Alice's father for president. She hadn't been nearly as gracious as Theodore in accepting Nick's political predicament and had made her pique at her husband quite plain. For all her many issues with her father, Alice had thrown herself wholeheartedly into his campaign. After all, she reasoned, to once again be the daughter of the president would give her a much greater platform from the one she currently enjoyed as the wife of an Ohio congressman.

Alice hadn't forgotten how she had ruled Washington society as First Daughter. It seemed she could do anything back then. Soon after her marriage, she had announced her intention to dispense with the long-cherished tradition of "calling," a ritual of visiting politicians and wives in their homes, several in the course of a day, and one that Alice found tedious. Some were shocked by the First Daughter's announcement; others, thrilled. "If young Mrs. Longworth takes the lead and flings these customs to the winds, there will be great rejoicing in the Dupont Circle contingent," one newspaper wrote. "No one except the daughter of the chief executive would dare to start such an enterprise."

Yet in the three years her father had been out of office, Alice had lost much of her influence. Nick was just one of 394 representatives in the House, after all; nothing set Alice much apart from the rest of the wives. She performed her duties, and even now, during Nick's reelection campaign, she showed up at his side in his district as he fought to keep his seat. Still, she despised spending any more time than was absolutely necessary in "Cincin-nasty," as she called her husband's hometown, where Nick's mother resented her and was openly hostile toward her.

On the morning of the fifteenth, after hearing of the assassination attempt, Alice fled them all and rushed to her father's bedside. Nick arrived sometime later, "a little intoxicated," Alice observed in her diary with disdain.

Her marriage had started off well enough, with the glamorous White House wedding that Eleanor had declined. Alice came down the stairs on her father's arm, her brothers, "with their hair plastered down, smirking at the bottom," as she'd remember. How happy she had been finally to be able to escape the control of her parents, and she was never more so than when Edith, bidding her good-bye, blurted out, "You have never been anything but trouble." Her stepmother's words left Alice startled. "It was quite fantastic," she'd recall. "It just came out like that."

Yet if Alice had hoped that her new home life with Nick would provide her with the embrace and acceptance she had long craved, she was disappointed. Soon after it began, her marriage soured. An anonymous letter arrived detailing Nick's infidelities and the fact that he'd fathered an illegitimate child. "Dear girl," the mother of the child wrote to Alice, "he loves me in a way in which he and you do not share . . . but ambition seized him, he met you and desired 'notoriety,' which he has obtained at the sacrifice of his love." The woman pledged never to cause a scandal, as Nick had "liberally provided" for her and their child, but she thought Alice should know the truth about the man she had married.

To separate from Nick over this news would have caused a scandal beyond any Alice had yet weathered, so she soldiered on with the marriage. Nick had been inconstant since she first met him, when he flitted back and forth between Alice and Maggie Cassini.

Always there seemed to be another woman in Nick's sights, just as there had always been another sibling in Theodore's. Once again, Alice was isolated, living as an outsider in her marriage much as she had in her childhood. So she kept up her own life, with her own friends, and made sure she never got pregnant by Nick: motherhood was not part of her plan, especially not now. Unlike most women of her time, Alice used contraception, "one of those cunning labor devices," as she called it, provided by her doctor, a woman. She'd remember Nick's sister begging her for such a device after she gave birth to her third child, in order to save her "tottering reason." Alice made sure she'd never lose hers.

For six years now the Longworths had kept up appearances, even finding, at times, some tenderness. Still, the tension over Theodore's campaign exposed the fault lines in their marriage. That summer, Alice made plain to her diary her increasing irritation with her husband's lack of support: "Was rather unpleasant this morning to Nick," she wrote on August 6. It was one thing to not actively support her father, but quite another to campaign fervently for Taft, as Nick was doing. For the sake of peace in the household, though, Alice mostly held her tongue. "I should be mad," she told her diary after Nick left to stump for the Republican ticket in Toledo, "but some things I shan't fight."

At least not yet. At the end of the line, Alice scrawled her favorite refrain: "*Revenge.*"

By the end of August, feelings between husband and wife had become impossible to disguise. "He hates me," Alice wrote plainly, "and I hate him." Her old nemesis, her father, was looking better and better to her. Theodore had to win. Otherwise, Nick would be unbearable. With an eye to the history that was about to unfold, Alice had, on February 12, 1912, her twenty-eighth birthday, begun writing in her diary again after several years of inactivity. The record of her father's triumph she intended also to be hers.

Several times, Alice expressed a desire to do "professional, practical work" on the campaign, but was stymied by both her father and Nick, who insisted she not appear at various events because of the awkwardness it might involve. Other women, such as Jane Addams, played key roles in her father's effort, but Alice was left cooling her heels, which made her further resent Nick and the position he'd put her in. "It is torture not to be doing something," she wrote in her diary. "If I let myself think at all, I go nearly crazy," she wrote. "I don't want to be too disappointed or sad November 6." During these weeks, she went frequently to get her "head rubbed" in order to relieve the stress.

Yet, to her great satisfaction, her father had begun to ask her for her opinion on his speeches. At long last Theodore seemed to appreciate the political acumen his daughter had developed during her decade in the public eye. "Shrug a shoulder, raise an eyebrow, and show a canine when necessary" was Alice's political motto—and now Theodore desired some of that shrewd practicality. He would "pass over the first draft of every sheet" of his speeches to Alice as he finished writing it. "There were no speechwriters in those days," she recalled. "Or at least he never used them. He just did it as a matter of course because we were good friends."

Good friends. It was a sea change from seven years earlier. Before the family moved out of the White House, Alice had buried a voodoo doll in the garden: a talisman for bringing her back there someday. At the time, she likely imagined returning across that columned portico with Nick. Now she hoped the spell she had cast would recall her father to his rightful place—the father who now trusted her, who considered her a friend, whose legacy meant everything.

Also hurrying to his father's bedside was Ted, now twenty-five and a slender, frog-eyed fellow in round spectacles, carrying much less baggage with him than Alice. For Ted, his father had always been, without reservation, his hero. No matter how much Theodore pushed him or bullied him, Ted had accepted it as his due, as the mark of how a good parent *should* raise his children. Living up to Theodore's example was always going to be a challenge. Ted had graduated from Harvard without much distinction, which was par for the course for him; but he had, nonetheless, done it. After being on probation for low grades during his final year, he'd buckled down (once Theodore applied some pressure) and passed all his courses, which was also standard for the stalwart Ted.

Fresh out of college, he'd been determined to find "a job with-out the help of his family and to live with no allowance," as his wife would later tell the story. With the same kind of single-mindedness that had driven him to try to excel (not always suc-cessfully) in swimming, hunting, boxing, and football, Ted set to work charting a career for himself. What drove him, his wife said, was his "feeling that he must prove worthy to his father." To family friend and former Rough Rider John Campbell Greenway, Ted wrote that he desired an occupation that would allow him to do "a man's work" (an echo of his father's words still resonating from his childhood) and to "rise on his own merits and nothing else."

Through a Porcellian Club connection, Ted found work as a mill hand at the Hartford Carpet Company in Thompsonville, Con-necticut—an odd choice for a Harvard grad, but Ted had a plan. His first day in the mills was October 1, 1908. The local newspa-per reported that the mill hands were paid eight dollars a week and toiled from sunrise to sundown. From all across the country, newspapermen descended on tiny Thompsonville and packed the one hotel in order to report on the First Son's working-class ad-venture. Ted was described as wearing a black shirt, white tie, blue overalls, white canvas shoes, and a straw hat as he walked to the mill. The company put out a statement that Ted would "ad-vance from one department to another until the art of manufac-turing carpets has been learned."

Clearly there was more to Ted's career choice than simply prov-ing to his father that he could make it on his own (though, as always, that was part of it). Ted was taking the long view: if he were ever to follow in his father's footsteps and enter politics, which most expected, he would need to lay some groundwork. He'd done nothing at Harvard to distinguish himself; he wasn't going on to law school as his father (or Franklin) had done; he had no practical experience in anything. Ted's life so far had been one of privilege, in which everything had been handed to him. So it wasn't only to his father he'd need to prove himself, but to everyone.

This was especially true now, as the American population

shifted and changed, and the ruling classes were increasingly being challenged on their presumption to lead. In the past decade, immigration into the United States had skyrocketed: in 1907, the peak year, 1.2 million people arrived on American shores, most of them laborers from eastern and southern Europe. Many of these people were becoming citizens and voting: if Ted hoped ever to rally the kind of populist support his father had enjoyed, he'd need to roll up his sleeves and go to *work*.

By all accounts, he worked very hard in the mills. He was put "at the tubs," the local paper reported, "and must keep his end up with the man on the other side of the box." He learned how to sort wool and master the loom, to weave and stitch, to bundle and package. He spent time in the clerical office as well, learning about accounting, payroll, and inventory. "I am in the mills now," he reported to Greenway after a couple of months on the job. "We work ten hours and a half a day." Still, he was having "fun," he declared, "because I am accomplishing something."

What he was accomplishing, in the long run, was the basis for his claim to be his father's successor. "Theodore Roosevelt Junior," reported the Associated Press, "who started at the foot of the ladder in Thompsonville a few months ago to learn carpet making has been advanced to the loom." Hard work paid off— that was the message Ted wanted to get out. His father clearly understood the importance of his son's venture and his desire to make it on his own. "Ted's boss was in touch today," Theodore wrote to Kermit, "and evidently thinks Ted is doing well." After seeing his namesake briefly at Sagamore, he told Ethel how "delightful" it was to witness Ted so "absorbed in his business."

Yet for all his undeniable hard work, low pay, and long hours, Ted Roosevelt wasn't exactly in the same boat as the majority of his coworkers. When he started the job, he lived not in one of the cramped mill cottages, but with the factory's vice president, Alvin Higgins, at his comfortable house on Pleasant Street. Later, he moved over to the mansion of the wealthy capitalist Robert King, who had servants to take care of his household and guests. Also, according to the local paper, nearly every weekend, Ted fled the backwoods town for the bright lights of Manhattan, where he stayed with friends or at a boardinghouse on West Twenty-Fifth Street. If, as his wife would later claim, he was really paying five dollars out of his seven- or eight-dollar-a-week salary to his hosts for room and board, then he must have had access to other money, as the cost of his weekend getaways alone would have more than depleted the remaining two or three bucks in his wallet. Also, unlike the Greek, Polish, and Italian immigrants Ted labored beside—many of whom, as census records would indicate, had large families to support—the president's son could have quit at any time. Theodore probably wouldn't have been pleased, but home was always there to go to.

That shouldn't discount Ted's effort: he worked hard to prove himself. Still, the endeavor, like so much in politics, was a bit of an illusion, a play being enacted to achieve something else. That there was a political element to all this weaving and twining was made clear soon after Ted's arrival in Connecticut, when he was appointed as aide-de-camp to the newly elected Republican governor, George Lilley. The position carried the rank of "major," which generated a whole new round of publicity: ROOSEVELT JUNIOR A MAJOR, read the headlines. Although Ted was scheduled to play a significant role in the governor's inauguration, once criticism was raised, his bosses made clear that he would be hard "at work in the carpet mills" during the inaugural parade.

In 1910, Ted married Eleanor Butler Alexander, the wealthy, socially conscious daughter of a prominent New York banker. The Hartford Carpet Company transferred him to its West Coast offices, and the newlyweds moved to San Francisco. It was there that Eleanor gave birth to their daughter, Grace, Theodore's first grandchild.

Ted had, by now, mastered the arts of business and manufacturing; his next education, if he planned to enter public life, would need to be in the world of finance. Accordingly, soon after his daughter's birth, he accepted a job as a bond salesman with the investment firm of Bertron, Griscom and Company, and relocated his family to New York. Once again, it was all with an eye to the future. "His business career was nothing but the means to an end," his wife recalled, "and his desire was to get it over and done with as fast as possible." The next stop after this one, Ted decided, would be public office.

Yet he remained insecure about filling the shoes of his father. "The disadvantages of being a great man's son far outweigh the advantages," his wife would say. Ted's career was "cloaked inevitably and perpetually by his father's fame." Usually a temperate, self-restrained sort of man, Ted, on occasion, buckled under the pressure. In fact, it was around the time Theodore launched his independent campaign that Edith began to worry that her son drank too much at his club. Nonetheless, Ted worked tirelessly at his father's election headquarters, and was the first to rush to Theodore's hospital room when he was shot. For Ted, his father remained the shining example of his life.

One of the great man's "bunnies," however, was missing from his hospital bedside—not counting the youngest ones, who were left behind in school. That was Kermit, who at the time his father took a bullet to his chest was fighting off his own attacks from poisonous snakes, fevers, and hostile natives in the jungles of Brazil. When he'd graduated from Harvard the previous spring, Kermit had wanted to emulate Ted in doing "real" work—but unlike Ted, there was no ulterior motive, no political theater involved. Kermit had never been primed to follow Theodore into public service, so his choice was fully his own. He indulged his dream to see and conquer the world, signing up with a railroad construction company. Kermit's mission: to cut through the rainforest and lay tracks across the tropics.

The young man's wanderlust had begun with the safari he took to Africa with his father three years earlier. Theodore had rightly sensed the trip was exactly the break his second son needed from the rigid framework of school life. Like his wayward cousin Jimmie, Kermit had always chafed against campus regimen; he never really fit in with his classmates. As a Harvard underclassman, he was blackballed from the Sphinx, one of the important clubs, and feared his father's disappointment. Theodore, however, was consoling: "You have had so much," he wrote to Kermit, "and *are* so much, that you needn't be sensitive about the clubs." He never pushed Kermit quite as hard as he did Ted, but in fact, by this point, Theodore was mellowing all around. If Kermit got into any clubs, he said, "I shall be neither over-elated nor over-depressed whichever way it turns out. There are too many things of real importance over which to feel sorrow or joy."

Too many things of real importance. This was indeed a new Theodore—but he remained enough of a disciplinarian to upbraid Kermit for skipping classes. "You must not give the impression that you care nothing for your duties," he told Kermit.

That was just it, though: Kermit *didn't* care. He was a dreamer not a scholar, a wanderer not a go-getter. He could sometimes fall into dark, contemplative moods, which made people leery of him. When he was younger, Edith had said of Kermit, "Very few outsiders care for him," but those who did "like him very much." Thankfully for his parents, he didn't rebel like his sister Alice had; as eager as Ted for his father's approval, Kermit rarely strayed too far out of line. All he needed, Theodore believed, was some inspiration and toughening up. So he'd decided to take him to Africa.

"It is no child's play going after lion, elephant, rhino and buffalo," Theodore wrote to his son in advance of the trip. "We must be very cautious; we must be always ready to back each other up; and we probably ought to have a spare rifle when we move in to the attack." Once in Africa, Kermit more than lived up to his father's hopes and expectations. Watching his son on those "hot, moonlit nights" as they stalked eland or hunkered down "in the white rhino camp, listening to strumming of the funny little native harp," Theodore saw the man take the place of the boy. He wrote home to his daughter Ethel, "The most wise Bavian [Kermit] is hunting by himself at the coast; I expect him back today, and on Saturday we start for Uganda. You will find him much older in every way, and he is a dear. I am very proud of him."

The one outcome from the trip that Theodore feared was that the adventure might "unsettle" Kermit when he returned to school. "I should want you to make up your mind fully and deliberately," he told his son before they set out, "that you [will] treat it just as you would a college course; enjoy it to the full; count it as so much to the good, and then when it was over turn in and buckle down to hard work; for without the hard work you certainly cannot make a success of life." His fears turned out to be real, though, and no amount of lecturing would change things: Kermit spent the next few years after the safari aching to get back out into the world, hating his studies, wanting to explore, and flinching from the rules.

No surprise, then, that after graduation he chose Brazil and set for himself a task (clearing the Amazon jungle) that was even mightier than shooting lions and rhinos. His brother Ted fully expected Kermit to come back from his adventure ready to go into business with him, but such a plan, Kermit told their sister Ethel, was "as inapt as anything to fit me." He had not gone to Brazil to fill up a résumé; he wasn't looking to make a mark and a name for himself for something later on. Nor did he have any desire to spend the rest of his life commuting into the city to some bank or investment firm. "I'm afraid that no matter what I did," he said, "I wouldn't be able to fit into that."

Kermit's South American adventure, then, was a purely personal one, and Theodore approved. With great satisfaction he read Kermit's letters. "I am very proud to think of you living in a box-car and bossing the steam-shovel gang way off in Brazil," he wrote from the campaign trail. "I am so glad that the second of my boys has gone manfully out to do his share of the world's work."

The fact remained, however, that Kermit left for Brazil on July 27, just as his father's campaign to win back the presidency was kicking off. Ted was running around managing the New York campaign headquarters while most of the various cousins were doing their parts as well. George, Philip, and Oliver Roosevelt "have worked like beavers for me," Theodore wrote to Kermit. "I have been very much touched." He couldn't entirely hide his disappointment that Kermit had not waited to depart until after the election. "I miss my side partner *very* much," Theodore wrote, making sure to underline the adverb.

If Kermit harbored any guilt, the feelings were likely aggravated that hot October day when a dispatch was brought to him by "a big, up-from-the-soil sort of foreman." The man told him indifferently, "I guess they've shot Roosevelt all right." Kermit was horrified, thinking his father dead, but telegrams soon set his mind at ease. A week or so after the shooting, he received a letter from Theodore himself, full of his usual bluster: "Well, this campaign proved as exciting and as dangerous as any of our African hunts!" Kermit knew then that his father was going to be fine. Still, Theodore and the family never forgot that he wasn't there.

When Theodore was released from the hospital after a short stay, his doctors ordered him temporarily off the campaign trail, a directive that was strictly enforced by Edith. Colonel Roosevelt reluctantly convalesced at Sagamore. He refused to accept the idea that Schrank was merely a lunatic. The hunter in Theodore had recognized a pattern in his would-be slayer: "The choice of the gun showed that he was an experienced man-killer," he wrote to Kermit. "He had followed me for some time but was evidently afraid to shoot me in the South, for fear he would be mobbed, and waited until he was in a state where there is no death penalty." Nonetheless, Schrank was found insane by a judge and spent the rest of his life (thirty-one more years) in a Wisconsin mental hospital. In all that time, never once did he have a visitor.

The wave of public sympathy for Theodore following the shooting convinced some political observers that the tide had turned in his favor. Ethel told Bye that "encouraging reports were coming in from all over" and that "things look better for us than they ever have." Edith noticed the "great change in popular feeling" and the belief among some on the campaign that "a Progressive landslide was possible." Theodore wasn't quite as ready to predict victory, but he did think that "one good thing" had come out of the attempt on his life. "The circumstances of the shooting have emphasized what really ought not to have needed emphasizing," he wrote to Kermit, "namely, that in this contest we were living up to our professions and our motto was 'Spend and be spent,' that we were not considering the welfare of any one of us but were battling for a cause in which we earnestly and zealously believed."

His purpose had become holy. No previous campaign had ever mattered as much to him, he said, "for the principles for which we are fighting make up a platform that really means an immense amount [and] we are wholly free from the repulsive type of politician." It was true that many of Theodore's letters, even those to his children, were written with the expectation that they'd some- day be read by a wider audience; he chose his words, therefore, with an eye to his legacy. Yet even such self-conscious posturing never fully undercut the sincerity of his beliefs, and that was es- pecially true now. Nearing the end of his public life, after two decades of personal glory, Theodore was genuinely committed to making a difference for the greater good. "Instead of my growing less radical," he told one audience, "I have grown more radical. This country will not be a good place for any of us to live in if it is not a reasonably good place for all of us to live in." Those were the sorts of words that inspired another Roosevelt, a hundred miles north, waging another campaign.

>——<

Franklin was now thirty. He'd passed the New York State Bar without even needing to complete his studies at Columbia, and was now running for his second term in the New York State Senate. His last name had guaranteed him attention. During his first campaign, he'd used his family connection to get a laugh from the crowds who flocked to see him as he crisscrossed the Hudson Valley in a red two-cylinder Maxwell touring car. "A little shaver told me the other day that he knew I wasn't Teddy," Franklin said from the podium. "I asked why, and he replied, 'Because you don't show your teeth!'"

There was another difference between the two men: Franklin was a Democrat. He'd chosen his father's party over his cousin's, surprising many by winning in the predominantly Republican district. The younger man's political apostasy didn't trouble The- odore overmuch. Franklin was "a fine fellow," he told Bye, though he did wish he held the "political views" of Joseph Alsop, the husband of "Little" Corinne Robinson and a progressive Republi- can state legislator in Connecticut.

In one significant way, however, Franklin had followed Theo- dore precisely: just as the former president had bucked the bosses in the Republican Party, now Franklin took on Tammany Hall, the corrupt, backroom-dealing cabal that controlled the Democratic Party. If the cousins were separated by partisan enrollment, they were united by the idea of reform. In his first term as a state senator, Franklin had derailed the election of Tammany's choice for U.S. senator and proven himself a force to be reckoned with. "With his handsome face and form of supple grace," one reporter observed, "he could make a fortune on the stage and set the matinee girls' hearts throbbing. But [his] quiet force and determination are now sending cold shivers down the spine of Tammany." The boy who'd told Franklin he didn't "show his teeth" was wrong. Franklin was a tiger. Party bosses bewailed "the second coming of a Roosevelt."

Yet as his reelection campaign got under way that summer, Franklin was faced with a choice: did he remain a maverick or toe the party line? Cousin Theodore had changed the political calculus by running with a third party. Franklin was ideologically in sync with the Progressives; his mother, Sara, thought that if the party were "true to its principles," it would endorse him. Eleanor was also drawn to the Progressives. Her uncle's party was promising affordable housing, fair wages, an eight-hour workday, the right for labor to organize, the abolition of child labor, and federal insurance for the jobless, elderly, and sick—all issues Eleanor had come to care about in her work with immigrants and the poor. "Uncle Ted's progressive ideas have fired so many of the young men to really work in this state," she wrote to her friend Isabella Ferguson, "that even if he doesn't win this time I feel a big work will have been accomplished." Her sympathies were clearly with the Progressives, even if her husband was a Democrat. "I wish Franklin could be fighting now for Uncle Ted," she confided to Ferguson, "for I feel he is in the party of the future."

Yet Franklin had more immediate concerns than some far-off utopian future. If Wilson prevailed in the presidential race (as everyone, including Theodore, expected him to do), Franklin would need to be perceived as a loyal Democrat and party stalwart to reap any political reward from the new administration. Accordingly, he did not seek a Progressive endorsement. Also, that October, he withdrew his support for a team of insurgent candidates in the state elections and endorsed "the regular Democratic ticket."

For all his high-minded ideals, Franklin turned out to be more of a party man than his cousin. His shrewd political gamesmanship was his best shot at guaranteeing personal advancement. It was also, as time would reveal, the first salvo in the wars between the Hyde Park and Oyster Bay Roosevelts.

All the other nephews and nephews-in-law were either working on Theodore's campaign or running as Progressives themselves. Teddy Robinson had ditched the Republicans to run for reelection as a Progressive for the New York State Assembly. So had Joseph Alsop, "Little" Corinne's husband, who'd left the Republicans to become a firebrand Progressive leader, running for Congress in Connecticut as an alternative to both the major parties.

Franklin pointedly didn't follow their example. While Theodore was barnstorming across the country, shouting himself hoarse for the Progressive ticket, Franklin was motoring around Columbia and Dutchess Counties, rallying his constituents for Woodrow Wilson. "I am just back from a long day in which I have covered 150 miles in the machine," he wrote to Eleanor. He'd stopped in Claverack, Hillsdale, Copake, Pine Plains, Stanfordville, and Salt Point, and "ran straight [back] up to Columbia County, then turned East, and thence home." Even after Theodore was shot, Franklin continued stumping for the Democrats, impressing party leaders with both his eloquence and indefatigability.

Until, suddenly, he developed a mysterious fever and collapsed on the floor of his house on East Sixty-Fifth Street in Manhattan. Shades were drawn and servants spoke in whispers. Eleanor hustled up and down the stairs bringing her husband medicine and cool cloths. The diagnosis: typhoid fever. By now, Franklin and Eleanor had three children: Anna, six; James, four; and Elliott, two. They had to be moved out of the house for fear of contagion. In and out of delirium, Franklin tossed and turned on sweat-drenched sheets, worrying what would happen to his campaign. If he wasn't out there on the trail, how could he make a case for his reelection, when he had not just one but two opponents, the Republican and the Progressive?

The front door of their town house opened. There in the door-frame stood a small, skeletal, pockmarked man wearing a crumpled suit that looked (and smelled) as if it hadn't been laundered in weeks. By his own admission, he was one of the "four ugliest men in New York." The man's name was Louis Howe.

From his lips dangled a Sweet Caporal cigarette, pungent in its bitter, unfiltered aroma. He was constantly hacking from chronic emphysema. Everything about the man repulsed Eleanor. Still, she brought him up to speak with Franklin, who had asked him to visit. Howe was a newspaperman and a savvy observer of up-state New York politics: if anyone could save Franklin's imperiled campaign, it was he.

At this particular moment, however, Eleanor cared more about Franklin's health than his political ambitions, and the cloud of gray smoke Howe was puffing out in her husband's room certainly couldn't be beneficial. So she made sure to lurk nearby as the two men spoke, signaling her disapproval and generally making a "nuisance" of herself, as she'd remember. Then, shortly thereafter, Eleanor got sick, too. Sara confined her to her own room and took over the care of both of them—and if her beloved son wanted to talk with Mr. Howe, then Mama let it be so.

Eleanor and Sara had reached a sort of détente, which generally meant that Eleanor deferred to whatever her mother-in-law wanted. When they were at Springwood, Sara insisted Franklin reclaim his old position opposite her at the dining table, with Eleanor seated somewhere in the middle. Eleanor never complained, about seating arrangements or anything else. She made sure to call her mother-in-law "Mama," with the accent on the second syllable, a pseudo-British practice that her cousin Alice considered affected. "Cousin Sally," as Sara was called by the Oyster Bay branch, was a "domineering tartar," in Alice's words, from whom Eleanor had to "put up with a lot." Indeed, when Sara paid for a house to be built for the newlyweds on Sixty-Fifth Street, it came with an unexpected proviso: an adjacent town house was also constructed for Sara, and the two residences were linked by an inner door.

"My mother-in-law was a lady of great character," Eleanor

would say. "She always knew what was right and what was wrong"—so much so that Sara would correct Eleanor in everything, from social etiquette to child rearing. From the moment Eleanor's first child, Anna, was born, it was Sara who decided what was best for her grandchildren to wear, eat, read, and learn. "It was hard to differ with her," Eleanor recalled. "She never gave up an idea she had, whether it was for herself or for you. And her methods of achieving her own ends at times seemed a bit ruthless if you were not in accord. She dominated me for years."

Now twenty-eight years old, Eleanor had not matured into the sort of woman whom her mentor, Mlle. Souvestre, might have expected her to become. Her volunteer work for the poor and disadvantaged largely ended once she became a mother. "I was always just getting over having a baby or about to have one," Eleanor remembered. (A third son, Franklin Junior, had died at seven months.) Everything in her life, Eleanor said, was left to her mother-in-law and husband, including her opinions. She took "for granted," for example, "that men were superior creatures and still knew more about politics than women." Even on an issue of such personal relevance as women's suffrage, Eleanor deferred to Franklin, joining the cause only after he announced his support: "I realized that if my husband were a suffragist I probably must be, too."

What seemed to matter most to Eleanor was that she was finally part of a family, even if that meant deferring to the more powerful personalities in the household. Such submission was worth it to a woman who'd been lonely most of her life, bereft of a family structure, and who was still deeply in love with her husband. Franklin returned her devotion, addressing her as his "own dear Babs" or "Babbie" and writing to her with tremendous affection when he was away: "Loads of love, my dearest. I do hope that you are taking care of yourself and that the lambs are well."

How very different were Eleanor and Franklin from Alice and Nick. Alice might have enjoyed more personal independence in her marriage, but she lacked the love and intimacy Eleanor enjoyed, which was perhaps why she could barely tolerate being in her cousins' presence. "Eleanor and Franklin could be very boring together," Alice remembered, sneering at their "solemn little Sunday evenings where one was usually regaled with crown roast, very indifferent wine, and a good deal of knitting." Alice masked her envy as contempt.

Yet, without question, Eleanor *had* surrendered some stronger part of herself after her marriage to Franklin. The tradeoff was a certain homely contentment. By 1912 she'd achieved a sense of tranquility in her life that, while fragile, nonetheless held. That was about to change.

>––––<

As Eleanor fought her way back to health, she could hear the political strategizing coming from her husband's room. The ugly little man she'd let in the house, Louis Howe, had seized the reins of Franklin's campaign and, in doing so, the direction of the family's life for the next twenty years.

Howe had "enormous interest in having power," Eleanor came to realize, and if he couldn't wield that power himself, "he wanted it through someone he was influencing." She was deeply skeptical of this man's place and influence in their lives.

But Franklin trusted Howe implicitly. The shrewd newspaperman, for his part, had found the perfect client in Franklin Delano Roosevelt: someone as ambitious as he was. He called Franklin the "beloved and revered future President." He had a very particular endgame in mind for his candidate. The road to the White House began in the bucolic hills of the rural Hudson Valley.

From Franklin's sickbed in Manhattan, Howe motored back up into the district, stopping at the offices of local publications along the way. If the voters couldn't meet the candidate in person, Howe reasoned, they'd meet him in print. Newspaper and magazine ads were uncommon for local candidates, but Howe figured the media could be used to their advantage. Everyone read the newspapers, and there were dozens of them, including commercial circulars and pictorial flyers. In as many as he could, Howe placed little square boxes headlined HE IS PLEDGED TO SERVE THE PEOPLE, and underneath, he itemized the promises Franklin was making to his constituents. Among them: standardization of the size of apple barrels, reduction of costs for farm equipment and fishing licenses, and the repair of roads and bridges. As many voters as possible received a personal home visit from Howe, who handed out campaign letters that appeared to be individually addressed to them and signed by Franklin. The latest mimeograph technology was amazing. People were duly impressed.

Finally, as November approached, the two fallen candidates, Franklin and Theodore, rose from their beds and returned to the campaign trail. On the night of October 30, Theodore made a triumphant comeback at Madison Square Garden in front of sixteen thousand cheering fans. The auditorium was hung with hundreds of flags, a giant stuffed bull moose was lit by a spotlight, and the crowd chanted, "Four more years!" until they were hoarse. "We want Teddy!" they screamed as the candidate, looking more drawn than in the past, finally appeared on the stage. As one reporter would observe, "The moment his red face, gray moustache and eyeglasses showed up on the platform, the crowd lost all semblance of order. Perfectly respectable gray-haired matrons climbed on chairs with flags and handkerchiefs in their hands and forgot themselves for three quarters of an hour"—that being how long the room went on cheering before letting Theodore speak.

"We know that there are in life injustices which we are powerless to remedy," he said when finally allowed to proceed. "But we know also that there is much injustice which can be remedied . . . We intend to strike down privilege, to equalize opportunity, to wrest justice from the hands that do injustice, to hearten and strengthen men and women for the hard battle of life. We stand shoulder to shoulder in a spirit of real brotherhood. We recognize no differences of class, creed or birthplace.

"It is of little matter whether any one man fails or succeeds," Theodore concluded, "but the cause shall not fail, for it is the cause of mankind!"

The band struck up "Hail to the Chief" and "A Hot Time in the Old Town Tonight." The crowd was pumped with confidence. Even Theodore allowed that maybe the mood in the country had shifted, and he might possibly win.

Up in Dutchess County, another candidate was putting out his own statement. Franklin released a letter to the press he had written to Sen. Thomas Gore of Oklahoma, one of Woodrow Wilson's chief backers, in which he officially declared his support for the Democratic candidate. "From the human point of view," Franklin wrote, "Mr. Wilson has shown that he is keenly alive to the social and industrial welfare of the great body of workers." Wilson was "a practical student of government," Franklin pointed out, and not an ideologue—an indirect dig at the passion of Cousin Theodore. Under Wilson, Franklin declared, "a national administration will be, at last, a servant of the whole people." Even more than Franklin's superlatives for Wilson, it was the headline that appeared in dozens of newspapers around the country, NEPHEW OF T.R. IS FOR WILSON, that no doubt rankled his Oyster Bay relations.

They were already frantic as the campaign neared its end. Alice was hoping an influx of cash might push them past the finish line. She put six hundred dollars of her own into the effort—"all I can afford," she wrote—and convinced one donor to send a check for five thousand dollars in early November. At home in Cincinnati, she continued to spar with her husband. "Nick and I had a tremendous row after lunch," she wrote in her diary on November 3. "He accuses me of not being for him, not 'standing by' him." At issue was her appearance at a local Progressive rally in support of her father, which some of Nick's constituents took as a tacit endorsement of her husband's Progressive opponent. Alice acted surprised that anyone might have gotten that impression, but of course she was far too politically astute not to have realized the implication of her actions. "We are surely drifting apart," she wrote in her diary. "It is so sad—it will blow hot, blow cold, until we finally blow away from each other, final and all."

On the night of November 5, Theodore gathered with most of the clan at Sagamore to await the results of the election. Very early in the night, it was clear which way the country was going. New York and Massachusetts, traditionally Republican strongholds and big supporters of Theodore's in the past, went Democratic in large numbers. Wilson was declared the winner, with Theodore coming in a distant second; although he beat Taft, he didn't rack up anywhere near the margin he'd hoped for. "Well, we have gone down in a smashing defeat," Theodore wrote that very night to Kermit. "Whether it is a Waterloo or a Bull Run, time only can tell."

It was a Waterloo. Although his loss was not as bad as it seemed in the moment—he had formed a brand-new party and taken it to a second-place finish while ousting an incumbent president—not one Progressive candidate won nationwide. That meant Teddy Robinson and Joseph Alsop also went down with Theodore, while Franklin sailed to victory, even though his Republican and Progressive opponents together won more votes than he did.

In Cincinnati, it was a long night. Alice was downcast by her father's loss, but thought he'd made "a marvelous showing." Nick's fate, however, remained unclear. The vote was so close that precinct officials were still counting late into the night. In the midst of all this, husband and wife endured "a few unpleasant moments" between themselves, but then put on their smiling, public faces and stepped out in front of the crowd that had gathered at the local newspaper office. Nick then left to pay his condolences to Taft, while Alice went home alone.

The preliminary result the next morning had Nick winning by about 1,800 votes, but Alice wrote in her diary that she wouldn't "feel secure" until she heard "the official count." She was wise to wait: the next day, the final tally revealed that Nick had actually lost by 105 votes. Since there had been at least 100 voters at the Progressive rally Alice attended, Nick blamed his loss squarely on his wife's disloyalty. "I know he feels bruised and betrayed," she wrote in her diary. She did her best to keep out of his way.

A few weeks later, she made the trip home to Sagamore. Edith thought Alice looked "horribly ill and worn," and wrote to Kermit in Brazil that his sister had "had a dreadful time" with Nick since the election: "He can't seem to face his defeat." Stripped of their Washington residence, the Longworths were now exiled to Ohio; Alice was trapped in "Cincin-nasty," her worst fear.

Meanwhile, Franklin and Eleanor were on their way. Every other Roosevelt in public life had been routed, but Franklin, no matter how close his victory, had triumphed. That was made abundantly clear when President-elect Wilson asked him to join his new administration as assistant secretary of the navy, the very same position Theodore had once held. Wilson "rather liked the idea," Josephus Daniels, the navy secretary, recalled, "of having a Democratic Roosevelt fill the position from which Theodore Roosevelt was elevated to the governorship of New York. It intrigued him."

It intrigued Franklin as well. "Of course he is delighted," Eleanor wrote to Auntie Bye, "as it is the thing of all things he's most interested in." *The thing of all things.* Franklin's interest wasn't so much the navy as it was following his illustrious cousin's footsteps as closely as possible: Groton, Harvard, the New York State Senate, and now the navy.

The message was unmistakable: it was Franklin who would lay claim to Theodore's mantle, not any of the other nephews who had gone down in ignoble defeat that election season, and certainly not Ted Junior, the much-heralded namesake, who was, at the moment, scratching out a living in New York as a largely anonymous bond salesman. Indeed, when offered the navy position, Franklin made sure to sound very much like Theodore in his reply. "I'd like it bully well," he said. "It would please me better than anything in the world."

PART V

BELIEVING MORE THAN EVER BEFORE

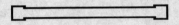

1918–1920

MANHATTAN

An unusually strong wind whipped her hair and skirt on the morning of September 19, 1918, as Eleanor waited on the pier for Franklin's ship, the *Leviathan*, to arrive. It was that strange sort of Indian summer day when the sun disappeared and the winds blew in off the ocean, but temperatures still hovered in the high seventies and thunderstorms threatened to crack open the sky. Such portentous weather fit Eleanor's mood. She was worried about Franklin, who, in his role as assistant secretary of the navy, was returning from a three-month tour of Europe. With war rampaging across the Continent, he'd been in danger from the day he departed, but it was a telegram Eleanor received just as her husband's ship set out for home that had most alarmed her. Franklin was seriously ill, the cable reported, with both pneumonia and Spanish influenza. Doctors advised that an ambulance be waiting at the pier to meet him.

Eleanor had arranged for one. Sara was there, too, in desperate distress over her cherished son. The Spanish flu had already claimed millions of lives around the globe, spread by wartime mobility. Closer to home, New York hospitals overflowed with stricken people. In neighboring New England, as the newspapers reported that very morning, the epidemic was claiming on average forty-eight lives a day. Franklin had always been very susceptible to illness; now his wife and mother stood waiting on the pier, fearing the worst.

Ever since the United States had entered the war the previous year, joining Britain, France, and Russia in the fight against Imperial Germany, Franklin had been away from home more often than not, overseeing naval troop movements and strategy. Raging since 1914, the war had brought death and destruction on an unprecedented scale; the influenza victims only piled more bodies atop an already unbearable number of casualties. Millions had been killed across Europe, and even more had been maimed, wounded, and displaced. Now that some four million American troops had been sent to fight in the trenches of France and Belgium, the war's terrible cost was being felt stateside.

No one was immune to the horrors of the war, not even those who bore the name Roosevelt. Eleanor's cousins had all joined the war effort. Ted and Archie were among the first to sign up after war was declared, serving under Gen. John J. "Black Jack" Pershing at Theodore's special request. Kermit, with less military training than his brothers, volunteered for the British Army, and was accepted as a favor to his father. The baby, Quentin, just nineteen at the time, dropped out of Harvard and signed up with the nation's first airplane combat division. All four quickly distinguished themselves, especially Ted, who led his battalion to the front lines during several battles. The bravery of the eldest Roosevelt son made his parents' "hearts glow," Theodore wrote to Douglas Robinson. Until the war was over, though, he knew "the hand of fate" might still weigh "heavy upon us."

He was sadly prescient. On July 14, 1918, Quentin Roosevelt's plane was shot down by enemy fire. He was just twenty years old.

Two months later, as Eleanor waited anxiously for Franklin's ship to arrive, she knew her Oyster Bay relatives viewed her husband with some scorn for his comfortable, sheltered role during the war. Theodore had initially been quite gracious when he learned of Franklin's appointment to the navy position. "It is interesting to see that you are in another place which I myself once held," he had written. He was sure that Franklin would do "capital work," and he urged Eleanor to be "particularly nice to the naval officers' wives." Once war was declared in Europe, Theodore continued to express his admiration, pleased that Franklin was keeping the navy prepared to fight even as his commander in chief, President Wilson, did everything he could to keep America out of the conflict. Theodore despised Wilson for his pacifism in the face of German aggression, and heartily approved of the often-clandestine maneuvers Franklin had to take in order to get the navy ready for war, if it came—and of course it did.

Yet when Franklin defended Wilson from Republican critics by charging that, in 1907, under a Republican president, American battleships were fitted with equipment recycled from older ves-

sels, Theodore took umbrage. The Republican president in question, of course, was himself, and he sent Franklin a curt response:
"My memory was not in accord with the statement as you made
it." Franklin duly apologized and promised to correct the record.

Whether Theodore still felt Franklin was "a fine fellow," as
he'd once written to Bye, wasn't so clear anymore. When war was
finally declared, he told the younger man, "You must resign! You
must get into uniform at once!" After all, that was what Theodore
had done when he was assistant secretary of the navy during the
war with Spain—and he'd had young children at home then, too,
just as Franklin had now. However, for the first time, Franklin
didn't follow his hero's lead. Although he did consider enlisting
late in the conflict, he stayed at his post, content to fight the war
from his desk in Washington.

He would, however, make much of his just-completed visit to
the front lines. Wearing a French helmet and equipped with a gas
mask, Franklin was given a tour of the battery of cannons pointed
toward the Imperial German Army, and he took tremendous thrill
in firing one of them. "I will never know how many, if any, Huns
I killed," he wrote in his journal. It was the closest Franklin ever
came to combat, a fact much derided by his Oyster Bay cousins,
especially with Quentin so fresh in his grave.

Even Ted's wife went to France, providing humanitarian aid
to the war-torn country through the YMCA. When news agencies
reported that President Wilson's son-in-law had gone to Europe to
work with the YMCA, Theodore tartly replied, "How very nice.
We're sending our *daughter*-in-law." Nobody beat the Roosevelts
of Oyster Bay.

All her life, Eleanor had known their fiercely competitive
drive. All her life, she'd been made to feel less than. Yet no longer
did she try to keep up with her cousins. She'd aged a great deal
in the last six years, looking much older than thirty-four; child-
bearing and motherhood could do that to a woman. Standing on
the pier waiting for Franklin, she was a tall, gangly, windblown
sentinel, her face drawn and dour, heavy bags under her eyes. She
was also exhausted from her own contributions to the war effort.
Volunteering for the Red Cross, Eleanor worked in various New

York canteens and hospitals. As the wife of the nation's assistant secretary of the navy, she'd been obliged to do something, but typically, she went above and beyond, pouring her heart into her work. One mother of a wounded soldier wrote to Eleanor with profound gratitude for "the kind words—the little favors—the interest" she had given her son: "He always loved to see you come in. You always brought a ray of sunshine with you." Eleanor also raised money for a number of projects that benefited disabled veterans returning home from the war. Yet when Uncle Theodore divvied up the cash from his 1906 Nobel Peace Prize among those relatives engaged in war work, not a single dollar was earmarked for Eleanor's efforts. In many ways, she was still the unwanted, vagabond niece to her father's family.

By 1918 the distance between Oyster Bay and Hyde Park had become noticeably pronounced. The cordiality that prevailed a decade earlier, when Uncle Theodore walked Eleanor down the aisle, had all but disappeared. Franklin and Eleanor, in the view of Oyster Bay, had gone over to the other side, choosing partisan politics over family. Accordingly, Eleanor saw very little of her father's family these days. "How I wish I saw you more often," Eleanor wrote to Auntie Bye, "for you are one of the people I love and admire and long to be with." Only Aunt Corinne kept up any sort of regular contact with their niece and her husband; Eleanor had recently attended the funeral of Corinne's husband, Douglas Robinson.

With Franklin gone and her family distant, Eleanor had busied herself with war work. She learned to drive an automobile. The family chauffeur gave her lessons, and she picked it up like a pro, zipping from home to market to hospital wards to Red Cross meetings in a battered Stutz Bearcat. She drove so fast that she often frightened her passengers. At Sara's summer house on the Canadian island of Campobello, just off the coast of Maine, Eleanor also learned to swim. She was no longer the terrified little girl shivering in the arms of her father on board the sinking *Britannic* or trembling at the end of the pier in Oyster Bay, needing to be goaded by her uncle and cousins into jumping. She'd spent a decade conquering her fears, but her strength was about to get its most rigorous test yet.

Finally, the *Leviathan* steamed into port. In great secrecy, as his wife and mother fluttered around in concern, Franklin was taken off on a stretcher and driven by ambulance to East Sixty-Fifth Street. Instead of his own house, however, which was being rented out while he and Eleanor made their primary residence in Washington, Franklin was carried up the stairs into his mother's house next door. Dr. William Draper was on hand to examine him, and later that afternoon the family physician, Dr. A. H. Ely, arrived as well. After consulting with the doctors, Sara stepped out onto the porch to assure the gathered reporters that her son's condition wasn't serious. He would still need several weeks' recuperation, however, before resuming his duties in Washington.

Eleanor was, of course, relieved by the optimistic prognosis. As it turned out, though, Franklin's illness would be the least of her worries that fall. Her thirteen-year marriage had sailed into choppy waters. Franklin's prolonged absences had worn Eleanor down, leaving her bored, lonely, and often depressed. Part of her melancholia grew out of lingering regret over not doing enough to take care for the little son who had died: "In some way I must be to blame," she thought. Yet another, even larger part of her depression was more existential. Eleanor would recall a harrowing moment at the house on Sixty-Fifth Street, when she sat in front of her dressing table and just wept. Her "bewildered young husband" asked her what was wrong, but Eleanor couldn't tell him; she couldn't fully understand her tears herself. "Being an eminently reasonable person," Eleanor said of Franklin, "he thought I was quite mad and told me so gently, and left me alone until I should become calmer." Eventually she convinced herself she was "acting like a little fool."

Yet deep down she knew why she was so sad: she was disappearing as a person. "I was simply absorbing the personalities of those about me," she said, "and letting their tastes and interests dominate me."

Eleanor was the mother of five young children. In addition to Anna, twelve; James, ten; and Elliott, seven, now there were also Franklin Junior, four, and John, two. Increasingly, Eleanor felt as if she were raising her brood with her mother-in-law instead of her husband, and she resented it. Franklin often even had to miss holidays at Hyde Park or Campobello, and he seemed strangely aloof to the concerns of his family. "I don't think you read my letters," Eleanor complained, "for you never answer a question and nothing I ask for appears!"

Eleanor's brother Hall was aware of his sister's loneliness. "Is F. paying any attention to his family this summer," he wrote a few seasons back, "or is the bee buzzing as hard as ever?" Hall suggested that Eleanor build a cell for him at Campobello "and tie him down," but Franklin was too slippery for that.

For a time, Eleanor had relied on her social secretary, Lucy Mercer, an efficient, pretty young woman of twenty-six, for news of her husband. According to Jonathan Daniels, the son of Franklin's superior at the navy, Lucy was "of assured social position" (meaning she came from the "best" of families), "but very insecure finances" (meaning her family had fallen on hard times). Franklin took an interest in Lucy, and frequently cajoled her into coming along on his excursions, such as the time he and a group of friends sailed down the Potomac to inspect the fleet. Eleanor appeared somewhat uneasy with their closeness, and in the spring of 1917, she let Lucy go. It was an amicable break.

Much to Eleanor's surprise, however, Lucy then enlisted in the navy as a yeoman and was assigned to Franklin's office. Eleanor's jealousy grew. At one point, she reacted in anger about something involving Lucy; Franklin wrote to assuage his wife's fears and asked Lucy to do the same. The incident left Eleanor deeply embarrassed. "Dearest Honey," she wrote to Franklin in response. "Why did you make [Lucy] waste all that time [answering my] fool notes?" She asked that "the results of [her] idiocy" be torn up "at once."

For his part, Franklin insisted that he truly regretted being away from the family. In one letter, after Eleanor and the children had headed off to Campobello for the summer, he lamented being left behind in Washington. "I really can't stand that house all alone without you, and you were a goosy girl to think or even to pretend to think that I don't want you here all the summer, because you know I do!" A summer alone in the heat and humidity of Washington, he predicted, would turn him into "a bear with a sore head." Still, he promised not to be so "unreasonable and touchy" as he had been of late.

Of course, as Eleanor knew full well, Franklin wasn't alone in Washington. He had many friends—such as "the Charlie Munns, the Cary Graysons, Lucy Mercer and Nigel Law," as he wrote to his wife.

Part of the reason Franklin was so "unreasonable and touchy" during this period was an ongoing scandal that had roiled the navy. A crackdown on off-hours sexual activity at the Newport naval base had been launched in 1914, leading to a series of high-profile arrests of several well-respected Rhode Islanders, including Samuel Nash Kent, an Episcopal priest who'd served as a navy chaplain. The entrapment of these men by naval investigators had been condemned by the local press, and Kent, fighting to exonerate himself, had subsequently exposed the navy's unorthodox method of actually having its investigators engage in sex with other men in order to catch those men in the act. The sordidness of the sting caused the operation to backfire, and the public tended to be far more sympathetic toward the accused "perverts" than their interrogators. Franklin, who'd given approval for the crackdown, was called before several congressional panels to explain the navy's actions.

Eleanor did her best to understand the stress Franklin was under. When in Washington, she was a very dutiful political wife. Rejecting her cousin Alice's embrace of a new, more casual etiquette, she adhered to the old protocol of calling on senators and their wives. Soon after Franklin's appointment to the navy post, Eleanor had written to Auntie Bye for "all kinds of information" about official Washington. "Will you tell me if there are any people I ought to go and call on at once as . . . I am afraid I'll make all kinds of stupid mistakes?" Quickly getting a feel for things, Eleanor was soon undertaking a regular round of calls, setting aside time each week to "sort and list" the cards she received, to keep track of all her social obligations.

For support, she increasingly leaned on Sara. "I was growing dependent on my mother-in-law," Eleanor would recall, "requiring her help on almost every subject, and never thought of asking for anything that I thought would not meet with her approval." For all her domination, Sara nevertheless offered a solid family structure that bolstered Eleanor in her loneliness. She was the stable parent figure Eleanor had never had. While Sara could be demanding and blunt, she also lacked disingenuousness and kept no secrets. At a time when Eleanor increasingly suspected that Franklin *did*, her mother-in-law's forthrightness was reassuring. Sara meant security. She still controlled the purse strings of the great Roosevelt wealth; without regular infusions of cash from Sara, Franklin's meager salary as assistant secretary of the navy would never have allowed his wife and children to live quite as luxuriously as they did.

Every summer, Sara headed to Campobello, sending the servants on ahead a week early to get the place ready. Eleanor and "the chicks," as Sara called her grandchildren, went along as a matter of course. Except for her war work, an opportunity she welcomed, the tasks that made up Eleanor's life had become not so different from the banal social and domestic obligations she had rebelled against after her return from London more than a decade earlier. "I did a great deal of embroidery during these years, a great deal of knitting," she remembered.

Her conscience itself seemed dulled: even after all her work with the disadvantaged, she could appear oblivious to the privilege she enjoyed. In an interview with a reporter from the *New York Times*, Eleanor attempted to convey an image of frugal wartime conservation, but something very different emerged instead: "The cooks see that there is no food wasted [and] the laundress is sparing in her use of soap." Each of the family's "ten servants," Eleanor told the reporter, had signed a pledge card to do his part. "Making the ten servants help me do my saving," she told the reporter, "has not only been possible but highly profitable." It was, of course, a classic Marie Antoinette moment, and Franklin quickly recognized that his wife's remarks had gone wrong. He teased Eleanor about it: "You have leaped into public fame," he wrote. "All Washington is talking." Once again, Eleanor was mortified. "Some of it I did say," she admitted. "I'd like to crawl away for shame."

Instead, she took refuge, as always, with Sara. "As I have grown older," Eleanor wrote to her mother-in-law, "I have realized better all you do for us and all you mean to me and the children especially." Of all the parts of her life Eleanor had ceded to Sara, none was quite so significant as the care of her children. Eleanor loved her daughter and sons unquestionably, and took pride in them: "Anna is going to be capable and dependable," Eleanor wrote to her friend Isabella Ferguson. "James already devours books and I think will have a quick and interesting mind. Elliott is just very lovable and sensitive and stormy"—words that could also have described the boy's namesake, Eleanor's father. Finally, she said, "The two babies [Franklin Junior and John] are very soft and adorable." For all her love and pride, though, Eleanor did not dote on her children; that she left to Sara. It was Sara who gushed over little James when he fell off his pony. Eleanor declared he wasn't hurt all that badly, but Sara laid him out on the sofa and pampered him for the rest of the day.

"We chicks quickly learned," James wrote, "that the best way to circumvent Pa and Mummy when we wanted something they wouldn't give us was to appeal to Granny." Sara was constantly interfering, fussing over the children, handing them treats, and allowing them to run wild. Eleanor came to understand that Sara wanted them to grow up just as she had raised Franklin: spoiled and indulged. As a result, Eleanor said, "Franklin's children were more my mother-in-law's children than they were mine."

Her forfeiture of motherhood, however, was as much her doing as it was Sara's. "It did not come naturally to me to understand little children or to enjoy them," Eleanor admitted. "Playing with children was difficult for me because play had not been an important part of my own childhood." Her view of parenting, as she outlined in an essay, consisted of a few key tenets, among them, "Furnish an example . . . stop preaching ethics and morals . . . stop shielding your children and clipping their wings . . . don't prevent self-reliance and initiative." Nowhere did she mention love, affection, or encouragement. The irony was obvious: the very qualities that had made her so revere her father she herself withheld when it came to her own children. "Sentiment," Eleanor's son Elliott recalled, was "rarely evident in Mother."

Eleanor lacked the easy, light, spontaneous touch that was needed with children. When Anna was very young, Eleanor tried having the girl lunch with her, "but after spending a solid hour over the meal on our first attempt I returned her to the nursery." She had expected the toddler to sit up straight and "never reach or ask" for "the forbidden goodies" on the table; when Anna didn't behave to her mother's expectations, she was sent away. So the children were brought up largely by nurses and governesses, under the supervision of their grandmother. Their father played with them when he was home, which wasn't often, but Eleanor consigned herself mostly to reading to them. "She felt a tremendous sense of duty to us," Anna would say, looking back. "It was part of that duty to read to us and to hear our prayers before we went to bed, but she did not understand or satisfy the need of a child for primary closeness to a parent." The irony, of course, was staggering.

Yet not all women find fulfillment in maternity, despite the myths hardwired into the culture. For Eleanor in that late summer of 1918, a whole universe of her humanity remained frustratingly unexplored, and no amount of maternal enterprise was going to satisfy that wanderlust. The small, homely securities with which she had contented herself for so long were suddenly no longer enough. Franklin's devotion had once sustained her, and made up for whatever else she didn't have, but now it seemed capricious and unreliable. All summer long, while he was in Europe, Eleanor had waited in vain for his letters, much as she had during the cruise Sara took him on just after their engagement. Similar insecurities arose now. "Much, much love dearest," Eleanor closed a letter to her husband on August 17. "I do long for letters and don't quite understand the delay." When at last one came, she replied, "I do hope there will not be such a long time again."

No one, of course, appreciates a hectoring spouse. Yet Eleanor had reasons for her fears. Not long before, probably sometime in the spring or summer of 1918, she visited the Capitol Building. Wartime paranoia permeated the place. Policemen stood at every entrance, even at the underground tunnels, stiff in their gold braid and brass buttons. Plainclothes officers also moved stealthily through the crowds. Anyone carrying a package was stopped before getting too close to the building, "in view of the present tense situation and the increasing number of cranks out there," as the newspapers reported. Since Eleanor was the wife of the navy's assistant secretary, she enjoyed more freedom of movement than most. So did her cousin Alice, the wife of the powerful congressman from Ohio. After his humiliating defeat in 1912, Nick had come roaring back two years later, reclaiming his old seat. Alice, with great relief, had packed her bags, bid Cincinnati good-bye, and returned to Washington.

That day at the Capitol, the two cousins ran into each other on Eleanor's way out. They paused in the doorway to exchange greetings on the marble terrace that surrounded the building. From Eleanor's account of the meeting, it would be clear she wasn't happy to see her cousin. After all, a long history of hurts and slights festered between them; they'd inherited all the enmity their fathers had felt for each other but none of the affection. "Now that I am older," Eleanor wrote to Isabella Ferguson, and "have my own values fixed a little, I can only say that what little I saw of [Alice's] life gave me a feeling of dreariness and waste. She's a born hostess and has an extraordinary mind but as far as real friendships and what it means she hasn't a conception of any depth." A short time before, Eleanor was furious to learn that Franklin had visited Alice in her hotel room while both were in Boston. "No one would know that you were her cousin," Eleanor complained to Franklin. "I think it would be a good idea if you and Alice didn't see each other for some time."

That was the context in which Eleanor encountered Alice at the Capitol. As she would detail in a letter to Franklin, her cousin was particularly viperish that day. With insinuation dripping like honey from her lips, Alice asked Eleanor if Franklin had told her any "secrets" lately. Eleanor stiffened. No, she replied, Franklin had not told her anything. Then again, Eleanor added, she didn't believe in knowing things that her husband did not wish her to know. "So I think," Eleanor concluded, trying to get away, "I will be spared any further mysterious secrets." She left Alice standing there on the terrace, probably smiling like the Cheshire cat.

Clearly the encounter rattled Eleanor, which was why she wrote to Franklin about it. His reply, most likely, did little to reassure his wife; from the few letters of his that would survive, Franklin usually responded vaguely to direct questions, never wanting to commit himself. So Alice's words lingered all that summer as Eleanor waited for Franklin's return and fretted over the long delays between his letters. The insinuation in her cousin's words would still have been fresh in Eleanor's mind as she unpacked Franklin's luggage during his convalescence at his mother's house.

A packet of letters dropped to the floor.

Eleanor bent down to retrieve them. The letters were from Lucy Mercer. Glancing through them, Eleanor realized they were written from one sweetheart to another.

All her old insecurities came rushing back to her. Aunt Pussie had told her she was too ugly ever to have any beaux. Eleanor had once cried on her cousin Ethel's shoulder, worried she'd never keep such a handsome man. Apparently, she'd been right.

"The bottom dropped out of my own particular world," Eleanor admitted to a friend, years later, about that day in September 1918. "I faced myself, my surroundings, my world, honestly for the first time."

WASHINGTON, DC

On the evening of November 19, 1918, at the offices of the U.S. Food Administration, at Vermont Avenue and K Street, Alice Roosevelt Longworth was putting on a show—not like the shows she used to perform at the White House, when she dazzled her father's advisers with parlor tricks. Nor was she entertaining the assembled crowd of government officials and newspapermen with any of her fabled bon mots or her sparkling repartee. Instead, on this night, Alice was *cooking*, hardly a skill she or any of her society friends was known for. Yet these were different times.

Elite Washington was bedeviled by "the servant problem": the vast majority of cooks, butlers, and footmen had been drafted into the war, while most of the female household employees had quit to take factory jobs. What was a society hostess to do? "The servant problem," one syndicated newspaper columnist opined, "has its root deep in Bolshevikism [sic] and is a part of the 'woman in industry' problem and the whole readjustment of our attitude toward 'domestic service.'" With increasing numbers of working-class people eschewing domestic work, a revolution of sorts was taking place in the parlors and drawing rooms of the aristocracy. Many affluent society ladies had barely ever set foot in the kitchens of their homes. How were they supposed to feed their families, let alone entertain as they had been brought up to do?

That night, the Food Administration promised a solution. Even with the war now officially over—an armistice with Germany had been signed by the Allies on November 11, 1918—the soldiers had yet to come home, and even when they did, few intended to return to their old lives and positions. With "food centers" being established all across the country, government planners hoped to distribute precooked and prepared meals to homes both wealthy and modest. To demonstrate, Alice and several other Washington hostesses were on hand to present the various offerings to the crowd. "Every article of the elaborate and delicious menu," one observer noted, "was found to be sufficiently hot for serving, even a hot pudding with sauce, while the salad, requiring a cold temperature, was found to be as crisp as the most exacting could require." No one could say Alice wasn't doing her part for the war effort.

She'd done other, more menial volunteer work, such as "dishing out ice cream to soldiers coming through and things like that," as she'd remember. Yet "nothing very serious," Alice would admit. She wasn't like her "do-gooder" cousin Eleanor, she said, slaving away at canteens and hospitals, feeding and bandaging men without arms or legs.

Alice's main contribution to the war, other than her cooking show, was in fact something she'd needed to keep secret. Among the very few people who knew about it, ironically, was Franklin.

Alice was friendly with a certain society woman who was suspected of having links to the enemy. That brought U.S. intelligence to Alice's door, inquiring whether she might help them bug the woman's apartment. Alice jumped at the chance to play spy. Accompanying the agents when they broke into the woman's place, she pointed out the best spots to bug. "We were doing a most disgraceful thing in the name of looking after the affairs of our country," she said, "but it was sheer rapture!"

The spy games didn't end there. Alice also passed on false military information to the woman, so that she'd pass it on, in turn, to her contacts in Bucharest, scrambling the enemy's intelligence about American military activities. As assistant secretary of the navy, it was Franklin who gave Alice the information, and he was very grateful for his cousin's cooperation. Of course, he kept Alice's involvement in the government's spying program top secret; it wouldn't be revealed until many years later, by Alice herself.

Alice, in turn, kept Franklin's secrets—when she wasn't hinting about them to Eleanor at the Capitol. Like much of official Washington, Alice knew all about Franklin's affair with Lucy Mercer. "And who could blame him for having an affair?" Alice asked, looking back. "He was married to Eleanor."

Alice had noticed Franklin driving through town in an automobile, sitting beside "a beautiful, charming, absolutely delightful creature." She made sure to bring it up with him later. "I saw you out driving with someone very attractive indeed," she said. "Your hands were on the wheel but your eyes were on her." Rather than deny it or make excuses, a besotted Franklin replied, "She is lovely, isn't she?"

With gleeful disloyalty to Eleanor, Alice invited Franklin and Lucy to her house on M Street on a number of occasions. She seemed pleased to provide the lovers with refuge from the prying eyes of Washington.

Alice would justify her actions by claiming that Franklin and Lucy were in love—and how could one object to true love? "Their relationship was very much a lonely-boy-meets-girl thing," she'd say years later. The affair, Alice insisted, was tender and romantic: "The rose behind the ear. The snipped-off lock of hair. That kind of thing."

Of course she knew how much this would hurt Eleanor. She would admit she knew exactly how "uncertain and insecure about affection" her cousin remained. Alice knew all that, yet still she invited Franklin and his mistress to her home.

She seemed, in fact, delighted by the troubles in her cousin's marriage. Alice's actions in regard to Franklin and Lucy exposed her own corroded heart: she seemed to conclude that if she had to endure a loveless charade of a marriage, why shouldn't Eleanor?

After the election debacle of 1912, Alice had wanted to divorce Nick. The love between them had dried up. He blamed her for his loss; she blamed him for his disloyalty, both to her father and to her, since all of Washington knew by now how Nick carried on with women behind Alice's back. She'd decided to put the marriage out of its misery, and announced to her family that she wanted a divorce. Yet divorce was unconscionable in polite circles. "There is nothing like the divorce court," decreed the *Chicago Tribune*, "to show up the petty weaknesses of the human spirit." So Theodore and Edith "exercised considerable pressure" to get Alice to reconsider. "I don't think one can have any idea of how horrendous even the *idea* of divorce was in those days," Alice said later. The "hullabaloo" that would have occurred had she and Nick split would have not only destroyed Nick's career but also damaged any chance Theodore might have had to make one more try for the White House, which he hadn't entirely ruled out. It might also even have affected brother Ted's ambitions. So Alice had glumly accepted a life of staged presentations and inauthentic smiles.

Remaining with Nick, however, did have another key benefit: it kept Alice relevant. As a divorcee, without any connection to the machinery of government, she would never have been able to establish herself as the Washington mover and shaker she had become over the last six years. She still didn't have the right to vote; Ohio, where she was officially a resident, had yet to extend suffrage to women, even if many other states, including New York, had already done so. (That meant Eleanor was a voter before Alice was.) Yet even with that handicap, Alice exerted tremendous influence in the capital. She'd become a shrewd observer and strategist; many legislators sought her opinion and support, much as an earlier generation had courted the wisdom of Alice's aunt Bye. Because of Alice's frequent presence on Capitol Hill, the rules regulating access to legislators' private galleries were changed to accommodate her: unrestricted access was expanded to include the immediate families of former presidents.

With an awareness of the eyes that followed her every move, Alice, wearing her large Rembrandt hat and carrying her long cigarette holder, climbed the marble steps inside the Capitol Rotunda, nodding to officers she remembered from her days as First Daughter. Unlike Eleanor, she had aged imperceptibly, looking younger than her thirty-four years. She was still lithe and serenely graceful, moving through the chambers of the Capitol like a cat.

As it had been for the last several months, her destination was the Senate Gallery. Her husband served in the House, but it was the Senate that held her interest these days. The Senate was where the real power lay. With a commanding view of the floor, Alice took her usual spot on one of the Gallery's hardwood benches, making sure to place a velvet cushion on the seat before she sat down. Who knew how long she might be sitting there, after all, watching some senator or another make an ass of himself?

One Washington insider left an eyewitness account of Alice's visits to the Senate Gallery. "In winter, a heavy beaver coat envelops a figure still slim and graceful. Her hat, no matter how becoming, is flung instantly aside." Genteel ladies usually left their hats on their heads, but not Alice: the brim might have obstructed her view. "Alice has big, dreamy eyes," the insider went on. "At least, they look dreamy until her interest is aroused. Then they light up with vivid intelligence. An interesting debate in the Senate was a lure she could not resist. When rubberneck tourists come chattering and clattering into the Senate chamber, and the barker points out the persons and places of interest, he has only to indicate the hatless woman leaning forward in the Senate Gallery, listening intently." Everyone wanted to see Princess Alice.

Alice, for her part, paid no mind to the tourists. She was too busy watching the senators. She judged and graded all of them. Only a few impressed her, and then, just so much. "Wasn't Mr. Lodge splendid the other day in the Senate?" Alice wrote to Auntie Bye about Theodore's longtime friend Henry Cabot Lodge. "There are moments when the crusty old object is a great comfort, though he is all wrong on a lot of things. On the whole they are such a stagnant lot, our 'statesmen,' that it is pretty depressing."

There was one senator, however, who'd caught Alice's attention and kept it: William Borah of Idaho, tall, barrel-chested, with a thick mane of dark, wavy hair on his "great leonine head," as Alice described him. Borah's voice was deep and melodious, and he had a reputation for transfixing his audiences and persuading them of his argument; the senator's voice, his admirers claimed, had the power to change the world. "Bill gets up on his feet in the Senate," wrote one observer, "tosses his head a mite, gives a sort of hitching twist to his hands as if his cuffs were too small for him, and says a few words about the last line of the fifth paragraph of the seventh section of the third whereas of the treaty between Poland and Afghanistan, and the next thing you know the Bank of England is hollering for help and Syria's sent an ultimatum to Tierra del Fuego."

For Alice, it was Borah's passionate denunciations on the Senate floor of Wilson's plan to ensnare the United States in a postwar international body called the League of Nations that left her exhilarated. Finally, a man not afraid to speak the truth! Alice hadn't been fond of Borah in 1912, when he declined to join her father in the Progressive Party, but he was more than making up for that now, offering a full-throated rejection of Wilson's policies. While the war was being fought, no word of criticism was publicly tolerated against Wilson: "politics is adjourned," the president liked to say, and like sheep, everyone followed his dictate. Now that the war was over, though, Alice was "delighted" to see that this attitude had been tossed "out the window." Wilson, she believed (as her father also believed) had waited too long to get into the war, and now that peace was at hand, he was waiting too long to get out, wanting to keep America embroiled in Europe's affairs. Down there on the floor of the Senate, Borah was saying all the things Alice would have said had she been a man.

Bill Borah intrigued her. Men of conviction always did—men, in other words, fundamentally different from her husband.

In the wilderness of her marriage, Alice had occasionally found some solace. Nick wasn't the only one who took lovers. A few years earlier, Alice had met Joseph Graydon, a lawyer from Cincinnati, whom she'd see when she spent time in Nick's district, and occasionally when Graydon visited Washington. Graydon was married, with two daughters, so his meetings with Alice in public were always proper and discreet. The letters they wrote to each other, however, suggested an intimacy that went much deeper than that. Graydon told Alice that they were defiant of conventional norms; they "refused to live in time and space." They discussed religion and Kant and materialism and immortality. The relationship may also have been physical. Although they were both too discreet ever to commit anything incriminating to paper, Alice was certainly sexually liberated enough—she used contraception, after all—to have an affair if she so chose. Graydon may well have hinted at this when he wrote to her that he would keep hunting for her missing earring "by night, to keep as a souvenir."

Eventually Alice's ardor for Graydon cooled, and for reasons that revealed a great deal about her: they parted over politics. Graydon resented Alice's "venting" about his support for "the President and administration for the course of the war." For Alice, support for Wilson was unforgivable. No amount of intellectual discussion, or physical gratification, could make up for that.

Bill Borah, on the other hand, spoke the truth as Alice saw it. Borah was so eloquent for the Republican cause that he'd been considered for president in 1916, and might someday be considered again. This only made Alice, of course, even more intrigued.

At the moment, though, as far as Alice was concerned, there was only one man who could salvage the country from the degradations imposed on it by Wilson. After eight long years, it was time for a Republican to take back the White House—not a conservative, Taftian sort of Republican, but a progressive, Rooseveltian sort.

In fact, Theodore himself.

Alice listened as the senators below her grandly made their points, their voices echoing up into the vaulted ceiling of the chamber. Hiram Johnson of California and Robert La Follette of Wisconsin, neither of whom Alice much cared for, were both being talked about as possibilities to lead the charge against whatever Democrat attempted to succeed Wilson. Yet some were waiting for a roar from the old lion at Oyster Bay that he wanted one more shot at the job.

That fall of 1918, Republican optimism was high: in the midterm congressional elections, the GOP had taken control of both houses of Congress, a stinging repudiation of Wilson and the Democrats. Most pundits predicted that the Republicans would reclaim the presidency in 1920, and a small but passionate minority of Republicans deemed their chances especially high if their standard-bearer were a figure as beloved as "Teddy." Others remained angry about Theodore's apostasy in running as an independent in 1912 and costing Taft the presidency. Others thought he was just what the party needed.

Alice was one of them, no surprise. Her father might not have been as strong as he used to be, and Quentin's death had unquestionably knocked much of the old bluster out of him, but he was nonetheless mulling the idea, listening to the arguments of his supporters, and acknowledging that he'd have to "get in this thing" by June of the following year at the latest. The voodoo doll buried somewhere on the White House grounds might finally be summoning the family back.

Alice knew that if Theodore could be made president once again, she'd regain the power and prestige she once had, and in far greater amounts than she possessed at the moment. That power had made up for the deprivations of her childhood, and now Alice believed it could soothe the deficiencies of her marriage as well. Nick might yet achieve his dream of becoming Speaker of the House, but that wasn't enough for the woman who'd once been America's princess. Alice knew the Speakership would be as high as Nick would ever get. He lacked the temperament and drive to go after the nation's top job—besides, he had all those skeletons rattling around in his closet. No one wanted a repeat of "Ma, Ma, where's my pa?" on the campaign trail.

So, for Alice Roosevelt Longworth, the best and surest route to power was still the same as it always had been: through her father, the man she'd both loved and hated, coveted and rejected, ever since she was a little girl.

MANHATTAN

An icy wind howled up the Gothic spires of Roosevelt Hospital at Ninth Avenue and Fifty-Ninth Street. Winter had struck hard and early that year. According to newspaper reports, the electric lights in the hospital's operating room sometimes flickered in unsettled weather. For forty-seven years, the brick structure had stood, named for and endowed by James H. Roosevelt, a distant cousin of both the Hyde Park and Oyster Bay branches of the family. On this day in late November 1918 a drama was taking place inside the hospital's wood-paneled walls with as much force as the winter wind outside—a confrontation between the founder's third cousin twice removed and an intrepid nurse wearing a stiff white pinafore and a frilly conical hat. The nurse had had the gall to suggest to her patient that he might be hereafter confined to a wheelchair.

"All right!" an irritated, defiant Theodore at last conceded. "I can live and work that way, too!"

Colonel Roosevelt in a wheelchair would be a sorry sight indeed, however. Theodore's decline had been rapid over the past month. On October 27, his sixtieth birthday, he had allowed a reporter onto the grounds of Sagamore Hill. The reporter had found the former president "the picture of activity and health," the impression that Theodore, no doubt, had been hoping to convey as he romped on the lawn with his four-year-old grandson, Richard Derby, Ethel's son.

The whole clan had been present for the birthday party, save for Ted and Kermit, who were still on the front lines. Archie was there, however, his arm and leg bandaged from war injuries. In some ways, Theodore had become the father of the nation; like many parents from coast to coast, he'd seen every one of his sons march off to combat, and one of them had made the ultimate sacrifice. The *New York Tribune* bannered Theodore's birthday as a national milestone: STILL VIGOROUS, the paper declared of the

former president, SPARTAN IN HIS BEREAVEMENT. Printed on the
front page was a long ode to Theodore's greatness, beginning with
the lines "Today your threescore years have tolled / And millions
fain would grasp your hand / And pray that you be never old /
You noblest servant in our land!"

Away from the eyes of reporters, though, America's noblest
servant was unsteady on his feet. At one point, Ethel noticed
him lose his balance and asked him what was wrong. He told her
that ever since he underwent an operation for a tooth abscess a
short time before, he'd had "queer feelings" in his head. His joints
ached from rheumatism; he was practically blind in one eye. Still,
Theodore wanted the world to know he was capable of running
for president once more if he wanted to.

In the meantime, he made sure to enjoy the autumn at his beloved Sagamore. "Fall has come," he wrote to Kermit. "The dogwood berries are reddening, the maple leaves blush, the goldenrod
and asters flaunt their beauty, and log fires burn in the north
room in the evenings." The sea turned darker and rougher in the
fall, with lots of whitecaps. At long last, Theodore had allowed
electricity to be installed in the house, so white electric light, soft-
ened by red silk lampshades with fringe, had replaced the glow
of gas lamps.

Theodore had done what he could to help the Republicans
in the midterm elections, mending his relationship with his old
party. At Carnegie Hall he'd summoned some of the old fire to deliver a stinging attack on Wilson and the Democrats. He'd taken
great delight in, and some credit for, the Republican sweep of both
houses of Congress earlier that November.

Then, on November 11, the same day the Armistice was signed
and the war officially brought to a close, the pain in his joints
became too much to bear. He was admitted to Roosevelt Hospital.
His doctors were never quite sure if in addition to the rheumatism
he also suffered from lumbago, sciatica, or gout. Perhaps it was
some combination of all of them. His increased debility was what
had led his stouthearted nurse to suggest he might spend the rest
of his years in a wheelchair.

Could he run for president if he couldn't walk? He seemed determined to try. Edith stood by, ready to support him if he made that decision, but she let slip to a visitor her true feelings. When the visitor mentioned their going back to the White House, Edith suddenly shivered and added, "Heaven forbid!"

Edith knew what lay beneath her husband's physical decline. He'd never recovered from the blow of Quentin's death that summer. Quentin had been his baby, not even twenty-one when he was killed. "I can see how constantly he thinks of him," Edith wrote to Kermit, "and not the merry happy silly recollections which I have, but sad thoughts of what Quentin would have counted for in the future." Family friend Hermann Hagedorn saw Theodore after Quentin's death and thought "the boy in him had died."

Nine years earlier, Corinne's son Stewart Robinson had died from a fall from a window while a student at Harvard. Corinne took Stewart's death very hard, and Theodore grew mildly impatient with her when her grief stretched over several months. "Evidently she is still unable to face or overcome her grief," he wrote to Bye. "If I were about to die, I should feel very sorry not to feel that those I loved would mourn me, but I should be still more sorry that they would be broken and beaten down by grief, and would not in any way strive to enjoy, and make the most of, life." Now, after his own loss, he seemed to understand what his sister had gone through. "Your burden was harder to bear than ours," he wrote to Corinne, "for Stewart's life was even shorter than Quentin's, and he had less chance to give shape to what there was in him." The death of the young, Theodore mused, "at the crest of life, in their golden morning," was the saddest fate of all.

Still, he carried on with fortitude. "As our lives draw towards the end," he told Corinne, "we are sure to meet bitter sorrow, and we must meet it undauntedly." He followed his own advice. Quentin was dead; Archie was wounded, with shrapnel still in his legs and his left arm paralyzed. In many ways, though, this was the place to which Theodore had been pushing his sons all their lives, pressing upon them the manliness and honor of the fight. When he learned that three of his sons had been sent to the front, he declared he wouldn't have them "anywhere else for anything in the world." To him, the public affirmation of their manhood was more important than having them safely home.

The ultimate sacrifice, therefore, became the ultimate expression of manhood. Quentin, Theodore told Archie, had died like "the heroes of old." So he bottled up his tears for Quentin: his sons had turned into the men he'd wanted them to be. In his stoicism, Theodore was joined by Edith. When word came that Ted, too, had been badly wounded, his survival uncertain, his parents did not rend any garments or utter any anguished cries. Instead, they took a swim. At length, Edith turned to Theodore and, quoting a favorite poem, said, "There is left the wind on the heath, brother." That was how they grieved.

How very much Theodore had wanted to go to war himself. He was very grateful when Franklin had helped arrange a meeting with the president soon after hostilities began; Wilson might have been repugnant to Theodore, but he was the commander in chief. With Alice at his side, Theodore had asked Wilson for permission to raise a division, much as he had done during the war with Spain. "Anything that has gone before," he said, "will be as dust in a windy street, Mr. President, if you will let me have this division." Wilson, however, could see that Theodore was no longer the physical specimen he'd once been; he also wasn't eager to make the Colonel a hero once again so soon before the elections. So he declined Theodore's offer. "It was a very bitter thing," Alice would remember, "when it was refused."

The bitterness, however, had been around for some time before that, originating with his defeat in 1912, which stung Theodore deeper than he anticipated. It also cast doubt, at least in his own mind, on his legacy. "It rather diminishes the sum of my achievement," he wrote to Kermit at the time, "which is the only heritage I leave you children."

The myopia of his class privilege trivialized what Theodore was in fact leaving his children: valuable properties, stocks, bonds, a $60,000 trust fund left by his father and still untouched, and other funds set up by such relatives as Uncle Jimmie Gracie. In all, Theodore's estate would be worth $810,607, or the rough equivalent of $11 million today. For a man of Theodore's class, however, that was simply not all that impressive; it wasn't the sort of fortune his cousin Emlen or Mr. James of Hyde Park had left his heirs. So what mattered most to Theodore in what he left behind was his legacy, and if Progressivism was in fact defeated, its gains rolled back, he'd feel as if he'd left his children nothing of real value. What had he fought so hard for these past two decades? Had it all been for naught?

If he ran in 1920, however, things might be different. Already the platform he'd campaign on was taking shape in his mind. According to progressives he spoke with, he planned to endorse an eight-hour workday, social insurance, an old-age pension—in other words, a full-throated expression of the social safety net espoused by progressives. The idea of another Roosevelt candidacy had some people giddy with excitement. "I tell you no secret when I say the cards are arranged for the nomination of T.R.," Hiram Johnson told a journalist. Yet anyone who saw Theodore at Roosevelt Hospital that winter would have had a difficult time imagining him crisscrossing the country stumping for votes.

Much of Theodore's pain could be traced back to the malaria he caught in the jungles of Brazil nearly five years earlier, when, to assuage his loss in the presidential race, he had accompanied explorers down the largely uncharted Rio da Dúvida, "the River of Doubt." With Kermit at his side, Theodore had made it through, but only barely: he cut his leg badly and came down with an extreme fever. He begged the others to leave him behind; he was ready to die there, he said, alone in the jungle. What a legacy that would have been: ROOSEVELT DIES WHERE NO MAN HAS GONE BEFORE.

Kermit had refused to abandon him, however. Shouldering his father up, he carried him along the rest of the way. It was a bond Roosevelt *père* and *fils* would share for the rest of their lives. In many ways, Kermit (the different son, the dreamer) became closer to his father than even his heir apparent.

Yet Ted was still the one to carry the family mantle. When he returned from the war, Ted began his political career in earnest— and Theodore fully expected his namesake to ensure his progressive legacy. At the moment, though, it was a very different

Roosevelt, from a very different party, who was in a position of power, who was being groomed for office the way Theodore had once been groomed.

Theodore had always been gracious and respectful of Franklin's rise. During the midterm elections of 1914, he had turned down an invitation from Sara ("Cousin Sally") to stay at Springwood when he passed through the area. "I shall be in the middle of a tour in which I am attacking the Administration," he wrote, "and I think it might well be an error, from Franklin's standpoint, if we stayed with you . . . I hope you understand, dear Sally, that it is the exact truth to say that I am only thinking of Franklin's interest." A year later he offered similar thoughts to Eleanor: "I am very anxious to see you and Franklin whenever the chance offers; but I do not want to compromise Franklin by being with him at this time. I wish you to tell him that from all quarters I hear praise of the admirable work he has done for the Navy under very difficult conditions."

Theodore had to wonder if any of his boys, who had greater experience than Franklin in uniform and in business, really possessed the skills to compete with him politically. Franklin was such a charmer. Only time would tell.

On Christmas morning 1918, Theodore was finally released from the hospital. A mix of snow and rain was battering Sagamore Hill when he arrived home. In most every room, a fire blazed to ward off the cold. Theodore was still too weak to move about much. He was once again the frail little Teedie: confined to a mahogany sleigh bed, watched over night and day by his wife and loyal servants the way his mother had once done.

His mortality was now impossible to avoid. "I wanted to see this war put through and I wanted to beat Wilson," Theodore told a friend. "Wilson is beaten and the war is ended. I can now say *Nunc dimittis*, without regret." He was not a deeply religious man, but he had achieved his goals. He had seen his god.

As the snow piled up outside against the house and Theodore remained bedridden, there was plenty of time to think. His main thoughts seemed to be of Edith, who'd been at his side through all his travails, who'd shared his ambitions and heartbreaks, his triumphs and defeats. A few years earlier, Kermit had married the socialite Belle Willard, and now Theodore wrote to his son to say that he hoped Kermit would, at sixty, still be "as much in love with Belle" as he, Theodore, was with Edith, "and will feel that you owe her as much."

He thought, too, certainly, of Quentin, but when a proposal was made to erect a memorial to the fallen airman on the site where he was killed, Theodore nixed the idea. Many other boys had died, he explained, and "Quentin was no more hero than they, and should not be honored above his merits because he was our son." His egalitarian public spirit won out over any personal comfort the memorial might have brought.

If he thought of his brother Elliott at all, or of Elliott's illegitimate son, no one would know. If Theodore ever had any regrets, they were fleeting: he'd always been a master at justifying his actions, and there wasn't any reason to think that had changed.

On Friday, January 3, 1919, Theodore spent the day dictating some articles for various publications from his bed and then wrote some letters. His joints were inflamed, and the doctor came to inject arsenic into the swollen areas. Nothing helped: the entire weekend, he was in pain. Little Teedie had gone farther than he had ever imagined possible, but at long last, he had reached his limit.

Desperate to alleviate her husband's pain and insomnia, on Sunday night Edith received permission from the doctor to administer some morphine. Gratefully Theodore nodded off to sleep. Checking on him at twelve thirty and finding him slumbering peacefully, Edith at last tiptoed off to bed herself. The fire crackled in the dark; outside, the winds kept up their howling and snow collected on the windowpanes. Around two o'clock, Theodore's valet was drawn to his employer's bedside by the sound of labored, intermittent breathing. The servant had no way of knowing that the great man had just suffered an embolism of the lung. Theodore's breathing became raspier, more guttural.

Shortly before four o'clock, Edith was summoned. By the time she got to his room, however, Theodore was gone.

BROOKLYN

The morning was overcast and cold. A barking newsboy caught the attention of a tall, dark, handsome man who looked down with some surprise at the paper the boy held out. The portrait on the front page was a familiar one: the serious demeanor, the pince-nez, the bushy mustache. It was the triple-tiered headline bannering across the top that was so startling:

ROOSEVELT DIES SUDDENLY WHILE ASLEEP;
SIMPLE FUNERAL WILL BE HELD TO-MORROW;
NATION, SHOCKED, IS FILLED WITH SORROW

As the family story would be told, Elliott Roosevelt Mann, now twenty-seven years old, devoured every word of every article about Theodore's death in that edition of the *Sun*, reading them as he rode the elevated train across the East River to his job at the National Bank of Commerce in downtown Manhattan. No one on the train knew, of course, that the young man was the late president's nephew. Nor did any of Elliott's coworkers at the bank know his personal history. They just knew him as the efficient young cashier who stood behind his slatted teller's window and counted out cash for his customers with rarely an error and always a smile.

The lives of Elliott and his mother hadn't been easy since Frank Weeks stole their money. Katie had scrimped and saved to feed and clothe her son. For a while, she worked as a dressmaker in Harlem; she and Elliott lived in a tenement on 146th Street. Katie's mother resided with them. In 1900 they moved back to Brooklyn, to Throop Avenue, where they remained for most of Elliott's childhood. Katie told her neighbors that she was a widow, and listed herself as "Mann, Catherine, widow of Elliott" in the city directories. She reported the same thing to census takers when they came knocking. It was her way of making her past "right." Her family said that Katie lived with a deep sense of "humiliation" for her circumstances.

At one point, "a man of good reputation and means" asked her to marry him. This man might have changed her life, made everything easier for her and Elliott. Yet Katie turned him down, unwilling to reveal the truth of her son's birth. She couldn't bear to disclose to a man she respected, and possibly even loved, what she perceived as shameful. It was also a fact that she had made a vow to Theodore never to divulge the truth. She kept that vow.

Elliott never went without; his mother saw to that. But it was an austere childhood. When he was seven, the boy wrote a letter to Santa Claus that was chosen by the Brooklyn postmaster to be published in the local newspaper, along with several others from poor children. "Please Santa Claus," Elliott wrote, "will you bring me a drum and a pencol [sic] box and two billy goats and a Christmas tree?" His dearest wish, however, was for a tricycle: "Please Santa Claus, will you bring me that?" But there were few gifts in that Brooklyn tenement, bereft of even a Christmas tree.

As a boy, Elliott did not fully comprehend his family circumstances. All he knew about his father was that he was dead. When he got older, however, Katie told him everything. She revealed who his father was. If she told no one else, she believed her son deserved the truth. The revelation affected the young man, and he came to share his mother's shame. "He was terribly embarrassed by his personal history," Elliott's granddaughter recalled. So he and his mother kept the secret to themselves. When asked what the *R* in his name stood for, Elliott replied, "Robert."

Their lives were very different from those of Elliott's half-siblings and cousins. While Theodore was entertaining heads of state at the White House and Edith was planning sumptuous menus for their daughters' coming-out parties, Katie was making one brisket of corned beef stretch for a week. While Eleanor was being sent to Allenswood, and Hall, Ted, and Kermit to Groton, Elliott was attending classes at Public School 55 on Floyd Street in Brooklyn. "This is one of the schools which has grown far beyond the capacity of the building," reported the *Brooklyn Daily Eagle* the year Elliott graduated. Sometimes fifty students were packed into a classroom. These were not the offspring of bankers and lawyers and robber barons, but of immigrants and laborers and factory workers. On Sundays, Elliott and Katie attended religious services not at a small, quaint Episcopal church set along a quiet country lane, but in the packed pews of St. Peter's Evangelical Lutheran Church at 457 Greene Avenue in Brooklyn, shoulder to shoulder with other working-class German and Scandinavian immigrants. Yet Elliott always "felt very connected and comfortable" in church, his family would recall.

Despite his private shame, Elliott was a cheerful, friendly young man. When he graduated from PS 55 in June 1906 (his photograph, along with his class, published in the newspaper) the quote he gave for the commencement booklet stood out for its sense of optimism and joie de vivre: "A very good piece of work, I assure you, and a merry." If Elliott was haunted by the secret of his birth, he was also free of the heavy expectations that weighed down and sometimes overwhelmed his cousins Ted and Kermit. He was free to be whatever he could make of himself, to pursue whatever dreams he might be lucky enough to latch on to. Even if his opportunities were more limited than Ted's or Kermit's (or even Eleanor's), it was Elliott, and no one else, who would be the master of his own destiny. No one was there to guide him, but no one was there to control him, either.

Around 1910, Elliott, his mother, and grandmother moved into an apartment in a large tenement building on Park Avenue in Brooklyn. Katie was still working as a seamstress. She made Elliott a suit he could wear when he pounded the pavement, looking for work. He set out, age fifteen, with nothing more than an elementary school education and a fierce determination to succeed. Ted and Kermit had Harvard; Elliott had drive. Always good at numbers, he landed a job as a clerk at a local bank.

There was no gamesmanship involved in Elliott's job choice, as there had been for Ted when he chose the carpet factory. There was no master plan to build up a reputation for some larger purpose. For Elliott, there was only the need to pay the bills. Before long, he had impressed his employers with his skill and found himself promoted to bookkeeper. Soon after that, he was offered the cashier job with the National Bank of Commerce in Manhattan.

For the illegitimate son of an immigrant seamstress, this was an extraordinary achievement. The NBC was one of only three banks in New York with capital of $25 million or more; its deposits totaled $356,446,602. If Elliott did his job well, he could rise through the ranks. So, every day, he donned his suit—Katie soon made him others—and rode the subway and the elevated train into Manhattan. The bank's offices were located at 31 Nassau Street, a building that also housed the offices of many prominent lawyers, including Elihu Root, once secretary of war under Theodore and chairman of the Republican National Committee. Theodore was known to visit his old friend at his office, so it was possible, and perhaps even likely, that at least once, when the building's tenants were all aflutter over a visit by the former president, that Elliott stepped out of his offices for a moment to catch a glimpse of his uncle. It was also possible that he saw his cousin Ted: the Business Man's Training Regiment, a group of businessmen preparing for America's possible entry into the war, and on whose board Ted sat, based its headquarters at 31 Nassau. If Elliott ever saw either of them, however, they didn't see him: they wouldn't have known him from anyone else.

The election of 1912 was the first in which Elliott was eligible to vote. He registered as a Republican. Just whom he voted for in that volatile three-way contest, in which his uncle played the role of spoiler, would never be known.

When the war came, Elliott registered for the draft, but he was excused, given that he was his mother's sole support. Regular raises in his salary meant that they could gradually move up in the world. By the middle part of the decade, they lived in a two-family row house on a quiet stretch of Madison Street in Brooklyn. By then, there was one fewer mouth to feed: Katie's mother had died in 1913, aged about ninety.

By the time of his uncle's death in January 1919, Elliott was on the move, making a name for himself at the bank and courting a woman seriously for the first time. The name of his lady-love was Lena Wilhelmina Prigge; she was twenty-three, pixyish, and pretty, and employed at a steelworks plant making kitchen knives. Her parents were immigrants from the same part of Bavaria from which Katie hailed. Her father had died, so Lena and her sister were supporting their mother. Elliott intended to marry Lena as soon as he'd saved enough money. Not even with Lena did he yet share his secret.

If anyone at the National Bank of Commerce had ever known Elliott Roosevelt, and there might well have been some, they would have been struck by the uncanny resemblance borne by the young clerk with the same first name. Except for his brown eyes, which were his mother's, Elliott Mann was the spitting image of his father: tall, slender, dark, and handsome. Detective Comstock, that "expert in likenesses," had seen the truth plain as day when Elliott was a baby. Now his Roosevelt blood was only more apparent.

Had he been born legitimately, or had his father's family embraced him, Elliott would have done the Roosevelt name proud. He would have been one of the family achievers, like Theodore, Bye, Franklin, and Eleanor. He was far more like his uncle Theodore than he was his father. Elliott's eyes were always focused on the goal; he was driven by a sense of duty and decorum. He saw life as a prize to be sought after and won, just as Theodore did. He was not like other cast-off members of the family, such as his father and Jimmie, who were noncompliant with the rules, resistant to expectations. Of course, Jimmie had had the financial means to shrug off his family's disapproval and disownment, a luxury not shared by either Elliott. Yet the trajectory of Elliott Mann's life went up; for Jimmie, it went steadily down.

By 1919, Jimmie was living as a recluse in Jacksonville, Florida. He was ridiculously rich: on his thirtieth birthday he'd received another installment from his mother's estate of three quarters of a million dollars. His marriage to Sadie, though, had irretrievably broken down. Living under such a cruel spotlight, husband and wife felt the inevitable tensions. While still in New York, Jimmie pursued various extramarital affairs, at one point indulging in "a public escapade of the most flagrant character," as reported in the gossip columns. There were nasty public brawls with Sadie. Despite all his money, Jimmie was negligent in paying his bills; at one point, he had a florist come after him for an unpaid balance of $104 and a jeweler demand $7,500 for Sadie's diamond collar.

The solution was to hightail it to Florida, a move insisted on by Jimmie's father, Rosy—and no doubt his uncle Franklin as well. There he was to live under an assumed name. In Florida, Jimmie sometimes called himself "King," other times "Sims." Finally Sadie left him, departing for Europe with a $10,000-a-year allowance; in 1917 there was a bitter, contested divorce suit. The saga of Jimmie and Sadie, which had started with such high drama and romance, fizzled out in a sad, pathetic conclusion.

Jimmie remained a very wealthy man—he paid the largest income tax of any man in Florida—but he was completely alone. Around this time, he visited Bye, who'd been his substitute mother for a brief time. He didn't drink, Jimmie told her, and Bye believed him. It wasn't alcoholism that had led Jimmie to defy convention, as some assumed, just a fundamentally different view of the world. He kept himself busy fixing cars, he told Bye, though too much time lying on a cement floor underneath the vehicles repairing brakes and springs had left him with a bad back. At least Jimmie was doing something he loved, which wouldn't always be as readily apparent with Theodore's sons.

Over and over, there would be those Roosevelts who did not follow the family drummer, who marched to their own beat, and paid the price for it. Two of Corinne's sons also dared to deviate from the prescribed path. The accident that claimed Stewart's life had seemed suspicious to many: Harvard officials gave a wildly improbable account of the young man falling out a window whose sill was more than four feet from the floor. The coroner quickly ruled the death accidental, but conflicting stories among Stewart's friends and family ensured that a question mark would always hover over the tragedy. Was it a drunken accident? Was it suicide?

As it turned out, Stewart hadn't been the bright, dedicated student his obituaries portrayed him as being; private letters would reveal a far more complicated portrait. "Poor Stewart has now been expelled from Harvard for good," Theodore wrote to Kermit a year before the young man's death. Obviously the expulsion wasn't "for good," since Stewart would be back on campus the following semester, but clearly there were problems. "He just did not seem able to make himself pay attention and work," Theodore wrote. "He was always mooning about something else instead of paying attention to his lessons." Like Jimmie, Stewart didn't fit in a classroom. He was more at home playing hockey or befriending stray dogs; at one point he rounded up seventeen of them.

Stewart's younger brother, Monroe, was another awkward and restless student. While "very able in his studies," one teacher reported, Monroe was easily distracted and "very fractious and short of temper." As a teenager, he incurred the wrath of his parents for indiscreet, and probably drunken, exhibitions in public, prompting Theodore to write Corinne that he was "ready and eager to do anything whatever that you think will help." Monroe graduated from Harvard, but only barely. He had the soul of an artist, a poet, but was pushed toward business, as all Roosevelt sons were if they didn't go into politics. By 1919, Monroe's drinking was a scandal throughout New York, invoking comparisons to his uncle Elliott. Like Elliott, too, he eventually separated from his wife and was seen with other women. Alcoholism was (and is) of course a disease, but Monroe's management of it was certainly not helped by his family's expectations and pressure.

For people such as Theodore—and others in positions of power in their extended clan—it was difficult to grasp that not every young man was capable of following the same path. Stewart's death didn't make Theodore rethink his worldview; indeed, he saw it as a cautionary tale. "Youth is elastic," he told Corinne at the time. "I can only hope the bent blade is straightened by time." In other words, he hoped others similarly "bent" would heed the lesson of Stewart's fate. It was a worldview that simply could not comprehend that the ability "to pay attention and work" in the classroom was not the only criterion for success in life, or that "mooning" about things might lead to results just as positive as scholarly achievement. What if Jimmie had been allowed to pursue his interest in mechanics and marry whom he loved? What if Stewart and Monroe hadn't been pushed into Harvard? What if Elliott (the first Elliott) had been left alone to repair his marriage and his life?

Such questions would, of course, never be answered. In retrospect, though, one fact became clear: the one member of the family they never accepted, the one who was never granted membership in their exclusive tribe, would have followed their rules far more stringently and successfully than Jimmie, Stewart, or Monroe—or his own father.

In the months after Theodore's death, Elliott Roosevelt Mann was promoted yet again, this time to mortgage officer. He also found a little house for his mother and himself at 354 Hart Street in Brooklyn. They no longer had to share walls with other tenants. From abject poverty to the solid middle class—Elliott's achievement was as great as (or even greater than) anything Theodore's sons had yet accomplished, given their relative starting points. One could only wonder what else Elliott Mann might have achieved in life had he been born into the same privilege as his cousins.

NORTH ATLANTIC OCEAN

At the start of the second week of January 1919, the naval ship *George Washington* cut through frigid ocean waters, still a few days off the coast of France. Its deck was windswept and ice-encrusted, its shuffleboard courts deserted, its lounge chairs folded up and stored away, but below, the ship was thrumming with life. From the portholes lining the hull, golden light spilled out onto the dark ocean. From the ballrooms and dining rooms, a discordant symphony wafted upward into the night: an orchestra, a jazz band, and the simple strings of a violin quartet all blending together. High above it all, perched in the crow's nest, a sentry kept his eyes peeled for icebergs.

Franklin and Eleanor were heading to France and then to England, where, now that peace had been achieved, Franklin would oversee the navy's demobilization. In the meantime, he was having a grand time on board the ship. Theodore's death, relayed via wireless late on the sixth, had made Franklin the most prominent Roosevelt on the world stage. The nation was in mourning, but the news from Oyster Bay hadn't dampened Franklin's spirits. "The crossing has been a fortunate one," he wrote to his mother on the tenth, "though the sea was heavy for two days, this ship is the steadiest I have ever crossed on." In the ship's movie theater, he and some friends laughed uproariously at Charlie Chaplin in his war spoof, *Shoulder Arms*. "Funniest movie I ever saw," one of Franklin's pals recorded in his diary. Another night, Franklin attended a musical play put on by the crew. "You would have loved the sailors dressed up as chorus girls!" Franklin wrote to Sara. "This is what we call in the Navy a 'Happy Ship.'" His appreciation of the sailors' cross-dressing was ironic, since back in Newport, he'd approved efforts to uncover and discharge homosexual personnel. Here on the ship, however, he was applauding those gay men who'd found a degree of refuge and authenticity as performers in military theatricals.

For her part, Eleanor kept a lower profile on the ship. Although she engaged in some lively discussions, conducted in French, with the Mexican and Chinese delegations on their way to the peace talks in Paris, she mostly kept to her stateroom, reading *The Education of Henry Adams*. Those who knew her would have noticed how wan and weary she looked during the voyage. A photograph taken shortly before she left New York showed her looking almost cadaverous. Eleanor seemed to be carrying the weight of the world on her shoulders. Shortly before the trip, she told a friend that she felt "breathless" and "hunted."

The death of her uncle was not the cause of Eleanor's melancholy; nor did it seem to add to it much. Eleanor expressed little grief over Theodore's passing in the letters she wrote back home. She did spend one moment in a letter to Sara considering Aunt Edith, who would now be "very much alone." Otherwise, Eleanor's only comment about Theodore's death was one that could have been made by any political observer: "Another big figure gone." It was hardly the expression one might have expected from a supposedly favorite niece. To Auntie Bye, with whom Eleanor would have felt comfortable enough sharing personal feelings, she merely wrote, "You have been very constantly in my thoughts ever since we heard of Uncle Ted's death for I knew what a shock and sorrow it would be for you." That was all: the rest of her letter went on to describe the interesting trip she and Franklin had had so far. Presumably, Eleanor wrote a note of condolence to Aunt Edith, and possibly was more expressive of her grief. Yet that letter did not survive.

Eleanor's relationship with her uncle, no matter how future mythmakers would try to frame it, had been complicated and conflicted. One of her last encounters with Theodore, in fact, was decidedly unpleasant. At Douglas Robinson's funeral the previous September, the Colonel was still pressuring Eleanor to coax Franklin into enlisting. He should be in uniform, Theodore insisted. Once again her uncle was attempting to impose his morals and standards on her family, and Eleanor resented it. No matter what Franklin had done to hurt her, she did not want him to risk his life on the front lines.

On January 11, the *George Washington* arrived at Brest. Eleanor and Franklin disembarked to the cheers of the jubilant French, who were grateful that the long years of fighting were over. From Brest, the Roosevelts went on to Paris, where they paid their condolences to Ted and Kermit, who were still waiting to be sent home from war duty. The two brothers had, in fact, missed their father's funeral. Toward the end of the month, Franklin and Eleanor left Paris for London, just missing Aunt Edith's arrival in the French capital—to their "great regret," as Eleanor wrote to Bye.

Even if she had been inclined to comfort her aunt, however, Eleanor was hardly in a frame of mind to offer much empathy anyway. The discovery of Franklin's affair with Lucy Mercer had left reverberations that were still being felt. That the Roosevelts were even making this trip to Europe together was a bit of a miracle: two months earlier, such an outcome had not been clear at all. Eleanor's sense of hurt and betrayal cut very deep. She had loved Franklin effusively, completely. That was her pattern. She either loved with all her being (as she loved her father, her brother Hall, Franklin, her children when they were babies) or she withdrew, keeping herself guarded and removed. "If she really loved somebody," her niece Eleanor Wotkyns would say years later, "she just gave her whole love to them." Also, Wotkyns added, she would be hurt if her love "wasn't returned in that same way"—as, in fact, she had been hurt by Franklin.

Yet beyond the personal hurt there was also the public pain.

Eleanor knew she'd been held up for ridicule in front of official Washington. If Alice knew about the affair—and from the innuendo Alice dropped that day at the Capitol, she certainly *did* know—how many others were in on the secret? Tongues had been wagging for some time, much to Eleanor's mortification. Auntie Bye's son, Sheffield Cowles, had seen Franklin and Lucy together a little "too often," he said. Mary Patten, who volunteered with Eleanor at the Red Cross, saw them, too, and wasn't above passing on to other people what she'd seen. The "worst talkers," however, according to Bertie Hamlin, the wife of Charles Sumner Hamlin, the chairman of the Federal Reserve, were the even bigger names: Lois Marshall, the wife of the vice president, and James McReynolds, associate justice of the Supreme Court. Eleanor's humiliation was complete.

For his part, Franklin would always enjoy subterfuge; it was why he'd so enjoyed the caper with Alice when she'd bugged that woman's apartment. Likewise, slipping in and out of Alice's house with Lucy on his arm was devilish fun. At thirty-six, the Lothario he'd been so briefly during college returned in full force, making up for all those teenage years spent dedicated to his mother—and, in many ways, the past thirteen years spent dedicated to his wife. Cousin Corinne Alsop thought that the marriage of Franklin and Eleanor had been, up to that point, "a good one," but that it had never been "délicieux"—by which she seemed to mean that the marriage lacked any passion that was worth savoring. Eleanor's "very good mind" had been enough to attract Franklin, but not enough to keep the spark alive between them after thirteen years.

For all her noble attributes, Eleanor was undeniably stiff and prudish. At the Democratic National Convention in 1912, Franklin had originally been pleased that his wife wanted to accompany him, showing an interest in politics. Yet Eleanor had instinctively recoiled from the merrymaking in the hall. During a spontaneous demonstration by the supporters of House Speaker Champ Clark (Wilson's chief rival for the nomination), Clark's fifteen-year-old daughter, Genevieve, happily climbed up onto the shoulders of the delegates to be carried around the room. The spectacle left Eleanor appalled. "Such things simply did not happen to ladies, in my code," she said. So she packed her bags and left. "I decided my husband would hardly miss my company," she said—and she was right.

Arthur Schlesinger, the Harvard professor and progressive intellectual who became friends with Franklin during this period, would later write that Franklin's emotional involvement with Lucy occurred in reaction to his wife. Eleanor was "gawky and insecure," Schlesinger said, "sternly devoted to plain living, invincibly 'sensible' in her taste and dress, oblivious—and to some like her brilliant cousin Alice Longworth, it seemed humorlessly, even self-righteously so—to the gaieties of existence. Her husband loved her. But he liked the pleasantness of life a good more than she did."

When Lucy showed up in his life, Franklin saw a very different sort of woman. Like Eleanor, Lucy was tall—Franklin liked tall women—and she possessed similar striking blue eyes. Yet where Eleanor's voice was high-pitched, reedy, and often shrill, Lucy spoke in a low, husky whisper. She was warm and nonjudgmental; Franklin's children, especially Anna, had loved Lucy when she worked in their household. Best of all, Lucy enjoyed having fun, whether it was kicking back with Franklin on a yacht down the Potomac or sneaking off for impromptu getaways from Washington. Franklin had fallen madly in love.

His feelings were returned, as Lucy's family would remember. "She and Franklin were very much in love with each other," Lucy's cousin Elizabeth Cotten declared. Lucy would confide to her cousins how she loved Franklin's "ringing laugh" and longed for "his beloved presence." The love and affection she offered him was uncritical. She made none of the demands of a wife consumed with family and household. Lucy could make Franklin forget his responsibilities for a few hours or, when he was very lucky, a few days or even weeks. As Alice would point out, every June, "Washington wives and their children went off to the country or the seashore," and "all the nice old politicians accumulated a little summer wife of sorts." Franklin, Alice said, was "delighted to have Eleanor away." Yet Franklin did more than just forget his responsibilities. By carrying on the affair so indiscreetly, he also left his wife open to humiliation, condescension, and pity—a particularly lethal mix.

After finding the letters, Eleanor had gathered her strength to confront Franklin. He didn't try to deny the affair, not with the proof in his wife's hands. So, as her Aunt Corinne would reveal years later, "Eleanor offered Franklin his freedom." With her self-esteem utterly evaporated, such an offer probably seemed the only course to her. How could she expect him to stay married to her when he so clearly loved another woman?

Possibly, at least for a moment, Franklin considered her offer. Lucy, according to her family and friends, was hoping for just this outcome. She was "no mere placid figure in this situation," said Jonathan Daniels, the son of Franklin's navy superior, who knew Lucy well. Daniels felt that Lucy would have made her wishes very clear to Franklin. Although Lucy was a Catholic, she was aware that dispensations to marry divorced men weren't all that difficult to obtain, especially if the man's first marriage hadn't taken place in the Church.

Yet if Franklin's love for his mistress was indeed so strong that he actually contemplated divorce—which even Alice Longworth had rejected for herself and Nick as too "horrendous" to imagine—then his wiser nature didn't take long to reassert itself. According to those who had the inside track on the story, that wiser nature was forcibly awakened by the sharp and timely intervention of Sara.

When Franklin's mother learned of the affair, and of her daughter-in-law's offer to step aside, she called an emergency "family conclave," according to Corinne Alsop. Flush with indignation, she confronted her son. If Franklin wanted to leave his wife and children for another woman, Sara declared, and bring scandal to the family and destruction to his career, she could not stop him—but she would "not give him another dollar," and would disinherit him from Springwood. That was how outraged Sara was. She would cut off her beloved only son from his inheritance.

It was also likely that Eleanor's own offer, carefully phrased, convinced Franklin as much as his mother's threat. Eleanor did not ask him to choose between Lucy and her. According to Sheffield Cowles, she described his choice as between Lucy on one side and his children and career on the other. "If she'd put it as a choice between the two women," Sheffield said, "she wouldn't have stood a chance."

So it was decided. There would be no divorce. Franklin and Lucy would part. Franklin and Eleanor would carry on as if nothing had happened. Eleanor would do her best to hold her head high and ignore the gossip. "Everybody behaved well" in resolving the issue, Corinne Alsop believed, "and exactly as one would expect each of the protagonists to behave."

Franklin, however, didn't behave quite as well as Eleanor or Sara. According to Lucy's family, the reason he gave his mistress for ending the affair was that Eleanor had refused to give him a divorce. In other words, he took the coward's approach, and blamed it on his wife. Lucy's cousin Elizabeth Cotten would always believe that a marriage would've taken place between Franklin and Lucy but for one fact: "Eleanor was not willing to step aside." Not until many years later would Lucy's family learn that Eleanor had, in fact, offered Franklin his freedom and that it was his mother's ultimatum that finally settled the issue.

Throughout the fall of 1918, everyone did his or her best to ensure that the affair was erased from history. At some point, Sara would go back through her diaries and expunge that year from her collection. Likewise, Eleanor made sure no record of her feelings was left for posterity. She stopped writing to people with whom she'd previously corresponded regularly. If any letters referenced the affair, Eleanor evidently destroyed them.

One fragment remained, however, that revealed her state of mind that fall. Among her papers she kept a newspaper clipping of a poem by Virginia Moore, with "1918" written across the top in her handwriting. The poem read, in part, "The soul that has believed / And is deceived / Thinks nothing for a while / All thoughts are vile." Yet, after some time, the sun, by "mute persuasion," inspires the soul to consider "the pull of breath / Better than death," and the soul "Ends by believing more / Than ever before."

The heartbreak and crisis of Franklin's affair was transformative for Eleanor. In her memoirs, she'd write only indirectly and obliquely about this period, but her catharsis would nonetheless be apparent. When she was younger, she'd write, she had no "appreciation for the weakness of human nature." Only when she accepted "how fallible human judgments are" did she come to truly understand "what being in love or loving really meant."

Eleanor did love Franklin, and she did her best to continue loving him and to make the marriage work. It wasn't always easy. For several months after her discovery of the affair, she started her letters simply "Dear Franklin," but by July 1919 she was back to addressing him as "Dearest Honey." Though their correspondence would never again ring with the romance and passion of their earlier years, a mutual affection and respect between them remained evident. Throughout their trip to Europe, Franklin was very solicitous of his wife, making sure she was comfortable; he always included her on his various excursions through Paris and London. For all the pain they'd been through, their relationship was far more cordial than the stiff, insincere interaction endured by Alice and Nick after their own marriage crisis.

Still, forgiving was one thing; forgetting was another. Eleanor made it a point to tell people she had the memory of an elephant. "I can forgive," she said, "but I cannot forget."

The pain made her stronger. Just before she and Franklin left for Europe, sickness had once again descended on the Roosevelt household. Nearly everyone (Franklin, all the children, and three of the servants) came down with the flu. Only Eleanor remained impervious. She took charge, rushing from room to room, taking care of them all. "There was little difference between day and night for me," she recalled. Keeping busy, however, seemed to be what she needed: in addition to caring for her own family, Eleanor volunteered at the local Red Cross clinic, where hundreds of other flu patients were hospitalized. She brought food prepared by her own cook and "tried to say a word of cheer to the poor girls lying in the long rows of beds." Caring for other people seemed to be the balm Eleanor needed to keep the memory of Lucy's love letters at bay and to heal herself.

She would go on loving her husband and her family as best she could; she would do her duty by them. She would stand by Franklin and take care of the children when they were sick. Increasingly, though, it was not her family from whom Eleanor would seek fulfillment. As a child, she learned that her family did not sustain her. That lesson had been brutally underscored by Franklin. While Eleanor would always insist that it was "the sense of being really needed" that gave her "the greatest satisfaction," from this point on, she looked away from her family and out toward the world for that satisfaction—to the girls in the Red Cross hospital, to the poor children huddled in orphanages, to the nameless faces who could love her and be grateful to her, but who would never have the power to hurt her.

WASHINGTON, DC

A cloud of gray tobacco smoke hovered just below the ceiling. The waistcoats of the men sitting around the table were unbuttoned. Cigars were clenched between their teeth. The women puffed at long slender cigarettes in pearl-encrusted holders, and at everyone's elbow sat a tumbler of whisky.

Alice shuffled the well-thumbed deck of cards, a pile of poker chips at her side. Starting at her left, she dealt the cards around the table.

Alice Longworth's poker games were famous. Nick was usually there, as were other high-level legislators and Cabinet members. A number of Alice's girlfriends showed up, too, most often her old pal and rival Cissy Patterson, who'd since married and divorced a Polish count. Whoever played cards with Alice had to be good, since she was an ace: she'd once won ten thousand dollars in a single night, even after paying off Nick's debt. "It began as an amiable game," Alice recalled, "and then it got higher and higher." She usually won, she said, because she had "no curiosity." Never did Alice push her luck; never did she take a risk if she was ahead, hoping for more. She played to win.

These days, one of the most frequent cigar puffers around her table was Sen. Bill Borah, a leader of the so-called "Irreconcilables" in the Senate, who were opposed to Wilson's League of Nations. Alice had lent her own name to the effort and was impressed with Borah's willingness to stand up to President Wilson and play hardball politics. He was a man after her own heart—literally.

Nick had what Alice called his "girls," mistresses such as Alice Dows, a wealthy woman with a gorgeous mansion in Georgetown and a complaisant husband who mostly kept to their country estate in Rhinebeck, New York; and Marie Beale, the much-younger wife of the former ambassador to Greece. Alice had just one man, and that man was Bill Borah.

Their affair began, most likely, during their passionate crusade to stop the League. Borah was even older than Nick, by four years, but Alice had always liked older men, and at thirty-five, she could feel like a young woman again with her fifty-four-year-old lover. Bill was also far more handsome than Nick, with wavy dark hair starting to turn silver at the temples. Alice was utterly enthralled by him. Her passion came through even when she tried to speak of Bill as merely "a great friend." She gushed over how he "could hold one spellbound for hours with tales of labor disputes in Illinois at the turn of the century. Unusual subjects like that." He certainly had her spellbound: friends noticed a more "carnal" side of Alice in public these days. At one party, the hostess recalled, "She ate three chops, told shady stories and finally sang in a deep bass voice: 'Nobody cultivates me, I'm wild, I'm wild'"—lyrics to the popular song "I'm a Little Prairie Flower." It could have been Alice's theme song.

She and Bill conducted their affair like teenagers. In their letters to each other, they used code, in case the letters were ever intercepted. But the code was patently obvious: "Hello" stood for "I love you." So Bill's letters to Alice began with "Hello, hello, Alice, more than you know" and ended with "Hello every minute. I wish you understood fully how Hello." He'd send her copies of his speeches, underlining various letters to spell out messages to her: "Darling I am so lonesome," read one hidden message. "I want my own sweet girl. You are more to me than you have dreamed. I am counting the days until I shall see you."

At first Alice had had to fight Cissy for Bill's attentions, just as she'd once had to fight her for Nick's a decade and a half earlier. After Cissy and Bill disappeared into another room during one party at Alice's house, a suspicious Alice searched for evidence the next morning and found some of her friend's hairpins in the library. She returned them to her with a note: "I believe these are yours." Cissy didn't deny anything. In fact, she asked Alice to look in the library's chandelier: "I think you will find my garter."

The story of the hairpins and the garter became a favorite along the Washington grapevine, even if it might have been apocryphal or simply a joke between friendly rivals. Nonetheless, it illustrated the sexually liberated, polyamorous culture of much of official Washington then. Except for Cissy, who was a divorcée, most of the players were married. Husbands and wives carried on indiscriminately, often with each other's knowledge. Everyone respected the open secrets of the capital.

Borah was married as well. His wife, Mary, lived with him in his apartment on Wyoming Avenue, a mile away from Alice on M Street. The Borahs had no children. Mary spent much of the winter in California, and when she was in town, she wasn't very social. Her name appeared infrequently in the society pages; in 1919 only a handful of teas and luncheons recorded her as being present. The most news Mary had made lately was her acceptance of a Pomeranian puppy given to President Wilson and then passed on to others. The Borahs had given the animal a home despite its name, League of Nations.

Whether Mary knew of her husband's affair with Alice was never known, but Washington was a small town. Just as with Franklin's dalliance with Lucy Mercer, people talked, and Bill and Alice were only marginally more discreet. They were seen riding through Rock Creek Park and conferring intensely in the halls of the Senate. Bill's automobile was often spotted outside Alice's residence in the evenings, even on nights when Nick was still on the floor of the House.

They had a cover for their interaction: both were plotting against the League, and by the spring of 1919, they seemed to be winning. To join the League, Wilson needed the approval of two thirds of the Senate. Thanks to Bill, with a healthy assist from Alice, it appeared he'd come up short.

Bill's opposition to the League was rooted in his interpretation of the Constitution. While Wilson argued that the world, bloody and weary from four years of war, was depending on America to join the League to help resolve future conflicts and ensure peace, Bill and his allies believed that the League threatened American sovereignty. On the Senate floor, he cited statements opposing American involvement in world affairs from some of the great leaders of the past, including Washington, Jefferson, Lincoln, and, significantly, Theodore Roosevelt. "Their company," he thundered, "is safe enough for me."

Alice's reasons for opposing the League were a little less lofty and a lot more personal. Wilson had defeated Theodore, so the Roosevelts of Oyster Bay opposed every initiative Wilson ever made. "We were against the League of Nations because we hated Wilson, who was a Family Horror," Alice would admit. "He couldn't do any good in our eyes because he had beaten Father."

The Irreconcilables used Theodore as a sort of rallying cry, implying that the nation's late, beloved Colonel had been opposed to the League. In fact, Theodore had long envisioned such an international body. "We all of us desire such a league," he wrote in an editorial shortly before he died, "only we wish to be sure that it will help and not hinder the cause of world peace and justice." Only his qualifications, however, and none of his support did the Irreconcilables quote now. Alice was aware of the hypocrisy at work, but she didn't care. Although she admitted that her father "had advocated the idea of the League of Nations in his Nobel Prize acceptance speech," she "didn't like other people's Leagues muscling in on our own." Years later she'd declare unapologetically, "It was entirely personal politics designed purely to annoy."

Revenge had, after all, always been a favorite word of hers, from the time she kept her diary as a teenager. Now revenge and personal politics helped defeat an organization many thought might have prevented another world war.

For Alice, politics was a game; as in poker, she took great satisfaction in winning. Her middle name, she declared, was "Detached Malevolence." What she enjoyed most was causing trouble for people she disliked. "I've an antihero complex," she'd admit. "I am always anti-something."

She was certainly pro-Borah. Bill had a future, Alice believed. He still aspired to be president, and he'd be a good one, Alice thought. He was a Progressive Republican, and Theodore was one of his personal heroes; Alice could definitely get behind any campaign her lover wanted to run—and, increasingly, her backing was important.

All the possible GOP nominees for the 1920 presidential election had paid calls on her by now; they all wanted the Colonel's family's blessing, and Alice was the one to dispense it. She maintained her daily presence in the Senate Gallery, keeping track of everything and everyone. Democrats and Republicans alike could find themselves on the receiving end of a blistering attack from Alice. After one debate in the chamber, she wrote furiously to Auntie Bye, "I hated the way they sentimentalized our Father, and then proceeded to do what never would have been done had he been alive. It was a combination of folly and perfidy that was pretty unpleasant to see successful."

Alice had become, quite against all odds, Theodore's legatee in Washington. It was ironic, given how she had always felt so separate from him, and how he had rarely deigned to give her much credit for anything. Yet, with her brothers still finding their feet after returning from the war, Alice was the one to keep the flame burning. "As time goes on, we miss him more, if that were possible," she wrote to Bye. "Think of this week, the peace treaty debate, the issues of that sissie in the White House . . . yet Father in everyone's mind, his name on their lips and his memory in their hearts."

Ultimately Alice wasn't her father's true heir, though, and she knew that. The crown prince had always been her brother Ted, and by the spring of 1919, she was already grooming him to take his rightful place. She wasn't just a powerbroker in Washington; she intended to be a kingmaker as well.

If a Republican didn't win the presidency in 1920, or if the *wrong* Republican did, Alice, as a clear reading of her various letters and memoirs would reveal, had a very specific long-range plan in mind. She was still the same woman who had buried the voodoo doll on the White House grounds; she still intended to get back there one day. She'd do so first, she hoped, through her lover. Yet if Bill became president, Alice's presence at the White House would always have to be shadowy and behind the scenes. If her brother Ted became president, however, she could assume the very public role that Auntie Bye had played for their father: the shrewd older sister sought out for advice and favors, and who, everyone agreed, would have been president herself if only she'd been a man.

Bill could take care of himself getting ready for a run. Ted, on the other hand, would need a little help. So Alice began inviting her brother to Washington to get him acquainted with how the capital worked. "It was a delight to have Ted here with me," she told Bye. "His energy, resourcefulness and capacity for work are fine to see. We have great times of all sorts together." Ted would be a fine candidate for office. His chest was full of ribbons. In March 1919 he was awarded the Legion of Honour, the highest accolade of the French government. Maj. Gen. Charles Summerall also cited him personally for his bravery; another citation commended Ted's gallantry during the Battle of Cantigny. Despite being gassed in the lungs and the eyes, Ted "refused to evacuate and retained command of his battalion under heavy bombardment." He was every bit the war hero their father had been upon his return from the Spanish-American War, and by remaining in the Army Reserves, Ted had been promoted to a full colonel. He was now, quite literally, the new Colonel Roosevelt.

In addition, Ted spent much of 1919 advocating for the American Legion, which kept the name "Theodore Roosevelt" in the newspapers. In every way, Ted was an ideal candidate to groom for bigger things. Alice heartily approved when he rented a house near Council Rock in Oyster Bay in order to run for the New York State Assembly that fall—a campaign timed to coincide with the publication of his memoir and paean to national duty, *Average Americans*. Col. Theodore Roosevelt, war hero, of Oyster Bay, would begin his political career in Albany. It was as if their father had come back to life.

Alice hoped Ted's path to power would proceed just as quickly.

For her other siblings, she held less interest, though she did her best (despite being a very inconsistent correspondent) to keep up with them. Ethel's husband, Richard Derby, a surgeon, had, like his brothers-in-law, returned from the war with honors for bravery. The Derbys lived in Oyster Bay with their two children, Richard Junior and Edith. Archie had taken a position with the Sinclair Oil Company (a longtime supporter of his father) and moved out to New Trier, a suburb of Chicago. He was married to the former Grace Lockwood and also had two children, Archibald Junior and Theodora. The Roosevelts liked keeping names in the family.

Kermit, meanwhile, had settled in Manhattan. His wife was the former Belle Willard, the very wealthy heiress and daughter of Joseph Willard, the U.S. ambassador to Spain and a prominent Democrat. By 1919, Kermit and Belle had three children: Kermit Junior, called "Kim," age three; Willard, one; and a newborn daughter, Clochette. While Kermit fought honorably in the war, he hadn't come home with the same sort of glory the other male members of his family had: Quentin had sacrificed his life; Ted, Archie, and Dick Derby had all been wounded. Unlike them, Kermit had been ambivalent about the war; before enlisting, he wrote to his father that the only way he'd want to fight was under his command. "I could go off with you again," he wrote, a reference to their adventures in Africa and Brazil, "and try for the malevolent hyenas with the courage of samba." As Theodore was denied the chance to raise a division, though, Kermit was left behind as his brothers trooped off to fight; unlike them, he had no National Guard or other military training prior to the war. Enlisting at that late date would have meant being forever behind his brothers, and that would have diminished him in his father's eyes. "I've never been behind before," he insisted to Theodore, "and I don't like to begin." The only way to see combat immediately was to sign up with the British Army, so Theodore went straight to the top on his son's behalf. Writing to British prime minister David Lloyd George, the former president sang Kermit's praises: "He was my companion through Africa and South America. He is very hardy and cool and resourceful . . . I pledge my honor that he will serve you honorably and efficiently." Kermit was quickly appointed an honorary captain in the British Army and shipped off to the Middle East.

From the days when he'd sat daydreaming in the windowsill, or taken refuge at Edith's side rather than chase after his father on one of his "scrambles," Kermit had been the unusual brother. "Odd and different," Edith called him as a child, and odd and different he remained. Kermit wrote poetry; he preferred to sit and write in a café than run around demonstrating the sort of robust, rigorous manhood Theodore always propagated. He was, nevertheless, as tough as rawhide and as resilient as rubber; his time in the jungle proved that. He saved his father's life on the Amazon, after all. Yet while Kermit sought out adventure and challenge, he did so for the thrill and pure wanderlust of it, not from some compulsive need to prove himself to his father, in the way his brothers sometimes did.

That attitude made him seem, to some, "far less ambitious than the rest of the family," Kermit's younger brother Quentin had once said. To his fiancée, Quentin had observed about Kermit, "Work, so far, hasn't meant anything to him and what he has been doing has been merely because he felt he had to. That's the trouble with Kermit. His life's aim was accomplished when he married."

Even once Kermit was in the war, his service was very different from his brothers'. Sitting in a Mesopotamian coffeehouse, largely out of danger with the British forces, he read letters from his father describing Ted as "the best battalion commander in his brigade." Once more it was clear who was fulfilling Theodore's wishes and who was not. Eventually Theodore got Kermit transferred into the American army. "I'm sincerely pleased," he wrote to Archie. "Now all my four sons are fighting under our own flag."

Only at the very end of the war did Kermit see real combat, when he joined up with Ted's regiment. "I can't say how pleased I am that you got into action with your battery," Theodore wrote to him, "and took part in the last three weeks' victorious drive." It was one of the last letters Kermit would receive from his father, who died a month later. Kermit could at least console himself that, at the eleventh hour, he finally did the sort of thing his father could wholeheartedly applaud.

Of course, Kermit had never needed to return home with the sort of fame and glory that Ted had; it wasn't Kermit, after all, who was set upon the road to greatness. Smoking his pipe and sipping whisky in the company of poets and pretty women evoked Uncle Elliott more than it did his father. Kermit was always more comfortable in salons and clubs than assembly halls and political rallies. What had kept him mostly on the straight-and-narrow path so far was the simple, omnipresent fact that he was the son of Col. Theodore Roosevelt.

Now that the Colonel was dead, though, Kermit no longer had anyone to please but himself. So, instead of running for office or making speeches around the country, he opened a coffeehouse. Coming across an old pal from South America, Alfredo Salazar, who ran a coffee establishment on Wall Street, Kermit had been impressed with the venture's success. Salazar had hooked hordes of businessmen on his Brazilian brew; for many, it was now impossible to start the day without a hot cup of joe. Inspired, Kermit teamed up with Salazar to launch a chain of coffeehouses, corralling nearly his entire family to invest in the business. Ethel and her husband, Dick Derby, together owned the largest share of stock, but Ted, Archie, and Belle's brother were investors, too. Second cousin Philip Roosevelt was named president of the new company.

The first Brazilian Coffee House opened in the fall of 1919 at 108 West Forty-Fourth Street. The timing was fortuitous. With the passage of the Volstead Act, the Eighteenth Amendment was empowered to ban the sale, production, and importation of alcohol starting on January 16, 1920. "The effect of Prohibition," Philip Roosevelt told a reporter, "was to make our enterprise more useful and important. What we desire to do is afford a place for people to come, where they can talk, write letters, eat sandwiches and cake, and above all drink real coffee." With its doors open until one o'clock in the morning, the coffeehouse was the new saloon. Kermit's plan was to expand to Chicago, Philadelphia, and Boston.

Like Ted, Kermit also wrote a book about his war experiences, called *War in the Garden of Eden*. Unlike Ted's chronicle of military campaigns and political strategy, though, Kermit's tome was more of a travelogue, a sensory celebration of the exotic flavors and fragrances of the Middle East. "I used to sit in one of the coffeehouses and drink coffee or tea and smoke the long-stemmed water-pipe, the narghile," he wrote. "Besides smoking and gossiping, we also played games, either chess or backgammon or munkula," an ancient Arab board game. This was the kind of laid-back, easygoing, nonaggressive, contented experiences that Kermit wanted to offer the public with his coffeehouses—a very different bill of goods from what the rest of his family sold.

Notably, the one sibling who was not on the board of Kermit's coffeehouse was Alice. "Sister" had much bigger, much more dynamic plans. With Ted as her proxy, she was planning to claim their father's mantle and restore their family to the pinnacle of power. Kermit could smoke all the hookahs he wanted in his coffeehouse. Ted was going to be president of the United States, and Alice was going to put him there. At least, that was what they all thought as 1919 turned into 1920.

ALBANY, NEW YORK

On the night of March 31, 1920, Assemblyman Theodore Roosevelt, thirty-two years old, steeled himself as he walked up to the rostrum and looked out over his colleagues seated in the vaulted chamber. All eyes were on him. Ted knew his future might very well hang on what he was about to say.

He was a small figure, standing there at the lectern, and not just because of the vastness of the assembly hall. Ted was slenderer than his father ever was, not quite as tall, and his voice was reedier and less likely to resonate. His bulging eyes still had a tendency to cross. His nose was crooked from his college football injuries. Still, with such exemplary war service, Ted was nonetheless a figure of considerable stature, so the Assembly waited eagerly to hear what he had to say about an issue that was rending them in two, one with ramifications for the entire nation.

Ted had been elected to the state legislature the previous November. He campaigned on "constructive liberalism" and against the "old guard" of the Republican Party. To the frustration of some, he seemed less concerned about local Nassau County issues than about the wider, national progressive platform his father had championed. The Democrats had charged that the Assembly was merely a stepping-stone for Ted, and that his constituents on Long Island would be better represented by someone who planned to stay there and fight for them for many years to come. That was the mantra adopted by Ted's opponent, Elias Raff, a twenty-six-year-old lawyer from the town of Seacliff and the son of a longtime local tailor. "My hat is in the ring," said Raff, "and it is not my father's hat"—implying, not so subtly, that Ted's was.

In the end, the doubts about Ted were unfounded: it became clear, early on Election Day, that the Republicans were cruising to easy victories throughout the state. When told the news, Ted replied, in front of a reporter: "How perfectly fine! Great! Bully!" He had double cause for excitement: his wife, Eleanor, had delivered a baby boy that same afternoon, and they named him Quentin. By the time the votes were all tabulated, Ted had won with the largest majority ever given to a candidate from that district. He even beat Raff in Seacliff by 193 votes. That night, huge celebrations broke out all over Oyster Bay. Marching bands paraded through the streets; bonfires were lit on the beaches. A sense of Teddy Roosevelt redux pervaded the district. "It was a big day for my family," Ted told reporters. "It will be my earnest endeavor to stand fearlessly for the principles of justice and order, and to aid in the solution of the vital problems of economic readjustment with all that lies in me."

Ted was still speaking like his father and pursuing his father's goals, which was perhaps appropriate, since it was clear that it was Theodore's exalted memory that had gotten his son elected, or had at least provided him with his overwhelming margin of victory. Still, there may have been something else at play in those staggering election results. Elias Raff was a Jew. His parents were born in Lithuania. With the end of the war, a creeping xenophobia had infected much of the nation's political discourse. A repugnance for further involvement in European affairs, exemplified by the reaction against the League of Nations, had led many politicians, Republican and Democratic, to adopt "America First" policies. Immigrants became suspect, especially non-Anglo-Saxons. It was not, therefore, the most favorable time for Elias Raff to run for political office.

Along with the rising nativism came an intense paranoia over the threat of Bolshevism. Ever since the Russian Revolution of November 1917 and the rise of various domestic Communist parties, fears of a similar insurrection on the streets of America had grown. Even the decades-old Socialist Party, which took a full 6 percent of the American vote for president in 1912, was now considered untrustworthy. The Socialists had opposed the war, after all; that was seen by many now as evidence of their treason.

Just home from the war, Ted tended to agree with such talk. In his book *Average Americans*, intended to introduce him as a major player in American politics, he resorted to a little Red-bashing of his own. "All over the country," he writes, "you will find the servicemen keen to put down [Bolshevist] demonstrations of this sort." He tells the story of a serviceman who heard about a "red-flag meeting" in his town. "That ain't the flag we know anything about, or fought for," the serviceman said, before exhorting his friends, "Let's go down and bust them birds up." Ted tells the story approvingly, as an example of manliness and patriotism, even though it presumably ended in violence and in an abridgment of freedom of assembly.

When he ran for office, however, he thought better of such talk. He was unnerved by the rising intolerance. At the National Republican Club, Henry W. Taft, brother of the former president, railed against Socialists and Bolsheviks, claiming that too many educators were "wild-eyed" in their sympathies for the "Reds" and therefore influencing America's children. Ted, also on the docket to speak, was asked for his views on the subject. Wisely, he chose not to continue the rhetoric, replying instead, "The way to [recruit] teachers who don't run wild-eyed is to pay them proper salaries." America was a very wealthy country, he said, with the means (and the responsibility) to take care of all its citizens. His statement was one that the Socialist Party itself might have made.

The fearmongering wasn't going away, though. In fact, it seized control of the State Assembly in Albany after Ted's election. On the night of March 31, standing at the rostrum in the cavernous chamber, Ted faced it head-on.

Since noon that day, a fierce debate had been raging. Now, with the hour closing in on midnight, the legislators were tired and angry. In front of Ted sat the five young men at the heart of all this discussion, five duly elected assemblymen from the City of New York: Charles Solomon of Brooklyn, Samuel DeWitt and Samuel Orr of the Bronx, and Louis Waldman and August Claessens of Manhattan. They were all Socialists, and House Speaker Thaddeus Sweet had called for their expulsion from the chamber on grounds of sedition.

A full investigation of the men had been carried out. No evidence of any crime was turned up, but the mere fact of their publicly stated allegiance to Socialist principles was considered enough to expel them. In the heat of the debate, members of both parties conflated support for expulsion with patriotism; one was either "for America and for expulsion" or else a collaborator with treason. Tempers flared. Legislators pounded the lectern with their fists to make their points, their faces and necks turning beet red above their high, stiff, white detachable collars. The rhetoric turned ugly. "As a true American, I will refuse to sit here any longer with members whose hearts are touched with treason," shouted one Democrat, before hinting darkly about citizens taking the law into their own hands, as with the lynchings that still occurred down south.

Amid all this tension and rancor, Ted stepped up to speak. He had never before delivered a speech to the entire body. He'd been biding his time, building alliances, learning his way, forming his opinions. He was well liked, and many saw a great future ahead for him. The leaders of the Republican Party envisioned him as governor in four years, and possibly, four years after that, as president. So when Ted got up to speak about the Socialists, everyone in the room quieted and listened intently to what he had to say.

He began by admitting that the legislature had the right to expel any member who committed treason, but, he added, "as this power is subject to no external control, it is doubly necessary for us to exercise it only with self-control, because the greater the power, the more dangerous the abuse.

"To expel the Socialist Party from our Assembly we must condemn it as a conspiracy. If we so expel it, we must in all logic set about expelling all Socialists from every office they hold through the length and breadth of this state and, to bring the expulsion to its logical conclusion, as the right to vote in general entails the right to hold office, we must disenfranchise every dues-paying member of the Socialist party."

Groans began rumbling through the Assembly. Ted's views weren't a surprise; he'd expressed his discomfort with the witch hunt over the past few months, but many had hoped, at the moment of expulsion, when all the charges were made and an overwhelming number of assemblymen were in favor of kicking the Socialists out, that he would have changed his mind. Yet not only had he remained fixed in his opinion, but he was making an extremely cogent argument against what the Assembly was trying to do.

Ted acknowledged that the official position of the Socialist Party had been against the war, but he reminded his colleagues about the cherished American value of freedom of speech. None of the investigations, he said, had uncovered any evidence of treasonous activity. The Assembly might "abhor the doctrines of the Socialist Party," Ted said, and claimed that he shared their abhorrence, but such disapproval should not allow them "to commit a crime against representative government."

Boos and catcalls erupted as he finished his speech. He made no acknowledgment of the hostility. He kept his head high, his eyes averted from all gazes, including those of the five Socialists, as he returned to his seat.

Ted didn't really abhor Socialist doctrine. The Socialists might sometimes go too far, in his opinion, but he shared their underlying conviction that the true power of a nation rested in its workers. Earlier, when asked what he considered the most important problem facing America, he replied that, "without question," it was the conflict between "capital and labor." Remembering those men he'd worked with in the carpet factory, he wanted to create a real partnership between employer and employee. Profit sharing and "representation of labor in management" were among his primary goals as a legislator. Unlike many Republicans, he was supportive of unions. "The working people need unions," he argued, "to protect them and to represent them, especially in collective bargaining." Such positions left him open to being called a Socialist himself, and made many Republican bosses nervous. Once again, a Roosevelt was challenging party orthodoxy.

There was another element to the expulsion debate that no doubt left Ted uneasy, and that fueled his opposition to it. All five assemblymen being investigated were Jewish. In many ways Ted was an extension of his father: the policy positions he espoused grew directly out of Theodore's Progressive campaign of 1912. He differed from his father in one key aspect, though: Ted was not afraid of a multicultural America. Theodore had worried about the old Anglo-Saxon stock not breeding fast enough to keep its majority and hegemony. Ted, on the other hand, embraced the changes that were coming. When writing his book *Average Americans*, he made it a point to celebrate the diversity of his regiment during the war. He named Sergeants Braun, Schultz, and Cramer, born in Germany; Privates Belacca, Kalava, and Rano, born in Italy; Sergeants Murphy, Hennessy, Leonard, Magee, and O'Rourke, born in Ireland; Sergeant Hansrodoc, born in Greece; Sergeants Masonis, Crapahousky, and Zablimisky, born in Poland; and Sergeant Mosleson and Privates Brenner and Drabkin, "of Jewish extraction." Many of these men had been wounded in battle, and some had been killed. "All of these men," Ted wrote, "were straight Americans and nothing else."

Still, fear of foreigners was bubbling over that night in the State Capitol. Among the legislators, there were very few names suggesting a non-Anglo-Saxon background: for every Patryzkowsky and D'Amico, there were dozens more Cosgroves and Chamberlains and Harringtons and Smiths. When one of the accused, Assemblyman Solomon, attempted to take the floor, he was barred by the sergeant-at-arms. Solomon then made formal application to speak under Assembly procedures, but Speaker Sweet ruled him out of order.

Once the boos and hisses had died down following Ted's speech, Speaker Sweet stepped from the rostrum and made a speech directly from the floor, exciting his supporters. Sweet was forty-seven years old, a wealthy paper manufacturer, and the scion of an old Oswego County family dating back to Colonial times. He had been extremely welcoming of Ted when the freshman legislator first arrived in Albany. Even during the debate over the Socialists, relations between Ted and Sweet had remained cordial. Now, however, the Speaker was about to deliver a particularly low blow.

"This day," he said from the floor, his voice ringing through the chamber, "while we are making legislative history, we must surely feel with us the presence of that indomitable, country-loving statesman Colonel Theodore Roosevelt, who in these chambers only a few years ago, laid the foundation of his noble, self-sacrificing labors in the interest of this Republic he so dearly loved."

Ted burned with anger and resentment.

"Deep in the heart of every true American," Sweet went on, "is a reverence for his words and a regard for his deeds." Theodore's example, Sweet declared, empowered him to condemn the traitors in their midst. It was time to place "the seal of doom" upon the Socialist Party, he averred, "which had long masqueraded as a political party." The Assembly needed to expel the Socialists posthaste.

This time, the chamber responded with cheers. "Throw them out!" the body began chanting in unison. The demonstration went on until 3:00 a.m.

The next day, the newspapers all picked up on Sweet's "implied censure" of the son of the great Roosevelt. For Ted, this public shaming was excruciating. All his life, he had lived with the "fear he would not be worthy" of his father, as his wife, Eleanor, had so painfully observed time and time again. Ted was always being "compared with his father and found wanting, accused of imitating his father in speech, walk and smile," she said. Now, before the entire legislature, he had been tarred as a false son, an inadequate substitute, a fraud.

At home, Ted's wife was steaming mad at Sweet. "How many

people think they know just what Colonel Roosevelt would have done in any situation!" she huffed. Yet what *would* Theodore have done? He certainly had held contempt for pacifists, which the Socialists had become. Still, many Progressive positions dovetailed with Socialist doctrine, such as social and health insurance and the rights of workers. Theodore had displayed more ire at old-guard Republicans than he ever had at Socialists. Indeed, he called himself "a fellow radical" in a letter to Russia's new Bolshevik leaders, and congratulated them in their "great movement for democratic freedom." Yet he also cautioned them against "unbalanced extremists" who might undermine democratic aims.

The world was different now, of course. Democracy had, as Theodore feared, been overrun in Russia, and anarchists and Communists were openly calling for revolution in this country. Raids of political meetings, led by U.S. attorney general A. Mitchell Palmer in late 1919 and early 1920, had resulted in charges of conspiracy against hundreds of immigrants, many of whom were then deported. Most everyone believed that the threat posed by these agitators against the United States was real, even if few charges were ever proven. Theodore, always jingoistic but even more so as he grew older, might well have viewed the new breed of Socialists, sympathetic to the dictators in Russia, as traitors. At least, that was what people such as Thaddeus Sweet argued.

Ted didn't buy it. His father had pushed, prodded, and sometimes humiliated him into being the man he was. The manhood he'd inherited was partly grim and austere, intolerant and aggressive, but another part (the better part) was founded on honesty, justice, and character. For all his bombastic exhortations to fight and to win, Theodore had also stressed to his sons the importance of fair play. "I would rather have a boy of mine," he wrote, "show real character than show either intellect or physical prowess." Character, Theodore said, most made the man.

Thaddeus Sweet, however, defined character as being sufficiently patriotic to throw the Socialists out of the legislature. Ted rejected that equivalence. If his father had stood for anything, it was for democracy, and those Socialists had all been legally elected, chosen by their constituents to represent them. On the morning of April 2, after a twenty-three-hour session, Ted cast his vote against expulsion, saying "the consequences be damned." He was one of only 28 to do so, out of a total of 144.

Charles Solomon was the only Socialist assemblyman present to witness the vote. Afterward, he gave a statement to the press: "Treason has been committed in the New York Assembly, with few honorable exceptions. A bipartisan combination has over-thrown representative government. The Constitution has been lynched."

What made things worse was the timing: Sweet had held off the vote until one day after April 1, which was the deadline for the governor to set new elections. That meant that the five districts would remain unrepresented for almost a year, until the next election could send new legislators to Albany. Ted was outraged, but there was nothing more he could do.

Ted was never the sort to rant and harangue; in this he was also different from his father. He didn't go on lecturing his colleagues; he simply put his head down and went back to work. His was a steady, deliberate character. One week after his vote against expulsion, he submitted a key piece of legislation for consideration, a bill bearing his name and giving employers the ability to include their employees on their boards of directors. It was voted down 87 to 28.

Speaker Sweet was having his revenge. "Theodore Roosevelt has begun to 'take his medicine' for opposing the ousting of the Socialist assemblymen in opposition to the decree of Speaker Sweet," the *New York Times* reported the next day. In voting against Ted's bill, one of Sweet's lieutenants declared, "Minori-ties in directorates should be protected." That led Ted's ally as-semblyman William Pellett to quip, "I thought minorities had no rights." Ted himself said nothing. "Colonel Roosevelt," the *Times* reported, "took the defeat of his bill with a grin."

If Ted had hoped his first term in office would set him up as an influential leader of his party, he was badly disappointed. This 1920s version of Theodore Roosevelt couldn't even get a bill passed. "Ted's vote was extremely unpopular," his wife would recall, "not only in his own district but throughout the state. He received so many abusive letters that we thought his political career might be over before it began." For all his sincere insistence on character and fair play, Ted's father had also been a shark, able to dodge cutthroat politicians and cut back when necessary. During the Spanish-American War, he'd charged up San Juan Hill, slaughtering the enemy right and left to make it to the top. Ted, however, had won his war accolades not for the number of men he killed but for the number he saved. Ever since he was a boy, swimming like a frog after being tossed off the pier to prove he could swim, he had been trying to demonstrate that he was as tough as his father. His proving time, it seemed, had just begun.

HYDE PARK, NEW YORK

Some eight thousand people thronged the lawn of Springwood on the afternoon of August 9, 1920, congregating under the ancient oak trees and along the grassy banks with the sweeping views of the Hudson River Valley. Above them the Roosevelt mansion stood in all its gray-stucco glory, its architecturally incongruous wings and porches displaying eccentric charm. The weather that day was exquisite: "a very fine temperature," Sara recorded in her diary. Everyone who'd come out for the celebration was in the most buoyant of spirits. Friends, political allies, and Democratic Party loyalists from all over Dutchess County rambled across the grounds, excited for the upcoming election. Uniformed footmen moved in and out of the crowd, serving lemonade and cake. "Very fine and impressive," Sara declared, taking a look around.

All those feet trampling her lawn, however, did make her a little queasy. For Franklin, though, Sara could endure anything. The proud mother was overjoyed to host this "notification" gala. Her son had just been nominated to run for vice president of the United States.

Inside the house, another five hundred guests were being served lunch. Some of the Democratic Party's biggest names were there, including New York governor Al Smith and treasury secretary William McAdoo, who'd vied for the chance to succeed Woodrow Wilson. In the end, however, the Democratic nomination for president had gone to Governor James Cox of Ohio. Originally this gathering at Springwood was supposed to have been much smaller, for about two hundred, but then Franklin kept inviting more and more, most of them middle-class party workers eager for a chance to see the Roosevelt estate. Sara looked on, biting her tongue, as district captains and precinct officials with last names such as Murphy and Schwartz shouldered their way into the great house, where, as Eleanor observed, "for so many years only family and friends were received." At one point, Sara walked into the dining room to find "a little tailor from Poughkeepsie with his fat, good-natured wife" munching sandwiches. Still, these were the people who could get Franklin elected, so she greeted them as graciously as she did Smith and McAdoo.

For his part, the candidate was as sunny as the afternoon, expressing abundant optimism as he addressed the crowd from the terrace. "Our eyes are trained ahead," Franklin trumpeted, "forward to better new days! America's opportunity is at hand!" As if to punctuate his point, an airplane flew low over the crowd, the sound of its propellers momentarily drowning out Franklin's words. He paused before continuing. "We can lead the world by a great example!" he shouted. "The Democratic program offers a larger life for our country, a richer destiny for our people. It is a plan of hope."

Applause and whistles followed his remarks. Franklin had been hearing a lot of that over the past few weeks. The delegates at the national convention in San Francisco had loved the tall, handsome assistant navy secretary who'd become their dashing, eloquent vice-presidential nominee. Franklin was so much more dynamic than Cox, their standard-bearer. "Hurrah for the Democrats!" Rosy wrote to Eleanor when word reached Hyde Park of Franklin's nomination. "Won't Ma have to buy a whole set of new hats to contain her head! Seriously I am awfully proud of him and so must you be." To Franklin, his brother wrote, "Tell Ma when they ask for photographs of you at an early age for publication not to give out the one in a kilt and scotch bonnet!" Yet there was no suppressing Sara in her pride: she made sure that picture got out there.

During the convention, Eleanor and the children had been at Campobello; they learned of Franklin's nomination only the next day. Fourteen-year-old Anna wrote to her father that she liked his "nomination pretty well," and twelve-year-old James assured Franklin that the locals were "planning a great holiday" for him. Eight-year-old Elliott, meanwhile, wrote to his grandmother to say how much he looked forward to seeing his father when he got home, as it had been "a very long time." About Franklin's ambitions, the children were ambivalent; on the one hand, there was great pride; on the other, there was a continual sense of disappointment at his absence. They directed their resentment at Louis Howe, the grumpy little man who was constantly taking their father away and who lived in their house and monopolized Franklin's time whenever he was at home.

Like Theodore's children a generation earlier, Franklin's brood craved their father's attention, waiting impatiently for him to take a break from his official duties and return to them. Unlike Theodore's children, however, Franklin's offspring were frequently let down. Theodore might have pushed his children too hard at times, but at least he always came home to them; he never failed to make time for his bunnies. Franklin, in contrast, would drop in for a few days and then be off again. That summer of 1920, when he was off running for vice president, his five-year-old son, Franklin Junior, taught himself how to ride a bicycle. Theodore would never have missed such a milestone.

Even when Franklin was home, there was little of the "romping" that had gone on between Theodore and his children; Franklin was never the roughhouser that his cousin was. Still, he rode horses with the children when they were together at Springwood, and took them ice-boating on the frozen Hudson River in the winter. In those rare moments when they were together, Franklin was warm and effusive. He indulged his children, coddled them, even, and loathed ever having to scold them. Discipline was left to their mother and grandmother. Once, when Eleanor insisted that Franklin punish Elliott for some misbehavior, he took the boy into another room, spoke a few words to him, and then told him to cry out, so that his mother would think he'd been spanked. Franklin's love for his children, James would remember, was "both detached and overpowering," but at least, Anna said, they could always count on his "consistency of affection," whereas their mother was aloof and distant.

When his children were young, Franklin was at his most ambitious; he was constantly on the move, climbing the political ladder, cultivating friends in high places. Springwood, while dear to his heart, never had quite the emotional pull on him as Sagamore Hill had for Theodore. Springwood meant status to Franklin. Indeed, he'd remodeled the house in ways that were inconsistent with its original structure, an architectural sin hard to imagine Theodore committing. Franklin, however, needed a grander home than the original, quaint nineteenth-century mansion offered. So he tore off the old clapboards, demolished the porches where his father had so enjoyed reading, and constructed a second tower. He raised the front roof to add a third floor, built wings on both sides of the house, and tacked on a new entrance with an elaborate balustrade and columned portico. Springwood, of course, needed to be bigger to accommodate Franklin's five children when they were there, but more important, it needed to match Franklin's emerging place in the world.

Among the political class, Franklin had assembled a sterling reputation. He was seen as the ideal combination of ruling-class commander and selfless champion of the average man. "One of the bright spots in Washington," *McClure's* magazine had called the young assistant secretary of the navy. "His eyes are on the doing of the job and not on Franklin Delano Roosevelt." That, of course, was the impression every good politician wanted to give, and Franklin, by 1920, was a very good politician indeed.

Vice president, however, was a thankless job, and Franklin hadn't been pleased when Cox rebuffed his request that the position be made more than a placeholder and that he be allowed to sit in on Cabinet meetings. Cox declared that such a move would compromise Franklin's appearance of neutrality when, as part of his constitutional duties, he would have to preside over the Senate. So, for the time being, he had to content himself with hoping the vice presidency might lead to greater things down the road.

Surely most everyone at his "notification ceremony" that day on the grounds of Springwood envisioned the same thing. The laughter and high spirits continued into the early evening, but once the speeches were over and many of the guests had departed, the smiles on the faces of the party bigwigs inside the house faded. Underneath all the happy talk, an undeniable sense of doom festered. The country had soured on the Democrats and the progressive movement. What the Republican nominee Warren Harding was promising was a return to "normalcy," to that simpler, less stressful time before the war. In many ways, Cox and Roosevelt were being put forth as sacrificial lambs. Only the most dedicated party loyalists actually thought they could win. "I suppose he would have rather gone to the Senate," Rosy wrote of Franklin in his letter to Eleanor after the convention. "But he is young enough, even if beaten, for this to be a splendid stepping stone in future politics. It is not like an old man who might be shelved by it."

Still, Franklin was determined to do what he could. The day after the notification party, he left to barnstorm through the West. By the first of September he was back in New York; then he immediately headed up to Maine and down through New England. On September 6 he delivered a rousing speech at the Brooklyn Navy Yard. Then he was off to campaign through the Midwest.

For much of it, Eleanor accompanied him. It was important, Franklin felt, for his wife to be seen at his side on campaign stops. They needed to project the image of a happy, devoted couple. James Cox was divorced and married to a second wife, which many Democrats feared would hurt his chances, although the other side had its problems. Mrs. Warren Harding was also divorced, and "if the Cox divorce is made a factor by the opposition," Franklin vowed to a friend, "you may be sure that the Harding divorce will be brought out." Most insiders were also aware that Harding had two mistresses. The best strategy to offset such marital disarray, Franklin realized, was for him and Eleanor to radiate domestic bliss. With Eleanor always a few steps behind him, smiling from under her wide-brimmed hat, they succeeded in their goal.

In fact, it wasn't all acting. The couple had regained a level of equanimity. If the old fire between them was never going to be relit, Eleanor and Franklin did at least enjoy each other's company. At the convention, Franklin had written with sincere longing to his wife, "I miss you so, so much. It is very strange not to have you with me in all these doings." Eleanor replied asking for all the news. Franklin was once again her "dearest dear honey."

Of course, it helped that Lucy Mercer seemed permanently out of the picture. On February 11 of that year, Franklin's former mistress had married a wealthy New York widower. "Did you know Lucy Mercer married Mr. Wintie Rutherfurd two days ago?" Eleanor wrote in a postscript to a letter to Sara. She said nothing more than that; she didn't need to. Both women, presumably, breathed sighs of relief.

Eleanor's appearance on the campaign trail drew the attention of the press. Zoe Beckley, one of the more prominent female reporters of the period, was sent out by the New York *Evening Mail* to get the distaff side of the coming election. Beckley found Eleanor very articulate on the themes her husband was campaigning on. "The Democratic candidates stand for progress, for going ahead," Eleanor told her. "The present leaders of the Republican party stand for inaction. So far as I can see, they are looking backward." To another reporter, she was even plainer about the difference between the parties: she'd become a Democrat not because her husband had requested it, Eleanor said, but because the Democrats were "the most progressive." The Republicans, on the other hand: "Well, they are more conservative, you know," Eleanor opined, "and we can't be too conservative and accomplish things."

In Washington, Alice burned. Eleanor's speaking out against the Republicans was bad enough, but nothing would have ticked Alice off more than Beckley's observation that Eleanor resembled Theodore. "In appearance she is a Roosevelt of the Oyster Bay branch," Beckley wrote, "including the dental Rooseveltian smile." The observation likely cut very deep.

Much to Alice's chagrin, Eleanor was in the papers all summer long, her portraits gracing the society pages, her story being told alongside those of the other candidates' wives in special newspaper supplements. "Mrs. Franklin Roosevelt is of the grande dame type," the Washington *Evening Star* society columnist wrote, "and is of the cosmopolitan order, whereas all three of the others are what is called the small-town type, even Mrs. Cox." Reading reports of her former lady-in-waiting described as a "grande dame" and being of "the cosmopolitan order" probably made Alice's skin crawl.

Yet Eleanor was right in her assessment of the political situation: the Republicans, led by Harding, had abandoned the progressivism of Theodore and their last nominee, Charles Hughes, in an attempt to distance themselves from the unpopular Wilson and his policies. The Democrats, meanwhile, had picked up the progressive mantle. Harding, Franklin warned, would return the country to "the financial domination of the eastern, tariff-protected, moneyed interests of the Republican Party"—the very forces Theodore had worked so diligently to disempower. In the words of one newspaperman, Theodore had been "an essential and fundamental democrat [small *d*] and an exponent of liberalism and progressivism," but now it was "the Democratic Party, inspired by Wilson," which stood "for everything the great Roosevelt represented."

With this turn of events, Alice was not at all pleased. After all, her father was supposed to have been at the top of the ticket this time; after his death, the family had thrown their support to Gen. Leonard Wood, former army chief of staff and a veteran of Theodore's Rough Riders. Then, when the convention deadlocked between Wood and Governor Frank Lowden of Illinois, party bosses hunkered down in the quintessential smoke-filled room and selected Harding as a conciliatory candidate. When Alice received news of the nominee, she blanched. "To call [Harding] second rate," she declared, "would be to pay him a compliment." Against the Ohio senator she nursed "a personal grudge": Harding had opposed her father in 1912. Cornering George Harvey, the editor of *The North American Review* and one of the behind-the-scenes men who'd selected the nominee, Alice asked why they hadn't picked someone with higher qualifications. Harvey replied that ability didn't matter. Harding would "go along"—meaning, as president, he'd do what the party wanted him to do. Mulling over that bit of information, Alice decided to pay her own call on the presidential candidate.

Harding's campaign was conducted largely from the front porch of his home in Marion, Ohio, a brilliant bit of hokum engineered by the crafty head of the Republican Party, Will H. Hays. Alice was in Ohio herself, doing her part for Nick's reelection campaign, plastering a fake smile on her face as she shook hands with constituents and counting the days until she could get back to Washington. She took advantage of her proximity to Harding, though, to meet him in person. No doubt the senator was cautious, even apprehensive, when the sharp-tongued Alice Longworth swept into the room. Their last interaction, eight years earlier, when he opposed her father, hadn't been pleasant.

Yet Alice was all smiles this day. She'd come with an offer from her family, she told Harding. They'd support him, she explained, if he promised to back Ted for governor of New York when he chose to run. Since the support of the Oyster Bay Roosevelts was essential, Harding agreed.

Yet what Alice had just done was trade ideals for personal fortune and ambition, one of those sins her father had so often warned his children about, and against which he had railed in one of his most famous progressive speeches: "I am far from underestimating the importance of dividends," Theodore had thundered, "but I rank dividends far below human character."

Progressivism, for Alice, had always been a means to an end. What she really cared about was power. It didn't seem to matter to her that Harding would utterly repudiate Theodore's progressivism; what mattered was that she and her family would stay in power—and get a chance to stop that upstart Franklin and his timorous little wife, Eleanor, in their tracks.

All the political prognosticators predicted a Harding victory. The senator was simple, down to earth, the sort of fellow one might like to have a beer with—if beer were still legal. (Prohibition had been in effect since January of that year.) Harding was about as different from the effete, intellectual, wooden Wilson as possible. He appealed to the American electorate's weariness with big-city immigrant problems and its yearning for a simpler, small-town past. "America's present need," Harding said, "is not nostrums, but normalcy; not revolution, but restoration . . . It is one thing to battle successfully against world domination by military autocracy, because the infinite God never intended such a program, but it is quite another thing to revise human nature and suspend the fundamental laws of life and all of life's acquirements."

The need for nostrums and revolution, and for the sharing of "life's acquirements," had, of course, been Theodore's battle cry. That cry was now sounded by Franklin and Cox, both of whom, unlike Harding, traveled the length and breadth of the nation with their message. "Some people have been saying of late, 'We are tired of progress,'" Franklin declared at his nomination party at Springwood. "We want to go back to where we were before, to go about our business, to return to 'normal conditions.' They are wrong. That is not the wish of America. We can never go back. The 'good old days' are gone past forever; we have no regrets."

Based on ideology alone, the Oyster Bay Roosevelts should have supported the Democrats in the 1920 election. Yet there was simply no way they could ever vote for Franklin. The animosity had seeped in too deeply.

For all her venom, Alice was at least honest about her motives, if only in retrospect. "We behaved terribly," she admitted. "There we were—*the* Roosevelts—hubris up to the eyebrows, *beyond* the eyebrows, and then who should come sailing down the river but Nemesis in the person of Franklin. We were out. Run over."

What made things more "complicated," as Alice explained, was that Theodore's real son and heir was out there doing his best to take wing himself, but he had found himself frustrated that his cousin was grabbing all the attention. "My brother Ted had been brought up by my father to follow in his footsteps," Alice said, "which was very tough, and then to see Franklin follow in those same footsteps with large Democratic shoes on was just too terrible to contemplate!"

Still, Ted had complicated his own chances by alienating much of the Republican Party, especially in Albany, where he still hadn't been fully forgiven for his heresy in siding with the Socialists. He'd also angered many ardent Prohibitionists by voting for a bill that would have permitted the drinking of beer in hotels and restaurants in cities with populations of 175,000 or more—a bill now in limbo as Governor Smith put off signing it, fearing the courts would overturn the law. Both parties wanted to avoid Prohibition as a campaign issue, arguing that it was now settled law. Yet fervent "wets" (anti-Prohibitionists) in the Democratic Party refused to give up pushing for nullification laws. The Republican "drys" considered Ted a traitor to their cause—a Republican, they said, "in name only."

So when he considered throwing his hat in the ring for governor that summer, there simply wasn't enough support from the party—which was why Alice had secured Harding's promise to back Ted in either 1922 or 1924. Ted knew there was only one way to win back his party's trust and support. He had to do all he could to ensure that the Republicans regained the White House in November—and in so doing, he might also win back the legacy that was supposed to be his.

So he'd set out on the campaign trail to stop Franklin and the Democrats in their tracks. From the rear platform of a train pulling out of Pennsylvania Station in New York, through the clouds of smoke and soot, Theodore Roosevelt Jr. waved to the throng that had come to see him off on his great journey west. Handkerchiefs flew; men shouted, "Give them bully hell!" Ted planned to shadow Franklin as he stumped for votes, offering a countermessage to the Democrats' spin and a reminder of who the *real* Roosevelts were. If Ted could do that, all would be forgiven in the GOP ranks.

The venture was not without its risks. As one newspaper editorialized, "The best evidence of the success of Franklin D. Roosevelt's speaking tour throughout the West is the fact that the Republican committee has scurried around and drafted Theodore Roosevelt, Junior, in an effort to offset his influence." Ted wanted to offset Franklin's message, but Franklin, as the paper pointed out, was only offering praise of "young Teddy's father when he scored the Harding bunch of reactionaries." This was Ted's dilemma. "Will young Teddy try to discredit this praise of his father by denying his progressive father's deeds? Will he say Harding was right and his father was wrong in 1912?"

Mostly, Ted avoided the issue altogether. He chugged through the Midwest and then to the far West, rallying Republicans from the rear platforms of trains and the stages of community halls. Rarely did he mention the Democrats by name; mostly he just praised Harding and said "bully" a lot. In Keokuk, Iowa, he ate fried chicken prepared by the wives of Iowa farmers and rallied the crowd at the Grand Opera House. Newspapers called him "a chip off the old block." At Burlington Train Station in Omaha, Ted clambered up on a special platform next to the tracks and roused a crowd of several hundred. One observer thought he "resembled his father in a number of ways and has adopted mannerisms to make the likeness still more striking." He confined his remarks to attacks on Wilson and the League of Nations.

Not until he got to Wyoming did Ted let fly with a direct assault on Franklin. When asked specifically about his cousin, Ted called Franklin "a maverick" who didn't "have the brand of our family." Clearly, the Democrats' continued manipulation of the media, especially the effort to sell Franklin as close kin to Theodore, had left Ted frustrated. When the public thought he was Theodore's son or nephew, Franklin did not correct them, leaving the Oyster Bay clan seething in rage. Nick Longworth went so far as to call Franklin "a denatured Roosevelt," which understandably left Sara hopping mad.

In the middle part of September, the family attempted to set the record straight once and for all. They issued a statement making clear that they had never endorsed Franklin and were backing Harding. Ted, the statement declared, was stumping for the Republicans out west, Alice was doing her part in Ohio, Archie in Chicago, and Corinne in New York. "Governor Cox and Franklin D. Roosevelt are going about the country invoking the name of Roosevelt and claiming to represent the Progressive policy of the revered Republican," one editorial declared. "Who has a better right to speak for Theodore Roosevelt in this campaign: his sons, his daughter and his sister, or the fifth cousin?"

The Democrats *were*, in fact, representing Theodore's progressive vision (an eight-hour workday, workers' rights, social insurance) far more specifically than the Republicans, who largely

avoided the word *progressive* and offered only vague policy promises along those lines. Also, while Corinne had somehow been
roped into that family statement, she quickly made sure to let
Franklin and Eleanor know that she wasn't taking sides. She sent
her "love and interest" in Franklin's "adventure," and while she
wished they were of the same political party, she was "so proud"
of all they had done. "Politics or no politics," she concluded,
"I am always and affectionately your Auntie Corinne." Eleanor
promptly sent her a list of Democratic women's organizations, perhaps in the hope of getting her to join—what a coup that would
have been!—but Corinne didn't bite.

Until now, Franklin had chosen to ignore the attacks from
Oyster Bay, but Ted's salvo from Wyoming got under his skin.
While he might not have supported Theodore in 1912, Franklin
said, he didn't personally attack him the way Harding (the man
Theodore's children were now so strenuously backing) did. "Senator Harding called Theodore Roosevelt first a Benedict Arnold and
then an Aaron Burr," Franklin said at a stop in Salina, Kansas.
"That is one thing at least *some* members of the Roosevelt family
will not forget."

Democratic-leaning papers pointed out the hypocrisy of Oyster
Bay. Ted was "prostituting the prestige that is his because he is
the son of his father," wrote the *Kansas City Post*. The editorial
writer wished that Theodore were still alive "to take his obstrep-
erous offspring by the ear and lead him to the woodshed." In Hyde
Park, one friend of Sara's was so put off by "the self-revealing
sneer of young T.R." that he wanted "Franklin to tweak his nose."
The friend went on: "Poor chap, bitterness will be his pastime for
he cannot go far and yet the farther he goes the louder will come
to him the jeers of those who discover that he is not his Dad."
(When she received the letter, Sara wrote across the envelope in
large, clear script: "to be kept.")

Ted was not a shrewd politician like his sister; his tongue was
not so quick or sharp. Nor did he possess the keen honing instincts of the hunter Theodore: while the younger Roosevelt had
bagged his share of wild beasts, he always seemed to be trying
to keep up, to prove he could take down a lion or a bear (or a

political opponent) as effortlessly as his father. That summer, like so many times before in his life, Ted was faced with the task of proving his worth. Attacked from the left by Democrats and from the right by members of his own party—one Albany Republican told a reporter that Ted's vote on Prohibition had made him a "traitor to much that the father stood for"—there seemed no other recourse but to fight back.

When he was at Harvard, stalked and harassed by photographers and newspapermen eager for a scoop on the president's athlete son, Ted had turned to his father for advice on how to survive the onslaught. "Blessed old Ted," Theodore replied. "The thing to do is to go on just as you have evidently been doing . . . You can never in the world afford to let them drive you away from anything you intend to do . . . This is just an occasion to show the stuff there is in you. Do not let these newspaper creatures and kindred idiots drive you one hair's breadth from the line you had marked out in football or anything else."

The line Ted had marked out was, in truth, the line his father had marked out for him: to carry on the Roosevelt name and legacy. So, facing a similar offensive as he had in college, Ted followed Theodore's advice once again, traveling by train across the country and doing his best to yank the spotlight back to himself—a spotlight unfairly stolen, he believed, by usurpers. His cousin Sheffield Cowles would call Ted "mad for publicity" and "an exhibitionist," recalling a prizefight at Madison Square Garden where Ted fumed after not being introduced from the ring, despite having paid a publicity man to arrange it. In fact, Ted was only fighting for what he felt was rightly his. If he didn't fight, he believed, he would let his father down. Even at thirty-three years old, his father a year in the grave, Ted was still, with every step he took, every speech he made, every train he boarded, trying to win Theodore's approval.

On another train, sometimes crossing tracks with Ted's, someone else was on a proving course of her own. As wife of the vice-presidential candidate, Eleanor was enjoying this crash course in the nuts and bolts of electoral politics. Before setting off with Franklin on their national tour, she'd agreed to meet with Bertrand G. McIntire, the Democratic nominee for governor in Maine, "who is trying to get the Democratic Women organized," as she wrote to her husband. Later that campaign season, Eleanor made news by donating one hundred dollars of her own money (and in her own name) to the League of Nations Fund. In Bowling Green, Indiana, she was buoyed by the rally of more than a thousand eager supporters who'd come to hear Franklin speak. "F.'s voice is all right," she wrote to Sara, though "yesterday he must have talked to at least 30,000 people." Perhaps nothing in Eleanor's life since her days at Allenswood had been as intellectually stimulating as these animated policy conversations with progressive-thinking people all across the nation.

One day, as their train rattled through the heartland, kicking up dust and soot and lulling many to sleep with the constant clack of its wheels, Eleanor heard a rap at her compartment door. She opened it to find Louis Howe (still at the helm of Franklin's campaigns) standing there with a stack of papers in his hand. Howe explained that he was writing a speech for Franklin, and he wondered if Eleanor might take a look at it and give him her thoughts.

Eleanor stood there in the doorway stunned. She had never really liked the little gnome and his smelly cigarettes, but there he was, smiling up at her, asking for her help—and not in planning a tea for reporters or a meet-and-greet for donors. Rather, he wanted her opinion on policy and issues. Flattered, Eleanor took the speech, read it, and returned the pages with some notes about its content and Franklin's delivery.

While Franklin was pleased to have his wife along on the journey, it turned out to be Louis Howe, the man Eleanor had once despised, who encouraged her the most. That first collaboration led to others. "Before long," Eleanor recalled, "I found myself discussing a whole range of subjects." Howe thought she was "worth educating," she'd say, "and for that reason he made an effort on this trip to get to know me." One morning, as the campaign took a break during a swing through upstate New York, Howe impishly suggested to Eleanor that they run off together on an adventure. For once she let go of her timidity and rigid sense of propriety, and off they motored to Niagara Falls. Having never been to the

Falls before, Eleanor was awed by their grandeur. That day, standing in Niagara's majestic spray, Eleanor saw Louis Howe in a new light. He wasn't just a pugnacious little politico; he was also an artist who painted watercolor landscapes and read poetry to her. For Eleanor, the unlikely romance of the mind she enjoyed with Louis Howe was an utterly unexpected and absolutely delightful ancillary benefit of the 1920 campaign.

Eleanor was smart enough to know, of course, that altruism alone did not motivate Howe's pursuit of her. If he were ever to succeed in making Franklin president, Howe would need the support and commitment of the candidate's wife. The campaign manager knew that Eleanor would need to feel as if she were an integral part of the effort. So they discussed everything from labor law to child welfare to international relations, and the positions Franklin should take. Just as important, Eleanor learned the ins and outs of politics from a master strategist. "This was a field I had carefully shunned," she recalled. "But little by little, I found myself beginning to understand why certain things were done and how they came about." The homely little man Eleanor had once judged solely on the basis of his appearance (an offense many people had committed against her) became one of her closest friends.

For Eleanor, so long in the background when it came to politics, this was a whole new world. Passion might have fled her marriage: she wasn't blind to the way Franklin looked at all the pretty women who came out to hear him speak, with a gleam in his eyes he had not shown her in years. Yet she might just find some ardor for herself once again in a pursuit of policy and politics. "Shall I vote the Democratic ticket?" she asked in response to journalist Zoe Beckley's question. "I certainly shall! I am an enrolled Democrat and have been since I cast my first ballot under New York state law three years ago."

Interviewing her, Beckley found Eleanor "modest, retiring and unassuming—backing as quickly and as far away from the limelight as possible." Somehow, though, the journalist persuaded her to open up. An articulate, confident career woman, Beckley was the sort Eleanor had always admired since the days of

Mlle. Souvestre. Divorced, Beckley would later live in Greenwich Village within a community of women, several of whom were lesbians. Perhaps it was Beckley's sense of self-sufficiency, her independence and her disregard for men's rules and men's interests, that inspired Eleanor to talk. A few years earlier, Eleanor had been embarrassed when a reporter used her words to make her look patrician and out of touch with ordinary people. Now, to Beckley, she spoke seemingly without filter about her emerging political views.

"I have always been for woman suffrage," she said, a bit of an exaggeration, as her later statements would reveal, but the passion of the moment seemed to direct her words. "I regard it as much a duty for women to vote as for men to. Neither my home nor my five children will suffer because I take an interest in my country's affairs." In fact, Eleanor suggested, her children's lives might even be made better if she helped elect to office the right people with the right positions. She was confident the Democrats would win in November: she'd take great satisfaction, she predicted, watching "the tide rise to success."

Still, the doubts over the Democrats' chances had only deepened by the fall. The campaign had turned decidedly nasty. In early October, a pamphlet written by William E. Chancellor, a professor of history at the College of Wooster in Ohio, was mailed to thousands of households across the country. A racist Democrat, Chancellor claimed to have historical proof that Harding had Negro blood. Just who funded the printing and mailing of Chancellor's pamphlet was never clear. When the story erupted, President Wilson was quick to condemn the effort to besmirch Harding's reputation—it was a time when such an allegation could still be seen as defamatory—and ordered a quarter million of the pamphlets seized at the San Francisco post office and destroyed. Nonetheless, Harding's camp blamed Cox. While there was no evidence to back this up, Democrats hadn't been unhappy when the pamphlet started showing up in people's mailboxes. Franklin's own personal secretary, Charles McCarthy, had been eager for the news to break; when it did, he assured Franklin, "you and Cox are going to win the election."

Yet the scandal was quickly contained by Wilson's prompt action and by newspaper editors refusing to print anything about it; to those who did receive the pamphlets, the allegations seemed like a Democratic dirty trick. Certainly the Republicans thought so. Turnabout, they decided, was fair play.

On Saturday night, October 23, Franklin had just come out of a gathering of supporters at the Hotel Palatine, in Newburgh, New York, about twenty-five miles south of Hyde Park. Crossing the gold-gilt and red-velvet lobby, he was approached by a man he vaguely recalled as being a reporter; the man handed him a thick sealed envelope and quickly walked away. When Franklin read the documents inside the envelope, he panicked. He felt, in fact, how Harding must have felt when he first learned of Chancellor's pamphlets.

The cover letter inside the envelope was from John R. Rathom, the editor of the *Providence Journal*. Ever since the entrapment scandal of homosexual men at the Newport naval base some two years earlier, Rathom had been waging war against Franklin and his superior in the navy, Josephus Daniels. One of the ways in which the navy had sought to distance itself from the Newport fracas had been to reduce, and in some cases dismiss, the sentences of several men accused of sodomy. Franklin had also approved the appointment of his old friend Thomas Osborne as warden of the Portsmouth Naval Prison in Kittery, Maine, despite being aware that he was homosexual and, in Rathom's words, "unqualified to handle any body of men, large or small, in any station of life." Rathom accused Franklin of "destroying or sequestering" records that might prove embarrassing to the navy in "a cowardly and clumsy subterfuge."

Rathom had been nipping at the navy's heels for the past two years; as recently as the previous May, he told a naval judge that Franklin and Daniels sought to "injure and degrade" him for his persistent investigations into the 1918 entrapment episode. These new charges, however, made just ten days before the election, were clearly political, timed to hurt the Democrats at the polls.

The allegations were criminal. They were also as deeply personal as the whispers about Harding had been. What Rathom was implying about Franklin was particularly unnerving for a man who'd grown up being called "nancy" and a "feather duster" and derided for his love of fine clothes. Rathom hinted broadly that Franklin's protection and advocacy of known homosexuals signaled some secret degeneracy of his own.

As fast as possible, Franklin motored back to Hyde Park. A similar packet of accusations had been delivered to various newspapers, so time was of the essence. With Louis Howe, he prepared a simple, straightforward, three-paragraph statement for the press. Before the sun rose that Sunday morning, telegraph machines in nearly every major American daily were furiously tapping out Franklin's response to Rathom's allegations.

"A reading of this letter convinces that it is libelous *per se* in the view that statements contained therein are false," the vice-presidential candidate told editors. "I have placed this letter in the hands of my lawyers with instructions to immediately commence suit upon its publication. My reason for issuing this statement is that I deem it only fair to call attention to the fact that any paper printing this letter will do so on its own responsibility." In other words: print Rathom's words and face a lawsuit.

The headlines that greeted Franklin in Sunday's and Monday's newspapers weren't as bad as they might have been, had editors chosen to go with Rathom's accusations, but they were damaging enough. ROOSEVELT IN LIBEL CASE; ROOSEVELT WOULD JAIL PROVIDENCE, R.I. EDITOR; and ROOSEVELT ASKS U.S. PROSECUTION FOR ALLEGED LIBEL. Readers were left in the dark about just what sort of libel Rathom had committed; whatever it was, however, Franklin considered it terrible enough to sue. He filed in New York State Supreme Court on October 28, 1920, just six days before the election, asking for half a million dollars in damages. "Unfortunately," his lawyer said in a statement to the press, "Mr. Roosevelt cannot have his day in court before the election. Until then, he can confidently rest upon public knowledge of his character, based upon years of public service, and upon the good opinion and affection of his hosts of friends."

For all that, Rathom probably didn't siphon off too many votes from the Democrats; voters seemed to have made up their minds a good while before then. The Republicans, confident of a win, formally ended their campaign on October 27 with a "Theodore Roosevelt Rally" in Washington, honoring the late president's birthday. They had spent $3,042,892.32 on the presidential campaign by that point; the Democrats, by contrast, had spent a total of $878,831.24, with Cox contributing $5,000 of his own money, Franklin $3,000, and Eleanor $100. If money could buy elections, the Republicans had already made the sale.

A steady downpour of cold rain on Election Day, November 2, seemed to fit everyone's mood. Franklin, Eleanor, and Sara arrived at the Third District polling station in Hyde Park at 10:45 a.m. Franklin voted first, followed by his wife and mother. Then they returned to Springwood, where a special telegraph wire had been installed to bring in the returns that night. The house was filled with important Democratic Party donors and boosters (in her diary, Sara calls them "Franklin's friends," as if they were classmates from Groton) who planned to stay through the following morning. So it was with a crowd of people around him, instead of the small family gathering Theodore had always preferred, that Franklin learned the election results. Harding and Coolidge had crushed Cox and Roosevelt with the largest percentage of the popular vote on record, 60 percent to 34 percent. Progressivism, Theodore's holy cause, was not only dead, but had been bludgeoned to death, and probably for some time to come.

"Harding and Coolidge elected," Sara wrote in her diary, "quite a landslide for Republicans." She added: "Franklin rather relieved not to be elected Vice President."

No doubt that was true. He would've spent four years in limbo, for little return. There was not a great track record of vice presidents going on to the presidency except when the chief executive died in office. It was actually better for Franklin this way, some argued. He'd proven to the party leaders his strengths on the campaign trail, he'd secured loyalties all across the country, and he was now free to plan for another run, four years from now, at the top of the ticket.

Meanwhile, Alice and Ted were celebrating the victory they'd fought so hard for, smiling broadly in Election Night photographs at Republican Party headquarters. Yet victory was bittersweet, and Ted, at least, must have felt it. With his and his sister's permission and facilitation, their father's legacy had been co-opted by big-money, antilabor, probusiness, backroom conservatives—the very type whom, in 1912, Theodore called "the repulsive type of politician."

Eleanor was perhaps the only one who truly grieved the loss of 1920. After months of stimulating conversations and interactions, she was now expected to return to her duties as wife and mother. There was no longer any need for her to be seen in public—at least not until Franklin ran his next campaign. Once all the concession speeches were made, she was expected to fade back into a routine of domestic chores and social obligations. Her husband, meanwhile, would get back on the train and continue the journey on his own.

Except, he wasn't on his own. After everyone left Hyde Park, two people remained behind to plan and strategize with Franklin. As Sara wrote in her diary, they were "Mr. Howe and Miss Le Hand." Marguerite "Missy" Le Hand was Franklin's pretty young secretary, who'd proven indispensable to him during the campaign and who was never far from his side.

Eleanor was shrewd enough to see where that was going. She had two choices, as she saw it. She could go home quietly, return to her old life, and wait to be trotted out again when Franklin needed her—or she could take matters into her own hands and transform her world.

PART VI

ROUGH STUNTS

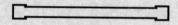

1924–1925

HAMILTON, NEW YORK

The afternoon of October 21, 1924, was a cold one in upstate New York. Pinwheels of snow eddied in the air, fading away before reaching the ground. A vast sheet of gray stood in for the sky, now pregnant with winter.

A copper-colored steam locomotive slowly pulled into the station at Hamilton Village. Beside the tracks, about a hundred people had gathered, most of them bundled in heavy woolen coats. A delegation of football players from nearby Colgate University stood out from the crowd in their green caps and bright yellow oilskin coats. The train continued clattering through the station until its rear car was alongside the crowd. When the man they had come to see stepped out onto the back platform, the crowd let out a roar of welcome.

Ted beamed. His wife, Eleanor, stood by his side, nodding to the crowd. They were on a tour of the upper part of the state, an important leg of Ted's campaign to become governor of New York. At these various whistle-stops, Ted's appearance was often unintentionally comical. His froglike eyes would scan the crowd, sometimes crossing like film comedian Ben Turpin's did. In contrast, Eleanor looked regal beside him, her cheeks rosy under a lace bonnet, her hands clasped inside a fur muff. At every stop, they were cheered. Ted might not have looked like his father, but he was Theodore Roosevelt's son and namesake nonetheless, and in the five years since his death, the late president had become perhaps even more beloved in the American mind than he had ever been in life.

At Hamilton, Ted launched into his usual spiel about how it was time to end the Tammany-controlled administration of Democratic governor Al Smith, and how he pledged to bring honesty and clean government to Albany. The whoops from the college football players that day sent him off script, though, making him punchy with nostalgia. For the thirty-seven-year-old Ted, who'd tried so hard to shine on the football field but who had never made the varsity squad, these young athletes were what he'd once wanted to be and, in some ways, what he was still trying to become.

Hoping to connect with these youths, Ted said jauntily, "As I recall it, there was a football game in which Colgate participated not long ago. The score was very satisfactory from your standpoint." When no immediate cheer erupted as he'd expected, Ted asked, "The Cornell game. Didn't you play Cornell?"

"No!" a student shouted from the crowd.

"Who told me that, then?" Ted grumbled, casting his eyes behind him into the train as if to find the offending aide. He looked back out at the crowd. "I was misinformed. What was the last game you played?"

"Nebraska," came the answer, "and it wasn't very satisfactory, either."

"Who told me that?" Ted muttered again. He tried a different tack. "I do remember way back in the old days," he said, meaning the days of his own youth, "when you pounced down and beat Yale to a frazzle."

Yet there were more recent Colgate triumphs of which he was clearly unaware. "How about Syracuse last year?" someone shouted.

Ted squirmed. "I played on Harvard second," he said, making one more effort to win over the crowd. "I never got as far as the first. I played against Yale in the freshman game, and in that game they converted from a handsome aquiline nose to the one you see I have today. Also I broke two ribs and a finger." He paused. "And the score was not satisfactory from my standpoint, either."

That got him a laugh, and a smattering of cheers, but surely Ted was eager to move on. Already the newspapermen covering the event were snickering among themselves and mimicking Ted: "Who told me that?" Even as he kept talking, he gave the signal to head out of town.

At each of Ted's campaign stops, a bit of stagecraft was employed: before he was quite finished with his speech, the engines would kick in and the train would start chugging away slowly down the tracks. Ted would have to shout the last of his speech, giving the impression that he would have stayed longer if only he'd had the time. As the train moved away, Eleanor would toss campaign buttons at the little boys who inevitably chased after them, bringing a frantic, upbeat ending to each whistle-stop. At Hamilton, however, Ted was no doubt very glad when he felt the train start to move. Once they were safely away from the village, whoever had given him the erroneous information about the Colgate football game surely got a reprimand.

Ted was not the smooth campaigner his father had been—or, for that matter, his cousin Franklin was. He sometimes stammered, stepped on the punch lines of his own jokes, told stories wrong just as he had done this day. Yet despite his blunders, he was feeling optimistic about his chances of becoming governor. He expected 1924 to be a repeat of 1920, a strong year for Republicans. A few months earlier, there'd been some panic over the Teapot Dome scandal, which had engulfed the Harding administration and caused some to fear for the party's prospects in 1924. Yet Harding had died, and the investigation into the potentially illegal government transfer of oil reserves at Teapot Dome, Wyoming, had narrowed to just a few individuals, and Republicans as a whole seemed no worse for the wear. Ted, who'd been appointed by Harding to his father's (and Franklin's) old position of assistant secretary of the navy, had come under scrutiny himself by congressional investigators, but he had been completely vindicated. No one could possibly link him to the scandal—at least, Ted believed that to be the case.

So, as he campaigned across the state that summer and fall, he was filled with confidence and high spirits. His time had come, he believed; he would finally begin to fulfill his father's dream of legacy. All signs pointed to success. Political observers thought Ted's chances of victory had steadily risen as he'd proven "his winning way with political audiences." In addition, the top of the ticket, Harding's successor, Calvin Coolidge, was untainted by scandal and, moreover, had struck a balance between the conservative and progressive wings of the party. As a result, Coolidge was a much stronger candidate than his Democratic opponent, John Davis, the former ambassador to Great Britain. In Ted's view, Davis wasn't nearly progressive enough to carry progressive voters; as Ted calculated it, that bloc would either vote for the independent candidate, Robert La Follette, or stick with Coolidge. The math seemed to add up to a huge Coolidge win, and Ted expected to ride his coattails.

There also, significantly, wasn't another Roosevelt in the race this time, as there had been in 1920. Cousin Franklin had been sidelined from politics, felled by infantile paralysis. It was a terrible tragedy, and one that had scuttled any plans Franklin might have had to run for the presidency, or any office, this year.

When he heard the news, Ted had expressed his sympathy and his hopes for Franklin's recovery in a letter sent on official navy stationery, the same stationery Franklin would have used just a year before. Although Ted's note hadn't been effusive—how could it have been, after the bruising campaign of 1920?—he was a decent enough man to be sincere in his sympathy. Still, he was also shrewd enough to take advantage of Franklin's absence, and reclaimed the position of the most prominent Roosevelt on the national scene.

In addition, just as Ted's campaign for governor kicked off, Scribner's published a collection of Theodore's letters to his sister Bye that reminded the public of the wisdom and fortitude of the late president, qualities now presumably handed down to his son. Even Franklin's well-received appearance at this year's Democratic convention, in which he dramatically ascended the podium on his crutches, wasn't enough to stop Ted's momentum. They might share the name Roosevelt, but only Ted possessed the "Theodore" and the "Junior."

By the fall of 1924, there was a growing sense that Ted was on his way. A cartoon in various New York newspapers showed Ted literally following in the very large footsteps of his father, with a sign pointing to "The Presidency," via the "state legislature," the "assistant secretary of the Navy," and "Governor of New York." The cartoon was headlined HE'LL HAVE TO BE SOME STEPPER. By all appearances that fall, he was indeed—so long as Teapot Dome remained well and truly buried.

Some New York Republicans worried that the scandal might

flare up again as a campaign issue. The transfer of the oil reserves from the navy to the Interior Department, and then to private control was significant (and possibly criminal) because the private companies had paid thousands of dollars to the interior secretary, Albert Fall (and possibly to others), giving the appearance of bribery. At the time of the transfer to Interior, Ted had been assistant secretary of the navy; he had facilitated the leases on the oil reserves being turned over to the new department. In many ways, however, the most embarrassing detail for him was the fact that one of the private companies leasing the oil reserves was the Sinclair Oil Company, on whose board he'd once sat. His brother Archie had also, until very recently, been a high-ranking Sinclair executive. The Sinclair connection, Ted feared, could upend all his dreams.

"My political career is over and done with," he'd lamented to his wife, Eleanor, when the scandal first broke, bursting into their Washington home at 1601 Twenty-First Street, Northwest. "The Sinclair Oil Company stock has jumped ten points on the strength of the lease, and we own a thousand shares! I can never explain it. People will think my price is ten thousand dollars and will never believe the truth."

Eleanor tried mightily to get a word in edgewise, but Ted was too distraught to listen. Finally, she managed to silence him: "For heaven's sake, it's all right!" Several months earlier, she explained, she'd sold their Sinclair stock to help pay their taxes. At the time, Eleanor hadn't been happy that they'd lost money on the sale; now, of course, she couldn't have been more pleased. The sale of the stock and the loss they took on it, several months *before* the scandal emerged, removed any appearance of impropriety on Ted's part. Eleanor would never forget the look of relief she saw pass across her husband's face.

Eleanor was often Ted's rock. Unflappable, methodical, and fiercely loyal to her husband's goals, she was in some ways the better politician. She kept her head when he despaired; rarely was she at a loss. When Ted was appointed to his navy post, some had called for Eleanor to replace him in the New York State Assembly. She was all for it: "I would feel highly honored," she said. Instead, the party went with Frederick Trubee Davison, a young war hero and the son of a noted financier. A female candidate, party bigwigs argued, was still too risky.

So, for now, Eleanor contented herself as the power behind Ted's career. She'd saved the day with her revelation about the Sinclair stock. She believed they'd completely distanced themselves from any scandal. She was wrong.

Just as Ted took his first steps to explore a run for governor, Archie rang from New York. He admitted to his brother that he had, in fact, known of the money Sinclair paid to Secretary Fall. That was a bombshell that could directly implicate the Roosevelts in Teapot Dome. Archie maintained, however, that he learned of the payment only after the fact, from another employee. Given this development, Ted told Archie he should resign from Sinclair immediately, return with him to Washington, and testify before Congress. Archie agreed. On Monday, January 21, 1924, Archie told what he knew, and investigators seemed satisfied. Once more, Ted breathed a sigh of relief.

Yet the nightmare still wasn't over. It was an election year, after all, and Democrats weren't about to let this likely Republican gubernatorial, and possible presidential, candidate off that easily. On March 15, Congressman William F. Stevenson of South Carolina had delivered an impassioned speech on the floor of the House calling for Ted's resignation from the navy. "Mr. Roosevelt approved of the leasing at two or three different times," Stevenson charged, "and when pinned down, said, 'I approved of this general policy.'" Ted's superior, Secretary Edwin Denby, had recently been forced to resign over the scandal; Stevenson declared that Ted should be obliged to do the same.

All at once, the House exploded into shouts, jeers, and calls for order. Stevenson smirked. A florid, vowel-dragging, white-haired man of sixty-three, he seemed to take great delight in the commotion he'd caused. The former Speaker of the South Carolina House, Stevenson had come to Washington seven years earlier, sweeping in during the height of Woodrow Wilson's war popularity; he'd never quite adjusted to being in the minority. When Nick Longworth jumped up to defend his brother-in-law's honor and to charge Stevenson with making a false statement, the Democrat gleefully suggested they take their argument outside. No matter if none of his charges could be proven, Stevenson had successfully planted suspicion of Ted in the public mind.

Ted was especially angered that Stevenson had dragged Eleanor's name into the debate, revealing how she had been the one to hold stock in Sinclair. Ted told his wife he planned to find the congressman and beat him to a pulp—"and to bloody hell with the consequences." Before Ted could leave to find Stevenson, however, Eleanor placed a call to Alice. "I hear you're going to beat up Stevenson," his sister said when Ted took the phone from his wife. "Of course he deserves it," Alice went on. "I know he's a rat. By the way, he's a little elderly man and wears glasses. Remember to have him take them off before you hit him." After that, Ted gave up the idea of physical assault.

Even if the story is apocryphal, it demonstrates Ted's lack of political armor. Personal attacks didn't just roll off him; he felt them as acutely as his war wounds, and just as in the war, his instinct was to fight back, to settle things fair and square, without any consideration of publicity or image. Ted was far too authentic ever to feel entirely comfortable in the artificial world of politics.

Stevenson's charges meant that Ted was now obliged to address the questions that still swirled: Why had he not come forward sooner to tell what he knew about the oil leases? After all, he'd helped transfer them from the navy to Interior; knowingly or not, he had assisted Fall in his money-making scheme. So, on May 13, he testified before the congressional panel himself. He swore under oath that he did not know that "these leases were being considered until after they had been decided upon," and that while he had made a protest to his superior, Denby, the protest had been "made too late." Certainly, Ted insisted, he had not benefited financially in any way. His wealth was entirely earned, he told the panel: "I did not inherit my money. I made it myself before the war. I was making before the war more than twenty times my present salary [as assistant secretary]. I gave it up and went into political life for exactly the same reason I went to the war." By that he meant: to commit himself to serving the public and the nation. Investigators thanked him for his time; they had no further questions. Ted hoped he'd spoken his last words on Teapot Dome. So far, as he toured the state during his campaign for governor, those hopes had held up.

The ordeal, however, had taken its toll. Ted was uneasy on the campaign trail, distrustful of the press and of fellow politicians. Insults he felt deeply; ever since he was a child, he never believed he truly measured up, so he was forever sensitive to slights. Consequently, he found it difficult to unwind or relax; he'd never been one for much gaiety or culture. After one White House dinner, he sat with Alice and Sen. Frank Brandegee of Connecticut through a musical presentation. "Both of them enjoyed it," Ted wrote in his diary. "I wish I liked music." He also loathed the theater, finding he could get through the first part of a production by observing the audience; the second part was pure hell.

He was also far too uptight to indulge in the sort of flirtations on the campaign trail that Franklin so enjoyed. When women showed up batting their eyelashes at him, Franklin usually made a beeline in their direction. Ted, on the other hand, looked straight through them. Of all the Roosevelt marriages, that of Ted and Eleanor seemed the most content; Ted would make it a point in his diaries to record just how faithful he was to his wife. Of course, he expected that Eleanor and his children would read his diaries someday; like his father, he recorded even his most personal thoughts with an eye to how they might be read by history. Still, he was genuine in his abhorrence of sexual license; in this, he was very much his father's son. In his diary, he complained about one man Alice frequently invited to dinner: "He is one of those character combinations you run into in both men and women. He is devoted to his wife and children, and he will run after any girl he sees. He can never quite make up his mind that I am not the same type of man. He merely thinks I am clever in concealing it."

Ted was, at heart, a deeply honorable man. When the Fox Film Corporation asked him to place a wreath on George Washington's tomb for a film commemorating the first president's birthday, he hesitated; even after he agreed to do it, he remained distinctly uncomfortable. Another politician might have jumped at the free publicity and the association with the nation's beloved founder. Not Ted: "I had an instinctive reaction against it," he wrote in his diary. "It seems to me that it is not natural and would be largely a stage play." Likewise, at Christmastime, it was only with the greatest reluctance that he accompanied the other assistant secretaries to have their photos taken with the president at the White House. "This is right in line with the other fool things they do," Ted wrote.

Yet, for all his honor and all his loathing of dishonesty, Ted was forced to tell lie after lie as he rambled the state asking for votes. In his heart, he was not in favor of Prohibition; no one in his family was, with his mother defiantly serving alcohol at Sagamore Hill just to make a point about personal liberty. Yet a Republican candidate had to be "dry" because the Republican base demanded it. With the Democrats calling for "modifications" in the Volstead Act, Republicans could not alienate the considerable "dry" demographic. Accordingly, Ted had to recite all the standard talking points about supporting and enforcing Prohibition laws even if he saw all too clearly that they were not working. Many of the fiercest "drys," however, recalling his vote in Albany, doubted his sincerity and attacked him as a closet "wet." Fred B. Smith, the former national secretary of the YMCA, denounced Ted as an untrustworthy "fop" in the meetings he held around the country promoting "Christian citizenship." Ted couldn't take on Smith honestly—or punch him in the nose, for that matter. Rather, he had to attempt to placate him, while denying his own principles in the process. It was precisely this surrender of integrity, so expected, so necessary, that made Ted so ill at ease in politics.

Perhaps that was why he had tried, at the eleventh hour, to find a different path ahead. A Cabinet position might have served his ambitions to be president just as well, and allowed him to avoid the petty politics of the campaign trail, at least for a while. So he'd met with President Coolidge in July 1924 and made the request. "I told him I thought the time had come when I should get recognition of some type," Ted recorded in his diary. "I was absolutely frank. I said both administratively and politically I felt I ranked a cabinet position." If not, he told Coolidge, he would "run for governor of New York." Coolidge nodded his head and said he agreed with Ted. "I don't know whether this did good or not," Ted wrote, "but at least he knows perfectly frankly what I feel."

Ted's entire life had been one long, mostly futile attempt to "get recognition of some type"; and once again, he was disappointed. Coolidge made no move to appoint him to anything. As in that long-ago letter from his father advising him to keep striving because he had yet to achieve his maximum potential, the message Ted received now from Coolidge was that he was still not good enough.

He'd show Coolidge. He'd show everyone. He'd win the race to be the next governor of New York, and from there, it would be an easy reach to claim his maximum potential: the presidency, at last.

"I am deeply sensible of the honor that has been conferred upon me," Ted told the crowd when he accepted the nomination for governor at the Republican convention in Rochester. In his speech, he seemed to acknowledge there had been some moderation of his father's progressivism: "We have married common sense to idealism. Our heads may be in the clouds, but our feet are on the earth. Since the birth of our party, we have stood for sane, constructive liberalism." What the Democrats were offering, Ted said, wasn't liberalism, but "windy promises for an unrealizable Utopia."

His opponent was the incumbent governor, Al Smith, whose nomination at the Democratic convention had been seconded by Ted's cousin Eleanor. "Of course" Smith was going to win, Eleanor told reporters afterward. "The Republican convention yesterday did everything it could to help him"—meaning nominate Ted. The appearance of meek little Eleanor at his adversary's side, openly denigrating her cousin, was a slap in the face. Ted could hardly have been surprised, however, given how he had campaigned against Franklin in 1920.

The family rivalry had deepened; only Corinne remained neutral in the war between her nieces and nephews, a stance that sometimes proved maddening to the opposing sides. Back in 1921 in his diary, Ted wrote, "I received a thoroughly irritating letter from Auntie Corinne," but whatever feelings he gave vent to after that would be scissored out later by his wife Eleanor. In this way, Ted's reputation was safeguarded. Indeed, his diary would end on September 24, 1924, just after his nomination; almost certainly, he kept a campaign diary, but it would not be included among his effects. His fiercely protective wife made sure that Ted's personal thoughts on his political enemies, including those from his extended family, would not be left for posterity.

In truth, Ted's politics were still quite close to those of Eleanor and Franklin. He might have accepted a certain moderation to his party's progressivism, but he was still a progressive at heart. A couple of years earlier, he had sat with Alice waiting for news of a Republican primary for governor in Pennsylvania; when it was clear that the progressive candidate, Gifford Pinchot, had beaten the conservative, George Alter, Ted was overjoyed: "It is a remarkable victory and I believe indicates in general that the people want to go progressive. Of course this feeling is inconsistent. They don't know exactly what they mean by progressive, but nevertheless they do vaguely desire progress rather than stagnation or retrogression." After President Harding died in 1923, Ted expressed hope that the party would "assume a more liberal complexion." As Teapot Dome exemplified, however, he was badly disappointed.

In fact, Ted was the only progressive left among the Oyster Bay branch. Alice, as always, was primarily concerned with power over policy; Kermit was emphatically apolitical; and Archie had turned so far to the right that he was now more conservative than even some of the "standpats," as the strongest conservatives in the Harding and Coolidge administrations were called. Before Ted launched his campaign for governor, Archie had sent him several articles clipped from newspapers, encouraging him to rethink some of his more liberal positions. One piece was written by the new Fascist prime minister of Italy, Benito Mussolini, who posited that liberty had become "an obsolete ideal" since the war and should be replaced by "the ideal of hierarchy." Archie called it "an interesting premise," and told Ted, "he might be right." Ted, no doubt, was horrified.

So, entirely on his own, the eldest Roosevelt brother endeavored to be the sort of progressive candidate his father would have approved of. He fired up the crowds in town halls and railroad stations all across the state. On the campaign trail, his opponent, Governor Smith, was making fun of him, picking up the reporters' parody of his mistake with the Colgate students. After reciting a list of what he called Ted's errors in judgment, Smith would say, "Who told me that?" His audiences would then join in, entire auditoriums chanting, "Who told me that?"

Ted knew he was being laughed at, but he soldiered on—because that was what he was: a soldier, not a politician. It was the discipline he'd learned during the war that kept him from breaking down now on the stump. By all accounts, he remained focused for the entirety of his campaign. Yet he displayed none of the confidence and command he'd shown on the battlefield as he motored through the state looking for votes. This was a different kind of war, with none of the honor and integrity he'd known among his troops and even his enemies in France. In September 1924, when he marched in a parade honoring America's defenses, he reclaimed, for one brief, shining moment, his true power. "This morning I got into my uniform as a colonel of infantry," he wrote in his diary. "I loved getting into it. It fitted me very well. My decorations, my wound stripes, my Croix de guerre pleased me as if I were about ten years old. I wanted to strut up and down"—and so he had.

Now, however, the battlefield was the State of New York, and the enemy combatants were the troops of Governor Smith—including one new recruit. After shouting himself hoarse delivering a speech in Troy, Ted learned that Cousin Eleanor had officially joined the opposing army. She was now following Ted around the state, much as he did to Franklin four years earlier. Also like Ted, Eleanor was making speeches, challenging Republican positions. How extraordinary: little Eleanor, who had once been afraid to jump off the pier, making speeches, firing up crowds! Yet there was even more to it than that, Ted learned: Eleanor was doing something that even Al Smith had declared off-limits. Eleanor was bringing up Teapot Dome.

That was outrageous enough, but it was *how* she was invoking the scandal that really left Ted flabbergasted. A supporter provided the startling account. To follow Ted around the state, Eleanor was sponsoring an automobile *in the shape of a teapot*, a vehicle that reportedly spouted real steam from its roof! Politics, Ted must have thought, had gone completely mad.

NEWBURGH, NEW YORK

Most of the autumn foliage was gone from the trees by the first of November 1924, and the hills of southeastern New York were blanketed in hues of red and gold. The air was crisp and the skies a bright cyan blue as Eleanor met up with her caravan somewhere east of the Hudson River, in the environs of Newburgh. She was flushed with excitement, her cheeks as red from her own high spirits as from the brisk fall weather. She'd just come from Middletown, where she delivered a rousing speech to the Women's Democratic Organization of Orange County in which she called for revolution. She might not have used that exact word, but her message came across loud and clear, ringing through the rafters of the old Elks' Home and followed by round after round of applause and whistles.

"I cannot stress in too strong urgings," Eleanor said, "the necessity for the vote of the women on November 4." Women, she declared, had the power to change the political structure in this country. Republicans were touting a sharp drop in unemployment and an economy on the move, but Eleanor argued that prosperity had not reached down to the lowest levels of society, where a disproportionate number of those living in poverty were women. That was why change was needed, and change, she said, started by voting out the status quo. Full equality for all women, Eleanor declared, could come about only through radical action—through a "new relationship for women with their husbands and with their world." The crowd cheered.

Two decades earlier, Eleanor had walked a few steps behind her cousin Alice, terrified of small talk, awkward and uncomfortable in the limelight. Now, having just turned forty, she held entire auditoriums in thrall, exhorting her listeners to action and then basking in the waves of applause. She was full of confidence, and it showed on her face: the exhausted, jowly look of six years earlier was gone, and she now radiated youthfulness and her own special beauty. Photographs taken of Eleanor in the past had usually shown her with her face cast downward; now she stared straight into the camera, her gaze filled with passion and self-assurance— and perhaps a little bit of revenge.

At Newburgh, her caravan awaited. Eleanor greeted the drivers, all of them women, exhausted after completing a two-week, thousand-mile ring around the State of New York, led by a vehicle the likes of which no citizen had ever seen before and that had drawn hundreds of spectators everywhere it parked. The newspapers were calling it the "Singing Teapot." It was "a canvas design fastened on a wooden frame and attached to a seven-passenger touring car . . . so arranged that the top is collapsible and is let down when those traveling in the party stop to make their campaign speeches." The automobile had been donated by Buick, and the costs of the trip underwritten by Elinor Morgenthau, of the wealthy upstate farming and real estate family.

This was the device that would keep Ted from realizing his dream, and repay him for his attacks on Franklin four years earlier. The makeshift teapot could blow real steam, thanks to a lid on the top and an oil burner in the backseat of the car. "The Singing Teapot will boil with Republican corruption," announced Caroline O'Day, from the Democratic State Committee, when the vehicle was launched on October 17. Departing from Manhattan, the Teapot had traveled to Poughkeepsie, Albany, Plattsburgh, Potsdam, Oswego, Fulton, Buffalo, Olean, and other towns before completing the circle in Kingston. At each stop, a saxophone player honked out some jazz to get the townspeople's attention, and then a puff of steam from the top of the Teapot announced that day's speakers, usually women from the Democratic State Committee who eagerly tied the Republican candidate for governor to the Teapot Dome scandal.

Although Eleanor hadn't accompanied the Singing Teapot on its tour of the state, her endorsement of its mission was common knowledge, and in the press, the outlandish vehicle was called the "automobile of Mrs. Franklin D. Roosevelt." The Teapot had been the brainchild of Louis Howe, and at its wheel, at least for much of the trip, was Eleanor's spirited daughter, Anna, now eighteen.

Eleanor knew it was dirty politics. She'd later admit that she knew Ted "had had nothing to do" with Teapot Dome. The Singing Teapot, she said, was "a rough stunt." Even Ted's opponent, Governor Smith, declared that smearing him with the scandal was off-limits. Still, "in the thick of political fights," Eleanor reasoned, everything was fair game. Coolidge had to be defeated, and Smith had to win; the Republicans were holding back progress, Eleanor believed. So the end justified the means, even if it meant slandering her cousin.

Besides, this was personal. As Louis Howe made clear, if Ted won the governor's office, he'd likely displace Franklin, already delayed by his illness, on the road to the White House. So Eleanor wasn't fighting the good fight just for women and progressive causes. She was also taking out her husband's chief rival for the throne.

In the past four years, Eleanor had become one of the leading Democratic and women's rights activists in the state; in the process, she'd also become ruthless. The revolution couldn't come soon enough for her. That fall, she'd led the charge demanding that women receive equal representation with men on the state Democratic Committee. She'd also advocated for a plank in the party's platform against child labor. At the state convention in Syracuse on September 25, she'd seconded the nomination of Smith in a rousing speech, exhorting women to vote; their very lives depended on it, she insisted. When reminded by reporters that the Republican candidate would be her own cousin, Eleanor snarled, "Well, I'm voting for Al Smith."

It wasn't just for Franklin that Eleanor was fighting her cousin, however. It was also for a lifetime of slights from her father's family: the childhood taunting; the condescension from Uncle Theodore about Franklin not being in uniform; the years of put-downs from Alice and, worse, Alice's facilitation of Franklin's trysts with Lucy Mercer. The Singing Teapot was nominally aimed at Ted, but in actuality it was taking on all of Oyster Bay. In her newfound power, Eleanor was not gracious. She was not merciful. She had scores to settle, debts she wanted paid. She behaved, in fact, like Alice: she was out for blood. At heart, Eleanor was "kind and compassionate," her friend Marion Dickerman observed, "but when certain matters touched her personally, she could be very hard and sometimes cruel."

That campaign season, she was also fighting without her husband's help. Franklin was still mostly waylaid by the infantile paralysis that had struck him down during the summer of 1921, although he'd just risen magnificently to the occasion at the Democratic National Convention, giving a powerful speech and letting the delegates know they shouldn't count Franklin Roosevelt out quite yet. At the moment, though, he was taking the healing waters in Warm Springs, Georgia, the latest promised remedy for his affliction. So it was up to Eleanor to stop Ted on her own, and she embraced the challenge enthusiastically.

Franklin's condition had ensured Eleanor's activism and fired her independence. In order for the political ambitions they both shared to prevail, she would need to go out into the world and bring it back to her husband; as she'd later point out, she needed to become Franklin's eyes, ears, and legs. "His illness finally made me stand on my own feet," she'd remember. "The alternative would have been to become a completely colorless echo of my husband and mother-in-law. I might have stayed a weak character forever if I had not found that out."

No longer did Eleanor check in with Sara before scheduling her own calendar; no longer was she quite as vulnerable to the guilt the older woman tried to impose on her. Over the past several years, she'd stood up to her mother-in-law more and more, and on at least one occasion she told Sara off. "Mama and I have had a bad time," Eleanor wrote to Franklin afterward. "I should be ashamed of myself but I'm not." Sara's snooty upper-class pretension made Eleanor want "to squirm and turn Bolshevik."

The deaths of her grandmother and Aunt Pussie had also changed her. Grandmother Hall, that grim, austere figure of her youth, died in 1919, and Eleanor was left musing about her life. "I wondered if her life had been less centered in her family group, [would] that family group have been a great deal better off? If she had had some kind of life of her own, what would have been the result? Would she have been happier?" Soon afterward, Aunt Pussie, high-strung but also talented and ambitious, died, along with her children, in a fire. A wasted life, in many ways. Eleanor believed that "given greater discipline, the drive of necessity and wider opportunities," Aunt Pussie "might have been an artist of real quality." Eleanor was not about to live with those sorts of regrets. Her motto became "The life you have is your own."

What ultimately held her grandmother back, Eleanor believed, was her primary focus on her "family group." So the most important changes Eleanor needed to make in her life lay outside the home. Soon after the 1920 election, she ramped up her political work. While she and Franklin were still living in Washington, she volunteered for the International Congress of Working Women; after Franklin's defeat, when the couple was based mostly in New York, Eleanor became actively involved as a board member for the League of Women Voters. As part of this work, she helped assemble a manual for the use of female politicians and campaigners—"an aider of women," as it was described, "in their determination to stand for progressive measures and candidates."

Winning the vote, Eleanor came to believe, was only the first step in the fight for women's rights. "We have now had the vote for four years," she told one audience. "I have been wondering whether it occurs to the women as a whole that, if they expect to gain the ends for which they fought, it is not going to be sufficient simply to cast a ballot. They must gain for themselves a place of real equality and the respect of the men."

Feminist politics transformed her. Women had a unique opportunity, she believed, to make the world a better place for everyone, whether that was ensuring the rights of workers or putting an end to war. One of Eleanor's heroes was the suffrage leader Carrie Chapman Catt, whom she'd heard speak at a League of Women Voters convention. "Men were born by instinct to slay," Catt had said. "It seems to me God is giving a call to the women of the world to come forward, to stay the hand of men, to say: 'No, you shall no longer kill!'"—or oppress, or cheat, or deny equal opportunity, Eleanor would have added.

"Women are by nature progressives," Eleanor declared in one speech. Politically speaking, she no longer thought it was possible to be both "a Republican and a progressive." Once upon a time, "all the radical leaders" had been Republicans, she said, but then "they slipped," and now the party was "a bulwark against radicalism." That was her message as she toured the state that summer and fall of 1924, boosting Smith and denouncing Ted.

Joining the caravan of women behind the Singing Teapot as they headed east for the last days of the campaign, Eleanor found herself embraced by a company of like-minded souls. Florence "Daisy" Harriman was a firebrand advocate for the rights of the poor and had fought hard for the League of Nations. Harriet May Mills was a suffragist who, like Eleanor, had turned her energies toward advancing progressivism through the Democratic Party. Caroline O'Day, in addition to being part of the New York State Democratic Committee, was active in the Women's Trade Union League.

Friendships with women such as these shaped Eleanor's transformation. With the attorney and author Elizabeth Fisher Read, she worked shoulder to shoulder developing policy and positions on the League's national legislation committee. At first, Eleanor had felt somewhat "humble and inadequate" collaborating with Read, a graduate of Smith College. Indeed, many of the women Eleanor befriended were college graduates—the first generation of women to emerge from the rise of female-only institutions in the late nineteenth and early twentieth centuries. Self-conscious about not having attended college, Eleanor was put immediately at ease by Read, who helped build within her "a sense of confidence."

Eleanor's most influential friend, however, was Nancy Cook, the executive secretary of the women's division of the state Democratic Committee. Their first contact, soon after the 1920 election, was by telephone, as Cook tried to inveigle Eleanor into speaking at a fund-raising luncheon. The intense phone conversations left Eleanor dazzled. She agreed to speak at the luncheon, and arrived clutching a bouquet of violets for the woman who had invited her. "Where is Miss Cook?" she asked, seeming smitten. The violets, of course, harkened back to Eleanor's days at Allenswood, where the younger girls would bring them as gifts to the older girls on whom they had crushes. Now Eleanor was bringing them to Cook, two years her senior and light-years ahead of her in self-awareness.

The daughter of a farmer from Massena, New York (way up north on the Canadian border), Cook graduated from Syracuse University before volunteering for the Red Cross in London during the war. Small but athletic, with classic good looks and short, curly hair, she had a buoyancy to her movements and an easy, irreverent laugh. She was also as authentic as any woman Eleanor had ever met, living by no one's rules but her own. She wore men's jackets and trousers and refused to disguise her committed, romantic relationship with Marion Dickerman, another Democratic activist.

The violets may have been intended for Cook, but very soon Eleanor was devoted to both women. Dickerman was eight years younger than Cook, and a fellow graduate of Syracuse. The two lived together on West Twelfth Street in Greenwich Village, in a community of artists and bohemians. In 1919, Dickerman ran for the State Assembly against Thaddeus Sweet, the same Speaker of the House with whom Ted would tangle in 1920 over the expulsion of the Socialist legislators. While she didn't win, Dickerman's strong showing against Sweet (despite a misogynist campaign against her in which she was described as an "escaped nun") ended any talk of the Speaker running for governor.

By the summer of 1924, no one was closer to Eleanor than Nancy and Marion. The three spent time together on political campaigns but also in quiet evenings in the Village, talking philosophy, reading poetry, and making one another laugh. Nancy and Marion were frequent guests at Hyde Park as well, where even Sara warmed to them: Nancy especially, with her wit and geniality, was hard to dislike. In 1923, Nancy stayed at Springwood six times, three of them with Marion. So far during the summer of 1924, the two women had been guests on the estate on two occasions, and more visits were planned. Although few letters would survive among the three friends, those that did attested to how much Eleanor enjoyed their company and how much she longed for them when they were away. "I feel I'd like to go off with you," she wrote to the couple around this time, "and forget the rest of the world existed."

For Eleanor, Nancy and Marion represented a world that could have been hers. They had made choices she'd never even known were options. They'd gone to college, forgone marriage, refrained from children, and devoted their lives to their own interests. (Nancy was a woodworker, Marion a teacher.) They also championed those political issues that were important to them. In Eleanor's devotion to her friends, there was as much envy as admiration.

Of course, had she made the same decisions as Nancy and Marion, there would have been no Franklin and no children. Eleanor might not have been very demonstrative with her family, but she did love them; in none of her letters would she ever express any regret about the path she had taken. There would be, however, a certain wistfulness to her words, a longing for what might have been. At one point, on board Franklin's houseboat, in the company of her husband and children, Eleanor penned a note to Dickerman that spoke volumes: "Much love to Nan and to you. Life is quite empty without your dear presence."

She was cognizant and respectful of the nature of her friends' relationship. "Providence was particularly wise and farseeing when it threw these two women together," she wrote, "for their gifts complement each other in a most extraordinary way. From their association has come much good work which has been of real service in a good many causes." There were many lesbians among the activists Eleanor befriended during this period; Elizabeth Read's life partner, Esther Lape, a journalist and researcher, became another close associate of Eleanor's. Like Nancy and Marion, Elizabeth and Esther often invited Eleanor to their home, where talk tended to focus on culture more than politics. Eleanor started to dress like them, wearing flat shoes instead of heels, trousers instead of dresses, and string ties instead of pearls. At one event, she and Nancy Cook showed up dressed in matching tweed knickers.

Such a sartorial transformation caused comment. "If you think Eleanor looked bad in skirts," her cousin Sheffield Cowles quipped, "you should have seen her in those pants!" Cousin Alice derided Eleanor and her friends as "female impersonators." The implication was clear. Although as yet there was no construct of being "openly gay," the more sophisticated set knew exactly what Nancy and Marion, and Elizabeth and Esther, were to each other. So, quite naturally, they began to gossip about Eleanor. Helen Robinson (Rosy's daughter, Franklin's niece, and the wife of Teddy Robinson, Aunt Corinne's son) was at one point in a hotel room that adjoined a room shared by Eleanor and her friends. Helen walked in on the group of them having a pillow fight and "leapfrogging" all over each other. Helen found it "horrible," she wrote to Alice, who was delighted by the insinuations. Eleanor had had such an unhappy childhood, Alice later mused, that "it was nice for her to have some vigorous companions who adored her. More strength to all of them." Pillow fights, Alice declared, "were obviously as jolly a form of communication as any." The implication was that since Eleanor wasn't getting any sex from Franklin, at least she was having some fun with the girls.

If Eleanor's friendships with any of these various women ever became sexual, no letters give evidence of the fact. Still, rarely was sex, homo or hetero, ever directly mentioned even in the correspondence of the participants themselves. What would become clear from Eleanor's letters, however, was that her association with these friends, especially Nancy and Marion, was emotionally intimate and fulfilling. Female friendships sustained and nurtured her, and gave her life meaning in a way she had never known before. By 1924, Eleanor Roosevelt was a very different woman from who she'd been just four years earlier, and profoundly different from how she was at the time of her wedding.

Her intimate friendships with women did not, however, pull her away from her husband. Ironically, they allowed Eleanor's marriage to Franklin to grow and thrive in unexpected and unconventional ways.

By 1924, Franklin was in debt to Eleanor for many things. Yet he was especially grateful for her unwavering support during his illness. Sara had wanted him to retire from public life after the infantile paralysis struck him down, but Eleanor and Louis Howe had kept pushing him, not allowing him to give up on his dream. Eleanor brought him newspapers and kept him up to date on current affairs. She debated him on the issues and goaded him into getting angry in order to keep his passions alive. Now, after his dramatic speech at the Democratic convention, Franklin was once again considered a viable political prospect, no matter his paralysis. Eleanor could take much of the credit for that—and she was continuing on her mission to restore her husband's political power by campaigning to defeat Ted that fall.

Still, husband and wife led mostly separate lives now. Though they wrote to each other with frequency and affection, for only a few weeks out of the year did they spend any unbroken time together. Eleanor still called Franklin her "Dearest Honey," but gone were the old expectations of traditional fidelity. Safe and content with her female friends, Eleanor no longer needed to be first for Franklin. During the 1920 campaign, she saw the way women flocked around him, and the irresistible appeal Franklin had for the opposite sex. She learned to make light of the "lovely ladies who served luncheon for my husband and who worshipped at his shrine." Afterward, Eleanor recalled, "They would get behind me and ask if I wasn't jealous." If she was, she had found a way to swallow her jealousy and move beyond it. When some cheeky reporters in Jamestown, New York, joshing Franklin about his female admirers, slipped a note under Eleanor's door pretending to be from the Burns Detective Agency and offering to investigate her husband's infidelity, Eleanor laughed gamely.

All the while, there was Missy Le Hand, Franklin's pretty, twenty-two-year-old secretary, constantly at his side. Missy had proven especially valuable to Franklin after his illness. If anyone did more than Eleanor to keep his spirits up and his body strong during that period, it was Missy. At the moment, she was with Franklin in Warm Springs. In fact, she was with him constantly, seeing him much more often than his wife did.

Eleanor was fond of Missy. She'd accepted the young woman's place in Franklin's life. Indeed, having Missy there to take care of Franklin, to help him out of bed, to read to him, to exercise with him, freed Eleanor to do the sorts of things she now wanted to do, activities that her old role as traditional wife and mother had prevented. There was also a growing acceptance of Franklin's need for a softer, more conventional woman in his life. If Eleanor felt some sadness about that, it was more than made up for in the freedom she now enjoyed.

A more mature relationship had blossomed with Franklin in the wake of his illness. With each accepting the other's life, they forged a successful alternative family. During one weekend in June 1923, all five of them (Franklin, Missy, Eleanor, Nancy, and Marion) spent a delightful time together at Springwood. To Franklin, his wife's friends were "the girls," whose company he thoroughly enjoyed. Once, when Nancy and Marion couldn't join him and Eleanor and Missy on a holiday, he wrote them a note expressing his hope that next year they could "make it a real family party." Missy added a postscript: "Dear Nan and Marion, I just want to send my love to you both, too. I wish you both were coming."

The feeling was mutual. "Never in my life," Nancy wrote, "had I met so utterly charming a man." She would devote herself "heart and soul" to Franklin's political career.

Yet for all the camaraderie, the need for separate spaces for husband and wife became apparent. Eleanor had never felt at home at Springwood. It was her mother-in-law's house. "For over forty years," she'd recall, "I was only a visitor there." It was still Sara and Franklin to command opposite ends of the dining table; likewise, mother and son occupied the two chairs that flanked the fireplace, while Eleanor "sat anywhere." Even the house Eleanor and Franklin shared in Manhattan had been bought for and designed by Sara, and could be accessed from her home. Eleanor craved a place that was hers alone.

In the summer of 1924, therefore, with Franklin's blessing, work began on a cottage for Eleanor, Nancy, and Marion on land not far from Springwood. According to Marion, it was actually Franklin's idea. They'd all been sitting on the banks of a rocky stream when the women remarked how sad they'd be to lose their

Hudson Valley retreat once Sara closed Springwood for the winter. Franklin replied, "But aren't you girls silly? This isn't Mother's land. I bought this acreage myself. And why shouldn't you three have a cottage here of your own, so you could come and go as you please?" Soon afterward, he wrote a contractor he knew: "My missus and some of her female political friends want to build a shack on a stream in the back woods." Plans were soon drawn up; Nancy got to work building the furniture for the house herself.

Eleanor never intended to move out of Springwood entirely, but having her own cottage to spend time in with her friends would, almost certainly, detach her even further from her children. In fact, her personal independence grew in direct proportion to her distance from them. Of this dynamic, Eleanor was not unaware; it was a choice she made consciously. The lessons of her grandmother's life guided her. "I determined that I would never be dependent on my children by allowing all my interests to center in them," she wrote years later.

So she left them to their own devices, rationalizing that it was better for them than the sort of rigid parental control wielded in most families of their class. Ironically, even as she spread her own wings, she did not advocate for her children to do the same. Anna was now eighteen; James, sixteen; Elliott, fourteen; Franklin Junior, ten; and John, eight. As per their father's wishes, the two oldest boys were at Groton, and the younger two were slated to follow, even though none of them particularly wanted to go. Significantly, their mother did not take up their cause. Nor did she speak up for Anna when the teenager was expected, like all Roosevelt women, to come out to society. Desperately opposed to the idea, Anna appealed to her mother for help. Yet, despite how much she'd hated the ordeal herself, Eleanor deferred to Sara in the matter, telling her daughter, "Yes, you must."

Anna was a shy, withdrawn teenager with masses of golden hair. Years of transferring between different schools in Washington and New York had left her lonely and largely friendless. Eleanor should have been able to relate to her, to empathize with her, but rarely did she advocate for her. "My mother made me go to Newport for what they call 'Tennis Week,'" Anna remembered.

"She didn't help me a bit." Neither did Eleanor ever suggest that Anna go to college, despite her own fervent wish that she had done so herself. "College for me was never even discussed," Anna would remember. On that point, Sara held the deciding vote. She argued that "girls who went to college were very apt to be 'old maids,'" an obvious slap at Eleanor's friends.

For all her regret at not having had more options at a young age, Eleanor did not champion her children's prerogative to make their own choices. She seemed almost frightened that, if she pushed too hard on their behalf, she might find her own freedoms taken away by her husband and mother-in-law. Franklin could countenance his wife living by her own set of standards, but he and his mother were not about to permit the children to play by anything other than society's traditional handbook.

For their part, her sons looked upon Eleanor as some sort of exotic character who droned on about women's rights and trade unions on their outings together. They regarded her "dutifully and affectionately," Eleanor told Marion, but they considered her to "hold queer opinions that can't be considered seriously as against those of their usual male environment." Still, Eleanor exerted some influence, at least in the political sphere. From Groton that fall she received a letter from James that must have made her smile: "It is very funny up here because nobody can understand why I am against T.R." The campus was very excited, James wrote, that Ted, "a Groton boy," might be elected governor. Yet, as James wrote his mother, who was off on the campaign trail doing her best to prevent that outcome, "I fear they will be rudely awakened."

Eleanor's withdrawal from the daily lives of her children allowed her to travel the state with the League of Women Voters and to spend time with her friends in Greenwich Village. It also delivered some heartbreak. She had always hoped to show the children Europe, as her father had shown her. In the summer of 1924, however, without telling Eleanor ahead of time, Sara announced that she would be taking Anna and James on a grand tour of the Continent the following spring. Eleanor was crushed. Yet the reality was, she simply didn't have the time to take them.

Besides, the children were more used to spending time with their grandmother anyway.

Eleanor had made a choice, and now she had to live with it, even if it broke her heart at times. Once, reading to the youngest boys, Franklin and Johnnie, she suddenly started to cry. The boys stared up at her dumbfounded. Elliott then walked in to see his mother crying; terrified, he ran off, and was quickly followed by his brothers. For the rest of the night, Eleanor "sobbed and sobbed" until no more tears were left. Yet the trade-off—family for personal independence—was unavoidable.

Eleanor's detachment from familial involvement extended to her brother Hall as well. She had seen him through school and beamed in pride when he got married, and in 1918, when Hall's newborn son got sick, she hurried up to her brother's home in Boston intending to make everything right. She'd found a household in chaos. The place was small, and Hall and his wife, Margaret, took in roomers to help pay their bills, since Hall, a brilliant engineer, was nonetheless frequently out of work. He also drank too much, and his marriage had soured; the couple bickered constantly, and the threat of separation hung in the air. Eleanor realized that the situation was beyond her ability to fix. After "weeks of anxiety," she recalled, "the baby died without our ever being entirely sure what was wrong with it." Despite her guilt over her long-ago promise to her father to take care of her brother, Eleanor gradually faced the fact that she had done as much as she could for Hall, and it was time now to focus on herself.

At the moment, that meant ensuring that her cousin Ted went down in defeat. In Washington, Alice was outraged by Eleanor's campaign shenanigans. Clearly her mousy little cousin had finally "developed a tougher side of her character," but Alice didn't believe that Eleanor's newfound strength brought "much enjoyment to anyone, least of all herself." That was Alice's bitterness speaking, because, in fact, Eleanor was having a grand time on the campaign trail, suffering no real pangs as yet over what she was doing to Ted's reputation, a common response of the bullied who become bullies themselves. Two days before the election, Eleanor debated Frances Parsons, the author and Republican Party activist, at New York City's Town Hall. Parsons pointed out that the Senate investigation had cleared Ted of any involvement in Teapot Dome, and it was "neither fair nor sincere to attempt by intimation of any sort that he is disqualified from holding high office." Parsons was clearly referring to the Singing Teapot. Eleanor offered no apologies. Ted, she said, was "a personally nice young man whose public record shows him willing to do the bidding of his friends."

Again, that wasn't true: Ted's stand in support of the Socialist legislators was just one example of his principled positions that put him at odds with the leadership of his party. Still, this was politics, and Eleanor had learned how to play the game very well.

Just before Election Day, Eleanor and her friends piled into the Singing Teapot for one last trip. This time they rumbled across the border of New York and into Connecticut. Just why Eleanor would want to visit Auntie Bye at Oldgate, her country house, especially at this particular moment, was unclear. She must have known that Bye would be torn by the rift among her nieces and nephews. Perhaps Eleanor wanted her aunt to witness how strong she had become; perhaps she wanted her to meet her friends, all resourceful, independent women of the kind Eleanor imagined Bye once had been, before she got married and gave up her influential role of Washington adviser. Yet Bye was now sixty-nine years old, a widow, and more disabled than ever, needing to be carried up and down the stairs of her house. It had been a very long time since she took part in politics, wooing the Japanese ambassador or the Speaker of the House to help advance her brother's policies. Now she was an old woman completely befuddled by the new generation. In horror, she gaped as Eleanor and her friends paraded into her house in their tweed knickers and men's jackets.

"I just hate to have Eleanor let herself look as she does," Bye wrote to Corinne Alsop after her guests had left. "Though never handsome, she had to me a charming effect, but alas and lackaday! Since politics have become her choicest interest all her charm has disappeared, and the fact is emphasized by the companions she chooses to bring with her." When Eleanor asked her aunt for some political insights, the only advice Bye had to offer was that, in public, "her front hair should be becomingly arranged." From Eleanor's point of view, Bye had turned away from revolution, from the power and independence she once possessed, and toward the traditional role of wife and mother she once thought could never be hers.

Rolling down the long driveway at Oldgate in the Singing Teapot, Eleanor didn't look back. She was undoubtedly glad for the refuge of her friends. Once more her family had proven as alien to her as she was to them.

WARM SPRINGS, GEORGIA

"Dearest E.," Franklin wrote that October from his little cottage surrounded by pine trees. "Life is just the same day after day and there is no variety to give landmarks. The mornings, as you know, are wholly taken up by the pool and four of the afternoons we have sat on the lawn."

For a man used to luxury, Warm Springs was exceedingly primitive. Squirrels ran across the roof of Franklin's small white-washed cottage; wind and sunlight slipped in between the slats in the walls. The concrete that surrounded the adjacent pool was cracked and stained bright orange from the sulfur in the water. The mineral waters, however, were warm, soothing, and buoyant, allowing Franklin, for the first time in three years, to stand upright on his own without the aid of braces. The joy that this gave him more than made up for the pervasive odor of rotten eggs.

He'd been lured to Warm Springs by a sympathetic newspaper columnist named Tom Loyless, who hoped not only that Franklin would benefit from the healing waters, but that his support might turn around the once-thriving resort. Accompanied by Eleanor and Missy Le Hand, Franklin was less than impressed upon his first arrival earlier that fall, but after a few days in the mineral pool, he was convinced that this was the way to get back on his feet—and back on the path to the White House. "The legs are really improving a great deal," he reported to Eleanor after she returned to New York. "The walking and general exercises in the water is fine [sic]—and I have worked out some special exercises also. This is really a discovery of a place, and there is no doubt that I've got to do it some more."

As Eleanor motored around New York campaigning for the Democrats, and the Singing Teapot spouted its steam across the state in an effort to bring down Ted, Franklin concentrated on strengthening his spindly, wasted legs. Day in and day out, he worked his legs in the pool. In the afternoons, dried off and tired, he would join Tom Loyless and his wife for a drive through the peach orchards and pine trees of the Georgia countryside. Missy Le Hand would accompany them. "I like him ever so much," Franklin wrote to Eleanor about Loyless, "and she is nice but not broad in her interests. She chatters away to Missy in the back seat and I hear an occasional yes or no from Missy to prove she is not sleeping." To any local, they would have appeared to be two married couples out for an afternoon drive.

What struck Franklin more than the beauty of the countryside, however, was "the great deal of poverty and neglect" that lay just beyond the resort, as he wrote to his mother. Once, perhaps, the spoiled scion of Hyde Park wouldn't have taken much notice of ramshackle houses and barefoot children, but Eleanor had taught him to see the world as it really was and had made him want to do something about it. Franklin's ambition was personal. He wanted very much to beat back all his rivals, especially his cousins, who thought his illness had taken him out of the running, but another part of his motivation, just as it had been for Theodore, was the desire to make a difference in the world.

He'd been poised to do that, too, after his vice-presidential defeat. He'd entered a law partnership in New York and set his eyes firmly on 1924. Then the paralysis struck. One morning in August 1921, while he was at Campobello, he got out of bed and noticed that his left leg dragged behind him. He'd been swimming the day before and, he believed, had caught a chill. "I tried to persuade myself that the trouble with my leg was muscular," Franklin said, "that it would disappear as I used it," but over the next few days the paralysis spread to his right leg and then up his chest. The pain started then, too.

At first, Louis Howe kept the news from the public. Franklin was variously reported in the newspapers as recovering from pneumonia or some unspecified illness. "I am telling everybody who asks," his half-brother, Rosy, wrote to Franklin, "that you have had a very severe rheumatic attack from 'excess bathing' which makes it very difficult for you to move." Trying to boost Franklin's spirits, Rosy said it was "too silly for you to have an 'infantile' disease. Anyway I don't half believe in it yet, and think still you will be well and over it long before the doctors think. Unless it develops into whooping cough or measles!"

On September 16, however, the *New York Times* bannered the truth: F.D. ROOSEVELT ILL OF POLIOMYELITIS, a variant name for infantile paralysis. As the newspaper reported, there'd been a rise in recent months in the number of those suffering from the disease; the city's total of 269 was the highest in five years, and the fatality rate stood at 20 percent. "Polio," as the disease was called, was caused by a virus that could be present in lakes and communal swimming areas—and Franklin had always been very susceptible to viruses.

Rosy was wrong: Franklin did not recover right away. For three long, arduous years he suffered and fought. People whispered that the once-promising political career of Franklin D. Roosevelt was over. Yet Franklin had beaten the odds before. He'd won his second term in the New York State Senate, after all, without ever moving from his sickbed, which led Rosy to joke that it was a "pity" Franklin wasn't running for election that season. "Judging by the last time," Rosy wrote to his half-brother, "when you were in bed, what a majority you would run up without legs!"

Franklin would forever be grateful for Eleanor's support and encouragement. Both his wife and Louis Howe had never let him give up, and eventually he was back on his feet, albeit with the help of braces and crutches. He learned to walk by swiveling his hips. He also had a car fitted with hand controls so he could drive. The disability became integrated into their lives, less a hardship to overcome than an everyday reality to be lived with. "We had tried so hard to ignore any handicap he labored under," Eleanor remembered, "that I'm sure the two youngest boys had never even thought about what their father could not do, and I had taken it for granted that he himself had also come to ignore his disabilities."

In fact, even as ambulatory as he had become, Franklin had not accepted his condition. Mobility was not enough; if he were ever to reenter public life, he had to appear strong and vigorous. Wilson's last years were marked by frail health; Harding died in office. Americans were not going to elect a man who appeared in any way feeble. Franklin could never be seen to struggle. That was what had sent him to Warm Springs in search of a cure.

Exercising in the water, pushing his endurance even further than he had in the past, he was doing his part to ensure that his grand plans came true. Meanwhile, he'd sent Eleanor back to New York to do hers.

"It is too bad that Eleanor has to leave so soon," Franklin wrote to Sara after his wife departed Warm Springs, "but she and I both feel it is important for her not to be away the rest of the campaign." He was as aware as Eleanor of the need to take Ted out. As a politician, Ted inspired little respect from Franklin; his cousin's sense of self-importance made Franklin laugh, and he didn't disagree when Rosy called Ted's public speeches "inane." Ted might have "a splendid war record," Franklin later declared, but he couldn't escape "a wretched record in public office." Under Ted's leadership, Franklin would claim, the navy had suffered from low morale and too many ships lost. "The assistant secretary," Franklin said, in one of his few direct attacks on Ted, "showed the most charming and complete ignorance about his job that any government official has ever displayed."

Once Ted was neutralized, Franklin believed he'd have a clear path to the White House. Louis Howe now had his eye set on 1928. After the successful speech Franklin delivered at the Democratic National Convention that past summer, such a plan seemed eminently possible, a scenario none of them could have imagined in the darkest days after the polio first struck.

The crowd at Madison Square Garden in New York City that warm June night in 1924 had "fairly lifted the roof" when Franklin appeared at the podium, according to one news report. The packed auditorium reeked of cigar smoke, roasted peanuts, and sweat. American flags dangled from the rafters, and giant electric fans rattled back and forth, doing nothing to alleviate the heat. A brass band was playing "America the Beautiful," though the music was barely audible above the din of the crowd. Franklin was brought in through a side door, to avoid being seen in his wheelchair. His son James, sixteen, as tall as his father, accompanied him. As they entered the hall, James locked Franklin's braces and helped him stand upright. The wheelchair was hidden away. Then Franklin, using just one crutch, held onto James with his other hand and began the slow, painful, twist-and-turn movement to the podium.

"His fingers dug into my arm like pincers," James recalled. "I doubt that he knew how hard he was gripping me. His face was covered with perspiration." An aide walked on the other side of Franklin, in case he fell; a policeman kept watch as well. They all made a great show of laughing and carrying on, calling out to friends as they passed, in order to disguise the agony of the effort.

Those at the convention weren't entirely fooled. One reporter compared the striking athletic figure Franklin had cut four years earlier with his current diminution. "Today the same young man," the reporter detailed, "still rich in the vigor of his mind, but fighting gamely against the creeping inroads of infantile paralysis, was assisted to the platform in Madison Square Garden . . . With a husky negro on one side and a two-hundred-pound New York copper on the other, Mr. Roosevelt was virtually carried up to the speaker's platform and placed in a chair. But he was laughing and smiling all the time and when the effort was over, the policeman stood beside Mr. Roosevelt's chair and applauded."

Franklin had come to the convention to nominate Al Smith, the governor of New York, for president. Smith was not the choice of the majority of the delegates; eventually the convention would reject him, sending him back to Albany to run for reelection against Ted. Yet that didn't stop the throng packing the Garden that night from embracing Franklin. When he got to his feet, with the assistance of James, and walked the short distance across the podium, propping himself against the lectern and tossing away his crutch, the crowd burst into cheers. "The roaring demonstration continued," the same reporter described, "until Mr. Roosevelt himself quieted it."

The entire hall sat rapt as he spoke. "We need as president not a man who will satisfy some one section or some one class. The relationship of labor and capital, the farmer and the city dweller, the manufacturer and consumer, the rich and poor, have become so complex in our national life that problems have arisen acute beyond our forefathers." He was placing the name of Smith into nomination, but for many, he might also have been describing the kind of president he himself would be. When Franklin concluded his speech with a call for "overwhelming victory this year," the audience roared again, louder than ever. The crowd "just went crazy," Eleanor's friend Marion Dickerman remembered. "It was stupendous, really stupendous!"

The band struck up "The Sidewalks of New York" as the delegates paraded through the aisles, waving flags and signs, blowing bullhorns. Franklin, meanwhile, was left clinging to the lectern, fearful his legs might collapse under him. While he was eased into his wheelchair, a group of supporters stood in front of him to block the view of the crowd. Once home, Franklin was exultant. Marion Dickerman visited him in his room, where he was propped up in bed. "Marion," he exclaimed, opening his arms wide, "I did it!"

Franklin's speech was the highlight of the convention. "Franklin Roosevelt made a good speech when he put Al Smith's name before the convention," the *Syracuse Herald* observed. "In the long record of political convention oratory, there are names that shine with more effulgence, but none equaled him in gameness, in the triumph of will over physical distress." He was a Roosevelt, the paper said, "which explains all"—a claim of family legacy that surely must have left Ted irate. Yet the *Herald Tribune*, while declaring Franklin "easily the foremost figure on the floor or platform," insisted that his name had nothing to do with it. Franklin deserved the attention, the paper editorialized, for his eloquence and rousing articulation of the challenges the party and the country faced. Even his Republican cousin-in-law Teddy Robinson couldn't help but send a word of praise. "I have listened to a lot of nominating speeches of all kinds of descriptions and in most of the parties," he told Franklin, "and yours beat them all." He and his family had listened to the speech on the radio, Teddy reported, "and we were all thrilled."

Franklin's speech offered progressivism for a new era. Conservatives might hold sway at the moment, but times were changing, and fast. Every year, America became more different than the year before. Since Franklin's birth four decades earlier, the population of the country had more than doubled, and was now more diverse than ever. The older, whiter, Protestant demographic was shrinking; for the first time in the nation's history, more people lived in cities than in rural areas. Most were immigrants from the more Catholic areas of Europe (Irish, Italians, Poles), in contrast to the Anglo-Saxon origins of earlier citizens. Now nearly 20 percent of the population was Catholic, and a growing number of Jewish immigrants were arriving as well. This new body politic would need to be accommodated, as Franklin well understood.

Al Smith was, in fact, a Catholic. For that reason, many Democrats were opposed to his nomination, fearing he was unelectable. The Ku Klux Klan was mobilizing hatred of Catholics, blacks, and foreigners, and would be a significant factor in voter turnout. One prominent Democrat worried to Franklin that "the money interests of Wall street," as represented by the Republicans, along with "Klanism and religious issues," would spell defeat for the Democrats that fall. Indeed, a number of party loyalists were furious over Franklin's support for Smith. "The people are very much surprised at you—a Protestant and an Episcopalian—trying to have a Romanist elected president," one letter writer castigated him. Another called him "a disgrace" to the name he carried, and wondered why Theodore's Rough Riders did not appear to strike him "down dead." Another felt Franklin had brought shame "to the former President of the United States" who shared his name.

Yet Franklin had the foresight to recognize that by supporting Smith, he was a hero to Catholic voters, whom he would need when he ran again himself. He was also galvanizing the old progressive base. The noted author and journalist Hendrik van Loon was at the convention, and until Franklin's speech, he observed little he could be proud of in "the political machinery of our good land." Then Franklin made his way to the podium and inspired the crowd, and van Loon was left wishing he'd brought his sons to see and hear the momentous event. "I have witnessed many heroic deeds," the author wrote in a piece that was syndicated to newspapers across the country, but never "so fine a display of high mental courage as when Roosevelt carried himself to the front of the speaker's tribune." To his readers nationwide, van Loon declared that if Franklin ran for president himself, he would "stand on the corner of every street" to shout his support. "Once upon a time," van Loon went on, "there was a Roosevelt who spent his life killing everything he met that walked on four feet and calling everything he met on two feet a liar. We now have one who is fair to his opponents and who with sublime courage makes his mind triumph over that mortal matter which so often kills the spirit of our soul."

For the first time, a writer was suggesting that Franklin wasn't just equal to Theodore as a leader, but in fact surpassed him. Certainly Franklin's convention speech had positioned him precisely where he needed to be. It didn't matter that ultimately John Davis, the former U.S. ambassador to Great Britain, was chosen over Smith as the nominee; nor did it even matter all that much whether the Democrats won or lost that coming November. Franklin had his eye set squarely on four years down the road. "I am philosophic enough to think that even if Coolidge is elected," he wrote to Eleanor, "we shall be so darned sick of conservatism, of the old-money-controlled crowd, in four years that we get a real progressive landslide in 1928." His half-brother, Rosy, ever his booster, concurred: "I believe if Davis is beaten, as I think he will be, all being well, you will have a walk over for the nomination in 1928."

For now, all Franklin could do was wait—and exercise his legs as hard as he could in the warm mineral springs. His walk to the podim to accept the nomination, Franklin vowed, would be done without any help or crutches.

Until then, he relied on Missy for his day-to-day support. Marguerite "Missy" Le Hand was, like Eleanor and Lucy, tall with blue eyes, but unlike them, she had dark hair and hailed from much more working-class origins. Missy's father was an Irish-Catholic gardener from Boston who'd run off on his family, leaving his wife to raise their children on her own. The young woman, now just twenty-five years old, had come to Franklin's attention when she worked on his 1920 campaign, where she proved her efficiency. At the end of that effort, Franklin offered her a job as a secretary at his law firm. "I deeply appreciate how nice you were to me and that working for you and with you was a very great pleasure," Missy wrote. "I will let you know about coming back . . . just as soon as I have talked with my people. You were very nice to ask me."

Her people evidently gave her a yes, as Missy was working for Franklin by early 1921. They developed a close, affectionate, joking rapport with each other. She teased him in her letters, calling him "Your Majesty" and reporting on the regular appearances of their office mouse. Then everything changed when a letter arrived from Eleanor that summer from Campobello, where the family was vacationing: "Mr. Roosevelt had a severe chill last Wednesday which resulted in fever and much congestion and I fear his return will be delayed," Eleanor wrote. She asked Missy to break any engagements Franklin had before Labor Day.

As Missy would soon learn, her employer's illness was far more serious than a chill. He would need much more from her now than just letter writing and appointment scheduling. Perhaps in anticipation of this, Franklin instructed Eleanor in her letter to Missy to advise his secretary that he was requesting a raise in her salary, from thirty dollars a week to thirty-five.

Missy proved up to the task. When, after many months away, Franklin finally returned to the law office, his loyal secretary kept his mobility challenges in mind. For one luncheon, she chose the Bankers Club in the Equitable (the same building where Frank Weeks had once had his office) because of the ease of access it afforded. "You can get your elevator (express and alone) direct to the club," Missy wrote to Franklin, "and you do not have to go through the public dining room to your own private room."

For such consideration, Franklin was extremely grateful. He

grew to depend on Missy, giving her more and more responsibility in his life. She learned how to help him stand, to ease him
back into his wheelchair, to lock and unlock his braces. Eleanor
was devoted and encouraging throughout the ordeal, but she did
not possess the soft, gentle, tender touch of Missy. The young secretary sympathized, commiserated, *listened*. She was always there
with a gentle smile, a wry laugh, a mood-lightening joke. The two
of them shared a love of the absurd, often working out silly word
puzzles together—hardly an activity Eleanor would ever have
had the time for. Their intimacy allowed Missy to become "the
frankest of [Franklin's] associates," one political adviser observed,
"never hesitating to tell him unpleasant truths or to express an
unfavorable opinion." By 1924, Missy had won Franklin's complete and absolute trust.

Taking charge of most aspects of her employer's life, Missy
became, in many ways, Franklin's "office wife—quote, unquote,"
his daughter Anna would quip. Yet Missy's wifely involvement
extended beyond the office. "*Please* have the dentist come down
if the tooth is not all well," she admonished Franklin at one point.
She also helped choose his clothes and monitored his guests, and
when they were apart, she missed him terribly: "Gosh, it will be
good to get my eyes on you again," she wrote after one separation. Observing Missy and Franklin together, one reporter proved
quite perceptive: "She watches her man so closely that she can see
the slightest changes in his emotional attitude before they have
become apparent to anyone else. She knows when Roosevelt's
thick layer of Dutch stubbornness is coming to the surface before
he knows it himself. She knows when he is really listening to the
person who is talking to him and when he is merely being polite."

When Franklin purchased a yacht so that he could swim—the
best sort of exercise, his doctors felt—Missy became the unofficial mistress of the vessel. She decorated the deck, organized the
meals and the games, and regularly threw out a fishing line with
Franklin and sat there with him, shoulder to shoulder, for hours
at a time. As the sun set, Missy broke out the liquor and mixed
up some cocktails for Franklin and any of their guests, proving
they were "wets" in deed as well as in name. How different, yet

again, from Eleanor, who retained her stiff-backed disapproval of alcohol.

Once, while on the yacht, Franklin's son Elliott witnessed Missy, in her bathrobe, sitting on his father's lap. Elliott would come to believe the relationship was romantic and sexual. His siblings weren't so sure, however, pointing out that their father was paralyzed from the waist down. Yet physical and emotional affection and intimacy could take many forms, and it was clear to everyone that the couple was devoted to each other. One of Franklin's cousins on his mother's side would declare Missy "the only woman Franklin ever loved," although Lucy Mercer's relatives would say the same thing about her.

No matter the exact nature of their relationship, the association of Franklin and Missy was intense and constant, far more constant than the one with Eleanor, and it raised suspicions in Sara. The formidable lady, now seventy, disapproved when her son's secretary accompanied him to Hyde Park.

Eleanor, however, raised no such objections. "I haven't told Mama that Missy is back," she wrote to Franklin a few months before the 1924 campaign season began in earnest that year, "because I think she has more peace of mind when she doesn't know things." Eleanor was now light-years removed from the insecure wife she'd once been, making accommodations for her husband's lady friend and helping him keep up appearances with his mother. Franklin, of course, had given Eleanor the freedom to pursue her own interests. While no public embarrassment could ever be countenanced for either of them, in private, husband and wife gave each other extraordinary room to lead separate lives.

WASHINGTON, DC

In Washington, Alice was seething. The various New York newspapers delivered to her in the nation's capital so she could keep up with Ted's campaign were spread all around her, and she was outraged by the reports of Cousin Eleanor gallivanting across the state in that contraption people were calling the Singing Teapot. Eleanor's increasingly shrill speeches against the Republicans, published verbatim in many newspapers, had left Alice furious.

Yet Alice was not one to let her anger get the better of her. Her attacks and put-downs were always delivered with a smile and a heaping dose of irony, a skill that Eleanor, so earnest, so humorless, had never learned. Alice's best line of attack against Eleanor had always been to belittle her by imitating her: she'd thrust out her upper teeth, pull in her chin, and speak through her nose. Alice called Eleanor's high-pitched speech "the voice of well-brought-up little brownstone-front girls." Her imitations made everyone laugh.

Yet, inside, she was still seething.

Her venom for her cousin wasn't difficult to provoke. "She was always so good and so nice about everybody that it became quite intolerable," Alice said about Eleanor, "especially as one knew she harbored quite a lot of well-hidden resentments." Alice, of course, was resentful, too, but she was far too clever to show it. As Eleanor increasingly became a well-known public figure, advocating strongly for progressive causes, other journalists followed up on Zoe Beckley's observation that she resembled her uncle Theodore, especially in her passion for reform. "Some writer," Alice recalled, "once stated that I was frightfully put out because Eleanor was so much more like my father than any of his own children." When she made that statement years later, Alice, significantly, did not deny that she'd been put out; nor did she take issue with the idea that Eleanor was more like Theodore than she was. She admitted, in fact, that "In some respects, she probably *was*." After all, her father had had "a do-gooding side to him, too."

That was what burned at her. After spending most of her life trying to win her father's attention and respect (and repeatedly failing), it was no surprise that Alice was "put out" when Eleanor was called Theodore's heir. The fact that Alice might have brought that on herself, by abandoning her father's progressivism for the sake of political expediency, never seemed to occur to her.

In one important measure, however, Alice was unquestionably following her father's wishes: she was doing all she could to make Ted president. Their nemesis Franklin had, at least for the moment, been sidelined, and finally Alice saw their best chance to grab what they wanted. If Ted won the governor's race, his sister reasoned, he could be the Republican candidate for president in 1928. Even if Franklin somehow managed to run for the White House himself that year, offering the nation a choice between Roosevelts, voters would surely opt for Ted, Alice believed, since he would have had four years of executive experience at that point. And his very presence on the ticket would undermine the absurd claims people made that Franklin was Theodore's true successor.

How sweet victory would be when she had it. "All the fun of having it," Alice believed, "is *taking* it."

What very few knew, however, was just how desperately Alice needed Ted to win that fall. To an outside observer, she would have appeared to be very secure in her power in the nation's capital. Nick was on the verge of achieving his long-held goal of becoming Speaker of the House. With the Republicans widely expected to retain and even expand their control of the House in the coming election, and with current Speaker Frederick Gillett most likely to be elected to the Senate, Nick was next in line for the Speakership—if, as one political columnist estimated, "the political wiseacres are guessing right." There was no guarantee of that, however, and according to another writer, Nick's chances were really dependent on Alice's influence: "The congressman is his wife's political creation. Left to himself, he might not have taken the trouble to climb. His wife provided the ingredient of ambition. She provided also a quality of cooperation such as few public men ever have had."

The wife of the Speaker commanded considerable clout in the nation's capital, but it was more social status than an actual political career. That wasn't what Alice wanted. She had never had much interest in hosting functions and receiving diplomats if there wasn't some payoff in it for her. She also knew that Nick's career would top out at Speaker; he was never going any higher than that. That was why she was still counting on Ted to win her the top prize.

So she threw everything she had that fall into making Ted— "my darling Ted, whom I adored"—governor. As children, they had fought and scraped; Ted had teased her and brought attention to Alice's outsider status. Yet now he was her ticket back to the top.

Alice had been grooming Ted for years. During her brother's time in Washington as assistant secretary of the navy, she made sure he became friends with senators such as Frank Brandegee, James Wadsworth, and Eugene McCormick. She frequently hosted dinners for them all to scheme and plot. Even more fruitful were the poker games she would set up after dinner, giving Ted an up-close view on how these hotshots maneuvered their way. Alice was one of the first to push Ted toward running for governor of New York; his diary would reveal how frequently he placed long-distance calls to Washington to get advice from "Sister."

In another era, of course, Alice wouldn't have been pushing anyone: she would have claimed her father's mantle as her own and run for office herself. Certainly she was the shrewdest, most capable politician in the family; in that regard she was very much her father's daughter. Yet in 1924 a female candidate was still a novelty, and a risk. Only four women had been elected to the House, one succeeding her father and another her husband. Only one woman had been appointed to the Senate, and that only for a symbolic one-day term. No woman had ever been elected governor. Alice didn't feel slighted by Ted's primacy in any way. She loathed public speaking and preferred to work her magic behind the scenes. Still, the fact remained that, despite her superior abilities, only much later would anyone even think of her as a potential candidate: the spotlight was always on Ted, the first son, the namesake, the heir to the throne.

Yet Alice had always wielded more power than Ted. CAPITAL POLITICIANS BOW TO WILL OF TEDDY ROOSEVELT'S DAUGHTER, ran the headline of a syndicated article that fall of 1924, written by Charles P. Stewart of the United Press, a well-respected veteran political journalist. "Mrs. Alice Roosevelt Longworth," Stewart wrote, "is considered the most influential individual, politically, in Washington today. Not being a public character, though, like her father, she has not the sort of influence with the mass of voters he had, but doubtless she could obtain it if she chose." Alice's method, Stewart reported, was to "pull the strings and when she pulls them she gets results in Congress and the executive offices." He added, "She gets most anything she wants."

Alice had watched the game long enough to play it far better than most. Her expertise in political affairs she credited to a "simian ability to catch on." Indeed, ever since helping to defeat the League of Nations, she had been one of Washington's most influential powerbrokers. "The country's ablest and most powerful men listen and pay attention when she speaks," Stewart revealed. She was involved in nearly every political battle on the Hill; her guests became used to her receiving phone calls in the middle of dinner parties and then dashing off. "Grabbing a hat, and hurling an abrupt apology at her guests, Alice left the astonished crowd to finish the party without a hostess," one partygoer revealed to a newspaper reporter. Another time, she skedaddled out of a holiday party in New York to return to Washington in order to watch a vote on an economic conference proposed by Bill Borah. "Fancy staying in New York with all this happening here," Alice explained, with a wave at the Senate floor.

Other women had power in Washington, but their power was located in their dining rooms and their gardens; it derived from the dinners and parties they gave. Alice threw some of the capital's most successful parties, but her power was much more extensive—from the poker games she hosted after her dinners to the deals she made, face-to-face, with politicians in the Senate chambers. Never in her nineteen years of marriage to Nick had Alice been the "garden-party" congressional wife. "She's always done so very much as she pleased," one observer wrote. "Never mind about making calls; never mind about heading committees; never mind about anything outside." Instead, Alice cut her deals in smoke-filled backrooms with the boys.

Her deal making, however, was usually more about politics than policy. When it was time for nominations and appointments, whether for president, Senate, the House, or the Cabinet, Alice's support could make or break a candidate. She'd made Republicans sweat by not declaring her support for Coolidge, who'd never been her man, until fairly late in the campaign season. Her point was clear: by reining in her family's progressive impulses and becoming a loyal Republican partisan, she expected to be repaid with the same loyalty. Henceforth, only those she approved would carry the Republican banner; there should be no more Hardings, she made clear.

The power Alice held over Washington insiders was often personal. As one friend observed, she knew "a good many of their secrets," and she wasn't above letting people think she might spill a few. That month of October 1924, a rumor spread that Alice was writing her memoirs. "The more this rumor gains belief," one columnist wrote, "the more keyed up everybody is getting about it." A large segment of the public, the columnist said, was "eagerly anticipating the gossipy revelations which Alice Roosevelt Longworth can so easily make of Washington social and political life." HOW MUCH WILL ALICE ROOSEVELT LONGWORTH TELL? the newspapers wanted to know. "It is doubtful there is any living person, either man or woman, who knows the inside story of Washington for the last twenty years as thoroughly as Mrs. Longworth," the columnist went on. "Prominent society matrons would have to admit that she has facts where they have only gossip; graybearded senators would be forced to acknowledge that she has been to the bottom of countless political problems while they have only skimmed the surface."

Holding so many cards, Alice could exact enormous concessions for herself, her husband, and her brother. Yet by making a threat of her memoirs, she was playing an increasingly dangerous game—because, that fall, she had her own secret to protect, a secret that had changed all her political calculations, a secret that many would have loved to discover and use against her.

Once, Alice had possessed another route back to power besides Ted. For a while it had seemed as if her lover, Bill Borah, might go all the way to the White House. Yet Bill missed his best chance the previous spring when he failed to launch a primary challenge to President Coolidge, as some supporters had urged him to do. And by the time Coolidge asked him that summer to run as his vice president, Alice's secret made it impossible.

At the convention in Cleveland, Ted had lobbied hard for Borah as vice president. He thought it was a done deal until a telephone conversation with Sister suddenly dashed his hopes. "She told us that Borah had talked to her and would not take the vice presidency under any circumstances," Ted wrote in his diary. Of course, he couldn't convey that news to the convention floor, because to explain where he'd gotten his information would have "involved Sister," and even though most everyone knew of the Longworth-Borah affair, appearances had to be kept up.

So why had Bill refused the vice-presidential nomination? One answer, which undoubtedly held some truth, was that the vice-presidency was a thankless, often dead-end post. Still, being vice president of the United States nonetheless carried considerable honor and clout, and could have made Bill a front-runner in 1928. Undoubtedly, then, there was more to his refusal than that. Bill refused, most likely, because of the secret he shared with Alice.

The secret was not, of course, their affair, since that wasn't a secret at all. In libertine Washington, an extramarital affair was hardly enough to exclude someone from the presidency; if it were, a good number of candidates would never have thrown their hats in the ring. Rather, the secret that changed all their calculations was that Alice was pregnant, and Bill was the father—and, quite radically, Alice was planning to keep the baby.

Sometime in the late spring or early summer, just as Bill was being mentioned as a candidate for vice president, Alice had discovered that she was expecting a baby. She was forty years old; Bill was fifty-nine. For a woman who prided herself on her use of contraception, who had kept herself from getting pregnant for nearly two decades now, this was unlikely to have been the result of an accident. Even if it was, the decision to keep the baby was deliberate. While abortions were illegal, they weren't difficult to come by for women of means. The danger of the procedure, however, was perhaps enough to keep Alice from going that route; in 1930, the first year for which there are records, almost three thousand women would die of abortion-related complications. Indeed, Bill's wife, Mary, according to rumors, may have been permanently injured by an abortionist some years earlier.

Whatever the reasons, Alice's decision to keep the baby almost certainly derailed Bill's ambitions to be president. After all, enough of Washington knew about his affair with Alice to be able to see through the fiction that the child was Nick's. Bill's opponents could easily mount a whisper campaign against him, and even the mainstream press might pick it up if it involved "Princess Alice." Bill seemed to understand the reality he faced. The timing of Alice's pregnancy and of his refusal to run for vice president were simply too close to be written off as coincidental. Alice would have realized she was pregnant by early June; on June 12, after playing coy about his decision for so long, Bill officially turned down Coolidge's offer of the vice-presidential slot. And it was Alice who relayed that news to Ted at the convention.

Her only hope now to reclaim her power was through her brother.

Much later, when an interviewer tried to get her to talk about Borah, Alice was playful. "Well, if you really want to know," she said, "I suppose you could say that I was adept at skating on thin ice and playing with fire. Nice image, don't you think?" Playing on the edge had always been Alice's favorite pastime, ever since her days of slinking off with her boyfriends or up to the roof to smoke. That fall of 1924, despite the implications to Bill's career, she seemed to enjoy being the subject of rumor and gossip. If people ever stopped talking about her, Alice might have ceased to exist.

Yet, underneath her gaiety, her joy in making people squirm, there seemed something still of the teenage girl who cried in her room and poured out her loneliness and lack of human connection in her diary. She loved Borah, but she was using him as much as she used Nick (and as much as they both used her). Their worldly, tolerant, nonchalant approach to open marriages was not, in essence, all that different from the arrangement worked out between Eleanor and Franklin. Yet what Alice and Nick seemed to lack was the mutual respect, affection, and caretaking that defined the relationship between Alice's cousins. For all Eleanor's rigid morality, she seemed to detect what it was in Alice that drove her escapades: "Life seems [to Alice] to be one long pursuit of pleasure and excitement," she wrote to a friend, "and rather little real happiness either given or taken. The 'blue bird' always to be searched for in some new and novel way."

The bluebird was, in fact, flying farther and farther out of Alice's reach. Everything depended now on Ted's being elected governor. It was the first step in her long-range plan—but, in fact, she had run out of time.

COVE NECK, NEW YORK

On November 4, 1924, a stunningly beautiful day, with temperatures soaring into the seventies and voters flocking to the polls in droves, Ted, his wife, and his mother cast their ballots at Watson's candy store in Oyster Bay, then returned to their home in Cove Neck. Friends and family gathered that evening to hear the results. Kermit came by to pay his respects, but didn't stay; Archie was also in and out during the evening. Ted's five-year-old son, Quentin, whose birthday it was, seemed to think that everyone had come for him. Grandmother Edith sat stiffly in a chair, listening to radio reports. Alice rang twice from Cincinnati, where she'd gone to vote herself, and inquired how things were going.

They were going well, it seemed. An early report that Ted had lost Buffalo was overturned with a report that he'd won, and while it seemed that Al Smith had taken the City of New York, Ted was outperforming him above the Bronx. "The atmosphere in the house took on a cheerful tone," a reporter observed.

Ted was heartened. His time had at last arrived.

Yet, as the night wore on, the news coming in by telephone and telegraph became grimmer. The family ate dinner in silence; afterward, the children were sent up to bed. Soon after midnight, Ted was informed that he had lost.

Over the campaign's last days, the momentum had shifted decidedly to Smith—due in no small part, Ted fumed, to Eleanor and her shenanigans. When the final votes were tallied, Ted's loss was humiliating: Republicans had swept to victory all across the nation, but somehow he'd been left out. All around him there was rejoicing. In Connecticut, Ted's cousin Corinne Alsop was elected to the State Assembly, one of the first women to win elected office in that state. Ted was the only Republican, it seemed, not to be celebrating at a victory party.

All through the night, until the sky began to turn pink in the east, Ted tried to make sense of the returns. In New York, the GOP had carried every statewide office except for governor. Most embarrassing of all, Seymour Lowman, Ted's lieutenant governor candidate, had been elected without him, collecting some eight thousand more votes than his running mate. In unprecedented numbers, voters had split their tickets, but only to cut out Ted.

In Cincinnati, an irate Alice started casting about for excuses. "We naturally said it was because they did something to the ballot boxes in New York," she remembered. "We had to say a thing like that." Ted's wife, Eleanor, agreed. She would always believe that the forces of Tammany Hall stole the election from her husband. "Lack of voting machines in the city made it easy to juggle figures," she said.

Ted didn't buy it. Tammany hadn't beaten him; if anything, it was Cousin Eleanor and her dirty tricks. He lost by a little more than one hundred thousand votes, about as many as had come out to see the Singing Teapot, according to the Democrats' claims. The family would never forgive Eleanor: both Ted's wife and Alice would come to believe that their cousin herself had been at the wheel of the Singing Teapot, and described her that way in their memoirs.

Ted was angry, too, but he was more resigned in his anger: the main reason he'd lost, he believed, was because yet again he hadn't been up to the task. It was an old refrain. "I just didn't do enough," he told his wife. The same curse that had hounded him all his life had struck again. For a few blissful years, the nation had seen Ted as a shining war hero. Now he was perceived as a second-rank candidate who'd traded on his father's memory and come up short.

"Poor T.R. Junior," Alice concluded. "Every time he crosses the street someone has something to say because he doesn't do it as his father would—and if he navigates nicely, they say it was just as T.R. would have done it."

There was still hope, of course, that Ted could try again in 1926 or 1928. His father didn't win the office until he was forty, and Ted was still three years short of that. Still, his stunning rejection at the hands of New York voters left him badly damaged and disillusioned. There was also a growing expectation that Franklin, after his stirring convention speech, would run for office himself, for either the governorship or, possibly, the presidency in 1928. If there was a moment when Ted might have eclipsed Franklin before his cousin got back on his feet, that moment had passed.

Meanwhile, Alice tried to salvage the family's ambitions. On November 21 she announced her pregnancy and was greeted with an uproar of surprise and excitement. "No similar event in Washington official and social circles has so piqued the interest of the capital as has the report that the stork shortly will pay a visit to the home of Nick and Alice Longworth," one newspaper reported. "The arrival of an heir" was thought to give a boost to Nick's ambitions to be Speaker. "Should the stork time its arrival propitiously," the same newspaper speculated, "the House might be minded to hand Nick the Speakership, for which he is a candidate, as a token of its felicitations."

Not everyone was so excited, however. At Sagamore Hill, Edith wrote one word in her diary on the day she learned her stepdaughter was expecting: "Bouleversé"—meaning she was "stricken" or "shattered." To Bye she wrote, "Alice's news was rather a blow." Even if Alice hadn't revealed her baby's paternity to her stepmother, Edith was smart enough to have figured it out. No doubt she'd heard the rumors, and she'd been wise to Alice's ways for an awfully long time.

On February 14, 1925, Valentine's Day, and two days after her forty-first birthday, Alice gave birth to a daughter at the Chicago Lying-In Hospital. It wasn't easy. Having a baby, Alice declared, was "like trying to push a grand piano through a transom." In Congress, Nick was greeted with an ovation, and his colleagues trooped up to the podium to make speeches in his honor. The Democrats seemed especially eager to add their own warm wishes though their motives seemed suspect. "If legislative business were not so pressing," declared congressman William D. Upshaw of Georgia, "it might be fitting, in the name of the Continental

Congress and the great God Almighty, to declare a holiday in the House to commemorate the perpetuation of the name of Theodore Roosevelt, Nicholas Longworth [Nick's father] and Nicholas Longworth Jr."

Upshaw was probably being sarcastic. Many in the chamber had heard the rumors that Paulina was not Nick's child. Wags were calling Alice "Aurora Borah Alice," while a rumor made the rounds that she originally wanted to name the child "Deborah," or "of Borah." For the Democrats, this was an opportunity to embarrass the man who hoped to lead their opponents. Their congratulations to Nick on the birth of his daughter ring down through history as disingenuous. Upshaw was one of the most socially conservative members of Congress, a fundamentalist Christian and an ardent supporter of Prohibition. When he declared that Nick's family line had been perpetuated by Paulina's birth, the mockery in his words would have been evident, especially his quip about declaring a national holiday in honor of the event. Known as "the dryest of the drys," Upshaw had been apparently unable to resist the opportunity to needle Nick, well known as a "wet." Nick, meanwhile, surrounded by his peers, the public, and the press, had no choice but to play along with his adversaries' nasty little game. The *New York Times* reported that "his face grew crimson" as he listened to the praise and congratulations from his colleagues.

Yet even Nick seemed to be speaking with tongue thrust firmly in cheek. "I'm a little bit jealous, of course," he told a reporter after seeing the child for the first time, "because she looks so much more like a Roosevelt than a Longworth." He added, "But she's young yet."

If Nick resented his wife for bearing another man's child, he never let Paulina know it. He treated the little girl, who would grow up calling him "Father," as his own, doting on her and spending a considerable amount of time with her. That was more than she got from her mother, who, although bewitched by the pretty little creature she'd brought into the world, was eager to get back to her political maneuverings and quickly found a nanny to take the lead in child rearing. With their household grown, the

Longworths purchased a stately Beaux Arts town house at 2009 Massachusetts Avenue, just west of Dupont Circle, where Alice's father's uncle, Robert B. Roosevelt, a Democrat like Franklin, had once lived. It was here that Alice would hold court as she tried to keep her family's ambitions alive.

On February 27, less than two weeks after the child's birth, Nick was chosen as Speaker of the House. That, however, was as far as he'd ever go, as Alice understood all too well. Somehow she had to get Ted elected before Franklin beat them both.

CHICAGO

A light snow powdered the streets and an icy wind whipped down Michigan Avenue on the evening of February 16, 1925. The wintry weather didn't deter a group of women from congregating on the corner of Monroe Street, where the doorman outside the twelve-story University Club did his best to keep them back and the sidewalk clear. At any moment, the club was expecting a distinguished visitor. Kermit Roosevelt, the son of the former president, was slated to deliver that month's "Ladies' Night" lecture, about big game hunting and his travels through exotic lands. The topic was exciting enough, but for the ladies on the street, it was a chance to meet "the handsome brother," as Kermit was called, that had brought them out. What a dashing, romantic figure Teddy's second son had turned out to be.

Kermit arrived in a car with officials from the Field Museum of Natural History. The women called his name as he stepped out onto the sidewalk. He waved and blew a kiss. Kermit was indeed good-looking—not as handsome as his cousin Franklin, perhaps, but more rugged, more devil-may-care. Thirty-five years old, with thick dark hair, blue eyes, and a well-trimmed moustache— rather like the one worn by movie star John Gilbert—Kermit resembled his father in body if not in face. He stood five eleven, and his shoulders and legs were thick with muscle, the result of many years' laboring and adventuring through jungles and deserts. His skin was as tough as leather, though remarkably uncreased.

He shook hands all around. Escorted upstairs to the club's

ornate Cathedral Hall, which was ringed with stained-glass windows and the insignias of Harvard, Yale, Princeton, and other Ivy League schools, Kermit, almost certainly, before doing anything else, knocked back a drink; it was the way he operated. If the drink wasn't poured from the club's private bar, then it came from his own flask, carried inside his jacket. For playboys like him, Prohibition was an inconvenience, but there were always ways to get around it.

He was probably exhausted. He'd kept to a busy schedule since his arrival in the Windy City the day before, "feted to within the proverbial inch of his eyebrows," as one columnist put it. In addition to tours and meetings, he was the guest of honor at a luncheon hosted by the Field Museum, after which he lectured on the terrifying trip he'd taken with his father down the Amazon. Later that day, Kermit gave a public talk on "Hunting and Collecting in Many Lands," and finally, he was delivering this evening's presentation to the ladies' auxiliary of the University Club.

Kermit had never run for any public office. He'd never held any government position. Yet suddenly he was in demand to speak at museums and clubs all across the country. In an era enthralled by the exploits of Richard Byrd, Robert Flaherty, and other explorers, people wanted to hear stories of high adventure, and Kermit, the world traveler, could deliver. With his brother Ted licking his wounds in seclusion after his electoral loss, it was Kermit, for the first time in his life, who had become the most prominent Roosevelt brother.

"There is always something fascinating and romantic about anyone of the name Roosevelt to us Americans," a reporter for the *Chicago Tribune* wrote, but Kermit, she thought, was especially exciting: "This son of the great man was with the latter on his famous African tour when . . . they collected a fine gathering of representative fauna which may be seen today in the national museum in Washington." The ladies at the University Club hoped to hear more stories like that. Kermit, probably loosened up by a couple of whiskies, was only too happy to oblige. He told a tale of photographing lions with his father. One great cat, he recalled, was reclining while Theodore watched from a thicket nearby.

"His fascinating, ferocious smile" was visible through the leaves. Distracted, Kermit finally whispered, "Father, I do wish that you would get away from those bushes. I can't tell which is you and which is the lion." The women howled.

By now, Kermit had been around the world several times. He'd hunted tigers in India and black bears in Korea; explored the temples of Japan; ridden the Trans-Siberian Railway across the frozen tundra; and witnessed arrests by the Bolshevik secret police in Moscow. He could speak Swahili, Urdu, Portuguese, and Hindustani. Whenever he returned to the Knickerbocker Club in New York after one of his trips, "all the old gentlemen immediately put down their papers and sat on the edge of their chairs," eager to hear Kermit's latest exploits, as one friend remembered.

Now, this year, a new adventure beckoned. The Field Museum had enlisted him to travel through Asia to bring back specimens of the big mammals of the Central Plains; in particular, the museum hoped he could snare the *Ovis poli*, the rare giant sheep described by Marco Polo. Some people doubted the animal's existence, comparing it to the unicorn or the phoenix, but Kermit vowed he'd bring one home. The expedition would be underwritten by James Simpson, president of the Chicago department store Marshall Field's—and as his partner in the journey, Kermit chose his brother Ted.

In accepting the offer, Ted was once again following in his father's footsteps: after his devastating loss in 1912, Theodore attempted to restore his manhood with the trip down the Amazon. For Kermit, the decision to include Ted was a chance to repair some fractured family ties. Close as boys and as students at Groton and Harvard, the two brothers had drifted apart in recent years, their life paths diverging sharply and sometimes conflicting. What better way to heal their broken bond than by killing some giant sheep together?

In many ways, all this was history repeating itself: two brothers, one aggressively ambitious and making a name for himself in public life, the other blithely apolitical and committed to a life of travel, adventure, and high living. The analogy wasn't perfect: Ted had lost the governorship of New York while Theodore had won it, and Kermit was far more successful in his various endeavors than Elliott had ever been. In addition to his thriving coffeehouse, Kermit had also launched the Roosevelt Steamship Company, an international freight concern with offices at 44 Beaver Street in New York City. Yet, personally, the comparison couldn't have been more exact. Ted abided by the same rigid moral code as his father, in business, politics, and sex; Kermit was a rogue who preferred knocking back whiskies at the club and flirting with pretty girls to debating politics or discussing policy, and if he could cut a deal on the side for some business venture without adhering to all the rules, he was glad to do it.

Like Elliott, too, Kermit had spent a lifetime in his older brother's shadow. It was Ted who'd come home from the war covered in ribbons and trailing clouds of glory; it was Ted who'd chased after elected office, emulating Theodore's career in the Assembly and in the navy. To avoid the inevitable comparisons, Kermit had largely kept his distance during his brother's rise, traveling the world and stalking wild beasts—the one way he knew to impress his father. Now that his father was gone, though, Kermit seemed to have embraced the bon vivant he was born to be.

Just as his uncle Elliott had done thirty years earlier, Kermit was demanding the right to make his own life choices, even when his family didn't approve. From his mother and siblings came much clucking over the way he and his wife, Belle, raised their children: in addition to Kim, Willard, and Clochette, a baby boy named Dirck had been born the previous January. Both parents were frequently absent from their children's lives. While Kermit was off globetrotting, Belle, one of New York's most prominent socialites, was busy with her clubs and functions. She was an heiress in her own right, with plenty of money, so a squadron of nursemaids and governesses was always around to keep an eye on the youngsters. Still, the lack of regular parental supervision led Edith and Kermit's younger brother Archie to intervene on occasion, spiriting the children away to Sagamore for a dose of discipline.

Kermit's diary would reveal just how frequently he stayed in the city, dining at the Knickerbocker and sleeping at his club,

instead of trekking out to Oyster Bay, where his family now resided. He was always restless, constantly on the hunt, even when
his guns were packed away and he was dressed in his finest
Oxford trousers and fashionable double-breasted waistcoats. Kermit's life, one friend thought, was "a work in progress"; he was
always searching for and assembling something new. If Ted was
the striver and Archie the loyal caretaker, then Kermit was the
romantic dreamer, just as he'd been as a little boy, sitting in the
windowsill and staring up in wonder at the moon.

Among his friends, he counted some of the most sparkling figures of the period. Backed up by saxophones and trumpets and
the sizzle of hot jazz, Kermit made his way through the salons
and speakeasies of the Roaring Twenties. He dined with novelist
Elinor Glyn, smoked cigars with Rudyard Kipling, read poetry
with Edwin Arlington Robinson, and drove popular comedian
Will Rogers out to Oyster Bay in his flashy blue roadster. His closest celebrity pal, though, was boxing promoter George L. "Tex"
Rickard, whose picaresque life, from prospecting for gold in
Alaska to running gambling houses in Nevada, appealed greatly
to Kermit. Rickard was one of the investors in Kermit's coffeehouse, and through him Kermit obtained tickets for all the biggest prizefights at Madison Square Garden. At restaurants, the
two men often shared a table, surrounded by pretty girls, most of
whom were very young, as per Rickard's taste.

That predilection got Rickard in trouble during the fall of 1921,
and put Kermit's reputation at risk as well. Alice Ruck, fifteen,
the daughter of a laundress, charged the promoter with sexual assault. The district attorney then located another girl, aged eleven,
who made a similar claim. Fearing what might come next, Rickard took two other young friends, ages twelve and fifteen, for a
ride around the city, threatening them with reform school if they
spoke to the police. To further ensure the girls' silence, a third-
rate boxer named Nathan Podd kidnapped one of them, twelve-
year-old Nellie Gasko; she was found a couple of weeks later by
police and persuaded to bring charges against Rickard.

His trial, held in March 1922, brought out all the news photographers. A parade of witnesses was called to testify to Rickard's

character: the novelist Rex Beach, millionaire A. J. Drexel-Biddle, former Nevada governor Denver Dickerson. Yet the one whose photograph adorned many of the articles about the trial was Kermit. Teddy's famous adventurer son insisted on the stand that his pal Rickard was an honest man. Even as a gambler, Kermit said, Rickard made sure all his clients got a "square deal," a phrase strongly associated with his father. Indeed, Kermit made sure to tell the jury that Theodore had thought very highly of Rickard, though the judge ordered some of Kermit's comments about his illustrious parent stricken from the record.

Despite all the evidence against him—the precise consistency of the girls' stories and the flimsy alibi for his whereabouts on the night of one of the assaults—Rickard adamantly maintained his innocence. His lawyers claimed he was the victim of a "frame-up," though they offered no evidence of who might be doing the framing. As was the case in many similar trials of wealthy men accused of rape, some court watchers argued that the working-class victims were at least as culpable as the alleged perpetrator. All the accusers, they pointed out, came from desperately poor families; all admitted to accepting money and gifts from the promoter. Not yet was such victim blaming called out by the press.

Perhaps Kermit truly believed his friend wasn't guilty, or perhaps, like others, he felt Rickard's life shouldn't be ruined by a quartet of gold-digging girls, the daughters of illiterate immigrants from Poland and Germany. That seemed to be the jury's opinion. Largely on the strength of the testimony given by Kermit and the other celebrity witnesses, Rickard was acquitted. All further charges against him were dropped. The girls, against the pleas of their parents, were remanded to the Society for the Prevention of Cruelty to Children.

Rickard's career wasn't harmed by the scandal. Indeed, with Kermit on board as an investor, he'd announced plans to build a new Madison Square Garden at Fiftieth Street and Eighth Avenue, currently the site of old streetcar barns. The old Garden was set to be razed in the spring.

Lacking Ted's commitment to social justice, Kermit had little empathy for the sort of lives his friend's accusers lived. Martin

Gasko, the father of little Nellie, worked odd jobs as a concrete laborer and gardener to support his six children and pay the forty-five-dollar-a-month rent on their tenement apartment on West Eighth Street, in the Gravesend section of Brooklyn. Kermit, in contrast, left much of the running of his two businesses to others as he traipsed around the world shooting tigers. When he was actually in New York, he could be found most nights cheering ringside at high-profile prizefights. During his friend's trial, Kermit and Belle watched Harry Greb beat Tom Gibbons in fifteen exciting rounds at Madison Square Garden; their companions were Mr. and Mrs. Vincent Astor.

One comment Kermit had made at the trial was as telling about him as it was about Rickard. He was asked if anything could be inferred about Rickard's character since he had once run a gambling house. "A man who runs a gambling house," Kermit said, "isn't necessarily a bad character, anymore than a man who runs a church isn't necessarily a good character." Those same words might have served as a motto for his own life. Kermit disregarded convention and rejected old bromides. The trappings of society bored him: he preferred prizefights to horse shows and Broadway to Newport, and when his peers cheered on a yacht race, Kermit yawned. "I wish I cared for yachting," he wrote to a cousin. A generation earlier, a similar worldview had turned Elliott's family against him, but this was a new era: women wore their dresses above their knees and traveled unchaperoned with men in automobiles. Society wasn't as easily scandalized as it had been in 1891. Still, Kermit's family was wary of him. It was possible, they knew, for rule breaking to go too far.

Most of his family had invested money in Kermit's enterprises. Quite naturally, then, they took an interest in how things were run. Although the coffeehouse—now called the Double R, signifying the entrance of cousin Monroe Robinson to the venture—was always packed, no one had yet seen a dime from it. "The Coffee House, from all reports, seems to be making money hand over fist," Ted recorded in his diary. "However, I am always doubtful of it. It no sooner makes the money than it spends it, and after it spends the money, there is nothing to show for it." Nonetheless,

Kermit and his partners had opened another establishment, at 726 Lexington Avenue, and there would be still another one, at 11 South William Street. The original Double R was then leased for five thousand dollars a month under a different corporation, in order "to avoid excessive taxation," as Kermit explained to Ted, while their cousin Monroe launched a fourth coffeehouse, at 166 West Forty-Fifth Street. These technically separate operations all shared board members, including Kermit. It was a new world of conglomerates and subsidiaries that the trust-busting Theodore would have loathed.

Even greater ethical concerns were raised about the Roosevelt Steamship Company. Kermit had organized the business in late 1920, chartered under the more flexible laws of the state of Delaware. The business was incorporated with capital of one million dollars, much of it from Tex Rickard. Right from the start, Kermit relied heavily on his family's history of national service: "No vessel has a better right to fly the American flag than a Roosevelt boat," read the newspaper articles announcing the inaugural fleet. When Albert Lasker, chairman of the U.S. Shipping Board, embarked on a reform of the U.S. Mail Steamship Company, he found it expedient to hire ships belonging to the son of America's exalted former president Roosevelt, the name alone supposedly guaranteeing ethical standards.

Yet Kermit was a different sort of Roosevelt. He wasn't averse to using friends and family in high places to get what he wanted. He was frequently in touch with brother-in-law Nick Longworth, a member of the House Ways and Means Committee, to discuss trade bills and tariffs on fruit, iron ore, or South American beef— anything that might negatively affect Kermit's import business. In return, he made sure his brother-in-law got ringside seats for prizefights, including the "fight of the century," between Jack Dempsey and Georges Carpentier. Archie proved helpful as well. While still employed at Sinclair Oil, the youngest living Roosevelt brother was able to hire Kermit's ships to transport some of the company's oil. "That was grand of you," Kermit wrote his brother. Since then, Archie had become one of Kermit's partners in the shipping business.

It was only when he asked for help from Ted (he of the ironclad principles) that Kermit ran into conflict. In March 1923, Archie prevailed upon Ted, then still assistant secretary of the navy, to help the shipping company woo a Japanese steamship firm, Kokusai Kisen Kaisha. The agent, Takashi Komatsu, regarded their father highly for negotiating the peace after the Russo-Japanese War. "Like all Japanese," Archie wrote, "he is very proud of his acquaintance with our family. It is most desirable that all of us are very polite to this little bird." Archie asked Ted to meet with Komatsu and "flatter the little fellow to think that we are pleased to have Kermit in with him." Ted appeared reluctant about a meeting, but he did write to Komatsu, and several months later the press announced the partnership between the Roosevelt Steamship Company and Kokusai Kisen Kaisha. The alliance allowed Kermit to offer round-the-world freight service, and significantly boosted the company's stock.

The next time Kermit asked a favor, however, Ted was not as accommodating. Just before launching his bid for governor and in the last weeks of his navy position, Ted received a distressing phone call from his brother, pleading with him to meet with T. V. O'Connor, Lasker's successor on the Shipping Board, to pressure O'Connor into accepting a bid from the Roosevelt Steamship Company. Ted was infuriated. "He apparently totally failed to see the impropriety thereof," he wrote in his diary. "If Kermit can't see the impropriety, after what has happened this past winter [the Teapot Dome scandal] and after having been brought up in a family of politicians, you can't expect other people to see it. I am sorry to say that it comes down, I am afraid, to a question of self-interest."

Ted had good reason to be irked with his brother, but in his words echoed the indignation and sense of moral superiority that Theodore had felt over Elliott. This condescension came through to Kermit, who reacted with his own outrage. After stewing over Ted's refusal to help, he rang his brother again. Kermit, Ted wrote in his diary, was "totally unable to understand my point of view. . . . He feels that I have insulted him by doubting the propriety of the proposition he is making and refusing to back him."

In a huff, Kermit told Ted to forget the favor; he'd ask Nick for help instead. Yet Ted got to Nick before Kermit did, and Nick also turned down the younger Roosevelt brother. "His feelings were badly hurt," Alice told Ted afterward.

Kermit had in fact been nursing hurt feelings toward his family for years. They resented his independence, he believed. He was never a joiner, always missing in action during political campaigns dating back to their father's failed run in 1912. Unlike Alice, who coordinated every step of Ted's gubernatorial effort, and Archie and Ethel, who lent their support in the days leading up to the election, Kermit kept his distance from his brother. He did motor out to Oyster Bay to vote, and saw Ted for a few minutes to wish him well, but unlike the others, he didn't stick around for the returns to come in. Instead, according to his diary, he got the news at the opulent home of telegraph millionaire Clarence MacKay on East Seventy-Fifth Street. MacKay, a prominent Catholic layman, was almost certainly backing Al Smith; his children had publicly declared their support for the governor. So rather than consoling Ted with the family in Oyster Bay, Kermit spent the evening with supporters of his brother's opponent. He wrote dispassionately in his diary, "Gov. Smith defeated Ted. Coolidge walked in." Then he left on the midnight train for Boston.

Kermit simply did not care about the family sport of politics. The only political issue he ever really expressed an opinion about was the overthrow of Prohibition. When he attended a rally of the American Federation of Labor, it was only because Samuel Gompers was calling for an end to the law and a return of the right of every American to buy himself a drink.

Soon after finishing his lectures in Chicago, kissing pretty girls on their proffered hands and making sure they got his card, Kermit headed to Washington. At the State Department, whose offices at the time were right across the street from the White House, Kermit's former home, he secured the paperwork for his trip to Asia. As a reporter watched, Kermit's sister Alice pulled up in her car to meet him so he could see his new niece. Leaning over the backseat of Alice's car, Kermit laid his eyes on baby Paulina, swaddled in a market basket that her mother joked to the reporter had set her back sixty-five cents. Unlike others in the family, Kermit had been delighted when Alice announced she was pregnant: "That is the most amazing news about Sister," he told his wife, Belle. He seemed unaware that Paulina wasn't Nick's child—or, if he had any inkling of the truth, it didn't matter to him.

That spring of 1925, what mattered most to Kermit was to repair the relationship with Ted. A journey into wild, unknown lands, he expected, would do the trick, just as the adventures he'd taken with his father had bonded the two of them. Yet the troubles between the brothers ran deep. After their argument the previous summer, Ted had written in his diary, "The real problem, I think, with Kermit was that he felt I was not interested in his work." That, indeed, was the crux of their problem, and had been so all their lives. No matter what Kermit did, no matter how much attention he got (whether on the football field at Harvard, on the battlefronts during the war, or in the competitive world of business), it was always Ted whom people took more seriously. Even their father, despite the closeness Kermit felt to him, had always looked to Ted as the leader, as the achiever in the family. Getting elected to high public office, maybe one day the highest office in the land, was always going to mean more than anything Kermit could do, no matter how many coffeehouses he ran or how many ships he sent around the world. And when Kermit sensed Ted's disinterest in his work, he took it as condescension.

Not without reason, either. As Ted wrote in his diary after patching things up with Kermit, he found his brother once more "as delightful and inconsequential as ever." *As inconsequential*: Like Elliott before him, Kermit was weary of his family not valuing the choices he had made in his life. Yet it seemed he was always giving them reasons to judge, as developments late that fall of 1924 proved.

On November 23, Kermit was named as a defendant, along with Tex Rickard, in a lawsuit filed by a representative of the government of Guatemala. The Roosevelt Steamship Company was charged with reneging on a contract for an oil concession, an agreement that stemmed back to Archie's time at Sinclair Oil. Just when they thought they were past it, Kermit's business practices had summoned back the specter of Teapot Dome to haunt the family. Lawyers got to work building a defense, but it was clear that a case of this magnitude, involving a sovereign nation, would not go away anytime soon.

It was in this atmosphere filled with tensions and misgivings that Kermit and Ted embarked for Asia, when one point of conflict perhaps loomed larger than the rest. Kermit had always been more cordial with Franklin than his siblings were. Yet, over the past year, a closer friendship had blossomed. Franklin had written a letter to the *New York Times* raising concern over the financial loss incurred by the government each year with its shipping fleet. Kermit, ever hopeful for more government leasing of private ships like his own, immediately wrote to Franklin suggesting they team up on a campaign to boost the U.S. Merchant Marine. His cousin had been receptive to the idea. "I wish you would run in and see me," Franklin wrote back, advising Kermit to call ahead so that he could shoo the politicians out of his office.

Of course, for Ted, for Alice (for all of Oyster Bay, including Kermit's mother, who doted on him), such a partnership would be akin to collaborating with the enemy. Lawsuits, influence peddling, and improper favors on Kermit's part could all be managed—but an alliance with Franklin?

That would be unforgivable.

PART VII

THE FUTURE AND
THE PAST

1932

QUEENS, NEW YORK

Like machine-gun fire, a heavy rain assaulted the iron framework of the Queensboro elevated station on the evening of November 9. Passengers returning from their jobs in Manhattan stepped off the train, popping open a battalion of umbrellas before rushing headfirst into the storm. By the time they got home, they were wet and tired. But they were the lucky ones. They still had jobs. All around them on the streets, they passed the unemployed, panhandling for coins in the rain.

The day before, a new president had been elected who promised to get America working again. "These unhappy times," he had said during his campaign, "call for the building of plans from the bottom up and not from the top down, that put their faith once more in the forgotten man at the bottom of the economic pyramid."

One of those workers heading home from the train station that night had followed the presidential election with keen personal interest. Elliott Roosevelt Mann was no longer at the bottom of the pyramid. He'd worked hard to get ahead, to buy a neat, comfortable home for his family at 88–79 Commonwealth Boulevard, valued at $7,500 in the 1930 census. The nation might have been enduring the worst of times, engulfed by what economists were already calling the Great Depression, but Elliott had held on to his job in the midst of it and had even been promoted yet again. He'd been on the bottom once, however. He knew all too well what it meant to be a forgotten man.

Once at home, Elliott settled into his chair to wait for dinner, opening the newspaper his family remembered he always brought from the city. On this night the headlines were enormous. ROOSEVELT WINNER IN LANDSLIDE! DEMOCRATS CARRY 40 STATES. ELECTORAL VOTES 448. Inside the paper, there was a photograph of the president-elect and his tall, beaming wife, Elliott's sister Eleanor.

Elliott hadn't voted for Franklin Roosevelt. At least, his family would never believe he did. He was a loyal Republican. Most of the men he worked with at the bank were also Republicans, and while the bank hadn't taken an official position on the presidential race, many of the bigwigs had actively campaigned for local Republican candidates. Yet nearly every Republican had been beaten in the Democratic landslide. After twelve years of Republican rule, the nation had woken up this morning to a brand-new world.

Elliott had done all right in the old one, however. Now forty-one years old, he was a firm believer in hard work and self-sufficiency. The kind of government programs the Democrats were talking about could easily turn into perpetual handouts, he felt, destroying any motivation for people actually to work for a living. That way of thinking went against everything Elliott had built his life on. Against the greatest of odds, he'd made something of himself. Not a single cent had he received from his father's family. In fact, he'd never accepted a handout from anybody, growing up with only his own (and his mother's) determination to succeed.

And succeed he had. Five years earlier, he had packed up his family and moved from Brooklyn to Queens. For many upwardly mobile New York families in the mid- to late 1920s, this was the pathway to a better life. Developers in Queens could barely keep up with the demand for middle-class residential lots, most of them offering small, private yards. Paraphrasing Horace Greeley, county judge Frank Adel had marketed the area: "Come east, young man, to Queens, the borough of opportunity, the gateway to the sunrise homeland. Here you can establish your home or business among pleasant, healthful surroundings and, as Mr. Greeley said, 'grow up with the country.'" Adel praised the borough's schools, the modern buildings, the fine stores and theaters, and the chance to know one's neighbors. In Manhattan, there were 137 persons per acre; in Brooklyn, that number was 42; in Queens, it was only 9. Elliott had given his family room to breathe and grow.

In the Bellerose area he'd chosen, the streets were quiet and tree-lined. The newly built homes still smelled of fresh-cut wood. They were fitted with the latest indoor plumbing and electrical fixtures. While the train made the city easy to reach, Bellerose retained the sense of being a part of Long Island: lots of trees, lots of sky, easy access to the beach. For Elliott, the area may have held a more ironic appeal. The home he purchased was just six miles away from his father's former sprawling estate at Hempstead, and just nineteen miles from Sagamore Hill, the heritage he had been denied.

Some of those who had bought homes in Bellerose before the stock market crash of 1929 were now facing foreclosures; on Elliott's block alone there were five. Because Elliot worked for the bank, his mortgage was safe. He'd also, quite fortuitously, left the now-struggling National Bank of Commerce for Chase National, one of the largest and most stable banks in America. At Chase's main building, at 18 Pine Street in downtown Manhattan, he worked as an auditor. His keen mathematical mind and efficient record keeping impressed his new employers as much as they had his last. No doubt Elliott's bosses were surprised when they learned their crackerjack auditor had only an eighth-grade education. Elliott was living proof of the American dream.

As he sat reading his paper in the evenings after work, his little house was usually filled with the aroma of pinkelwurst, kale, and boiled potatoes, his family remembered, being cooked on the stove by his wife, Lena. Elliott's mother no longer lived with them, having remained behind in Brooklyn, but she often visited on Sundays. As fiercely independent as always, Katie continued to take in work as a seamstress.

There were new members of Elliott's family now. After eleven years of marriage, he and Lena had two daughters. Mildred was eight, born with a curvature of the spine that made sitting and walking difficult. Her parents had tried using a brace to correct the problem (no small expense), but the device proved too uncomfortable for the little girl to tolerate. Not until much later would Elliott discover that Millie suffered from a condition similar to his Auntie Bye's; nor did he know that his sister, Eleanor, and his cousin Alice had been born with less extreme bone conditions, and that they had benefited greatly from more advanced braces, equipment that was surely far beyond Elliott's financial means. Millie would have to endure her condition for the rest of her life.

Elliott's second daughter was five. Unlike her sister, this little girl was a bundle of energy, running up and down the stairs and into the yard. Already a charmer, she had blonde hair and hazel eyes. Elliott had named her Eleanor, after his sister.

He hadn't voted for Franklin, but he respected Franklin's wife a great deal. Over the past few years, Elliott had followed Eleanor's emerging public persona in the newspapers. He'd seen the photographs of her at political conventions. He'd taken great interest in Eleanor's calls for equal treatment for women. What she was proposing, Elliott realized, would make his daughters' lives better. He grew to admire his sister very much—and now his sister was about to become First Lady of the United States.

Only his wife, his mother, and his mother's brothers' families knew Elliott's secret. He'd been hiding the truth of who he was all his life, and he was tired of it. For his own children's sake, he wanted some acknowledgment of where he'd come from. Not public acknowledgement, of course: he knew the damages the stain of illegitimacy could cause, not only to the new First Lady but also to him and his children. Yet, privately, Elliott wanted some understanding, some closure—an end to the secrets. His daughters' aunt was going to live in the White House. Little Mildred and Eleanor should know the truth of their family heritage, and their cousins should know them. After four decades, Elliott decided the time had come to act.

On November 26, a Saturday, he sat down at his desk and composed his thoughts. On a piece of paper marked MEMORANDUM (likely a sheet he used at the bank), he drafted a letter, doing his best to adhere to proper letter-writing style and the correct forms of address. "To the Honorable Mrs. Franklin D. Roosevelt," he wrote. His spelling and grammar were not always perfect, but his penmanship was neat. "In behalf of mother and myself I wish to convey our most sincere good wishes and congratulations for the esteemed honor conferred upon you as the 'First Lady of the Land.' May you long cherish and enjoy this great privilege bestowed upon you by the citizenry of this country."

The next few lines were more difficult to write. Elliott scratched words out and inserted others. He needed to let Eleanor know who he was without saying too much; he did not want to embarrass her if the letter were seen by the wrong eyes. He told her about the photograph his mother possessed from "many years past," which Eleanor had "so kindly sent to her as a gift of remembrance" from Bad Reichenhall, Germany. "Mother informs me that she was known as 'Katie' in your parents' household," Elliott wrote, hoping that this would be enough to jog Eleanor's memory. A closing line identifying his daughters, including the one he'd named Eleanor, was reconsidered and crossed out. Elliott signed the letter, "Yours very respectfully, Elliott Roosevelt Mann."

He copied the draft onto more formal stationery. As he did so, he apparently decided that one more detail was needed. In case it wasn't obvious, he told Eleanor that he'd been named for her father. Then he sealed the envelope, affixed a stamp, took it to the post office, and waited for a reply.

>——<

Elliott's letter, of course, was just one of thousands pouring in to Eleanor and Franklin that month. Overnight, their lives had been transformed. The nation now looked to Franklin to solve its overwhelming problems. Will Hays, former Republican National Committee chairman and now head of the Motion Picture Producers and Distributors of America, observed that the public looked at the new president "as a drowning man looks at a life saver . . . one eye on him and one eye on God." The pressures on Franklin to succeed were enormous.

The president-elect felt up to the task. He had triumphed over the odds before. He'd achieved his dream to be president at last, a goal whose realization he and many others had begun to doubt a decade earlier as he struggled through the first difficult stages of his polio. Yet even in braces and a wheelchair, Franklin had done what Ted could not: he'd won the governorship of New York and pivoted from there to a successful bid for the White House.

Franklin had waited until 1928 to make his move; when encouraged to try for the Senate in 1926, he demurred: "Not until I can throw away my props. Not until I can stand upon my own legs." Two years later, he still wasn't quite able to stand on them, but he decided the time had finally come. For both his successful campaigns, for governor in 1928 and president in 1932, the crafty Louis Howe made sure the candidate was always carefully propped at a lectern or at the back of a train; only a rare few ever saw Franklin hobble along on his crutches. Candid photographs of the candidate were discouraged, an agreement the newspapers largely respected. To make up for that, Howe provided the press with photographs from the campaign trail: Franklin standing with his family or driving his car, with the hand controls discreetly hidden.

As governor, Franklin had responded to the Depression with a rousing, unapologetic resurgence of progressivism: "Progressive government by its very terms must be a living and growing thing . . . If we let up for one single moment or one single year, not merely do we stand still but we fall back in the march of civilization." State assistance was provided to beleaguered farms and families, and New Yorkers approved of their governor as a strong, dynamic leader. His polio seemed almost forgotten—but would the nation at large react the same when he ran for president?

To reassure any doubts about Franklin's vitality, his old friend and navy superior Josephus Daniels penned an article for the *Saturday Evening Post* in September 1932, at the outset of the presidential campaign. "The fact that conservative and nonpolitical life insurance executives," Daniels wrote, "after thorough examination by medical experts, insured his life for $500,000, thus demonstrates by the highest testimony that physically he is sound."

While not perceived as cured, Franklin was generally regarded by his physicians as having overcome the worst of his disability; his foundation of the Warm Springs Rehabilitation Institute for other polio sufferers seemed to be evidence that the therapy he'd undergone worked. In fact, Franklin could get around only moderately better than he could a decade earlier; what the springs had done was strengthen his upper body and, more important, his spirit.

For it was that indomitable spirit, that can-do attitude, that drew such large crowds to hear him speak during the campaign and that had changed so many minds about what government could, and *should*, do for its citizens. It was the campaign Theodore had tried in 1912 but had failed to sell. Progressivism had largely fallen into disfavor during four consecutive Republican administrations; private enterprise was seen as the means to address social problems. Franklin predicted that the public would tire of such rigid conservatism; they did, eventually, but it took a while. With the economy still booming, voters in 1928 had elected yet another Republican, Herbert Hoover, as president; Franklin had been wise to set his sights on the governorship before the presidency. Yet after the stock market crashed and the economy imploded, Americans were desperate and clamoring for their government to help them.

The misery in the country was unprecedented. Nearly a quarter of the workforce was unemployed; savings had been wiped out; thousands of family farms suffered foreclosures. Meanwhile, President Hoover remained ideologically opposed to government relief programs, a position that ended up sealing his doom, especially as Franklin barnstormed the country promising aggressive assistance of the kind he'd supported in New York. In his inaugural address as governor three years earlier, Franklin had articulated his vision for America: "To secure more of life's pleasures for the farmer; to guard the toilers in the factories and to insure them a fair wage and protection from the dangers of their trades; to compensate them by adequate insurance for injuries received while working for us; to open the doors of knowledge to their children more widely; to aid those who are crippled or ill; to pursue with strict justice all evil persons who prey upon their fellow men; and at the same time, by intelligent and helpful sympathy, to lead wrongdoers into right paths."

It was, in essence, Theodore's vision of a progressive utopia warmed up for a new generation. Disillusioned by twelve years of free-market conservatism that had failed to protect them from the Depression, voters were once again receptive to the Democrats' vision. Franklin restored the moribund Progressive brand, made it a viable force in American politics again—and as before, he wasn't shy about using one of the best tools in his arsenal: invoking the name of his revered predecessor. When people shouted, "I loved your father!" Franklin rarely corrected them, and once again

Oyster Bay seethed. "I do see how annoying it must be to have people saying and thinking Franklin is a near relation of Uncle Ted's," Eleanor admitted to Aunt Corinne. But, she added, "I do hope they realize we personally never sail under false colors."

They realized no such thing. The bitterness between the two sides of the family calcified as the returns came pouring in on Election Night. Franklin won the White House by some seven million votes. He had stolen, his cousins believed, what was rightfully Ted's. They would never forgive him.

>---->

At the time of Franklin's election, Ted was serving as the governor-general of the Philippines, a position he had been pleased to accept when President Hoover offered it to him less than a year earlier. (That it was his sister Alice's name, and not his, first mentioned for the post was a slight that he swallowed; he had experience, after all, with swallowing slights.) "I had a letter from Ted yesterday written on the steamer," Kermit reported to Ethel during their brother's voyage to the islands. "Naturally he was thrilled and said that he couldn't believe he was actually on the way." The Philippines had been won from Spain during the war of 1898, the conflict Ted's father would forever personify; Theodore established a military base there in 1901, launching a new imperial thrust in American foreign policy. For Ted, then, getting the Philippines was compensation for his loss of New York.

His bruising defeat left him gun-shy about undertaking another political campaign, though neither he nor Alice entirely gave up hope. In the fall of 1927, Ted commissioned a report on what went wrong in his 1924 campaign, with an eye to doing things differently in the next election. Evidence was uncovered that in certain districts, the total population (as reported by the 1925 state census) "was less than the total number of votes cast in 1924," suggesting that Ted's wife might have been right in her belief that the election was stolen by Tammany. The report concluded that if Ted were to run again, he'd need to insist on voting machines, so the tabulation of ballots couldn't be tampered with, and to examine each and every election official to ensure he wasn't in collusion with Tammany.

Yet corruption was hard to prove, and old nagging self-doubts likely influenced his decision not to seek another shot at the governorship. Another loss at the hands of the voters would have been devastating. Ted figured there were other routes to the White House. In 1929 he was appointed by Hoover as governor of Puerto Rico; that gave him the executive experience he needed. Still, the real prize was the Philippines. If he could excel at governing the islands, he could cast his eye confidently on 1936. Under this plan, his patron, President Hoover, would serve out his second term and Ted could claim to be his successor.

Yet Franklin, as ever, had gotten in the way. First, he ran for governor once it was clear Ted wouldn't be a candidate. Then he ran for president, getting a jump on Ted by four years. Ted felt blindsided and frustrated. "Ted always felt that Franklin was getting everything he was entitled to," his cousin Sheffield Cowles observed. Yet the Depression had fundamentally altered the political calculus: Franklin's progressivism suddenly made him the ideal candidate that campaign season. Even before any votes were cast, most political observers felt certain he'd trounce Hoover. Also, even if he only moderately improved the economy, Franklin would prove a formidable opponent for Ted to beat in 1936.

Far away in boiling-hot Baguio City, as ceiling fans clattered in constant rotation and the palm trees outside the governor's white Spanish Colonial mansion dripped with humidity, Ted finally accepted the cold truth that he would never be president. His Philippine post would be his apogee. Just as he'd failed to make the varsity team at Harvard, he simply wasn't good enough to go all the way to another white mansion eight thousand miles across an ocean and a continent away, in Washington, DC. That fall, he wrote to his mother to say that he'd reached the end of his political career; he'd done his best, he told her, and his governorships of Puerto Rico and the Philippines had given him "enough in the way of accomplishments" to leave to his children.

If Ted was willing to step off the seesaw he'd shared with

Franklin these past two decades, however, Alice did her best not to let him.

><———<

In Washington, Alice Longworth paced the parquetry floors of her house on Massachusetts Avenue, stopping only when her phone rang, to fret, plot, and commiserate with likeminded partisans who were "similarly shaken by the dramatic shift in the political landscape," as a newspaper reporter observed. In the weeks leading up to the election, Alice had been a bundle of nervous energy, increasingly distraught at the idea of Franklin claiming the brass ring they'd all been vying for. If he won, she would lose all her relevance. Nick was dead, succumbing to pneumonia the year before at the home of one of his mistresses. The bitterness between husband and wife had mostly evaporated, replaced by benign indifference; Alice had been grateful at least for Nick's embrace of Paulina. The worst effect of his death, in fact, was her own diminution: she'd already lost her status as Speaker's wife when the Democrats won control of the House in 1930, but with Nick's death, she lost any chance of ever reclaiming it. Franklin's forthcoming presidency, of course, only made Alice's irrelevance complete.

Life as a Washington powerbroker was the only life she knew. "She obviously liked being the daughter of a very popular President, the wife of a Speaker of the House, and the perennial belle of the Washington social scene," one friend said. Over the past three decades, Alice had created for herself a "unique vantage point . . . in the front row of the circus," and occupied that place "far longer than anyone else." Franklin's victory meant she'd have to move out of the front row and take a seat farther in back. That was something she could never abide.

So she'd thrown herself into the effort to keep Franklin from winning, even if she must have known, smart as she was, that it was all in vain. Although she would claim that she undertook her mission on account of her brother Ted, who'd been brought up by their father "to feel he must be in politics and carry on the tradition," she was really fighting for herself.

It was a matter of survival. By 1932, Alice was alone. Her relationship with Bill Borah had dimmed, partly because they hadn't wanted to give the gossips more fodder than they already had. ("What does the Longworths' new parquet floor have in common with their daughter?" one joke went. "There's not a bit of a 'nick' in either one.") But Bill was also older now, and far less influential. As a consequence, the ardor Alice used to feel for him had cooled. Ambition had been their aphrodisiac. Without it, as a couple, they withered away. By 1932, Bill was sixty-seven; Alice was forty-eight. In the end, the lover she once hoped would be president had proven simply not ambitious enough for her. "There was a withdrawn, rather secretive quality about him," she would say many years later, "which seemed to hold him back." Once again, all she had left was Ted. With Franklin's win, however, Ted had turned his back on electoral politics. Alice was adrift. What was a kingmaker without her king? She still never seemed to consider that she could have taken the lead on her own.

It could have happened if she'd let it. A year earlier, in 1931, Rep. William Williamson of South Dakota, responding to rumors that Vice President Charles Curtis might decline to seek reelection, floated Alice's name as Hoover's running mate. "The Alice Roosevelt Longworth boosters seem to think that she would add color and pep to the race," Williamson said. All at once, the capital was abuzz with the idea. "Ever since her husband died," one reporter for the Associated Press opined, "faint rumors have been heard his widow might run for the Senate or the House." That wasn't uncommon: half the women who had served in Congress over the past fifteen years had followed in the footsteps of a husband or father who served before them. Alice had acted as an unofficial campaign manager for one of them, Ruth Hanna McCormick.

Yet Alice wasn't being primed for Congress. Williamson wanted her higher than that: a heartbeat away from the presidency itself.

Eleven years after women gained the right to vote, Alice Roosevelt Longworth was the first woman to be seriously mentioned for a spot on a presidential ticket. The idea was taken seriously by the press and the public: she was considered as capable as, and perhaps more than, any other candidate. "Senators and other high officials cluster around her in the White House Blue Room during receptions," the *Boston Globe* reported. "She has displayed shrewd political sense in her comments and suggestions."

Yet before the idea of a female vice president (and, therefore, a female president) could get a serious hearing in the press, Alice withdrew her name. She did so for the same reason she'd rebuffed earlier efforts to appoint her Philippine governor-general or to persuade her to run for Nick's congressional seat. She was afraid. The capital's most ferocious wit was simply too terrified of speaking in public and debating her opponent to risk running for office. In private, she could argue her case brilliantly. In front of a group of people, though, she turned into a shy schoolgirl. Whatever old insecurities lurked in her subconscious rushed straight to the fore whenever she was on a stage.

She was also, as she pointed out, "never any good at remembering names, and that's fatal in politicians." Alice was unquestionably a master political strategist; she was *not*, however, a natural politician like her father, being neither warm nor congenial. She would have made "a rotten candidate," one reporter agreed. "She doesn't like people and she won't shake hands. Can you imagine Alice Longworth going around kissing babies?"

So, as Franklin's campaign had accelerated, Alice fell back on her brother as the only force able to prevent their "feather duster" cousin from winning the White House. She encouraged Ted to return from the Philippines and campaign against Franklin. President Hoover seconded her request, but Ted balked. "No previous American Governor General had ever left his post to take part in partisan politics," his wife, Eleanor, recalled. Ted knew such a move would not play well. The *New York Times* opined that Ted's return would merely "continue the political feud in the Roosevelt family." Another newspaper wrote, "Teddy . . . has tried to build up on his father's reputation and made a flop of everything he has undertaken in that direction." He was "a weak sister by comparison with his illustrious father and distinguished sixth cousin."

Stung by the backlash, Hoover told Ted to stay where he was. Instead, the Philippine governor general addressed the American public by radio, arguing that the country should not "be made a

At the start of her husband's political career, Eleanor played the dutiful wife, smiling at Franklin's side at campaign events. *(Franklin D. Roosevelt Presidential Library and Museum)*

Alice married the much older and ambitious congressman Nick Longworth of Ohio. She intended for him to become Speaker of the House—and maybe president. *(TR Center, Dickinson State University)*

Alice's real love, however, was Senator William Borah, and their affair was an open secret in Washington. *(Author collection)*

Theodore's 1912 comeback was sidelined briefly by the bullet of a would-be assassin. *(TR Center, Dickinson State University)*

Ted proved his leadership skills in World War I—talents not seen as readily in politics or business. *(TR Center, Dickinson State University)*

Eleanor and Franklin with their two eldest children, James and Anna. *(Franklin D. Roosevelt Presidential Library and Museum)*

Theodore wrote that he was still as much in love with his wife, Edith, at age sixty as he was thirty years earlier. *(Author collection)*

Elliott Mann, looking remarkably like his father (inset), married Lena Prigge in 1921. *(From the collection of the Biles family / Franklin D. Roosevelt Presidential Library and Museum)*

The Crown Prince
of Sagamore Hill
and his family: Ted,
Thedore IV, Cornelius,
Eleanor, and Grace.
(TR Center, Dickinson
State University

Intelligent, capable,
and deeply honorable,
Ted spent his life
trying to fill his
father's extraordinarily
large shoes.
(Author collection)

Alice and her daughter, Paulina. Insiders knew the father was Borah, not Longworth. *(Author collection)*

Kermit was the handsome, adventurous brother whose safaris in Africa and hunting trips across Asia made him a popular lecturer. *(Author collection)*

Mrs. Franklin D. Roosevelt

INTERNATIONAL PHOTO

ife of the Democratic nominee for the Vice-Presidency, long has been popular in Washington society.

Eleanor was still looking down in photographs (and had encouraged her daughter to do the same) by the time Franklin ran for vice president in 1920. *(Franklin D. Roosevelt Presidential Library and Museum)*

During the 1920 campaign, she was sold as a fashionable society wife, an image that never quite took hold. *(Author collection)*

Lucy Mercer's affair with Franklin changed Eleanor's life and her view of herself, her marriage, and her world. *(Author collection)*

By 1924 Eleanor was a different woman, confident and outspoken, thanks in large part to the friendship of Marion Dickerman and Nancy Cook. *(Franklin D. Roosevelt Presidential Library and Museum)*

Franklin and Eleanor in the White House. They changed all the rules. *(Franklin D. Roosevelt Presidential Library and Museum)*

Franklin with two of his most important advisers: his political guru, Louis Howe, to his right, and Nancy Cook, to his left, who eventually became closer to him than to Eleanor. *(Franklin D. Roosevelt Presidential Library and Museum)*

Franklin was always careful never to appear unsteady on his feet, but someone was always holding on to him, in this case Eleanor. Behind them is Earl Miller, with whom Eleanor developed an intense friendship. *(Franklin D. Roosevelt Presidential Library and Museum)*

THE GREAT IMPERSONATOR

F.D.R. LIKENED TO T.R. AT OPENING OF ROOSEVELT MEMORIAL.

F.D.R. LIKENED TO ANDREW JACKSON AT JACKSON DAY DINNER.

Franklin's Oyster Bay cousins accused him of being an unsuccessful imitator and false heir to Theodore. *(Author collection)*

LEFT: Lorena "Hick" Hickok helped create the "personage" of Eleanor Roosevelt, but said she preferred the "person." *(Author collection)* RIGHT: Eleanor at the river at Val-Kill with Missy Le Hand, Franklin's secretary and intimate companion. For a while they all maintained a very enlightened, sophisticated, alternative family. *(Author collection)*

The new First Family in 1932. Back row: Franklin Junior; James; John; and Anna's first husband, Curtis Dall. Front row: Franklin, Eleanor with granddaughter Sistie Dall, Anna with son Buzzie Dall, and Sara. Missing: Elliott. *(Franklin D. Roosevelt Presidential Library and Museum)*

Elliott Mann's rise from poverty to a solid middle-class life in Queens was as remarkable as any of his cousins' achievements. *(From the collection of the Biles family)*

Elliott named his daughter Eleanor after the sister he never got the chance to meet but much admired. *(From the collection of the Biles family)*

After a lifetime of disappointments and near-misses, Ted became a hero at Normandy in World War II. *(TR Center, Dickinson State University)*

Kermit looked to the military at the end to provide some discipline and order in his life. *(TR Center, Dickinson State University)*

Once touted as the nation's first vice presidential candidate, Alice became a newspaper columnist and cigarette pitchwoman in the 1930s.
(Author collection)

Alice Roosevelt Longworth

tells how Senators choose a light smoke…
considerate of their throats

"*I often lunch in the Senate restaurant at the Capitol. Nearly every Senator and Representative there smokes, and the number I see take out a package of Luckies is quite surprising. Perhaps surprising is not the word. Because off and on, ever since 1917, I myself have used Luckies for this sound reason: They really are a light smoke— kind to the throat. It's simply common sense that these Senators and Representatives, whose voices must meet the continuous strain of public speaking, should also need a cigarette that is considerate of their throats . . . a light smoke.*"

Alice Roosevelt Longworth

In a recent independent survey, an overwhelming majority of lawyers, doctors, lecturers, scientists, etc., who said they smoked cigarettes, expressed their personal preference for a light smoke.

Mrs. Longworth's statement verifies the wisdom of this preference and so do leading artists of radio, stage, screen and opera, whose voices are their fortunes, and who choose Luckies, a light smoke. You, too, can have the throat protection of Luckies—a light smoke, free of certain harsh irritants removed by the exclusive process "It's Toasted". Luckies are gentle on your throat.

THE FINEST TOBACCOS—
"THE CREAM OF THE CROP"

A Light Smoke
"It's Toasted"–Your Throat Protection
AGAINST IRRITATION–AGAINST COUGH

Elliott Roosevelt Mann with his granddaughter Debra in 1961.
(From the collection of the Biles family)

Eleanor's apotheosis as "the mother of us all" and "First Lady of the world." *(Author collection)*

laboratory for wholesale experiments in government ownerships, tariff tinkering or currency inflation." He ended with a rousing admonition to reelect Herbert Hoover. Few took his advice.

The bitterness was now pervasive throughout Oyster Bay. The *Saturday Evening Post* article by Josephus Daniels particularly incensed Ted's wife, Eleanor. "Did you see Dear Cousin Franklin's attack on Father in the *Saturday Evening Post*, via Josephine Daniels?" she wrote to her son Cornelius, who, like so many other Roosevelt boys, was now attending Groton. Eleanor's slur on Daniels referenced the navy scandal in which he and Franklin were accused of protecting homosexual employees. What really set Eleanor off was Daniels's assertion that under Ted's leadership, morale in the navy had plummeted. "I can't understand their attitude," Eleanor told her son. "First they say they are blood brothers, then they insinuate a family row in such shocking bad taste, then they turn around and are the ones to make the most nasty and vicious remarks." She expected Ted would be relieved of his Philippine post "just as soon as Dear Cousin Franklin can get around to it." When that happened, she said, they were planning "to go home the other way around," which would keep them away "until well along in the summer." That would allow them, thankfully, to miss all the postinauguration hoopla.

"Dear Cousin Franklin" was how Ted's wife would henceforth refer to the new president; she took to abbreviating it in her letters. "Well, the election certainly was decisive," she wrote to Cornelius. "I thought of the excitement at Groton, as of course D.C.F. is the first Groton boy to be President, and I knew it must have been rather annoying to you. The thing I am afraid of is that business will gradually improve, and that D.C.F. will get all the credit when it was really Hoover who was responsible for starting the machinery working."

Franklin had not yet officially announced whether he'd ask Ted to stay on in the Philippines, though few expected him to do so. Asked by a reporter just how he was related to the new president, Ted sardonically replied, "Fifth cousin about to be removed."

Back in Washington, Alice had fallen into an uncharacteristic silence. For days after the election, the Longworth house on Massachusetts Avenue was dark. Barricaded inside, Alice could not have helped hearing the all-night parties that went on for days in the neighborhood. Bootleg whisky suddenly flowed freely, since the new president had given every sign that he would seek the repeal of Prohibition.

The world was changing, and for no one more than Alice. The new elites scorned her; even her old friendly rival Cissy Patterson, now the editor of the *Washington Herald*, had felt the shift in the wind and enthusiastically endorsed Franklin. In the nation's capital, "a decided change" was coming, one society columnist predicted. Franklin would be sworn in on March 4, 1933, and "Alice Roosevelt Longworth will disappear from the picture." Alice and her family, another columnist reported, were "going into decline." The long reign of Princess Alice was over.

How Alice hated to lose. Right before the election, she'd endured one final humiliation. An item in several foreign newspapers read, "If Mr. Roosevelt wins the election it will be owing largely to the merits of his wife, who is known in America as the Princess Alice. She is not only the daughter of the former President, but she is also the wife of the Democratic candidate this year. Her life ambition is to return to the White House as First Lady of the land." To be confused with Eleanor was likely the final straw for Alice. She put away her poker chips, stopped inviting people in, and made no comment after the election, merely stewing by herself in the privacy of her house.

She'd never written the memoirs many had predicted; she would start on them now. The money she made might come in handy, as Nick had left her with some debt. As for politics, however, it seemed she was through. Some wondered if she would retreat into quiet private life, the way Auntie Bye had done. The announcement of Bye's death the previous year had been relegated to the inner pages of the newspapers. Had Bye died in her prime, when she was a Washington powerbroker, her obituary would have made the front page. Was Alice Roosevelt Longworth really ready to settle for page 19?

Not likely. For now, Alice fell silent. Yet no one truly expected her to stay that way. She needed attention almost as much as she needed air.

><

The celebrations continued. For the last two months of 1932, excitement about the new president bubbled over—in the streets, in the newspapers, on the radio, in movie newsreels. Hope and change were everywhere. Franklin was only the third Democrat to occupy the White House since the Civil War, when Lincoln made the GOP the party of most Americans living outside the Deep South. Yet America was a fundamentally different place now. The cities were largely immigrant and non-Protestant; African American voters were leaving the South and settling in the North and the West; and after two decades, women were finally achieving parity with men in the electorate. These new demographics skewed overwhelmingly Democratic. For those who had been shut out of the American Dream, or those who had come to this country looking for it, only to be stymied at every attempt to achieve it, Franklin's prescription to heal the country's problems gave them hope. For working-class, native-born Americans, too, who'd discovered the perilous lack of foundation beneath their dreams, Franklin seemed to have the answers. "As I see it," he said, "the object of government is the welfare of the people." He was not opposed to private initiative, the *New York Times* pointed out. Yet "in the event of a grave emergency," such as the Depression, "private initiative may not have the last word."

Franklin's theme song (craftily chosen by Louis Howe) was "Happy Days Are Here Again," and people truly believed they were—or, at least, that they were right around the corner.

One of those swept up in all the excitement was Kermit. After the election, he sent a note to Franklin. "I can say with absolute truth that although I have been a Republican all my life, I am tremendously relieved and pleased that you were elected," he wrote. Whether he had actually voted for him, however, Kermit didn't say. Still, over the past several years, he and Franklin had continued to be chummy. As governor of New York, Franklin had facilitated some meetings for Kermit, such as an introduction to Herbert Odell, another shipping magnate and the son of a previous governor of New York. Friendly notes and family memorabilia passed between them, and when Kermit's daughter, Clochette, was diagnosed with a mild case of polio in the mid-1920s, Franklin was extremely supportive and helpful. He'd kept in touch with the girl through the years. "I don't think anything has ever touched me more deeply than your visit to Clochette," Kermit's wife, Belle, wrote to the new president at one point. "It was really so kind and so imaginative and so unselfish—it's easy to understand your hold on the American public." The girl, Belle reported, had "improved steadily" since his visit. "It gave her a great lift."

The favors in fact went both ways. In 1931, Franklin's son Elliott, twenty years old, was working as a salesman for Albert Frank and Company, an advertising firm at 165 Broadway. Elliott had bucked family tradition and refused to attend Harvard, deciding to try business instead. So he approached "Cousin Kermit," who may have recognized a kindred independent spirit. Though he couldn't get out of the contract Roosevelt Shipping had with another advertising agency, Kermit did his best to give Elliott "a part of the account." As this would have been one of Elliott's first commissions for Albert Frank, Franklin was no doubt grateful for Kermit's efforts.

The friendship with Franklin, of course, deeply displeased Kermit's family. Kermit claimed to be apolitical, but his letters to Franklin suggest he wasn't quite as clueless about or indifferent to politics as he professed. In Franklin's new policies, Kermit evinced great interest, seeming to feel they might benefit his business, which had been hit hard by the Depression. Just six months after the stock market crash, he tried to expand his operations by acquiring the International Mercantile Marine Company, and two ships, the *Minnetonka* and the *Minnewaska*, previously part of the Atlantic Transport Line. For three decades, the ships had carried only first-class passengers. Kermit's plan was to refit them both, reduce the cost of fares, and increase the number of passengers. "The Roosevelt name certainly intends to be heard on the high seas," wrote Cousin Monroe, Kermit's partner in the coffeehouse business. Yet, just two years later, Kermit was making plans to scrap both ships. His business was in deep trouble. "Due to the lack of passengers and freight," he wrote Franklin, "we have been obliged to lay up many of our vessels, and it is all we can do to try to keep people who have been with us for years."

The coffeehouses, too, had gone under. Monroe, drinking heavily and cheating on his wife, had been unable to manage the various businesses. They were sold, and Monroe was committed for a time to the Battle Creek Sanitarium, in Michigan. The Roosevelt coffeehouses turned out to be a huge financial loss for all their investors.

Despite his financial worries, though, Kermit considered himself something of an expert on business, and he attempted to counsel the new president. "I believe that I can be of real service to you and this without pay and without a political job," he wrote to Franklin. His study of economics all over the globe had taught him that "trade and business activity is [sic] dependent not only on the basic supply of money but also on confidence and the velocity of credit." He believed that Franklin had discovered this "great truth" as well. In one letter to Franklin, Kermit included a brief outline of his economic theories. "If I can be of any service now or at any other time, I trust you will call upon me," he wrote. "You can trust me to keep my mouth shut and, as I said before, I don't want any pay or office." Among the policy papers authored by Kermit and sent to Franklin was one titled, "How to Raise Prices and Still Keep the Integrity of the Dollar."

Kermit was a shrewd operator. There had always been a bit of the huckster in him, ever since the days when he maneuvered himself out of the family scrambles or convinced his father to let him see the world instead of working on the 1912 campaign. No doubt he was sincere in offering Franklin his help, and certainly he was cheeky enough to believe he actually had something to offer. Yet he also knew that, while proclaiming he wanted no recognition or pay, a close, friendly, and seemingly mutual friendship with Franklin could only work to his benefit. Franklin had helped him out as governor, and now that he was going to be president, the possibilities were boundless.

Yet Franklin was even shrewder than his cousin. There was little that Kermit could offer the president of the United States in the way of business or advice. Personally, however, he could offer Franklin a great deal. Kermit's friendship was a way of politically embarrassing and perhaps, to a degree, neutralizing Franklin's Oyster Bay adversaries. So the president-elect decided to issue quite a high-profile invitation to his new best friend Kermit.

"Something to amuse you," Kermit wrote to Ted in the Philippines. He'd been invited by the millionaire playboy and philanthropist Vincent Astor to join him on board his yacht, the *Nourmahal*, for a Caribbean cruise the following February. That was neither amusing nor unusual: Astor was an old friend of Kermit's, and they often traveled together. What made the invitation significant was that Franklin would also be on board. The yacht trip was to be the president-elect's last holiday before assuming office in March. No doubt the newspapers would cover the excursion, and that was why Kermit was telling Ted about it ahead of time, trying earnestly to make it all appear very innocent and amusing.

Ted wasn't laughing. Kermit argued that it was too late for him to back out of the trip without looking "stupid." He tried to insist that the cruise would be "a little bit awkward," but concluded, with an unconvincing air of self-sacrifice, "I guess I can pull through." Likewise, to Edith, Kermit said that he wished Astor hadn't invited him. No one was buying his fabrications, however. Kermit was clearly thrilled to be included in the presidential party on board what the *New York Times* called a "super yacht . . . an ocean liner in miniature . . . the biggest and fastest ocean-going motor yacht ever built." Undoubtedly Kermit had known right from the start that Franklin would be there, as Astor had made it plain that they were sailing in honor of the new president.

Learning that Kermit would be on board, the newspapers proclaimed the end of the long family feud. ROOSEVELT ENDS ROOSEVELT ROW, read an item syndicated by the United Press: "Pres.-elect Franklin D. Roosevelt, announcing the guests who will accompany him on his vacation cruise, included in the list Kermit Roosevelt, son of 'T.R.' and brother of Theodore Roosevelt Jr., who once called Franklin Roosevelt a 'maverick.'" Another news item reported, "There has been no affection evident between the Republican Roosevelt line and the Democratic Roosevelts until now."

There still wasn't much affection. The feud had now escalated.

"I do not remember anything that hurt Ted as much as this," Ted's wife, Eleanor, would write at the bottom of Kermit's light-hearted, disingenuous letter explaining his part in the yacht trip. Vigilant about her husband's place in history, Eleanor was not about to let her brother-in-law's deceit go unchallenged for posterity. The brothers had grown close again over the last few years, ever since they returned from their hunt with several *Ovis poli* carcasses for the Field Museum. A second Asian hunting expedition was undertaken by them a few years later, during which they snared a giant panda and other exotic animals. Any problems between the two brothers seemed completely erased.

No longer. Kermit had accepted the invitation to the yacht knowing full well how his family would react. He'd agreed to go because it served his interests; his family's interests seemed irrelevant to him. Of course, he could have argued that it was time to let bygones be bygones; and if he'd been more political, he might have pointed out that Franklin intended to put in place many of the reforms Theodore had wanted to implement if he'd been elected in 1912. Still, too much water had flowed under the bridge for the Oyster Bay clan to respond to reason now. So they turned their backs on Kermit—much as Theodore had done to Elliott almost half a century earlier.

The rift was particularly hard on Edith, now a brittle seventy-one-year-old woman. Kermit had always been her favorite, her strange and different child. Now she hardened toward him. Visiting Ted in the Philippines before he vacated his post, she sat like a dowager queen in her chair during an official lunch at Malacañang Palace. When someone asked Ted why Kermit had accepted an invitation from Franklin, "the whole table stopped talking," as Eleanor Butler Roosevelt would remember. Then, "quick as light," Edith chimed in with a reply. "Because," the dowager said, "his mother was not there to forbid him!"

It wasn't just Kermit's association with Franklin that troubled the family. Kermit had always done things his own way, but over the last few years his behavior had become increasingly shady. The lawsuit brought by the Republic of Guatemala against him, Archie, and Tex Rickard had dragged on, with a judge finally ordering all three to stand trial. This was Kermit's worst fear: he'd hoped the judge would dismiss the case. Now he'd be forced to testify about the fifty thousand dollars he failed to pay Humberto Blanco-Fombona, a Guatemalan consul, for his efforts to "persuade the government of Guatemala to change its constitution in order to open large tracts to oil exploration," as the *Chicago Tribune* would report. They'd also have to reveal their connections to Sinclair Oil, the main villain of the Teapot Dome scandal. To avoid being put on the stand, Kermit and the others settled for an undisclosed amount. Yet the headlines had an effect. Kermit was seen as a wheeler and dealer in a family of straight shooters.

Strolling through the streets of Lenox Hill, as one newspaper would describe him, Kermit wore a pinstriped suit and a fedora. He sometimes flipped a coin in his right hand like George Raft in the movie *Scarface*. Kermit was forty-three, the age at which his father became president. He hadn't achieved anything in his career close to that, but while such a fact might torture Ted, the younger brother merely shrugged it off. He wasn't unhappy with his lot, even if his business was struggling; who wasn't finding it tough these days? Yet Kermit had friends in high places. He was going on a yachting trip with the soon-to-be president of the United States and some of their best, well-connected chums.

Kermit was part of a well-heeled, hard-drinking crowd that included Astor, the publisher Nelson Doubleday, the philanthropist William Rhinelander Stewart, and the financier Winthrop Aldrich, president and chairman of the board of Chase Manhattan Bank. The men met at a private club on Sixty-Second Street they called "the Room." Sometimes the members of the Room invited celebrity guests. There was the time the author Somerset Maugham kept them all on the edge of their seats with his tales of working as a secret agent during the Great War. Other nights were less high-minded. While "ladies should not be brought in as guests," Vincent Astor told Kermit, the prohibition extended only to "society ladies." Other sorts of ladies were permitted. The club had several rooms where its members could spend the night.

Kermit, not infrequently, availed himself of the privilege rather than walk the few blocks up to the house he shared with his wife and children on East Sixty-Ninth. Other nights, he hunkered down at the Knickerbocker. It was better, he seemed to reason, to pass the night elsewhere than to go home and risk the children smelling whisky on his breath or get a scolding from Belle. After eighteen years, Kermit's marriage was showing some strains. Although Belle was often at his side at prizefights and other events, she also increasingly busied herself with society balls and charity functions, occasions that bored Kermit to tears. In his letters to her, Belle remained Kermit's "darlingest Buddle," but they were growing apart, even as their younger children struggled with their father's absences.

For as long as Theodore had lived, Kermit mostly kept to the rules, but now he was testing the limits of his family's patience—to his peril. The Roosevelts' record was clear when it came to dissent within their ranks.

>——<

By agreeing to include Kermit on his yachting party, Franklin appeared willing, perhaps even keen, to antagonize his Oyster Bay relatives. Just what Eleanor thought about the situation, however, was not quite as apparent, but it seemed at least possible that she enjoyed watching them squirm.

For her, the last straw in her long, fraught relationship with her father's family had probably been Aunt Edith's behavior in the final days of the campaign. On Halloween night, Eleanor waited in a cab outside Madison Square Garden—the new one, on Eighth Avenue between Forty-Ninth and Fiftieth Streets, built by Tex Rickard—for a reporter friend, Lorena Hickok, who was inside covering a rally for Herbert Hoover. When Hickok at last slid into the backseat beside Eleanor, she asked, "What do you suppose your Aunt Edith did tonight?"

"I can't imagine," Eleanor replied.

"She introduced Herbert Hoover."

Eleanor grew quiet. "How very interesting" was all she said. Not yet did she know Hickok well enough to share any more with her than that.

In fact, she was stung. Later she would learn the details of her aunt's actions. Edith had known her appearance at the Garden would be major news. The former First Lady, the widow of the legendary "T.R.," was coming out of seclusion to speak to them this night. Edith's appearance had been kept secret until that day; Lorena Hickok had learned of it only at the last minute. "I shall never forget the murmur that ran through the crowd," Hickok recalled, "as Theodore Roosevelt's widow, dressed all in black, walked out on the rostrum and was introduced." Edith had to be introduced, Hickok explained, because she'd been out of the public eye so long that few recognized her anymore.

As the former First Lady ascended the podium, the band struck up "Auld Lang Syne." Edith's white hair caught the light and contrasted starkly with the solid blackness of her clothes. Her voice was so soft that few beyond the first couple of rows could hear her, but she drew applause when she lauded Hoover for the "sleepless nights he has spent in service of his country." Hickok thought the old woman made "an unforgettably dramatic picture as she stood there before that wildly cheering audience, gesturing with her black-gloved hands." In the end, Edith received "more applause than President Hoover." The aunt who had once deemed Eleanor not good enough to associate with her stepdaughter, Alice, now stood up in public to declare Eleanor's husband not good enough to be president.

Not all of Eleanor's family was against her. "You would of course have a perfect right to do anything you felt right," Eleanor wrote to Aunt Corinne that summer, "but I think it is 'swell' of you not to do it when all the rest of the family seem to feel so very much more active than usual." Corinne's neutrality wasn't due to any lack of coaxing from the other side, however. "Sometime I must tell you," she wrote to Sara, "of the endless offers of 'high jobs' I have had if I would only speak against Franklin. Oh, [politics] is a strange game."

Yet the long family contest seemed finally settled when, on the night of November 8, in the grand ballroom of the Biltmore Hotel in Manhattan, the results on the big board showed that Franklin had won, and by a large margin. Only Connecticut, Delaware, Maine, New Hampshire, Vermont, and Pennsylvania had gone for Hoover. The old days of quiet election nights, with the candidate at home receiving the returns with his family by telegraph after dinner, were dim memories of a quaint past. Now the giant board lit up as each state's results came in, transmitted by crackling radio reports. Cheers from the crowd filled the ballroom as all awaited the appearance of the president-elect and his family. Yet, until victory was absolutely certain, Franklin remained sequestered with a few close advisers.

For most of the night, Eleanor was at the house on Sixty-Fifth Street, hosting a small dinner party for some key supporters. She was edgy and uncomfortable. Her entire life was about to become very different, and suddenly she wasn't sure she was ready for it. When Lorena Hickok showed up, Eleanor seemed glad for a friendly face, greeting her friend at the door with a kiss. "It's good to have you around tonight, Hick," Eleanor said. Not until well into the evening did she head over to the Biltmore, accompanied by her son James's wife, Betsey. Eleanor, wearing a striking blue gown, waved nervously to the well-wishers. Soon afterward, her daughter, Anna, and son Elliott arrived, both in formal evening wear.

When, finally, Franklin emerged to bask in the roar of the crowd, holding tightly to the lectern and surrounded by his attractive children, people got their first good look at their new First Family. Thirty years earlier, Theodore's clan of rowdy youngsters boosted his popularity. Franklin's children were older— the youngest, John, was now sixteen, and three were already married—but they were tall and lithe, with movie-star good looks. Asked why the Oyster Bay branch so resented their Hyde Park cousins, Sara allegedly quipped, "I can't imagine, unless it's because we're better looking."

For Eleanor, the jitters she felt on election night only got worse over the next several weeks. What was going to happen to her privacy? Things had been bad enough as the governor's wife; now the eyes of the whole nation were upon her. She wasn't sure she could adjust to living in the public eye. "She likes to go places and hates being recognized," Hick wrote about her in an article soon after the election. "She does most of her walking alone. She spent a whole morning going about Chicago accompanied only by a couple of friends, and not a soul recognized her, although the night before she had ridden in a car behind her husband in one of the biggest parades the loop ever saw."

Such anonymity was going to be impossible now.

After Franklin was nominated back in July, panic set in for his wife. Over the last eight years, Eleanor had blossomed, creating for herself a fulfilling life and career outside her husband's influence. She did not want to give that life up now. The cottage built for her in 1924 to share with Nancy and Marion in the deep pine forest of Hyde Park had become the symbol of Eleanor's independence. The friends christened it Val-Kill, a name taken from the Dutch name for nearby Fall Kill Creek. Val-Kill was Eleanor's first home of her own.

During much of the 1920s, even during Franklin's time as governor of New York, Eleanor retreated to Val-Kill for rest and renewal. Her battered automobile would navigate along a dirt road beside a creek, crossing a rolling-log bridge to arrive at the small, double-chimney stone cottage. When Eleanor would step out of the car, greeted by Nancy and Marion, she could let down her guard and be herself in a way she couldn't anywhere else. At Val-Kill, she chopped her own wood, made her own meals. She took long hikes and refreshing swims. Although her husband and children visited her at Val-Kill, this was her refuge, a place where she and her friends set the pace and the rules. On the towels, linens, and tablecloths were embroidered the initials "E.M.N." Franklin called the place the ladies' "honeymoon cottage."

Sara, not surprisingly, disapproved of Eleanor's new home, and couldn't understand why her daughter-in-law preferred to live in "that hovel" rather than with her at Springwood, with all its comforts and luxury, attended to by servants. Yet Eleanor had long ago stopped caring what Sara thought.

At Val-Kill, Eleanor sat at her desk, which was piled high with papers and books, and edited the *Women's Democratic News*, a feminist journal that had achieved a wide readership. In another first, Eleanor was earning her own income, bringing in several thousand dollars annually by writing about women's issues for popular magazines. Other income-generating projects developed. In a second building on the property, Nancy built furniture, with the aid of local craftsmen, that was sold throughout the state of New York. Often "E.M.N." was engraved on the furniture. A visit to Val-Kill meant walking through a perennial carpet of sawdust, serenaded by the music of hammers and saws.

Another mark of Eleanor's new, independent life was the Todhunter School, at 66 East Eightieth Street in Manhattan, which the three Val-Kill partners had purchased together in 1927. Unlike most girls' schools of the era, the Todhunter program was college preparatory, with a rigorous academic curriculum, and drew from New York's most privileged families. Marion served as principal. Eleanor taught history, government, and literature classes; she was at the school Monday and Wednesday mornings and all day on Tuesdays. She wore a stately, dark red tailored gown with low-heeled oxfords, the same uniform the girls were required to wear.

Teaching invigorated Eleanor. For once, she was embarking on an enterprise dependent entirely on her own abilities. "It is the one thing that belongs to me," she told a reporter after a couple of years of teaching. Although she remained self-conscious about not having a college degree, she brought two decades of political activism and experience to her classes. For her first year of teaching, she took no salary, reasoning that she was on as much of a learning curve as her students.

She had become Mlle. Souvestre. Although Marion was the principal, and other teachers were popular as well, Eleanor personified the school. Girls flocked to sign up for her courses. She inspired them to strive for the same sort of independence she had found in her own life. Her lectures were warm and filled with passion, and they left their mark. One student would say, many years later, "I never forgot a damn thing she ever taught me."

Like Souvestre, Eleanor made no secret of her progressive

views. Among the exercises on her final exams were these: "List the ways in which your government touches your home. Do you know of any way the government protects women and children? What is the object today of inheritance, income and similar taxes? Why is there a struggle between capital and labor? How are Negroes excluded from voting in the South? Who is Mahatma Gandhi?"

Here was the dilemma Eleanor faced. Could she really give up the active, deeply satisfying, independent life she'd created for herself to live like a caged bird in the White House?

>——<

For Eleanor, the saving grace of the campaign had been the friendship of Lorena Hickok. If anyone could help her make it through the transition, it was Hick, a stout, cherub-faced, thirty-nine-year-old native of Wisconsin whose insight and sharp wit delighted everyone, especially Eleanor.

The friendship had blossomed in the fall of 1932, when they both accompanied Missy Le Hand to her mother's funeral in Potsdam, New York. Eleanor graciously allowed Missy to take the only drawing room compartment available, while she and Hick slept in a pair of lower berths elsewhere in the car. When Hick arose in the morning, the train had stopped at a station. "When I'd finished dressing," Hick recalled, "I found Mrs. Roosevelt seated, her berth made up for the day, and set out on Pullman towels on the seat opposite her were cardboard containers filled with coffee and orange juice and some rolls." Since there was no dining car on the train, Eleanor had gotten up early to buy some provisions at the station during the layover.

"I thought you'd like some breakfast," Eleanor told Hick. This was the wife of a candidate for president of the United States, running about on her own through a train station to buy breakfast for a reporter. Hick was touched.

Later that day, after the funeral, the two women drove up to the Canadian border to see the planned Saint Lawrence Seaway and then motored through upstate New York, chattering all the while. That night, back on the train, only one berth was available, so Eleanor gave it to Hick. She took a couch. "I'm longer than you are," she said, adding with a smile, "and not quite so broad!"

As it turned out, neither woman was sleepy. They stayed up late into the night getting to know each other. Outside, a steady rain beat against the windows as the train chugged back toward Manhattan. In the hushed, darkened train car, Eleanor found herself sharing her life story: her "strict grandmother," her "odd sort of childhood," her "first taste of freedom" at Allenswood, her work at the Rivington Street Settlement, the early years of her marriage. She disclosed to Hick how she'd "sit and listen by the hour, fascinated," as Franklin and Louis Howe and other politicians plotted strategy in another room. "But it never occurred to me to enter it," she told her new friend. When Hick asked if she could use what Eleanor had told her in an article, Eleanor smiled. "If you like," she said. "I trust you."

From that point on, the two women were inseparable. They made an odd-looking pair, Eleanor tall and slender, Hick short and plump. Certainly the worlds they came from couldn't have been more different. Hick was the eldest daughter of three of an itinerant farmworker, a cruel and violent man who could never hold a job for very long. Working as a teamster, he moved his family around Wisconsin, Minnesota, and South Dakota. After her mother died, Hick took off on her own; she was just fourteen. Working as a housemaid, she was able to finish high school only with the help of a cousin. Eventually she landed a job at the *Evening News* in Battle Creek, Michigan, earning seven dollars a week covering train arrivals and departures. That experience led to a position at the *Minneapolis Tribune*, where Hick managed to break out of the rigidly defined "woman's beat" to cover sports and politics. She won an Associated Press award for her articles about President Harding's funeral train.

In Minneapolis, Hick also fell in love. For eight years she maintained a relationship with another reporter, Ella Morse. The two women lived together, entertained together, and were acknowledged as a couple by their colleagues. When Hick was diagnosed with diabetes in 1926, she and Morse moved to San Francisco to simplify their lives; Hick planned to write a novel. Their idyll was shattered, however, when Hick discovered Morse's infidelity with an old boyfriend. Hick was heartbroken.

Although they came from very different social classes, Hick and Eleanor could relate when it came to the scars of betrayal and abandonment by family and loved ones. For both women, the heartbreak had changed their lives. Hick had gone on to her acclaimed career at the Associated Press. Eleanor had become an advocate for women. When the two of them met in late 1932, both had already remade their lives. Both, however, were also alone.

"Every woman," Eleanor wrote, "wants to be first to someone sometime in her life." For so long—since the early years of her marriage, really—Eleanor had not been first to anyone, and she had no one who was hers alone. Franklin had Missy, Nancy had Marion, Esther had Elizabeth, her children had their spouses or inamoratas. For a brief time, while Franklin was governor, Eleanor had turned to her bodyguard, the loyal, burly, plainspoken Earl Miller, for support and companionship. Earl had been devoted to her, calling Eleanor his "Lady." He believed she "would have made a better president" than Franklin because she had "a keener insight into what the people of the country needed." Earl's companionship empowered Eleanor for a while—but eventually, and reluctantly, they'd had to cool things down, since people were talking. It wasn't seemly for the wife of a presidential candidate to take off on motor trips with another man.

With Hick, however, there'd be no such talk. What possible objection could anyone have to two ladies spending time together?

Hick showed up just at the moment when Eleanor was feeling the most vulnerable: bereft of Earl, who'd recently married, and terrified about what might await her if Franklin won the White House. So when she kissed Hick on Election Night, and whispered that it was good to have her with her, she was being heartfelt. The fortuitous arrival of Hick in Eleanor's life gave her the courage to face the role of First Lady. As the weeks flew by, and they drew closer to Franklin's inauguration, Eleanor was far more grounded than she had been, readier to embark on this new chapter in her life.

She was also putting some closure on an old chapter. With Aunt Corinne's help, Eleanor had gone through her father's letters and assembled a chronicle of his life, from his childhood through his Indian hunting trip to his last, heartbreaking notes to her. As she prepared to take her place on the national stage, she seemed to want to reclaim her father's life and give him a place of honor, too. To Corinne, she wrote, "I was going to have it printed just for the children, but several people think it is interesting and I might as well see if a publisher would be interested."

Indeed, Scribner's was, but wouldn't commit. Louis Howe pressed Charles Scribner for a reason. As Eleanor communicated to Corinne, the publisher was "very nervous" to publish Elliott's letters "on account of being great friends with Alice, Aunt Edith and you." Scribner feared that if "he published them at this time, they would in some way be considered a political document and he would be accused of playing up the enemy camp." So while Scribner's went ahead and published the book, which Eleanor was calling *Hunting Big Game in the Eighties: The Letters of Elliott Roosevelt, Sportsman*, it did so without any publicity, holding back until after the election.

Eleanor's intent in publishing her father's letters wasn't financial. It was unlikely she'd ever earn any royalties off the small printing. Rather, it was deeply personal. "I want my children and my brother's children and the grandchildren in the family to know a little of the man who was my father and their grandfather," she wrote in the book's preface. "They will read much in many books of their uncles and aunts, especially in history of their uncle, Theodore Roosevelt, but no less important in our daily lives are the things and the people who only touch us personally; therefore, though Elliott is not important historically, I am publishing these letters . . . in the hope that his short life may have something of value as a human document not only for my own children but for other people as well."

It was around the same time that Eleanor received her first copies of *Hunting Big Game*, still fragrant with printer's ink, that she also received in the mail the letter from Elliott Roosevelt Mann.

><———<

In behalf of mother and myself I wish to convey our most sincere good wishes . . .

Although Elliott had sent the letter to Sixty-Fifth Street, Eleanor most likely read it in the privacy of her cottage at Val-Kill. The reply she eventually sent would be postmarked Hyde Park.

Mother informs me that she was known as "Katie" in your parents' household.

A name out of the mists of her past. Did Eleanor remember her father sending Katie the photograph from Bad Reichenhall? Even if not, she must have known who Katie was. If not Aunt Pussie, then someone, sometime, must surely have told her enough of what had happened forty-one years ago for her to be able to figure things out now.

Yours very respectfully, Elliott Roosevelt Mann.

If Eleanor had been seeking some closure by publishing her father's letters, her half-brother in Queens was looking for the same by writing to her. Together, Elliott seemed to believe, they might find what they both were so desperately seeking. If they sat down together and looked into each other's eyes, they might learn a great deal about their father, and themselves.

For a brief moment, Eleanor seemed to consider doing just that.

"My dear Mr. Mann," she replied on December 3. "I was very interested to receive your letter and to learn that you were named after my father. It was very nice of you and your mother to congratulate us, and both my husband and I deeply appreciate your good wishes. I shall hope sometime to see both you and your mother." She signed it, "With all good wishes, I am very sincerely yours, Eleanor Roosevelt."

She did not dodge when addressing her reply. She typed out clearly, "Elliott Roosevelt Mann," the name Dr. Wynkoop had withheld on the birth certificate all those years ago in the hope that no one would ever learn it.

In Queens, the arrival of the envelope with the Hyde Park postmark caused considerable excitement in the Mann household. Lena had it waiting for Elliott when he came home from the bank. He read the note eagerly. He immediately informed Katie that Eleanor was willing to meet with them. They planned what to say, what to wear. Then Elliott sat back at his desk and carefully composed a response to his sister.

"I am deeply greatful [*sic*] to receive your esteemed communication to which I am indeed happy to reply," he wrote. "I wish to express my sincere appreciation for your graciousness to Mother and I of your desire to see us both. I am well aware of the countless duties and requests you are called upon to perform and with due consideration of all these events, I am only too happy to await your wishes in this respect when it becomes most convenient to you." He ended his note with "sincere good wishes of the Yuletide season" to her and to "his Excellency, Mr. Franklin."

He stamped the envelope and put it in the mail.

Christmas came and went. There was no reply.

For several months, Elliott and his family waited, their hopes resilient. Yet, when the New Year passed and then winter turned into spring and still no response arrived, they came to the realization they would never hear from Eleanor.

She had changed her mind—fearful, perhaps, of a scandal just as Franklin was sworn in, and just as her father's published letters were being reviewed in the newspapers; fearful, perhaps, that Elliott's motive in contacting her had been for money, and that she would find herself at the mercy of a blackmailer. Yet her fears most likely went deeper than that. What Eleanor really couldn't bear was this final confirmation of her father's transgressions. She had just enshrined his memory in print, and to see him now from someone else's perspective was likely just too difficult to contemplate. By publishing her father's letters, she had finally shaped his image into what she wanted it to be. Her father belonged to her now, and to her alone. Her brother Hall didn't remember him—but Katie Mann did. Katie knew a side of Eleanor's father unknown to anyone. In the end, Eleanor simply could not share her father with anyone else, least of all those he'd abandoned even more grievously than he'd abandoned her.

Had she met with Elliott Roosevelt Mann, however, she might have had the chance to see her father again, looking back at her, from her brother's eyes.

PART VIII

CHANGING THE WORLD

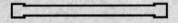

1936–1938

WASHINGTON, DC

Despite a cold, steady rain, people began queuing up outside the Capitol Building early on the morning of January 3, 1936, hoping to get a seat for the big show that night. By noon, the crowd had swelled to over a thousand. Women huddled under umbrellas; university students with upturned collars and hands jammed deep into pockets bounced up and down in place, trying to keep warm. Once they made it inside, they were corralled behind a red-velvet rope set up by Capitol police to separate them from the parade of legislators and staff heading in the same direction. Everyone wanted to be in the House chamber that evening.

Not since Woodrow Wilson had a president addressed a joint session of Congress at night, and that was to request entry into the war. Also, never before had a State of the Union address been scheduled outside daylight hours. That was the reason so many people had turned out to hear it: the president must have something extraordinary to say. Yet his opponents suspected this was just President Roosevelt's mastery of political theater. The year before as well, he had broken tradition, calling a joint session of Congress to veto a bill in person, in front of those who had passed it, the first president ever to do so.

Now, after Republican leaders watched the National Broadcasting Company and the Columbia Broadcasting System rig up their equipment, dragging wires and antennas through the halls of Congress, they hurried out front to demand equal time. Clearly this president was not simply exercising his constitutional duty to report to Congress the conditions of the country. Henry P. Fletcher, Republican National Committee chairman, argued that Franklin was delivering "a political speech" paid for by taxpayers and broadcast for free by the radio companies. At the very least, Fletcher demanded, the opposition party should be given equal time to broadcast its own view of the nation. CBS rejected the demand outright, and while NBC agreed, the company offered only to broadcast opposition speeches "from time to time," without the prominence given to the president's address.

Republicans steamed. How much more autocratic could this president become?

Back inside the House chamber, as aides arranged chairs and NBC and CBS set up microphones, a small figure wearing a blue halo hat cut through the crowd. Guards stepped aside when they recognized her, tipping their own hats in greeting. Even though the House was now firmly in the hands of the Democrats, this Republican had not lost her seat in the Speaker's Gallery. As they'd been doing for the past twenty-five years, spectators craned their necks to get a look at Alice Roosevelt Longworth as she entered the Gallery and grandly took her usual place up front to watch the drama unfold below.

Alice's fears had been groundless. She hadn't lost her ringside seat. Moreover, she was no longer merely a spectator in the Gallery. She was an active participant. Once settled in her seat, she opened the copy of the president's speech she had received in advance and withdrew her pencil from her purse. Alice was now a journalist.

A few weeks earlier, she'd been hired by the McNaught newspaper syndicate, best known for the "Joe Palooka" comic strip and columns by Jimmie Fidler, Walter Winchell, and Will Rogers. Alice was being positioned as a counterpoint to First Lady Eleanor Roosevelt, who'd just started her own column, for the rival United Feature Syndicate. Alice's first assignment was to respond to the president's State of the Union address. She'd always had plenty to say after one of Franklin's speeches. Now she just had to put it down on paper.

Alice sat there in the Gallery, aware of all the eyes upon her. In a month, she would turn fifty-two. She was still attractive and fashionable, in the latest designer dresses and hats. She wore her dark hair short, and her toothy smile could still dazzle and terrify. She liked to tell people there was "plenty of kick in the old horse yet." She could still dance the hula, she boasted to one reporter, which she'd learned during a stopover in Hawaii during her famous youthful Pacific excursion. Yet her face had turned hard. Her mouth was pinched; her eyes seemed forever suspicious. For all Alice's glamour, for all the prominence she still held in the Speaker's Gallery, life had not turned out the way she'd hoped.

Franklin had been president for three years now. His administration had exceeded the worries of conservatives. In his zeal to get the economy moving again, he had, according to his critics, overreached his executive authority. The New Deal was unconstitutional, they argued. The banking acts were nothing more than power grabs by the federal government over private financial institutions. The Federal Emergency Relief Administration and the Civil Works Administration represented government spending at its most unrestrained, and the Wagner Act had deprived business owners of the right to forbid unions on their property. The Works Progress Administration, meanwhile, had turned the federal government, already swollen in the eyes of conservatives, into the single largest employer in the nation. Worst of all, to some, had been the Social Security Act, which seemed like socialism to many. Congressman James Wadsworth of New York argued that the president was creating a federal government "so vast, so powerful, as to threaten the integrity of our institutions and to pull the pillars of the temple down upon the heads of our descendants."

Thankfully for conservatives, the Supreme Court had stepped in to correct some of the worst of the president's excesses. Last May, the justices had ruled unconstitutional Franklin's National Recovery Administration, which he'd put into place by executive order to give the federal government a voice in setting work hours, pay rates, and prices. Other parts of the New Deal were coming up before the Court. Conservatives remained hopeful that the judiciary could rein in an out-of-control executive.

Now here the president was, calling this extraordinary night session of Congress, hooking up his radio transmitters and going over the heads of legislators and justices to appeal directly to the public. In the Gallery, Alice stewed. She and her confederates had always known that Franklin was unscrupulous, but they hadn't counted on his being a dictator.

The sounds of applause filled the chamber. Alice's eyes moved over to the Executive Gallery. The First Lady was entering, accompanied by her daughter, Anna Boettiger, who, as gossips liked to point out, was already, at twenty-nine, on husband number two. They were followed by Eleanor's son John, nineteen and a senior at Groton, and her son James's wife, Betsey. Scampering alongside and waving at the crowd were Anna's two children, eight-year-old Anna Dall and five-year-old Curtis Dall, the White House grandchildren known affectionately as "Sistie" and "Buzzie," and whose exploits were followed by the public the way an earlier generation had followed stories of Alice and her siblings.

Alice had once imagined herself in that Gallery: first, perhaps, as the wife of President Nick Longworth; then, when those hopes faded, as the esteemed guest of President Bill Borah; and finally, as the sister and close adviser of President Theodore Roosevelt Jr. Yet it was Eleanor, little Eleanor, too scared to jump off the pier, who was receiving the applause of the chamber.

Then the House sergeant at arms announced the president of the United States.

The Republican legislators mostly stayed in their seats as the rest of the chamber leaped to attention, whooping and hollering like spectators at a football game. Franklin, assisted by his son James and flashing that Roosevelt smile, made his way to the Speaker's lectern. Alice waited for him to begin his oration, her pencil poised above the copy of his speech.

It didn't take long for him to say something that sparked her ire. When the president assured the Congress that no new taxes were "advisable or necessary," Alice scribbled, "Said last year." When Franklin spoke of putting an end to "dollar diplomacy, to money grabbing, to speculation for the benefit of the powerful and the rich, at the expense of the small and the poor," Alice wrote in the margin, "Soak 'em!" Indeed, many old-money families considered Franklin a traitor for taxing the highest incomes while providing handouts to the lowest. When the president vowed never to let the country return to the sort of "individualism" that had once fueled the economy, Alice scrawled "benevolent despotism" and "fascism."

The 1936 State of the Union speech was unprecedented for

more than just its evening schedule. So fervid were most of the Democratic lawmakers in their support of this president's policies that they broke tradition, and House rules, to cheer wildly at several points during the address. Even more extraordinary were the bursts of dismissive laughter that regularly erupted from the other side. Alice recorded that the president's opponents booed him when he said, "Under these policies we approach a balance of the national budget," noting that the jeers began at the word *approach*. The partisan rancor that was expressed that night would not have been tolerated in Theodore's time.

Yet Franklin, Alice believed, had brought it on himself. Such a divisive figure could never be reelected to a second term, she felt certain—and, as always, she would do her part to defeat him, this time with the power of the pen.

Back home on Massachusetts Avenue, Alice sat down at her desk and scratched out her first column. She wrote in longhand first, in an atrocious scribble that passed for handwriting, then typed up her thoughts before handing them off to her secretary to polish. Her first column was published in newspapers across the country on January 6. "Now that the Klieg lights are off and the thrill of the beautiful voice has vanished," it read, "Congress faces the job of carrying out such suggestions as it can find in the state of the union." In his speech, Franklin had warned about the rise of despots in Germany, Italy, and Japan. Alice used his comment to draw a comparison to what was happening here. "There can be no despotism at home," she wrote. "There is a hint the Administration would like to have powers of the lower courts curbed. Is it possible that Congress will be asked to say that future New Deal legislation must not be interfered with by any but the highest court?" She warned, "There are vistas of despotism in the thought," echoing a recurrent trope in Republican circles.

She also went after Franklin's continued calls for sacrifice. "The President ended in a sad note suggesting the hair shirt and the lash," Alice wrote. "What has happened to the old 'Happy Days Are Here Again'?"

While she might rile up the opposition, however, she was in fact no longer backed up by giants. Men such as Henry Cabot

Lodge and Frank Brandegee were dead, and Bill Borah was but a husk of his former self. Alice lamented the disarray of the Grand Old Party, which was led by the hapless Henry Fletcher. "The opposition has found no real David to sling the big stone at the White House Goliath," she wrote in her second column. "Merely spattering Goliath with showers of pebbles may rouse him to the point of making another speech, and then what will Mr. Fletcher do?" They all knew that whenever Franklin spoke directly to the public, as in his radio "fireside chats," he seemed to get whatever he wanted.

The conservative opposition needed a strong, national voice. Many hoped Alice, through her column, could be it. The McNaught Syndicate promised Alice's column "six times a week by wire or airmail." Eleanor's competing column was titled "My Day," but the name of Alice's column depended on local prerogative. In some newspapers, it was called "Chatting with Alice"; in others, "Capital Comment" or "Alice Roosevelt Says." Some papers were more creative: "Alice Longworth's Terse Comment," "The Other Roosevelt Says," and perhaps the best and most popular, "Alice in Blunderland."

A few days after the State of the Union address, Alice was gratified by the Supreme Court ruling that struck down Franklin's much-heralded Agricultural Adjustment Act (AAA). The decision unraveled New Deal control over crop production and left Congress leery of passing more of the president's controversial initiatives. "The Senators, in a sudden attack of realism," Alice crowed in her column, "refused to consider a bill that was no more within the Constitution than the AAA it was supposed to supplant. The Administration's strategy is to continue passing laws that the Supreme Court is bound to turn down. Thus it hopes to create the impression that nothing can be done for the farmer under the Constitution as it stands." That just went to prove, Alice wrote, that New Dealers really wanted to amend the Constitution.

Alice was now the most public face of Franklin's opposition, but that didn't mean she expected to be left out of the glitz and glamour of White House gatherings. She was Princess Alice, after all, and still demanded to be treated as such. Even as she railed against Franklin's policies, questioned his motives, and called him a despot in the newspapers of America, she accepted his invitations to the White House—and used them whenever possible to undermine his initiatives. On January 9 she attended a White House reception for the judiciary, where she cornered the notoriously private justice Benjamin Cardozo. Some wondered if she was chastising him for having dissented in the AAA case and encouraging him to think differently in the future. "He's a dear!" was all Alice would say when asked by reporters about their conversation.

Alice had also attended Franklin's inauguration in 1933, despite how vicious she'd been during the campaign, and dined afterward with her cousins. No matter how distressed she was by their victory, the idea of being excluded from the action was far worse. Eleanor told her after the election, "You are always welcome here but never feel you *have* to come." That was a laugh. Armed sentinels couldn't have kept Alice away.

In the past three years, no matter how much she criticized the administration, Alice attended every White House function she could, with "great alacrity and enthusiasm and had a lovely, malicious time," she said. She'd sit with like-minded souls and dish the proceedings under her breath. "There was always a sufficient number of people who didn't like Franklin and hovered around me," Alice would remember. According to Eleanor, Alice would act as if she couldn't understand "why any of us should mind anything she has said." For Alice, politics was a game, a ruthless one, but a game nonetheless. For Eleanor, it was deeply personal.

No surprise, then, that when Eleanor heard that Alice called dinners at Franklin's White House "boring," she wrote to her cousin saying, in that case, she wouldn't impose on her by inviting her again. Alice immediately wrote back, not to deny or apologize, but merely to lament that anyone would have passed the story on to Eleanor, "trying to make more trouble than there already is between us." So the invitations continued, at least for the time being.

For his part, Franklin enjoyed needling Alice. At one reception, just as Alice was leaving, the president said, "Do you know that after this is over I'm going upstairs and, by signing my name, I'm going to save the country fifty million dollars?"

Alice didn't miss a beat. "That's a drop in the bucket compared to what you are *costing* the country," she replied.

While she'd insist she had "a lot of laughs" bantering with Franklin, the enmity was deep-rooted and often cruel. Alice refused, for example, to call Franklin "Mr. President" to his face, showing an utter disregard for his office by sticking to a first-name basis even in front of others. Also, she was well aware that her newspaper column really got under his skin, "because in it," she admitted, "I said some rather mean things about him."

In private, she could be even worse. "He has the cripple's psychology," Alice wrote to a friend. "He puts his disability out of his mind and makes the most of what is left to him. He treats the American people in the same way, distracting them with anything which he thinks will keep them happy for the moment, but without any deep thought behind it." In later years, she was even more brutal. "He was trying to adjust this great lusty country into the same condition as his own," she told an interviewer. Alice acknowledged that such a comment was "pretty nasty," but she stood by it.

Her cousins, however, never stooped to her level, which left Alice frustrated. "They should have been better winners," she griped. "They could have said, 'Look here, you miserable worm, of course you feel upset because you wanted this—you hoped your brother Ted would finally achieve this, and now he hasn't—but after all, here we are. Just come if it amuses you.' But they took it all seriously. They took the meanness in the spirit in which it was meant." In other words, they took her attacks seriously, even personally, yet, still, they never retaliated. Politics wasn't any fun, Alice believed, if people didn't fight back.

Alice's bark was actually worse than her bite. Ted's retirement from politics meant she lacked a serious electoral challenger to promote. Bill Borah was being touted again as a presidential candidate, but Alice had lost faith in her former lover. If she'd seen Borah as a viable contender, she would have used her column to boost his candidacy; in fact, she did just the opposite. Senator Borah's campaign, Alice implied, was a relic of the past. "If you shut your eyes," she wrote, "you would think you were back twenty-four years." The senator, she said, was fighting "the League of Nations all over again to a standstill." Now seventy years old, Bill lacked the fire in his belly to win, and Alice knew it; somebody like Alf Landon, the forty-eight-year-old governor of Kansas and a progressive Republican in the mold of Theodore, stood a better chance. A friend wrote to Alice that Landon was the best shot to beat Franklin, as "Grandpa Borah" could never unite the party. Alice evidently agreed. She gave Landon considerable ink in her column—but in fact she had no skin in the game anymore.

One route back to power did remain for her, but as always, she refused to entertain it. After Franklin's election, conservatives had looked around for a savior, and many turned to her. In April 1934, Thomas Latham, a former Ohio state senator, launched a movement to draft Alice for the U.S. Senate, hoping she'd provide a conservative antidote to Franklin. Yet just as she had several times in the past, she quickly made it clear she would not run. Her dread of public speaking remained too disabling.

The best Alice could do, then, was rally the base, and her columns (short, pithy, to the point) succeeded very well in that goal. "I enjoy your articles in the Chicago *Daily News*," wrote a fan from Illinois. "You are certainly hitting them 'between the eyes' just like your father." From Idaho, a correspondent praised her "keen and clean-cut grasp" of the situation facing the country, adding, "I hope there are wise people enough left in the country to save us from dictatorship." One man from Ohio couldn't contain his surprise over his enjoyment of her columns. "Lordy!" he wrote. "When I find myself liking a woman columnist better each day, really, it shocks me into action. Frankly speaking, my appreciation for what women can do and how well they do it has been, and is, in the majority of cases, very, very low. You bring it up a little bit for women. As for yourself, way, way up."

Eleanor's column, often run alongside Alice's, was considered more lightweight. "Her column on 'coughing at concerts' is the Ne Plus Ultra on what *not* to write about," an editor from the *Idaho Statesman* wrote to Alice. Eleanor herself thought Alice the better writer, admitting to a friend, "She certainly writes well. I wish I were as free as she, though I do not wish ever to be as bitter."

Alice was less confident in her ability. "They want me to be bright, and I am very, very trite," she told a friend. "I am not a wit or a wisecracker and I haven't got a sense of humor. What I have is a measure of irony and that is neither easy to get across nor endearing." Earlier requests to write a newspaper column she had turned down, "too aware of my quarter horse limitations." Now, however, Alice persevered, because the income the columns generated was welcome. She'd finally penned her memoir as well, a volume she called *Crowded Hours*, with just enough settling of scores to make it amusing. "I wrote for profit," she later admitted, "not literature." She'd also signed a contract to pitch Lucky Strike cigarettes in newspaper and magazine advertisements, perhaps the first presidential offspring to market his or her celebrity in this sort of way. "Ever since 1917," Alice was quoted in the ad, "I myself have used Luckies for this sound reason: they really are a light smoke—kind to the throat."

The revenues she brought in from all this activity kept her living according to the standard she'd grown used to. Also, in this way she could remain squarely in the public eye, a place she absolutely refused to surrender just because her cousins had taken over the White House.

During the third week of January 1936, Alice traveled to New York with her daughter, Paulina, now almost eleven, for the dedication of the Theodore Roosevelt Memorial Hall at the Museum of Natural History. On the afternoon of January 19 a blizzard hit, sending sheets of snow whipping down the corridors of the city. Hats tumbled in the wind, and shopkeepers struggled to clear paths to their doors. Taxicabs got stuck in the middle of Central Park West, and above the buildings, the sky was growing ominously dark.

With the exception of some legislators coming from out of town, most of the fifteen hundred invited guests braved the blizzard and made it to the ceremony. The $3.5 million hall was a shining monument to the late president, with walls of dark green marble and a one-hundred-foot-high vaulted ceiling. The pink granite entrance was modeled on the arches of ancient Rome, complete with granite columns supporting figures of Lewis, Clark, Audubon, and Boone. Over the entrance was carved the dedication to the man deemed an even greater explorer and naturalist than they. Theodore's "love and conservation of nature and of the best in life and in man" was chiseled into the marble to be known for all time.

As the guests took their seats in the cavernous hall, the wind whipped outside the building. Alice and Paulina sat on the dais, along with Governor Herbert Lehman and Mayor Fiorello La Guardia. Ted and his wife, Eleanor, were there, as was Ethel Roosevelt Derby. Edith Roosevelt could not be present, as she'd broken her hip and was still convalescing in the hospital. So, in a place of honor, sat Franklin's eighty-one-year-old mother, Sara. Not on the dais, but in a section of the audience reserved for family, were Kermit and Belle, Archie and Grace, Corinne Alsop, Monroe Robinson, and other cousins.

Once everyone was settled, the museum's band struck up the ruffles and flourishes that led into "Hail to the Chief." The crowd stood. Alice watched as Franklin and Eleanor made their entrance onto the dais from a conveniently short distance away—Franklin, as usual, on the arm of their son James.

Outside, the day grew nearly black as night. Icy gales lashed against the three large windows overhead.

Franklin opened the ceremony by quoting Theodore: "A great democracy must be progressive or it will soon cease to be great or a democracy." Slowly and emphatically he made his points. Alice was no doubt clever enough to quickly realize where he was going with his speech: he was using Theodore to justify his own policies. Of his predecessor, Franklin said, "It is his warning to us of this day and generation that eternal progress is still the price of liberty." He extolled Theodore's support of a "Square Deal" for all Americans, clearly drawing a parallel with his own New Deal. Theodore had not been afraid of federal power; he had harnessed it to achieve great things. "He was able to see great problems in their true perspective, because he looked at the nation as a whole. There was nothing narrow or local or sectional about that man."

Many in the audience were surprised that Franklin would use a personal, nonpartisan ceremony to score some political points against his adversaries. It was, apparently, an opportunity he'd been unable to resist—and once again, he'd made sure it was all broadcast to the public by radio.

Sitting on the dais just a few feet away from him, Alice boiled—and just at that moment, the room shook with thunder. Later, the Weather Bureau could offer no explanation for the phenomenon. One meteorologist "was extremely skeptical of thunder during a snowstorm and indicated he had never heard anything like it."

Inside the museum, though, Alice was suppressing enough rage to shake heaven and earth. How dare Franklin try to compare himself to her father? While the mood in the hall was congenial and smiles dominated all around, the president's message had come through loud and clear. He believed he was finishing the work Theodore started, and if Theodore's heirs thought otherwise, it was they and not he who had failed to live up to their father's standards.

After tenor Roland Hayes sang "The Battle Hymn of the Republic," it was time for Ted, the family spokesman, to speak. Slipping his glasses on, he walked over to the lectern. Ted had never been a passionate speaker, but now all the political fervor seemed beaten out of him. As chairman of the board of the American Express Company, he had become buttoned-down and restrained. He did manage, with a little smile, to remark that those extolling Theodore's courage that day had not been "on the same side of the fence with him when he was alive." For the rest of his talk, Ted was amiable and bland, focusing only on his father's "warm humor and humanity."

If only Alice hadn't been so fearful of speaking in public. She likely would have had a few other, more pointed things to say.

How she despised the way Franklin had claimed her father's mantle. The father who was never truly hers in life had, in death, become Alice's defining purpose, the emblem she wore, the source of her power. In death, she, like Eleanor, possessed her father completely—except for when Franklin started talking about policy.

On some level, Alice must have known Franklin had a point. His political methods and flagrant power grabs might not have been Theodore's, but his goals and his aims (and, critically, his views on the role of government) were not dissimilar.

Yet the truth was Alice could never reconcile herself to Franklin and Eleanor's having stolen the place that should have been hers. "There we were, swelling with pride and security," she'd admit later, "and what happens? Along comes Franklin, called by many in the family 'Feather Duster,' and hops into the presidency." For all the policy arguments she tersely articulated in her columns, Alice's real issue with the president of the United States was far more personal. She remained, as ever, contrarian: a lonely, middle-aged woman who was always "anti-something" simply for the sake of being "anti." She took a certain sad satisfaction in that—and she was too old to change now.

NASSAU, BAHAMAS

Kermit's head emerged from the clear waters several yards from shore. Scuba diving had become one of his favorite pastimes now that stalking white tigers and panda bears seemed firmly relegated to his past. As he slipped off his headgear and waded up toward the beach, anyone could have seen that the forty-four-year-old was no longer the lean, muscled hunter who once prowled the plains of Central Asia. He was heavier these days, softer, and his eyes seemed forever tired. The past few years had not been easy on him.

Waiting for him at their lodgings was his loyal wife, Belle, still as delicately pretty as she was the day he married her twenty-two years ago. Kermit adored Belle, who'd given him four children and stood by his side through every up and down of his business. Lately, however, he had been traveling so much for his shipping business that he hadn't spent much time with his wife. This jaunt to the Bahamas, sandwiched in between the museum dedication to his father and Kermit's upcoming trip to Europe, was a moment for reconnection.

It was also, no doubt, a chance for him to take stock of himself.

His business continued to bleed money. Much of the capital he'd used to build up Roosevelt Steamship, which had now merged into the conglomerate United States Lines, had come from Belle, and now most of that money was gone, evaporated in the Wall Street crash. Guilt compounded Kermit's stress. When his son Willard wrote to him from Groton asking for a raise in his allowance, Kermit sent back an agonized letter laying out his financial difficulties. "Don't speak of this to Mother or anyone," he told his son. "I confide my troubles to you so that you may understand."

He'd chosen shipping as a career because he'd figured it would enable his wanderlust, but balancing books and managing staff had never been among Kermit's strengths. Years ago, he'd told his sister Ethel that he and business would make an "inapt" fit. No matter what he did, he said, he wouldn't be able to adjust to a regular daily routine. He was twenty-three when he made that observation. He was nothing if not prescient.

On February 22, 1936, Kermit and Belle packed their bags and bid the Bahamas adieu, boarding a small airplane to Miami. Neither could have been much looking forward to the life they were returning to. In addition to everything else, they worried about their children, especially the two youngest. A year earlier, Clochette, who struggled with the lingering aftereffects of childhood polio, had suffered a fall over a staircase bannister that left her with several broken bones; she was still in physical therapy. Son Dirck, now eleven, was proving to be different from his older brothers, a moody dreamer not unlike his father at that age.

Kermit threw himself back into work. He remained a strong advocate for the U.S. Merchant Marine within the administration, recently speaking at a White House conference on the topic. His friendship with Franklin had deepened these past three years. The president had asked him to help organize a conference on North American wildlife, and frequently invited him and Belle to the Executive Mansion. Kermit, one reporter noted, was "the only one of the Oyster Bay branch of the family whose hat is welcome at the White House."

Items like that, of course, only inflamed the wounds between Kermit and his family. Ever since a photo of him standing beside the president-elect on Vincent Astor's yacht graced newspapers across the country three years earlier, Kermit's siblings had been cold to him. Although Alice was in and out of the White House even more frequently than Kermit, her loyalty was never in doubt, since daily she tore apart Franklin's policies in her column. Kermit, on the other hand, was clearly a friend of the administration. A chill settled over Oyster Bay, and visits between the siblings tapered off.

Family tensions only grew when Kermit became a target of Franklin's Republican opponents, who questioned whether the president's fishing trips with Kermit and Vincent Astor were hauling in more than white marlins and yellowfin tuna. The Senate Special Committee to Investigate Air Mail and Ocean Mail Contracts subpoenaed copies of radiograms Kermit received onboard the yacht from his shipping interests "containing instructions on information to be conveyed to the President." No specific indiscretion was ever proven, but once again Kermit was embroiled in a scandal that embarrassed his family and kept them aloof from him.

Because 1936 was an election year, Franklin was also keeping a bit of distance from his cousin, deciding against a fishing trip with Kermit and Astor this season and sticking to his own yacht. Kermit wouldn't have been much company, in any event. In the spring of 1936, his friends began to note a marked change in his demeanor. Once, he'd been the devil-may-care playboy, hosting society maven Elsa Maxwell's Halloween party and scavenger hunt, but now he tended to grow quiet in crowds. He no longer fit in, his friend the financier Goodhue Livingston recalled: "He didn't like the type of life he was leading but didn't quite know how to get out of it."

The problem was his drinking. "My father always thought he could handle liquor," his son Willard would reflect, "and when it dawned on him he couldn't, he reacted with bewilderment." Edith called it "the curse of the Roosevelts," fearing that the affliction that had bedeviled Elliott and Monroe Robinson (as well as her own father) had now attached itself to her son. Kermit's drinking may have indeed been genetic, a family disease, but it was certainly not helped by the stress he was under, or the physical pain he endured. A series of warts on his hands had been treated with radiation, but the cure turned out to be worse than the complaint. Eventually his left thumb was so badly burned and withered that it had to be amputated. Drinking dulled the pain.

Soon after he returned home from the Bahamas with Belle, he was stopped by police after blowing through a traffic signal at the corner of West End Avenue and Seventy-Third Street. He paid a five-dollar fine in traffic court. Later that spring, when the explorer Adm. Richard Byrd, back from his latest expedition to Antarctica, gave a guest talk at the Room, Kermit got so drunk he passed out in a corner and wasn't found until the next day.

Just as it had been with his uncle Elliott, Kermit's problems only worsened after his family turned their backs on him. Belle was furious with the way Kermit's brothers kept their distance. All they had to do, she felt, was "look at him to see the agony of mind and body he was suffering." Yet they did nothing. To their way of thinking, Kermit had gone over to the other side, to Franklin, and that was simply unforgivable. For Kermit, to be expelled from Theodore's clan, his tight-knit, loyal band of bunnies, was excruciating. So he clung only more fiercely to Franklin as a result—and drank all the more.

He had never really fit in anywhere: not in his family, not in business, not in the war. Perhaps the closest he ever came to finding work that suited him had been the coffeehouse, where he could sit back, smoke, drink, and chew the fat with his friends all day—but even that had meant balancing spreadsheets and keeping track of inventory, and such tedium bored him to death. Theodore had ruined him in a way: by taking him to Africa and South America, he showed his son a life where ambition meant stalking a lion or navigating through rapids. Back home, however, achievement was defined very differently, and Kermit was expected to adjust.

So long as his father lived, Kermit had maintained some semblance of order and enterprise. After Theodore's death, however, Kermit's disguise gradually fell away, revealing the Elliott or Jimmie he was inside, recoiling from the expectations of his society and class. He'd always been the square peg, and no amount of pounding ever got him into that round hole, though the years had badly damaged his edges in the attempt.

Beginning in 1936, Kermit would no longer make the effort. He seemed to decide he would reclaim the dreams of the young boy he'd once been, sitting in the windowsill looking up at the moon—and as so often happens for middle-aged men in personal and professional crises, the catalyst for his life change was a younger woman.

Just how Kermit, scion of a great family, met Carla Peters, immigrant masseuse, would never be entirely clear. Yet when she first arrived in the United States from Germany in 1930, Carla worked as a maid for the family of Robert E. Miller, a vice president of the Bank of New York, at his house in Queens. Kermit likely knew Miller, since his cousin Emlen Roosevelt was on the board of directors for the bank. Carla was twenty-five, blonde, and naturally unpretentious, which Kermit found refreshing after a life spent with society ladies.

Born Herta Peters in Bockhorn, Lower Saxony, she arrived in America with her father and younger brother, both farm laborers, on board the *Majestic*. At some point, Carla received some form of occupational therapy training, for by 1933 she was working as a nurse, possibly at St. Mary's Hospital for Children. On her petition for citizenship in 1935, she described herself as a masseuse. She was likely a good one, too, standing five foot eight and weighing one hundred fifty pounds. When Kermit met her, she had recently become an American citizen, her naturalization papers having been issued on February 10, 1936.

Up the stairs to Carla's studio in a high-rise building on Eighty-Fifth Street, just off Broadway, Kermit trudged regularly for a massage. One session led to another, and soon he and Carla were spending a considerable amount of time together, inside and outside her massage studio. Her earthiness drew him—the way Elliott had been drawn to Mrs. Evans, perhaps, and Jimmie drawn to Sadie. Like those women, Carla carried none of the affectations or inhibitions Kermit expected in ladies of his own class. During the summer and fall of 1936, Carla loved going to movies with him, and riding along the Delaware shore with the top down on the car. Together, she and Kermit sneaked away for little holidays, where they'd register at hotels as Mr. and Mrs. Hilton, a nod to James Hilton, author of one of Kermit's favorite novels, *Lost Horizon*, about the search for Shangri-La. With Carla, Kermit seemed to have found it.

He'd spent a lifetime doing what he was supposed to do, or feeling guilty if he didn't. Now, suddenly, breezing down the old coast road in Delaware with Carla, the wind in their hair, Kermit was liberated from all that. Once, Carla asked him what he saw in her. "Relief," he replied, without missing a beat.

HYDE PARK, NEW YORK

At eleven o'clock in the morning on Tuesday, November 3, 1936, three black cars pulled up in front of a small, white wooden structure in the center of Hyde Park. Originally the building had been a nickelodeon screening silent movies, but now it served as the town hall, where election officials braced for the arrival of the president and his family.

Out of the first car stepped the president himself, assisted by his son Franklin Junior. Behind them emerged the president's mother, Mrs. Sara Roosevelt, eighty-two years old, her white hair offset by a royal purple cape and her customary black velvet hat. Sara seemed oblivious to the unusually warm weather (mid- to high sixties), though the gray skies portended rain.

The second car was driven by the First Lady, who wore a blue tweed suit and was accompanied by Nancy Cook, identified by the newspapers as "a close friend and resident of Val-Kill, the President's farm." Eleanor's retreat was often referred to in that way by the press, obscuring the independent lifestyle the First Lady pursued. Alighting from the third car were several Secret Service agents; the president's daughter, Anna Boettiger, and her husband; Eleanor's secretary, Malvina Thompson; and the president's secretary, Missy Le Hand.

A crowd of about 150 people was waiting to greet the First Family. Cheers broke out when the president was sighted. Franklin waved, beaming his famous broad smile, chin always up. Eleanor's face, however, betrayed her anxiety over how the election would turn out. Polls were all predicting a close race between the president and Governor Landon. Yet Franklin sailed into the town hall on the arm of his son with a look of supreme confidence on his face.

Inside, clerks were forced to work around newsreel cameras, glaring electric lights, and radio microphones clamped to their tables. A score of newspaper reporters was there to record the moment the president cast his vote, but the stiff-backed election inspector seated at the registration table wasn't about to show anyone preferential treatment. After asking the president to state his name, she checked him against the register and only then gave him permission to proceed to the voting machine.

Afterward, the president's entourage returned to Springwood to await the results that night. Telegraph instruments had been set up in a room on the ground floor, and a battery of telephones installed. Franklin maintained his composure all day, sanguine in his expectations of victory. He'd barely campaigned; he'd never taken his opponent seriously, even as Landon crept up in the polls. While Franklin "smiles and fishes," his close adviser and secretary of the interior, Harold Ickes, wrote in his diary, "the rest of us worry and fume. The whole situation is incomprehensible to me." The problem, Ickes felt, was that Louis Howe had died the previous April, and Howe had been "the only one who dared to talk to [the president] frankly and fearlessly." Now Franklin did not take "advice from anybody."

That Franklin was able to remain so upbeat even in the midst of a campaign that had turned nasty and personal was extraordinary. Big business, and the influential newspaper magnate William Randolph Hearst, had spread the fear of socialism, alleging that Franklin wanted to turn the United States into a Soviet-style republic. Meanwhile, Eleanor's outreach to African Americans and labor movements was derided as an attempt to disempower white rural voters, whose electoral dominance had continued to recede. For the first time, African American delegates (including the first black female delegate) made up a sizeable bloc at the national convention. When a black preacher gave the opening prayer at one session, one longtime southern Democrat stormed out, growling, "My God, he's black as melted midnight."

While Eleanor was worried that the loss of traditional Democratic white voters in the South might imperil Franklin's reelection, she believed the loss could be offset with new voters, often nonwhite or urban. Racists reacted by popularizing a reprehensible campaign song that they said illustrated the First Couple's strategy: "You kiss the niggers, and I'll kiss the Jews, and we'll stay in the White House as long as we choose!"

Franklin made the unprecedented decision not to play to the middle, but rather to embrace a radical sense of a new America. Fired with the sort of messianic purpose that drove Theodore in 1912, he left handlers such as Ickes worried that he'd suffer the same fate, defeated on Election Day, relegated to history before he had a chance to implement his ideals fully. Yet Franklin was undeterred. He ended the campaign on Halloween night with a fiery speech at Madison Square Garden, the same place where, exactly four years earlier, Herbert Hoover made his last stand, Edith Roosevelt standing smugly at his side. Categorically rejecting the conservative argument that the best government was the one that was "most indifferent," Franklin declared that government had a great role to play in the lives of its citizens. Government should protect them against "business and financial monopoly . . . reckless banking . . . class antagonism [and] sectionalism." He described the conflict they faced in the starkest "us versus them" terms. The "us," of course, consisted of him and ordinary Americans—quite an evolution for a man who'd grown up riding around in the Empress Eugénie's sleigh, but he pulled it off, brilliantly.

"Never before in all our history," Franklin bellowed, "have these forces been so united against one candidate as they stand today. They are unanimous in their hate of me—and *I welcome their hatred.*"

He went on: "I should like to have it said of my first administration that in it, the forces of selfishness and of lust for power met their match. I should like to have it said of my second administration that in it, these forces met their master."

It was a stunning political speech: incautious, boastful, defiant. Franklin made no attempt to find common ground with his adversaries. He depicted them as standing in the way of progress, so they must be defeated.

To those on the other side, however, Franklin was a despot and a demagogue intent on remaking America in ways they did not recognize. His Oyster Bay cousins, while no longer leading the opposition, were very much in agreement with the expressions being voiced against him, and they did their part, as always, to ensure his defeat.

Not surprisingly, Alice was the most aggressive, especially now that she had the platform of her newspaper column. She made sure to hit all the standard Republican talking points. When Franklin pointed to a rainbow at a campaign event, Alice said he was promising voters "a handout of government checks" instead of a pot of gold. She trivialized the achievements of the Works Progress Administration as "beautifying the insane, teaching mountaineers to write poetry [and] stopping malaria in Westchester County, New York, where there has never been a case of malaria." The "nationalized giving" under Franklin, she said, was "destructive of the true spirit of charity." Red-baiting was a particular specialty of Alice's. The Communist Party, she said, didn't really need to organize in America: "Those who would like to see a change in our form of government don't have to look any further than the New Deal."

Ted, too, trooped out once more to campaign against Franklin. Reversing his famous quip from four years earlier, he now declared that it was Franklin who was the "fifth cousin about to be removed"—to the great cheers of his Republican audiences. Yet Ted didn't hate the New Deal the way Alice did. Even his wife, Eleanor, who had no love for "Dear Cousin Franklin," admitted that her husband shared in the policy's stated objective of "a more abundant life for all." After Franklin's election, in fact, Ted argued that unless Republicans returned to being a party of "constructive liberals," they would continue to see "disastrous" electoral returns. The party needed to "reorganize along modern progressive lines," he wrote in a letter published in the *National Republican Club Review*, and become "liberal in that we would search for solutions to every problem with an open mind, recognizing the failures in our present social structure and striving to correct them."

Yet the "out-of-season" Roosevelts, as the Oyster Bay crowd was called, no longer had the nation's ear. Newspapers were, in fact, dropping Alice's column right and left. After less than a year, only a handful of papers remained as platforms for her attacks. Her conservative contrariness no longer fit the country's mood.

So, on Election Night, only laughter and shouts of joy were heard at Hyde Park as the returns came in by telephone and telegraph. The president had defied the pollsters and won by a landslide. Eighty-three percent of eligible voters had cast their ballots, and Franklin won nearly 63 percent of them, the largest presidential victory up until that time. Taking forty-six states (losing only Maine and Vermont), he had an even more impressive Electoral College triumph, garnering 523 votes to Landon's 8. The House and Senate remained in Democratic hands as well, and actually increased Democratic control to 75 percent. All his critics who'd warned about socialism were stunned into silence.

A crowd of well-wishers gathered around Springwood as red and white flares were shot into the sky in celebration. The president stepped onto his front porch to thank his supporters, who let out a cheer when they saw him. Smoke from the flares billowed up onto the porch. Franklin joked, "I'm swallowing a lot of red fire," complaining lightheartedly that he was about to start off his new term "with a cough."

That was when some supporters spotted Eleanor behind him. "Three cheers for Mrs. Roosevelt!" someone in the crowd shouted. Franklin reached out to touch her shoulder as Eleanor shyly took her place beside him, listening to the cheers from the crowd.

"Again in 1940!" someone shouted.

That would mean an unprecedented third term, the Republicans' greatest fear. Would Franklin dare?

WARM SPRINGS, GEORGIA

Alone in the cottage he'd built for himself near the rehabilitation center and mineral waters, Franklin read the reports from his military advisers. His great victory behind him, he now understood that the next four years would prove even more daunting than the last. The situation in Europe was becoming more dangerous. Nazi Germany and Fascist Italy had signed a treaty of cooperation, sending waves of fear across the rest of the Continent. Almost certainly a decision was going to have to be made soon about war. So far Franklin had been able, by and large, to sell his vision to the nation. He hadn't ended the Depression, but he'd brought some relief, and was promising more. He enjoyed tremendous goodwill entering his second term, but would the nation follow him into war?

Just as he'd done when he was assistant secretary of the navy, before America entered the war in Europe in 1917, Franklin started building up the military, ensuring that troops and equipment were ready to fight in the event that war became inevitable. "I'm praying that the European situation does not get any more acute than it is now," his daughter, Anna, wrote to him, but it seemed her prayers would go unanswered. Already Franklin's critics were regrouping to oppose him should he start advocating for war. His first term, he expected, would be a cakewalk compared to his second.

As a father, of course, he would find any decision to go to war wrenching, not only politically but personally as well. If Americans were called up to fight, the president's sons would be expected to enlist, just as their Roosevelt cousins had been a generation before. Yet Franklin's sons were not as civic-minded as Theodore's. Nor had they given him the sort of positive public relations copy that Ted, Kermit, Archie, and Quentin (with their boisterous, good-natured, all-American hijinks) had provided their father. Instead, for the past four years, Franklin's sons had only stirred up controversy.

James, now twenty-eight, the father of two young daughters,

was Franklin's right-hand man, especially since Louis Howe died. Yet the liquor import business he ran with Joseph P. Kennedy— the repeal of Prohibition meant business was thriving—drew charges of illegal kickbacks. Critics also accused James of steering business to his private insurance firm through his access to the president. Yet both James and his father seemed utterly indifferent to any impression of impropriety. Just days after his reelection, Franklin gave James a direct commission as a lieutenant colonel in the Marine Corps, a rank he felt appropriate for his top aide. Republicans blustered about nepotism, but in the afterglow of his overwhelming electoral victory, Franklin brushed off the charges of his critics, acting at times like the dictator they accused him of being.

Franklin Junior had also caused his share of problems for his father. A couple of years back, the president's namesake, then nineteen and a student at Harvard, struck a woman while driving a car in the Jamaica Plain neighborhood of Boston. Despite the multiple injuries the woman suffered, police made no arrest, claiming that Franklin Junior was not at fault. The woman sued for $25,000, charging that police had shown the president's son preferential treatment. Eventually, Franklin settled his son's case for $4,500.

So far, John, the youngest son, had managed to escape any public scrutiny, but that wouldn't last long. In the summer of 1937, on a visit to France, he let his high spirits get the better of him. During the annual "Battle of Flowers" in Cannes, in which festivalgoers toss flowers in the streets, John and a buddy shoved an entire bouquet of flowers into the mayor's face and then squirted him with a bottle of champagne. The mayor declined to press charges, but noted to the press that his suit had been ruined.

The biggest headaches, however, arose over Elliott, Franklin's middle son, now twenty-six and as restless as the grandfather he was named for. He'd shunned Harvard to go into business, but his career as a salesman turned out to be short-lived. Abandoning his wife and newborn baby, he headed west, his duties as a father proving no match for his wanderlust. "Betty has just made up her mind she'll hate it out here," he told his mother about his decision to leave his wife, "so there isn't much to be done about it. I know I won't try anymore." The couple was divorced soon after, a move unthinkable a generation earlier. From the El Paso Club, Elliott wrote, "Gosh but this is what I should have done three years ago!" He claimed to have found himself: "Nothing could pay me to go back East again." Heading through Dallas, he was lured to see the rodeo in Fort Worth. "Of course I couldn't resist," he said when offered the chance to ride in the rodeo. He was made a Texas Ranger "under the hand and seal of Ma Ferguson," the colorful governor of Texas, Elliott wrote to his mother. "I'm really awful happy!"

Here was another Roosevelt unable to fit into the prescribed role his family expected. While his brother James maneuvered his way to power through political favors, Elliott rejected the entire system. In an essay he tried to get published during his father's first term, he wrote, "I have endeavored to avoid one topic of conversation almost from the day I opened my little blue eyes on the world. I was born to a father and mother whose main purpose in life seems to be that of serving the masses of this country." Elliott, like his namesake grandfather, refused to apologize for not sharing the family commitment to duty. "I dislike politics, politicians and the machinations of the great," he wrote. "Why? Probably because familiarity breeds contempt." Both political parties, Elliott averred, were made up of "a lot of die-hard old fossils," and both were "chock full of graft." In his essay, he made the sort of heartfelt plea that might also have come from the lips of his grandfather, his paternal cousin Jimmie, or his maternal cousin Kermit: "I really own and operate a mind of my own. Please be gentle with me. After all, I am a child in arms, still groping my way around this cruel, cold world, trying to find the truths of life."

Remarkably, he was given that gentleness, that freedom. This time, a Roosevelt was neither expelled nor punished for his nonconformity. Franklin fretted over the negative publicity of a son running out on his family and riding in rodeos, but he allowed Elliott to live his life as he chose, even when his choices were increasingly unorthodox. After his rodeo adventure, Elliott became an airplane pilot, serving on the Aeronautical Chamber of Commerce. Living in Texas, he also started buying up radio stations, eventually owning twenty-three of them. Just days after his divorce came through in July 1933, he got married again, in a rock garden overlooking the Mississippi River, blithely telling reporters he was "not interested" in what the Episcopal Church thought about divorce and remarriage. Although his parents weren't present for the ceremony, they told the press they'd sent their sincerest congratulations. Not long afterward, Elliott was dancing the hula as he was inducted into the Circus Saints and Sinners Club, and submitted himself to a shower of dried peas onstage. When photographers tried to snap pictures of him and his new wife, he grabbed their cameras and smashed the plates on the ground. No official reprimand came from his father.

Neither did Franklin move to curtail his son's aviation activities when Republican senators, during the waning days of the 1936 campaign, alleged that Elliott was in the midst of brokering a deal for airplane manufacturer Anthony Fokker with the Soviet Union. If the deal went through, the senators charged, Elliott stood to reap half a million dollars in commission, and Fokker had other "high foreign officials" eager to meet with the president's son. Elliott denied he was trading on his father's name, and Franklin apparently did not press him further on it.

He'd never been the fearsome patriarch Theodore was, keeping his sons in check. These days, Franklin seemed only to want peace in the family, and to isolate no one. He'd grown up, essentially, an only child; Rosy had been so much older than Franklin that he was more like an uncle than a brother. When Rosy died (nine years before), Franklin had been genuinely bereft. Never having many family members to start with, he now had even fewer, which was perhaps part of the reason he so warmly embraced Kermit.

For intimacy, Franklin continued to turn to Missy. Despite his very active public persona, in private, Franklin found that his physical limitations were still a defining aspect of his life, so it was up to Missy to bring people and activities to him. Card games and cocktail parties, all arranged by her, were frequent entertainments at the White House. Missy acted as the president's hostess more often than his wife did. "As Miss Le Hand lived in the White House," Eleanor would remember, "she very often . . . invited people she thought my husband would enjoy, or whom she personally wanted."

Eleanor continued to accept Missy's place in Franklin's life. "To me, she was always kind and helpful," Eleanor said, "and when I had to be away she took up without complaint the additional social responsibilities thrust upon her." Of course, it wasn't just when Eleanor was away that Missy was called upon to play a wifely role for Franklin, but also when the First Lady was just down the hall in the White House. No one had more daily intimacy with the president than Missy, and Eleanor respected that. "If I should outlive FDR," Eleanor wrote to Hick, "I know Missy would be the one I should worry about"—making it plain that Missy's grief and loss would be more intense than her own.

Yet if Franklin could be grateful that his wife and his secretary-companion were accommodating of each other, there was a third woman in his life whom neither knew about, and whom neither would have abided if they had known. Sometime over the last few years, Lucy Mercer Rutherfurd had discreetly returned to Franklin's life.

They had never stopped loving each other. Nothing had been strong enough to "dismiss a lasting devotion," as one friend would write. The former lovers had been corresponding since at least the late 1920s. Franklin sent Lucy a copy of one of the first speeches he made after returning to public life following his paralysis. Without letting his wife, his secretary, or his mother know, he arranged for a limousine to pick Mrs. Rutherfurd up and bring her to his first inauguration in 1933. Also, when, on January 20, 1937, on the portico of the U.S. Capitol, he was sworn into office for the second time, he reportedly did the same.

On that cold, wet day, Eleanor did not know that somewhere out there in the crowd, huddled under a makeshift tent to ward off the driving rain, stood Lucy Mercer, a woman who had once upended her life, and might still have the power to do so again.

Upsetting his wife in that way once more, however, was a risk Franklin could not take, because he'd come to depend on Eleanor politically a great deal. If anyone deserved credit for his re-election, it was Eleanor. She wasn't just his eyes, ears, and legs anymore, but also his conscience—and sometimes his attack dog, too. Late in the campaign, an article appeared with the headline HIS MOLLYCODDLE PHILOSOPHY IS CALLED TYPICAL OF ROOSEVELT. (It was not authored by Alice Longworth, though some would later attribute it to her.) The piece contrasted Franklin's supposed "mol-lycoddling" of Americans (providing government handouts to re-lieve the suffering of the Depression) with Theodore's philosophy of the "strenuous life," which had exhorted people to work hard for success. Reading it, Eleanor saw red.

Until that point, her daily newspaper columns had been largely slice-of-life stories, little morality tales or warmhearted anecdotes. All that changed with her column of October 5, 1936. Reacting to the newspaper article, Eleanor wrote, "No man who has brought himself back from what might have been an entire life of invalid-ism to strength and activity, physical and mental and spiritual, can ever be accused of preaching or exemplifying a mollycoddle philosophy." In a dig at her own affluent cousins and friends, El-eanor went on: "My acquaintances who exemplify the philosophy of the mollycoddle are not amongst those to whom my husband is trying to bring greater security and ease of life. Most of my mollycoddles have had too much ease, too much dependency, too much luxury of every kind."

Such a full-throated defense and articulation of his political philosophy was what Franklin had come to rely on from his wife, and why Eleanor was indispensable to his presidency. Not in many years had she possessed his heart, but his wife still had a very strong hold on his mind.

WASHINGTON, DC

On the evening of February 15, 1937, Hick was feeling quite gay. She was staying at the White House as the personal guest of the First Lady, and that night she was attending an elegant party at the Mayflower Hotel, wearing a new black velvet gown bought just for the occasion. Not very often did Hick get the chance to spiff up quite as fancy as this. For the daughter of a farm laborer, who got her start as a housemaid and as a reporter covering train arrivals, all this Washington hoopla was quite heady. These days, Hick moved among world leaders and sat in on national policy discussions. She now worked as a publicist for the upcoming New York World's Fair; before that, she was an investigator for the Federal Emergency Relief Administration, appointed by the president on the First Lady's recommendation.

Hick's friendship with Eleanor had changed her life. She had also changed Eleanor's. For the past four years, ever since their tender, makeshift breakfast that morning on the train, Hick and Eleanor had been inseparable. Even when they were physically apart, they sent each other long letters (sometimes fifteen pages) filled with their daily activities and most intimate thoughts.

"Hick darling," Eleanor wrote at one point during a separation, after finally getting a chance to speak with her on the telephone. "Oh, how good it was to hear your voice. It was so inadequate to try to tell you what it meant. Jimmy [Eleanor's son] was near and I couldn't say *Je t'aime et je t'adore* [I love you and I adore you] as I longed to do but always remember I am saying it and that I go to sleep thinking of you and repeating our little saying." What that little saying was would be left to history's imagination, but it was evident that Eleanor had fallen in love.

"My dear," Eleanor wrote to Hick before one press conference, "may I forget there are other reporters present or must I behave? I shall want to hug you to death." Hick endured the same sort of longings. When they were apart, she admitted to Eleanor that she sometimes cried herself to sleep, thinking of those others (husband, children, friends) who had their own claims on her beloved's time and heart. Eleanor reassured her: "Remember one thing always. No one is just what you are to me. I'd rather be with you this minute than anyone else." She ended with this affirmation: "I've never enjoyed being with anyone the way I enjoy being with you."

The fear that Eleanor had had of being left alone and adrift once Franklin moved into the White House had proved groundless, because Hick had been at her side. The relationship between Eleanor and Hick flowered in full view of the world.

In the exhilaration of new love, Eleanor seemed sometimes to enjoy pushing the envelope, testing the limits, seeing how far she could go. She would do so that night at the Mayflower Hotel. Nearly two thousand Democrats were gathering to pay tribute to Postmaster General James Farley, who'd run Franklin's enormously successful reelection campaign. Eleanor was seated with the president, but she frequently found her way back to visit Hick, who was seated with Mary "Molly" Dewson, head of the Women's Division of the Democratic National Committee, and Molly's life partner and fellow women's rights activist, Mary "Polly" Porter. At one point, Eleanor spotted Dewson (tall, well-built, masculine) bending down, pinning a rose on Farley's lapel, and giving him a kiss on the cheek. The First Lady clearly got a kick out of the sight. Dewson, Eleanor wrote after the event, was "not accustomed to embracing gentlemen, and I think she must have had some coaching—but it was profitable coaching[,] for it went off very well."

Many Washington insiders knew very well that Dewson and Porter were lesbians, and saw them as a couple. The truth of the women's relationship, however, was understood as an open secret, as something that was never spoken of in public. Even when mentioned in private, it was likely uttered in whispers or in code. Yet Eleanor, after a decade of friendship with Nancy and Marion and others, saw it all as quite natural, so she dispensed with such tiresome reticence. A month after the event, her undisguised delight in describing Dewson's kissing Farley was printed for all to read in the *Democratic Digest*, and those "in the know" got her meaning when she said Dewson was "not accustomed to embracing gentlemen."

Eleanor was having fun tweaking convention. For once in her life, she was in on the joke. Being "in the know" (cosmopolitan, sophisticated, modern) was an empowering experience for a woman who'd grown up feeling like an outsider, awkward in society and clueless about the ways of the world. The sisterhood Eleanor had found with her female friends had been transformative. She was, for the first time, a member of the club.

Ever since Allenswood, Eleanor had drawn strength from the

nurturing company of women. Yet, until now, she had remained apart in one important way. With fond eyes and likely some envy, she had observed the closeness, intimacy, and trust between Nancy and Marion, Esther Lape and Elizabeth Read, and other couples, even as she herself remained alone. There had been so much to admire in Nancy: her independence, her politics, even her sartorial style. Perhaps most of all, Eleanor had admired the commitment and devotion of Nancy's relationship with Marion, that one-on-one sense of belonging to someone else, of being first in their eyes. Yet that had been the sole aspect of Nancy's life that Eleanor had been unable to model for herself—until now. Now she had her own Marion.

The extent of the physical intimacy between Eleanor and Hick, of course, would be known just to them. Yet only those with the narrowest views of the world and sexuality and women's lives could read the letters that survived and not recognize a profound, passionate, and at times physical love. "You have grown so much to be a part of my life," Eleanor wrote to Hick at one point, "that it is empty without you." Wearing a ring that Hick had given her, Eleanor wrote, "I look at it and think, 'She *does* love me, or I wouldn't be wearing it!'" One particularly heartsick night, she penned, "I wish I could lie down beside you tonight and take you in my arms."

Hick was equally love-struck. "I've been trying to bring back your face," she wrote to Eleanor after one parting, "to remember just *how* you look. Funny how even the dearest face will fade away in time. Most clearly I remember your eyes, with a kind of teasing smile in them, and the feeling of that soft spot just northeast of the corner of your mouth against my lips."

On the night of Jim Farley's tribute at the Mayflower Hotel, Eleanor was fifty-two and Hick forty-three—although, when their romance began, they were both four years younger. Yet the sheer youthful joy they took in much-anticipated holidays bouncing around the country in Eleanor's little roadster would give the lie to those who, later on, denied or expressed doubt about the vibrancy of passion in older women. As Eleanor and Hick motored along the back roads of America, they were like a couple of teenagers, laughing and getting lost and eating at roadside stands. With Hick, Eleanor rediscovered a sense of fun. Too often, she was the serious, earnest creature Alice loved to poke fun at; but she could also sometimes once again be the little girl who finally let go and had fun plunging down Cooper's Bluff, laughing from the exhilaration.

During Franklin's first summer in office, Eleanor took off with Hick on a driving holiday through New England and Canada—albeit with a carload of Secret Service men following behind. The women drove up to the summit of Mount Mansfield, in Vermont, then hiked the two miles to the "chin" of the famously human-profiled range. In Maine, the "famous blue roadster," as the newspapers called it, was spotted zipping alongside the Saint John River; tourists were surprised to spy the First Lady and her friend camping alongside them at Dyer Brook. Whenever she was recognized, Eleanor graciously shook hands and told people how much she was enjoying seeing the beautiful American countryside. At Old Town, a delegation of Penobscot Indians performed for her and Hick in full headdress.

In the spring of 1934, Eleanor and Hick went to Puerto Rico on a fact-finding trip for Franklin, who was interested in learning firsthand about the effects of the Depression on the island territory. At the time, Hick was a FERA investigator, so she had an official role in the trip as well. On the train from Washington to Miami, where they were scheduled to depart by plane, Hick was at Eleanor's side as a guitar-accordion-saxophone trio entertained the passengers. They sang "When You and I Were Young" and "Let Me Call You Sweetheart" while Eleanor, knitting away, bobbed her head to mark time.

That summer, the friends took off on another getaway, this time to California, where they tried, without success, to evade the pack of journalists following them. With a nationwide manhunt under way for gangster John Dillinger, Eleanor joked to the intrepid newsman who'd tracked them down, "If I had charge of the Dillinger search, I would call off the police and send reporters after him. They would be sure to find him."

Standing outside a little diner in the dry, dusty railroad town of Roseville, where they'd pulled over for some food, Eleanor was in a reflective mood. "I'm just out on a vacation," she told the reporter. She and Hick had no destination, she explained; it was all about the journey. "I'll know [where to go] in a couple of days if I can lose myself and get away from being the President's wife," Eleanor said. "I'm willing to be the President's wife when I join him, but I'd like to get away from that while on this holiday."

That was an extraordinary thing for any wife to say in the 1930s, let alone the First Lady of the United States. Eleanor was an anomaly. One newspaper feature, chronicling various presidents' wives, noted that "Mrs. Franklin D. Roosevelt is the first to be a public figure and personage in her own right." She was not only "mistress of the White House" but also a "lecturer, writer [and] civic leader . . . unique in the long line to which she belongs."

She had inaugurated a tradition unthinkable before her own time in the White House: regular Monday morning press conferences, not with the president, but with the First Lady, and to a press corps composed solely of female journalists. The topics were not dinner parties or White House menus, either, but policy: the impact of Social Security, the rights of workers, child welfare laws. At her press conferences, Eleanor was always informed, articulate, and unflappable. "I'd never have believed it possible for a woman to develop after fifty as you have," Hick wrote to her in awe. "My God, you've learned to do surprisingly well two of the most difficult things in the world—to write and to speak."

Praise came from other, more surprising sources. A year into Franklin's first term, Aunt Edith sent Eleanor a letter commending her for the way she handled her responsibilities: "I am quite sure I did not deal with them as efficiently as you have done." The note was likely both gracious and somewhat disingenuous, as Eleanor was about as far from Edith's ideal of a First Lady as could be imagined. For Eleanor, however, it was the only way she could survive the job.

By 1937, she was doing more than just surviving; she was thriving. With Hick at her side, Eleanor had, for the very first time in her life, achieved a balance between personal fulfillment and her sense of public duty. Sitting with her children at the Jim

Farley tribute, with Hick and other close female friends at a table close behind her, listening as Franklin delivered the evening's key address, Eleanor couldn't have been happier. She was doing good work, the sort of work Mlle. Souvestre had encouraged her to do. She was making a difference.

Yet, behind the scenes, her relationship with Franklin was not always so sanguine. Although he shared more policy with her than most previous presidents had done with their wives, Eleanor wished he'd discuss even more and allow her greater leeway in the development of ideas. His files were stuffed with memos from Eleanor, typed up by her secretary Malvina "Tommy" Thompson, stating her opinions on the important issues of the day. After getting a letter from a citizen telling her that she "poked her nose" into too many things, Eleanor laughingly called herself the "First Nuisance." She took the criticism as a compliment.

Franklin did allow her to spearhead a few projects on her own, such as a subsistence farming community in Arthurdale, West Virginia, that Hick had helped engineer. (Eleanor hoped Arthurdale might become a model for the nation.) Still, she played no official role in public life other than as her husband's goodwill ambassador.

Had Louis Howe lived, however, that might have changed one day. Howe was the first man truly to recognize Eleanor's inherent gifts and political skill. He had devoted twenty years to making Franklin president, and soon after that goal was reached, he'd told Eleanor that, within the next ten years, he'd make her president as well. The notion seemed wild, absurd. Perhaps it was uttered in the adrenaline thrill of victory. Yet Howe had never been a man to make idle promises or engage in improbable speculation. If he said that he could make Eleanor president, he believed it. But would anyone else?

Even with all the talk in recent years of Alice Longworth running for vice president, the public seemed unwilling to accept the idea of a female chief executive. A Gallup poll in 1937 showed that only 33 percent of Americans were open to voting for a woman as president. The times were constantly changing, though. Sixty percent were now willing to vote for a Catholic, a concept unimaginable when Eleanor was young.

One of the last essays Howe wrote before he died was about women in politics. "Forty years ago," he observed, "a woman interested in politics was as scarce as an Irish snake." Now women had forced male politicians out of their "peaceful sloth" and transformed the playing field. Howe gave much of the credit to Eleanor and such activist friends as Nancy Cook, Molly Dewson, and Polly Porter. "Once tasting a sense of political power," women had made "many sweeping changes," he wrote, "and are now rapidly approaching an equal power with men." He argued that women were in fact superior political creatures, better campaigners and more intelligent policy makers. Soon, he predicted, the nation would be faced with "not only the possibility but the *advisability* of electing a woman as President of the United States."

No other woman, Howe believed, was as qualified for that job as Eleanor Roosevelt. "He always wanted to 'make' me President when FDR was through," Eleanor wrote to Hick after Howe's death, "and insisted he could do it."

Was she interested? Eleanor had never sought the kind of acclaim Franklin had hungered for since he was a young man. She'd never been motivated by the same sort of personal ambition. Certainly, when she first joined Franklin on the political road back in 1920, an elected position for herself was not on her mind. Yet now, after all they'd been through, after all she'd done to prove herself on the campaign trail, on the lecture circuit, in the convention halls, did Eleanor ever imagine a greater future for herself?

Certainly she was not hindered by a fear of public speaking the way her cousin Alice was; Eleanor had become a natural in front of groups, able to charm an audience and disarm a heckler. Confronted once by a group of men determined to disrupt a talk she was giving in Eau Claire, Wisconsin, she refused to become rattled, and instead answered the men's questions with the sort of dignity that made them look petty. She could handle herself on any stage.

Louis Howe was right. If any woman could have run for president and won, it was Eleanor. Yet once Howe was gone, Eleanor shot the idea down when a reporter asked her about it. Would she run in 1940, at the end of her husband's current term? "To elect anyone president," Eleanor replied, "the candidate has to be willing. And there would be strenuous objection on my part." Of course, she *had* to say such a thing. Franklin's opponents would have jumped all over him if they'd thought he was grooming his wife to be his successor. Besides, there was always the possibility, however remote, that Franklin might run for a third term himself.

Yet the second part of her answer to the reporter's question suggested where her thoughts really lay. While a woman was "capable of being president," she said, "they could never get the backing," so, "under the circumstances[,] to nominate any woman would not be a service to the country."

Under the circumstances.

Circumstances could change.

Hick knew this as well as anyone. By 1937, she sensed Eleanor moving away from her, toward a greater national destiny. Finding time to spend with Eleanor had become increasingly difficult ever since Hick left her job at the Federal Emergency Relief Administration. There, working under Harry Hopkins, one of the president's closest advisers and friends, she'd always been in close proximity to the First Lady. Now, working for the World's Fair, Hick was in New York more often than not. Eleanor had taken a New York apartment, in a house owned by Esther Lape, but when she was there, she was usually consumed with duties. The two friends were definitely feeling the distance.

Hick had sorely needed to make the change, however. She had become desperately unhappy in her work at FERA. For a former journalist, Hick turned out to have surprisingly thin skin. When *Time* magazine described her as "a rotund lady with a husky voice, a peremptory manner [and] baggy clothes," she was very hurt. There was also the implication that she'd gotten the job because of her friendship with Eleanor, which Hick "bitterly" resented. "I love Mrs. Roosevelt dearly," she wrote to a colleague at FERA. "She is the best friend I have in the world. But sometimes I do wish she was Mrs. Joe Doaks of Oelwein, Iowa!"

How different indeed things might have been if the woman Hick loved hadn't been the wife of the president of the United States. Yet that was a fact of her life, and after three years at FERA,

Hick longed to return to journalism, and to some semblance of her old life. She considered becoming a foreign correspondent covering the Spanish Civil War. Eleanor, however, wasn't keen about letting her go that far. "I'd hate to go to Europe and see a war," she wrote to Hick. Accordingly, she pushed her friend in the direction of the World's Fair job; New York, after all, was a lot closer than Madrid.

Their time together had become more precious because it was less frequent. In April 1937 the two women set off in Eleanor's little roadster once more, heading into the Great Smoky Mountains of Tennessee and North Carolina. Up to the top of Clingmans Dome they drove, and then out toward Bryson City for an exhibition of Cherokee pottery. In Asheville, they stopped for provisions and were caught by a reporter. "I have no plans," Eleanor said, much as she had on earlier trips. "I just go."

She and Hick ended their holiday in Charleston, South Carolina. "The trip has been really beautiful," Eleanor wrote to Anna. They'd taken fewer hikes this time, since Hick had been "in an office all winter," but they did walk four miles "to see some wonderful trees and she bore up nobly."

When they got home, Hick returned to her office in New York, and Eleanor found herself increasingly alone. The balance she'd achieved so belatedly in her life now seemed fleeting. When Franklin got angry with her over an offhand comment she made in one of her columns about his displeasure with White House food—a remark Eleanor had found "amusing and human"—she began to count the days until they were out of office. "Will I be glad when we leave the White House," she wrote to Anna, "and I can be on my own!" Left unsaid was whether she ever contemplated coming back.

VICTORIA, BRITISH COLUMBIA

The reporter from the Associated Press found Mrs. Theodore Roosevelt Jr., currently the country's most famous war refugee, seated on an upturned suitcase in her stateroom on the SS *President Jefferson*. She was furiously dictating the account of her ordeal to her seventeen-year-old son, Quentin, whose fingers were flying over the keys of a portable typewriter positioned on his lap.

"If the national administration takes the attitude Americans should stay at home," Eleanor Butler Roosevelt snapped, "then why the Asiatic fleet?"

The *President Jefferson* had just made it safely across the Pacific, one of the last ships out of war-torn China, steaming into Victoria Harbour on September 7, 1937, for a short layover on her way to Seattle. Eleanor, fuming over an experience she couldn't wait to let the world know about, seized the opportunity to get her statement out to the press.

When she was done dictating her account, she instructed Quentin to pull the paper from his typewriter and hand it over to the reporter. Eleanor intended that her story would be in all the evening papers. She was spitting mad. She and Quentin had just been through a terrible nightmare, and she blamed it all (as she blamed most things) on Dear Cousin Franklin.

Eleanor's ordeal had started the previous spring. She'd needed a change of environment and a bit of an adventure after furnishing and decorating the new house that she and Ted had built in Oyster Bay, not far from Sagamore Hill. Months of overseeing the installation of upholstery and curtains had left her simply exhausted, and Ted feared she'd work herself "to death" over the house. "Why don't you go to China?" he'd suggested, as any helpful, upper-class husband might. "A month on the sea going out, a month there, and another coming back would do you a lot of good." In fact, he suggested, Eleanor ought to take Quentin with her. What "a splendid trip" it would be for him, Ted thought, before the boy started Harvard in the fall.

They didn't seem too worried about mounting tensions between China and Japan, despite warnings from Washington to Americans traveling there. After all, Ted and Eleanor had friends in high places in China. They were well acquainted with Madame Chiang Kai-shek, the wife of the Chinese president; Ted, in fact, in his latest employment venture as an editor at Doubleday (a position secured for him by his friend Nelson Doubleday), was publishing Madame Chiang's memoirs. So mother and son had packed their bags and boarded a train to Chicago, where they transferred onto the "Gangplank Special," a fast train commissioned exclusively by wealthy East Coast travelers heading to West Coast seaports. From Seattle, on July 4, they set sail for the Far East on the *President Jackson*. On July 7, while they were still at sea, Japan invaded China.

For people with money and connections, such as the Roosevelts, the war proved only a minor inconvenience. Routes were still open to them; hotels and restaurants still waited to accommodate them. All they needed to do was to use common sense and avoid problem areas. "We had planned to go to Peking," Eleanor remembered, "but our ambassador, Joseph Grew, an old friend, mentioned the trouble that had broken out near Tientsin between the Chinese and the Japanese and said to me, 'If you went to Peking, you might get into trouble, and you might get us into trouble getting you out. Now be good. Go back on your steamer and land at Shanghai." Eleanor followed his advice.

While hundreds of people, civilians and combatants, were being killed in Peking (the contemporary English spelling of Beijing), Eleanor and Quentin toured Chengdu and flew on to Chongqing, where they were the guests of an executive from Standard Oil. They stayed at his palatial home atop a mountain overlooking the city. At another point, Eleanor lunched with Madame Chiang, picking up the manuscript Ted planned to publish. She was having, Eleanor would recall, a "remarkable time."

Yet Japanese troops were pushing onward, taking over parts of Shanghai. The death toll mounted. Eleanor and Quentin were staying in a suburb of the city, only a few miles from the fighting. In her statement to the press, Eleanor would insist that she had no idea the war had gotten so close. She told of having dinner with the American banker William P. Hunt, at a restaurant where they were entertained by a troupe of Hungarian gypsies. They laughed and drank and tipped the gypsies. "No one had the faintest idea of what was to happen in the next forty-eight hours," Eleanor would say.

Except, of course, people *did* have an idea. The State Department had been issuing travel advisories for Americans in China

for the past week. Even as they applauded their gypsy trouba-
dours, Eleanor and Hunt were wondering just how close the fighting might get. "Between courses," Eleanor remembered, "we kept
going outdoors to see if we could hear firing, but everything was
quiet."

Impulsively, recklessly, they decided on a little war tourism.
Rousing Quentin—Eleanor knew her son "would never forgive"
her if she went without him—they made for the Hongkou part of
Shanghai, where Japanese soldiers were guarding the streets with
bayonets. Eleanor hadn't had time to change before setting out.
"I had on my best evening dress of pale organza with a full skirt
trimmed with black lace," she said, as she stepped over broken
glass and debris. Whole blocks of buildings ahead of them were
on fire. Smoke filled the air, and the sound of gunfire echoed
through the streets. When they headed back to Hunt's house for
the night, the trio of American sightseers passed "thousands of
refugees sleeping on the ground," as Eleanor would recall.

A few days later, the Japanese flagship *Idzumo*, anchored in the
Huangpu River, began shelling Shanghai. After lunch, Eleanor
and Quentin hurried over to the Cathay Hotel, where, from the
eighth floor, they could see the river and watch the show. When
the signal lights on the *Idzumo* started to blink, Eleanor turned
to Quentin and said, "Watch now, it is going to begin." Her husband had been assistant secretary of the navy, after all; she knew
about such things. In fascination they watched as the city was
bombarded, and turned away only when the hotel was evacuated.
Before leaving, Eleanor "left a note with the telephone boy telling him where we were going in case friends wanted to find us."
Twenty minutes later, she'd recall, "our friends stepped over the
boy's body." Perhaps it was time, Eleanor decided, to go home.

That was easier said than done by this point. More than four
hundred American evacuees were forced to cram onto a small
tender that would take them down the Huangpu to the port
of Shanghai. To proclaim their neutrality, a few U.S. Marines
stretched an American flag in front of the smokestack. "We were
jammed in the tiny cabin so that it was literally impossible to
move," Eleanor said in the statement that Quentin would type

up for the press recounting their ordeal. She was outraged that American battleships, anchored nearby, did nothing to assist them. "Why did not one of them," she asked, "convey us as a visible guard?"

Now that she was safely back on this side of the Pacific, that was the question she wanted put to Washington. How gutless was Dear Cousin Franklin, unwilling to defend American citizens at risk! Eleanor intended to expose Franklin's cowardice. If Ted had been president, surely he wouldn't have given an order to his fleet to stand down when Americans were in danger.

When the *President Jefferson* finally arrived back in American waters, docking at Seattle around 6:00 p.m. on September 7, Eleanor was no doubt pleased to discover that the newspapers on the pier had printed her indignant statement. Her words indicted Franklin in stark black and white. "What does all the talk from the State Department mean about protecting American citizens when, in a case of real danger like this, nothing is done? If our ships are not used to guard us, why are they kept in anchorage in the Whangpoo [Huangpu] River where bombs and shells are falling like hailstones?"

Of course, she seemed not to consider the chance that even one fired cannon might have plunged America into the Sino-Japanese War. Such concerns were utterly beside the point. Eleanor was angry, and she intended to let Franklin (and the entire world) know just how much. She and Quentin were *refugees*, she insisted, just like those people sleeping on the sides of the road.

Yet, of course, not entirely like them. When the *President Jefferson* had stopped in Kobe, Japan, Eleanor realized that they'd lose a lot of money if she changed her Chinese currency back into dollars. So she exchanged it for Japanese yen and went on a shopping spree. "It was lovely being forced to spend all that money in order to save it!" she remembered. She and Quentin bought bronzes, porcelains, rolls of brocade, and fifteenth-century Buddha sculptures—and as she noted in her memoir with great satisfaction, she got them at a discount because tourist season had passed. When they debarked in Seattle, Eleanor recalled, "We were followed by a procession of coolies carrying our well-packed purchases."

Once back home in Oyster Bay, Eleanor simmered down, probably on orders from her husband. Ted was no fan of Franklin, but he would have understood the geopolitics that kept those battleships idle. Congress had voted nearly unanimously to remain neutral in the conflict; as Sen. Lewis Schwellenbach of Washington declared, in the only official response to Eleanor's complaints, the president was merely following the law. If U.S. troops had been forced to fire against a Japanese ship, America might have found itself not just at war with Japan but in conflict with Japan's ally Germany, and that was something Eleanor's husband felt very strongly against.

Ted remained fiercely opposed to America becoming embroiled in any foreign war, even as Japanese aggression spread across China. So, almost certainly, when Eleanor got home, he told her to mute her criticism of Franklin; she apparently complied, as the issue was not raised again. Most likely, though, she did not button her lip happily, since the bitterness toward her husband's Hyde Park cousins had seeped in very deep.

A year earlier, on a lecture tour about life in the Philippines intended to replenish the family coffers as they planned their new house, Eleanor accepted an invitation to speak at the town hall in Fort Worth, Texas. Yet when she learned that Elliott Roosevelt, Franklin's son, had been asked to introduce her, she balked. Immediately she shot off a letter threatening to renege on her agreement to appear unless Elliott were canned from the event; her husband's politics, she said, "differed in every aspect" from those of Elliott's father, and "it would be embarrassing for all concerned" if the young man were present. When contacted by the organizers, Elliott withdrew, as per her wishes, but he also made sure to leak the story to the press, no doubt knowing how petty Eleanor would appear. She seemed utterly unfazed.

Eleanor believed these people had cheated her husband out of his rightful place in history. When James Roosevelt, Franklin's eldest son, was taken to the hospital for an operation, Ted wrote a very gracious note of support to the young man's mother, who replied equally as graciously that no matter how old children got, their parents continued to worry about them. She was sure she worried about her son Elliott in Texas just as Ted "must be anxious about Cornelius," his son who had gone to Mexico to work. It was a perfectly innocuous communication between parents, but Ted's wife, Eleanor, would scrawl "Not for the same reasons!" across the bottom of the letter, wanting to make clear for posterity that their son wasn't as wayward and shifty as Franklin's.

If Eleanor was bitter, Ted was more "gloomy and depressed" during this period, as Kermit observed. His positions at American Express and Doubleday had failed to inspire him; at fifty years old, he was dissatisfied with what he had achieved in life. Considered for an international position assisting Jewish refugees from Europe, he was ultimately not chosen. Mentioned as chairman of the National Republican Committee, he never had the votes. Even his governorship of the Philippines was no longer an unqualified triumph. When he left the post, he trumpeted his achievement of turning a budget deficit into a two-million-dollar surplus. A few months later, however, an auditor discovered that his report had been based on estimates and that, in fact, Ted had left the Philippines worse than he'd found it, to the tune of five million dollars in debt. The resulting headlines were deeply embarrassing.

Ted was also, by the mid-1930s, homeless. What fifty-year-old man of his rank and class did not own his own home? Kermit and Archie had theirs, but Ted and Eleanor had, in effect, been waiting for Edith to die. Sagamore Hill was supposed to be theirs. When Edith broke her hip a couple of years earlier, many predicted she'd never return to Oyster Bay and that she'd deed the property over to Ted. Yet the old warhorse surprised them all by recovering and reclaiming her house and her life. Ted grew cold toward his mother. "As far as he is concerned," Edith wrote to Kermit, "it had been better if I had been dead."

In their mother's standoff with Ted, Archie sided with Edith; he had no desire to see Sagamore Hill, so rich with the memory of their father, taken out of the reach of his own children. Ted fired off a letter to Archie bewailing how he (Ted) had "never known what it meant to . . . plan and work on improvements on your own home." So he gave up on his dream of making Sagamore his own and purchased the land adjacent to it, tearing up Alice's

Fairy Apple Orchard and building his own Georgian mansion. His daughter Grace's husband, William McMillan, was the architect, giving the place all the grandness Ted requested, from wide corridors to high ceilings. When it was finished, the walls were hung with portraits of Roosevelts stretching back into the eighteenth century. Just as his father had done, Ted lined the floors with bearskins and arrayed the walls with the heads of beasts he had killed. There were mementos and souvenirs from the world war, from Puerto Rico, from the Philippines, from the campaign trail. One friend, after a visit, would privately comment, "It looked like a museum of past dreams."

That fall, while Ted's wife recuperated from her Chinese misadventure by exhibiting her needlework at a Park Avenue gallery, Ted had a new enterprise. He and his sister Alice were putting the finishing touches on *The Desk Drawer Anthology*, a book of American poetry they'd compiled for Doubleday. Alice had some time on her hands at the moment. Her column had been dropped by the McNaught Syndicate. Within the industry, Alice's declining readership had become a joke: "The cigarette advertisement lady, Alice Roosevelt Longworth," one pundit observed, referring to Alice's tobacco ads, "also writes a column, but it may be less widely read." The loss of her column also deprived her of the best platform from which to needle Franklin.

Both she and Ted hoped for more success with *The Desk Drawer Anthology*. Billed "as American as Indian corn," the book came out just in time for Christmas, and Ted traveled a bit promoting it. Although the *New York Times* didn't get around to reviewing it until the following August ("some is fine poetry, but more is tangy, homely verse"), it did get one prominent mention before the end of the year: in First Lady Eleanor's "My Day" column—which, to Alice's chagrin, had continued to thrive.

"No two people I know," Eleanor wrote, "are better fitted to do a book of this kind. They were brought up on poetry. I don't remember much about Ted's memory, but I have always regarded Alice's with awe." That line must have made Alice guffaw.

The First Lady's memoir, titled *This Is My Story*, had also recently been published, in November 1937. It was immediately reviewed by the *Times* and praised as "candid, unaffected and courageous." Ted read it, and was apparently grateful for one passage: Eleanor offered a mea culpa for the "Singing Teapot" episode, admitting that Ted had "had nothing to do" with Teapot Dome. Ted seemed to feel such an admission was better late than never, because he sent Eleanor a copy of *The Desk Drawer Anthology*, inscribed, "Dear Eleanor, I bought your book and liked it very much. This book comes to you as a present. Merry Christmas."

The gift of Ted's book seemed to touch a nerve for Eleanor. In her column dated December 30, 1937, she acknowledged feeling some guilt—for not sending Ted a copy of her own book, she said, but maybe there was a little more to her self-reproach. In print, for the whole world to read, she promised her cousin, "I'll be more thoughtful next time."

For all the antagonism that roiled the Oyster Bay family during this period, however, none was as painful as the war they fought with Kermit. No longer was it just his fraternization with Franklin that perturbed his family; now his affair with a masseuse and the threat of scandal it posed left them outraged. Belle, they learned, had suffered a nervous breakdown while traveling in Europe, and Kermit had placed her in a Swiss sanitarium for a period. Yet, as Belle's later letters would indicate, no one reached out to help them.

In response to Kermit's behavior, the family was doing what Roosevelts nearly always did when one of their own broke the rules. They iced him out. Kermit's absence from the family broke his seventy-six-year-old mother's heart. He was Edith's favorite son, and the family matriarch declared herself willing to defy the others if Kermit only said the word. "Dearest Kermit," she wrote that October. "I am always thinking about you, and should you ever want to see me, I will appear." He never put her in that position, however. He simply accepted his exile without protest.

The same would not be true, however, for his wife.

MANHATTAN

Christmas lights still twinkled around the doors of the River Club on East Fifty-Second Street, at the bank of the East River, as Belle

Roosevelt, one of the city's most popular socialites, arrived in typically grand style, gesturing to friends, blowing kisses, supremely confident that all eyes were on her. It was soon after the New Year, 1938. As usual, Belle was dressed to the nines. Her plumed hats and couture fashion were the envy of many club women. While most nights Belle was accompanied to the club by other glittering ladies, this evening her companion was more plainly dressed, and seemed distinctly ill at ease with the doormen holding doors open for her and the waiters fluttering around, offering flutes of champagne on silver platters.

The two women settled themselves at the bar, a mix of Art Deco platinum and tropical wicker and bamboo. Belle ordered for both of them. Beyond, through the large windows, the lights of the city sparkled off the dark river. During the summer, the adjacent tennis and squash courts were jammed with Astors and Rockefellers working up a sweat, and the marina was filled with their yachts. Many times, Belle and Kermit had stepped off Vincent Astor's *Nourmahal* right there and strolled up to the club for dinner. For a time, Kermit had been the president of the River Club. Tonight, however, he was nowhere to be seen. This was a night out for Belle and her new friend.

When club members stopped by the bar to greet her, Belle introduced them to the modest, quiet woman sitting beside her. A friend of the family, Belle explained. Her name was Carla Peters.

Some of the club members surely knew, or at least suspected, just what sort of friend Carla was. In New York society, word got around quickly when a man as prominent as Kermit took a mistress. In addition, just before the New Year, there'd been a bit of embarrassment in the newspapers when one of Kermit's ships, the *City of Hamburg*, collided with an Italian steamer in the North Sea. While the ship was a freighter bound for New York, wireless reports revealed that there was in fact one passenger on board: a "Miss Herta Peters of New York." The disabled ship made its way back to Germany while passage was arranged for Miss Peters's return to New York on the SS *Washington*. For those with some knowledge of the situation, it wasn't difficult to figure out what had likely happened: as fear of a European war escalated, Kermit arranged for his mistress to discreetly visit her homeland via a freight vessel, sailing under her original German first name. If not for the collision of the *City of Hamburg*, no one would have been the wiser.

In response to her husband's indiscretion, Belle might have done what other wives had always done: hid her face, disappeared from the scene for a while, or, perhaps, carried on stoically. Yet Belle had never been like other society wives: She'd hunted with Kermit across Asia, learning how to fire a gun. She'd cheered herself hoarse at prizefights, getting splattered with sweat and blood. Belle, in other words, was no shrinking violet, her breakdown in Europe the previous year notwithstanding. In fact, she'd entered the Swiss sanitarium on the advice of Kermit, who seemed to hope that some quiet contemplation on his wife's part would make her accept his peccadillos. Yet no amount of time away could persuade her to give up on her marriage.

Their four children were pretty much all grown by now. Kim was an associate professor of history at Harvard, his alma mater, married and with a baby son, Kermit III. Willard was also at Harvard, approaching graduation, and had all the makings of a brilliant musician. Clochette, eighteen, was still recovering from her injuries but was making great strides; and Dirck, thirteen, had just entered Groton. Belle was fighting for them as much as for herself: she knew how gossip spread in social circles, and she simply could not abide what it would do to her children.

At forty-five, she'd lost the piquant beauty that first attracted Kermit, but she remained a fashionable, good-looking woman, the kind called "handsome" in those days. Returning from her stay in the sanitarium, she tried laying down the law with Kermit, asking him to give up his mistress for the sake of the family. What she did not do, however, was offer him his freedom, as Eleanor had done with Franklin. That left them at an impasse, since Kermit, increasingly smitten with Carla, refused to break off the affair.

So Belle had embarked on a strategy few others in her place would ever have had the strength or the chutzpah to pull off: she took Carla under her wing. Her reasoning went this way: if the woman spotted with Kermit was known to be his wife's protégée, and seen as frequently with her as she was with Kermit, then the gossip might be mitigated, even managed.

It was a bold plan, but really Belle's only option if she wanted to save face. Kermit was becoming less and less discreet about the affair. Even Franklin, on Belle's urging, had advised his cousin to cool things down. "Why can't you keep your women on the side like the rest of us?" the president asked Kermit, as Carla would remember.

Franklin's intervention did no good. Kermit brought his mistress to his various clubs, and to restaurants where they were seen by all the busybodies in town. His behavior to the wife he insisted he still loved was uncharacteristically cruel, yet he seemed incapable of stopping himself. He was, as one family member speculated, weary of playing the part of the "dutiful son, brother and husband." Carla offered him "a taste of the life he could have lived" had he not been a Roosevelt. The alcohol, of course, contributed to his impropriety. Kermit was drinking more than ever—the family curse his mother so feared. Yet it seemed to have given him the courage to break out of his stultifying routine.

One winter day, he brought Carla to his father's grave in the little cemetery at Oyster Bay. Sitting together on the frozen grass, they spoke very little, just looked out through the bare branches of the trees toward Long Island Sound, where his father had taught Kermit to swim. With Carla, Kermit could be a little boy again, the daydreamer in the windowsill. Still, real life always beckoned, with its rules and obligations. When Carla suggested they plant some crocus bulbs around the grave so there would be color in the spring, Kermit demurred. "Mother wouldn't like that," he said.

Theodore had convinced his sons that the world could be theirs if only they worked hard enough to grab it. Kermit had believed it, and did indeed work very hard, but by the start of 1938 he had very little to show for it. All his shipping companies were in debt; he could barely pay the bills. His income for the last year had been $16,585, two dollars less than Cousin Eleanor had made that year from her newspaper columns alone. Kermit wanted out—out of his business and out of his life. The bottle, and Carla, provided his escape.

In the past, a renegade Roosevelt was ostracized. When Elliott took a mistress, Theodore insisted that his wife, to be honorable, should no longer live with him. Belle didn't see it that way. She embraced the emerging consensus that alcoholism was a disease, not a personal failing; its solution was not condemnation and exile, but treatment. She tried to get Kermit to see a psychiatrist; when he refused, she went herself, dragging Carla along with her. She tried to enlist Kermit's brothers in an effort to help him, but their judgmental attitude only "caused trouble and unnecessary pain," as Belle would describe it. The previous spring, when Belle and Kermit were in Alaska on a combination business and hunting trip, Ted and Archie had failed their brother in some way, possibly by not helping him out in a financial crunch. Belle would later bitterly refer to this period as "the Alaska episodes." The Roosevelt brothers still held to what Belle considered an outmoded view of social correctness; they had, apparently, washed their hands of Kermit. Belle considered herself her husband's only hope.

For all her good intentions, Belle was no saint. She could get angry and frustrated, phoning Carla in the middle of the night and growling, "If I can't sleep, I don't want you to sleep either." Once, at the Waldorf-Astoria, she bit Carla on the arm when she refused to cooperate in some face-saving plan. Also, Belle hadn't entirely given up on the idea of separating the lovers permanently. In the spring of 1938, she arranged for Kermit to get away for a while on Vincent Astor's yacht, in the hope that he'd forget Carla. In addition, to boost his sense of family responsibility, she sent Clochette along.

Father and daughter set sail with Astor for the Pacific. For several weeks they cruised through idyllic blue waters, tacking back and forth through the atolls and coral reefs of the Gilbert and Ellice Islands. They docked at Honolulu on April 29 for a weeklong Hawaiian sojourn, but as soon as they arrived, Kermit abruptly changed his itinerary and hopped onboard the SS *Matsonia* for Los Angeles; Clochette was left to sail back to the mainland by herself. Almost certainly, the reason Kermit was heading to LA was to meet Carla, who had arrived out west shortly before.

Belle came to the realization that she could not end the affair. If she wanted to stay married to Kermit, she could only accept it.

Clochette was not the only child Kermit left unattended. Back home, his youngest son, Dirck, was struggling in school, his father's absences and alcoholism not helping the boy's outlook on life. Dirck was very much Kermit's son, the different child, the one with the poetic soul, the one without the ambition of his brothers—yet another Roosevelt who chafed against the rigid structures and expectations of his class. "Groton disappoints me greatly," Dirck's first letter back home read. "Groton disappoints me still more," his next letter echoed. He ran away from the school more than once, and despite his pleas to his parents, he was always sent back.

As later events would reveal, Dirck was homosexual, and his differences made him the target of jeers, pranks, and slurs from his classmates. In the spring of 1938, he bolted the school once more, this time with a friend, Henry Distler, also thirteen, the son of a Baltimore industrialist. As an adult, living as a bachelor in Sweden and making occasional visits back to the United States, Henry would style himself Henry Von Distler-Dircksen or Henry Distler zu Dircsen. It's tempting to imagine that the "Dircksen," which apparently existed nowhere else in his family, was in honor of his boyhood friend Dirck Roosevelt.

The two runaways were traced to Springfield, Massachusetts, where police just missed them but found an essay written by one of the boys left behind at their hotel. "If a man feels it necessary to take his own life, should he be condemned?" the essay read. Eventually the boys turned up at Henry's house in Baltimore. They were immediately put back on a train to New York, where Henry's father was waiting with Belle. When they arrived at the train station, a fight broke out between their waiting chauffeurs. The fracas was reported widely in the press but never satisfactorily explained—just like so much of Dirck's life.

Despite the evidence of suicidal thoughts, the despondent teenager was returned to Groton. Belle might have been willing to make accommodations for her husband's nonconformity, but not her son's.

Kermit, even if he had wanted to intercede on Dirck's behalf, could not have done so. He was drying out at Doctors Hospital on East End Avenue in New York City. On May 28 he wrote to his sister Ethel that he was making satisfactory progress. By May 31, he was out of the hospital, paying another fine in Traffic Court, but by the early part of June, he'd suffered a "relapse" and was back at Doctors Hospital, as reported by Walter Winchell in his column. The relapse was claimed to be a recurrence of the malaria Kermit had picked up in South America more than two decades earlier. Most everyone knew better.

When he was finally discharged, Kermit understood that the responsible path forward was to remain with his wife, tend to his troubled family, and do what he could to make his shipping lines profitable again. It also meant breaking off with Carla. Surely that was what his father would have done. Yet Kermit was not like his father—not in the least.

CINCINNATI, OHIO

On a warm autumn day in 1938, Eleanor's chauffeur steered the car along the road that ran adjacent to the meandering Ohio River, a route freshly paved and tarred by the Works Progress Administration, a fact the First Lady would make sure to point out in her column when she wrote about her trip to the Buckeye State. The year before, Cincinnati suffered severe flooding after heavy rains, with water levels rising to eighty feet, the worst in the city's history. On this bright, sunny day, however, the devastation of just a year earlier was nowhere to be seen. "It is such a sleepy, quiet river," Eleanor would write in her column, "one can hardly imagine that it ever gets out of hand." That was because federal assistance had poured into the region, and the U.S. Army Corps of Engineers was now hard at work building a system of storage reservoirs to reduce the impact of future floods. Under Franklin, this kind of response had become the norm after national disasters, a far cry from the days when Theodore could only offer a sympathetic tour by his daughter after the ravaging Baltimore fires.

The First Lady was not in Cincinnati just to inspect the rebuilt

Ohio River, however. On a lecture tour through the Midwest, she'd decided to pay a call on her cousin Mrs. Longworth, who, as she always did at voting time, had temporarily relocated to her Ohio residence. The congressional elections had seen a number of Republican gains. While Democrats maintained control of both houses of Congress, their majority had been significantly whittled down, suggesting that Franklin needed to give the opposition more consideration in setting policy. A cordial visit by Eleanor to the most prominent Republican Roosevelt was therefore a prudent move at this particular time.

When Eleanor arrived at Alice's home, she was greeted by her cousin's daughter, Paulina, a quiet, pretty thirteen-year-old and "a born horsewoman who loves animals," Eleanor wrote. Among her pets were a horse, a Jerusalem donkey, and a fat little pony "whose usefulness is long past," all meandering across the grounds freely without any enclosures.

In her column, Eleanor made a point to compliment Alice's house. The place hadn't been changed since the 1880s, she wrote, retaining many fine old pieces of furniture and the era's beautiful woodwork. "It is a comfortable house . . . made bright and livable with light walls and chintzes," Eleanor wrote. Still, she seemed unable to resist a subtle dig: "Open fires burned in every room and, though the period of the Eighties is not at present our ideal of architectural beauty, still we must acknowledge that it had quality and real comfort." Without actually coming out and saying it, she implied that Alice lived in the past.

The two cousins greeted each other. There were likely kisses and smiles and cups of tea, accompanied by pleasant words that could be taken any number of ways. Eleanor and Alice didn't like each other, but on some level they needed each other. The previous spring, the press made a big deal over the fact that Alice had not been invited to the wedding of Eleanor's son John. Now, as the political pendulum seemed to be swinging back toward the Republicans, it was time for Eleanor to reach out to Alice, just as she had reached out to Ted. "I always enjoy my cousin," Eleanor wrote in her column, "for while we may laugh at each other and quarrel with each other's ideas or beliefs, I rather imagine if real trouble came that we might be good allies. Fundamental Roosevelt characteristics gravitate toward each other in times of stress."

That was malarkey. In times of stress, the fundamental Roosevelt characteristic was to tear one another to shreds. Going forward, though, it would be helpful if that dynamic changed; Franklin still had two years left in his term, and some bipartisan support, even at the eleventh hour, would legitimize his legacy. There was also the possibility that he might actually run for a *third term*, breaking all precedent; peace with Oyster Bay would certainly be helpful in that case. Still, a third term was something Eleanor didn't like to contemplate.

As 1938 drew to a close, Eleanor's world was changing. Within the past eighteen months, not only John but Franklin Junior had married; now all her children had left the nest, starting families of their own. In addition, James was resigning his post as his father's assistant and moving to Los Angeles to work for Samuel Goldwyn's film studio. Eleanor had never been pleased by James's White House position, feeling it left him and the family open to too many conflicts of interest; but now that he was leaving, bitter at his mother for her lack of support, she was quite sad. "James has not said one word to me about his plans," Eleanor lamented to Anna. As ever, her children remained enigmas to her.

The stress and isolation of being First Lady were taking their toll. In addition to the distance with her children, Eleanor had lost some of her family of choice as well. The friendship with Nancy and Marion, once so sustaining, had been growing more distant as Eleanor spent more time on the road and with Hick. A series of incidents over the past few years had driven the wedge between the friends deeper. Eleanor frequently invited reporters, labor activists, grandchildren, and others to Val-Kill, and Nancy and Marion resented their loss of solitude. Also, when Marion held a fund-raiser for the Todhunter School, she was stung by Eleanor's apathy for the project. "I am terribly sorry," Eleanor wrote. "I do not intend to make the school one of my major interests." It was quite the change from just a few years earlier.

The final break came that summer. Eleanor and Nancy had a terrible row during which both said things they regretted. Nancy implied that she and Marion had made Eleanor what she was. While her friends had unquestionably assisted her, Eleanor resented not being given credit for her own transformation—and not receiving credit had been a lifelong pattern for her. The friendship would never be fully repaired. "Eleanor never forgot a hurt, never," Marion would write. "There was forgiveness in Franklin in many instances but I never found it in Eleanor." The most altruistic of women, Eleanor had also learned how to hold a grudge.

Nancy and Marion could be snobs; they could be possessive and judgmental. They had also grown closer to Franklin, and seemed to have become more supportive of his issues than Eleanor's. Yet their worst crime, for Eleanor, was that they had failed to love and support her unconditionally. That was what she had always longed for from family and friends since she was a lonely child in her grandmother's house.

"Such damned fools!" Hick wrote to her after the rift with Nancy and Marion, trying to be supportive. "I hate to see you disillusioned that way."

In fact, the distance was growing with Hick as well. Bored in her new life shilling for the World's Fair after a career spent traveling the country, Hick had turned into a recluse: "I do so need to be alone—my temper and state of mind are so uncertain," she wrote to Eleanor. She was also resentful that Eleanor called all the shots in their relationship. Back when she was in Minneapolis, she and her then lover, Ella, made a home for themselves, entertaining friends and living with a degree of freedom and authenticity. Now Hick was alone, unable to spend time with, or even fully acknowledge, the woman she loved. Nothing was dependable in the relationship with Eleanor; nothing seemed sacred. Eleanor would blithely cancel their getaways whenever duty called, which was often at the last minute. "Dearest, you are going to think me an unmitigated ass and I deserve it," Eleanor wrote to Hick when a lecture got in the way of a planned vacation together. "I know how upsetting my uncertainties have been and this is the worst of all and I am so sorry, please try to forgive me." Hick always did, though she did so less and less graciously.

From her letters, it was clear that Eleanor understood Hick's need to call someone her own. She'd felt the same way for much of her life, and it had been Hick who'd given her, for the first time, a love she didn't have to share. Hick loved her exclusively; Eleanor was the center of her world. Yet Eleanor, bound by her duty and her position, was no longer the woman she was when she and Hick first met. Now she had causes to pursue, an image to maintain. Her public life increasingly defined her. So she found herself pulling back, and Hick's love went from being nurturing to possessive. That, of course, only made Eleanor pull back more.

That past spring, the hurt feelings had reached the boiling point. Hick accused Eleanor of simultaneously controlling her and distancing from her. Eleanor had, after all, been unwilling to let Hick move on in her life, dissuading her from going to cover the war in Spain. Yet at the same time, she was no longer as present in the relationship, and Hick felt adrift. After their argument, Hick apologized for her outburst, but significantly she did not take her words back. "I'm sorry I talked to you with such bitterness," she wrote. "It wasn't fair, but since I did say it—it's true. I've felt this way for nearly a year."

To outbursts such as these, Eleanor responded patronizingly. "You poor child," she wrote at one point, her choice of words revealing. "Stop worrying . . . and enjoy what you can."

Shortly before Eleanor's trip to Cincinnati to see her cousin Alice, she had met Hick at the latter's cottage on Long Island. Finally the two friends could spend some time together. Yet Eleanor had confided to Esther Lape that she didn't really want to go; the "gaiety," she said, had departed from her relationship with Hick. "I am afraid," she told Lape, "it departs from all of us as we grow older and encounter more and more of the difficulties of life, but if we keep even a few snatches of it, it is a great help to our friends as to ourselves." She went to Long Island, then, as a help to her friend, and in the hope that maybe some small part of their former intimacy might still be salvaged.

Yet Eleanor was wrong. The gaiety did not, in fact, depart from all relationships, and she'd immediately had to concede the point when making it to Lape, since Lape and Elizabeth Read had maintained it in theirs. While the gaiety had certainly departed for Eleanor and Franklin, and for Alice and Nick, and Alice and Bill Borah, and Kermit and Belle, and Hall and both his wives, it had remained intact for Theodore and Edith, Ted and Eleanor, and a select group of others. It had certainly remained constant for Eleanor's half-brother, Elliott Mann, and his wife, Lena, who'd just celebrated their sixteenth wedding anniversary and whose photographs from Coney Island showed a couple still very much in love. Of course, Eleanor wasn't aware of their example. She saw only the gradual deterioration of her own relationships and called it inevitable.

Eleanor had grown up without any accommodation from her family; now she demanded accommodation as a condition from those friends who wanted to be in a relationship with her. Franklin, after their crisis, accommodated her, providing the balance they needed to continue on in their relationship with each other. Yet Franklin had been looking for *less* of Eleanor, not more, just as she had with him, so their needs had dovetailed. Hick, on the other hand, wanted more, not less, so she and Eleanor faced a conundrum. To assert one's own needs, as Nancy, Marion, and Hick had done, risked making Eleanor feel unsupported and only conditionally loved. It risked, in the end, driving her away. After years of being abandoned, Eleanor preferred doing the abandoning herself.

After all, as her niece would observe, when Eleanor "really loved somebody," she gave her all. The moment she felt her love "wasn't returned in that same way," however, she withdrew.

The friendship with Hick did not end, as the friendships with Nancy and Marion did, but, going forward, Eleanor erected a barrier between them. "If only you weren't the President's wife," Hick wrote to her that fall, "with all the fuss and pushing and hauling that goes with it—how I should love to travel with you! It would be a lot of fun if someday we could just go off bumming, looking at things, visiting all sorts of funny little towns."

In the past, Eleanor might have responded with equally rapturous daydreams, but now she felt the need to keep Hick's fantasies in check. "I doubt, dear, if I'll ever have the money to travel except on a money-making basis such as lecturing or writing," she responded matter-of-factly. "I cannot imagine that you would enjoy it even if I were not the president's wife, for one does of necessity so much one does not want to do."

So Eleanor filled up her loneliness with public works. Her secretary, Tommy Thompson, was now closer to her than anyone. Much more than a secretary, Tommy was also confidante and companion, living in an apartment at Val-Kill. At the end of the day, though, she was still a paid employee. Until Eleanor could escape from the White House, this was perhaps the best the First Lady could hope for when it came to friendship and intimacy.

Yet when would that escape take place? The refusal of Franklin to rule out a third term was increasingly unnerving for Eleanor. When supporters of a third term declared they'd make their plea public at an upcoming forum sponsored by the *New York Herald-Tribune* in the summer of 1938, Eleanor sent a memo to her husband stating clearly, "You know I do *not* believe in it." Franklin answered in vague generalities. He never renounced the idea.

Another movement was swirling out there. The New York League of Business and Professional Women was urging Eleanor to run for governor of New York. Her work as First Lady had been so effective that they felt it was time for her to assume an official elected position. The *New York Times*, so often snide and critical of Eleanor in its past coverage, noted that she was "so patently sincere and unpretentious in all she says and does, so ebulliently a part of every activity she undertakes, so good-humored even in the face of criticism, that she remains today one of the most popular women who ever lived in the White House." If she were to run for "Mrs. America," the newspaper concluded, "she could command a landslide of votes."

Other newspapers picked up that idea and went further, urging Eleanor to run for her husband's position at the end of his term. It would spare Franklin a controversial third-term decision while keeping his policies intact. It was more than that, however, one editorial concluded: Eleanor deserved "the presidency on the basis of her own personality and performance." Citing some of the great warrior queens of the past, the newspaper demanded of its readers, "What sound reasons can be advanced against a woman for President of the United States?"

If Eleanor ever gave serious thought to what she might be able to accomplish as governor, or as president, she could never have expressed it while Franklin remained undecided on what his own plans were for 1940. As always, she was auxiliary to him, her ambition dependent on his.

SAN FRANCISCO

Trolley cars jangled down Battery Street as Kermit met with reporters out in front of his new office. He'd been full of surprises that summer of 1938, stunning employees and stockholders in July by resigning from the International Mercantile Marine Company (IMM), the business he built from scratch nearly two decades earlier. At the time of his resignation, Kermit said that he wanted the freedom to pursue "other plans," though just what those plans were wasn't clear. Now, two weeks later, on a typically cool, foggy morning in August, he was back in the news, announcing his new position as vice president of the Kerr Steamship Company, which was actually a subsidiary of IMM.

The downsizing of his role, Kermit explained, was deliberate. Running the larger concern simply took up too much of his time, and because he wanted a change of scenery, relocating to the beautiful, slower-paced Golden Gate City was just what he had in mind.

What Kermit didn't say, but what many insiders knew, was that he had effectively run himself out of New York. He'd chosen his mistress over his wife, and no one in polite society could be seen with him anymore.

The final break with his company came abruptly. After speaking with Belle, one of Kermit's partners had insisted, for the good of the company, that he give up both his drinking and his mistress. Furious, Kermit resigned on the spot and headed to California, where Carla was waiting for him. "He seems to have broken down nervously into pieces," Archie wrote to a friend.

The position at Kerr was not as prestigious as Kermit made it out to be. Rather, it was the gift of an old friend to keep him busy a few days a week. He earned just enough money to keep himself afloat. He and Carla took a small house forty miles outside the city, in Palo Alto, where they hoped to settle into comfortable anonymity. Half a century of living up to the demands of being a Roosevelt was enough for Kermit. It was time for a new life.

Or so he thought. One night at a restaurant, a reporter recognized him. After all, Kermit had once been a very famous world explorer, and even the puffiness of his face and the dark circles under his eyes could not entirely hide his Rooseveltian features. The reporter asked him if he had plans to give any "lectures or public appearances." Kermit said he did not. Those days were over. Other sorts of days were beginning.

On the warm, sunny afternoon of Tuesday, October 4, the squeal of brakes rent the air as an automobile struck a seven-year-old girl at the corner of Gough and Grove Streets in the working-class Hayes Valley neighborhood of San Francisco. Bystanders came running. The driver of the car stepped out to look back at the damage he had caused. The little girl was alive, but bleeding and terrified, and seemed to have broken some bones. Some of her friends ran up to Octavia Street to summon her mother, Mrs. Elsie Johnson, whose husband was a deliveryman for a bakery. When the mother arrived on the scene, the driver of the car took her aside and assured her that he would pay for all hospital treatment. He gave her his card. Mrs. Johnson looked down at the name: Kermit Roosevelt. The son of the great T.R.

When the cops showed up, Kermit was not arrested. His name did not make the newspapers. But attorneys for the Johnsons did press charges, and despite fulfilling his promise to pay for the girl's treatment at Mary's Help Hospital, Kermit accepted an out-of-court compromise settlement, awarding the girl's parents an additional $550. The settlement, unlike the accident, did make the papers. Kermit was unlikely to have settled if he had not been at fault.

As with his uncle Elliott, Kermit's drinking got worse after his banishment from his family. Also as with Elliott, the shame his family felt was as much about his cohabitation with a woman far below his class as it was about his drinking. It was his refusal to give up Carla that ultimately forced Kermit out of the family.

Belle never pursued a divorce; nor did Kermit apparently want one. His wife remained his "soul mate," as he wrote in various letters, even if he could no longer live with her or keep up the masquerade of the life they'd once lived. To people who asked, Belle explained that Kermit was just off exploring business possibilities in California. She continued to write her husband cheery letters about life back east. Belle was living in a dream world in which the separation from Kermit was only temporary and due to business, instead of being her husband's choice. When she had to sell their brownstone on Sixty-Ninth Street and auction off its furniture for income, she did not blame Kermit. Whenever she faced a problem, she never wrote to trouble Kermit with it, terrified that she might send him off on a bender. Even with Dirck still threatening to kill himself ("I fear I shall have to go so far as to leave the world by violent methods such as falling off a building," he wrote to his mother—reminiscent of the way his cousin Stewart Robinson had died), Belle kept mum to Kermit. When Dirck was finally expelled from Groton, Belle wrote to her sister that the most difficult thing was how to explain it to Kermit "so that he will not be worried or frightened."

For Belle, the crisis with Dirck, followed by the little girl's injuries in San Francisco, proved to be too much. Exhausted from carrying on alone, she turned at last to the Roosevelt family for help. Kermit, she argued, could not be allowed to languish forever in California. He needed to be welcomed back into the family, for only with his family's support and respect, she said, could he ever regain a sense of self-respect and self-confidence. She was echoing the appeal that Anna had made to Theodore on Elliott's behalf forty-seven years earlier, when she asked him to write to his brother and restore his sense of self-worth. Theodore had refused then. Ted and Archie refused now.

When Belle tried to set up a meeting with them to talk about Kermit, she got the runaround, and finally she exploded. She addressed her words to Richard Derby, Ethel's husband, but they were intended for the entire family. "I cannot help but feel that, had the family so desired, they could have agreed upon one hour to have given us," Belle wrote. Clearly, she believed, her brothers-in-law had written Kermit off. Although there were outstanding bills that needed to be paid (possibly the settlement to the Johnsons), the issue went deeper than money, Belle insisted. "We who love Kermit," she told the family, "hope and believe that he will get well. The family, however, have said to me, as well as to others, that they didn't believe, even that they did not hope. I cannot express to you what this attitude has done to me and to Kermit's children spiritually. It will serve no purpose to enumerate the times when the family's attitude has caused unnecessary pain. Neither my sons nor I can longer tolerate the loose fashion in which Kermit's family discuss him and condemn him." She was therefore ending her relationship with the family, as were her sons, "until we are assured that such talk is at an end."

Ted denied speaking ill of Kermit. But they had all talked behind his back, cold-shouldered him, distanced themselves from him, ever since he had showed up on Vincent Astor's yacht with Franklin five years earlier. The shunning had gotten only worse after Carla Peters appeared in his life. No one could deny that.

"Whatever Kermit's feelings for me now are," Belle told the family, "nothing can erase the memory of more than twenty years of love and devotion."

Her words were remarkable. Belle wasn't perfect; her lack of understanding of Dirck's troubles showed that. Nonetheless, she was revolutionary in the history of the Roosevelts. For the first time, someone was standing up to the family tradition of exile. The shaming and expulsion of those who departed from the established path, Belle declared, was wrong, cruel, and destructive. The frilly little society bride whom Kermit married more than two decades earlier had turned out to be made of fire.

Shortly before he died, Theodore had written to Kermit to say he hoped that, in the future, he'd still be "as much in love with Belle" as he, Theodore, was with Edith, "and will feel that you owe her as much." Whether Kermit was still in love with Belle was unclear, but after this, he knew he owed her everything.

PART IX

TERRIFIC RESPONSIBILITY

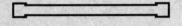

1943–1945

From the back terrace of Springwood, with the leaves off the trees, one could spot the Hudson River snaking through the valley. Temperatures hovered in the low twenties on Valentine's Day, February 14, 1943. Fires blazed in all the rooms of the house to ward off the chill.

In a red embroidered satin dress, slit on the sides, wrapped in a mink coat even indoors, Madame Chiang Kai-shek, the wife of China's beleaguered leader, paraded through the house like a queen. For her visit, she'd brought an army of servants and her own silk sheets to place on her bed. Wellesley-educated, Madame Chiang spoke perfect English, but in all other respects, she retained traditional Chinese style. Her makeup was heavy, and her fingernails were long and lacquered red. Franklin found her fascinating.

He had, of course, a way with women. When Madame Chiang read the things the newspapers printed about him, she was appalled. In China, she said, such slander would not have been tolerated. To demonstrate, she drew one of her long red fingernails across her throat. Franklin laughed.

Madame Chiang may have behaved like a queen, but authentic royalty also had stayed at Springwood over the past few years. The guest book read more like a ledger from Westminster Abbey than from the residence of the leader of the democratic United States. Prince George, Duke of Kent, the brother of the king of England, had stayed there in August 1941, a year before he was killed in a plane crash. Juliana, Princess of the Netherlands, was a guest in November 1941, and her mother, Queen Wilhelmina, in July 1942. Zita, the former empress of Austria, was welcomed in August 1942. Crown Prince Olav of Norway was there in May of 1942, while his wife, Crown Princess Märtha, and six-year-old son, Prince Harald, had been living with the Roosevelts since fleeing to the United States shortly after the German invasion of Norway in April 1940.

These weren't exactly the huddled masses the Statue of Liberty promised to take in, but the United States had become the place of last refuge for many people fleeing the war-ravaged Continent, from princes to proletariat. Moreover, Europe's fight was now America's as well. After the Japanese attack on Pearl Harbor on December 7, 1941, Franklin led the nation into war, with virtually all those who had previously opposed America's involvement falling silent.

He had become a man consumed. Even the toughest battles over the New Deal had not been as profound as the burdens of a commander in chief during a world war. American casualties were already unbearable, and there was every belief that before the war was over, the tally of the dead and wounded would be in the hundreds of thousands.

"No wartime President has ever carried such terrific responsibility," the esteemed journalist William H. Lawrence wrote in the *New York Times*. "He is determined to come through the great test with flying colors . . . He believes that history will hold him largely responsible for the war's outcome. Those who are closest to him say that it never crosses his mind that we can lose."

When the war began, Franklin was the symbol of the nation's optimism, his blue eyes sparkling, his chin thrust out jauntily. Even in the way he gripped the lectern he appeared as if he were grabbing the bull by the horns—when in reality he was holding on for dear life. In a country still beaten down by a decade of depression, he'd instilled a vibrant confidence. Now, as the toll of duty began to show on his face and body, it was usually Franklin's voice to keep public spirits high, coming through the radio as millions of Americans worried about their husbands, fathers, sons, and, in some cases, daughters risking their lives far from home. Fear, the president said during his first inaugural address, was all they had to fear, and the nation took his message to heart.

To see him now, though, one might wonder if he still believed his own words. Franklin was a pale shadow of the man he'd been when he first took office: often sick, with liver spots discoloring his skin, his shirts and jackets hanging loosely from his shoulders, the upper-body muscle he'd worked so hard to achieve through swimming and exercise deflated from disuse. He was now sixty-one years old and rarely out of his wheelchair. Belle, a regular guest at Hyde Park and the White House, worried in her diary about the president's health. "His face was gray, his voice lifeless," she wrote after one visit. "There was no real spark, no pickup, though one felt the gallant effort."

Often Franklin was up all night, on the phone with generals in the Pacific and then taking calls from Europe at the break of dawn. The war never retreated. In his zeal to win, he sometimes went too far, as with his executive order to incarcerate tens of thousands of Japanese residents of the West Coast, most of them American citizens, in military camps. The president did not question the inherent racism in the military opinion that these people posed a security risk to the nation; nor did he ask for any kind of judicial review of the policy. The planet was on fire, he believed, so he tolerated extraordinary measures even when they seemed to stand on shaky legal ground, with the power to stain his legacy. That winter of 1943, all he could see was the advance of the Germans across Europe and the Japanese across Asia. Stories of unbelievable atrocities (the widespread extermination of Jews, the enslavement of Chinese) were reaching the White House. So the need for security trumped everything else. Fear acted like acid, burning a hole straight through the Constitution.

On this Valentine's Day, though, the mood had brightened, and hopes had lifted. The Battle of Stalingrad was the first major defeat of the Nazi forces, with the Soviet Army driving the Germans out of the city after a five-month occupation. So Hitler's armies were no longer quite so invincible as they'd once seemed. In addition, Franklin had recently returned from Casablanca, where he and British prime minister Winston Churchill mapped out a plan for victory. In a radio address just two nights before, on February 12, Franklin declared that they would accept nothing less than the "unconditional surrender" of Germany, Italy, and Japan. "We mean no harm to the common people of the Axis nations," he said. "But we do mean to impose punishment and retribution upon their guilty, barbaric leaders."

American forces had also just achieved a major victory on the

Pacific island of Guadalcanal, where the Japanese occupiers were defeated after months of intense fighting. Franklin's son James, now thirty-five and a commander of a battalion of Marine Raiders, had been training to fight at Guadalcanal when he got malaria, losing thirty pounds before being sent back to a hospital in San Diego for treatment. Still, he had fought at the Battle of Midway and on Makin Island. All Franklin's sons were now in harm's way. Elliott, thirty-two, was a reconnaissance pilot and navigator in the Army Air Corps; Franklin Junior, twenty-eight, was a naval officer who'd "dodged torpedoes from Iceland to Minsk," according to his brother James, and was now the executive officer of the USS *Mayrant*, cruising the Mediterranean off North Africa. Both Franklin and Elliott had been with their father at Casablanca. John, twenty-six, was now serving in the navy on an aircraft carrier.

His sons were frequently on Franklin's mind, and he invoked their names at dinner that Valentine's Day with Madame Chiang. Among the others present were Eleanor, Cousin Belle, and Harry Hopkins, who'd taken Louis Howe's place as Franklin's closest adviser and confidant. As the windows rattled against the wind and the temperatures outside dropped into the teens, the president rolled up to the table in his wheelchair and, clasping the hand of the person on each side of him, said grace.

Franklin had known war was coming. That was one reason he'd taken the unprecedented step of running for a third term, and why there was already speculation he'd stick around for a fourth—even if his tally this last time wasn't as impressive as his previous wins. His opponent, the corporate lawyer Wendell Willkie, won eight states, compared to Alf Landon's two and Herbert Hoover's six, and lowered Franklin's margin of victory to 54 percent from previous highs of 60 and 57 percent. Still, it was enough of a mandate that he felt justified when he made the decision for war.

If war had never threatened, Franklin might have retired at the end of his second term, in 1941, and he might have been living quietly right now at Top Cottage, the Dutch Colonial house he'd built in Hyde Park as a refuge from "the mob" at Springwood, living like a country squire like his father, instead of hosting Madame Chiang and discussing military strategy.

One face was missing at their dinner table that night. Sara had died, two weeks before her eighty-seventh birthday, in September 1941. "Mama had been rather frail all summer," Eleanor told Corinne Alsop, "and the end came peacefully and suddenly." Franklin was at Hyde Park when his mother died, and enjoyed "a good day with her before this sudden turn came."

For Eleanor, Sara's death was the anticlimactic end to their long struggle. She'd loved, loathed, feared, and eventually overcome the old woman. "I couldn't feel any emotion or any real grief or sense of loss," Eleanor wrote to her daughter, Anna, "and that seemed terrible after thirty-six years of fairly close association." She was left to pick through the residue of her mother-in-law's eight decades, saving some things, donating others, tossing still more in the trash. "Cousin Sally's closets are beyond all belief," Belle understood from her conversations with Eleanor. On a brisk day in April 1942, the First Lady, wearing a black dress, black hat, and a silver fox cape, was spotted directing the move between the town houses on Sixty-Fifth Street, which were sold to Hunter College, and a new apartment Eleanor had taken for herself in Washington Square. If war hadn't come and Franklin had retired in 1941, he likely would have gone to Hyde Park and Eleanor would have based herself at her place in Manhattan, perhaps to launch a political career of her own.

Yet war *had* come, which meant both Roosevelts remained in their current roles, possibly for some time. Franklin could not abandon the ship of state as long as the conflict endured. He and Winston Churchill were committed to a victory for the Allies and, just as important, building a postwar world order. Churchill had been to Hyde Park twice; the two men had great respect and affection for each other, even if their aides were continually jostling one another, each trying to make sure their side's flag came out on top.

During the last war, Franklin had wrestled with his conscience, and endured the taunts of his cousins over his not being in uniform. Now he was commander in chief to those very same cousins who, despite their advanced ages, had all reenlisted. After being opposed to American involvement in "Europe's war" for most of the previous decade, Ted had finally recognized the inevitable and rejoined his old army regiment in the summer of 1941. Franklin promoted him to brigadier general a week after the attacks on Pearl Harbor. Kermit, welcoming the opportunity for some discipline in his life, had signed up even earlier than that, in the fall of 1939, with the British Army, much as he did during World War I. When Kermit's various health troubles led to a discharge from the British forces, Franklin helped him obtain a commission in the American army. He also assisted Archie in getting back into uniform, for which the youngest Roosevelt brother penned a gracious note of thanks. War had a way of making old grievances seem rather pointless.

After the dinner with Madame Chiang, the president and his guests moved to the presidential lounge, where they spoke of the Allied bombing in Munich and Vienna, and Madame Chiang made promises for a more democratic China once the war was over. Eventually they all retired to their bedrooms, Eleanor making the short drive to Val-Kill. An aide wheeled Franklin to his room.

In those moments at the end of the day, Franklin was lonelier than he had been in many years. Part of it was the singular burden of the presidency, especially during wartime. Another part, however, was a far more mortal kind of loneliness, the ache that came from the absence of a loved one.

One more familiar face had disappeared from the president's side. Two years ago, not long before the war began, Missy suffered a series of strokes that left her paralyzed on her right side and unable to speak. Great secrecy surrounded her condition; just as when Franklin was first struck with his paralysis, the initial news reports played down the direness of the situation. Missy had gone to the hospital with a case of neuritis, the papers said; her condition was "reasonably good" and "not serious." In fact, she was nearly unrecognizable. Visiting her at the hospital, Franklin had been unable to speak. He was looking at himself, two decades earlier, prostrate, paralyzed, frustrated, and frightened.

Back then, however, Missy had been there to urge him up,

fasten his braces, and push his wheelchair. None of these things could Franklin do for Missy once she was similarly afflicted. Feeling helpless, he visited her infrequently, whereas Eleanor was at her bedside almost daily. Their son Elliott mused, "The strange thing was that Mother was more protective and upset about Missy's illness than Father." The president's seeming indifference to the plight of his longtime companion angered secretary of the interior Harold Ickes. "He is cold as ice inside," Ickes complained.

Franklin was not, in fact, cold; he was shattered. He took care of Missy the only way he could, paying her medical expenses out of his own pocket. In addition, when he realized she would never fully recover, he changed his will to leave her half of the income from his estate. The children "could care for themselves," Franklin told his lawyer, but Missy could not. His loyal secretary had never been paid very much. Her salary had risen in the White House, but given the hours she worked, five thousand dollars a year didn't come out to a lot, and was only half of what the male secretaries made. Franklin was ensuring that Missy, who'd taken such exemplary care of him, would always be taken care of herself.

He also arranged for her to receive rehabilitation at Warm Springs, and once she'd regained some mobility, he brought her back to the White House, nine months after her first stroke. Missy's return, however, was a disaster. Unable to get around or fully communicate, she became despondent. Once, she'd overseen the entire affairs of the president and the Executive Mansion; life as a bystander proved impossible to endure. Eventually she went to live with family in Massachusetts. On her last day in the White House, Franklin stopped by to wish her Godspeed, but he spent only ten minutes with her. It was simply too hard to say good-bye.

Missy was irreplaceable in his daily life. Yet a man like Franklin needed female companionship. His son James thought he was always "at his sparkling best when his audience included a few admiring and attractive ladies." So it was no surprise that, once Missy was gone, the president continued to surround himself with fawning women. There was Belle, who thought Franklin walked on water after the repeated times he'd helped Kermit. There was also his cousin Laura Delano, who visited frequently to entertain the president with witty conversation. Laura usually brought along her friend and very distant cousin Margaret "Daisy" Suckley. Laura was close to Franklin in age, but Daisy was fifty-one and looked younger. They'd been friends since the early days of his polio, and Franklin especially enjoyed her company.

Once, some years earlier, the two of them had shared a kiss. Although that appeared to be the extent of any physical relationship, Franklin and Daisy spun an elaborate fantasy life as they laughed and flirted. They imagined a cottage for themselves at the top of what they called "Our Hill," filled with books for what they called "Our Library." Such coquettishness sustained Franklin through trying times. Adoring women paying attention to his every word gave him great comfort. It was how he'd been raised, after all—and his wife had long ago stopped playing that role.

Franklin also very much enjoyed the company of "the pretty little Norwegian princess," as Belle described Princess Märtha, who was living right there under his roof. The princess and her four-year-old son, the heir to the throne of Norway, were attended by a gentleman and a lady-in-waiting; Belle thought they brought "an incongruous touch of old-world ceremony" to the White House. Although Märtha was married, Franklin flirted with her just as he did with most every attractive woman who crossed his path—and the princess, like most every other woman, flirted right back.

"Märtha would sit and simper and tell him how wonderful and beautiful he was," one observer described. Because she went months without seeing her husband, who was in England with the Norwegian government-in-exile, Märtha took great pleasure in her friendship with the president, and made little effort to hide their flirtation. Franklin's son James thought it was possible that "a true romantic relationship" developed between princess and president. If so, it was unlikely that it ever moved beyond flirtation and conversation. Franklin was very focused on shaping the balance of power in a postwar world; he would hardly have risked alienating an ally such as Prince Olav, Märtha's husband, who would one day be king of Norway, by having an affair with his wife.

Besides, while Eleanor might not have been around all the time, she was there enough, and she never felt any threat from this latest sycophantic woman at her husband's side. As she put it succinctly, "There always was a Märtha."

Still, the loss of Missy left a huge void in Franklin's life. All the banter and laughter and winking and occasional hand patting that went on with the likes of Daisy and Märtha came nowhere near to filling it. That was probably why, during the fall of 1942, Franklin made an extraordinary request of his wife.

He and Eleanor had settled into comfortable, parallel coexistences, with only the occasional, strategic intersection. They'd pursued other lives, other lovers, other goals, other relationships, but had always maintained their political alliance. Despite differences, arguments, and resentments, they'd also maintained a degree of goodwill and respect. Now, Franklin wondered, might they come back together? He was sixty-one; Eleanor was fifty-eight. With Missy gone, he seemed to want to grow old with someone at his side.

The idea came to him as they traveled together on a tour through the South, stopping in Fort Worth, Texas, where their son Elliott was stationed. While there, they visited the Consolidated Aircraft factory, watching "the longest assembly line in the world" (three thousand feet) roll out B-24 Liberator airplanes. The assembly line employed 8,500 people, 20 percent of them women. The presidential party was driven inside the cramped, smoky, noisy room in a special car from which they could observe the men and women at work.

Eleanor took particular satisfaction in the work of the women. Consolidated officials admitted that the rate of production had skyrocketed once they brought in more female workers. The work had seemed to transform the women as well. "I never did anything more mechanical than replace a worn-out fuse," one female laborer said. "But after the war broke out I wasn't satisfied with keeping house and playing bridge." Eleanor was thrilled. Such reports justified her long years of working for greater opportunities for women. Yet the sight of so many strong women seemed to impress Franklin nearly as much. Women, he came to understand, had become a vital piece of the war effort; the conflict, he realized, could not be won without them.

So perhaps it was not a coincidence that he chose that particular moment, late one night while they were still on the road, to ask Eleanor to stay by his side, to spend more time at the White House, to be with him when otherwise he would be alone.

"I think he was really asking her to be his wife again in all aspects," their son James believed. "He had always said she was the most remarkable woman he had ever known, the smartest, the most intuitive, the most interesting, but because she was always going somewhere he never got to spend time with her. But now that Missy was gone and his mother was dead . . . he was lonely and he needed her." Son Elliott also recalled this pivotal moment between his parents. Franklin told him, "I think that your mother and I might be able to get together now and do things together and take some trips, maybe learn to know each other again." Elliott, like James, was astounded.

It was quite the overture. Franklin was, in essence, asking Eleanor to take a trip back in time with him, to before Lucy, to before the betrayals, to before Louis Howe and the presidential campaigns, to before Missy and Nancy and Marion and Hick, to before separate bedrooms and separate compartments and separate holidays, back to a time when they were young. Eleanor was thunderstruck by her husband's request. Yet, according to her son Elliott, she did not entirely rule it out. "I hope this will come to pass," she told Elliott.

Nonetheless, she held off giving Franklin a final reply. Since she was scheduled to head west, she suggested they talk more when she returned. What Eleanor was thinking, no one knew.

On the night of October 9, husband and wife had dinner alone at the White House. Franklin's request hung in the air. For as long as possible, they talked around it. Waiters brought in their courses. Almost certainly they discussed Franklin's recent speech against prejudice toward women in the workplace. "Within less than a year from now," he had said over the radio, "there will probably be as many women as men working in our war production plants." Eleanor was likely exuberant in her praise of the speech.

Still, they could avoid the subject for only so long. Their conversation quieted. Franklin waited for Eleanor to speak.

When she did, she made a request of her own. She wanted to take a trip to England, she said, to visit the American troops stationed there. The boys in uniform needed to know they were not forgotten. A visit, Eleanor insisted, would do wonders for their morale.

So that was her answer, and Franklin heard it loud and clear. He gave her permission to go to England. Eleanor had made her choice. Now he would make his.

Less than two weeks after Eleanor took off in a military plane for London—the first wife of a president to fly the Atlantic and the first to visit Europe unaccompanied by her husband—Franklin invited an old friend to join him for a private dinner at the White House. In the official visitor register, the friend was listed as "Mrs. Johnson," but she was in fact Lucy Mercer Rutherfurd.

In the fullness of time, the visitor's identity would be determined by historian Doris Kearns Goodwin by comparing Lucy's schedule with Mrs. Johnson's visits, the first of which occurred in August 1941, at a time when Winthrop Rutherfurd, Lucy's husband, was a patient at Walter Reed Hospital in Washington, having suffered a stroke. Franklin had assisted Lucy in getting her husband admitted. "Mrs. Johnson" returned a couple of times after that, in November of that year and then in the spring of the next, accompanied by her daughter. On her most recent visit, however, she came alone, and returned the next day for tea. She would return again.

Once more, Lucy could sit in Franklin's "beloved presence" and hear his "ringing laugh," two attributes she had described so lovingly to her family. To Franklin, Lucy seemed as lovely as ever. The only thing that had changed about her was her hair, which was now snow white. Her voice remained low and husky, like warm syrup. Her eyes were still blue, but filled now with the wisdom of experience. For many years she had loved and cared for her older husband, and she had raised a daughter who was now married. Franklin was enchanted.

Bereft of Missy, and rejected by his wife, he could take comfort in the companionship of a woman who truly loved him, which, for all his dreams of power and glory, seemed to be what he wanted most of all.

OYSTER BAY, LONG ISLAND

Winter held its grip longer than usual that year. Out at Oyster Bay, the marshlands were still frozen, the beaches eroded by wind. On the morning of April 4, 1943, temperatures barely climbed above freezing as a man slowly made his way up Sagamore Hill. Once, he was a boy there, chasing his dogs, roughhousing with his father. He'd been the most agile of Theodore's sons, but now Kermit moved slowly. At fifty-three, he looked older, his once-muscled body bloated and sore. His skin was blotchy. He was losing his hair.

The house in front of him showed its age as well. The winter winds had torn shingles from the roof, and the fanciful pink trim had been beaten into gray by four decades of furious weather. Beyond the house, the apple orchard was gone, razed so his brother Ted could build his house. The scent of the sea remained, though, tangy and sharp, and the gulls still soared overhead in the white winter sky.

Inside, the house was as it ever was, even if the odor of mold was more prominent than anything else. His mother had refused to change or move a thing. No matter where Kermit looked in the house, he saw his father. In the entrance hall, the skin of an African antelope lay across the floor. Just beyond, a pair of elephant tusks was mounted as gong supports. In the living room sat a tobacco jar made from a hippopotamus foot, and on the wall hung a giant silk American flag inscribed "Presented to President Roosevelt by the Colorado Society of the Daughters of the American Revolution." A set of Japanese miniature armor stood in a glass case, given to Theodore by Adm. Heihachirō Tōgō in 1910. Now Tōgō's grandson was fighting U.S. forces in the Pacific.

The stairs creaked with every step Kermit took. Up in her room, Edith awaited. This could not have been an easy reunion for Kermit. He was aware of how much he'd disappointed his mother over the years, and even more, how much he'd worried her.

It had been a rocky few years for Kermit. When Germany invaded Poland and the war in Europe officially began in September 1939, Kermit was still living with Carla in California. Ted and Alice were supporting the "America First" campaign, trying to keep the U.S. out of the fight, but Kermit saw things differently. "Franklin is quite right," he told Carla. "We'll have to go after Hitler some day, and you know of course that I'll have to be a part of it." He told Ted the same thing in a letter: "I don't see how we can keep out of it without heaping up more and worse trouble for ourselves and our sons in the future."

Kermit also saw the war, ironically, as a chance for salvation. His life had only further devolved after the car accident involving the little girl. A pariah from his family, he was drinking more than ever. The military offered him the discipline he needed to straighten out his life; more than that, it could give him a mission, a sense of direction, something he'd never really had in his life, except perhaps for those times on his safaris and adventures. So, pushing fifty and in the worst physical shape he'd ever been, Kermit went to war. Since America was not yet involved, he reenlisted in his old regiment in the British Army with a little assistance from Winston Churchill.

His decision caused a flurry of publicity in his native country, and a chance for him to needle his antiwar siblings. The European conflict, he insisted, was "a clear-cut moral issue," and it was the duty of all freedom-loving men to fight. Trained as a machine-gun specialist and promoted to major, Kermit instructed new recruits at a camp in Middlesex. SON OF U.S. PRESIDENT TEACHES BRITISH HOW TO FIGHT, read a United Press headline. Ted, the war hero of World War I, must have burned a little when he read the reports.

In April 1940, Kermit was sent to Norway on a reconnaissance mission. There he found what he'd been hoping to find: purpose. In the Battles of Narvik, he carried wounded men on his back. One of his comrades later wrote to him, "It was a great asset to me to have a chap like you there, who did not mind how many bullets cracked around his head or how many hours a day he had to work." When Britain withdrew its troops from Norway, Kermit was sent on to Egypt, but there he caught malaria. He was still, after all, a middle-aged man, looking and feeling far older than his years; his constitution was frail, his nerves shot. He was honorably discharged for medical reasons, despite his pleas to Churchill to be allowed to return to his regiment.

In the spring of 1941, Kermit arrived back in the United States. Belle met him in Boston, and from there they flew to New York. A group of reporters met them at La Guardia Field. Kermit gave a brief account of his time in Norway and tried to fudge his discharge from the British forces. He was "sort of on furlough," he insisted. He seemed unwilling or unable to imagine what his life would be like from that point on. "I don't know what I'm going to do," he admitted. "We live from day to day. I'm awaiting my orders."

His orders never came. While Belle was thrilled to have him home, he was soon out at the clubs again. He had tried staying to the path, but he'd become too weak. He had tried keeping to his father's admonition to always go Over, Under, or Through, but life had just become too difficult, and so he had, to his lasting shame, started going Around.

Soon after his arrival home from Britain, Kermit became sick, "shaking like a leaf [with] his teeth chattering around in his head," Belle wrote to a friend. It might have been a recurrence of his malaria; it might have been syphilis, which a later report would note he suffered from. It might also have been delirium tremens: with Belle around, Kermit was doing his best to keep from drinking.

He agreed to check himself into a hospital known for treating "overindulgence in alcoholics," as an FBI investigation into his activities would divulge. On June 30, Belle placed him in a cab with the understanding that he would go directly to the hospital. Yet he never showed up there. Through the grapevine, Belle learned that Carla was back in New York, and Kermit had gone to stay with her. In desperation, Belle turned to Eleanor.

Belle was now very close to the First Family. A frequent guest at the White House and Hyde Park, she was trusted enough to be invited to private gatherings for such world leaders as Madame Chiang and Lord Halifax, the British ambassador. Eleanor was sympathetic to Belle's plight. "I understand what you are going through," she wrote in reply to Belle's plea for help, and promised she'd enlist Franklin's assistance. The goal, Eleanor communicated to her husband, was to find "something which will take Kermit out of the country immediately." Only the disciplined regimen of the military seemed able to save Kermit from himself.

Yet the military didn't want him. When Franklin asked that something be found for his cousin, he was told by his assistant chief of staff, Gen. Sherman Miles, that, after investigation, there was "no hope of getting [Kermit] fit to travel as long as his woman retains her hold on him."

Once again, Carla was seen as the real villain. Just as the general consensus had been to blame Katie Mann and Elliott's other women for his troubles, so, too, did everyone now blame Carla for Kermit's. Carla carried the double offense of being German in wartime. Kermit could only get well, the family believed, if he were separated from his mistress. Carla, not the alcohol, was the toxin that was destroying him. So Franklin appealed to the American Museum of Natural History to find "a mission or line of investigation" that would take Kermit to South Africa—about as far away from Carla as they could imagine.

Beside herself with gratitude for the president's efforts, Belle wrote, "You are the most wonderful person in every way. You have restored a faith that has been missing, and with your infinite understanding and support we will win—no matter how dubious others are."

Still, they needed to find Kermit first. Franklin put both the Federal Bureau of Investigation and his old friend Vincent Astor on his cousin's trail. At this point, Franklin had real reason to worry: if Kermit was truly this out of control, he might cause a scene in public or get arrested and prove quite the embarrassment to the administration. He was known to be close to the president, after all, a fishing buddy; surely the Republicans would revive questions of impropriety over Kermit's shipping businesses and his presidential yachting trips. Franklin had also, at one point before the war, asked Kermit and Astor to scope out the South Pacific for Japanese activity. Was this the sort of man, Republicans might ask, the president trusted? Finding Kermit therefore became imperative.

In July 1941, Vincent Astor phoned FBI director J. Edgar Hoover. "I want to talk over this little problem of ours," the millionaire said, according to Bureau transcripts. When Hoover pleaded ignorance of what problem he meant, Astor told him it was the case "the Big Chief is interested in," meaning the president. Hoover resented putting Bureau time and resources on Roosevelt family problems, but he did as he was ordered. "Everything is being done on that, Vincent, that can be done," he told Astor. He reported that the New York office had been instructed "to put everybody on it that they possibly can with the effort of trying to find out where this fellow is."

Yet Astor was insistent. "We've got to be careful that it doesn't get out," he told Hoover. "A story like this, if it got out, would just be terribly embarrassing to the Big Boss."

Astor's determination, in fact, proved more effective than the FBI's in locating their quarry. A week or so later, he spotted Kermit at one of their old haunts, having a drink with Carla. He tried shaming Kermit into accepting Franklin's offer of South Africa, telling him he'd be doing a service to the government. Carla became angry. "Can't you see that Kermit's sick?" she asked.

Like everyone else, Astor blamed Carla for Kermit's condition, and told her to mind her own business. This only angered her more.

"You!" Carla shouted. "With the millions you inherited from your German ancestors and you try to tell other people what to do!" She grabbed hold of Kermit and whisked him away, much to Astor's frustration.

Afterward, Kermit told her, "That was wonderful, darling. I don't think anyone has ever talked to Vincent like that."

Their escape was temporary, though. Driving Carla's car not long afterward, Kermit rammed into a taxicab and got into a fistfight with the driver. He took himself to get stitched up at the same hospital Belle had originally tried to admit him to; hospital personnel recognized him and notified FBI agents, who showed up just moments before Kermit could get away.

"Roosevelt had such an odor about his person," read the FBI report, "that he almost turned the stomach of the agents when they got in an elevator with him." Barely able to walk, Kermit agreed to the agents' demands that he check himself into the hospital. Now that he was located and confined, plans could be made to ship him off to South Africa.

Once again, however, he wriggled out of the noose. Disappearing from the hospital, he, along with Carla, took himself entirely off the grid. No one could find them—not Belle, not Astor, not the FBI. So, for the summer of 1941, the family lived in constant fear of Kermit's next calamity.

It came that fall. So incoherent had Kermit become that Carla, not knowing where else to turn, phoned Archie for help. Archie arranged for his brother to be transferred to the Hartford Retreat, in Connecticut.

The preferred sanitarium for millionaires and movie stars, the Hartford Retreat was set on thirty-five lush acres landscaped by Frederick Law Olmsted in the 1860s. Patients were referred to as "guests," and lessons were offered in painting, sculpting, and dancing. The grounds could be used for horseback riding and other sports. Belle made sure to send Kermit "a squash racket, sneakers, heavy socks, [and] some sweaters," though she couldn't find "the Norway one with the reindeer," apparently a favorite he had requested. It seemed rather like a stay at a country club.

The reality was very different. When Edith came up to visit in November, she was deeply disturbed to see Kermit among the other residents, some of them far worse off than he. "Cannot write" was all she was able to record in her diary afterward. Two nights later, she was still troubled: "Too tired when I went to bed for prayers." She couldn't "put Hartford away," Edith wrote. She simply couldn't get out of her mind the image of her favorite son confined to an institution.

Kermit wasn't any happier. For all its amenities, the Hartford Retreat held no appeal for him. Perhaps the lobotomy room, still in frequent use, frightened him. When he was discharged at the end of January 1942, he declared he would never return. He knew he wasn't cured, he knew he still needed help, but from now on, he intended to make his own health care decisions.

A few weeks after leaving the Retreat, Kermit brought two

doctors with him to see his mother at Sagamore. The doctors explained that Kermit needed more treatment. "A hard blow" was all Edith wrote in her diary that night. She'd apparently allowed herself to believe that her son's problems were over.

Clearly Kermit was making an effort to get better, in his own way and with his own doctors. His uncle Elliott had tried to do that, too, but with little success. Kermit expected a different outcome. On February 11, 1942, he checked himself into Overlook Hospital in Summit, New Jersey, for what the newspapers called a "general check-up." Overlook was not a mental health or substance abuse facility; Kermit evidently wanted to focus on his physical troubles before anything else, perhaps the reason he'd resented the Hartford Retreat's more psychological approach. Whether his reasoning in this decision was sound, he was declaring that he, and not his family, had the right to make his medical choices.

Kermit wasn't ignoring his addiction. Once he checked out of Overlook, he immediately checked into the Shannon Lodge in nearby Bernardsville, a "health resort" founded by Dr. William Lawrence, who also ran Overlook. Shannon Lodge offered a refuge for those suffering from substance abuse and emotional breakdowns. Yet it was a very different sort of place from the Hartford Retreat. While Shannon Lodge was also situated on lush property (the virgin forest of the Somerset Hills, on a seven-acre lake), and while its "guests" had the chance to play tennis and golf on the grounds, it was much more a rest home than a medical facility. A nursing staff did make the rounds, but residents lived on their own in furnished bungalows, with minimal oversight. Significantly, that meant Carla could move in with Kermit. No surprise, then, that he chose this place over the Retreat.

Once word got out that Carla was living with him, however, his family decided to overrule his choice. In a series of events uncannily similar to Elliott's ordeal, the decision was made to recommit Kermit to the Hartford Retreat against his wishes. A court-ordered conservatorship was obtained, and power to control his person and his affairs was vested in his brother—in this case Archie, since Ted was in the war. All this was done, just as it had been with Elliott, with the regretful consent of the wife.

The night of April 22, 1942, was unseasonably warm and muggy. The grounds of Shannon Lodge were quiet, the sounds of spring peepers and bullfrogs the usual night chorus. Through open windows and doors came the fragrance of the blooming ash trees that covered the rolling hills. In his bungalow, Kermit was playing cards with Carla. At around 9:30 he heard the sound of automobiles pulling up outside. Before he could even get to the door, two orderlies in white coats rushed in carrying a stretcher and seized him. Carla screamed. Kermit tried to fight back, but the men were strong. He demanded to know what was happening, but they did not speak to him.

Another figure then stepped into the doorway. It was Archie. Kermit asked his brother what was going on, but Archie didn't answer him, either. He just calmly instructed the orderlies to strap Kermit down to the stretcher.

With Archie was Dr. Samuel Feigin, a psychiatrist from New York's Bellevue Hospital. In his hands, Archie held the court order granting Feigin the power to commit Kermit against his will. For the nearly five-hour ride to Hartford in the ambulance, Kermit thrashed and cursed and demanded to be released. Once in Hartford, he signed the voluntary commitment only because Feigin told him that to refuse would mean a forcible commitment, under which Kermit would lose all rights and powers.

Meanwhile, Carla called Kermit's lawyer, Hugo J. Frankl. A week later, in Hartford Probate Court, Frankl forcefully contested Archie's conservatorship of his brother. Taking the stand, Kermit insisted that his agreement to the commitment had been made "under duress," but a panel of four psychiatrists ruled him "in need of institutional treatment," and Kermit was put away for four months. If he left the facility before then, he was told, the court would commit him indefinitely.

The actions taken against Kermit, like those taken against Elliott, were done with the noblest of stated objectives: Kermit needed to be committed because he was going to hurt himself or someone else. His family could point to the little Johnson girl in San Francisco as proof of that. Yet there was no denying that political considerations drove the campaign against Kermit, just as they had half a century earlier with Elliott. Kermit's family was convinced that there was "real danger of a nasty scandal," as Archie wrote to Franklin—and that danger menaced not just Oyster Bay but also Hyde Park. "There was a distinct possibility that the little Shyster [Kermit's attorney Hugo Frankl] would try to involve you in some kind of litigation," Archie wrote to the president, revealing the ugly anti-Semitism that sometimes appeared in his letters.

Yet Kermit, hunkered down and hiding out at Shannon Lodge, had been at no imminent risk to anyone when he was kidnapped by his brother. He had, in fact, embarked upon a course of treatment for himself, even if his family did not approve of the treatment plan he'd chosen. They'd overruled his decision and taken control of Kermit's life—the only way, they believed, to separate him from "that woman." Ironically, the Hartford Retreat would end up allowing Carla to visit, because Kermit kept asking for her, and because she seemed to be the only one able to get through to him.

In the meantime, the family planned what came next. Only the discipline of the military could keep Kermit on the straight and narrow—and away from Carla. Clearly too frail to send into actual combat, Kermit was commissioned a major in the U.S. Army upon his discharge from the hospital in July, and sent to Alaska: a low-danger, isolated position, courtesy of the president.

The Alaskan assignment wasn't all pretend, however. The Japanese had taken the islands of Attu and Kiska, in the western Aleutians, and could use them as bases to attack the mainland. Kermit knew the territory from having hunted in the state five years earlier, so he was included on a reconnaissance mission, largely to give him a sense of purpose.

For the most part, Kermit merely served as a lookout, which left him alone with his thoughts on the barren tundra. Forcibly separated from Carla, he'd turned for support to the wife who'd been so loyal to him. Belle wrote him almost daily; indeed, she'd kept in touch with him through all his travails, never chiding him, always boosting him. She was prepared to wait forever for him, she made clear. "Time means nothing to me these days," she wrote to him at one point, "and one understands the significance of Eternity."

To keep his spirits up, Belle sent him carbons of her typewritten diary entries, stuffed with details of her visits with Franklin and Eleanor: the meetings with world leaders, the state dinners, the latest Washington gossip. For Kermit, the diaries read like a serialized novella. "I am glad you find the diary interesting," Belle told him. She was determined that Kermit not miss a single moment of her life.

In December 1942 their daughter, Clochette, married. Belle provided Kermit with all the details. "The wedding was all that we could have wished . . . simple and beautiful, and very solemn." The president and First Lady attended, which meant the world to Belle. "Franklin was too darling," she wrote to Kermit. "It would obviously have been impossible for him to come into the house and stand during a reception line which took a good hour, but he, himself, decided that he would get out of the car and have his picture taken with Clochette and Johnny, as well as speak to the family and bridesmaids."

Kermit seemed to rediscover some of the old feeling for his "darlingest Buddle" as he sat at his desolate, windswept post reading her letters. "Darling, I feel your shadow everywhere," he wrote to her. "How odd—and how lovely to have so dear a ghost so far from home."

At the start of 1943, he got sick again, and was sent home for treatment. He wouldn't hear any talk of discharge. The shame of coming home now, with both his brothers and two of his sons in the war, would have killed him. He was also, surely, smart enough to know that he'd start drinking again the moment he was no longer in the army. Once he got out of the hospital, he insisted on going back to Alaska. But first, he announced, he would say good-bye to his mother.

At Sagamore Hill, mother and son at last sat face-to-face.

Edith looked him over. Kermit was nearly unrecognizable. Each time he had visited over the past few years, his mother had written in her diary some version of *Miserere nobis*—"Have mercy on us." Yet this time, at least, Kermit's eyes were clear and his skin looked good. That meant he wasn't drinking. Still, he was winded from his walk up the hill, and the firm muscle that had once reminded Edith of Theodore's was now covered in layers of fat.

Once Kermit had been her "Fiddler of Dooney." Yeats's poem had always seemed to capture Kermit's spirit for his mother: "For the good are always the merry / Save by an evil chance, / And the merry love the fiddle / And the merry love to dance . . ."

Kermit was no longer merry. He had put away his fiddle. After their visit, so short, so bittersweet, he left to return to Alaska, and Edith felt endlessly sad. She moved through the old house touching things that were associated with him: a redwood tray he had sent her, a pink stuffed rabbit that had once been his. Sitting at her desk, she penned a note to him: "In each room, I can think of you." Mother and son would never see each other again.

Now another stanza of Yeats's poem would carry more resonance. "When we come to the end of time / To Peter sitting in state / He will smile on three old spirits / But call me first through the gate."

MANHATTAN

The audience of wealthy Upper East Side white ladies, in their little veiled hats and pearled gloves, waited excitedly for the arrival of the keynote speaker for this year's launch of Harlem Week, a series of forums and lectures designed "to solve the special problems of our Negro citizens," as the *New York Times* wrote in an editorial. Some of these ladies, liberal and Democratic in their politics, had never actually been above Ninety-Sixth Street, but they knew about the problems the Negro residents of Harlem faced: the *Times* had itemized them as "segregation, high rents, low incomes, overcrowding, bad housing, a tuberculosis rate nearly four and a half times that of the city as a whole, discrimination in employment," and much more.

On this day in May 1943, the ladies had gathered at the brand-new, ultramodern home of Edward A. Norman, the wealthy securities trader turned philanthropist, and his wife, Dorothy, on East Seventieth Street, to hear several speakers discuss what could be

done to help the American Negro. At the podium would be Alger-
non D. Black, head of the New York Society for Ethical Culture;
Mark Starr, educational director of the International Ladies Garment Workers' Union; and New York State assemblyman William
T. Andrews. Yet the person they'd all really come to hear was
First Lady Eleanor Roosevelt, whose arrival caused the ladies to
crane their necks as they turned to get a glimpse of her.

Eleanor made her way up to the podium, a small smile on her
face to acknowledge the audience's applause. After a decade as
First Lady, she no longer found much novelty in events like these,
but for many of the older ladies in the audience, it would have
been impossible to imagine Lou Hoover or Edith Roosevelt head-
lining a forum promoting Negro rights surrounded by so many
Jews. Their host that day had been born Nussbaum, and Alger-
non Black was not only Jewish but headed an organization that
preached "faith without God." Starr, the union organizer, would,
in an earlier day, have been labeled a rabble-rouser. Eleanor Roosevelt certainly kept company with a very different crowd from
that of any of her predecessors.

Assemblyman Andrews was the only African American on
the roster to speak that day. He was a great admirer of the president and First Lady, having once, on the floor of the statehouse,
compared Franklin to Abraham Lincoln, earning angry rebukes ‑
from Republican colleagues. Eleanor made sure to greet Andrews
warmly, shaking his hand firmly—a gesture that, if made down
South, could have barred both of them from the stage.

Eleanor had become an audacious public figure. She spent her
life now in the public eye, working for the public good, as if there
were no longer any private woman at all. She was taking a risk
every time she appeared at events like this, riling up conservatives
and forcing her to fend off accusations of socialism. Yet the public
arena had become safer for her than the private one. Here she
might be criticized or censured, but she was rarely disappointed
or hurt. At the podium, she became supreme, untouchable. "I
hope that when the war ends," she said that day at the Harlem
Week kickoff, "all the strength and energy that has gone into
fighting the war will go into fighting for the peace." Only on "a

real foundation," Eleanor told her rapt audience, could they build the future. "We face in this country questions of prejudice—of race and creed. We have to face them after the war. The patterns we set here will build the foundations for the future."

This was the message she carried with her wherever she spoke these days. Earlier that week, she'd addressed two thousand students at the School of Business at City College, many of whom were going off to war after graduation. "Being in the war is not enough," Eleanor told them. "If we want a better world, we have to go on working for it. Before the war is over there will be great losses, grief and sorrow. The one justification for that sacrifice and sorrow will be for us to accomplish something for the common man."

She stood there at the lectern so straight, her shoulders so square. Her voice was so steady and somehow, despite its reedy pitch, infinitely comforting. It was easy to believe, listening to her, that the world she envisioned might actually come about, that her dream of peace and freedom and equality for all might in fact be just around the corner. Eleanor's public mission had become her life.

No longer did she take vacations as she did with Hick a decade ago, when she fled from her public role, pleading with reporters to leave her alone. That woman was gone; the public creature seemed all that remained. Eleanor's gaze was now firmly set outward, away from herself.

This was the role she chose for herself when she turned Franklin down. He had wanted her to come back to him, to be his wife, his hostess, a more conventional First Lady. He had offered his companionship in return. At one time, Eleanor might have accepted his offer gladly. Indeed, some part of her, the part that still loved him deeply, may have wondered, if only for a moment, what a more constant relationship with him might have been like. Yet she knew if she had agreed to his request, if she had gone back to him in the way he wanted, she would not have been here, standing at this lectern, exhorting her audience to plan for a better world. She would not have been able to continue traveling the country, firing up the crowds, raising such inconvenient truths as racism and economic inequality and urging the nation to over-come them—or at least, she could not imagine doing both.

For, in Franklin's loneliness, he would have expected her to be like Missy, or like Eleanor herself had been in the first years of their marriage—and that she could never do. That was not who she was anymore, if she ever truly was that to begin with.

Eleanor was now the woman Mlle. Souvestre had wanted her charges to become. She was upending the status quo, question-ing authority, probing convention, and challenging her own pre-sumptions. Only when she did this, she had come to understand, did all her old fears depart. This was "a life intelligently lived." Anything else was inadequate.

Yet, like Mlle. Souvestre, she seemed to have ended up alone. Eleanor was now completely severed from her past. Two years ear-lier, in September 1941, her brother Hall died, his alcohol-soaked liver finally giving out on him. Hall, like Kermit, had become im-possible to control. He'd grab Missy's knee under the table and make her squeal at state dinners. His visits terrified Eleanor's grandson Buzzie, who feared that one of the times his grand-uncle threw him up in the air he'd forget to catch him on the way back down. Hall was one more Roosevelt nonconformist—although, unlike so many of the others, he'd been pretty much free to live his life as he pleased, even if he did leave the wreckage of failed marriages and fractured relationships in his wake.

Yet, bound by history, Eleanor had cherished her brother, the last link to their father, even if Hall didn't remember him. Her father had asked her to take care of Hall; she often felt as if she'd failed. Perhaps it was her father whom Eleanor was thinking of when she sneaked a bottle of gin into the hospital for Hall while he was suffering from delirium tremens on his deathbed. She wasn't always so rigid and inflexible, as it turned out.

"My idea of hell, if I believed in it," she told a friend later, "would be to watch someone breathing hard, struggling for words when a gleam of consciousness returns and thinking, 'This was once the little boy I played with and scolded. He could have been so much and this is what he is.'" Eleanor sat at her brother's bed-side until he drew his last, agonized breath. "In spite of everything," she told her friend, "I loved Hall." She admitted to being rather remiss in that love at times, but declared, "He is part of me."

Overcome by grief at her brother's death, Eleanor had made her way back to the White House. Hick was staying there now, but it was not Hick she sought out. Nor did she look to confide in her friend and secretary Tommy Thompson. She went, instead, to Franklin.

The president looked up when his wife came through the door. Their son James was there as well, and he observed the stricken look on his mother's face.

"Hall has died," she announced.

In stunned silence, James watched as his father put down what he was doing, grabbed hold of his crutches, and struggled across the room toward her, swinging his legs with his hips. "Sit down," he whispered tenderly to Eleanor—so tenderly that James could still hear it, decades later, in his mind. Eleanor sat in a chair, and Franklin "sank down beside her," James remembered, "and hugged her and kissed her and held her head on his chest."

Eleanor did not cry. "I think Mother had forgotten how to cry," James said. Still, she took great solace in her husband's embrace. "There remained between them a bond that others could not break," James said.

Yet that bond was no longer central to Eleanor's life. No longer did she look to either friends or family for fulfillment. Hick was living in the White House because she'd started working with Harry Hopkins on the Democratic National Committee, but the old intimacy with Eleanor was gone. For Hick, it had become too agonizing to settle for scraps of Eleanor's time. "It would be so much better, wouldn't it," she asked Eleanor at one point, "if I didn't love you so much sometimes? It makes it trying for you."

It did, indeed. As the conflict between them grew, Eleanor had found herself setting boundaries with her friend. She was no longer the free spirit she was when Franklin first took office. Two terms as First Lady she might have been able to endure and still find something of herself left at the end of them. Yet three terms, with a fourth possibly looming, seemed to calcify her. Eleanor had become as distant, as formidable—as iron-like—as the Statue of Liberty.

Not surprisingly, the physical intimacy between her and Hick, in whatever form it had taken, came to an end. Hick evidently missed that special connection a great deal. "I know you have a feeling for me which for one reason or another I may not return in kind," Eleanor wrote, "but I feel I love you just the same." Still, Hick went right on longing for it—for that "one thing," as Eleanor called it, that "never made anyone happy." Physical intimacy, after all, had never been as fulfilling to Eleanor as intellectual or cerebral interaction.

The bohemian Eleanor of the 1930s gave way to a self-sacrificing paragon of tradition. Now she made it clear to Hick that she was not "that way," or not that way anymore—or, in any event, not that way in the same way Hick was. "You should have had a husband and children," Eleanor lectured her former inamorata, "and it would have made you happy if you loved him, and in any case it would have satisfied certain cravings and given you someone on whom to lavish the love and devotion you have to keep down all the time." Eleanor had gone from longing to lie down beside Hick and take her in her arms to chastising her for never having considered marriage to a man.

Hick once lamented that she helped create the "personage" of Eleanor Roosevelt, First Lady, out of the raw clay of the "person" of Eleanor. While she admired and respected the personage, Hick said, "I still prefer the person."

Although she continued to live in the White House, increasingly Hick had business elsewhere. Eventually, she fell in love with someone else, a judge in the U.S. Tax Court, an ambitious, thirty-nine-year-old Berkeley graduate named Marion J. Harron. Known as a liberal "New Dealer," Harron was appointed to the court in 1936 and quickly proved herself an efficient, no-nonsense jurist. So frequently was she Hick's guest at the White House that the guards stopped asking her for identification. When Hick eventually moved out of the Executive Mansion, she moved out of Eleanor's life as well.

Eleanor's closest companions now would be the younger activists who were drawn to her through her words and teachings. Chief among those protégés was Joseph Lash, a young man who had captured Eleanor's fancy and who, as her biographer, would ensure that the public creature she became was immortalized and venerated.

Eleanor first met Joe Lash in 1939, when he was twenty-nine and the executive secretary of the American Student Union, a coalition of radical student organizations. Joe called himself "a full-time revolutionary" with the goal of bringing about a socialist revolution in America. Summoned before the House Un-American Activities Committee in 1939 to answer questions about Communist involvement in the nation's student groups, he was counseled ahead of time by the First Lady to keep his cool and not appear defensive.

Idealistic, committed, passionate for change, Joe was what Eleanor wished her sons had become; he may also have reminded her of the visionary young husband whose social conscience she'd awakened some forty years earlier. Joe had been sympathetic to the aims of communism, but he became disenchanted with the American Communist Party after it refused to condemn the 1939 Nazi-Soviet alliance. In response, and with Eleanor's encouragement, he founded the International Student Service, a liberal student organization that made clear its opposition to both fascism and communism.

Eleanor became fascinated by the intense young firebrand. She invited Joe to spend time with her both at Val-Kill and at her apartment in Greenwich Village, where they talked ideas, goals, strategies, and politics. Joe's affiliated student organizations worked hard for Franklin's 1940 reelection campaign. Frequently Eleanor turned to Joe for advice on her speeches, and after a radio address by Franklin, she'd sometimes check in with her young friend to see how he thought the president had come across.

Joe's own lectures and writings received encouragement from the First Lady as well, boosting the young man's confidence. When she met him, Joe, the son of Jewish immigrants, was shy and hesitant, stumbling over his words at the HUAC hearing. Eleanor nudged him toward greater self-assurance, recognizing in his struggle her own development. They shared, as Joe would observe, "insecurity, shyness, lack of social grace." By helping him overcome those things just as she had, Eleanor "filled a deep, unquenchable longing to feel needed and useful."

Joe was, at first, bewildered by the attention. He was just a student organizer, after all, and she was First Lady of the United States. Yet he had appeared in Eleanor's life just as she was becoming a national institution, an untouchable figure, and when the intimacy with Hick was in decline. Joe allowed Eleanor to stay in touch with her idealism, and with her own youthfulness, which she wasn't quite ready to surrender.

She also, most likely, fell a little bit in love with the young, handsome radical whose passion to change the world matched her own. "I'd like you to feel you had a right to my love and interest," she wrote Joe, "and that my home was always yours when you needed it or anything else which I have."

Eleanor's critics took note of her friendship with Joe. When "Mrs. Roosevelt's protégé" was appointed to the Office of Civil Defense in 1942, the federal agency was accused of favoritism and "frills and furbelows." Lash's socialist past continued to make him suspect to many people, and his association with Eleanor only made her more vulnerable to criticisms of extreme left-wing sympathies. When war was declared and Joe wasn't immediately inducted into the military, some thought the First Lady was angling to get him a comfortable commission. Joe was forced to tell the press that he "would be proud to serve with the millions of other young Americans in this great struggle for human freedom." Not long after that, he enlisted in the army, and Eleanor worried over him as much as she did her sons. She wore around her neck a charm in the shape of a tiny horseshoe that Joe had given her. "I like having something from you very near me always," she wrote him.

For all her affection for him, however, Eleanor was also aware of the reality of the situation: she was old enough to be Joe's mother, and was married to the president no less. So when Joe began courting Trude Pratt, a fellow activist, Eleanor encouraged the romance. Trude was married at the time, and Eleanor warned Joe against settling for only a part-time relationship. "Don't accept a compromise," she told him. "Trude must be all yours, otherwise you will never be happy." As an afterthought, she added, "Someday I'll tell you why I'm sure that is so."

So Eleanor forged on alone. She took sustenance from her work for social justice. When the Daughters of the American Revolution refused to allow African American opera singer Marian Anderson to sing at Constitution Hall, Eleanor arranged for Anderson to sing at the White House and, later, at a groundbreaking concert at the Lincoln Memorial. Soon after her Harlem Week speech, Eleanor published a manifesto adding some freedoms to her husband's famous "four freedoms" for the world. Now, in addition to "freedom of speech, freedom of religion, freedom from want and freedom from fear," Eleanor added "equality before the law," guaranteeing equal treatment regardless of race; "equality of education"; "equality in the economic field"; and "equality of expression." That last was a direct challenge to the Jim Crow laws that threw up obstacles to black voters' casting ballots. "There should be no impediment," Eleanor wrote, "which prevents any man from expressing his will through the ballot."

In private, she lobbied Franklin for more assistance to the Navajos of northeast Arizona, whose farms were struggling due to lack of irrigation. "If the irrigation system cannot be pushed through," she argued one day at Hyde Park, when Belle was present to preserve the exchange in her diary, "then you will have them on relief, which obviously you don't want." The average Navajo income, Eleanor said, was not even enough for food and clothes.

Franklin wasn't taking her seriously. "Let them go without clothes!" he quipped. "Greatest mistake ever adopting that mark of civilization. They'd be happier—you'd be happier—I'd be happier—with only a G-string."

Eleanor scowled. The idea of herself or her husband in a G-string wasn't even remotely amusing to her. She told Franklin to be serious. Did she have his permission "to work out a plan" to assist the Navajo that might avoid "too much inter-departmental feeling and red tape?"

"Yes, of course," Franklin told her, as he usually did about such things.

Another time at Hyde Park, the president and First Lady sat with their guests, who included the Duke of Kent, and discussed what the world order should look like after the war. Once again, Belle was there to record the evening in her diary. "Fascinating conversation by Kent and FDR on policies for post-war," Belle wrote. "Disarmament by armament. America and England will have to police the entire world, not on sanction basis but in trust."

Eleanor was having none of it. "Do you think you could ever sell that idea to the American people?" she challenged the men.

Franklin insisted he could. "There will be complete economic and commercial and boundary liberty, but America and England will have to maintain peace," he told her.

"That's fraught with danger," Eleanor argued. "You have more faith in human nature than I have." She, the idealist, was being the pragmatist here. "Even Anglo-Saxon races," she said, "will become drunk with power and will use this power to bring economic pressure on the smaller nations for the things they want." After that, everyone started talking at once, Belle wrote. Eleanor had clearly touched a nerve.

Eleanor was, apparently, the only one there wise enough to understand that the nobler instincts of human beings could not be achieved through force or coercion, but rather, had to be nurtured through example. Louis Howe hadn't been whimsical when he imagined Eleanor as president.

Once, at Val-Kill, Joe Lash told her that someday her name and work would be as highly recalled as her husband's. "Nonsense," Eleanor scoffed.

In fact, the shy, awkward, friendless little girl had been transformed into a messenger of hope for the downtrodden all over the world. People chanted her name when she made appearances. At one speech, before a crowd of eight hundred people, Eleanor was introduced as "the mother of us all." It was as if she had become Gaia, Hera, Athena—a mortal woman no more.

ANCHORAGE, ALASKA

Green army trucks rumbled down E Street on the evening of June 3, 1943, and despite the nightly blackouts, the sidewalks were thronged with men in uniform. The war had transformed the sleepy coastal Alaskan town. In the shadow of the snowcapped Mount Susitna, the place had become a beehive of people. In 1940 only a hardy three thousand souls called Anchorage home; by the time of the next decennial census, the population would skyrocket to forty-seven thousand. Much of that growth was military. Soldiers and sailors seemed to be everywhere, from sprawling Fort Richardson to the recently paved roads leading to Elmendorf Air Force Base to the battleships docked off the coast.

On nights off from guard duty or reconnaissance missions, packs of servicemen would wander into the darkened downtown looking for some entertainment. They found little to do in Anchorage, however, but drink.

Two men in uniform entered Nellie's café on E Street and took seats at the bar. Nellie Anthony, the forty-eight-year-old proprietor, knew them well. They were Marvin "Muktuk" Marston and Kermit Roosevelt, both regular customers. Kermit ordered a glass of wine. "I think wine was the only alcoholic beverage he could take," Nellie recalled. Kermit seemed to like the Australian-born proprietor. "He always sat at the counter," Nellie said, "so he could talk with me."

They were out "making the rounds," Marston said. Kermit had always enjoyed his drinking buddies, but his pals were no longer Astors and Doubledays. Marston was the son of a teamster; he'd worked as a miner, a gas operator, and a grocery store manager before the war. A Seattle native, he was about the same age as Kermit, and the father of a daughter and two sons. Despite not having a drop of native Alaskan blood, he'd acquired the nickname Muktuk because he loved the taste of whale blubber (*muktuk*). In charge of thirty thousand Alaskan native troops known as the "Tundra Army," Marston would, after the war, develop Alaskan real estate and turn a profit on the territory's jade deposits. He possessed the sort of entrepreneurial spirit Kermit had once cultivated in himself—but that seemed eons ago.

Kermit sipped his wine at Nellie's bar. His usefulness to the war effort, always tangential, had come to an end. Days before, American troops had expelled the Japanese from the island of Attu. Those stationed in Alaska were now just defending a remote frontier, unlikely to see any more action. Meanwhile, Ted and Archie were in the thick of the conflict, Ted in North Africa and Archie in the South Pacific. Kermit's sons were also in the midst of fighting, while all he could do was sit on a stool at Nellie's and sip wine.

What would his father have thought of him now?

Kermit had avoided much of the self-flagellation Ted endured, largely because he was always more confident that he'd won his father's admiration in Africa and South America. Yet his father would not have admired him these past eight years, and Kermit was aware of how far he'd fallen. He was now whispered about in the family the way he'd heard them whisper about others. After her brother Hall died, Eleanor wrote to their cousin Corinne Alsop, who struggled with her own alcoholic brother, Monroe. "I know you realize better than most people," Eleanor wrote, "that there is something we cannot understand in men like Hall and Monroe and Kermit. They start with so many wonderful qualities and so much ability, and yet this weakness causes them and many others so much unhappiness."

If Edith was right and "the Roosevelt curse" of alcoholism had been passed on to these unlucky recipients, then it provided an easy out for the family, an excuse against considering the family's role in these personal tragedies. No one ever stopped to question whether exile, shame, and judgment were the best responses, or how such reactions might exacerbate the situation. No one, that was, except Belle, who had gone above and beyond to fight for her husband.

Since his return to Alaska, Kermit had been sick again, and reports of his hospitalization had left his mother a nervous wreck. "You are scarcely out of my thoughts," Edith told her favorite son, "and please never worry about me . . . It was but a short goodbye we had! 'Perhaps t'was better so.'"

In letters to his wife and daughter, Kermit expressed happiness at being back in Alaska, at being able to do his part, but the charade was impossible to maintain, especially that dark night of June 3.

Leaving Nellie's, Kermit and Marston continued making the rounds of Anchorage watering holes. Perhaps there was another glass of wine (or two or three) or maybe something stronger. They returned to the base in the wee hours of the morning. Marston announced he was going to get some sleep.

"I wish I could sleep," Kermit replied.

He was a major in the U.S. Army, but Kermit was many years away from the man he had been. Once, he'd lectured around the country, smooth and suave with the ladies. He'd been the merriest storyteller at the Room, the darling of Broadway, the well-heeled pal of Tex Rickard. Now he was shunned by his brothers, pitied by his sisters and his cousins. He was a disappointment to his mother, a failure to his wife and children, and he'd shamed the memory of his father. At least, that's what he had possibly come to believe.

Lying there in bed, alone with his thoughts, Kermit lifted his .45 revolver. Placing the muzzle under his chin, he pulled the trigger and shot himself through the head.

OYSTER BAY, LONG ISLAND

Alice's car pulled up alongside the front porch of Sagamore Hill, where a lifetime ago her father used to arrive home on horseback, his satchel filled with presents for his bunnies. It was a cold, gray day in February 1944. Alice stepped out of the car, dressed as fashionably as ever, her hair mostly silver now that she had just passed her sixtieth birthday. Sagamore seemed to have grown smaller since those long-ago days. Back then, Alice wasn't very fond of the woman she'd now come to visit and whom she still called "Mother." These days, though, Alice was feeling more affectionate. Edith was, after all, a survivor. Just like Alice herself.

Inside, her stepmother had lunch waiting. As Edith would record in her diary, they spoke of politics and congressional rejection of the president's tax bill. Finally, Alice believed, the legislative branch had discovered a spine.

They probably discussed Paulina, since Alice had just come from a trip to visit her daughter, now a student at Vassar, for her eighteenth birthday. Relations between mother and daughter were difficult; perhaps the struggles Alice endured with Paulina made her see Edith with a bit more empathy. Paulina was shy and reclusive, with none of the wit and charm Alice expected a daughter of hers to possess. Katharine Graham, the daughter of the publisher of the *Washington Post*, considered Paulina "a rather sad girl, not terribly prepossessing and sort of pale." Paulina rarely wore makeup or fashionable clothes, a source of annoyance to her mother, who believed she was deliberately acting out to defy her. When she was a young girl, Paulina developed a stutter; the impediment still acted up from time to time, especially when her mother was around. Alice had been happy to send the girl away for her studies, first to the Madeira School in McLean, Virginia—"she made up her own mind about it," Alice wrote to Ted, "and for many reasons I think it is wise"—and then to Vassar. Still, from all reports, Paulina was miserable at school.

Sipping from delicate demitasses with their pinkies raised, Alice and Edith also likely spoke of Ted and the glorious news just in from Europe. He was to be awarded the Croix de Guerre for his service in North Africa. Once again, he was distinguishing himself on the battlefield in ways he had never seemed able to do in politics or business. Yet, as Alice and Edith no doubt noticed, no mention of the tribute to Ted had been mentioned in the newspapers. It could only have been Franklin's doing, the family believed.

The one topic, however, that Alice and Edith almost certainly did *not* speak about—in fact, probably studiously avoided—was Kermit. It had been eight months since Kermit's death. The army's official explanation for his suicide was that he'd suffered from depression due to "exclusion from combat duties." Edith knew nothing about any of that, however. She'd been told simply that Kermit had suffered a heart attack and died peacefully in his sleep. This, the family decided, was the kindest thing to do. Belle wrote to Edith to say that Kermit "was found with his head on his pillow, gone." She didn't mention that the pillow was covered in blood and brain matter.

Still, one fact couldn't be hidden: when Kermit's will was read, it revealed that he had left one fifth of his estate to Carla Peters—"otherwise unidentified in the document," the *New York Times* reported, "but described by Major Roosevelt's attorneys as 'a friend of the Roosevelt family.'" In a handwritten attachment to his will, Kermit stated, "If feelings are permitted in the hereafter, you will honor my wishes regarding Miss Peters."

Belle didn't contest the will. The long, sorry comedy was over, and she wanted peace. She received the pathetic bric-a-brac Kermit had left behind in his bunk: a couple of pinochle decks, a backgammon set, an engraved silver napkin holder, and a corncob pipe—maybe the one Alice presented to him all those years ago. Since then, Belle had carried on as if Kermit had died a hero.

Archie, however, suffered some pangs of guilt, at least for a while. "For about two weeks or so," he wrote to Franklin, "I felt as though I had been responsible for Kermit's death." Since then, he'd convinced himself that "the old Kermit" would never have come back to them "all normal," so, he concluded, "what happened in Alaska was probably the best that could have happened for him."

The best that could have happened. Any possibility of family culpability in Kermit's problems was resolutely pushed aside. Archie wrote to Franklin that they could now simply remember "the grand times Kermit gave us" and not dwell on the "trial and tribulation he caused us all."

Archie had gone off to war himself, and was stationed as a battalion commander in New Guinea. He'd recently been promoted to lieutenant colonel. When the same leg he'd injured during the first war was wounded by a grenade, his wife, Grace, wrote to Franklin asking him for help. "Archie is too old [forty-nine] to be able to stand the rigors of another campaign," she wrote. "It must be some terrible mixture of New England and Roosevelt which makes him feel his duty always lies in doing the most dangerous and disagreeable job." That was exactly the mix, and it had been ever so.

Sitting that day with Edith, Alice would have quickly grown bored with war talk. Her brothers were flag-waving patriots, but

she saw nothing but death and destruction in the conflict—and a
way for Franklin to prolong his power. Before Pearl Harbor, Alice
and Ted had both campaigned vigorously to keep America out of
the war. Alice told Ted that she'd just sit back and enjoy the fight
from afar, not rooting for either side—"a good deal the way I used
to about Dempsey and Carpentier," a reference to the prizefights
they attended with Kermit and Tex Rickard. She was incensed
when Franklin wrote to Hitler after the invasion of Poland,
"clanking the ball and chain of the Versailles treaty, which is Hitler's red rag." The president, Alice charged, was "needling the
Fuhrer," which proved to her that he wanted war. "He realizes
that war is the only way he can retrieve his power which has been
slipping away so rapidly, that only war can divert attention from
his sweeping failures," she wrote to Ted.

Some of Alice's pacifism undoubtedly grew out of a genuine abhorrence for war: her brother Quentin, after all, and too
many other young men she'd known, had been killed in the last
one. Years later, in fact, Alice would explain her attitude against
America's joining World War II in this way: "We've tried that
thing. Let's see if we can keep out this time." Yet she would also
admit that the greater part of her opposition was her continued
bitterness toward her cousins in the White House. "Of course,
a great deal was entirely mischief and dislike of Franklin," she
said. "Family feeling enters into it, you see—anything to annoy
Franklin."

What made it worse was that she had lost any semblance of
her old power. Her newspaper column kaput, she was rarely in
the news about anything anymore. Over the past year, the biggest story about Alice had been a quip she'd made at a cocktail
party to Vice President Henry Wallace, generally perceived as a
far-left daydreamer. "How are things in never-never land?" she
asked Wallace, to which he replied, "Oh, about the same as in
wonderland, Alice."

Most egregious of all, Alice no longer had any clout in the Republican Party. The woman once courted for her support and considered by some for vice president was now utterly irrelevant. To
a new generation of politicians, her father was but a dim memory;

some of the younger ones didn't remember him at all. The great
T.R.'s progressive policies had become anathema to current party
leaders, who felt no loyalty or obligation to Theodore's children,
who had, after all, failed to hold back the Democratic tide. As
William Allen White told Belle, the Republican Party was divided
between "those who hate all damn Roosevelts and those who hate
all *god*-damn Roosevelts."

Had Alice possessed the courage to run for office, as she'd been
urged to do several times, maybe things would have been different for her. She might have become a member of Congress; she
might have been on the floor of the Senate even now, with the
power actually to do something about those policies of Franklin's
she so opposed. As it was, she could no longer do anything to stop
or hurt him; all she could do was rant and rave to whoever would
listen. Yet fewer and fewer were listening these days.

Alice's contrarian nature had always been more personal than
philosophical. Her fear of public speaking had stopped her from
running for office, but surely she'd also been astute enough to
know that a political career based on personal spite would never
last. In few things was Alice actually fired by conviction. Rather,
it was the lust for power that had motivated her; later, bitterness
and the desire for revenge became the fuel to keep her going. Her
bitterness had now seeped in so deep that it was almost a sickness,
a fact she would tacitly acknowledge. "I don't think anyone has
ever properly diagnosed the distress an Oyster Bay or Sagamore
Roosevelt felt about the Hyde Park Roosevelts," she said.

Alice was particularly galled that Franklin had dared to run
for a third term, something her father had been unable to achieve.
"I'd rather vote for Hitler," she spat when Franklin announced
his intentions to run. Now, in the spring of 1944, there was every
indication that Franklin would run yet again, for a *fourth* term. In
her column, Alice had tried to warn America about the dictator in
its midst, but like sheep, voters kept following him.

Her resentment had come to define her, as an incident at the
wedding of Kermit's daughter, Clochette, in December 1942 illustrated. After snubbing Franklin and Eleanor at the ceremony,
Alice was taken aside for a scolding from Belle. The family feud

had gone on long enough, Belle said. She told Alice about "the warmth [Franklin] had always shown" Clochette since her early brush with polio. Listening to Belle's words, Alice seemed to melt a little, telling her sister-in-law she'd just had "the first nice feeling she had had [about Franklin] for a long time." So, at the end of the reception, Belle nudged Alice into Franklin's car "for a few minutes' conversation," hoping "there might be a rapprochement."

That, however, was never going to happen. Mere moments later, Alice stepped out of the car, her expression smug as she walked away. Belle hurried to the car to ask Franklin what had happened. It seemed Alice had never intended to use the opportunity to mend fences as Belle had hoped, but rather, to harangue Franklin up close and face-to-face. Alice was "pretty acid," Franklin told Belle, who lamented the "wasted effort."

Acid was apparently all that Alice had left to sustain her. It seemed to have replaced the blood in her veins.

Bidding her stepmother good-bye that cold February afternoon, Alice continued on her way to Washington, where she shut herself inside her house, estranged from her daughter, cut off from her siblings, unwelcome at the White House, abandoned by her party, and waiting for the war to end. If she'd come around to rooting for America, she did so halfheartedly, because a win would mean yet another triumph for Franklin in the history books, and Alice could never root for that.

THE ENGLISH CHANNEL

On a night in June 1944, the sixteen-thousand-ton warship *Bayfield* moved slowly, almost silently, through the waters off the coast of France. In a cramped cabin, a small, slender general was writing a letter to his wife.

"The ship is dark," he told her. "The men are going to their assembly stations. Before going on deck they sit in darkened corridors to adjust their eyes. Soon the boats will be lowered. Then we'll be off."

Nearly every day, Brig. Gen. Theodore Roosevelt wrote his

wife, Eleanor, and she did the same to him, though weeks often passed before the letters reached their recipients. Ted had no idea if this particular missive would ever make it to his wife. He was out at sea, and with every knot, he was drawing closer to the enemy's front lines. If he were killed in the upcoming battle, perhaps someone who survived would find his letters on the ship and send them on to Eleanor. If the ship were captured by Axis forces, then most likely all his letters would be destroyed, and all trace of Ted's thoughts and movements on this top-secret mission to Normandy obliterated.

The pacifism he once avowed had been abandoned the moment war was declared. While Alice seemed to make a fetish of her bitterness toward Franklin, Ted told reporters plainly, "It is our country, our war and our president." When Franklin promoted him to a temporary position of brigadier general, Ted was honored, but he was also shrewd enough to see the promotion from the president's point of view: "It will do something to make people feel in this war the hatchet has been buried," he wrote to his mother.

Ted first saw action in North Africa. After several battles, he was decorated for courage under fire, enduring "intensive shellfire and repeated air attacks while supervising the forward elements of the division," as his wife would record for posterity. His son Quentin, a member of the same division, was wounded at Tunisia, and was sent home for a brief time to recover. From there Ted had moved on to Sicily, Sardinia, and Corsica, where he helped liberate the islands from Axis control, losing a few teeth when a mortar exploded in his face.

He also now walked with a cane. Arthritis in his hip had flared up painfully as he scrambled over the "rugged hills" of the Mediterranean coast, "the valleys between filled with smoke and echoing with the rumble of artillery and the rattle of small-arms," as he described it to his wife. The sight of Ted, fifty-six years old, never tall and now hunched over a cane, hobbling in front of his troops, exhorting them to stay strong, was one that many soldiers would never forget.

This was where Ted belonged, where he found the confidence

that had eluded him in most other aspects of his life. This was where his power came back to him, and in that power, he became less driven, less discontented, and more reflective. With the death of Kermit, and with his three sons now putting their own lives at risk in the war, Ted seemed to shake off old resentments and focus on things that truly mattered. In his letters to his wife, he didn't write about any grand ambitions for after the war, or any lingering political grudges, but rather about taking her and the children to dinner. He wrote to her about "the quality of fortitude" that he witnessed on the battlefield: "Men who fall—pick themselves up and stumble on—fall again—and are trying to get up when they die." He could have been describing his own life.

No longer desperate to prove himself, Ted could now be magnanimous toward his former foes and even, possibly, a little bit repentant. He wrote to Franklin that he supported his "anti-inflation war economy program," which he was sure was bringing the president a lot of heat from "those whose toes have been pinched." Still, it was the right thing to do, Ted believed. "You have put it squarely to the people that it is their war and that all must sacrifice if it is to be won," he told Franklin. "That's the truth and the way to unite a nation." A decade before, it would have been unimaginable for Ted to write such a complimentary letter to Franklin. He ended with, "Don't bother to answer this note. It's written to relieve my mind, not yours."

His wife, Eleanor, however, wasn't quite so ready to bury the hatchet. For a while now, she'd been grumbling that Ted's war efforts went largely unheralded in the press, while Franklin's sons drew headlines for their achievements. Elliott had won the Flying Cross for his own service in North Africa; James was given the Navy Cross and the Silver Star for his actions in the Pacific; Franklin Junior had won the Purple Heart after being wounded on board the *Mayrant* off Palermo. All these honors were covered in the nation's newspapers, and often on the front page. (In his widely syndicated column, Walter Winchell raved about the "magnificent soldiery" of the president's namesake.) Meanwhile, barely a word had been printed about Ted. Eleanor had been keeping track, clipping out news stories about actions her husband had taken part in that failed to include his name. Something, she suspected, was up.

For much of the duration of the war, Eleanor lived in London, where, just as she'd done during World War I, she volunteered for the Red Cross. She took her suspicions about her husband's lack of press coverage to a British military official, who found for her a copy of a confidential memo from the British Ministry of Information. The memo ordered "a specific stop" on naming three individuals in news stories: Ted, his son Quentin, and Henry B. Wallace, the son of the vice president. The order came from top "U.S. advisors."

Eleanor was irate. To her, this was just one more example of Franklin's rivalry with Ted. For who else could have approved such censorship? The order, Eleanor believed, made Ted "the hero America kept hidden."

Of course, the inclusion of Wallace suggests that the censorship rule was due less to any political bias than to a genuine precaution against enemy combatants learning the movements of high-profile American targets. To capture the vice president's son, for example, would have been a huge coup for Axis forces. Yet the fact that the names of the president's own sons were not included in the ban seemed to turn that argument on its head. And if the names of Ted and Quentin were included in the ban because they were cousins of the president, why were Archie, Kermit, and their sons' names not included? Could it be because there was no chance of Archie or Kermit ever running on the Republican ticket for president? The names of Ted's other two sons, Theodore IV and Cornelius, were also not banned; was Quentin's included because he was part of his father's regiment and could therefore provide some reflected glory if he were named?

Eleanor was convinced the censorship rule was a plot against Ted, but in fact it wasn't always followed. Ted's heroism did receive some stateside coverage. Official press releases from the War Department mentioned him a number of times. When he arrived in Tunisia, the *Chicago Tribune* ran a story on the front page, noting, however, that it was "the first time that the press has been permitted to mention Roosevelt." Quentin's injury in the subsequent battle was also widely reported in the press, and his heroism noted favorably. A major headline along with photographs—GENERAL AND CAPTAIN ROOSEVELT FATHER-AND-SON HEROES IN AFRICA— ran in the *New York Times* in May 1943, when both Ted and Quentin received Silver Stars. While the coverage was late, Ted's Croix de Guerre did make the news that following July, and in August a photograph of "Young Teddy," victorious on the beach at Sicily, was run by papers all across the country.

Yet the evidence did seem to suggest that someone at the top wanted at least to control what was written about Ted and his son. Franklin had no way of knowing that Ted's political ambitions had evaporated as he made his way across the battlefield. For all he knew, Ted could come home the conquering hero, as he had in the Great War, covered in medals and ribbons, and this time he'd be a general. A war hero would prove much harder to beat than the hapless Alf Landon or Wendell Willkie. Even if Ted didn't challenge Franklin directly, what was to stop a highly decorated general like him from running for president against another Democrat in the near future?

After so many years, Franklin had become an extremely shrewd political animal. He knew very well how to keep his rivals at bay. It was not difficult to see some political calculation in the censorship order against Ted. Yet the number of times it was overruled, clearly with the consent of the president, suggested that politics was not its only aim—or, perhaps, that Franklin mellowed on the subject as time went on. Ted's wife, Eleanor, of course, blinded by years of resentment, could not see the order as anything other than a device to keep her husband, yet again, from receiving his due.

For his part, Ted shrugged off the dearth of news reports. He wasn't in the war for publicity, he said. Once, he'd been obsessed with getting publicity for himself, furious when he wasn't announced at prizefights. Now, as he steamed slowly toward the coast of France, he seemed liberated from all that.

His destination was Utah Beach, the code name for one of five planned Allied landings on the coast of Normandy. The objective was to secure a beachhead and cordon off the peninsula, the first step in breaking the German hold on France. It would be a massive undertaking, a direct surprise assault on the enemy's front lines, and would undoubtedly cost the lives of thousands (more likely tens of thousands) of American and British soldiers. Gen. Omar Bradley had advised his officers that "those present would have ringside seats at the greatest fight in history." Turning to the men with him, Ted whispered, "Ringside, hell! We'll be in the arena!"

At first, Bradley had been unsure whether Ted was right for the invasion. Was he tough enough to lead his beloved troops into what would be, for many, certain death? "The men worship Ted," Bradley told Gen. Dwight Eisenhower, "but he's too soft-hearted to take a division—too much like one of the boys." Ted asked to be given the chance. To Gen. Raymond Barton, he wrote, "The force and skill with which the first elements hit the beach and proceed may determine the ultimate success of the operation. You should have, when you get to shore, an overall picture in which you can place confidence. I believe I can contribute materially on all of the above by going in with the assault companies. Furthermore, I personally know both officers and men of these advance units and believe that it will steady them to know that I am with them." To General Bradley he wrote, "If you ask me, I'll swim in with a 105 [a howitzer] strapped to my back. Anything at all."

Bradley would recall, "Because the Fourth Division was green to fire, it was difficult to anticipate how it might act on the assault. If Ted would go in with the leading wave, he could steady it as no other man could. For Ted was immune to fear. He would stroll casually about under fire while troops about him scrambled for cover . . . he would banter with them and urge them forward."

His superiors finally agreed to let him lead the charge. Bradley asked Ted to take the first wave onto Utah Beach. "Show those green troops how to behave under fire," he said, before adding, gravely, "You'll probably get killed on the job." Ted accepted the mission regardless.

Just past midnight on the morning of June 6, 1944, the *Bayfield* reached its position opposite the beach. Ted had spent the night writing one last letter to Eleanor. "We are starting on the great venture of the war, and by the time you get this, for better or for worse, it will be history. We are attacking by daylight the most heavily fortified coast in history, a shore held by excellent troops. I go in with the assault wave and hit the beach at H-Hour [the first wave of assault]. I'm doing it because it's the way I can contribute most. It steadies the young men to know I am with them, to see me plodding along with my cane. We've got to break the crust with the first wave or we're sunk, for the following groups won't get in." Quentin would go ashore an hour later, Ted told his wife, which he feared might be an even more dangerous time to invade.

There, on the dark ship, the night passed in a sort of time-lessness. In his letter to Eleanor, Ted looked back on his past. "We've had a grand life," he wrote, "and I hope there'll be more. Should it chance that there's not, at least we can say that in our many years together we've packed enough for ten ordinary lives. We've known joy and sorrow, triumph and disaster, all that goes to fill the pattern of human existence. Our children are grown and our grandchildren are here. We have been very happy." Few Roosevelt couples could make that claim.

Shortly after sunrise, the call came. Ted, the oldest soldier to go onshore in the invasion's first wave, strapped on his helmet and his weapons. Then he and his men piled into the landing craft. The young soldiers, some still teenagers, shivered with terror. Ted remained cool, focused. The craft took them to the sandy beach, but very soon after they arrived Ted realized they had drifted more than a mile south of their planned target. Stomping up onto the beach, his cane puncturing the sand, a pistol gripped in his other hand, General Roosevelt quickly surveyed the scene. Then he turned and announced to his troops, in words that would become famous, "We'll start the war from right here."

And start it they did. The Germans quickly discovered them. Suddenly bullets and shells rained from the sky. As each new wave of troops arrived on the beach, Ted was there to instruct them on their altered objectives. To some, he quoted poetry; to all, he gave words of encouragement. Once again, the image of the general, leaning on his cane, brushing off sand and mud thrown at him by exploding shells, inspired his men. When General Barton finally came ashore, he met Ted on the beach and was overcome with emotion. He'd felt certain that Ted would be dead by then. General Bradley would later write about Ted, "He braved death with an indifference that destroyed its terror for thousands upon thousands of younger men. I have never known a braver man nor a more devoted soldier." Asked for the most heroic action he'd ever witnessed in combat, Bradley said, without hesitation, "Ted Roosevelt on Utah Beach."

Although more than ten thousand Allied soldiers were killed in the invasion of Normandy, casualties among the 21,000 troops of the Fourth Division that landed on Utah Beach that day were held to just 197. Ted's decision to start the battle from where they landed may have kept casualties low, since the Germans were preoccupied elsewhere. Under Ted's command, his division secured the beachhead; within days, much of the Normandy coast was won, and by the middle of the following month, the Allies had pushed the Germans back and broken their hold over France.

The war had reached a turning point. The Allies were on the offensive. Axis forces were in retreat—and Ted had made it through alive.

"Well, now," he wrote jovially to his wife on July 10, "I've got a little home in a truck. It was captured from the Germans by one of our units and given to me." He had a desk and a bed, and his crew had even rigged up an electric light. "I feel positively a softie," he told Eleanor.

Since the invasion, he'd been "a pretty sick rabbit," he added. "The Doc came and said with a little embarrassment that my troubles were primarily from having put an inhuman strain on a machine that was not exactly new."

On the night of July 14, Quentin came to visit Ted in his little truck. "We talked about everything," Quentin later wrote to his mother. "Home, the family, my plans, the war—just a swell time." Finally, Ted told his son that he was "very tired." Quentin left him so he could get some sleep.

Alone in his truck, listening to the rain tap incessantly on the roof, Ted was no longer the unlucky candidate laughed at on the campaign trail, or the reviled state legislator standing for principle only to be harangued by his own party, or the "out-of-season" Roosevelt eclipsed by his showier cousin. He was, at long last, not just the son of a great man. He had become a great man himself.

Ted closed his eyes. That night he died of a heart attack, peacefully in his sleep.

WASHINGTON, DC

The stillness in the House chamber was eerie, the sort of stillness that catches small sounds (the shuffling of feet, a wayward cough, the banging of a chair) and tosses them around the room. The chamber was packed—nearly every legislator was present—and the galleries were filled, all anticipating the arrival of the president. Uneasiness hung in the air. This address to a special joint session of Congress, on the afternoon of March 1, 1945, seemed different from those the president had given in the past. It should have felt triumphant. The war in Europe was almost over. Instead, it felt momentous and heavy. The exhaustion of the past three and a quarter years was palpable.

Just how different the occasion was became apparent the moment the president entered the chamber. "For the first time since he became President," the *Chicago Tribune* reported the next day, "Mr. Roosevelt permitted himself to be wheeled into the House to address the joint session." Throughout his speech, Franklin remained seated. Gone were the theatrics, the army of supporters at his side, giving the appearance that he could walk. On his withered legs there were no braces. The president opened by apologizing for not standing, and in another public first, he acknowledged the relief he felt not "having to carry about ten pounds of steel around the bottom of my legs." After more than a decade in office, the illusions were fading.

Franklin had won his fourth term the previous fall, against New York governor Thomas Dewey, by his smallest margin yet, 432 electoral votes to 99, collecting 53.4 percent of the popular vote to Dewey's 45.9 percent. He'd lost twelve states. Yet, although his mandate was getting smaller with each successive return to office, he still commanded the majority of the country, and that small, fragile figure in the wheelchair in the well of the House made clear that he was still shouldering the people's work with all the strength he had left.

He'd just returned from Yalta, in the Crimea, where he, Winston Churchill, and Soviet leader Josef Stalin set the vision for the postwar peace. Italy had surrendered, and Germany was in retreat; terms were now being laid down for the United Nations, a new world organization born the previous fall at Dumbarton Oaks in Washington, DC, to take over and manage the peace. "There can be no middle ground here," Franklin told his somber listeners. "We shall have to take the responsibility for world collaboration, or we shall have to bear the responsibility for another world conflict."

Unlike his raucous nighttime State of the Union address of nine years earlier, there were no cheers or jeers interrupting his speech. The occasion was just too serious, and the president clearly too frail, to endure such tumult. The legislators were struck by how thin and drawn he looked sitting there under a battery of floodlights, how he fumbled at times with his words. "His voice doesn't have the resilience it once did," opined Georgia senator Walter George. The president looked tanned from his travels, but his collar was loose on his neck and his hands moved with an uncharacteristic lassitude.

Franklin was sixty-three but appeared much older. He seemed not to have fully recovered after a long stretch of influenza the previous year. "I am really feeling no good," he wrote to Daisy Suckley at the time, "don't want to do anything [but] sleep." In fact, his doctor, Howard Bruenn, had diagnosed him with congestive heart failure, though the exact diagnosis was withheld from the president. Franklin was just ordered to take some green pills, digitalis, and to reduce his cigarettes from twenty a day to ten, and his cocktails from several to no more than one and a half per day.

Not surprisingly, that treatment plan hadn't done much to restore Franklin's vigor. The past December, when his son Elliott was home on leave to marry the Hollywood actress Faye Emerson (his third marriage), he was shocked when he saw the changes in his father's appearance. "Well," Franklin asked him irritably, "what did you expect?" The war was imprinted on his face.

Although the mood in the House chamber was solemn, the president's message was upbeat. "Never before," he said, "have the major allies been so closely united not only in their war aims, but also in their peace aims." That included, he said, the Soviet Union, which many still distrusted. Yet Franklin had convinced Stalin to become part of the United Nations. He'd also secured an agreement that the Soviets would join the fight against Japan once Germany officially surrendered. The war in the Pacific raged on, but here, too, Franklin sounded an optimistic tone. "The Japs know what it means to hear that the United States Marines have landed." Citing the recent American victory at Iwo Jima, the president assured the Congress, "The situation is well in hand." That statement brought one of the few bursts of applause from the chamber.

The Yalta Conference, he said, was "a turning point" for not only the United States but, he hoped, the world. "Certainly I don't want to live to see another war." At last Franklin put down his speech and looked up at his audience, his eyes sunken. "And that, my friends," he concluded, "is the only message I can give you."

Amid the applause, the small gray figure of the president was rolled out of the chamber. A limousine waited outside to take him back to the White House. With him was the First Lady; their daughter, Anna, and her husband; and Prince Olav and Princess Märtha of Norway. It was only a matter of time now before the royal couple could return to their country and their throne.

Back inside the Capitol, the reception to the president's speech was positive, even from Republicans. "On the whole," said Rep. John Vorys of Ohio, one of Franklin's chief foreign policy critics, "the speech was presented with great earnestness. It had a friendly and almost intimate tone. The President's approach and attitude were good." Minority leader Joseph Martin of Massachusetts thought the address would be "well received by the country."

For the moment, partisan bickering was out of favor. Gone were the days when Alice Roosevelt Longworth loomed large in the Senate chamber, with reporters waiting for the caustic pearls to drop from her lips. Alice hadn't been seen on Capitol Hill for some years. In fact, now that Ted had died, the whole Oyster Bay clan seemed like curious antiquities from another time.

Yet Franklin could not have delivered his speech that day in Congress had it not been for the men who won the invasion of Normandy. Sadly, Ted had died without ever knowing that he was about to be promoted to major general. On a day in September 1944, his wife and children gathered at the newly built Pentagon across the Potomac in Arlington, Virginia, and accepted the Congressional Medal of Honor on his behalf. Franklin sent his own personal letter of congratulations.

Theodore's one remaining son, Archie, had recently returned from combat and was feeling quite grateful to the president his family had once demonized. With the fifty-year-old Archie's health starting to decline, his wife, Grace, had pleaded with Franklin to find a way to keep him stateside. Accordingly, Franklin ordered a full medical examination for his cousin, but Archie ended up passing it. The only way to keep him from going back into combat was to discharge him "by direction of the President," Franklin was told. That, of course, was unthinkable; Archie's pride would never have allowed for it. So Franklin arranged for one more medical exam, and lo and behold, the chills Archie reported were diagnosed as recurrent malaria. He was reassigned to Camp Gordon, in Georgia, for the duration of his service.

Archie came to see Franklin at the White House after that. The two men had a pleasant conversation, old family enmities apparently forgotten. As he was leaving, Archie reached into his jacket and withdrew a metal cigarette case he'd "carried all through the Southwest Pacific." He wanted Franklin to have it.

Franklin was touched. One front in the Wars of the Roosevelts, it appeared, might be coming to a close.

"It seems to me," Archie wrote to Franklin, "regardless of the bitterness that many people feel toward the 'Hyde Park' Roosevelts or the 'Oyster Bay' Roosevelts, they have to admit that the whole clan has turned out to a man." What he meant was they'd all done their part for the war effort—both sides of the family, liberal and conservative, fathers and sons and daughters and wives. Even Kermit. All of them had put everything aside (personal grudges, family rivalries, selfish ambitions) and done their part for the war.

In fact, they'd done more than that. It wasn't just the war. The "whole clan," Hyde Park and Oyster Bay, had indeed "turned out to a man" (and to a woman) to shape the story of America for the first half of the twentieth century. "I think," Archie told Franklin, "we can take a certain amount of pride." He was right.

Archie's words were fresh in Franklin's mind on the day in late March when the presidential party left Washington for the "Little White House" in Warm Springs. It would be Franklin's first vacation in some time. He needed to rejuvenate himself. The war, after all, still had to be won, and then the hard work of peace would begin. This was no time to slow down. His daughter, Anna, had moved into the White House to look after him, to be with him when he needed someone. Eleanor, as ever, had other priorities.

Soon after Franklin's speech to Congress, Eleanor delivered her own speech, to the Southern Conference for Human Welfare, calling for the dismantling of racial barriers and a new beginning for the South. On March 20 she spoke at the annual Homemaking Institute, in Greensboro, North Carolina, along with Mary McLeod Bethune, president of the National Council of Negro Women. A week later, she was honoring blind veterans at Carnegie Hall, declaring that their disability should not be cause for discrimination. She also dedicated a new Negro community center in the Bronx, a gift from the National Council of Jewish Women. Now, as Franklin returned to his beloved Warm Springs, Eleanor was out advocating for the upcoming United Nations conference in San Francisco.

Franklin took comfort from others. With him at Warm Springs that March and April were Laura Delano and Daisy Suckley. They offered their usual cheer and sparkling conversation to offset the melancholy in the house, which had hung there since Missy died the previous summer. A cerebral embolism finally took her after three years of suffering. "Memories of more than a score of years of devoted service enhance the sense of personal loss which Miss

Le Hand's passing brings," Franklin said in a statement to the press. "Faithful and painstaking, with charm of manner, inspired by tact and kindness of heart, she was utterly selfless in her devotion to duty." Devotion to *him*, he meant, but he couldn't say that in public.

"The death of Marguerite Le Hand," observed the *New York Times*, "whom the President and everyone used to call Missy, severs a shining link between these grim times and the exciting days when the New Deal and the administration was young." Back then, the columnist wrote, "Washington hummed like a dynamo, of which the center was the White House, not the War and Navy Departments, and the vigorous young men of the administration under the buoyant leadership of the President were gaily making America over." Only the war, it seemed, could inspire nostalgia for the depths of the Depression.

Yet the idealism Franklin brought with him to the White House back then had been special, startling, revolutionary. He wanted to change the country, and he had. While it was true that, for all the New Deal's programs and innovations, it was the war economy that made America prosperous again. Franklin had instilled in the public's mind the belief that government could play a role in their lives—a positive role for change and for advancement. The boy who grew up rich and pampered, the inheritor of great fortune and privilege, had convinced America's poorest that they were entitled to a share of the national wealth. This would be Franklin's greatest legacy—Eleanor's, too, for it was she who first showed him the "other side." That night more than forty years earlier, when Franklin carried a sick little girl back to her tenement home, he looked at Eleanor and said he'd never known anyone lived that way. He determined then and there to make a difference in people's lives, and while the wisdom and effectiveness of his social policies would be debated for the next eighty years, few could argue that he hadn't made a difference in the lives of people like that little girl he met so long ago on New York's Lower East Side. Like Theodore, Franklin had left his mark.

At Warm Springs, he was sitting for a portrait being painted by the New York artist Elizabeth Shoumatoff. For the first time in many months, Franklin seemed relaxed. Laura and Daisy attended to his every need, as did his secretary, Grace Tully. Franklin was always happiest when surrounded by indulgent women, and that April he was even happier because another woman arrived to join their cheerful compound: Lucy Mercer Rutherfurd.

The visits with Lucy had continued. Her husband had died in March 1944, so Lucy found more time to spend with Franklin. They were no longer quite so clandestine. For at least one event at the White House (in honor of financial adviser Bernard Baruch), Lucy was seated at Franklin's immediate right, and the guests included other notable Washington and military figures. Franklin convinced his daughter, Anna, to facilitate Lucy's visits. "What would you think," he had asked the previous summer, "about our inviting an old friend of mine to a few dinners at the White House?" A simple enough request, but there was a stipulation: "This would have to be arranged," Franklin said, "when your mother is away and I would have to depend on you to make the arrangements."

Anna knew all about the affair that had nearly broken her parents' marriage. When she first learned the story, she had been on her mother's side, so she resented her father asking her to collaborate with him now. In the end, though, she did what he requested because, as she'd explain later, he was so frail, so lonely, so crushed by the responsibilities of being a president in wartime. Anna wanted him to experience a few evenings here and there, she wrote, that were "lighthearted and gay."

So she greeted Lucy at the Southwest Gate of the White House (away from too many prying eyes) and escorted her inside. Each time Lucy visited, Anna made sure the guest list for that night was not given out to the press. Recalling Lucy fondly from her time all those years ago as Eleanor's secretary, Anna surprised herself by becoming friends with her father's longtime love.

Lucy would tell Anna about a drive she took with Franklin during a visit to Warm Springs. It was just the two of them, except for the carful of Secret Servicemen a discreet distance away. After motoring up to the top of a hill with a panoramic view of the valley below, Franklin stopped the car, and the two of them talked. "He just sat there," Lucy described the moment to Anna, "and told me some of what he regarded as the real problems facing the world now. I just couldn't get over thinking of what I was listening to, and then he would stop and say, 'You see that knoll over there? That's where I did this-or-that.' And we just sat there and looked."

Anna was struck by Lucy's story. "I realized Mother was not capable of giving him this," she said. "Just listening."

Maybe not—yet, in the letters between Eleanor and Hick, there were many examples of quiet, happy moments such as these. Eleanor, when she felt safe and valued, could be contemplative. She could listen. She hadn't always been as closed off and solemn as she was now, consumed and transformed by her duty. That had become her mask, her defense, the stockade she erected around herself to survive Franklin's four terms as president.

Franklin, of course, needed someone softer, more pliable, and Eleanor seemed to understand and accept this. Long ago she had given him license to pursue his own life, as she could pursue hers, but it was always with the understanding that he would never do anything to hurt or embarrass her again, as he had back in 1918. She was not, in fact, as invulnerable as she seemed.

So far, Franklin had respected that. Nothing he ever did with Missy or with any of his other women ever crossed that line—until he started again seeing Lucy.

Lucy had been the one to commission the presidential portrait being painted by Shoumatoff. During those warm, sunny days of early April, they all sat around the little house: Franklin, Lucy, Laura, Daisy, Shoumatoff. The radio was playing, cocktails were flowing, laughter was bubbling. Perhaps Franklin passed around some of "Uncle Joe's Bounty," his name for the Russian caviar sent from Stalin. Daisy thought that the president looked more rested than he had in some time, and that he seemed to be putting on weight. Shoumatoff found him "full of jokes." Warm Springs was restoring him.

How Franklin loved the place. This was where he'd first reclaimed his life after the paralysis. Warm Springs would always mean renewal to him. Eleanor had Val-Kill, which was just hers;

Franklin had Warm Springs as his own personal refuge. He had designed the rustic cabin himself, "flush with the ground in front," as he described it, with a porch out back over the ravine "as high as the prow of a ship." The house was "wonderful for sunsets," he said. "A home for all the time I'll spend there."

On the night of April 11 there was likely a magnificent sunset to be seen, with the skies clear and the temperatures warm. The little house was filled with slanting rays of red and gold. An old friend, Henry Morgenthau, stopped by that evening and stayed for dinner. Franklin had two cocktails—a half more than he was allowed, but after all, he was feeling so much better. After Morgenthau left, they all gathered around as Shoumatoff told ghost stories, but then Dr. Bruenn arrived—he was never far away when the president traveled—and suggested that Franklin get some sleep. "The President, like a little boy," Shoumatoff would remember, "asked to stay up longer, but finally consented to retire."

The next day was hot. The windows were open, letting in air and the fragrance of pine. Still, Franklin got dressed in a double-breasted gray suit and red tie to continue sitting for his portrait. Dr. Bruenn stopped by at around nine thirty that morning and found the president in good spirits. After breakfast, Franklin took his place in front of Shoumatoff's easel. The women milled about the house, occasionally peeking in on the portrait session. As lunchtime approached, the butler began setting the table.

At one o'clock, Franklin told Shoumatoff that they'd break in about fifteen minutes. She agreed. Moments later, however, she noticed that the president was rubbing his head in "a strange, jerky way." Across the room, Daisy looked up to meet Franklin's gaze. "I have a terrific pain in the back of my head," he told her. Then, all at once, he slumped down in his chair.

Dr. Bruenn was called as the butler and Franklin's secretary, William Hassett, carried the stricken president to his bed. When Bruenn arrived at about one thirty, he realized that Franklin had suffered a cerebral hemorrhage. The family should be summoned, he told Hassett, who placed an urgent call to the White House. The First Lady, he said, needed to come quickly.

Lucy knew she and Shoumatoff needed to disappear. The two

women packed as fast as they could and departed, leaving no trace that they'd been there.

From Franklin's room came the sound of labored breathing. His friends and staff waited in silent anguish in the living room. More doctors arrived.

A little past three thirty, Franklin struggled for one last intake of air. His heart gave out before he could do so. The doctors pronounced him dead.

Later that day, when Lucy heard the news, she wrote to Anna, "The world has lost one of the greatest men that ever lived. To me, the greatest. Now he is at peace—but he knew even before the end—that the task was well done."

MANHATTAN

Clouds were moving in, obscuring the sunset and turning everything a dark shade of gray as Eleanor's train steamed back into the city on a chilly evening in April 1945. New York would once again be her home, her only home.

The former First Lady sat alone. Everything had been done. Franklin was buried, the reins of power handed over, the White House packed up and emptied. At that very moment, twenty army trucks were rolling toward Hyde Park, crammed so full with family belongings that "there wasn't enough room left in any of them for even a teaspoon," as one White House guard put it. The memorabilia would be put on display, Eleanor decided, and Springwood would be donated to the nation as a museum. It had never felt like much of a home to her anyway.

She had fulfilled every one of her obligations. She stood by as Harry Truman, Franklin's third vice president, was sworn into office. She introduced his wife, the new First Lady, to her Monday morning newspaperwomen, but the shy Bess Truman announced that she wouldn't be carrying on Eleanor's tradition of meeting with the press. So much for the role of the president's wife in public affairs.

The reporters asked Eleanor if she'd still hold regular press conferences in New York. No, Eleanor told them. From now on, she "would be simply a working newspaper woman" just like the rest of them, writing her columns and the occasional article, and "not a source of news."

Outside the train, the gray dusk faded into blackness. Eleanor's face reflected in the window back at her.

Just a little more than a week earlier, her calendar had been filled with events and appointments. How abruptly that life had ended. When she got the call from the White House informing her that the president had taken ill at Warm Springs, she was at a Washington charity benefit. She left immediately, without a word to anyone, and learned of her husband's death when she got back to the Executive Mansion. A plane was quickly arranged for her. She flew through the darkening skies to Georgia and was driven up to the little house in Warm Springs just before midnight.

Franklin's women—or some of them, at least—were sitting up waiting for her. Eleanor was composed as she entered the house, and calm as she spoke with the ladies, hearing first from Grace Tully and then from Daisy Suckley the chronology of her husband's last day.

Then she turned to Laura Delano. Franklin's cousin told her in the most casual way that Lucy Mercer Rutherfurd had been there. Later, when she was criticized for doing so, Laura would insist, "Eleanor would have found out anyway."

Eleanor did not react to what Laura told her. She remained steady and unflappable the entire time. After speaking with the household, she made her way to her husband's room. Once inside, she closed the door behind her.

For fifteen minutes Eleanor remained in the room, alone with her husband's body. This, then, was where their journey ended. They had come a long way together, been through a great deal, from that first reconnection on the train through their heady courtship and all the political battles that followed. Franklin had hurt her; she had forgiven him; they had formed a new partnership, but he had hurt her again, and this time he wasn't there to make amends.

When she came back out of the room, Eleanor was as composed as she'd been when she went inside—but then, she'd become an expert at masking her pain.

For the next few days, Eleanor felt "caught in a pageant," she'd recall. Not once was the former First Lady observed to cry. In rituals of public mourning, she explained, "You become part of a world outside yourself and you act almost like an automaton. You recede as a person. You build a façade for everyone to see and you live separately inside the façade." She could have been describing the past five or six years and not just Franklin's funeral.

Tens of thousands of people lined the tracks to catch a glimpse of their fallen president's funeral train. For the youngest among them, Franklin was the only president they had ever known. Some were kneeling in prayer as the train passed. The casket had been placed in a window, lit at night, in order that the people could see it and pay their respects.

Only once did Eleanor's emotions break, and then for just a moment. She asked Grace Tully if Franklin had ever spoken of his burial. Her voice caught on the word, before she quickly steadied herself. The secretary replied that Franklin had left instructions in a memo. His wish was to be buried at Hyde Park, the memo read, and he hoped "my dear wife on her death would be buried there also." Eleanor made no promise of that.

Condolences poured in from all over the world: Churchill, Stalin, other world leaders, senators, congressmen, Republicans as well as Democrats. Belle struggled to find the right words, going through many drafts and finally settling on one that started, "Darling Eleanor my heart is heavy . . ." From Sagamore Hill came "love and deep sympathy" from eighty-three-year-old Aunt Edith, who somehow still managed to hang on even with three of her sons dead. Eleanor kept herself busy replying to the condolences. To Edith she wrote, "I am glad he died working, without pain or long illness."

At the White House, Franklin's casket was placed in the East Room before its final trip to Hyde Park. Eleanor asked that it be opened one last time. According to the usher who accompanied her to see her husband's body, Eleanor removed a ring from her finger and placed it on the corpse's hand. She did not linger long. She told the usher to close the casket, then turned and left, eyes dry.

Inside, however, her anger grew. She confronted Anna, who insisted that every meeting between her father and Lucy had been "aboveboard" and always with others present. Conveniently, kindly, she did not mention the drives Franklin and Lucy took by themselves. Still, Anna's explanations did not assuage Eleanor's hurt. She'd remain cool toward her daughter for some time.

Her children could not offer her solace. Her sons were still in the service, but their own myriad family problems meant there was little empathy there. Eleanor had never really been there for them, either, which saddened her: "I've certainly not succeeded in giving my children much sense of backing," she admitted to Trude Pratt Lash (now married to Joe Lash). So how could she expect them to back her now?

All her life, sadness had seemed to be encoded in Eleanor's every gesture, her every word. Belle once said that mingled with her great admiration for Eleanor was "great sadness, for I do not think she has now—or ever had—much pleasure." Yet Eleanor *had* known pleasure, happiness, love: those early days with her father, strolling along a beach in Italy; those romantic early courtship days with Franklin, when they would lie under the trees at Springwood; those thrilling first times when she walked out onto a stage, encouraged by Nancy and Marion, to fire up a crowd in calling for the rights of women; those long, meandering trips with Hick in her little roadster, camping under the stars; and those nights when Hick would kiss her on that soft spot just northeast of the corner of her mouth.

Happiness, when it came, was a rare, wonderful gift Eleanor cherished. Her niece, Hall's daughter Eleanor Wotkyns, once watched her aunt and father dance, and caught a glimpse of pure joy on Eleanor's face: "When she saw happiness, you could almost feel her touching it and liking the warmth of it." Both siblings, Wotkyns believed, had been basically unhappy all their lives. "He hid his unhappiness with a jolly demeanor; she hid hers with hard work. And in the end, she hung on to work as tightly as he hung on to drink."

Indeed, it was work that carried Eleanor through the hurt and the grief she felt in the immediate aftermath of Franklin's death.

Packing up the White House took all her time and thoughts. She went through each room, organizing what stayed and what went and onto which truck it should be placed. Once that task was done, though, she couldn't wait to leave. "I never did like to be where I no longer belong," she wrote Joe Lash. To Hick, she wrote, "Nearly all that I can do is done."

She meant, of course, her settling of the president's estate and the process of turning the White House over to the Trumans. But in fact, Eleanor also believed her public work was finished. Once Franklin was buried, the pageant was at last complete. Leaving the White House for the last time, she boarded the train to New York with "something of uncertainty" smoldering in her mind and heart. For the first time in seventeen years (the period Franklin was governor and president), she had no public role to play. For the first time in her life, she was accountable to no one—not her mother, not her grandmother, not her teacher, not her husband. From now on, Eleanor realized, "I would be on my own."

At Penn Station, the train came to a halt. Eleanor stepped onto the platform, carrying only one small suitcase. A car was waiting to take her to Washington Square. Although clouds blocked the moon and the stars, the city was ablaze with light as Eleanor was driven down Seventh Avenue. The night was warm. People filled the sidewalks. Life went on.

Even as she held firm to the idea that her work was finished, her mind was racing with thoughts about the United Nations conference scheduled for San Francisco. There was no need to delay it, she'd told reporters. The mission was too important. Even as she packed up the White House and attended to funeral duties, she'd jotted down notes about what should be raised at the world gathering. Some things just continued to come naturally.

At the moment, however, with her pain and grief still so raw, Eleanor wanted nothing more than to just close herself behind the door of her apartment and shut out the world. She was planning to head up to Val-Kill the next day and spend several weeks by herself. Her job was done, she kept insisting.

Still, she went on making notes. Probably even in the car ride downtown, she was thinking of issues that should be raised in San Francisco.

The car pulled up in front of her apartment in Washington Square. Several reporters were waiting for her. Eleanor stepped out of the car. The scribes lunged for her, volleying questions one after another. What was next for her? What did she plan to do? Eleanor remained silent until she reached the top step and turned back to face the reporters.

"The story," she told them simply, "is done."

EPILOGUE:
THE LAST SORTIE

1962

The low, mournful sound of a bugle playing taps drifted across the muddy grounds of Springwood, through the bare limbs of the ancient oaks and tulip trees, as the president of the United States and his wife, along with two former presidents and one future president, stood in the rain in front of the casket waiting for burial. The bugle call was reserved only for those who had served their country with distinction. It seemed especially appropriate here.

After suffering from the aplastic anemia for a couple of years, Eleanor had died on November 7, 1962. The contributing causes were tuberculosis and heart disease. She was seventy-eight.

The revised autobiography she'd been working on as her health declined had come out a year earlier. Reviewers hailed the book's conclusion: "Life was meant to be lived, and curiosity must be kept alive. One must never, for whatever reason, turn his back on life."

Despite what she told those reporters in 1945, Eleanor's story had been far from over. If it had been over, if she had died merely the widow of a president, her funeral would never have drawn the more than two hundred mourners it did, many of them notable world leaders, all standing in the pouring rain as the Episcopal priest said a few words over her casket. President and Mrs. John F. Kennedy were in front. At their side stood former presidents Harry Truman and Dwight Eisenhower; behind them was Vice President Lyndon Johnson. New York governor Nelson Rockefeller was there as well; so was New York City mayor Robert Wagner; Supreme Court chief justice Earl Warren; Supreme Court justice Arthur Goldberg; Muhammad Zafarullah Khan, president of the UN General Assembly; Ralph Bunche, UN undersecretary for special political affairs; UN ambassador Adlai Stevenson; Roy Wilkins of the National Association for the Advancement of Colored People; opera singer Marian Anderson; and dozens of others. From the Soviet embassy came a large spray of flowers. Delegates from several West African nations came dressed in their native mourning attire.

"In the death of Eleanor Roosevelt," the priest intoned, as the rain fell even heavier, "the world has suffered an irreparable loss. The entire world becomes one family orphaned by her passing." They were words few could ever have imagined being spoken in honor of the shy, awkward, unwanted little girl whose father was a pariah to his family and whose future was so despaired over by her relatives.

Standing in the rain along with the president and world leaders were Eleanor's children and their families. Some were not speaking with each other; some had not spoken to their mother much in her last few years. Farther in back stood Eleanor's cousins, among them Alice Roosevelt Longworth—though Princess Alice had retreated so far in the public's mind by now that she wasn't even mentioned in any of the newspaper accounts of Eleanor's funeral.

Eleanor, by contrast, was world-famous at her death. Just nine months into her widowhood, she'd been appointed by President Truman as a delegate to the UN General Assembly. In early 1946 she was named the first chairperson of the UN Commission on Human Rights, for which she helped draft a groundbreaking document she'd call an "international Magna Carta for all men everywhere." The Universal Declaration of Human Rights established fundamental rights to life, liberty, and freedom of movement, association, thought, conscience, and religion. In September 1948, Eleanor delivered a powerful speech at the Sorbonne in Paris, calling for human rights to be the guiding principle of all nations. "The basic problem confronting the world today," she said, "is the preservation of human rights for the individual and consequently for the society of which he is a part. We are fighting this battle again today as it was fought at the time of the French Revolution and the American Revolution."

The speech would one day be included among the most inspiring and significant of the twentieth century. The Declaration of Human Rights was adopted by the UN General Assembly on December 10, 1948.

In her role as U.S. Representative to the United Nations, Eleanor became an ambassador to the world. Throughout the 1950s her globetrotting was monumental. She visited Hiroshima, where the United States had dropped the atomic bomb at the end of World War II, and met with Japanese emperor Hirohito. She visited Yugoslavia and met with Josip Tito. She undertook several tours of Europe, sometimes twice a year. In 1955 she journeyed to Bali and to a United Nations gathering in Bangkok. Two years later she met with the sultan of Morocco, and in 1957 she finally visited the Soviet Union, where, for her still-running newspaper column, she interviewed Nikita Khrushchev about the arms race. A second visit was made to the Soviet Union in 1958; and the next year, she visited Israel and Iran. In 1960, Eleanor attended the UN World Federation meeting in Poland. She had become, in the words of President Truman, "the First Lady of the World."

At home, however, she wasn't always quite as beloved. For all her talk of unity, she could be a divisive figure. Just because she played on the world stage now did not mean she'd suddenly become nonpartisan in domestic politics. Indeed, conservatives charged that she'd become even more blatant in her socialist tendencies. Eleanor argued that only "liberal-minded Democrats" could move the country forward. Lecturing around the country on behalf of women's rights and racial equality, she also denounced McCarthyism.

Even as she turned seventy, she was averaging one hundred fifty lectures a year. When she tried to retire, President Kennedy appointed her to chair the newly formed Presidential Commission on the Status of Women. "We need to use in the very best way possible," Eleanor wrote in her column, "all our available manpower—and that includes womanpower." She helped draft the commission's report, but died before it could be issued.

Yet, for all her influence, she never ran for office herself, despite frequent encouragement to do so. Repeatedly, she was mentioned for governor, vice president, and—as suggested by what she called "some particularly humorous souls"—"the first woman President of the United States." Modestly, she expressed surprise that anyone would think her "fitted to hold office." It was true, Eleanor acknowledged, that Louis Howe had encouraged her to make a political career of her own, but she gave the impression in her columns that she'd never taken the idea seriously.

Was that really so?

If there had been a moment when Eleanor might have run for office, and claimed for herself the mantle of her uncle and her husband, then it was lost the moment Franklin decided to run for a third term in 1940. He ended up staying in the job for twelve years—long enough to effectively extinguish any real chance for his wife to pursue an electoral political strategy of her own if she had wanted it. By the time Franklin died in 1945, she believed the idea was no longer even worth considering.

"The plain truth, I am afraid," Eleanor wrote in 1946, "is that in declining to consider running for the various public offices which have been suggested to me, I am influenced by the thought that no woman has, as yet, been able to build up and hold sufficient backing to carry through a program. Men and women both are not yet enough accustomed to following a woman and looking to her for leadership."

Then she admitted what appeared to be the real truth: "If I were young enough," Eleanor mused, "it might be an interesting challenge, and we have some women in Congress who may carry on this fight. However, I am already an elderly woman, and I would have to start in whatever office I might run for as a junior with no weight of experience in holding office behind me. It seems to me that fairly young men and women should start holding minor offices and work up to the important ones, developing qualifications for holding these offices as they work."

Had things been different, in other words, she might have enjoyed taking on the "interesting challenge" of elected office. Yet things were what they were; history couldn't be changed—and she had done well enough regardless.

At the end, politics no longer commanded Eleanor's most private thoughts. She had spent the latter part of Franklin's time in office almost as an automaton, her personal life subsumed by her public role. What interested her at the end of her life—what had compelled her to rewrite her memoirs and reconsider her past—was the possibility of finding a sense of personal closure, of giving some meaning to everything she'd been through. In her sixties and seventies, Eleanor tried to grab some of the happiness that had so often eluded her. She did this in big and small ways.

She nurtured a circle of intimate friendships with younger people, intellectuals such as Joe and Trude Lash, Dr. David Gurewitsch, and Adlai Stevenson. She became, by all accounts, a more interested and involved grandmother than she had been a mother. She never quite returned to being that free-spirited bohemian she was in the 1920s and '30s—running around in tweed trousers with Nancy and Marion, taking off on love trips with Hick—but she did manage to recapture some of the joy she lost during those years caged up in the White House. She learned to drive at age sixty-three. After a car accident, she had her teeth fixed to finally give herself "a better-looking mouth," something she'd always resisted for fear of seeming vain. After finishing her work on the Declaration of Human Rights, she celebrated by getting a running start and then sliding down the highly polished marble floor of the Palais des Nations in Geneva, arms outstretched and laughing—a playfulness reminiscent of her run, half a century earlier, down Cooper's Bluff.

Still, she was never able to fully draw close to her children, who remained at a distance and whose lives seemed forever in turmoil. Some were on their second or third marriages; all of them were uncertain in their careers. "Mother yearned to see all her children settled into happy, useful lives," Elliott would write, but "there seemed to be no end to her heartache." Both James and Franklin Junior served as congressmen, from California and New York, respectively, but quarreled with their mother politically. Elliott found himself mired in another influence-peddling scandal at the Defense Department. Anna's newspaper business went under, and she divorced her husband, who then committed suicide. John became a Republican, actively working for the election of Dwight Eisenhower. Among the siblings, fierce feuds broke out; some didn't speak to each other for years. At one point, during the height of the McCarthy witch hunts, Franklin even tried to finger Elliott as a Communist sympathizer. On some fronts, the Wars of the Roosevelts still raged.

Peace, however, had been found between Eleanor and Hick, whose friendship revived, even if the intensity of the past was long gone. Together, in 1954, they authored *Ladies of Courage*, profiling women in politics and predicting that among the grand-daughters of the book's readers would be a future president of the United States. Hick also wrote *The Story of Franklin D. Roosevelt* and *The Story of Eleanor Roosevelt*, both aimed at children. She survived Eleanor by six years, dying in 1968 at the age of seventy-five. Hick left her papers to the Franklin D. Roosevelt Presidential Library at Hyde Park, with the stipulation that her correspondence with Eleanor not be opened for ten years after her death.

A few key players in the long Roosevelt saga passed away before Eleanor. Edith died in 1948, at the age of eighty-seven. Lucy Mercer Rutherfurd succumbed to cancer that same year. Eleanor Butler Roosevelt, Ted's wife, died in 1960. Most of the others, though, outlived Eleanor by many years. Ethel Roosevelt Derby died in 1977, at the age of eighty-six. Archie died in 1979, at eighty-five, after repudiating his family's progressive heritage by joining the John Birch Society and leading a movement to rout Communists from the nation's universities.

Belle Roosevelt died in 1968. Her troubled son Dirck, after being arrested in Spain on a morals charge (code, in those days, for having sex with another man), had finally succeeded in taking his own life, in 1953. He was twenty-eight. The lives of the Roosevelt apostates did not, as a rule, end happily. Jimmie lived as a recluse after Sadie left him. He died at the age of seventy-eight in 1958, leaving all his millions to the Salvation Army. His sister, Helen, however, allowed his burial in the family plot in Hyde Park, finally rescinding Franklin's decree that Jimmie was no longer a Roosevelt.

One old warhorse, however, wasn't ready to lay down her arms. Even as old feuds and rivalries were settled by time or death,

Alice kept up the fight. She was not unlike one of those Japanese soldiers marooned on a Pacific jungle island, unaware that the war was over and still tossing grenades decades later. When reporters occasionally interviewed her, Alice kept up the insults of Eleanor and Franklin. In the 1970s she encouraged one interviewer to look into whether Franklin's Delano grandfather, a trader with China, had ever had dealings with opium. "Because, you see," Alice said, smiling the toothy grin that evoked her father, "that would make Franklin a *criminal*." For Alice, it was never too late to besmirch Franklin's reputation.

Alice's later life was marked by tragedy. Her daughter, Paulina, left a widow at twenty-six, took her own life six years later, still plagued by the depression of her youth. Alice raised Paulina's young daughter, Joanna Sturm, and like Eleanor, proved to be a far better grandmother than mother.

Despite latter-day myths that portrayed Alice as a relevant figure in Washington right up until her death, in fact she became a relic, someone invited to parties as a conversation piece—when she was invited at all. While politicians still liked having their pictures taken with Theodore Roosevelt's daughter, no one seriously sought advice from Alice Longworth anymore. She lived in her house on Massachusetts Avenue in Washington surrounded by the residuum of her colorful life: the animal skins brought back by her father from Africa, gifts from the empress of Japan, cartoons that belittled her Hyde Park cousins. Alice died in 1980, at the end of the Jimmy Carter administration, at the age of ninety-six. Her death, as she'd surely hoped, did at least make the front pages.

Yet the coverage of Alice's passing was nothing compared to what followed the death of Eleanor. The journalist Carl Rowan syndicated a multipart newspaper profile of the former First Lady entitled "The Most Remarkable Roosevelt," asserting that Eleanor had transformed the nation even more than Theodore or Franklin, on such fundamental issues as gender, race, and equal opportunity. While that argument could be debated, few denied the very real impact Eleanor had had on people's lives.

"We do not have to become heroes overnight," Eleanor once

wrote. "Just a step at a time, meeting each thing that comes up, seeing it is not as dreadful as it appears, discovering that we have the strength to stare it down."

Many times she had discovered the steel inside her that no one expected to be there, and in the process she had become a hero for the ages. Long ago, her father had told her to watch some men building a stone house. The stones were "ideas," Elliott said, and with the mortar of "persuasion," "instruction," "love" and "truth," Eleanor could build many things. She had done so, far more than her father could possibly have imagined.

Elliott had also suggested that the one building block in life that Eleanor would want most was the one called "love." Indeed, that was precisely what she had been seeking when she attempted to rewrite her memoirs at the end. Ideas and facts and instruction and truth—these would be the hallmarks of her life; but the loss of her father, the wellspring of all love for her, kept her forever guarded and easily disheartened. Family, husband, lovers—none could be depended upon to love her as unconditionally as her father had done. So, in the end, Eleanor took solace in the love of strangers, in the love of the world. Once Hick was gone, public works compensated for the lack of personal intimacy. The public would never let Eleanor down.

"There was a connection so strong between Mrs. Roosevelt and the people of this country that it could almost be felt," one longtime admirer of hers said, recounting a day when a group of citizens—"average New Yorkers, working people, black and white"—gathered around her after one of her appearances. "They kept calling out that they loved her, and it was almost as if their love was something solid, something weighty, something they could pass over their heads and straight into her arms."

How different Eleanor's story might have been if her father had never been taken from her. Of course, without the challenge his loss presented, she might never have found such reserves of inner strength. Or, possibly, she might have been even stronger, unhindered by doubt and fear.

Her father towered over her entire life. Among her treasures was an old, worn Bible that had been his. The year before she

died, Eleanor showed the Bible to a friend who was also an Episcopal priest, admitting, with some reluctance, that her father had
not been, "in strict religious terms[,] . . . morally correct" when he
died. The anguish on her face was evident to her friend. "Do you
think," Eleanor asked, "because of that, I won't see him? Do you
think it could be a bar to his being in heaven?"

About religion and an afterlife, Eleanor often seemed uncertain, but in that moment, she appeared to need some reassurance,
just in case. The priest was kind. God must be generous, he told
her, "or none of us stands a chance here."

Yet one fear remained unconquered, unaddressed, unexamined.
Eleanor had never found the strength to meet her brother, Elliott
Roosevelt Mann, despite the hand he had extended in friendship.

If she had met him, she might have found some truths about
love, commitment, and acceptance that she had missed. Sister and
brother held different political views, but they shared a fierce determination to survive. They had both triumphed over adversity,
and both had lived according to the values of hard work, honesty,
and integrity. Both had cared for loved ones facing physical challenges, although Elliott's daughter, Mildred, hadn't had the same
access to the care, treatment, and mineral waters that made such
a difference to Franklin. Also, while Elliott's mother, Katie, did
live long enough to see, and take pride in, her son's successes, she
did not have the privilege of living out her life in her own comfortable home, cared for by a staff of servants and nurses, as Sara
and Edith had.

By the fall of 1940, Katie had become senile, and Elliott was
forced to commit his beloved mother, who had done so much for
him, to the Creedmoor State Hospital in Queens, a crowded, un-
derstaffed facility. The family did not have the resources for anything else. Seven months after her admission to Creedmoor, on
April 13, 1941, Katie died at the age of seventy-eight. She was
buried with her mother in the Lutheran cemetery in Brooklyn.
On her death record, Elliott described her as a widow, listing her
father's last name as Köhler (in truth, her mother's maiden name).
He made it appear as if Katie had married a man by the last name
of Mann, thus saving her from that one last indignity.

They'd spent their lives in the shadow of this great secret, the secret Katie had promised Theodore never to reveal, and it had been life-draining for them. "It was quite an ordeal," Elliott's daughter, Eleanor, would say, "when a child was labeled 'illegitimate,' and to grow up with this stigma was truly a burden to bear." Even she, when asked to prepare a family tree in schools, pulled back "for fear someone would learn of this dishonor."

In 1968, Elliott retired from Chase Manhattan Bank. When offered a gold watch for his long years of service, he asked for the women's model. After so many years of frugality, he wanted his wife, Lena, to enjoy a little luxury for a change. They left Queens soon after his retirement, for the sunnier skies of Garden Grove, California, where their daughters had earlier relocated with their families. In 1971, Elliott and Lena celebrated their fiftieth wedding anniversary. Five years later, Elliott suffered a stroke; he died on December 20, 1976, at the age of eighty-five. Weary of a lifetime of obfuscations, Lena told the truth on his death certificate, naming Elliott Roosevelt of New York as his father. She survived her husband by fourteen years, dying in 1990.

Not long after, Elliott's daughter Eleanor decided it was time to claim her family's rightful place in the history of the Roosevelts.

Eleanor Mann Biles, named for her aunt, and with much of the same spirit and determination, had been corresponding with Roosevelt historians in order to piece together the puzzle of her family. According to her granddaughter Trisha Helland, she wanted to give "her now-deceased father some legitimacy where there had always been shame." She decided that the 1991 Roosevelt Family Reunion, to be held at Oyster Bay, was the perfect time and place to do it. John Gable, executive director of the Theodore Roosevelt Association, assured her that she and her family would be welcome.

Accompanying Eleanor to New York were her daughter and son-in-law, Debra and Jim Haberthur, and their ten-year-old daughter, Trisha, the great-great-granddaughter of Elliott Roosevelt and Katie Mann. "I was a young girl," Trisha remembered, "but well aware of the special nature of the vacation I was taking." A rough, delayed flight, combined with nerves, left her feeling sick when they arrived, and her grandmother comforted her with cold cloths on her face. "With all the excitement surrounding this trip," Trisha said, "I was reacting strongly" to what lay ahead. It was no surprise that she would be channeling some anxiety: exactly one century earlier, the drama between Elliott and Katie had torn the Roosevelt family apart. This moment had been a long time coming.

The reunion, as the Biles family had been told, was the first to include members of both the Oyster Bay and Hyde Park branches. By now, of course, the old family battles had faded into history. Theodore's children were all dead, and even several of his grandchildren had passed away. Likewise, the last of Franklin and Eleanor's children, James, had died that summer. So the descendants who gathered at the historic Seawanhaka Corinthian Yacht Club (grandchildren, great-grandchildren, and great-great-grandchildren of the two presidents) had no axes to grind. They were all just there to celebrate their connection to America's greatest political family, the same reason the Biles family had themselves come out from California.

Among the attendees at the reunion were Massachusetts governor William Weld, whose wife was a daughter of Quentin Roosevelt, Ted's son; Selwa Roosevelt, Archie's daughter-in-law and the chief of protocol under President Ronald Reagan; and various millionaires, businessmen, politicians, and British peers. Many had been to the Seawanhaka before; many more had yacht clubs of their own they belonged to.

Not the Biles family. When they arrived at the Seawanhaka, Debra Haberthur was self-conscious of being "the black sheep of the family"; her husband "expected to be talked down to." Their feelings of unease were compounded when they discovered, due to their late flight, that their table had been removed and had to be quickly reset. As they took their places, they were aware that the eyes of the room were on them—the descendants of Theodore and Edith taking stock of those of Elliott and Katie.

Trisha did her best to be "a good representative" for her mother and grandmother, demonstrating her knowledge of which fork and knife to use at dinner. "I wanted to do my part to prove them wrong about my family," she would remember.

To her great surprise, however, she never felt the need to do so. "They knew who we were," Trisha said, but instead of scorn, the other Roosevelts treated them with great respect and sincere interest. "I never felt shunned or looked down upon," Trisha remembered. A century earlier, and for some time thereafter, the story of Katie and Elliott had been the stuff of scandal, whispers, and shame. Now it was simply part of the shared story of the people in the room.

The formal dinner was followed by a much more casual gathering at the nearby home of P. J. Roosevelt, a grandson of a cousin of Theodore's. On the edge of the bay, the various kin all sat around in lawn chairs; children bounced on a trampoline. Eleanor Mann Biles sat on the veranda chatting with Tweed Roosevelt, Archie's grandson. There was a striking lack of pretension and formality. Among all the prominent names, there were also artists and writers and performers and musicians. Nonconformists were evidently now welcome among the sprawling Roosevelt clan. One grandson of Franklin and Eleanor's dropped his pants to show off a new tattoo on his thigh. Elliott and Kermit and Jimmie and Sadie and Dirck would have felt right at home. It was a very different world.

Off to the side, a cousin sat with Eleanor Biles, officially inscribing her father's line onto the family tree. "We were treated like we'd been there all along," Trisha said. And of course they had been.

The next day, they visited Theodore's grave, the descendants of Katie Mann come to pay their respects. Afterward, they took a tour of Sagamore Hill. Elliott Mann's little house in Queens hadn't been all that far away, but it might as well have been the other side of the world. Now his daughter was in Theodore's house.

On the last day of the reunion, the Biles family joined the others for a service at the church where Theodore and Edith used to worship. A chalice was presented to the priest as a gift from the Roosevelt family—all of them.

After a hundred years, the Wars of the Roosevelts had finally come to an end.

ACKNOWLEDGMENTS

My gratitude to the wise, diligent archivists and librarians who preserve our history and make it available for study, in particular those at the Houghton Library at Harvard University (with special thanks to Heather Cole, curator of the Theodore Roosevelt Collection); the Manuscript Division at the Library of Congress (in particular reference librarian Bruce Kirby); the Theodore Roosevelt Center at Dickinson State University (in particular digital library coordinator Pamela Pierce); the Franklin D. Roosevelt Presidential Library and Museum; and the Milford, Connecticut, Public Library.

I also want to acknowledge the wise counsel of Edmund Morris, whose three-part biography of Theodore Roosevelt is the definitive study of our twenty-sixth president. I am also deeply grateful to two members of the Roosevelt family who asked to remain anonymous for their insights, particularly about the life of Kermit Roosevelt.

The heart of this book was made possible by the kind cooperation of the family of Elliott Roosevelt Mann, who provided a window on a chapter of the Roosevelt story never previously chronicled. I am indebted to Eleanor Biles, Debra Haberthur, and Trisha Helland (Elliott Mann's daughter, granddaughter, and great-granddaughter), for providing memories, stories, and photographs, as well as a loving historical perspective. My dinner with Trisha, her husband, Ricky; and her two very smart and articulate boys, Jaxon and Rhett; was a highlight of writing this book. My only regret is that Eleanor Biles did not live to see publication; I can only hope that she would have felt her father's story had finally been told truthfully and respectfully. I am also grateful to Gary Miller and Dorothy Mann Miller, and to Pat Johnson, all three descendants of Katie Mann's brothers, for filling in other pieces of the family history.

Special thanks to Al Vinck, independent Roosevelt researcher, whose careful eye and expertise helped ensure this book was the best it could be. Any errors are mine alone.

I must also acknowledge my friends Jaffe Cohen and Michael Zam, for first inspiring my interest in the Roosevelt family struggles (and for coming up with the title); my enterprising and efficient assistants Collin Berill and Catherine Lindstrom; my original editor, Cal Morgan, who helped shape the idea and structure of this book; my current editors, Jonathan Jao and Roger Labrie, who helped polish the book; Sofia Groopman and John Jusino at Harper for expertly pulling all parts of this project together; Gregg Kulick for the gorgeous cover and Leah Carlson-Stanisic for the elegant interior design; my agent, Malaga Baldi, on this, our fourteenth book together; and my husband, Tim Huber.

ARCHIVAL COLLECTIONS

HOUGHTON LIBRARY, HARVARD UNIVERSITY
Alice Roosevelt Longworth Family Papers

Anna Roosevelt Cowles Papers

Archibald B. Roosevelt Family Papers

Corinne Robinson Alsop Cole Family Papers

Corinne Roosevelt Robinson Papers

Monroe Douglas Robinson Family Papers

Roosevelt-Derby-Williams Papers

Theodore Roosevelt Childhood Correspondence

Theodore Roosevelt Clipping Scrapbooks

Theodore Roosevelt Correspondence and Compositions

Theodore Roosevelt Diaries and Notebooks

Theodore Roosevelt Letters to Belle Wyatt Willard Roosevelt

Theodore Roosevelt Letters to Ethel Roosevelt Derby

Theodore Roosevelt Letters to Kermit Roosevelt

LIBRARY OF CONGRESS
Alice Roosevelt Longworth Papers

Archibald Roosevelt Papers

Kermit Roosevelt and Belle Roosevelt Papers

Theodore Roosevelt (1887–1944) Papers

Theodore Roosevelt Papers

FRANKLIN ROOSEVELT PRESIDENTIAL LIBRARY
Anna Eleanor Roosevelt, transcript of recording by George Roach

Anna Eleanor Roosevelt Papers

Doris Faber Papers

Esther Lape Papers

Franklin D. Roosevelt, Collection of Historical Manuscripts

Franklin D. Roosevelt, Collection of Speeches

Franklin D. Roosevelt, papers pertaining to the campaign of 1924

Franklin D. Roosevelt, papers pertaining to family, business, and personal affairs

Franklin D. Roosevelt, papers as vice-presidential candidate, 1920

Franklin D. Roosevelt, President's Personal File, 1933–1945

Franklin D. Roosevelt Papers, 1920–1928

Kermit and Belle Roosevelt Papers

Lorena Hickok Papers
Louis Howe Papers
Lucy Mercer Rutherfurd Letters
Margaret Suckley/FDR Letters
Marion Dickerman interview transcript
Marion Dickerman Papers
Roosevelt Family Papers, 1649–1962
Roosevelt Family Papers donated by the children
Sara Delano Roosevelt Household Book
Vincent Astor Correspondence

NOTES

ABBREVIATIONS OF ARCHIVES

FDRL   *Franklin D. Roosevelt Presidential Library and Museum*

HL   *Houghton Library, Harvard University*

LoC   *Manuscript Division, Library of Congress*

ABBREVIATIONS OF NAMES

ARC   *Anna Roosevelt Cowles*

ARL   *Alice Roosevelt Longworth*

BWR   *Belle Wyatt Roosevelt*

CRR   *Corinne Roosevelt Robinson*

ER   *Eleanor Roosevelt*

FDR   *Franklin Delano Roosevelt*

KR   *Kermit Roosevelt*

SDR   *Sara Delano Roosevelt*

TR   *Theodore Roosevelt*

TRJ   *Theodore Roosevelt Jr.*

Note: I have, in some cases, fixed grammar, spelling, and punctuation in original quotations, as well as dispensed with brackets and ellipses—*but only if the meaning or thrust of the quote was not changed by my doing so.* I have also eliminated ampersands from personal correspondence, replacing them with *and.*

PROLOGUE: THE LARGER PICTURE

1   *The old woman walked:* The *New York Times*, April 4, 1960; Lash, *Eleanor: The Years Alone*; ER, "My Day" column, April 5, 1960, transcripts, FDRL.

1   *"unite American women":* ER, "My Day" column, April 1 and 4, 1960, transcripts FDRL.

2   *She'd tell a friend the driver:* Lash, *Eleanor: The Years Alone.*

3   *"like a Picasso drawing":* Ibid.

3   *At the same time:* From Lash's diary, March 16, 1960, in ibid.

4   *"seemed necessary for a better":* ER, *The Autobiography of Eleanor Roosevelt.*

5   *"I can't work":* Lash, *Eleanor: The Years Alone.*

PART I: CAIN AND ABEL

9   *Theodore Roosevelt stomped:* The courthouse where the Civil Service Commission had its offices in 1891 was in the Old City Hall, which today stands in what is known as Judiciary Square. In an undated letter to his sister Bye, from early 1891 (probably January), he speaks of leaving the building "in a rage" over news of their brother Elliott's indiscretion (HL).

10 *"Quiet and tree-lined":* Teague, *Mrs. L.*

10 *"heart would beat a little faster":* TR admitted this in 1912; Stoddard, *As I Knew Them.*

10 *"It is a perfect nightmare about Elliott":* TR to ARC, January 24, 1890, HL.

11 *Anna . . . was "Chinese":* TR to ARC, May 2, 1890, HL.

12 *"the little gray man in the White House":* TR to ARC, February 1, 1891, HL.

12 *"civil service had a moral":* The *New York Times*, December 20, 1890.

13 *"thoroughly respectable," "I am very glad":* TR to ARC, February 1, 1891, HL.

13 *"a length of liverwurst":* TR to Henry Cabot Lodge, October 1886, quoted in Morris, *The Rise of Theodore Roosevelt.*

14 *Then, one day, his father:* Corinne Robinson Roosevelt [CRR], *My Brother Theodore Roosevelt.*

15 *"As athletes we are about equal":* TR Diary, July 3, 1879, quoted in Morris, *Rise.*

15 *A decade later, out on Long Island:* TR to ARC, August 5, 1888, HL.

15 *"All the girls":* TR to CRR, August 29, 1894, HL.

16 *"If I were to do something":* CRR to Douglas Robinson, March 19, 1881, HL.

16 *"eaten into her character like acid":* TR to ARC, April 30, 1890, HL.

16 *No matter that Dr. William T. Lusk:* For Lusk, see, among other sources, the *New York Times*, April 4, 1887; March 31, 1891; and June 13, 1897; and the *Hartford Courant*, February 4, 1892.

16 *"put himself completely in the hands":* TR to ARC, April 30, 1890, HL.

17 *"Most people know":* TR to ARC, January 25, 1891, HL.

17 *"Wynkoop is going to try":* TR to ARC, February 15, 1891, HL.

18 *"I do hate his Hempstead life":* TR to ARC, June 24, 1888, HL.

18 *"Live and let live":* Elliott Roosevelt unpublished story, "Was Miss Vedder an Adventuress?" FDRL.

18 *"Elliott has been a perfect angel":* Anna Hall Roosevelt to ARC, October 15, 1890, HL.

18 *"get away [from the] club":* TR to ARC, April 30, 1890, HL.

18 *"I am not going to speak":* Elliott Roosevelt to ARC, July 21, 1890, HL.

19 *from . . . Bad Reichenhall:* We know this from Elliott Mann's letter to ER, November 26, 1932, courtesy of Trisha Helland, granddaughter of Eleanor Mann Biles.

19 *"noble [and] beautiful":* Elliott Roosevelt to ARC, July 21, 1890, HL.

19 *"She is my only friend":* Elliott Roosevelt to Mary Livingston Ludlow Hall, June 2, 1891, FDRL.

19 *"kind and loving and charming":* ER, *Hunting Big Game.*

20 *"Tell Alice," Elliott wrote:* Elliott Roosevelt to TR, January 20, 1891, FDRL.

20 *"consideration and thoughtfulness":* ER, *Hunting Big Game.*

20 *in a series of fifteen bouts:* Morris, *Rise.*

21 *"You are right about Teedie":* Elliott Roosevelt to Theodore Roosevelt Sr., March 6, 1875, FDRL.

21 *he stood an inch taller:* My physical description of Elliott comes from his passport application, October 19, 1880.

21 *"the pride Theodore had taken":* Elliott Roosevelt to Martha Bulloch Roosevelt, August 1, 1881, quoted in ER, *Hunting Big Game.*

21 *Theodore published a catalogue:* Elliott eventually produced an essay, "The Description of the Ceylon Hunting," which was never published (FDRL).

22 *"very wicked" of him:* Anna Hall to Elliott Roosevelt, March 12, 1883, FDRL.

22 *"dissipated time buying dresses":* Elliott Roosevelt to ARC, June 9, 1887, HL.

22 *Writing to his brother:* Elliott Roosevelt to TR, January 20, 1891, HL.

22 *"a melancholy from which nothing":* Anna Hall Roosevelt to ARC, October 15, 1890, FDRL.

23 *"something dreadful":* Ibid.

23 *a very heavily pregnant young woman:* My description of the place and the circumstances of Elliott Mann's birth comes from several sources, including an interview with Pat Johnson, a descendant of Katie Mann's brother Bernhard. The address comes from Elliott Mann's birth record, March 11, 1891. I reconstructed the neighborhood using Manhattan property deeds, city directories (especially the 1890–1892 editions), census records, and various newspaper reports.

23 *"disorderly house":* The (New York) *Sun,* May 5, 1892; the place would also be raided a few years later (The *New York Times,* June 13, 1895).

23 *Dr. Gerardus Wynkoop, was attempting to rebuild:* New York Supreme Court papers, *Ann E. Wynkoop v. Mary S. Van Beuren, et al.,* May 9, 1890.

24 *more often he treated the likes:* The (New York) *Sun,* April 5, 1891.

24 *Clinton Roosevelt, a second cousin:* According to Manhattan property records, 32 East Thirteenth is part of Lot 22, Block 570. A study of the deeds shows there were at least two separate properties within Lot 22; the property inclusive of 32 East Thirteenth appears to have been part of the conveyance granted to Clinton Roosevelt from the Arden family on August 29, 1854 (Book 677, p. 26). According to a later record, this was "under a mortgage of James Roosevelt" (March 16, 1914, Book 229, p. 257). See also the *New York Times,* October 24, 1920, for a discussion of the property, and Whittlesey, *Roosevelt Genealogy.*

24 *gala society wedding:* The *New York Times,* February 3, 1889.

24 *C.V.S. had owned the entire end:* The *New York Times,* January 26, 1893. See also Morris, *Rise*; McCullough, *Mornings on Horseback.*

25 *whose friends called her Katie:* I have used the spelling "Katie" instead of "Katy" because this was how her son, Elliott, spelled the name in a letter he wrote to Eleanor in 1932. "Katy" was the spelling Theodore used in his letters to Bye. Theodore did not use exclusively "K.M." to indicate Katie, as Joseph Lash maintains in *Love, Eleanor.* Catherina Mann arrived into New York on the SS *Habsburg* from Bremen on October 27, 1884 (U.S. ship passenger lists). She was born September 26, 1862, in Grünstadt, Pfalz, Bavaria (German birth records online).

25 *Rudolph, a baker, and Bernhard:* Pat Johnson, U.S. census records, New York City directories. Rudolph Mann died in 1915; Bernhard Mann died in 1931. There was also another brother, Heinrich.

25 *"someone to marry":* Pat Johnson.

25 *"Katie Mann was the victim":* Eleanor Biles to Edmund Morris, July 6, 1981, used with permission of the Biles family. My account of Katie Mann's involvement with Elliott and the birth of her child is drawn from family remembrances told by Trisha Helland, Katie's great-granddaughter, and by Katie's third cousin Pat Johnson. The basic framework and timeline of the story are also documented in letters between TR and ARC, January–August 1891, HL.

25 *his "spiritual wife":* Pat Johnson.

26 *She held on to the letters:* Pat Johnson; Trisha Helland; also TR to ARC, February 15, 1891.

26 *Ten thousand dollars:* TR to ARC, July 8, 1891, HL.

27 *"Howe was the soul of honor":* The *New York Times*, April 12, 1914.

27 *All he reported was a male child:* Birth certificate, male child, son of Katie Mann, March 11, 1891, New York City Municipal Archives.

27 *Still, the girl wished:* Eleanor describes her frame of mind during her father's absence in *This Is My Story*.

28 *"shortcomings with a much more":* ER, "The Seven People Who Shaped My Life," *Look*, June 19, 1951.

28 *"I knew a child once":* Quoted in Lash, *Eleanor and Franklin*.

28 *"watching the gray surf":* Elliott Roosevelt to Mary Livingston Ludlow Hall, October 20, 1890, FDRL.

28 *His sharp words stung:* For Eleanor's reaction to her father's words, see ER, *The Autobiography*; her article "Conquer Fear and You Will Enjoy Living," *Look*, May 23, 1939; and its original draft in the Lorena Hickok Papers, FDRL.

29 *"hobbling out on crutches":* ER, *This Is My Story*.

29 *"should advise fighting her":* TR to Elliott Roosevelt, June 14, 1891, HL.

30 *He wrote Theodore and gave him:* TR to ARC, June 21, 1891, HL.

30 *"kept perfectly straight":* ARC to Edith Roosevelt, April 1891, HL.

31 *"Theodore rushed after Elliott":* CRR to ARC, August 1, 1888, HL.

31 *"perfectly limp and senseless":* TR to ARC, August 8, 1888, HL.

32 *"ecstatic half hour":* TR to ARC, March 29, 1891, HL.

32 *"a very pleasant dinner":* Ibid.

32 *Nearly two months earlier:* Although no record exists of Bye's transatlantic voyage, it can be deduced from TR's letters that she left New York sometime between the first and eighth of February. In his first letter, he worries over "the terrible trial" Bye is about to endure; in his second letter, he is all business and politics, without any mention of Elliott's troubles. Clearly this second letter was written with the knowledge that Elliott might intercept it and read it—so, evidently, Bye had already arrived in Paris, or was about to. A study of the ocean liners departing New York for French ports reveals only one in this period: *La Champagne* on February 7. Therefore, TR's letter of February 8 would have been waiting for Bye upon her arrival at Elliott's, and if Elliott read it, no suspicions would have been raised.

32 *"insane and should be confined":* TR to ARC, February 15, 1891, HL.

32 *"My dearest sister":* TR to ARC, February 1, 1891, HL.

33   *"useless as far as a permanent":* TR to ARC, March 1, 1891, HL.

33   *"evidently a maniac":* TR to ARC, June 17, 1891, HL.

33   *"Public opinion and the law":* TR, *Autobiography.*

33   *Bye suggested they speak:* That Bye had used Weeks's legal services comes from a letter written to her by TR on May 10, 1891, regarding Katie Mann: "She is to see Weeks, your lawyer" (HL).

33   *Anna had "no right":* TR to ARC, March 1, 1891, HL.

34   *"I regard it as little short":* Ibid.

34   *The lawyer who came:* My description of Weeks comes from newspaper engravings and from his admission register, Sing Sing Prison, November 9, 1893 (online).

34   *He introduced himself:* My description of Weeks's visit to Katie Mann is derived from a careful reading of the letters between Theodore and Bye and from family lore told by both Pat Johnson and Trisha Helland.

35   *The letter described:* The letter no longer survives but is referenced in correspondence between Theodore and Bye.

35   *"a houndsbreadth to a case":* TR to ARC, May 10, 1891, HL.

35   *In a letter to Bye dated:* The backstory of Weeks's involvement with Katie Mann, in which the lawyer was essentially a Roosevelt plant who displaced her real attorneys, has long been held as gospel by the Mann family, and seems confirmed in a letter from TR to ARC dated May 10, 1891: "Douglas is in much apprehension over the Katie Mann incident yet. She started to put her case in the hands of Howe and Hummel; he stopped this, and she is to see Weeks, your lawyer. There seems strong likelihood of an ugly scandal. I shall write you as soon as I get Weeks' report." Perhaps it was Douglas Robinson who convinced Katie to meet with Frank Weeks.

36   *At the moment, Weeks:* The *New York Times,* August 16, 1893.

36   *"chaffed her about Elliott's":* TR to ARC, June [nd] 1891, HL.

37   *"Even if Elliott does not drink":* TR to ARC, May 10, 1891, HL.

37   *"be shut up against":* TR to ARC, June 20, 1891, HL.

37   *"If we could get Elliott back":* TR to ARC, May 23, 1891, HL.

38   *On other occasions:* See Cook, *Eleanor Roosevelt, Vol. 1.*

38   *"Once here" he told Bye:* TR to ARC, June 7, 1891, HL.

38   *"a quitclaim" from her:* TR to Elliott Roosevelt, June [nd] 1891, HL.

39   *"out of the way":* ER, *The Autobiography.*

39   *"You have no looks":* ER, *This Is My Story.*

39   *"with scientific exactness":* TR to ARC, June 7, 1891, HL.

40   *"He was the only person":* ER, *The Autobiography.*

40   *Exultant, Bye wrote:* Because few of Bye's letters to Theodore survive from this period, one has to read his to her to assemble the chronicle of events and deduce what she was reporting from France. See, among others, TR to ARC, June 17, June 20 (two letters), June 28, July 2, July 8, and July 12, 1891, HL.

41   *Weekes, as Elliott's attorney, expressed:* TR to ARC, July 8, 1891, HL.

41   *"simply a selfish, brutal":* TR to ARC, June 7, 1891, HL.

41 *"Let Elliott know that"*: TR to ARC, June 17, 1891, HL.

41 *"judicially insane"*: TR to ARC, July 8, 1891, HL.

41 *"almost certainly shut Elliott up"*: TR to ARC, July 21, 1891, HL.

42 *"He went over to Brooklyn"*: TR to ARC, July 12, 1891, HL. I was able to identify Cosgrove through articles in the *New York Times*; see, for example, March 25, 1881; November 4, 1890; August 28, 1891; December 28, 1894; and December 30, 1894.

42 *"at all the right man"*: TR to ARC, July 21, 1891, HL.

43 *"the fastest schooner"*: The *New York Tribune*, June 23, 1893.

43 *"equipages and horses necessary"*: The *New York Times*, August 16, 1893.

43 *A network of clotheslines:* My description is based on photographs and histories of the neighborhood. Floyd Street no longer cuts across the block to Nostrand Street as it did in 1891.

43 *Katie had every reason to believe:* Pat Johnson.

43 *Frank Weeks had assured her:* If TR wrote a letter to Bye describing his visit to Katie and the baby, it has not survived. A careful reading of their correspondence, however, seems to indicate that he did make the visit, or at least was planning to do so, on July 13. Edmund Morris drew this conclusion as well in *The Rise of Theodore Roosevelt*. My description of their meeting is drawn from Mann family lore and from what we know about the agreement with Frank Weeks.

45 *The little girl's fear of water:* I have used eyewitness reports from newspaper accounts of the *Britannic* accident to describe the scene (The *New York Times*, May 22, 23, 24, 1887).

45 *Peeling Eleanor from his shoulder:* Eleanor wrote of the night on the *Britannic* in *Hunting Big Game in the Eighties*, including using the phrase "the person she loved best in the world" to describe her feelings about her father.

46 *"Where is Baby's home now?":* Anna Gracie to CRR, [nd], HL.

46 *"I come to settle the thing"*: TR to ARC, June 7, 1891, HL.

46 *in his anger, Elliott even asked:* Anna Roosevelt to ARC, July 1891, FDRL.

46 *"Elliott's hopeless misconduct"*: TR to ARC, June 17, 1891, HL.

46 *entered the facility willingly:* The exact details of Elliott's final removal from the family aren't clear, as most of Bye's letters do not survive; we have only Theodore's responses to hers. Still, enough can be gleaned from his letter to her dated July 10, 1891, to draw some conclusions. Elliott described being "kidnapped" in a letter to his mother-in-law, Mary Livingston Ludlow Hall, dated December 7, 1892, FDRL.

47 ELLIOTT ROOSEVELT INSANE: The *New York World*, August 18, 1891.

47 *"How far this was produced"*: Papers of the New York Supreme Court, in the matter of Elliott Roosevelt, Affidavit and Order for Commission, August 17, 1891.

48 *"If some frightful scandal arises"*: TR to ARC, June 21, 1891, HL.

48 *"Any poverty would be better"*: TR to ARC, June 26, 1891, HL.

48 *"loved everybody and everybody"*: Elliott Roosevelt to ARC, October 13, 1888, quoted in ER, *Hunting Big Game*.

PART II: EVERYTHING TO FEAR

51 *The path to the sea:* I have used several sources to describe and re-create the walk taken by the Roosevelt children out to Cold Spring Harbor, including ARL, *Crowded Hours*; ER, *This Is My Story*; and Archie Roosevelt, *A Lust for Knowing*. A letter from Theodore to Kermit Roosevelt, quoted in Joan Patterson Kerr, *A Bully Father*, also describes their route to the sea. A visit to Sagamore Hill and a hike along the area, so much of which is unchanged, gave me further insight.

51 *Only the child bringing up the rear:* I have determined that Eleanor's well-remembered visit to Oyster Bay, in which she was forced to jump into the harbor and was dunked by her cousins, most likely occurred in the summer of 1893. Hermann Hagedorn wrote in *The Roosevelt Family of Sagamore Hill*, without citing any evidence, that Eleanor was ten at the time of the dunking incident. Given a consideration of the 1894–1895 period, when she would have been ten, that seems unlikely, given what else was going on in that period. Still, it does suggest that Eleanor was not a very little girl when it happened. From Eleanor's own recollections, it would seem she was at least five or six; even the notoriously bullish Theodore wasn't likely to goad a four-year-old into jumping off a pier. Yet during the summers of 1890 and 1891, when Eleanor was five and six, she was in Europe with her family. That makes 1892 the first real possibility. That year, Theodore was only at Sagamore at the beginning of July and the beginning of August; nowhere in his letters to Bye during this period, when Elliott was a frequent topic, is there a mention of a visit from Eleanor. While he also does not mention Eleanor to Bye in his letters during the summer of 1893, he was at Sagamore for longer stretches that year (roughly July 2 to 17, July 28 to August 6, and August 26 to September 1). Finally, during the summer of 1894, Eleanor was at Tivoli and in Bar Harbor; there was no time for a trip to Sagamore that year. And after that, a visit of the kind Eleanor remembered seems increasingly unlikely: we know that after her father's death in August 1894, her visits to Sagamore stopped. (Edith Roosevelt's diaries are of no help here; there's no mention of a visit from Eleanor at all from 1892 to 1895, but then again, Edith recorded only the barest details in her datebooks.) So we are left with 1892 or 1893 as the only real possibilities. I've gone with 1893 because Theodore was there longer that summer; Eleanor was older; and it was a period of relative calm between Theodore and his brother, Elliott. (Indeed, Elliott had been invited to Sagamore for the Fourth of July that year, but he did not attend.)

51 *Only Eleanor remained on the pier:* Eleanor wrote about her fear of jumping off the pier, her uncle's insistence that she do so, and her cousins' "good-natured" dunking of her in *This Is My Story*.

52 *Ted had survived the experience:* "I remember Ted being tossed off the pier into the water way above his head, when up to that time he had only paddled about in the shallows. He was not the least bit frightened, took to it, and kept himself up and going like a little frog." ARL, *Crowded Hours*. Ted Jr.'s childhood illnesses, often exacerbated by strenuous play, are well documented in numerous Roosevelt letters.

53 *when Kermit was in the mood for fun:* The boy's antics are all described in letters written by his father. See also Morris, *Edith Kermit Roosevelt*.

53 *"Dive, Alicy, dive!":* ARL, *Crowded Hours*; Teague, *Mrs. L.*

54 *"I was a solemn child":* ER, *Hunting Big Game.*

55 *"mentally capable of transacting":* The *New York World*, August 16, 1894. The original commission had been ordered from the Supreme Court in Manhattan in August 1891 by Justice O'Brien. On October 26, 1891, Theodore entered a new petition at the Supreme Court in Brooklyn, and on December 3, Justice Willard Bartlett ordered a similar investigation (see the *New York Tribune*, December 4, 1891), and the commission was executed on January 18, 1892. The results were the same, however. Elliott was never found incompetent and so was never ordered committed to any asylum.

55 *"He is so sane":* TR to ARC, September 1, 1891, HL.

55 *"surrendered completely":* TR to ARC, January 22, 1892, HL.

56 *"He admits that he drank heavily":* TR to ARC, August 5, 1893.

56 *"desperately afraid":* ER, *This Is My Story.*

57 *Pans of ice melted quickly:* My description of Brooklyn's German neighborhoods in the 1890s comes from the (New York) *Sun*, August 10, 1894.

57 *the shoemaker who lived on the first floor:* This was John Loster. From 1892 New York State Census, Brooklyn city directories.

57 *anything elaborate:* Pat Johnson.

58 *The gold lettering on the door:* The *New York Times*, August 16, 1893.

58 *"He was quite a borrower":* The (New York) *Sun*, May 2, 1893.

58 *"meet every one of his obligations":* The *New York World*, May 2, 1893.

59 *"none of the securities belonging":* The *New York Tribune*, July 12, 1893.

59 *The house called Sagamore Hill:* My description of the house and grounds comes from *The Saturday Evening Post*, June 21, 1902, and various memoirs, particularly Hagedorn, *The Roosevelt Family of Sagamore Hill.* Also *Inventory and Appraisal of the Art, Literary and Other Personal Property Belonging to the Estate of the Late Theodore Roosevelt at Oyster Bay*, Theodore Roosevelt Jr. Papers, LoC.

59 *"The violets dotted the ground":* TR to ARC, May 20, 1888, HL.

60 *"Sagamore is the offspring of the years":* TRJ, *All in the Family.*

61 *"A life of slothful ease":* TR speech before the Hamilton Club in Chicago, April 10, 1899, available variously online and in print.

61 *"He wears big spectacles":* TR to Gertrude Carow, October 3, 1892, HL.

61 *"plays more vigorously":* TR to ARC, quoted in Hagedorn, *The Roosevelt Family of Sagamore Hill.*

61 *during one of the boy's illnesses:* When Ted rallied, coming out of his stupor to say "cunning things . . . in his changed, sick voice," it was about as much as Theodore could stand, he told Bye. TR to ARC, October 23, 1890, HL.

62 *"Sickness . . . is always a shame":* Mrs. TRJ, *Day Before Yesterday.*

62 *Over, Under or Through:* This game is described in various memoirs, including ARL, *Crowded Hours.*

62 *Competition was important:* For the "disinherit" quote, see Morris, *Rise.*

62 *"In so strenuous a household":* Hagedorn, *The Roosevelt Family of Sagamore Hill.*

63   "I'll have to have Ted and Kermit": TR to ARC, June 27, 1893, HL.

63   Later, Theodore would admit: Hagedorn, The Roosevelt Family of Sagamore Hill.

63   His father's cousin West Roosevelt: His actual quote was "the finest baby of the three physically . . . as bright as Ted but without his nervousness." Jean Paterson Kerr, A Bully Father: Theodore Roosevelt's Letters to His Children.

63   "A nice little moustache": Kerr, A Bully Father.

64   "pale and yellow-haired": Collier and Horowitz, The Roosevelts.

64   Far more likely to sit: Morris, Edith Kermit Roosevelt.

64   "Odd and independent": Edith Roosevelt to Cecil Spring-Rice, January 27, 1902, quoted in Cordery, Alice.

64   "sturdy little scamp": TR to Gertrude Carow, October 18, 1890, HL.

64   A preponderance of female births: Edith Roosevelt to TRJ, August 4, [1932?], quoted in Morris, Edith Kermit Roosevelt.

65   "announced a strong desire": TR to ARC, July 5, 1893, HL.

65   "Sissy had a sweat nurse": Teague, Mrs. L. See also Sally Quinn, "Alice Roosevelt Longworth at 90," Washington Post, February 12, 1974.

65   "Everything belonged to me": Teague, Mrs. L.

65   She took Alice to buy: Edith's diary, at the Houghton Library, documents all the small, mundane moments of Alice's childhood.

65   "withdrawn, rather parched": Teague, Mrs. L.

66   "it was just as well that": Ibid.

66   "blue-eyed darling": Rixey, Bamie. See also Anna Gracie to CRR, October 27, 1886, HL.

66   "And now . . . bang goes a torpedo": TR to Gertrude Carow, February 15, 1893, HL.

67   "I am fairly reveling": TR to ARC, July 3, 1893, HL.

67   Today, however, her companion: TR to ARC, July 25, 1893, HL.

68   "As far as my work": TR to Henry Cabot Lodge, July 4, 1893, Henry Cabot Lodge Papers, Massachusetts Historical Society, quoted in Morris, Rise.

68   "Mean, sneaking little acts": TR to Carl Schurz, June 25, 1894, HL.

68   "Mr. Roosevelt is a worthy example": The Chicago Journal, June 24, 1893.

68   "She was ambitious,": Rixey, Bamie.

69   "stretching from Gussie": Ibid.

70   "I hope you will not think me": James Roosevelt to ARC, March 31, 1878, HL.

70   Bye's grandfather C. V. S. Roosevelt: Comparative wealth estimates between Bye's family and the Hyde Park family were taken from the 1860 and 1870 censuses. In 1860, C. V. S. was worth half a million. Sylvia Morris, in Edith Kermit Roosevelt, cites the later seven-million-dollar figure from family letters. Mr. James, of course, became far wealthier after his marriage to Sara Delano.

70   "I am beaming over": James Roosevelt to ARC, August 1, 1880, HL.

71   "Mr. Roosevelt says that": The New York Tribune, May 24, 1893.

72   "Do not forget your Father": Elliott Roosevelt to ER, August 20, 1893, FDRL.

73   *"One fact wiped out"*: ER, *This Is My Story.*

74   *"but that cannot be"*: Elliott Roosevelt to ER, May [nd] 1893, quoted in ER, *Hunting Big Game.*

75   *"I do not eat between"*: ER to Elliott Roosevelt, [nd], 1891–1892, FDRL.

75   *"Because Father is not with you"*: Elliott Roosevelt to ER, October 9, 1892, FDRL.

75   *"I needed my father's warmth"*: ER, "The Seven People Who Shaped My Life," *Look*, June 19, 1951.

75   *"intoxicated by the pure joy"*: ER, *Hunting Big Game.*

75   *If socks were not darned:* Ibid.

76   *"desperately afraid"*: ER, *The Autobiography.*

76   *"They always tried to talk"*: ER, *This Is My Story.*

76   *"one stone after another"*: Elliott Roosevelt to ER, January 20, 1893, FDRL.

77   *"as ever of his love"*: Quoted in ER, *Hunting Big Game.*

77   *Elliott had leased a three-story:* The *New York World*, August 15, 1894; and the *New York Times*, October 20, 1883; and October 16, 1893.

77   *"taking the cure"*: The *New York Herald*, August 22, 1891.

78   *she followed the teachings:* See letter to Vivekananda from Sherman dated February 2, 1894, where she praises his "personal appeal . . . magnetism [and] powerful masterful presence." She was writing for both herself and her mother (vivekananda.net). In his suit against his wife, Roger M. Sherman charged her mother with being responsible for Florence's "misconduct" because of her "views on religion and morality" (New York *Sun*, March 29, 1884).

78   *Sherman's husband had accused her:* For Sherman's divorce, see the *New York Times*, October 13 and November 4, 1883; March 29 and May 15, 1884; and May 26, 1885; Washington (DC) *Evening Star*, October 20, 1883; the (New York) *Sun*, March 29, 1884.

78   *"unintelligent, petty, common, timid"*: Fragment from the diary of Florence Bagley Sherman, January 28, 1892, Anna Hall Roosevelt Papers, FDRL.

78   *"This morning, with his silk hat"*: Ibid.

78   *"I cannot understand"*: Elliott Roosevelt to Mary Livingston Ludlow Hall, December 7, 1892, FDRL.

79   *Her father, riding in the back:* CRR to ARC, October 11, 1893, HL.

79   *"We would go on"*: ER, *This Is My Story*; and the *New York Times*, June 16, 1946, in which Eleanor shared her "most vivid recollection" of her father for Father's Day.

80   *A crowd was waiting:* The *New York Times*, November 4, 1893.

80   *Weeks had been discovered:* The (New York) *Sun*, September 12, 1893.

80   *"the despoiler of women's"*: The *New York Times*, November 4, 1893.

81   *"The repair of the carriages"*: Morris, *Edith Kermit Roosevelt.*

82   *"Would it help if I came"*: Rixey, *Bamie.*

82   POOR LITTLE ROOSEVELT CHILDREN: The *New York Times*, August 11, 1894.

82 *pled guilty to embezzlement:* The *New York Times*, November 9, 1893.

82 *Eleanor tried to keep her mind:* Eleanor wrote in detail about her feelings on this day (albeit in the third person) in *Hunting Big Game*: "On this particular day there was suppressed excitement in every movement of the child."

83 *"I do wish Corinne could get":* TR to ARC, July 29, 1894, HL.

83 *"with averted gaze":* CRR, *One Woman to Another and Other Poems* (New York: Charles Scribner's Sons, 1914).

84 *"didn't seem quite certain":* The *New York World*, March 20, 1894.

84 *constitution remained "so marvelous":* TR to CRR, August 12, 1894, HL.

84 *"If only he could have died":* TR to ARC, July 29, 1894, HL.

85 *"not unnaturally":* TR to ARC, July 15, 1894, HL.

85 *"manly and very bright":* Ibid.

85 *He'd complained of pain:* TR to ARC, June 24, 1894, HL.

85 *"Little Kermit tends to be fretful":* TR to ARC, July 22, 1894, HL.

85 *A week later the boy:* TR to ARC, July 29, 1894, HL.

85 *"Both are entirely fearless":* TR to ARC, July 15, 1894, HL.

85 *"perfectly awful endurance tests":* Teague, *Mrs. L.*

86 *"I do feel quite sorry":* Edith Roosevelt to ARC, [nd] 1893–1894, HL.

86 *"I'm afraid I do not do rightly":* Edith Roosevelt to TR, August 15, 1889, HL.

86 *acknowledge both the "enormous effort":* Teague, *Mrs. L.*

86 *"Elliott has sunk to the lowest depths":* Edith Roosevelt to Emily Carow, August 10, 1894, HL.

86 *"I do not feel [Eleanor]":* Edith Roosevelt to ARC, [nd], 1892, HL.

87 *"I never wished Alice":* Edith Roosevelt to Gertrude Carow, November 4, 1893, HL.

87 *"look quite as forlorn as Eleanor":* Edith Roosevelt to Emily Carow, [nd], Sagamore Hill National Historic Site Archives, Oyster Bay, NY.

87 *"Her mouth and teeth seem to have":* Edith Roosevelt to ARC, May 18, 1884, HL.

87 *"doing the real work":* TR to Henry Cabot Lodge, June 29, 1891, HL.

87 *"the right career for a man":* TR to ARC, December 12, 1893, HL.

87 *"such a variety of indiscretions":* TR to ARC, August 12, 1894, HL.

88 *"I would literally have given":* TR to Henry Cabot Lodge, quoted in Morris, *Rise.*

88 *"ended in consequence":* ARC to Henry Cabot Lodge, quoted in Rixey, *Bamie.*

88 *"I cannot begin to describe":* Edith Roosevelt to ARC, September 28, 1894, HL.

88 *On a day that would forever:* It is not known exactly when Alice received the pages Auntie Gracie had written about her mother's death. A note was included among them asking that the pages be given to Alice if she, Auntie Gracie, died before being able to tell Alice the stories in person. This clearly suggests that the pages were delivered to Alice after Auntie Gracie's death, which occurred on June 9, 1893. I speculate that this occurred sometime in the 1893–1894 period, soon after Auntie Gracie's death and perhaps sometime

after Alice turned ten. It's possible, however, that they came at a later date. I believe they definitely came into Alice's possession before her acting-out, rebellious period of 1895–1899.

89   *"This lock of hair and this little piece"*: Note from Annie Gracie, dated 1884, 26 West Thirty-Sixth Street, HL.

89   *"What little I know"*: Teague, *Mrs. L.*

89   *"The light has gone out"*: TR Private Diaries, February 14 and 16, 1884, Theodore Roosevelt Collection, LoC.

89   *"My father obviously didn't"*: Teague, *Mrs. L.*

90   *From the schooners and yachts*: My description of Bar Harbor in the summer of 1894 comes from the *New York Times*, June 24, July 1 and 15, and July 29, 1894.

90   *"There are probably not many"*: The *New York Times*, July 29, 1894.

90   *"Don't you think I did well"*: ER to Elliott Roosevelt, July 30, 1894, FDRL.

90   *"to find the paths all alone"*: ER to Elliott Roosevelt, July 10, 1894, FDRL.

91   *"Father would write you"*: Elliott Roosevelt to ER, [nd] 1893, FDRL.

91   *"a return of my Indian fever"*: ER, *Hunting Big Game.*

91   *"whole bottles of anisette"*: TR to ARC, August 18, 1894, HL.

91   *Worse, he was using stimulants*: CRR to ARC, August 15, 1894, HL.

91   *He was "never still"*: TR to ARC, August 12, 1894, HL.

92   *"Katie Mann was again"*: TR to ARC, June 17, 1894, HL.

92   *"if Miss Eleanor Roosevelt"*: CRR to ARC, August 15, 1894, HL.

92   *"What must you think"*: Elliott Roosevelt to ER, August 13, 1894, FDRL.

92   *"My life has been a gamble"*: Elliott Roosevelt unpublished story, "Was Miss Vedder an Adventuress?" FDRL.

93   *Finally, at ten o'clock*: Elliott Roosevelt death certificate, August 14, 1894, New York City Municipal Archives. He did not die on the same day or "only hours after" he wrote to Eleanor, as some accounts have said, but rather the night of the following day.

93   *"a fearful shock"*: TR to ARC, August 18, 1894, HL.

94   *"[Roosevelt] lays down the singular"*: The *Nation*, May 14, 1891, quoted in Morris, *Rise.*

94   *"time will help him out"*: Quoted in Rixey, *Bamie.*

94   *"just as strange," "The absolute contradiction"*: TR to ARC, August 18, 1894, HL.

95   *"race suicide"*: Speech given by TR on March 13, 1905, before the National Congress of Mothers, transcript TRC.

96   *"I suppose"*: TR to ARC, August 18, 1894, HL.

96   *"I know it is best"*: CRR to ARC, August 15, 1894, HL.

96   *"stricken, hunted creature"*: TR to ARC, August 18, 1894, HL.

96   *"He was more overcome"*: CRR to ARC, August 15, 1894, HL.

96   *Edith did not accompany them*: Edith Roosevelt diary, HL.

96   *"a large number of relatives"*: The *New York World*, August 17, 1894.

97 *Theodore found it "grotesque":* TR to ARC, August 18, 1894, HL.

97 *Even in death:* Elliott's body was moved some years later, at the request of his in-laws, to rest beside his wife at Tivoli.

97 *"The woman" . . . had "a fair claim":* TR to ARC, August 25, 1894, HL.

97 *"five dollars for each night":* TR to CRR, September 5, 1894, HL.

98 *"mercy from his father's family":* Pat Johnson.

98 *He told Douglas that no further money:* That no money was ever paid to Katie was made clear by her family, and documented in the letter sent to Edmund Morris from Eleanor (Mann) Biles. I believe a message from Theodore to Douglas might reference this decision, coming as it did so soon after Katie's visit to Douglas's office: "Tell old Douglas I received his second letter. As he doubtless saw in my answer to his first, I entirely agree with him, and will act, and have acted, precisely as he advised. I am very much obliged to him for writing." TR to CRR, August 25, 1894, HL.

98 *"Katie Mann came in," "She was a bad woman":* TR to ARC, August 18, 1894, HL.

99 *"I did want to see Father":* Mary Livingston Ludlow Hall to CRR, August 25, 1894, FDRL.

99 *"The poor child has had":* Ibid.

99 *"He has broken his word":* ER, essay, [nd], FDRL.

100 *"He never accomplished anything":* ER, *Hunting Big Game.*

PART III: POPULAR AND POWERFUL

103 *"the sunshine of a perfect winter day":* The (Washington) *Evening Star,* January 1, 1903.

105 *"in his silk pajamas and barefoot":* Diary of Sara Delano Roosevelt (SDR), 1904, FDRL.

106 *"I want to know the name":* ARL and Helen Roosevelt (later Robinson) to FDR, September 10, 1897, FDRL.

106 *"[He] prefers it":* SDR to FDR, June 1901, FDRL.

106 *"systemize his time":* Quoted in Ward, *Before the Trumpet.*

106 *"retrouseé," or delicately turned up:* My description of Alice Sohier, including her height—she's described as six feet tall—comes from her passport application, dated October 1, 1902.

107 *The daughter of a wealthy Boston:* For the full story of Alice Sohier, see Ward, *Before the Trumpet.*

107 *"Miss Roosevelt and the younger":* The *Washington Times,* January 2, 1903.

107 *"so pleasantly calling attention":* The (Washington) *Evening Star,* January 1, 1903.

107 *Eleanor had a "very good mind":* Harrity and Martin, *Eleanor Roosevelt.*

108 *A few months later, Franklin was again:* FDR diary, November 17, 1902, FDRL.

108 *"Sat near Eleanor":* FDR diary, January 1, 1903, FDRL.

108 *"where the Empress Eugénie":* Ward, *Before the Trumpet.*

109 *On one transatlantic trip:* SDR diary, 1889, FDRL.

109   *"Mummie," he said:* Mrs. James Roosevelt (SDR), *My Boy Franklin.*

109   *"help the poor, the widow":* "Work," address given by James Roosevelt to the Guild of St. James Episcopal Church, Hyde Park, FDRL.

109   *"He did not have the 'common touch'":* Quote from Walter E. Sachs, in Ward, *Before the Trumpet.*

110   *"They are attacking us":* TR to ARC, August 20, 1887, HL.

110   *"The greatest disappointment":* Franklin told this to W. Sheffield Cowles, the son of Bye Roosevelt Cowles, who relayed it to Geoffrey Ward, in *Before the Trumpet.*

111   *"popular and powerful":* Quote from classmate Tom Beal, in Richard Thayer Goldberg, *The Making of Franklin Delano Roosevelt: Triumph Over Disability* (Lanham, MD: University Press of America, 1984).

111   *"long before they should have been":* SDR, *My Boy Franklin.*

111   *Six years before that New Year's Day:* TR to FDR, June 11, 1897, FDRL. See also Edith Roosevelt's diary, July 2–5, 1897, HL.

111   *"characteristically feminine":* Wehle, *Hidden Threads.* Childs is quoted in Ward, *A First-Class Temperament.*

112   *His initials, F.D.:* Alsop, *FDR.*

112   *"He was the kind of boy":* Lash, *Eleanor and Franklin.*

112   *"Very jolly!":* FDR diary, January 30, 1903, FDRL.

113   *"Every box in the Diamond Horseshoe":* Lehr, *King Lehr and the Gilded Age.*

113   *After the New Year's celebrations:* Eleanor's social schedule was chronicled in the newspapers, including the (Washington) *Evening Star,* January 3, 1903; the *New York Tribune,* January 3, 1903; January 21, 1903; January 28, 1903; and February 4, 1903; and the *Washington Times,* January 16, 1903; and March 14, 1903.

113   *"attracted much attention":* The *Washington Times,* March 14, 1903.

113   *Eleanor would remember watching with "great awe":* For ER's relationship with ARL, see ER, *This Is My Story* and *The Autobiography;* Lash, *Eleanor and Franklin.*

114   *"utter agony" for her:* ER, *This Is My Story.*

114   *"they were tribal friends":* The *New York Times Magazine,* August 6, 1967.

114   *"I knew that I was different":* ER, *The Autobiography.*

115   *"ugly duckling":* Quote from Corinne Robinson Alsop Cole in the film *The Eleanor Roosevelt Story,* dir. Richard Kaplan, 1965.

115   *"She probably went":* Teague, *Mrs. L.*

116   *"Her brilliant speech darted":* See Dorothy Strachey Bussy, *Olivia* (London: Hogarth Press, 1949).

116   *"a sort of hammering logic":* From the diaries of Beatrice Webb, quoted in Cook, *Eleanor Roosevelt, Vol. 1.*

117   *"I remember the day she arrived":* Lash and Roosevelt, *Love, Eleanor.*

118   *"one of the proudest moments":* ER, *This Is My Story.*

119   *"The purity of heart":* Marie Souvestre to Mary Livingston Ludlow Hall, [nd] 1900, FDRL.

119 *"She was beloved by everybody"*: Unpublished manuscript, Corinne Robinson Alsop Cole, HL.

120 *"never have the beaux"*: ER, *This Is My Story.*

120 *The Eleanor who finally returned:* Ship passenger lists, National Archives; the *Washington Times*, July 22, 1902.

121 *"the greater portion"*: The *New York Tribune*, July 12, 1903.

121 *"struggling through formal society"*: ER, *The Autobiography.*

121 *"Give some of your energy"*: Marie Souvestre to ER, July 7, 1902, FDRL.

121 *Thankfully, when she was in Washington:* For example, she stayed with Bye over the Easter holiday in March 1903 (the *New York Tribune* and the [Washington] *Evening Star*, March 21, 1903). There are other newspaper mentions as well.

121 *"Uncle Theodore made no major decision"*: ER, *This Is My Story.*

122 *That spring of 1903 alone, the newspapers:* The (Washington) *Evening Star*, April 8 and 21, 1903.

122 *"oversees the entire nation"*: TR to ARL, November 29, 1901, LoC.

122 *Yamei Kin, a well-known:* The (Washington) *Evening Star*, March 19, 1904.

122 *Eleanor was spending time:* The (Washington) *Evening Star*, March 1, 1904.

122 *"meant very little," "I loved to be with her"*: ER, *This Is My Story.*

123 *"I had a great curiosity about life"*: ER, *The Autobiography.*

123 *"Do not be bothered"*: *Ladies' Home Journal*, November 1944.

123 *when she told Henry Cabot Lodge:* Rixey, *Bamie.*

123 *"It seems so funny"*: ER to ARC: November 15, 1895, HL.

124 *When Eleanor was very little:* ER, *Hunting Big Game.*

124 *not quite accepted into the "inner clique"*: Bess Furman, *Washington By-Line* (New York: Alfred A. Knopf, 1949).

124 *"It was understood that no girl"*: ER, *The Autobiography.*

125 *"Eleanor is an angel"*: FDR diary, June 7, 1903, FDRL. His code actually translates to "E is an angel," but it's clear to whom he is referring.

125 *"and looking out over the beautiful Sound"*: TR to TRJ, August 25, 1903, HL.

125 *"I have seen a great many people"*: TR to CRR, September 23, 1903, HL.

126 *"I wish to make the rich man"*: TR to TRJ, October 24, 1903, HL.

127 *"Alice has been at home"*: TR to CRR, September 23, 1903, HL.

127 *"long-suffering Secret Service men"*: TR to KR, September 23, 1903, HL.

128 *"Teddy and the bear"*: See Jon Mooallem, *Wild Ones* (New York: Penguin Books, 2014).

128 *"a tendency to rheumatism"*: TR to TRJ, October 24, 1903, HL.

128 *"I feel rather aged and feeble"*: TR to KR, January 25, 1903, HL.

128 *"He can do better than I can"*: TR to Henry Cabot Lodge, September 15, 1903, HL.

129 *"Hereafter," he vowed:* TR to ARC, February 19, 1898, HL.

129 PRESIDENT'S SON STRICKEN: The San Francisco *Call*, February 8, 1902.

129   *"bundled in overcoats":* The *Washington Times*, February 23, 1902.

129   *including one from Kaiser Wilhelm II:* TR to Edith Roosevelt, February 26, 1902.

129   *not been "very sick":* TRJ to ARL, February 17, 1901, LoC.

130   *"I passed my swimming exam":* TRJ to ARL, [nd], postmarked June 3, 1901, HL.

130   *"There are from twenty to thirty":* TRJ to TR, [nd], HL.

130   *"I feel the trip will teach you":* TR to TRJ, August 25, 1903, HL.

131   *"hard as nails":* TR to TRJ, September 23, 1903, HL.

131   *"out of his class":* TR to TRJ, March 6, 1903, HL.

131   *"I greatly admire football":* TR to TRJ, October 4, 1903, HL.

131   *"I have sympathized":* TR to TRJ, October 24, 1903, HL.

131   *"I believe in rough, manly sports":* TR to TRJ, October 4, 1903, HL.

132   *"Indian summer":* The *Hartford Courant*, November 4, 1903. "Another wonderfully delightful day [added] to the many delightful fall days which have preceded it."

133   *Playing tennis at Sagamore:* TR to TRJ, August 25, 1903, HL.

133   *"I wish any of my boys":* TR to CRR, September 23, 1903, HL.

133   *"the ferocious scrap":* TR to TRJ, September 23, 1903, HL.

134   *"I enjoy being President":* TR to KR, October 2, 1903, HL.

134   *"As far as I can see":* TR to CRR, September 23, 1903, HL.

134   *"a colored archdeacon from North Carolina":* TR to TRJ, October 31, 1903, HL.

134   *"A live experience":* TR to KR, October 2, 1903, HL.

135   *President Roosevelt was sending:* The *Baltimore Sun*, February 13, 1904. Many newspapers across the country covered Alice's visit, including but not limited to the *St. Paul Globe* and the *Hartford Courant*, February 14, 1904.

135   *"I think you are divine":* Love letter dated November 23, 1905, LoC.

136   *"Miss Alice Roosevelt launched still":* The *Billings* (MT) *Gazette*, February 2, 1904.

136   *"a mistress of the occult":* The *Washington Times*, June 15, 1902.

136   *The event was memorialized:* See, for example, the *New York Tribune*, February 26, 1902.

136   *"did a little jig":* Teague, *Mrs. L.*

136   *"Lunch at Mrs. Congressman":* ARL diary, January 27, 1902, LoC.

137   *Alice regularly broke curfews:* For Alice's teenage rebellion, see Rixey, *Bamie*; and Stacy Cordery, *Alice.*

137   *Theodore rebuked his daughter:* See Cordery, *Alice*; and ARL, *Crowded Hours.*

137   *After a meal, she'd get:* William Howard Taft to Helen Taft, August 1, 1905, LoC.

137   *"The family remonstrated":* ARL, *Crowded Hours.*

137   *"Sweet cigarettes":* KR to ARL, [nd], 1907–1908, LoC.

137   *"hadn't the vaguest idea":* ARL to KR, October 9, 1901, LoC.

138   *"I can be President"*: The anecdote was told in Wister's *Roosevelt*, but had apparently been in circulation for some time.

138   *"fearfully naughty stories"*: ARL diary, December 31, 1902, LoC.

138   *"blessed girl"*: TR to ARL, May 27, 1903, LoC.

139   *"There was a village quality"*: Teague, *Mrs. L.*

139   *"He said I couldn't find out"*: ARL diary, January 20, 1904, LoC.

139   *"Sister continues to lead"*: TR to TRJ, January 20, 1904, HL.

140   *"I pray for a fortune"*: ARL diary, March 24, 1903, LoC.

140   *"gallivanting with society"*: Teague, *Mrs. L.*

140   *"a talking-to"*: ARL diary, July 20, 1902, LoC.

140   *"All the fun in having it"*: The *New York Times Magazine*, August 6, 1967.

140   *"You must keep Anna"*: Edith Roosevelt to ARL, [nd], LoC. Other quotes from Edith's letters to Anna are also not dated but come from the same period.

141   *"You say that you don't"*: George C. Lee to ARL, November 5, 1903, LoC.

141   *In Newport, her flamboyant behavior*: *Town Topics*, October 20, 1904; see also *Collier's*, November 11, 1905; and Mark Caldwell, *A Short History of Rudeness: Manners, Morals, and Misbehavior in Modern America* (New York: Picador, 2000).

141   *"Father doesn't care for me"*: ARL diary, January 27, 1903, LoC.

142   *"all more or less stupid"*: ARL diary, December 14, 1902, LoC.

142   *"I do not care for myself"*: Theodore Robinson to ARL, [nd], 1904, LoC.

142   *"No one ever comes"*: ARL diary, December 13, 1902, LoC.

142   *Sometimes Alice fantasized*: ARL diary, first page, 1902, LoC.

143   *The missive contained nothing*: ARL to Marie Souvestre, July 11, 1902, LoC.

143   *On the corner of 106th Street*: Unsourced clip, [nd], though it reads, "Mr. Roosevelt married his wife four years ago," so the date would be roughly mid-1904, FDRL.

144   *"Dutch Sadie" . . . in the red-light district*: The (New York) *Sun*, October 19, 1900.

144   *"American basement house"*: The *New York Tribune*, May 17, 1902.

144   *"a profusion of bronze hair"*: The (New York) *Evening World*, October 19, 1900. For more description of Sadie, see the (New York) *Sun*, October 19, 1900; and the (New York) *Evening World*, May 9, 1907.

145   *"[Franklin] had more on his mind"*: *Harvard Crimson*, December 13, 1957.

145   *Franklin and Taddy were more closely*: My description of Jimmie "Taddy" Roosevelt's early years comes from various correspondence at FDRL and from Ward, *Before the Trumpet*.

146   *"I have not heard from my father"*: James R. Roosevelt Jr. to ARC, May 2, 1897, HL.

146   *"much kinder to him"*: FDR to SDR [nd], FDRL.

146   *"A queer sort of boy"*: Ward, *Before the Trumpet*.

146   *"I have never heard"*: FDR to SDR [nd], FDRL.

147   *"troublesome, occasionally eccentric"*: Ward, *Before the Trumpet*.

147 "good-natured, well-intentioned": The (New York) Sun, October 19, 1900.

148 His mother's Astor fortune: I have calculated Jimmie's allowance based on the
     judge's ruling that he and his sister should split $7,500 a year from their inher-
     itance from their mother (the New York Times, August 11, 1894; and October
     19, 1900). Half of $7,500 divided by 12 comes out to be about $312 a month.

148 Now his best chum was Douglass Brown: U.S. Census 1880, 1900; New York
     State Census 1905; New York City directories.

148 "piquancy to her manner": The (New York) Evening World, October 19, 1900.
     Sadie's birthdate, as given in the 1900 Census, was June 1884; she was the
     third child (of six) of Martin and Esther (Newman) Messinger.

148 she was Jewish: 1900 Census; 1905 State Census; death certificates for Martin
     and Esther Messinger (1911 and 1912), New York Municipal Archives.

148 the Marriage Bureau clerk: See marriage certificate, June 14, 1900, Manhattan
     vital records; the New York Times, October 19, 1920; the (New York) Sun, Oc-
     tober 19, 1900; and the (New York) Evening World, October 19, 1900.

149 "flashy" and "not in the best": The (New York) Sun, October 19, 1900.

149 "to furnish the apartments suitably": The (New York) Sun, October 19, 1900.

150 "I'm just as good as any": Ibid.

151 "the dreadful and disgraceful business": SDR to FDR, October 25, 1900, FDRL.

151 "One can never again consider": FDR to SDR, October 30, 1900, FDRL.

151 in 1902 they sold the Eighty-Fourth Street: The New York Tribune, May 17, 1902;
     1905 New York State Census. Jimmie and Sadie did not immediately leave New
     York for Florida, but continued to live, quite openly, in the same city as their
     Roosevelt relatives until at least 1907. See the (New York) Evening World, July
     13, 1907, and many other references.

152 "think this matter over": ER, The Autobiography.

152 "I don't quite think your Mother": ER to FDR, [nd] 1904, FDRL.

153 "I cannot tell you": ER to FDR, January 27, 1904, FDRL.

154 "How do I love thee?": ER to FDR, December 18, 1903, FDRL.

154 "Fear nothing": ER to FDR, November 18, 1903, FDRL.

154 "Perhaps it is just as well": ER to FDR, February 12, 1904, FDRL.

154 "Dearest," she wrote to him: ER to FDR, December 19, 1903, FDRL.

155 "I loved him deeply": ER, This Is My Story.

155 "I want him to feel he belongs": Lash, Eleanor and Franklin.

156 "Her father wanted to give me": ER quote in Junior League commemoration,
     1935, quoted in Cook, Eleanor Roosevelt, Vol. 1.

156 "I can't say it was very important": ER, "My Day" column, March 23, 1960,
     collected at FDRL.

156 interested her "enormously": ER, The Autobiography.

157 "It had never occurred": ER quote in Junior League commemoration, 1935,
     quoted in Cook, Eleanor Roosevelt, Vol. 1.

157 "I was saved, but": FDR to Robert D. Washburn, August 18, 1928, FDRL.

158 Franklin was her "feller": ER, This Is My Story.

158 *"My God," he said; "I wanted him to see"*: Ward, *Before the Trumpet*.

159 *"I do so want you"*: ER to SDR, December 2, 1903, FDRL.

159 *"It is impossible for me"*: Ibid.

159 *"would never be able to hold him"*: Teague, *Mrs. L*.

159 *"I am so happy"*: ER to FDR, January 6, 1904, FDRL.

159 *the wedding of Helen Roosevelt and Teddy Robinson:* For details on the wedding, see the *New York Tribune*, May 27, 1904; and June 19, 1904; the (New York) *Evening World*, June 15, 1904; and the (New York) *Sun*, June 17, 1904.

160 *"From wearing costly lingerie"*: *Town Topics*, October 20, 1904.

161 *"the most degraded paper"*: *Collier's*, November 5, 1904.

161 *"Town Topics was supposed"*: Teague, *Mrs. L*.

161 *"Crazier than ever"*: ER to FDR, January 30, 1904, FDRL.

161 *"Town Topics said I did dance"*: The *New York Times Magazine*, August 6, 1967.

161 *Continually trying to outdo:* For the story of *Town Topics* and the *New-Yorker* and Theodore's involvement, see, among other reports, the *New York Tribune*, July 19, 1905; the (New York) *Evening World*, July 22, 1905; the *Washington Times*, July 20, 1905; and the *San Francisco Call*, July 25, 1905.

162 *The lawyers for* Town Topics*:* The (New York) *Evening World*, July 22, 1905.

162 *"a great friend" of Theodore's:* The *New York Times Magazine*, August 6, 1967.

163 *"scorched the paper"*: ARL, *Crowded Hours*. I have concluded that this letter was sent in response to, or at least around the time of, the *Town Topics* scandal, as Alice wrote that it arrived following newspaper coverage of her "motoring alone with another girl from Newport to Boston without a chaperone."

163 *"One of the greatest experts"*: Teague, *Mrs. L*.

163 *"She likes a strong drink"*: William Howard Taft to Helen Taft, August 1, 1905, LoC.

164 *the crunching of wheels on gravel:* Teague, *Mrs. L*.

165 *"Nobody can tell anything"*: TR to ARC, October 18, 1904, HL.

165 *"If things go wrong"*: TR to KR, October 26, 1904, HL.

165 *"be turned into a festival"*: TR to ARC, October 18, 1904, HL.

166 *"I am deeply sensible"*: The (Washington) *Evening Star*, November 9, 1904.

167 *"a few irate guests"*: ER, *The Autobiography*.

167 *"Very weak and looks like"*: SDR diary, December 4, 1904, FDRL.

167 *"A trip to Europe and an automobile"*: The *Minneapolis Journal*, December 6, 1904. The item erroneously reported "niece of Franklin"—which in fact backed up the point of the joke. I have made the correction here.

167 *"We are rejoiced"*: TR to FDR, November 29, 1904, FDRL.

168 *"You know how fond"*: TR to ER, November 29, 1904, FDRL.

168 *Three dates were best for him:* TR to ARC, December 12, 1904, FDRL.

168 *"Indeed I shall be very"*: TR to ER, December 19, 1904, FDRL.

168 *"My dear Eleanor, your uncle and I"*: Edith Roosevelt to ER, December 28, 1904, FDRL.

169   *Once Eleanor had declined:* Edith Roosevelt to ER, January [nd] 1905; January 12, 1905; and January 14, 1905, FDRL.

169   *On the day of the wedding:* My description comes from *Town Topics*, March 23, 1905; the guest list was excerpted in the *New York Tribune*, March 18, 1905.

170   *"Cheering and waving":* The *New York Tribune*, March 18, 1905.

170   *"the semblance of a 'National Event'":* The *New York Times*, March 18, 1905.

170   *"My father lived up":* Teague, *Mrs. L.*

171   *"Surprising for a Roosevelt":* *Town Topics*, March 23, 1905.

171   *"standing alone":* ER, *The Autobiography.*

171   *The largest crowd ever assembled:* My account of Alice's day at the Latonia Derby comes from the *Paducah* (Kentucky) *Sun*, June 2, 3, and 4, 1905; and the *New York Times*, June 4, 1905.

172   MISS ROOSEVELT IN LOVE: The *Burlington* (Iowa) *Evening Gazette*, April 15, 1905.

172   *"It is generally held here":* The *Norwalk* (Ohio) *Evening Herald*, June 3, 1905.

172   *"Lunch [with] Mr. Williams":* Notations taken from ARL diary, January 15 and 19, 1905.

173   *"My own beloved Nick":* ARL to Nicholas Longworth, February 15, 1905, LoC.

173   *"I love Nick more than I can think":* ARL diary, March 1, 1905, LoC.

173   *"His good head":* Clara de Chambrun, *The Making of Nicholas Longworth*, R. Long and Smith, 1933.

174   *"My darling little girl":* Nick Longworth to ARL, [nd] May–June(?) 1905, LoC.

174   *"warm friends":* The (San Francisco) *Call*, July 12, 1905.

174   *"a gigantic combination":* The (San Francisco) *Call*, February 8, 1906.

174   *"organize a mammoth company":* The (Stanford, KY) *Interior Journal*, October 13, 1905.

174   *Shubert theatrical syndicate:* The *Washington Times*, April 25, 1907.

175   *"Nick impresses no one":* William Howard Taft to Helen Taft, August 1, 1905, LoC.

175   *"a father complex":* Teague, *Mrs. L.*

176   AN INSULT TO MISS ROOSEVELT: Among others, the (San Francisco) *Call*, July 12, 1905. The piece in the *New-Yorker* ran on June 21.

176   *William Travers Jerome:* For his public support of President Roosevelt, see the *New York Times*, February 16, 1905.

176   SLUR AT MISS ROOSEVELT: The (New York) *Evening World*, July 11, 1905.

176   *"political advancement by introducing":* The (Washington) *Evening Star*, July 11, 1905.

177   *"Solicitors told the men":* The (New York) *Evening World*, July 22, 1905.

177   *No evidence would ever be found:* In 1909, Theodore testified that he had not known the photograph he provided had been for *Town Topics*, and that the whole matter had been left to his secretary, William Loeb. The Supreme Court of New York accepted his testimony as true. See the *New York Times*, March 31, 1909.

177   *unfairly "isolating" him:* The *New York Times*, February 16, 1905.

177   *On the night of August 3:* The *New York Times*, August 4, 1905.

177   *The libel investigation:* For more on the tabloid scandals and investigations, see the (New York) *Evening World*, July 11, July 22, 1905; the *New York Tribune*, July 19, August 5, 1905; the (Washington) *Evening Star*, July 11, 1905; the *Washington Times*, July 20, 1905; the (San Francisco) *Call*, July 12 and 25, August 5 and 7, 1905; the *Topeka* (Kansas) *State Journal*, July 24, 1905; and *Collier's*, November 11, 1905.

178   *"fantasized about what effect":* Teague, *Mrs. L.*

PART IV: A SHOT

181   *The man with the heavily lidded:* My account of John Schrank and the assassination attempt comes largely from the various testimonies, interviews, reports, and transcripts collected in Oliver E. Remey et al., eds., *The Attempted Assassination of Ex-President Theodore Roosevelt* (Milwaukee, WI: Progressive Publishing Company, 1912).

181   *"feeling like a bull moose":* The (New York) *Sun*, April 21, 1912.

182   *Back from Elba Club:* Edith Roosevelt to KR, November 28, 1909, HL.

182   *"Everything must be done":* TR to John Callan O'Laughlin, October 20, 1911, HL.

182   *"He made Taft president":* Henry Cabot Lodge to TR, December 18, 1911, HL.

183   T.R.'S NEPHEW BUCKS: The (New York) *Sun*, August 30, 1911.

183   *"I have sent Teddy":* TR to CRR, October 5, 1911, HL.

184   *"a fairly religious fervor":* TR to KR, July 13, 1912, HL.

184   *"Every corrupt boss":* TR to KR, October 11, 1912, HL.

185   *"I do not for a moment":* TR to KR, July 13, 1912.

185   *"full of animal spirits":* William Allen White, *The Autobiography of William Allen White.*

185   *"There is a very slight chance":* TR to KR, July 13, 1912, HL.

186   *"trying to get perpetual power":* Remey et al., eds., *Attempted Assassination*; the *Milwaukee Sentinel*, the *New York Times*, the *New York Tribune*, and the *Chicago Tribune*, October 15, 1912.

187   *"He did not come out," "A man that wants":* Remey et al., eds., *Attempted Assassination.*

187   *"possible contingencies":* TR to KR, October 19, 1912, HL.

188   *"Temperature and pulse":* Handwritten copy of telegram to ARC, [nd], HL.

189   *"Dearest Bamie":* Edith Roosevelt to ARC, October 29, 1912, HL.

189   *"If young Mrs. Longworth":* The *China Times*, September 7, 1906, quoted in Cordery, *Alice.*

190   *"a little intoxicated":* ARL diary, October 14, 15, and 16, 1912.

190   *"with their hair plastered":* Teague, *Mrs. L.*

190   *"Dear girl":* Anonymous letter to ARL, February 19, 1906, private collection quoted in Cordery, *Alice.*

191   *"one of those cunning":* Teague, *Mrs. L.* Curiously, Cordery discounts the possibility that Nick had a child, citing the fact that Alice never got pregnant and therefore concluding that Nick must have been sterile. That overlooks Alice's

direct statement to Teague that she used contraception, which I take as her way of explaining that her lack of children from Nick was a deliberate choice on her part.

191   *"I should be mad"*: ARL diary, August 24, 1912, LoC.

191   *"professional, practical work"*: ARL diary, October 4, 1912, LoC.

192   *"If I let myself think"*: ARL diary, October 4, 1912.

192   *"Shrug a shoulder"*: Teague, *Mrs. L.*

193   *"a job without the help"*: Mrs. Theodore Roosevelt Jr., *Day Before Yesterday.*

193   *"a man's work"*: TRJ to John Campbell Greenway, [nd] 1908, HL.

193   *"advance from one"*: The *Hartford Courant*, September 28, 1908.

194   *"at the tubs"*: The *Hartford Courant*, October 5, 1908.

194   *"I am in the mills now"*: TRJ to John Campbell Greenway, [nd] 1908, HL.

194   *"Theodore Roosevelt Junior"*: Associated Press report, as in the *Wenatchee* (WI) *Daily World*, February 6, 1909.

194   *"Ted's boss was in touch"*: TR to KR, October 22, 1908, HL.

194   *nearly every weekend:* "The townspeople see little of him as he spends his weekends in New York." From the *Hartford Courant*, February 11, 1910; and 1910 U.S. Census, Manhattan.

195   *If, as his wife would later:* Ted's wife, Eleanor, would make this claim in *Day Before Yesterday.* It's possible, even likely, that Ted received a pay raise with his various promotions; the *Hartford Courant* reported on May 2, 1910, that the pay grade for men in his position at the time of his departure from the mills was eighteen dollars a week. Even if he eventually earned that much, it would have been difficult to save any money (as Eleanor insisted he did) with all his travel expenses on top of room and board in Thompsonville and at the New York boardinghouse. Clearly he had access to other family cash.

195   ROOSEVELT JUNIOR A MAJOR: See, for example, the *Bemidji* (MN) *Daily Pioneer*, December 15, 1908.

195   *"at work in the carpet mills"*: The *Hartford Courant*, March 5, 1909.

196   *Edith began to worry:* "I realize that each child must lead his or her own life after leaving home and those who don't care to be the pearl in the satin box have at least the right of choice," she complained bitterly. ER to KR, November 17, and December 29, 1912, LoC.

196   *"You have had so much"*: TR to KR, October 15, 1910, HL.

197   *"You must not give"*: TR to KR, May 27, 1912, HL.

197   *"Very few outsiders"*: Edith Roosevelt to ARC, [nd], HL.

197   *"It is no child's play"*: TR to KR, June 6, 1908, HL.

197   *"hot, moonlit nights"*: TR to KR, September 27, 1912, HL.

197   *"The most wise Bavian"*: TR to Ethel Roosevelt, December 16, 1909, HL.

197   *"I should want you"*: TR to KR, April 23, 1909, HL.

198   *"as inapt as anything"*: TR to Ethel Roosevelt, September 9, 1913, HL.

198   *"I am very proud"*: TR to KR, October 11, 1912, HL.

198   *"have worked like beavers"*: TR to KR: September 27, 1912, HL

198   *"I miss my side partner"*: TR to KR, August 3, 1912, HL.

198   *"a big, up-from-the-soil"*: KR to Belle Willard Roosevelt (BWR), November 26, 1912, LoC.

199   *"Well, this campaign," "The choice of the gun"*: TR to KR, October 19, 1912, HL.

199   *"encouraging reports were coming"*: Ethel Roosevelt to ARC, October [nd] 1912, HL.

199   *"great change in popular feeling"*: Edith Roosevelt to KR, November 6, 1912, HL.

199   *"The circumstances of the shooting"*: TR to KR, October 19, 1912, HL.

199   *"for the principles"*: TR to KR, September 27, 1912, HL.

200   *"Instead of my growing less"*: TR speech at Point of Pines, MA, August 17, 1912, LoC.

200   *"A little shaver told me"*: Quoted in Ward and Burns, *The Roosevelts*.

200   *"a fine fellow"*: TR to ARC, August 10, 1910, HL.

201   *"With his handsome face"*: The *New York Times*, January 22, 1911.

201   *"the second coming of a Roosevelt"*: Gunther, *Roosevelt in Retrospect*.

201   *"true to its principles"*: SDR diary, August 1, 1912, FDRL.

201   *"Uncle Ted's progressive ideas"*: ER to Isabella Ferguson, September 28, 1912, quoted in Cook, *Eleanor Roosevelt, Vol. 1*.

201   *"I wish Franklin could be fighting"*: ER to Isabella Ferguson, July 24, 1912, quoted in Cook, *Eleanor Roosevelt, Vol. 1*.

202   *"the regular Democratic ticket"*: The (New York) *Sun*, October 5, 1912.

202   *All the other nephews*: For Robinson's campaign, see the (New York) *Sun*, October 27, and November 16, 1912; for Alsop's, see the *Hartford Courant*, August 1 and 12, 1912.

202   *"I am just back from"*: FDR to ER, July 7, 1912, FDRL.

203   *"four ugliest men"*: For more on Howe, see Ward, *A First-Class Temperament*.

203   *"nuisance" of herself*: ER, *The Autobiography*.

203   *When they were at Springwood*: SDR dinner party books, 1905–1906, FDRL.

203   *"domineering tartar"*: Teague, *Mrs. L.*

203   *"My mother-in-law was a lady"*: *Look*, June 19, 1951.

204   *"I was always just getting"*: ER, *This Is My Story*.

204   *She took "for granted"*: *Harper's*, October 1950.

204   *"Loads of love"*: FDR to ER, June 12, 1908, FDRL.

205   *"Eleanor and Franklin could be"*: Teague, *Mrs. L.*

205   *"enormous interest in having"*: Quoted in Ward and Burns, *The Roosevelts*.

206   *On the night of October 30*: For TR's Madison Square Garden speech, see the *New York Times* and the *New York Tribune*, October 31, 1912.

207   *"From the human point of view"*: Various papers, including the *Chickasha* (OK) *Daily Express*, November 5, 1912.

207   *Alice was hoping an influx*: ARL diary, October 10 and November 2, 1912, LoC.

207   *Very early in the night*: The *New York Tribune*, November 6, 1912.

208   *"Well, we have gone down"*: TR to KR, November 5, 1912, HL.

208   *"a few unpleasant moments"*: ARL diary, November 5, 6, and 7, 1912, LoC.

208   *"He can't seem to face"*: Edith Roosevelt to KR, December 1, 1912, HL.

209   *"rather liked the idea"*: *The Saturday Evening Post*, September 24, 1932.

209   *"Of course he is delighted"*: ER to ARC, March 10, 1913, HL.

PART V: BELIEVING MORE THAN EVER BEFORE

213   *Franklin was seriously ill:* The *New York Tribune*, September 20, 1918; and the
      New York Times, September 20, 1918.

214   *his parents' "hearts glow"*: TR to Douglas Robinson, December 18, 1917, HL.

214   *"It is interesting to see"*: TR to FDR, March 18, 1913, FDRL.

215   *"My memory was not"*: TR to FDR, May 26, 1916, FDRL.

215   *"You must resign!"*: Quoted in Ward, *A First-Class Temperament*.

215   *"I will never know how many"*: Ibid.

216   *"the kind words"*: Quoted in Lash, *Love, Eleanor*.

216   *"How I wish I saw"*: ER to ARC, [nd], HL.

217   *Finally, the* Leviathan*:* Franklin's return to New York and his illness and treat-
      ment were reported at length in the *New York Tribune*, September 20 and 22,
      1918; the (New York) *Sun*, September 20 and 22, 1918; and October 3, 1918;
      and the *New York Times*, September 20, 1918. Geoffrey C. Ward, in *A First-
      Class Temperament*, states that Franklin's condition was "grave," but cites no
      evidence for it; the newspaper coverage at the time agreed that he was not
      dangerously ill, and Eleanor confirmed that prognosis in her memoirs.

217   *"bewildered young husband"*: ER, *The Autobiography*.

218   *"I don't think you read"*: ER to FDR, July 24, 1917, FDRL.

218   *"Is F. paying any attention"*: Hall Roosevelt to ER, July 26, 1912, FDRL.

218   *"of assured social position"*: Jonathan Daniels, *The Washington Quadrille*.

218   *"Dearest Honey"*: ER to FDR, July 23, 1916, FDRL.

218   *"I really can't stand"*: ER to FDR, July 16, 1917, FDRL.

219   *A crackdown on off-hours:* See, among many other reports, the *New York Times*,
      April 26, 1915; July 29, 1917; and December 24, 1919; also Rupp, *A Desired Past*.

219   *"all kinds of information"*: ER to ARC, March 10, 1913, HL.

219   *"sort and list"*: SR to SDR, January 30, 1920, FDRL.

220   *"I was growing dependent"*: ER, *The Autobiography*.

220   *"I did a great deal"*: Ibid.

220   *"The cooks see that there"*: The *New York Times*, July 17, 1917.

220   *"You have leaped"*: FDR to ER, July 18, 1917, FDRL.

220   *"Some of it I did"*: ER to FDR, July 24, 1917, FDRL.

221   *"As I have grown older"*: ER to SDR, March 18, 1918, FDRL.

221   *"Anna is going to be"*: ER to Isabella Ferguson, November 13, 1917, quoted in
      Cook, *Eleanor Roosevelt, Vol. 1*.

221   *"We chicks quickly learned"*: James Roosevelt, *Affectionately*.

221   *"Franklin's children were more"*: ER, "I Remember Hyde Park," *McCall's*, Feb-
      ruary 1963.

221 *"It did not come naturally"*: Draft of an unpublished article, "My Children," by ER, FDRL.

221 *"Furnish an example"*: Unpublished essay by ER, "Ethics of Parents," quoted in Lash, *Eleanor and Franklin*.

221 *"Sentiment," Eleanor's son*: Elliott Roosevelt, *Mother R.*

222 *"never reach or ask"*: Draft of an unpublished article, "My Children," by ER, FDRL.

222 *"She felt a tremendous sense"*: Quoted in Lash, *Eleanor and Franklin*.

222 *"Much, much love dearest"*: ER to FDR, August 17, 1918, FDRL.

222 *"I do hope there will not"*: ER to FDR, August 19, 1918, FDRL.

223 *Policemen stood*: The *Washington Herald*, February 6, February 7, 1917.

223 *"Now that I am older"*: ER to Isabella Ferguson, [nd] 1916–1917, FDRL.

223 *"No one would know"*: Teague, *Mrs. L.*

223 *"So I think"*: ER to FDR, [nd] 1918, FDRL.

224 *A packet of letters dropped*: The affair with Lucy Mercer was first alluded to in print by Olive Ewing Clapper in her book, *Washington Tapestry*. It was discussed more specifically by Jonathan Daniels, the son of Franklin's navy superior Josephus Daniels, in his memoir, *The Washington Quadrille*. The affair was eventually confirmed by Eleanor's sons, Alice, and others.

224 *"The bottom dropped out"*: Lash, *Eleanor and Franklin*.

224 *"the servant problem"*: The *New York Tribune*, November 10, 1918.

225 *"Every article of the elaborate"*: The (Washington) *Evening Star*, November 21, 1918.

225 *"dishing out ice cream,"* Teague, *Mrs. L.*

226 *"We were doing a most," Alice's involvement with Franklin and Lucy*: Ibid.

227 *"There is nothing like the divorce"*: The *Chicago Tribune*, December 7, 1913.

227 *"exercised considerable pressure"*: Teague, *Mrs. L.*

228 *"In winter, a heavy beaver"*: Anonymous [Scanlan], *Boudoir Mirrors of Washington*.

228 *"Wasn't Mr. Lodge splendid"*: ARL to ARC, January 7, 1917, HL.

229 *"Bill gets up on his feet"*: *Collier's*, September 1932.

229 *"politics is adjourned"*: ARL, *Crowded Hours*.

230 *Joseph Graydon, a lawyer*: See Cordery, *Alice*.

231 *"get in this thing"*: White, *Autobiography*.

232 *"All right!" an irritated*: Morris, *Edith Kermit Roosevelt*.

232 *"the picture of activity"*: The (New York) *Sun*, October 28, 1918.

232 STILL VIGOROUS: The *New York Tribune*, October 27, 1918.

233 *"queer feelings"*: Ethel Roosevelt Derby to KR, October 27, 1918, HL.

233 *"Fall has come"*: TR to KR, September 13, 1918, HL.

234 *"Heaven forbid!"*: Wister, *Roosevelt*.

234 *"I can see how constantly"*: Edith Roosevelt to KR, October 29, 1918, LoC.

234   *"the boy in him had died":* Quoted in Morris, *Edith Kermit Roosevelt*.

234   *"Evidently she is still unable":* TR to ARC, October 17, 1909, HL.

234   *"Your burden was harder":* TR to CRR, August 3, 1918, HL.

234   *"As our lives draw towards":* TR to CRR, October 16, 1909, HL.

234   *"anywhere else for anything":* TR to KR, April 1, 1918, HL.

235   *"the heroes of old":* TR to Archibald Roosevelt, July 21, 1918, HL.

235   *"There is left the wind":* TR to KR, July 21, 1918, HL.

235   *"Anything that has gone":* Teague, *Mrs. L.*

235   *"It rather diminishes":* TR to KR, November 5, 1912, HL.

235   *a $60,000 trust fund:* This was finally distributed after Theodore's death. See the (New York) *Sun*, October 17, 1919.

235   *In all, Theodore's estate:* The value of TR's estate was reported in the *Washington Times*, October 26, 1919.

236   *Already the platform:* White, *Autobiography*.

236   *"I tell you no secret":* Hiram Johnson to Stanley Washburn, December 14, 1918, quoted in Morris, *Colonel*.

237   *"I shall be in the middle":* TR to SDR, October 2, 1914, FDRL.

237   *"I am very anxious":* TR to ER, March 15, 1915, FDRL.

237   *"I wanted to see this war":* Garland, *My Friendly Contemporaries*.

238   *"as much in love":* TR to KR, October 27, 1918, HL.

238   *"Quentin was no more":* Garland, *Friendly Contemporaries*.

238   *On Friday January 3:* My account of Theodore's last weekend and death come from accounts in the *New York Times*, the *New York Tribune*, and the (New York) *Sun*, and from the detailed research and descriptions provided in Morris, *Colonel*.

239   *The lives of Elliott and his mother:* Manhattan city directory 1899; Brooklyn city directory 1902; New York State Census 1905 and 1915; U.S. Census 1910 and 1920.

239   *"a man of good reputation":* Trisha Helland.

240   *"Please Santa Claus":* *Brooklyn Daily Eagle*, December 23, 1898.

240   *"This is one of the schools":* *Brooklyn Daily Eagle*, June 25, 1906.

241   *"A very good piece":* June 1906 commencement booklet, PS 55, courtesy Trisha Helland.

242   *The NBC was one:* The *New York Times*, March 19, 1918.

242   *Business Man's Training Regiment:* The *New York Times*, September 28, 1915.

242   *When the war came:* Elliott R. Mann draft registration, June 5, 1917.

242   *there was one fewer mouth to feed:* Death certificate, Elisabeth Mann, August 14, 1913. After her mother's burial in the Lutheran cemetery, Katie's secret slipped out, at least partially. Realizing mother and daughter shared the same name, the undertaker crossed out "Mrs." and wrote "Miss Mann" when recording who'd given him permission to bury the coffin.

242   *Lena Wilhelmina Prigge:* U.S. Census 1910 and 1920; Marriage record, Elliott Mann and Lena Prigge, June 10, 1921.

243 *By 1919, Jimmie was living:* Draft registration, James R. Roosevelt, September 12, 1918. For Jimmie's life in New York 1906–1908, see the (New York) *Evening World*, February 2, 1906; the (New York) *Sun*, February 27, 1906; the (New York) *Evening World*, July 13, 1907; unsourced clip [nd] 1911, FDRL.

243 *"a public escapade":* The (New York) *Evening World*, July 13, 1907.

244 *The solution was:* For Jimmie's life in Florida and the divorce suit with Sadie, see the (New York) *Evening World*, May 9, 1907; and February 24, 1917; the (New York) *Sun*, July 26, 1907; and the *New York Times*, February 24, 1917; and March 3, 1917.

244 *Jimmie remained a very wealthy:* The *New York Times*, March 3, 1917.

244 *Around this time, he visited:* Ward, *Before the Trumpet*.

244 *The accident that claimed:* The *Boston Globe*, February 22, 1909; the *New York Times*, February 22, 1909; and the *New York Tribune*, February 22, 1909.

244 *Was it a drunken:* Corinne Alsop insisted her brother had hit his head, gotten dizzy, and somehow fallen out the window four feet from the floor; her son Joseph Alsop believed Stewart and his friends had been reenacting the scene in *War and Peace* in which a group of rich young men dared one another to drink a bottle of rum while perched on a ledge. Interview with Corinne Alsop by Hermann Hagedorn, Robinson-Alsop Papers, HL; Joseph Alsop, *I've Seen the Best of It*.

244 *"Poor Stewart has now":* TR to KR, February 16, 1908, HL.

245 *"very able in his studies":* CRR to Douglas Robinson, October 2, 1902, HL.

245 *"ready and eager to do":* TR to CRR, September 8, 1913, HL.

245 *"Youth is elastic":* TR to CRR, October 16, 1909, HL.

246 *"The crossing has been a fortunate":* FDR to SDR, January 10, 1919, FDRL.

247 *"Funniest movie I ever saw":* Quoted in Ward, *A First-Class Temperament*.

247 *Here on the ship:* For the experience of gay men in navy theatricals, see Rupp, *A Desired Past*; Berubé, *Coming Out Under Fire*.

247 *"breathless" and "hunted":* ER to Isabella Ferguson, quoted in Ward, *A First-Class Temperament*.

247 *"very much alone":* ER to SDR, January 7, 1919, FDRL.

247 *"You have been very constantly":* ER to ARC, January [nd] 1919, HL.

248 *One of her last encounters:* see Ward, *A First-Class Temperament*.

248 *their "great regret":* ER to ARC, [nd] 1919, HL.

248 *"If she really loved":* Eleanor Wotkyns oral history, FDRL.

249 *Auntie Bye's son, Sheffield:* Ward, *A First-Class Temperament*.

249 *Mary Patten . . . The "worst talkers":* Daniels, *The Washington Quadrille*.

249 *"a good one," "délicieux":* Corinne Alsop unpublished memoir, HL.

249 *"Such things simply did not":* ER, *This Is My Story*.

250 *"gawky and insecure":* Ladies' Home Journal, November 1966.

250 *"She and Franklin were very much":* Daniels, *The Washington Quadrille*.

250 *"Franklin's ringing laugh":* See Ward, *A First-Class Temperament*.

250 *"Washington wives":* The *New York Times Magazine*, August 6, 1967.

251 *"Eleanor offered Franklin":* This was according to Alice Longworth, who told the story in the *New York Times Magazine*, August 6, 1967.

251 *"no mere placid figure":* Daniels, *The Washington Quadrille.*

251 *When Franklin's mother learned:* My description of Sara's intervention to save Franklin and Eleanor's marriage is drawn from Corinne Alsop's unpublished memoir, HL; Daniels, *The Washington Quadrille*; and the expert research conducted by Ward for *A First-Class Temperament.*

252 *"If she'd put it as a choice":* Ward, *A First-Class Temperament.*

252 *"Everybody behaved well":* Corinne Alsop unpublished memoir, HL.

252 *Franklin, however, didn't behave:* See Ward, *A First-Class Temperament.*

252 *"The soul that has believed":* Poem found in ER papers, FDRL, quoted in Ward, *A First-Class Temperament.*

253 *"appreciation for the weakness":* ER, *The Autobiography.*

253 *For several months after:* I made this observation after a careful perusal of her letters during this period. FDRL.

253 *"There was little difference":* ER, *The Autobiography.*

254 *"It began as an amiable":* The *New York Times Magazine*, August 6, 1967.

255 *"a great friend":* Teague, *Mrs. L.*

255 *"She ate three chops":* Graham, *Personal History.*

255 *"Hello, hello, Alice":* Quoted in Cordery, *Alice.*

256 *"I believe these are yours":* For the provenance of the hairpins and garter story, see ibid.

256 *Mary spent much:* The *Washington Herald*, May 13, 1918; the (Washington) *Evening Star*, October 22, 1917; and January 4, 1920; and the *Washington Times*, February 26, 1919; and March 8, 1919.

256 *Pomeranian puppy:* The (New York) *Sun*, December 21, 1919.

257 *"Their company":* Cordery, *Alice.*

257 *"We were against the League":* Teague, *Mrs. L.*

257 *"We all of us desire":* Written for the *Kansas City Star*, quoted in Morris, *Colonel.*

257 *"Detached Malevolence":* The *New York Times Magazine*, August 6, 1967.

258 *"I hated the way":* ARL to ARC, [nd] 1919, HL.

258 *"As time goes on":* ARL to ARC, October 27, [nd] 1919, HL.

259 *"It was a delight to have":* ARL to ARC, [nd] 1919, HL.

259 *"refused to evacuate":* American Expeditionary Forces citation, June 22, 1918, Sagamore Hill National Historic Site, Oyster Bay, NY.

260 *"I could go off":* KR to TR, June 4, 1917, LoC.

260 *"I've never been behind":* KR to TR, June 19, 1917, LoC.

261 *"He was my companion":* Quoted in Collier and Horowitz, *The Roosevelts.*

261 *"far less ambitious":* Quentin Roosevelt to Flora Whitney, August 8, 1917, HL.

261 *"the best battalion commander":* TR to KR, January 1, 1918, HL.

261 *"I'm sincerely pleased":* TR to Archibald Roosevelt, April 28, 1918, HL.

261 *"I can't say how pleased"*: TR to KR, December 3, 1918, HL.

262 *Ethel and her husband:* Dividends broken down in a letter from KR to TRJ, April 26, 1922, LoC.

262 *"The effect of Prohibition"*: The *New York Tribune*, December 7, 1919.

263 *"I used to sit in one"*: KR, *War in the Garden of Eden*.

264 *"constructive liberalism"*: Mrs. TRJ, *Day Before Yesterday*.

264 *"My hat is in the ring"*: Clipping, TRJ Collection, LoC.

264 *"How perfectly fine!"*: The (New York) *Evening World*, November 5, 1919.

264 *"It was a big day"*: The (New York) *Sun*, November 5, 1919.

265 *"All over the country"*: TRJ, *Average Americans*.

265 *"The way to [recruit] teachers"*: The *New York Times*, November 25, 1919.

266 *"As a true American"*: The *New York Tribune*, March 30, 1920.

266 *"as this power is subject"*: The *New York Times*, April 1, 1920. For Ted's position on the Socialist legislators earlier that session, see the *New York Times*, January 29, 1920, and others.

267 *"without question"*: Mrs. TRJ, *Day Before Yesterday*.

268 *When one of the accused:* The *New York Times*, March 31, 1920.

269 *"This day," he said:* The *New York Times*, April 1, 1920.

269 *"fear he would not be worthy"*: Mrs. TRJ, *Day Before Yesterday*.

270 *"a fellow radical"*: Quoted in Morris, *Colonel*.

270 *"I would rather have a boy"*: TR to KR, October 3, 1903, HL.

271 *"the consequences be damned"*: Quoted in Walker, *Namesake*.

271 *"Treason has been committed"*: The *New York Times*, April 2, 1920.

271 *"Theodore Roosevelt has begun"*: The *New York Times*, April 8, 1920.

272 *"a very fine temperature"*: SDR guest book, August 9, 1920; SDR diary, August 9, 1920, FDRL.

273 *"for so many years"*: ER, *The Autobiography*.

273 *"a little tailor"*: Quoted in Ward, *A First-Class Temperament*.

273 *"Our eyes are trained ahead"*: FDR speech, FDRL.

273 *"Hurrah for the Democrats!"*: James "Rosy" Roosevelt to ER, July 7, 1920, FDRL.

273 *"Tell Ma when they ask"*: James "Rosy" Roosevelt to FDR, July 8, 1920, FDRL.

274 *"nomination pretty well"*: Anna Roosevelt to FDR, July 12, 1920, FDRL.

274 *"planning a great holiday"*: James Roosevelt to FDR, July 12, 1920, FDRL.

274 *"a very long time"*: Elliott Roosevelt to SDR, [nd] 1920, FDRL.

274 *Franklin Junior, taught himself:* Anna Roosevelt to FDR, [nd] 1920, FDRL.

274 *Once, when Eleanor insisted:* Elliott Roosevelt oral history, FDRL.

275 *"both detached and overpowering"*: Quoted in Ward, *A First-Class Temperament*.

275 *"One of the bright spots"*: Reprinted in the *New York Tribune*, September 1, 1918.

276 *"I suppose he would have"*: James "Rosy" Roosevelt to ER, July 7, 1920, FDRL.

276 *By the first of September:* SDR diary, FDRL.

276 *"if the Cox divorce"*: FDR to Ellery Sedgwick, quoted in Morgan, *FDR*.

277 *"I miss you so, so much"*: FDR to ER, July 17, 1920, FDRL.

277 *"dearest dear honey"*: ER to FDR, August 27, 1920, FDRL.

277 *"Did you know Lucy Mercer"*: ER to SDR, February 14, 1920, FDRL.

277 *"The Democratic candidates"*: Syndicated article, as in the *Albuquerque Evening Herald*, August 19, 1920.

277 *"the most progressive"*: (Poughkeepsie, NY) *Eagle News*, July 16, 1920.

277 *Eleanor was in the papers:* Eleanor's photo was published in dozens of newspapers, including the (Washington) *Evening Star*, July 25, 1920, so Alice almost certainly would have seen it. Family portraits, some with Franklin and Sara, others with the children, also appeared in special photography features, including "The Camera News," which ran in a number of papers, including the *Washington Standard* (Olympia, Washington Territory), July 16, 1920.

278 *"Mrs. Franklin Roosevelt is of"*: The (Washington) *Evening Star*, August 1, 1920.

278 *"the financial domination"*: The (Washington) *Evening Star*, October 6, 1920.

278 *"an essential and fundamental"*: Quoted in Morgan, *FDR*.

278 *"To call [Harding] second rate"*: ARL, *Crowded Hours*.

279 *She'd come with an offer:* See ibid.; Teague, *Mrs. L.*

279 *"I am far from underestimating"*: Speech, "The New Nationalism," at Osawatomie, KS, August 31, 1910, FDRL.

280 *"America's present need"*: Speech by Warren Harding, May 14, 1920, transcript, FDRL.

280 *"Some people have been saying"*: FDR speech, August 9, 1920, FDRL.

280 *"We behaved terribly"*: Teague, *Mrs. L.*

281 *Both parties wanted to avoid:* The *New York Times*, May 2, 1920.

281 *"in name only"*: Unsourced clip, October 15, 1920, FDRL.

281 *"The best evidence"*: The *Washington Standard* (Olympia, Washington Territory), September 3, 1920.

282 *In Keokuk, Iowa:* The *Daily Gate City and Constitution-Democrat* (Keokuk, Iowa), September 30, 1920.

282 *"resembled his father"*: The *Alliance* (NE) *Herald*, September 10, 1920.

282 *"a maverick" who didn't:* The *New York Times*, September 9, 1920.

282 *"a denatured Roosevelt"*: ER to FDR, [nd] 1920, FDRL.

282 *"Governor Cox and Franklin"*: The *Laclede* (Michigan) *Blade*, September 17, 1920.

283 *"love and interest"*: CRR to FDR, August 16, 1920, FDRL.

283 *"Senator Harding called"*: The (Washington) *Evening Star*, October 6, 1920.

283 *"prostituting the prestige"*: Reprinted in the *Lexington* (MO) *Intelligencer*, September 10, 1920.

283 *"the self-revealing sneer"*: McLane to SDR, October 28, 1920, FDRL.

284   *"a traitor to much":* The *Daily East Oregonian*, August 19, 1920.

284   *"Blessed old Ted":* TR to TRJ, October 2, 1905, HL.

284   *"mad for publicity":* Quoted in Ward, *A First-Class Temperament*.

285   *"who is trying to get":* ER to FDR, August 27, 1920, FDRL.

285   *Later that campaign season:* The *Fulton County* (OH) *Tribune*, October 29, 1920.

285   *"F.'s voice is all right":* ER to SDR, October 3, 1920, FDRL.

285   *"Before long," Eleanor recalled:* ER, *The Autobiography*.

286   *"This was a field":* ER, *Look*, June 19, 1951.

286   *"Shall I vote the Democratic":* Syndicated article, as in the *Albuquerque Evening Herald*, August 19, 1920.

287   *Divorced, Beckley would later:* U.S. Census 1900, 1910, 1920, 1930, and 1940.

287   *"you and Cox are going":* Quoted in Ward, *A First-Class Temperament*.

288   *On Saturday night, October 23:* My description of the events leading up to Franklin's libel suit against Rathom come from a chronology in the file marked "Rathom Case," FDRL.

288   *"unqualified to handle":* "Rathom Case" file, FDRL.

288   *"destroying or sequestering":* United Press syndicate article, October 25, 1920.

288   *"injure and degrade":* The *New York Times*, May 28, 1920. A sampling of other news coverage about Rathom's complaints: the *New York Times*, January 20, 1918; February 28, 1918; February 19, 1919; January 23 and 27, 1920; and March 12, 1920.

289   *"A reading of this letter":* Press release, October 24, 1920, "1920 Campaign" file, FDRL.

289   ROOSEVELT IN LIBEL: Headlines from the *Hartford Courant*, October 25, 1920; the *Washington Times*, October 25, 1920; and the *New York Tribune*, October 26, 1920.

289   *"Unfortunately," his lawyer said:* The *New York Times*, October 26, 1920.

290   *They had spent:* Various news wire reports, as in the *Daily Ardmoreite* (OK), October 28, 1920.

290   *a special telegraph wire:* Topeka (KS) *State Journal*, November 2, 1920.

290   *"Franklin's friends":* SDR diary, November 1 and 2, 1920, FDRL.

PART VI: ROUGH STUNTS

296   *"As I recall it, there was":* The *New York Times*, October 22, 1924; the *Cornell Daily Sun*, October 22, 1924.

296   *At each of Ted's campaign:* Mrs. TRJ, *Day Before Yesterday*.

297   *Eleanor would toss campaign buttons:* The *New York Times*, October 20, 1924.

297   *"his winning way":* The *New York Times*, July 25, 1924.

298   *"The Presidency":* As in the *Daily Messenger* (Canandaigua, NY), October 18, 1924.

299   *"My political career is over":* Mrs. TRJ, *Day Before Yesterday*.

299   *"I would feel highly":* The (New York) *Evening World*, April 19, 1921.

300   *Archie rang from New York:* Ted described this sequence of events in his tes-

timony, May 13, 1924, as well as in his letter to Senator William Campbell, February 2, 1924, LoC.

300 *"Mr. Roosevelt approved"*: The *New York Times*, March 16, 1924.

301 *"and to bloody hell"*: Mrs. TRJ, *Day Before Yesterday*.

301 *"these leases were being"*: Testimony, May 13, 1924, LoC. Ted also stated this in a letter to Campbell, February 2, 1924, LoC.

302 *"Both of them enjoyed"*: TRJ diary, February 17, 1922, LoC.

302 *"He is one of those character"*: TRJ diary, August 25, 1922, LoC.

303 *"I had an instinctive"*: TRJ diary, February 14, 1923, LoC.

303 *"This is right in line"*: TRJ diary, December 10, 1923, LoC.

303 *denounced Ted as an untrustworthy "fop"*: TRJ diary, December 11, 1923, LoC; also see *Sandusky* (OH) *Register*, December 11, 1923.

303 *"I told him I thought"*: TRJ diary, July 16, 1924, LoC.

304 *"I am deeply sensible"*: The *Syracuse Herald*, October 1, 1924.

304 *"Of course" Smith was going:* The *Syracuse Herald*, October 2, 1924.

304 *"I received a thoroughly"*: TRJ diary, October 26, 1921, LoC.

305 *"It is a remarkable victory"*: TRJ diary, May 17, 1922, LoC.

305 *"assume a more liberal"*: TRJ diary, August 3, 1923, LoC.

305 *"an obsolete ideal"*: Archibald Roosevelt to TRJ, April 2, 1923, LoC.

306 *"This morning I got into"*: TRJ diary, September 12, 1924, LoC.

307 *A supporter provided:* The *Syracuse Herald*, October 24, 1924.

307 *Eleanor met up with her caravan:* Although Eleanor did not accompany the women of the Singing Teapot on its thousand-mile ring of New York State, she did join up with the group at some point for a side trip to see Bye in Farmington, Connecticut. A consideration of the route taken by the Teapot and its various stops, documented in newspapers, and consideration of Eleanor's speaking schedule in late October–early November, reveals the only time possible for a trip to Connecticut would have been *after* the Teapot completed its circle of the state in Kingston on October 30. As Eleanor spoke in Middletown on October 31, she could have been free to meet the Teapot crew only after that, and since we know she saw Bye before the election (November 4), the window for the visit would have to have been November 1–3. A check of the map indicates Eleanor's path from Middletown would have crossed the path of the Teapot from Kingston around Newburgh, and from there it was largely a straight line (and some ninety miles) to Farmington.

307 *"I cannot stress in too strong"*: The *Middletown* (NY) *Daily Herald*, November 1, 1924.

308 *"a canvas design"*: The *Olean* (NY) *Evening Herald*, October 28, 1924.

308 *"The Singing Teapot will boil"*: The *New York Times*, October 18, 1924.

308 *Departing from Manhattan:* For coverage of the Singing Teapot, see the *New York Times*, October 21, 1924; the *Dunkirk* (NY) *Evening Observer*, October 27 and 31, 1924; the *Olean* (NY) *Evening Herald*, October 28, 1924; and the *Kingston* (NY) *Daily Freeman*, October 29, 1924.

309 *"automobile of Mrs. Franklin"*: The *New York Times*, October 21, 1924.

309   *"had had nothing to do":* ER, *This I Remember.*

309   *At the state convention:* The *New York Times,* September 26, 1924.

309   *"Well, I'm voting for":* Wire reports, as in the *Billings* (MN) *Gazette,* September 26, 1924.

310   *"kind and compassionate":* Marion Dickerman oral history, FDRL.

310   *"His illness finally made me":* Look, June 19, 1951.

310   *"Mama and I have had":* ER to FDR, October 3, 1919, FDRL.

310   *"to squirm and turn":* Quoted in Lash, *Eleanor and Franklin.*

310   *"I wondered if her life":* ER, *This Is My Story.*

311   *"an aider of women":* The *Hope Penasco Valley* (NM) *Press,* October 10, 1924.

311   *"We have now had the vote":* The *New York Times,* April 15, 1924.

312   *"Men were born":* Quoted in Cook, *Eleanor Roosevelt, Vol. 1.*

312   *"Women are by nature":* ER speech, August 7, 1922, FDRL.

312   *"all the radical leaders":* The *Middletown* (NY) *Daily Herald,* November 1, 1924.

312   *"humble and inadequate":* ER, *This Is My Story.*

313   *In 1923, Nancy stayed:* Springwood guest books, 1922, 1923, and 1924, FDRL.

314   *"I feel I'd like to go":* ER to Marion Dickerman, August 27, 1925, FDRL.

314   *"Much love to Nan":* ER to Marion Dickerman, February 5, 1926, FDRL.

314   *"Providence was particularly":* ER, *This Is My Story.*

315   *"If you think Eleanor":* Quoted in Ward, *A First-Class Temperament.*

315   *"female impersonators," "leapfrogging":* Teague, *Mrs. L.*

316   *"lovely ladies who served luncheon":* ER, *This Is My Story;* and *The Autobiography.*

317   *"make it a real family party":* FDR and Missy Le Hand to Nancy Cook and Marion Dickerman, March 6, 1925, FDRL.

317   *"For over forty years":* McCall's, February 1963.

318   *"But aren't you girls silly?":* Dickerman oral history, FDRL.

318   *"My missus and some":* FDR to Elliott Brown, August 5, 1924, quoted in Davis, *Invincible Summer.*

318   *"I determined that I would":* ER, *This Is My Story.*

318   *"Yes, you must":* Quoted in Cook, *Eleanor Roosevelt, Vol. 1.* For Eleanor's lack of advocacy for her children, see also Lash, *Eleanor and Franklin;* and the various memoirs of ER's children.

319   *"My mother made me go":* Quoted in Cook, *Eleanor Roosevelt, Vol. 1.*

319   *"dutifully and affectionately":* Dickerman papers, FDRL, quoted in Cook, *Eleanor Roosevelt, Vol. 1.*

319   *"It is very funny up here":* James Roosevelt to ER, October 23, 1924, FDRL.

320   *Once, reading to the youngest:* ER, *The Autobiography.*

320   *"weeks of anxiety":* ER, *This Is My Story.*

320   *"developed a tougher side":* Teague, *Mrs. L.*

321   *"neither fair nor sincere"*: The *New York Times*, November 2, 1924.

322   *"I just hate to have"*: Quoted in Ward, *A First-Class Temperament*.

322   *"Dearest E.," Franklin wrote:* FDR to ER, October 1924, FDRL.

322   *"The legs are really improving"*: Ibid.

323   *"the great deal of poverty"*: FDR to SDR, October 1924, FDRL.

323   *Franklin was variously:* The (Washington) *Evening Star*, September 4, 1921; and the *New York Tribune*, September 10, 1921.

324   *"I am telling everybody"*: James "Rosy" Roosevelt to FDR, September 2, 1921, FDRL.

324   *As the newspaper reported:* The *New York Times*, September 18, 1921.

324   *"Judging by the last"*: James "Rosy" Roosevelt to FDR, September 2, 1921, FDRL.

324   *"We had tried so hard"*: ER, *This I Remember*.

325   *"It is too bad"*: FDR to SDR, October 1924, FDRL.

325   *public speeches "inane"*: James "Rosy" Roosevelt to FDR, September 2, 1921, FDRL.

325   *"a splendid war record"*: The *Saturday Evening Post*, September 24, 1932.

325   *"fairly lifted the roof"*: The *Syracuse Herald*, June 27, 1924.

326   *"His fingers dug"*: Roosevelt and Shalett, *Affectionately, F.D.R.*

326   *"Today the same young"*: The *Syracuse Herald*, June 27, 1924.

327   *"just went crazy," "I did it!"*: Dickerman oral history, FDRL.

327   *"Franklin Roosevelt made a good"*: The *Syracuse Herald*, June 27, 1924.

327   *"easily the foremost figure"*: The *New York Herald-Tribune*, June 29, 1924.

327   *"I have listened to a lot"*: Theodore Robinson to FDR, June 28, 1924, FDRL.

328   *"the money interests"*: C. V. Coffey to FDR, July 7, 1924, FDRL.

328   *"The people are very much"*: "Crank File, 1924 election," May 27, 1924; June 13, 1924; and May 26, 1924, FDRL.

329   *"the political machinery"*: The *Syracuse Herald*, June 27, 1924. Van Loon was not writing for the *New York Times*, as stated in Ward and Burns, *The Roosevelts*.

329   *"I am philosophic enough"*: FDR to ER, [nd] [October] 1924, FDRL.

329   *"I believe if Davis"*: James "Rosy" Roosevelt to FDR, July 1924, FDRL.

330   *"I deeply appreciate"*: Marguerite Le Hand to FDR, November 21, 1920, FDRL.

330   *She teased him:* Marguerite Le Hand to FDR, [nd] and August 1, 1921, FDRL.

330   *"Mr. Roosevelt had a severe chill"*: ER to Marguerite Le Hand, August 17, 1921, FDRL.

330   *"You can get your elevator"*: Marguerite Le Hand to FDR, "Sunday afternoon," [nd], FDRL.

331   *"the frankest of [Franklin's]"*: The *New York Times*, August 1, 1944.

331   *"office wife—quote"*: Ward, *A First-Class Temperament*.

331   *"Please have the dentist"*: Marguerite Le Hand to FDR, [nd], FDRL.

331   *"She watches her man"*: Quoted in Ward, *A First-Class Temperament*. Ward

provides a full consideration of the relationship between Franklin and Missy, to which my account here is indebted.

332 *"I haven't told Mama"*: ER to FDR, February 2, 1924, FDRL.

333 *"the voice of well-brought-up,"* *"She was always so good"*: Teague, *Mrs. L.*

334 *"the political wiseacres"*: The *Oakland Tribune*, November 9, 1924.

334 *"The congressman is his wife's"*: United Press syndicated article, as in the (Hanover, PA) *Evening Sun*, November 14, 1924.

335 CAPITAL POLITICIANS BOW: United Press syndicated article, as in the (Hanover, PA) *Evening Sun*, November 14, 1924.

336 *"simian ability"*: Teague, *Mrs. L.*

336 *"Grabbing a hat"*: Anonymous [Scanlan], *Boudoir Mirrors of Washington.*

336 *"She's always done"*: The *Oakland Tribune*, November 9, 1924.

337 *"a good many of their secrets"*: Teague, *Mrs. L.*

337 *"The more this rumor gains"*: Wire reports, as in *Anaconda* (MT) *Standard*, October 12, 1924.

338 *"She told us that Borah"*: TRJ diary, June 10, 1924.

338 *The secret was not:* Although neither Alice nor Borah ever officially admitted the truth of Paulina's paternity, the fact was confirmed to Stacy Cordery by Alice's granddaughter Joanna Sturm. Further proof is found in Borah's letters to Alice, where he refers to himself as "PMP" and Alice as "PFP," a code deciphered by Cordery as "Paulina's male parent" and "Paulina's female parent." See Cordery, *Alice.*

338 *almost three thousand women:* Rachel Benson Gold, "Lessons from Before Roe: Will Past Be Prologue?" *The Guttmacher Report on Public Policy*, 6, no. 1 (March 2003).

338 *Indeed, Bill's wife, Mary:* See Cordery, *Alice*, for full discussion.

339 *"Well, if you really want"*: Teague, *Mrs. L.*

340 *"Life seems [to Alice] to be"*: ER to Isabella Ferguson, [nd], quoted in Cook, *Eleanor Roosevelt, Vol. 1.*

340 *"The atmosphere in the house"*: The *New York Times*, November 5, 1924.

341 *"We naturally said"*: The *New York Times Magazine*, August 6, 1967.

341 *"Lack of voting machines"*: Mrs. TRJ, *Day Before Yesterday.*

341 *"Poor T.R. Junior"*: The *New York Times*, February 19, 1925.

342 *On November 21:* The *Daily News* (Hamilton, OH), November 21, 1924.

342 *"No similar event in Washington"*: The *Altoona* (PA) *Mirror*, November 28, 1924.

342 *"Bouleversé"*: Edith Roosevelt diary, November 12, 1924, HL.

342 *"Alice's news was rather"*: Edith Roosevelt to ARC, November 22, 1924, HL.

342 *"like trying to push"*: Teague, *Mrs. L.*

342 *"If legislative business"*: The *New York Times*, February 15, 1925.

343 *"I'm a little bit jealous"*: The *New York Times*, February 16, 1925.

344 *A light snow powdered:* My account of Kermit's trip to Chicago comes from the *Chicago Tribune*, February 7 and 16, 1925; unsourced clippings, LoC.

346 *"all the old gentlemen":* Unidentified memoir, Kermit and Belle Roosevelt papers, LoC.

348 *"a work in progress":* Quoted in Collier and Horowitz, *The Roosevelts*.

348 *Among his friends:* Various articles, LoC; see also Kermit Roosevelt diary, November 2, 1924.

348 *That predilection got Rickard:* My account of Rickard's trial and the charges against him comes from the *New York Times*, February 8 and 10, 1922; March 23 and 27, 1922; and June 26, 1922; and the *Chicago Tribune*, March 25 and 29, 1922. Also 1910, 1920, and 1930 U.S. Census; 1915 and 1925 New York State Census.

349 *Indeed, with Kermit:* The *Chicago Tribune*, January 10, 1925.

350 *Harry Greb beat Tom Gibbons:* The *Chicago Tribune*, March 14, 1922.

350 *"A man who runs":* The *New York Times*, March 27, 1922.

350 *"I wish I cared":* KR to George Roosevelt, September 1930, LoC.

350 *"The Coffee House, from all":* TRJ diary, November 8, 1921, LoC.

351 *"to avoid excessive taxation":* KR to TRJ, April 25, 1922, LoC.

351 *These technically separate:* The *New York Times*, December 10, 1923.

351 *"No vessel has a better":* For example, the *Public Ledger* (Maysville, KY), December 6, 1920; the *Carrizozo* (NM) *Outlook*, December 10, 1920. See also the *Bridgeport* (CT) *Times*, November 27, 1920.

351 *When Albert Lasker:* The *Chicago Tribune*, August 18, 1921.

351 *He was frequently in touch:* KR to Nicholas Longworth, August 24, 1921; September 5, 1921; January 21, 1922; and September 7, 1926, LoC.

351 *"That was grand":* KR to Archibald Roosevelt, July 27, 1922, LoC.

352 *"Like all Japanese":* Archibald Roosevelt to TRJ, March 29, 1923, LoC. See also Archie's letter of April 2, 1923, for Ted's contact with Komatsu.

352 *several months later:* The *New York Times*, January 30, 1924.

352 *"He apparently totally failed":* TRJ diary, July 10, 1924, LoC.

352 *"totally unable to understand":* TRJ diary, July 11, 1924, LoC.

353 *"His feelings were badly":* TRJ diary, July 14, 1924, LoC.

353 *"Gov. Smith defeated":* KR diary, November 5, 1924, LoC.

353 *When he attended:* The *Chicago Tribune*, May 4, 1922.

353 *Kermit's sister Alice pulled up:* The *Chicago Tribune*, March 13, 1925.

354 *"That is the most amazing":* KR to BWR, November 14, 1924, LoC.

354 *"The real problem," "as delightful and inconsequential":* TRJ diary, August 27, 1924.

354 *Kermit was named as:* The *New York Times*, November 25, 1924.

355 *over the past year:* Franklin's letter appeared in the *New York Times*, May 5, 1924. Kermit's letter to Franklin was dated May 5; Franklin's reply was dated May 9 (FDRL).

PART VII: THE FUTURE AND THE PAST

359 *"These unhappy times":* Transcript, FDR radio address, April 7, 1932, FDRL.

360 *actively campaigned for:* The *New York Times*, November 6, 1932.

360   *For many upwardly mobile:* For the development of Queens, see, as just a couple of examples, the *New York Times,* July 18, 1926, November 4, 1926.

360   *"Come east, young man":* The *New York Times*, May 2, 1926.

361   *Elliott's mother no longer:* U.S. Census, 1930. In that year, Katie lived at 354 Hart Street in Brooklyn, the same place she had resided with Elliott.

362   *"To the Honorable Mrs.":* Draft of a letter from Elliott Mann to ER, November 26, 1932, courtesy of Trisha Helland. The draft does not include a specific mention of Elliott being named for his father, although his signature was "Elliott Roosevelt Mann." Perhaps this was enough for Eleanor to comment, in her reply of December 3, how she was "very interested" to learn he'd been named after her father. Yet the wording of her letter makes me think Elliott stated it more precisely in the final draft of his letter to her, which has not survived.

363   *"as a drowning man looks":* Will H. Hays to James Wingate, March 13, 1933, Will H. Hays Papers, available on microfilm.

363   *"Not until I can throw":* The *Saturday Evening Post*, September 24, 1932.

364   *"Progressive government":* The *New York Times*, October 4, 1930.

364   *"The fact that conservative":* The *Saturday Evening Post*, September 24, 1932.

365   *"To secure more":* Inaugural speech, 1928, FDRL.

366   *"I do see how annoying":* ER to CRR, August 23, 1932, HL.

366   *That it was his sister:* The *Hanover* (PA) *Sun*, December 12, 1931, reprinted from the *Philadelphia Inquirer*.

366   *"I had a letter from Ted":* KR to Ethel Roosevelt Derby, March 12, 1932, LoC.

366   *In the fall of 1927:* Personal report prepared for the Honorable Theodore Roosevelt, October 28, 1927, LoC.

367   *"Ted always felt that Franklin":* Ward, *A First-Class Temperament*.

367   *"enough in the way":* TR to Edith Roosevelt, September 19, 1932; and October 14, 1932, HL.

368   *"similarly shaken by the dramatic":* Unsourced clip, November [nd] 1932, LoC.

368   *"She obviously liked":* Teague, *Mrs. L.*

368   *"to feel he must be":* The *New York Times Magazine*, August 6, 1967.

369   *"What does the Longworths'":* Cordery, *Alice.*

369   *"There was a withdrawn":* Teague, *Mrs. L.*

369   *"The Alice Roosevelt Longworth boosters":* The *New York Times*, October 27, 1931.

369   *"Ever since her husband died":* Associated Press report, as in the *Joplin* (MO) *Globe*, October 29, 1931.

369   *"Senators and other high officials":* The *Boston Globe*, October 28, 1931.

370   *"never any good":* The *Washington Star News*, February 12, 1974.

370   *"a rotten candidate":* The *Senator*, March 18, 1939, quoted in Felsenthal, *Princess Alice.*

370   *"No previous American":* Mrs. TRJ, *Day Before Yesterday.*

370   *"continue the political feud":* The *New York Times*, July 31, 1932.

370   *"Teddy . . . has tried"*: The *Johnson County* (IA) *Democrat*, September 1, 1932.

370   *"be made a laboratory"*: The *New York Times*, October 28, 1932.

371   *"Did you see Dear Cousin"*: Eleanor Butler Roosevelt to Cornelius Roosevelt, October 17, 1932, LoC.

371   *"just as soon as Dear"*: Eleanor Butler Roosevelt to Cornelius Roosevelt, October 28, 1932, LoC.

371   *"Well, the election certainly"*: Eleanor Butler Roosevelt to Cornelius Roosevelt, November 14, 1932, LoC.

371   *"Fifth cousin about to be"*: Although Ted said this in 1932 or 1933, the first direct use of the quote in the press was during the 1936 election, when Ted hoped it would now describe Franklin. The *Boston Globe*, October 21, 1936.

372   *"a decided change"*: Syndicated column, as in the *Lockhart* (TX) *Post-Register*, November 24, 1932.

372   *"going into decline"*: Syndicated column, as in the *El Paso* (TX) *Herald-Post*, December 24, 1932.

372   *"If Mr. Roosevelt wins"*: As reported in the *Boston Globe*, October 27, 1932.

373   *"As I see it"*: The *New York Times*, November 13, 1932.

373   *"I can say with absolute"*: KR to FDR, January 12, 1933, FDRL.

374   *Herbert Odell, another shipping*: KR file, FDRL.

374   *"I don't think anything"*: BWR to FDR, [nd], FDRL.

374   *he approached "Cousin Kermit"*: Elliott Roosevelt II to KR, January 14, 1931; KR to Elliott Roosevelt II, February 5, 1931, FDRL.

374   *Kermit claimed to be apolitical*: Kermit's only recorded active political involvement had been the campaign of Republican gubernatorial candidate William J. Donovan. He hosted a dinner for Donovan at Oyster Bay and made some radio speeches (*New York Times*, November 2, 1932). "I told Colonel Donovan that although I had always kept out of politics, I felt so strongly that he was the person for us to have as governor, that if his people wanted me to make a couple of speeches, I would do so" (KR to Kermit "Kim" Roosevelt, October 21, 1932). Belle also campaigned for Donovan. Donovan was beaten by Herbert Lehman (Franklin's lieutenant governor) by almost a million votes.

374   *International Mercantile Marine Company*: The *New York Times*, May 24, 1930; December 4, 1930; May 5, 1931; and April 6, 1932.

374   *"The Roosevelt name"*: Monroe Robinson to KR, August 4, 1930, LoC. See also George Roosevelt to KR, September 10, 1930, LoC.

375   *"Due to the lack"*: KR to FDR, September 2, 1931, FDRL.

375   *They were sold*: The *New York Times*, January 1, 1928; and July 15, 1931.

375   *"I believe that I can be"*: KR to FDR, January 12, 1933, FDRL.

376   *"Something to amuse you"*: KR to TRJ, January 13, 1933, LoC.

376   *Likewise, to Edith*: KR to Edith Roosevelt, January 18, 1933, HL.

376   *"super yacht"*: The *New York Times*, September 23, 1928.

376   ROOSEVELT ENDS ROOSEVELT: The *El Paso Herald Post*, January 25, 1933.

377   *"There has been no affection"*: The *Harrison* (AR) *Daily Times*, January 30, 1933.

377   *"I do not remember anything":* Notation from Eleanor Butler Roosevelt on letter from KR to TRJ, January 13, 1933, LoC.

377   *"the whole table stopped":* Notation from Eleanor Butler Roosevelt on letter from KR to TRJ, January 30, 1933, LoC.

378   *"persuade the government":* The *Chicago Tribune*, May 16, 1928; and the *New York Times*, May 16, 1928.

378   *"ladies should not be":* Vincent Astor to KR, December 19, 1927, LoC.

379   *"What do you suppose":* Hickok, *Reluctant First Lady.*

380   *"I shall never forget the murmur":* Hickok, *Reluctant First Lady.*

380   *"sleepless nights he has spent":* Associated Press report, as in the *Hartford Courant*, November 1, 1932.

380   *"You would of course":* ER to CRR, August 23, 1932, HL.

380   *"Sometime I must tell you":* CRR to SDR, [nd] 1932, FDRL.

381   *"It's good to have":* Hickok, *Reluctant First Lady.*

381   *"I can't imagine":* Quoted in Collier and Horowitz, *The Roosevelts*, and elsewhere. The remark may be apocryphal.

382   *"She likes to go places":* Associated Press, as in the *Hartford Courant*, November 10, 1932.

382   *"honeymoon cottage":* Dickerman oral history, quoted in Cook, *Eleanor Roosevelt, Vol. 1.*

383   *"It is the one thing":* The New Yorker, April 5, 1930.

383   *"I never forgot":* Cook, *Eleanor Roosevelt, Vol. 1.*

384   *"List the ways in which":* Final exam, May 1931, FDRL, quoted in Cook, *Eleanor Roosevelt, Vol. 1.*

384   *"When I'd finished dressing":* Hickok, *Reluctant First Lady.*

385   *Hick was the eldest daughter:* For Hick's background, see the papers prepared for a potential autobiography in the Lorena Hickok Papers, FDRL; Cook, *Eleanor Roosevelt, Vols. 1 and 2*; Faber, *Life of Lorena Hickok*; the U.S. Census, 1900 and 1920; and the South Dakota State Census, 1925.

386   *"Every woman," Eleanor wrote:* Lash, *A World.*

386   *"would have made a better":* Lash, *Love, Eleanor.*

386   *Eleanor had turned to her bodyguard:* For a detailed account of the relationship with Earl Miller, see Cook, *Eleanor Roosevelt, Vol. 1.*

387   *"I was going to have":* ER to CRR, July 22, 1932, HL.

387   *the publisher was "very nervous":* ER to CRR, September 23, 1932, HL.

387   *"I want my children":* ER, *Hunting Big Game.*

388   *"My dear Mr. Mann":* ER to Elliott Roosevelt Mann, December 3, 1932, courtesy Trisha Helland.

PART VIII: CHANGING THE WORLD

393   *Despite a cold, steady rain:* My description of the State of the Union address comes from the *New York Times*, January 3 and 4, 1936; *Chicago Tribune*, January 2, 3, and 4, 1936; the *Boston Globe*, January 4, 1936; and other contemporary newspaper coverage.

394 *"plenty of kick"*: The *Boston Globe*, February 11, 1934.

395 *"so vast, so powerful"*: Quoted in H. W. Brands, *A Traitor*.

396 *"advisable or necessary"*: FDR speech, January 3, 1936, with Alice's handwritten annotations, ARL Collection, LoC.

397 *"Now that the Klieg"*: The *Hartford Courant*, January 6, 1936.

398 *"The Senators, in a sudden"*: The *El Paso Herald*, January 27, 1936.

399 *"He's a dear!"*: The *Boston Globe*, January 10, 1936.

399 *"You are always welcome"*: Teague, *Mrs. L.*

399 *"great alacrity and enthusiasm"*: The *New York Times Magazine*, August 6, 1967.

399 *"why any of us should mind"*: ER to Anna Roosevelt Boettiger, January 10, 1937, FDRL.

399 *"trying to make more trouble"*: Teague, *Mrs. L.* Although Alice told Teague that after this Eleanor never asked her to the White House again, her statement is disproven by newspaper accounts of her many subsequent visits.

400 *Alice refused, for example*: The *New York Times Magazine*, August 6, 1967.

400 *"because in it . . . I said"*: Teague, *Mrs. L.*

400 *"He has the cripple's psychology"*: ARL to Arthur Lee, August 1935, quoted in Morris, S., *Edith Kermit Roosevelt.*

400 *"He was trying to adjust"*: Teague, *Mrs. L.*

400 *"They should have been better winners"*: The *New York Times Magazine*, August 6, 1967.

401 *"If you shut your eyes"*: The *Hartford Courant*, February 11, 1936.

401 *"the League of Nations all over"*: The *Hartford Courant*, February 25, 1936.

401 *"Grandpa Borah"*: "Constance" to ARL, February 25, 1936, LoC.

401 *In April 1934, Thomas Latham*: The *Boston Globe*, April 5, 1934.

401 *"I enjoy your articles"*: Arthur Atkinson to ARL, January 22, 1936, LoC.

401 *"keen and clean-cut"*: A. H. Clambey to ARL, January 24, 1936, LoC.

401 *"Lordy!" he wrote*: James Coleman to ARL, January 22, 1936, LoC.

401 *"Her column on 'coughing'"*: Margaret Aislee to ARL, January 21, 1936, LoC.

402 *"She certainly writes well"*: ER to Nan Honeyman, quoted in Lash, *Eleanor and Franklin.*

402 *"They want me to be bright"*: ARL to "Sam," [nd] 1936, LoC.

402 *"too aware of my quarter"*: ARL diary, July 15, 1917, quoted in Cordery, *Alice.*

402 *"I wrote for profit"*: Teague, *Mrs. L.*

402 *During the third week*: My account of the dedication comes from the *New York Times*, January 19 and 20, 1936; various wire reports; also reports on the strange weather conditions, the *New York Times*, January 20, 1936.

404 *"warm humor and humanity"*: Wire reports, as in the *Chester* (PA) *Times*, January 20, 1936.

405 *"There we were, swelling"*: The *New York Times Magazine*, August 6, 1967.

405 *This jaunt to the Bahamas*: Aircraft passenger records, Nassau to Miami, February 22, 1936, National Archives.

406 *"Don't speak of this":* KR to Willard Roosevelt, May 24, 1932, LoC.

406 *an "inapt" fit:* TR to Ethel Roosevelt, September 9, 1913, HL.

406 *He remained a strong:* The *New York Times*, January 12, 1936.

406 *The President had asked:* The *New York Times*, January 1, 1936.

406 *"the only one of the Oyster Bay":* The *Chicago Tribune*, March 6, 1936.

406 *a photo of him standing beside:* Wire photo, as in the *Alamogordo* (NM) *News*, February 23, 1933.

407 *A chill settled over:* It wasn't a complete frost, however. When Ted's daughter Grace made him a grandfather for the first time, he called Kermit "in a great state of excitement" to give him the news (KR to Ethel Roosevelt Derby, January 29, 1935, LoC).

407 *"containing instructions":* The *Boston Globe*, April 21, 1934.

407 *No specific indiscretion:* For more on how the scandal played out, see the *Chicago Tribune*, June 12, 1936.

407 *Elsa Maxwell's Halloween party:* The *New York Times*, November 2, 1933.

407 *"He didn't like the type," "My father always thought":* Collier and Horowitz, *The Roosevelts*.

407 *"the curse of the Roosevelts":* Morris, *Edith Kermit Roosevelt*.

408 *He paid a five-dollar fine:* The *New York Times*, March 26, 1936.

408 *"look at him to see":* BWR to Richard Derby, [nd] 1938, LoC.

409 *Yet when she first arrived:* Background on Carla Peters comes from U.S. Census 1930; ship passenger arrivals, March 11, 1930; naturalization petitions and declaration of intent, August 5, 1932, November 1, 1935, and February 10, 1936; and New York City directory, 1933.

409 *Carla received some form:* In the Manhattan directory of 1933, Herta Peters was listed as a nurse living at 52 West Seventy-First Street; this was a property owned by St. Mary's Hospital for Children, according to the *New York Times*, September 20, 1931. The hospital leased it to a Mrs. Florence Wolff through 1936.

409 *During the summer and fall:* I am grateful for a Roosevelt family member sharing stories about Kermit. See also Collier and Horowitz, *The Roosevelts*.

410 *"Relief," he replied:* Collier and Horowitz, *The Roosevelts*.

410 *At eleven o'clock in the morning:* My account of Election Day 1936 comes from the *New York Times*, November 4, 1936; and from various Associated Press reports and other wire services, November 3 and 4, 1936.

411 *"smiles and fishes":* Ickes diary, July 18, 1936, quoted in Ickes, *The Secret Diary*.

412 *"My God, he's black":* Cook, *Eleanor Roosevelt, Vol. 2*.

413 *"a handout of government":* ARL column, as in the *New Castle* (PA) *News*, September 14, 1936.

413 *"beautifying the insane":* ARL column, as in the *New Castle* (PA) *News*, September 19, 1936.

413 *"nationalized giving":* ARL column, as in the *New Castle* (PA) *News*, September 22, 1936.

413 *"Those who would like to see"*: ARL column, as in the *New Castle* (PA) *News*, October 3, 1936.

413 *"a more abundant life"*: Mrs. TRJ, *Day Before Yesterday*.

413 *"constructive liberals"*: The *Boston Globe*, December 5, 1934.

414 *A crowd of well-wishers*: The *New York Times*, November 4, 1936; wire reports, November 4 and 5, 1936.

415 *"I'm praying that the European"*: Anna Roosevelt Boettiger to FDR, October 5, 1935, FDRL.

416 *Yet the liquor import business*: For the questionable business deals and legal problems of Franklin's sons, see, among others, Burns, *Roosevelt: The Lion and the Fox*; Lash, *Eleanor and Franklin*; and Collier and Horowitz, *The Roosevelts*.

416 *Despite the multiple injuries*: The *Boston Globe*, March 31, 1934; and the *New York Times*, November 20, 1934.

416 *During the annual*: The *New York Times*, August 18, 1937.

417 *"Betty has just made up"*: Elliott Roosevelt II to ER, [nd] 1933, FDRL.

417 *"I have endeavored"*: Elliott Roosevelt II, "Rambling Thoughts of a Donkey on His Journeys," [nd], FDRL.

418 *After his rodeo adventure*: The *New York Times*, July 15 and 24, 1933; June 15 and 22, 1934; September 27, 1934; October 7, 1936; and August 18, 1938, among other newspaper reports.

418 *"high foreign officials"*: The *New York Times*, October 7, 1936.

419 *"As Miss Le Hand lived"*: ER, *This I Remember*. See also Cook, *Eleanor Roosevelt, Vol. 1*.

419 *"If I should outlive"*: ER to Lorena Hickok, April 20, 1936, FDRL.

419 *Lucy Mercer Rutherfurd had discreetly returned*: See Persico, *Franklin and Lucy*; Goodwin, *No Ordinary Time*.

419 *"dismiss a lasting devotion"*: Jonathan Daniels, *The Washington Quadrille*.

420 HIS MOLLYCODDLE PHILOSOPHY: Eleanor wrote about this article in her "My Day" column of October 5, 1936. She indicated that she had read it on a Sunday while going to church, presumably at some point not long before the column appeared. A search of hundreds of digitized newspapers from June to October 1936, however, did not reveal the article in question. When interviewed by Joseph Lash, Alice Longworth apparently claimed authorship of the piece (see Lash's notes, *Eleanor and Franklin*); indeed, Alice made similar arguments about Franklin's policies. Yet despite various assumptions in previous accounts (Cook, *Eleanor Roosevelt*; Peyser and Dwyer, *Hissing Cousins*; and others), Alice did not make the "mollycoddle" accusation in her column; an exhaustive search of all Alice's columns for 1936 disproved this possibility. It also seems unlikely that she wrote a separate piece with such a headline, as not one of the hundreds of digitized newspapers has record of it; usually a piece by Alice Roosevelt Longworth (and especially one as sensational and newsworthy as this would have been) was picked up by the wire services and carried (or at least mentioned) in many newspapers across the country. My own conclusion is that Alice had nothing to do with this particular attack on Franklin, though she later made a claim for it, either due to misremembering the facts or to her usual self-aggrandizement.

420   *Hick was feeling quite gay:* Lorena Hickok to ER, February 12 and 16, 1937, FDRL; the *New York Times*, February 16, 1937; the *Chicago Tribune*, February 16, 1937; and wire reports, February 16, 1937.

421   *"Hick darling," "My dear":* Quoted in Cook, *Eleanor Roosevelt, Vol. 2.*

421   *"Remember one thing always":* ER to Lorena Hickok, March 11, 1933, FDRL.

422   *"not accustomed to embracing":* The *Democratic Digest*, April 1937, quoted in Cook, *Eleanor Roosevelt, Vol. 2.*

423   *"You have grown so much":* ER to Lorena Hickok, March 5, 1933, FDRL.

423   *"I look at it and think":* ER to Lorena Hickok, March 7, 1933, FDRL.

423   *"I wish I could lie down":* ER to Lorena Hickok, [nd] FDRL.

423   *"I've been trying":* Lorena Hickok to ER, December 1933, FDRL.

424   *The women drove up:* The *Boston Globe*, July 12, July 19, 1933; and the *New York Times*, July 14, 1933.

424   *On the train from Washington:* The *New York Times*, March 6, 1934.

424   *"If I had charge":* The *New York Times*, July 13, 1934.

425   *One newspaper feature:* The *New York Times*, March 14, 1937.

425   *"I'd never have believed":* Lorena Hickok to ER, [nd] 1940, quoted in Goodwin, *No Ordinary Time.*

425   *"I am quite sure":* Edith Roosevelt to ER, November 17, 1933, HL.

426   *"First Nuisance":* The *New York Times*, April 9, 1937.

427   *Had Louis Howe lived:* For a full discussion of Howe's plans for Eleanor, see Cook, *Eleanor Roosevelt, Vol. 2*; Goodwin, *No Ordinary Time*; and Louis Howe, "Women's Ways in Politics," Mary Dewson Collection, FDRL.

427   *"Forty years ago":* Howe, "Women's Ways in Politics."

427   *"He always wanted to 'make' me":* ER to Lorena Hickok, April 20, 1936, FDRL.

427   *Confronted once by a group:* ER, "My Day" column, April 23, 1954.

427   *"To elect anyone president":* Associated Press story, as in the (Dubuque, IA) *Telegraph-Herald*, March 2, 1937.

428   *"a rotund lady with a husky":* *Time*, February 19, 1934.

428   *"I love Mrs. Roosevelt":* Quoted in Beasley, *One Third.*

429   *"I'd hate to go to Europe":* ER to Lorena Hickok, November 12, 1936, FDRL.

429   *"I have no plans":* The *Gastonia* (NC) *Daily Gazette*, April 15, 1937. See also April 13, 1937, and the *Hartford Courant*, April 14, 1937.

429   *"The trip has been really":* ER to Anna Roosevelt Boettiger, April 14, 1937, FDRL.

429   *"amusing and human":* ER to Anna Roosevelt Boettiger, March 3, 1937, FDRL.

430   *"If the national administration":* Associated Press report, as in the *Jefferson City* (MO) *Post Tribune*, September 7, 1937.

430   *"Why don't you go":* Mrs. TRJ, *Day Before Yesterday.*

430   *So mother and son:* The *Oakland Tribune*, July 3, 1937.

431   *"We had planned to go":* Mrs. TRJ, *Day Before Yesterday.*

431   *"No one had the faintest idea":* The *New York Times*, August 21, 1937.

432   *"Between courses"*: Mrs. TRJ, *Day Before Yesterday*.

432   *"Watch now, it is going"*: The *New York Times*, August 21, 1937.

432   *"We were jammed"*: Associated Press report, as in the *Jefferson City* (MO) *Post Tribune*, September 7, 1937.

433   *"It was lovely"*: Mrs. TRJ, *Day Before Yesterday*.

434   *Sen. Lewis Schwellenbach*: Associated Press, as in the *Hartford Courant*, September 10, 1937.

434   *"differed in every aspect"*: The *Boston Globe*, November 11, 1936.

435   *"must be anxious"*: ER to TRJ, September 18, 1938, LoC.

435   *"gloomy and depressed"*: KR to ARL, March 14, 1933, LoC.

435   *he was ultimately not chosen*: The *New York Times*, August 22, 1933; and the *Boston Globe*, October 13, 1933; and April 8, 1934.

435   *When he left the post*: The *Chicago Tribune*, March 27, 1933; and the *New York Times*, April 27, 1933.

435   *"As far as he is concerned"*: Edith Roosevelt to KR, June 19, 1936, LoC.

435   *"never known what it meant"*: TRJ to Archibald Roosevelt, [nd], LoC.

436   *"It looked like a museum"*: Collier and Horowitz, *The Roosevelts*.

436   *exhibiting her needlework*: The *New York Times*, December 26, 1937.

436   *"The cigarette advertisement lady"*: The *Daily News* (Middlesboro, KY), May 10, 1937.

436   *"some is fine poetry"*: The *New York Times*, August 7, 1938.

436   *"No two people I know"*: ER, "My Day," December 30, 1937.

437   *"candid, unaffected"*: The *New York Times*, November 21, 1937.

437   *Yet . . . no one reached out*: This is based on Belle's letter to Richard Derby, [nd] 1938, in which she blasted the family for their failure to help Kermit over the past several years. Their attitude, she insisted, was one of the things that harmed him the most (LoC).

437   *"Dearest Kermit"*: Edith Roosevelt to KR, October 24, 1937, LoC.

437   *Christmas lights still twinkled*: My description of Belle and Carla at the River Club comes from a conversation with a Roosevelt family member who asked not to be named, and from Collier and Horowitz, *The Roosevelts*. The description of the River Club comes from various *New York Times* contemporary accounts.

438   *wireless reports revealed*: The *Chicago Tribune*, December 22, 1937; and the *New York Times*, December 22, 1937. New York ship passenger lists, January 6, 1938. The *City of Hamburg* was a Baltimore Mail Line ship, a subsidiary of Kermit's Roosevelt Steamship Line (*New York Times*, January 7, 1931).

440   *"Why can't you keep," "Mother wouldn't like"*: Collier and Horowitz, *The Roosevelts*.

440   *"dutiful son, brother"*: Interview with Roosevelt family member.

440   *His income for the last year*: The *New York Times*, April 8, 1937.

441   *"caused trouble and unnecessary"*: BWR to Richard Derby, [November] [nd] 1938, LoC. The *New York Times* reported that Kermit and Belle were off to Alaska "on a trip that combined business and pleasure" (May 16, 1937).

441 *she sent Clochette along:* Three years later, Clochette was still in some kind of physical therapy, with her mother reporting to Kermit that she "has made the most stupendous strides and is developing magnificently" (BWR to KR, June 4, 1941, LoC).

441 *Father and daughter set sail:* Kermit's Pacific travels were re-created by a careful study of ship passenger arrival records. Both he and Clochette arrived in Honolulu on the *Nourmahal* on April 29. Kermit left the next day on the *Matsonia* for Los Angeles, and was listed as "transfer" from the San Francisco route. Clochette departed on the *Lurline* on May 7.

442 *"Groton disappoints me":* Dirck Roosevelt to KR and BWR, [nd] September and October 1937, LoC.

442 *He ran away from the school:* For one major incident Dirck caused, see the *Hartford Courant*, January 11, 1938; and the *Boston Globe*, January 11, 1938.

442 *Dirck was homosexual:* Dirck would later be arrested for homosexual activity in Spain (*New York Times*, July 4, 1951), and a family member agreed the struggle over accepting his sexuality was at the root of Dirck's emotional problems.

442 *In the spring of 1938:* My account of Dirck's escapade with Henry Distler and the subsequent fight between their chauffeurs comes from the *New York Times*, April 17, 1938; the *Hartford Courant*, April 16, 1938; and the *Chicago Tribune*, April 17 and 18, 1938.

442 *Henry Von Distler-Dircksen:* U.S. ship passenger arrival records.

443 *On May 28 he wrote:* KR to Ethel Roosevelt Derby, May 28, 1938, LoC.

443 *By May 31, he was out:* The *New York Times*, June 1, 1938.

443 *by the early part of June:* Winchell column, as in the *San Antonio Light*, June 14, 1938.

443 *"It is such a sleepy":* ER, "My Day," November 15, 1938.

445 *"James has not said":* ER to Anna Roosevelt Boettiger, October 23, 1938, FDRL.

445 *"I am terribly sorry":* Quoted in Davis, *Summer.* For the dissolution of the ER-Cook-Dickerman friendship in detail, see Cook, *Eleanor Roosevelt, Vol. 2.*

446 *"Eleanor never forgot":* Dickerman oral history, FDRL.

446 *"Such damned fools!":* Lorena Hickok to ER, November 17, 1938, FDRL.

446 *"I do so need to be alone":* Lorena Hickok to ER, June 16, 1937, FDRL.

446 *"Dearest, you are going":* ER to Lorena Hickok, July 27, 1937, FDRL.

447 *"I'm sorry I talked":* Lorena Hickok to ER, January 9, 1938, FDRL. For the conflict in the ER-Hick relationship in detail, see Cook, *Eleanor Roosevelt, Vol. 2.*

447 *"You poor child":* ER to Lorena Hickok, November 18, 1937, FDRL.

447 *the "gaiety" . . . her relationship:* ER to Esther Lape, August 11, 1938, FDRL.

448 *"really loved somebody":* Wotkyns oral history, FDRL.

448 *"If only you weren't":* Lorena Hickok to ER, October 12, 1938, FDRL.

449 *"I doubt, dear":* ER to Lorena Hickok, October 15, 1938, FDRL.

449 *"You know I do* not*":* ER to FDR, [nd] 1938, FDRL.

449 *Franklin answered in vague:* FDR to ER, August 12, 1938, FDRL.

449   *"so patently sincere":* The *New York Times*, October 13, 1938.

449   *"the presidency on the basis":* Quoted in Cook, *Eleanor Roosevelt, Vol. 2.*

450   *At the time of his resignation:* The *Oakland Tribune*, August 5, 1938; the *New York Times*, July 21, 1938; and August 6, 1938; and the *Reno Evening Gazette*, August 9, 1938.

450   *The final break with his company:* See Collier and Horowitz, *The Roosevelts*, for Carla Peters's account.

450   *"He seems to have broken":* Archibald Roosevelt to Arthur Lee, September 18, 1938, LoC.

451   *"lectures or public appearances":* The *San Mateo Times*, October 13, 1938.

451   *On the warm, sunny:* The *Oakland Tribune*, November 28, 1938; and the *San Mateo Times*, November 28, 1938.

452   *"I fear I shall have to go," "so that he will not be":* Quoted in Collier and Horowitz, *The Roosevelts.*

452   *"I cannot help but feel":* BWR to Richard Derby, [November] [nd] 1938, LoC.

453   *"as much in love":* TR to KR, October 27, 1918, HL.

PART IX: TERRIFIC RESPONSIBILITY

457   *In a red embroidered:* My account of Madame Chiang comes from BWR diary, LoC; the *New York Times*, February 18, 1943; and Elliott Roosevelt, *Mother R.*

457   *The guest book read:* Springwood guest book, FDRL.

458   *"No wartime President":* The *New York Times*, May 31, 1942.

459   *"His face was gray":* BWR diary, July 7, 1942.

459   *"We mean no harm":* "Casablanca Conference" radio address, February 12, 1943, transcript, FDRL.

460   *Franklin's son James:* Franklin wrote about James's training and illness in a letter to Archie Roosevelt, October 18, 1943, FDRL.

460   *"dodged torpedoes":* James Roosevelt, *My Parents.*

461   *"Mama had been rather":* ER to Corinne Alsop, September 16, 1941, FDRL.

461   *"I couldn't feel any emotion":* ER to Anna Roosevelt Boettiger, September 10, 1941, FDRL.

461   *"Cousin Sally's closets":* BWR diary, 1942, LoC.

461   *On a brisk day in April:* The *Boston Globe*, April 15, 1942.

462   *Franklin promoted:* Archibald Roosevelt to FDR, November 5, 1942, FDRL.

462   *"reasonably good":* The *New York Times*, July 3 and 10, 1941.

463   *"The strange thing":* Quoted in Goodwin, *No Ordinary Time.*

463   *"He is cold as ice inside":* Ickes diary, July 12, 1941, LoC.

463   *"could care for themselves":* For a full account of Missy's sad last days at the White House, see Goodwin, *No Ordinary Time.*

463   *He also arranged for her:* The *New York Times* of November 30, 1941, reported that Franklin had visited Warm Springs and visited Missy, and "was pleased to learn" that she was "able to be up and around again."

464   *some years earlier:* See Ward, *Closest.*

464   *"the pretty little Norwegian":* BWR diary, July 7, 1941, LoC.

464   *"Märtha would sit":* Goodwin, *No Ordinary Time.*

465 "the longest assembly line": The Fort Worth Star-Telegram, September 29, 1942.

465 "I never did anything": The Saturday Evening Post, May 30, 1942.

466 "I think he was really asking": For a full discussion of Franklin's request to Eleanor, see Goodwin, No Ordinary Time. Also see Elliott Roosevelt, Mother R; and James Roosevelt, My Parents.

466 "Within less than a year": Wire reports, October 3, 1942.

467 In the official visitor register: See Goodwin, No Ordinary Time.

467 "beloved presence": Ward, A First-Class Temperament.

469 "Franklin is quite right": Collier and Horowitz, The Roosevelts.

469 "I don't see how we can": KR to TRJ, April 14, 1939, LoC.

469 "a clear-cut moral issue": The New York Times, November 22, 1939. Also see the New York Times, September 21, 1939; and October 25, 1939; and the Boston Globe, September 21, 1939; and November 28, 1939; and the Chicago Tribune, November 4, 1939.

469 "It was a great asset": BWR papers, LoC, quoted in Morris, S.

470 "sort of on furlough": The New York Times, June 27, 1941.

470 "shaking like a leaf": BWR to Elizabeth Herbert, June 28, 1941, LoC.

470 it might have been syphilis, "overindulgence in alcoholics": FBI file, Kermit Roosevelt, July 7, 1941.

470 "I understand what you": ER to BWR, July 15, 1941, LoC.

471 "no hope of getting": Sherman Miles to Edwin Watson, July 29, 1941, FDRL.

471 "a mission or line": Edwin Watson to F. Trubee Davison, July 21, 1941, FDRL.

471 "You are the most wonderful": BWR to FDR, July [nd] 1941, FDRL.

472 "I want to talk over": FBI file, Kermit Roosevelt, transcript dated July 5, 1941.

472 "Can't you see that": Collier and Horowitz, The Roosevelts.

472 "Roosevelt had such an odor": FBI file, Kermit Roosevelt, July 17, 1941.

473 The preferred sanitarium: The Hartford Courant, April 2, 1943.

473 "a squash racket": BWR to KR, January 4, 1942, LoC.

473 "Cannot write": Edith Roosevelt diary, November 6, 1941, HL.

473 "Too tired": Edith Roosevelt diary, November 9, 1941, HL.

473 "put Hartford away": Edith Roosevelt diary, November 13, 1941, HL. There is a slight confusion of facts in Sylvia Morris's account of Kermit's stay at the Hartford Retreat in Edith Kermit Roosevelt. Kermit did not sue Archie until his second stay at the Retreat, in April 1942. See the Hartford Courant, May 1, 1942; also Hartford Probate court records, Kermit Roosevelt, April 30, 1942.

474 "A hard blow": Edith Roosevelt diary, February 14, 1942, HL.

474 "general check-up": The New York Times, February 13, 1942.

474 he immediately checked into the Shannon Lodge: Hartford Probate court records, Kermit Roosevelt, April 30, 1942.

474 Shannon Lodge offered a refuge: The New York Times, May 13, 1928; September 22, 1933; July 31, 1937; and June 9, 1939.

475 rushed in carrying: Details of Kermit's forced commitment come from the Hartford Courant, May 1, 1942, as well as an interview with a Roosevelt family member.

476 *"real danger of a nasty scandal":* Archibald Roosevelt to FDR, August 29, 1943, FDRL.

476 *a reconnaissance mission:* The *Chicago Tribune*, September 5, 1942.

476 *"Time means nothing":* BWR to KR, January 24, 1941, LoC.

477 *"I am glad you find":* BWR to KR, September 28, 1942, LoC.

477 *"The wedding was all that":* BWR to KR, December [nd] 1942, LoC.

477 *"Darling, I feel your shadow":* KR to BWR, [nd] 1942, LoC.

477 Miserere nobis: Edith Roosevelt diary, June 28, 1939, HL.

478 *"Fiddler of Dooney":* Edith Roosevelt diary, April 4, 1943, HL.

478 *"In each room":* Edith Roosevelt to KR, April 5, 1943, HL.

478 *"to solve the special problems":* The *New York Times*, May 29, 1943.

478 *the ladies had gathered:* The *New York Times*, May 23, 1943; and various wire reports, May 24, 1943.

479 *Their host that day:* U.S. Census 1930.

479 *having once . . . compared Franklin:* The *New York Times*, February 13, 1936.

479 *"I hope that when the war":* The *New York Times*, May 24, 1943.

480 *"Being in the war":* The *New York Times*, May 21, 1943.

481 *His visits terrified:* Goodwin, *No Ordinary Time*.

481 *"My idea of hell":* Lash, *Love, Eleanor*.

482 *"Hall has died":* James Roosevelt, *My Parents*.

482 *"It would be so much better":* Quoted in Streitmatter, *Empty Without You*.

483 *"I know you have a feeling":* Lash used this letter in *Love, Eleanor* as a refutation that Eleanor had ever had a physical relationship with Hick. To me, it suggests instead a change in their relationship.

483 *"You should have had a husband":* ER to Lorena Hickok, FDRL.

483 *"I still prefer the person":* Lorena Hickok to ER, [nd] 1940, FDRL.

483 *Berkeley graduate named Marion:* See Goodwin, *No Ordinary Time*; U.S. Census 1920, 1930, and 1940; the *Boston Globe*, June 3, 1948; and the *Chicago Tribune*, August 13, 1949.

484 *"a full-time revolutionary":* Lash obituary, the *New York Times*, August 23, 1987.

485 *"insecurity, shyness, lack of social grace":* From Anna Roosevelt Halsted's review of Lash, *Eleanor Roosevelt*, FDRL and quoted in Goodwin.

485 *"I'd like you to feel":* Lash, *Love, Eleanor*.

485 *"frills and furbelows":* The *New York Times*, February 9, 1942.

485 *"would be proud to serve":* The *New York Times*, January 24, 1942.

485 *"I like having something":* ER to Joseph Lash, April 22, 1922, FDRL.

486 *"Don't accept a compromise":* Lash, *Love, Eleanor*.

486 *"four freedoms":* The *New York Times*, July 15, 1943.

486 *"There should be no impediment":* The *Chicago Defender*, July 24, 1943.

486 *"If the irrigation system":* BWR diary, July 7, 1941, LoC.

487 *"Fascinating conversation":* BWR diary, September 28, 1942, LoC. Belle told Kermit "so much is verbatim" in these diaries that she could never get it published.

487   *Joe Lash told her:* Joseph Lash diary, July 17, 1940, quoted in Goodwin, *No Ordinary Time.*

487   *"the mother of us all":* BWR diary, July 7, 1941, LoC.

488   *"I think wine was the only":* Lyman Woodman, "A Roosevelt in Alaska," *Alaska Living* supplement to the *Anchorage Daily News,* June 2, 1968.

488   *Marston was the son:* U.S. Census 1900, 1920, 1930, and 1940; Rochester city directories, 1930–1940; the *Tucson Daily Citizen,* October 24, 1942; the *Mason City* (IA) *Globe Gazette,* May 26, 1944; and the *Kenosha* (WI) *Evening News,* January 17, 1948.

489   *"I know you realize better":* ER to Corinne Alsop, October 1, 1941, private collection.

489   *"You are scarcely":* Edith Roosevelt to KR, May 28, 1943, LoC.

491   *"a rather sad girl":* See Felsenthal, *Princess Alice;* and Cordery, *Alice.*

491   *"she made up her own":* ARL to TRJ, October 26, 1939, LoC.

491   *"exclusion from combat":* KR FBI file, June 6, 1943.

491   *"was found with his head":* Edith Roosevelt diary, June 27, 1943, HL.

492   *"otherwise unidentified":* The *New York Times,* July 28, 1943.

492   *"If feelings are permitted":* Collier and Horowitz, *The Roosevelts.*

492   *"For about two weeks":* Archibald Roosevelt to FDR, August 29, 1943, FDRL.

492   *"Archie is too old":* Grace Roosevelt to FDR, December [nd] 1943, FDRL.

493   *"a good deal the way":* ARL to TRJ, October 26, 1939, LoC.

493   *"We've tried that thing":* The *New York Times Magazine,* August 6, 1967.

493   *"How are things":* Drew Pearson syndicated column, as in the *Indiana Evening Gazette,* June 18, 1943.

494   *"those who hate all damn":* BWR diary, January 22, 1943, LoC.

494   *"I don't think anyone":* The *New York Times Magazine,* August 6, 1967.

494   *"I'd rather vote for Hitler":* Quoted in Felsenthal, *Princess Alice.*

495   *"the warmth [Franklin] had":* BWR to KR, December [nd] 1942, LoC.

495   *"The ship is dark":* Quoted in Mrs. TRJ, *Day Before Yesterday.*

496   *"It is our country":* The *New York Times,* December 23, 1941.

496   *"It will do something":* TRJ to Edith Roosevelt, December 15, 1941, HL.

496   *"intensive shell-fire":* Mrs. TRJ, *Day Before Yesterday.*

496   *"rugged hills":* TRJ to Eleanor Butler Roosevelt, quoted in Mrs. TRJ, *Day Before Yesterday.*

497   *"anti-inflation war economy":* TRJ to FDR, May 7, 1942, FDRL.

497   *Franklin's sons drew headlines:* See, for example, the *New York Times,* December 28, 1942; January 14, 1943; May 30, 1943; October 20, 1943; March 11, 1944; and November 19, 1943; the *Chicago Tribune,* August 7, 1942; and the *Hartford Courant,* March 4, 1943.

498   *"a specific stop":* Mrs. TRJ, *Day Before Yesterday.* The order, Number J.397, was reproduced in the book.

498   *"the first time that the press":* The *Chicago Tribune,* March 3, 1943.

498   *Quentin's injury:* See, for example, the *New York Times,* March 7, 1943; and June 5, 1943; the *Chicago Tribune,* March 7, 1943; and the *Boston Globe,* March

7, 1943. Quentin was also mentioned as being in the assault on Tunisia before his injury: the *New York Times*, February 6, 1943.

499   GENERAL AND CAPTAIN: The *New York Times*, May 7, 1943.

499   *While the coverage:* The *New York Times*, July 9, 1943; August 21, 1943.

500   *"those present would have":* Mrs. TRJ, *Day Before Yesterday*.

500   *"The men worship Ted":* Bradley, *Soldier's Story*.

500   *"The force and skill":* Quoted in Balkoski, *Utah Beach*.

500   *"If you ask me":* Bradley, *Soldier's Story*.

501   *"We'll start the war":* The quote may be apocryphal, but clearly the decision to stay where they were was made on the spot.

502   *"He braved death":* Bradley, *Soldier's Story*.

502   *"Well, now," he wrote:* Mrs. TRJ, *Day Before Yesterday*.

503   *"For the first time":* The *Chicago Tribune*, March 2, 1945. See also the *New York Times*, March 2, 1945.

504   *"I am really feeling":* FDR to Margaret Suckley, May 1944, quoted in Ward, *Closest Companion*.

504   *In fact, his doctor:* For Franklin's medical condition and treatment during his last year, see Goodwin, *No Ordinary Time*.

505   *"Well," . . . "what did you":* Elliott Roosevelt, *As He Saw It*.

505   *"On the whole":* For reactions to Franklin's speech, see the *Chicago Tribune*, March 2, 1945; and the *New York Times*, March 2, 1945.

506   *Theodore's one remaining son:* For the story of Archie's discharge and Franklin's role in it, see Archibald Roosevelt correspondence, FDRL, particularly the memo to Gen. Edwin Watson from Lt. Col. B. W. Davenport, November 11, 1944.

506   *"carried all through the Southwest":* FDR to Grace Roosevelt, November 27, 1944, FDRL. Franklin would later send the cigarette case to Archie's wife, Grace, because he thought she and their children should have "something so intimately associated with his second World War days."

506   *"It seems to me":* Archibald Roosevelt to FDR, March 25, 1945, FDRL.

507   *Eleanor . . . had other priorities:* The *New York Times*, March 7 and 28, 1945; and April 3, 1945; and the *Chicago Tribune*, March 17, 1945.

507   *"Memories of more than":* The *Chicago Tribune*, August 1, 1944.

508   *"The death of Marguerite":* The *New York Times*, August 1, 1944.

509   *The visits with Lucy:* The best account of Lucy's return to Franklin's life at this time is in Goodwin, *No Ordinary Time*.

509   *"What would you think":* Goodwin, *No Ordinary Time*.

509   *"lighthearted and gay":* Unpublished essay, Halsted Papers, FDRL, quoted in ibid.

510   *"He just sat there":* Asbell, *FDR Memoirs*.

510   *"full of jokes":* Shoumatoff, *FDR's Unfinished Portrait*.

511   *"flush with the ground":* Lippmann, *The Squire of Warm Springs*.

511   *"The President, like a little":* Shoumatoff, *FDR's Unfinished Portrait*.

511   *Lucy knew she and Shoumatoff:* Goodwin, *No Ordinary Time*.

512 *"The world has lost"*: Halsted Papers, FDRL.

512 *"there wasn't enough room"*: The *Boston Globe*, April 21, 1945.

513 *"would be simply"*: The *New York Times*, April 22, 1945.

513 *"Eleanor would have found"*: Bishop. *FDR's Last*.

514 *"caught in a pageant"*: Asbell, *When FDR Died*.

514 *"my dear wife on her death"*: Tully, *FDR: My Boss*.

514 *"Darling Eleanor, my heart"*: BWR to ER, April [nd] 1945, LoC.

514 *"I am glad he died"*: ER to Edith Roosevelt, April 17, 1945, HL.

515 *"aboveboard"*: For Eleanor's confrontation with Anna, see Goodwin, *No Ordinary Time*.

515 *"I've certainly not succeeded"*: Lash, *A World of Love*.

515 *"great sadness, for I"*: BWR to KR, April 4, 1942, LoC.

515 *"When she saw happiness"*: Eleanor Wotkyns oral history, FDRL.

516 *"I never did like to be"*: Lash, *Love, Eleanor*.

516 *"something of uncertainty"*: ER, "On My Own," *The Saturday Evening Post*, March 8, 1958.

517 *"The story"* . . . *"is done"*: The comment was reported in an Associated Press story, April 21, 1945, and the next day in the *New York Times*.

EPILOGUE: THE LAST SORTIE

519 *The low, mournful sound:* My account of Eleanor's funeral comes from the *New York Times*, November 11, 1962; the *Boston Globe*, November 11, 1962; the *Chicago Tribune*, November 11, 1962; and various Associated Press and other wire reports; and from Roosevelt, *Mother R.*; and more.

519 *"Life was meant to be lived"*: ER, *The Autobiography*.

520 *"international Magna Carta"*: The *Chicago Tribune*, December 10, 1948.

520 *"The basic problem confronting"*: The *New York Times*, September 29, 1948.

521 *"liberal-minded Democrats"*: *Look*, July 9, 1946.

521 *"We need to use"*: ER, "My Day," February 16, 1962.

522 *"some particularly humorous," "The plain truth"*: *Look*, July 9, 1946.

523 *"a better-looking mouth"*: Roosevelt, *Mother R.*

523 *After finishing her work:* Eleanor Wotkyns, "Life Lessons from Eleanor Roosevelt," FDRL.

525 *"Because, you see"*: Teague, *Mrs. L.*

525 *"The Most Remarkable"*: See, for example, the *Boston Globe*, November 11, 1962.

525 *"We do not have to become"*: ER, "My Day," November 27, 1960; also ER, *You Learn by Living*.

527 *"in strict religious terms"*: Unpublished interview with the Rev. William Turner Levy, quoted in Ward, *Before the Trumpet*.

528 *"It was quite an ordeal"*: Eleanor Mann Biles to Edmund Morris, July 6, 1981, quoted courtesy of the Biles family.

528 *Not long after:* Trisha Helland.

SELECTED BIBLIOGRAPHY

Alsop, Joseph. *FDR: A Centenary Remembrance*. New York: Viking, 1982.

Alsop, Joseph, and Adam Platt. *I've Seen the Best of It*. Mount Jackson, VA: Axios Press, 1992.

Anonymous [Nellie M. Scanlan]. *Boudoir Mirrors of Washington: With Sixteen Portraits*. Philadelphia, PA: John C. Winston Company, 1923.

Asbell, Bernard. *The FDR Memoirs*. New York: Doubleday, 1973.

———, ed. *Mother and Daughter: The Letters of Eleanor and Anna Roosevelt*. New York: Coward, McCann and Geoghegan, 1981.

———. *When FDR Died*. New York: Holt, Rinehart and Winston, 1961.

Bagby, Wesley M. *The Road to Normalcy: The Presidential Campaign of 1920*. Baltimore, MD: Johns Hopkins University Press, 1962.

Balkoski, Joseph. *The Utah Beach: The Amphibious Landing and Airborne Operations on D-Day, June 6, 1944*. Mechanicsburg, PA: Stackpole Books, 2005.

Baltzell, E. Digby. *The Protestant Establishment: Aristocracy and Caste in America*. New York: Vintage, 1966.

Beasely, Maurice. *One Third of a Nation: Lorena Hickok Reports on the Great Depression*. Champaign: University of Illinois Press, 1987.

Berubé, Allan. *Coming Out Under Fire*. Chapel Hill: University of North Carolina Press, 2010.

Bishop, Jim. *FDR's Last Year, April 1944–April 1945*. New York: Morrow, 1974.

Bishop, Joseph B. *Theodore Roosevelt and His Time*. New York: Charles Scribner's Sons, 1920.

Bradley, Omar N. *A Soldier's Story*. New York: Modern Library, 1999.

Brands, H. W. *T.R.: The Last Romantic*. New York: Basic Books, 1998.

———. *Traitor to His Class: The Privileged Life and Radical Presidency of Franklin Delano Roosevelt*. New York: Anchor Books/Random House, 2008.

Burns, James MacGregor. *Roosevelt: The Lion and the Fox*. New York: Harcourt, Brace, 1956.

———. *Roosevelt: The Soldier of Freedom*. New York: Harcourt, 1970.

Burton, David H. *Theodore Roosevelt and His English Correspondents: A Special Relationship of Friends*. Philadelphia, PA: American Philosophical Society, 1973.

Caroli, Betty Boyd. *The Roosevelt Women*. New York: Basic Books, 1998.

Chanler, Margaret. *Roman Spring*. Boston, MA: Little, Brown, and Company, 1934.

Clapper, Olive. *Washington Tapestry*. New York: Whittlesey House/McGraw-Hill, 1946.

Collier, Peter, and David Horowitz. *The Roosevelts: An American Saga*. New York: Simon and Schuster, 1994.

Cook, Blanche Weisen. *Eleanor Roosevelt, Vol. 1: 1884–1933*. New York: Penguin Books, 1992.

————. *Eleanor Roosevelt, Vol. 2: 1933–1938*. New York: Viking/Penguin Books, 1999.

Cordery, Stacy. *Alice: Alice Roosevelt Longworth, from White House Princess to Washington Power Broker*. New York: Viking/Penguin Group, 2007.

Daniels, Jonathan. *The Washington Quadrille: The Dance Beside the Documents*. New York: Doubleday, 1968.

Daniels, Josephus. *The Wilson Era: Years of Peace, 1910–1917*. Chapel Hill: University of North Carolina Press, 1974.

Davis, Kenneth. *FDR: The Beckoning of Destiny, 1882–1928—A History*. New York: Putnam, 1972.

————. *FDR: Into the Storm, 1937–1940—A History*. New York: Putnam, 1972.

————. *FDR: The New Deal Years, 1933–1937: A History*. New York: Random House, 1986.

————. *FDR: The New York Years, 1928–1933*. New York: Random House, 1985.

Davis, Kenneth S., and Marion Dickerman. *Invincible Summer: An Intimate Portrait of the Roosevelts, Based on the Recollections of Marion Dickerman*. New York: Atheneum, 1974.

Donn, Linda. *The Roosevelt Cousins: Growing Up Together, 1882–1924*. New York: Alfred A. Knopf, 2001.

Faber, Doris. *The Life of Lorena Hickok: Eleanor Roosevelt's Friend*. New York: William Morrow, 1980.

Felsenthal, Carol. *Princess Alice: The Life and Times of Alice Roosevelt Longworth*. New York: St. Martin's Press, 1988.

Flemion, Jess, and Colleen M. O'Connor, ed. *Eleanor Roosevelt: An American Journey*. San Diego, CA: San Diego State University Press, 1987.

Freidel, Frank. *Franklin D. Roosevelt: Launching the New Deal*. New York: Little, Brown, 1973.

Freidel, Frank. *Franklin D. Roosevelt: A Rendezvous with Destiny*. New York: Little, Brown, 1990.

Garland, Hamlin. *My Friendly Contemporaries: A Literary Log*. New York: Macmillan Company, 1932.

Goodwin, Doris Kearns. *The Bully Pulpit: Theodore Roosevelt and the Golden Age of Journalism*. New York: Simon and Schuster, 2013.

————. *No Ordinary Time: Franklin and Eleanor Roosevelt: The Home Front in World War II*. New York: Simon and Schuster, 1994.

Graham, Katharine. *Personal History*. New York: Alfred A. Knopf, 1997.

Gunther, John. *Roosevelt in Retrospect*. New York: Harper and Brothers, 1950.

Hagedorn, Hermann. *The Roosevelt Family of Sagamore Hill*. New York: Macmillan, 1954.

Harbaugh, William Henry. *The Life and Times of Theodore Roosevelt*. New York: Collier Books, 1963.

Harrity, Richard, and R. G. Martin. *Eleanor Roosevelt: Her Life in Pictures*. New York: Duell, Sloan and Pearce, 1958.

Hickok, Lorena. *Eleanor Roosevelt: Reluctant First Lady*. New York: Dodd, Mead, 1980.

Ickes, Harold LeClair. *The Secret Diary of Harold L. Ickes: The First Thousand Days.* New York: Simon and Schuster, 1953.

———. *The Secret Diary of Harold L. Ickes: The Inside Struggle.* New York: Simon and Schuster, 1954.

Keller, Morton. *Theodore Roosevelt: A Profile.* New York: Farrar, Straus and Giroux, 1967.

Kerr, Joan Paterson, and Theodore Roosevelt. *A Bully Father: Theodore Roosevelt's Letters to His Children.* New York: Random House, 1995.

Kraft, Betsy. *Theodore Roosevelt: Champion of the American Spirit.* New York: Clarion Books, 2003.

Lash, Joseph. *Eleanor and Franklin.* New York: W. W. Norton and Company, 1971.

———. *Eleanor Roosevelt: A Friend's Memoir.* Garden City, NY: Doubleday, 1964.

———. *Eleanor: The Years Alone.* New York: W. W. Norton, 1972.

———. *Life Was Meant to Be Lived: A Centenary Portrait of Eleanor Roosevelt.* New York: W. W. Norton, 1984.

Lash, Joseph, and Eleanor Roosevelt. *Love, Eleanor: Eleanor Roosevelt and Her Friends.* New York: Doubleday, 1982.

Lehr, Elizabeth Drexel. *King Lehr and the Gilded Age.* New York: J. B. Lippincott Company, 1935.

Leuchtenburg, William. *The FDR Years: On Roosevelt and His Legacy.* New York: Columbia University Press, 1995.

Lippmann, Theodore Jr. *The Squire of Warm Springs: FDR in Georgia, 1934–1945.* New York: Simon and Schuster, 1977.

Longworth, Alice Roosevelt. *Crowded Hours.* New York: Charles Scribner's Sons, 1933.

Martin, Ralph G. *Cissy: The Extraordinary Life of Eleanor Medill Patterson.* New York: Simon and Schuster, 1979.

McCullough, David. *Mornings on Horseback: The Story of an Extraordinary Family, a Vanished Way of Life, and the Unique Child Who Became Theodore Roosevelt.* New York: Simon and Schuster, 1981.

McKenna, Marian. *Borah.* Ann Arbor: University of Michigan Press, 1961.

Millard, Candice. *The River of Doubt: Theodore Roosevelt's Darkest Journey.* New York: Broadway Books, 2005.

Miller, Nathan. *FDR: An Intimate History.* New York: New American Library, 1983.

———. *Theodore Roosevelt: A Life.* New York: HarperCollins, 1992.

Morgan, Ted. *FDR: A Biography.* New York: Simon and Schuster, 1985.

Morris, Edmund. *Colonel Roosevelt.* New York: Random House, 2010.

———. *The Rise of Theodore Roosevelt.* New York: Random House, 1979.

———. *Theodore Rex.* New York: Random House, 2001.

Morris, Sylvia Jukes. *Edith Kermit Roosevelt: Portrait of a First Lady.* New York: Random House, 2009.

Mowry, George. *The Era of Theodore Roosevelt, 1900–1912.* New York: Harper, 1958.

O'Toole, Patricia. *When Trumpets Call: Theodore Roosevelt After the White House.* New York: Simon and Schuster, 2005.

Persico, Joseph. *Roosevelt's Secret War: FDR and World War II Espionage*. New York: Random House, 2002.

Peyser, Marc, and Timothy Dwyer. *Hissing Cousins: The Lifelong Rivalry of Eleanor Roosevelt and Alice Roosevelt Longworth*. New York: Doubleday, 2015.

Rixey, Lillian. *Bamie: Theodore Roosevelt's Remarkable Sister*. New York: D. McKay Company, 1963.

Robinson, Corrine Roosevelt. *My Brother, Theodore Roosevelt*. New York: Charles Scribner's Sons, 1921.

Roosevelt, Archibald. *For Lust of Knowing: Memoirs of an Intelligence Officer*. New York: Little, Brown and Company, 1988.

Roosevelt, Eleanor. *The Autobiography of Eleanor Roosevelt*. New York: HarperCollins, 2014.

—————. *Hunting Big Game in the Eighties: Letters of Elliott Roosevelt*. New York: Charles Scribner's Sons, 1933.

—————. *This I Remember*. New York: Harper and Brothers, 1949.

—————. *This Is My Story*. New York: Harper and Brothers, 1937.

—————. *You Learn by Living*. New York: Harper and Brothers, 1960.

Roosevelt, Elliott. *As He Saw It*. New York: Duell, Sloan and Pearce, 1946.

Roosevelt, Elliott, and James Brough. *An Untold Story: The Roosevelts of Hyde Park*. New York: Putnam Sons, 1973.

—————. *Mother R*. New York: G. P. Putnam's Sons, 1977.

Roosevelt, Elliott, and Theodore Roosevelt. *FDR: His Personal Letters, 1947*. New York: Duell, Sloan, and Pearce, 1947.

Roosevelt, James, and Bill Libby. *My Parents: A Differing View*. New York: Playboy Press, 1976.

Roosevelt, James, and Sidney Shalett. *Affectionately, FDR*. New York: Harcourt, Brace, 1959.

Roosevelt, Mrs. James. *My Boy Franklin*. New York: R. Long and R. R. Smith, 1933.

Roosevelt, Kermit. *War in the Garden of Eden*. New York: Charles Scribner's Sons, 1919.

Roosevelt, Theodore. *The Autobiography of Theodore Roosevelt*. New York: Macmillan Company, 1913.

Roosevelt, Theodore Jr. *All in the Family*. New York: G. P. Putnam's Sons, 1929.

—————. *Average Americans*. New York: G. P. Putnam's Sons, 1919.

Roosevelt, Mrs. Theodore Jr. *Day Before Yesterday: The Reminiscences of Mrs. Theodore Roosevelt, Jr*. New York: Doubleday, 1959.

Rupp, Leila. *A Desired Past: A Short History of Same-Sex Love in America*. Chicago: University of Chicago Press, 1999.

—————. *Worlds of Women: The Making of an International Women's Movement*. Princeton, NJ: Princeton University Press, 1997.

Schlesinger, Arthur. *The Age of Roosevelt, Vol. I: The Crisis of the Old Order*. New York: Houghton Mifflin, 1957.

—————. *The Age of Roosevelt, Vol. II: The Coming of the New Deal*. New York: Houghton Mifflin, 1959.

————. *The Age of Roosevelt, Vol. III: The Politics of Upheaval.* New York: Houghton Mifflin, 1960.

Shoumatoff, Elizabeth. *FDR's Unfinished Portrait: A Memoir.* Pittsburgh, PA: University of Pittsburgh Press, 1991.

Smith, Jean Edward. *FDR.* New York: Random House, 2007.

Steinberg, Alfred. *Mrs. R.: The Life of Eleanor Roosevelt.* New York: Putnam, 1958.

Stiles, Lela. *Louis Howe: The Man Behind Roosevelt.* New York: World Publishing, 1954.

Stoddard, Henry L. *As I Knew Them: Presidents and Politics from Grant to Coolidge.* New York: Harper and Brothers, 1927.

Streitmatter, Rodger, ed. *Empty Without You: The Intimate Letters of Eleanor Roosevelt and Lorena Hickok.* New York: Free Press, 1998.

Teague, Michael. *Mrs. L.: Conversations with Alice Roosevelt Longworth.* Ann Arbor, MI: University of Michigan Press, 1981.

Teichmann, Howard. *Alice: The Life and Times of Alice Roosevelt Longworth.* New York: Prentice-Hall, 1979.

Tully, Grace. *FDR: My Boss.* New York: Charles Scribner's Sons, 1949.

Walker, Robert. *The Namesake: A Biography of Theodore Roosevelt, Jr.* New York: Brick Tower Press, 2008.

Ward, Geoffrey C. *Before the Trumpet: Young Franklin Roosevelt, 1882–1905.* New York: Harper and Row, 1985.

————. *Closest Companion: The Unknown Story of the Intimate Friendship of Franklin Roosevelt and Margaret Suckley.* New York: Houghton Mifflin, 1995.

————. *A First-Class Temperament: The Emergence of Franklin Roosevelt, 1905–1928.* New York: Harper and Row, 1989.

Ward, Geoffrey C., and Ken Burns. *The Roosevelts: An Intimate History.* New York: Alfred A. Knopf, 2014.

Ware, Susan. *Partner and I: Molly Dewson, Feminism and New Deal Politics.* New Haven, CT: Yale University Press, 1987.

Wehle, Louis B. *Hidden Threads of History.* New York: Macmillan Company, 1953.

White, William Allen. *The Autobiography of William Allen White.* New York: Simon Publications, 1946.

Whittlesey, Charles Barney. *The Roosevelt Genealogy 1649–1902.* Hartford, CT: Press of J. B. Burr and Company, 1902.

Wister, Owen. *Roosevelt: The Story of a Friendship: 1880–1919.* New York: Macmillan Company, 1930.

Youngs, J. William. *Eleanor Roosevelt: A Personal and Public Life.* Boston: Little, Brown, 1985.

INDEX

ABOUT THE AUTHOR

WILLIAM J. MANN is the author of *Tinseltown: Murder, Morphine, and Madness at the Dawn of Hollywood*, which won the Edgar Award for Best Fact Crime in 2015; *Kate: The Woman Who Was Hepburn*, a *New York Times* Notable Book; and eleven other books of nonfiction and fiction. He is an associate professor of history at Central Connecticut State University and divides his time between Connecticut and Cape Cod.

TINSELTOWN

Available in Paperback and Ebook

"Mann tells his story expertly...When it's all over, Mann has argued so ably for his killer-candidate that he finally may have put this controversy to rest."

– Washington Post

"Mann's call sheet of colorful characters is so richly painted, they not only make the Roaring '20s come to life, they're so bizarre they seem like they could only exist in a movie."

– Entertainment Weekly

The Day of the Locust meets *The Devil in the White City* and *Midnight in the Garden of Good and Evil* in this juicy, untold Hollywood story: an addictive true tale of ambition, scandal, intrigue, murder, and the creation of the modern film industry. A true story recreated with the suspense of a novel, *Tinseltown* is the work of a storyteller at the peak of his powers—and the solution to a crime that has stumped detectives and historians for nearly a century.

Available Wherever Books Are Sold